Mathematics for Effective Management

Masoud Saravi
Shomal University, Iran

IGI Global
Scientific Publishing
Publishing Tomorrow's Research Today

Vice President of Editorial | Melissa Wagner
Managing Editor of Acquisitions | Mikaela Felty
Managing Editor of Book Development | Jocelynn Hessler
Production Manager | Mike Brehm
Cover Design | Phillip Shickler

Published in the United States of America by
IGI Global Scientific Publishing
701 East Chocolate Avenue
Hershey, PA, 17033, USA
Tel: 717-533-8845
Fax: 717-533-8661
Website: https://www.igi-global.com E-mail: cust@igi-global.com

Library of Congress Cataloging-in-Publication Data

Names: Saravi, Masoud, author.
Title: Mathematics for effective management / edited by Masoud Saravi.
Description: Hershey, PA : IGI Global, [2025] | Includes bibliographical references and index. | Summary: "This book explores some mathematical operators as leaders and functions as peace soldiers enter the faculty of management to teach managers how to think mathematically to build a future where the peace governs rather than war. Hoping to have a world of peace, this book is dedicated to all managers who act with mathematical thought"-- Provided by publisher.
Identifiers: LCCN 2024052933 (print) | LCCN 2024052934 (ebook) | ISBN 9798369336571 (hardcover) | ISBN 9798369351673 (paperback) | ISBN 9798369336588 (ebook)
Subjects: LCSH: Mathematics. | Management--Mathematics.
Classification: LCC QA37.3 .S26 2025 (print) | LCC QA37.3 (ebook) | DDC 510--dc23/eng/20241221
LC record available at https://lccn.loc.gov/2024052933
LC ebook record available at https://lccn.loc.gov/2024052934
British Cataloguing in Publication Data
A Cataloguing in Publication record for this book is available from the British Library.

To my Mother…she was a role model for the whole family.

Table of Contents

Preface

"*If I do a job in 30 minutes it's because I spent 10 years learning how to do that in 30 minutes. You owe me for the years, not the minutes.*" Pablo Picasso

It is not doubtful that mathematics is one of the fundamental manifestations of any culture, and little study proves that the cultural fertility of any society is without exaggeration a fundamental reflection of the flourishing of mathematics in that society. Even the richness of each society feeds on the soil that mathematics nourishes.

We must recognize the importance of mathematics without delving into it extensively here. We should only be reminded of the fear that the level of mathematical education in any society may decline, which itself indicates the hidden and fundamental (and sometimes obvious) importance of mathematics as the fundamental pillar of science, culture, art and the ability of a society.

The institutional ability of a society (whether governmental or non-governmental) is properly revealed when it has mathematical thought with it because mathematics is an orderly structure that can order the outside world.

Studying quantitative aspects of management requires a deep knowledge of the preliminary aspects of many mathematical topics. For this reason, I tried to start the mathematical methods from the basic principles and finish the book by mentioning many practical examples and avoiding proofs of theorems in such a way that it would be useful for management students.

This book is designed to meet the mathematical needs of students in management fields so that it can be useful even for students in economics, accounting, business, life and social sciences. The book itself has evolved from two semesters of management that I teach regularly at Shomal University of Amol. Both semesters form part of a B.Sc qualification in management. In the selection of materials for the course required of all undergraduates at the Faculty of Management and Accounting, I have been guided by the desire to choose topics of mathematical substance that have relevance for students whose major will be in one of the management-accounting areas.

Concerning the matter of selectivity, I would like to point out some of the dependencies that exist between the chapters.

Chapter 1, which is an introductory chapter, contains some basic concepts of mathematics, which are preliminaries and looks at the Methods of Reasoning and the counting techniques.

Chapter 2 is devoted to an introduction to sets and propositions. Apart from a few basic uses of sets, we can see more of their usefulness in other chapters. After an introduction to propositions and predicate logic, we discuss operations on propositions by use of truth tables.

Regarding the importance of differential and integral calculus, most of the existing chapters devoted to calculus, those that tackle many of topics in mathematical functions, limit and continuity, derivative and integral and their applications, respectively that contains the same content for parallel courses as Economics, Accounting and Business courses throughout Chapters 3-6.

In Chapter 7, I also presented the differential calculus of several variables functions which have nearly the same materials as Chapters 3-5. Besides that, the quadratic surfaces have been introduced and their graphs discussed.

Due to the importance of representing mathematical functions in the form of complex numbers, I dedicated Chapter 8 to introducing complex numbers and expressing some of their applications in solving algebraic relations and algebraic equations. Since usually the polar form of complex numbers are used in application, I devoted a large part of this chapter to this subject and shown the graphs of some specific functions in polar forms.

Since Ordinary Differential Equations (ODEs) and Difference Equations play an important role in modeling complex scientific, technological and economic processes, hence I added Chapter 9 which focuses on the solution of the first and second-ordered ODEs and Difference Equations for readers to get some basic knowledge about them and their applications.

In Chapter 10, after a brief introduction to vectors, I introduce matrix and different types of them then we discussed matrix algebra and show how the solution for the systems of linear equations can be determined by using them.

Chapter 11, deliberates the reliable tool for solving linear programming problems of the real world which would involve industrial and business problems. It contains some methods for addressing problems of optimization with some materials from the previous chapter. I added a section at the end of this chapter, namely Computer Station that can be useful in dealing with simplex problems.

Chapter 12 summarizes the probability and statistics with some of their applications.

Some chapters include optimal sections and examples which will gradually enhance the knowledge of readers. I added a section, namely Computer Station, to the end of Chapter, 7-8 to use for drawing the graphs of polar forms and quadratic surface equations and Chapter 11 for solving problems that are time consuming.

In the end of this preface I should mention that, unfortunately we are living in a disturbed historical time. Instead of training peace soldiers, we are forced to train war leaders. The expenses of killing humans are thousands times more than living cost.

On the cover of this book I designed a picture for most future managers of the world who may read this book. I chose some mathematical operators as leaders and function as peace soldiers enter the faculty of management to teach managers how to think mathematically to build a future where peace governs rather than war.

Hoping to have a world of peace, this book is dedicated to all managers who act with mathematical thought.

Masoud Saravi

Shomal University, Iran

Acknowledgment

The author acknowledges IGI Global Press for this opportunity and professional support. It has been a pleasure working with the IGI publication staff, in particular, my special thanks go to Ms. Melissa Wagner, Vice President of Editorial, for her offering on this book project and Miss. Nina Eddinger, Assistant Development Editor, patiently tolerated my writing emails and guided me well during this time.

I would like also to express my thanks to many of my colleagues at Shomal University, Dr H. Razavi, Dr M. Khorasani and Dr M.H. Rejaii for their valuable comments during our discussions, and my Irish friend Dermot O'Donnell, who read and revised the first section of the first chapter.

My particular thanks are due to the president of the university, Dr H. Ranjbar, for providing me with all the facilities I needed.

I must also express my gratitude to my wife, Mahnaz, for encouraging me during the writing of this book. Despite all the fatigue caused by her work in high school, she tolerated me as well as before, even though she knew very well that in our entire life together, I was never able to take a step forward from where I am to see, except pen and paper with a handful of books.

Finally, I wish to emphasize that any useful suggestions or comments for improving this book will be warmly appreciated and can be sent by email to masoud.saravi@shomal.ac.ir.

Chapter 1
Review of Basic Material:
Induction and Counting

ABSTRACT

In this chapter, we introduce some basic concepts of mathematics, which are preliminaries, in particular, some properties of integer numbers. After having a short marginal discussion about reasoning, we introduce some methods of reasoning, including the induction method, and present some results with this method. When we consider the outcomes of several experiments, we shall follow two basic counting techniques, namely sum and product rules that can be used to solve some types of problems in applications of counting. Using these rules, we introduce combinatorics, which is a branch of mathematics devoted to calculating the number of ways in which a specified process can be carried out.

1.1 PRELIMINARIES

Before we start this chapter, it is necessary to call some preliminaries on the following basic concepts which could also be useful for other chapters. We begin our discussion with an equation of line.

(a) The standard form of any straight line can be written as

$$Ax + By + C = 0. \tag{1}$$

If we rewrite (1) as $y = -\frac{A}{B}x - \frac{C}{B}$ and let $-\frac{A}{B} = m$and $-\frac{C}{B} = b$ then

$$y = mx + b. \tag{2}$$

This is another form of the line with slope m. By the Eq. (2), it is easy to find the slope of the line and y-intercept $(0,b)$ of the line.

DOI: 10.4018/979-8-3693-3657-1.ch001

If two points $P(x_1,y_1)$ and $Q(x_2,y_2)$ are given, then

$$m = \frac{y_2 - y_1}{x_2 - x_1}. \tag{3}$$

If $y_2-y_1=0$, ie., $m=0$ then we have the line $y=b$ which is a line parallel to x-axis, but if, $x_2-x_1=0$ then we have the line $x=0$ which is perpendicular to x-axis.

Another equation of a line passes through a point $P(x_1,y_1)$ with slope m is

$$y - y_1 = m(x - x_1). \tag{4}$$

If slope of two line L_1 and L_2 are m_1 and m_2 respectively. If $m_1=m_2$ then they are parallel. They are perpendicular if $m_1m_2= -1$.

Another form of equation of a line passes through two points $P(x_1,y_1)$ and $Q(x_2,y_2)$ is

$$y - y_1 = \frac{y_2 - y_1}{x_2 - x_1}(x - x_1). \tag{5}$$

Suppose a company sold a product for \$28, the number of sales was 1200. But when the company increased the price of the product to 35 dollars, the number of costumers decreased to 850 people. Assume that the relationship between the price p and the demand quantity q is linear we write the equation of this line.

We have two data points (1200, 28) and (850, 35). Therefore, from (5), we get

$$p - p_1 = \frac{p_2 - p_1}{q_2 - q_1}(x - q_1) \Rightarrow p - 28 = \frac{35 - 28}{850 - 1200}(x - 1200) \Rightarrow p = -\frac{1}{50}x + 52.$$

A typical demand and supply equations in linear forms are

$$Q_d = a+bP$$

$$Q_s = c+dP,$$

where Q_d and Q_s are quantity demanded and quantity supplied, and P is the price. In this set a,b,c,d are all parametric constants. When $Q_s=Q_d$, we say that equilibrium occurs in supply and demand analysis. By finding the point of intersection of these two linear equations, the equilibrium price and quantity can be found.

A linear equation with three unknowns which defines equation of a plane in a three-dimensional space coordinate takes the form

$$Ax + By + Cz = D.$$

We need two more equations to determine x,y and z. That is, we should have a system of the forms given by

$$a_1x + b_1y + c_1z = d_1$$

$$a_2x + b_2y + c_2z = d_2$$

$$a_3x + b_3y + c_3z = d_3.$$

Higher systems can be introduced similarly. We restrict our attention to system of equations having the same number of equations as unknowns. In Chapter 10, we will discuss the solution to such systems.

It can be shown that the distance between the two points $P(x_1,y_1)$ and $Q(x_2,y_2)$ is obtained from the following formula

$$d = \sqrt{(x_2 - x_1)^2 + (y_2 - y_1)^2}. \quad (6)$$

Similarly, the distance of point $P(x_1,y_1)$ from line $Ax+By+C=0$ is calculated with the following formula

$$d = \frac{Ax_1 + By_1 + C}{\sqrt{x_1{}^2 + y_1{}^2}}. \quad (7)$$

The relations (6) and (7) can be generalized in three-dimensional space coordinates by

$$d = \sqrt{(x_2 - x_1)^2 + (y_2 - y_1)^2 + +(z_2 - z_1)^2}. \quad (8)$$

$$d = \frac{Ax_1 + By_1 + Cz_1}{\sqrt{x_1{}^2 + y_1{}^2 + z_1{}^2}}. \quad (9)$$

(b) The standard form of a circle can be written as

$$A(x^2 + y^2) + Bx + Cy + D = 0. \quad (10)$$

Let's rewrite Eq. (10) in the following form

$$x^2 + y^2 + \frac{B}{A}x + \frac{C}{A}y + \frac{D}{A} = 0.$$

One may write it as

$$\left(x+\frac{B}{2A}\right)^2+\left(y+\frac{C}{2A}\right)^2-\frac{B^2}{4A^2}-\frac{C^2}{4A^2}+\frac{D}{A}=0 \Rightarrow \left(x+\frac{B}{2A}\right)^2+\left(y+\frac{C}{2A}\right)^2=\frac{B^2}{4A^2}+\frac{C^2}{4A^2}-\frac{D}{A}.$$

Since the left hand-side is positive, then the right hand-side must either be positive. That is,

$$\frac{B^2}{4A^2}+\frac{C^2}{4A^2}-\frac{D}{A}\geq 0,$$

that is

$$B^2+C^2 \geq 4AD. \tag{11}$$

The existence of the relation (11) guarantees the relation (10) denotes a circle.

The equation of the circle with a center in origin with radius r is

$$x^2+y^2 = r^2.$$

One may write this equation in the following form

$$\frac{x^2}{r^2}+\frac{y^2}{r^2} = 1.$$

We may say this is an equation of an ellipse with equal diameters. This leads us to introduce the equation of the ellipse with non-equal diameters, given by

$$\frac{x^2}{a^2}+\frac{y^2}{b^2} = 1, \tag{12}$$

with two diameters of length $2a$ and $2b$.

In general, the standard form of an ellipse is

$$Ax^2+By^2+Cx+Dy+E = 0. \tag{13}$$

With the same operations to obtain a relation (11), it can be shown that if

$$\frac{C^2}{A}+\frac{D^2}{B}\geq 4E, \tag{14}$$

then this relation guarantees the relation (13) denotes an ellipse.

In relation (10) if A and B are different signs then we get

$$Ax^2 - By^2 + Cx + Dy + E = 0. \tag{15}$$

which is the equation of a hyperbola. By this relationship we can write another form for hyperbola given by

$$\frac{x^2}{a^2} - \frac{y^2}{b^2} = 1. \tag{16}$$

We can also introduce a general equation for a second-order (or quadratic) surface given by

$$Ax^2 + By^2 + Cz^2 + Dxy + Exz + Fyz + Gx + Hy + Iz + J = 0$$

where *A, B, C, D, E, F, G, H, I* and *J* are real constant coefficients.

This equation represents a wide range of shapes, including spheres, ellipsoids, hyperboloids, cones, paraboloids, and cylinders. The coefficients determine the shape and orientation of the quadric surface in space. We encounter some of such equations in Chapter 7.

We may use polar coordinates, given by, $x=r\cos\theta$, $y=r\sin\theta$ to consider the graph of a function, because most of the times, the polar form of an equation can be easier to consider rather than its Cartesian's form. Even in some calculations, polar coordinates can be helpful, in particular in limit and integration problems. In Chapter 8, we devoted a section to the polar form of specific equations.

(c) The numbers 1, 2, 3, ... which are used in counting are called *Natural* or *Positive Numbers*. For such numbers we have two operations, namely, *addition* and *multiplication* with the following properties:

If *a, b, c* are arbitrary natural numbers, then

(i) $a+b=b+a$, (Cummutative Law of Addition)
(ii) $a+(b+c)=(a+b)+c$, (Associative Law of Addition)
(iii) $a.b=b.a$, (Cummutative Law of Multiplication)
(iv) $a+(b+c)=(a+b)+c$, (Associative Law of Multiplication)
(v) $a.(a+c)=a.b+a.c$, (Distributive Law)

If $b\neq 0$, then by $b|a$, we mean the number '*a*' is divisible by '*b*'.

If $b|a$ and $a|c$ then, $b|c$.

For two numbers *a* and *b,* there exist unique numbers *q* and *r* called *quotient* and *reminder* respectively, such that $a=bq+r$, $0\leq r<b$.

A natural number *p* is called a *prime number* if: $p>1$ and has divisor except 1 and *p*.

Every prime number greater than 2 can be written in the form $4n\pm 1$.

If $a=kc$ and $b=kd$, we say a and b has a common divisor k.
If the common divisor of two numbers a and b is '1' we write $(a,b)=1$.
The common divisor of two prime numbers is '1'.
If a/bc and $(a,b)=1$, then a/c.
(d) The following relations can be useful in calculation:
(i) For any positive integer, we have

$$x^n - 1 = (x - 1)(x^{n-1} + x^{n-2} + \dots + x + 1). \tag{17}$$

(ii) For any odd positive integer, we have

$$x^n + 1 = (x + 1)(x^{n-1} - x^{n-2} + \dots - x + 1). \tag{18}$$

In general,

$$x^n - y^n = (x - y)(x^{n-1} + x^{n-2}y + x^{n-3}y^2 \dots + xy^{n-2} + y^{n-1}). \tag{19}$$

$$x^n + y^n = (x + y)(x^{n-1} - x^{n-2}y + x^{n-3}y^2 \dots - xy^{n-2} + y^{n-1}). \tag{20}$$

(iii) Any polynomial denoted by $P_n(x)$ with a positive integer n, is given by:

$$P_n(x) = a_n x^n + a_{n-1} x^{n-1} + \dots + a_1 x + a_0. \tag{21}$$

where a_i, $i=0,1,\dots,n$ can be any number.
(iv) (1) – $(a^n)^m = (a^m)^n = a^{mn}$, (2) – $\sqrt[n]{a^m} = a^{\frac{m}{n}}$.

1.2 MARGINAL DISCUSSIONS

When someone asks us about mathematics, we often hear that it's the powerhouse of all sciences or the top dog ruling over everything else. People often compare it to Cyrano without a sword or James Bond without a gun – incomplete. But does this argument truly resonate? Certainly, mathematics is embedded in our daily routines, even in seemingly mundane tasks like counting objects. However, must we unequivocally view it as the reigning sovereign?

Tackling everyday problems involves a myriad of factors, many of which defy resolution through mathematics alone. Each scientific discipline possesses its own inherent value within its domain. Nevertheless, the indisputable importance of mathematics spans various sciences, encompassing physics, chemistry, biology, technology, engineering, and even the social sciences. This establishes mathematics in a category of its own. Its significance, at times overt and at times subtle, permeates numerous scientific fields, fostering cohesion and imparting meaning.

Mathematics plays an indispensable role in comprehending the developmental trajectory of scientific fields by expressing them in a mathematical language. Even commencing with the most basic integers, those intangible numerical entities, a comprehensive structure can be erected upon them. Some of these integers harbor concealed secrets that transcend their numerical identity, almost as if delineating the essence of our existence.

In addition to serving a very practical purpose, mathematics has been the core of major natural science theories. It has given direction and content to most of the philosophical thinking, reconstructed church teachings and cultivated economic and political theories. We may say that mathematics is the father of our logic and has provided us with the best answers in the field of fundamental issues related to nature of the universe. Therefore, mathematics can be considered one of the elements that shape the new civilization (Kline, 1964).

We're not advocating an exclusive commitment to mathematical perspectives here, but rather aiming to present a nuanced viewpoint that enhances the understanding of content and its applications. In this initial segment, let's delve into the methodologies of mathematical reasoning.

1.3 METHODS OF REASONING

Before introducing some arguments, we remind you that the collections of the numbers that we deal with in this introductory chapter are positive integers. Now, according to these choices, we are going to express and examine three types of arguments, which are not only in mathematics, but to prove what we claim, we need some kind of reasoning method.

One of the methods of reasoning is the use of *situations*. In this way, we examine the existing situations separately and prove that our claim is correct in each situation. Let's consider the following examples.

Example 1: Show that if n is a positive integer number, then $n(n+1)$ is an even number.

Solution: We consider two cases for n. (*i*)- n is an even number and (*ii*)- n is an odd number. In the first case, if n is even, we assume that $n=2k$ where k is any even or odd integer number. Then, the number $n= 2k(2k+1)$ is divisible by 2. That is, n is an even number. For another case, if n is odd, that means $n= (2k+1)\ (2k+2)= 2(2k+1)\ (k+1)$. This number is also divisible by 2 thus, n is an even number.

Another type of reasoning is *deductive reasoning*. In this way, we go from one partial verdict to another partial verdict. For example, if $a>b$ and $b>c$, then we conclude that $a>c$. But can it be said that if $a>b$ and $a>c$, then $b>c$? This result is not true in general. Therefore, in this type of reasoning, we may not have a definite result. In management systems, statistical comparison can be a good argument for the next results.

Example 2: Using example 1, show that if n^2+n+1 is an odd number.

Solution: We have $n^2 + n + 1 = n(n + 1) + 1$. But in example 1 we showed that $n(n+1)$ is an even number. Hence,$n^2 + n + 1 = n(n + 1)+1 = 2k + 1$.That is, n^2+n+1 is an odd number.

The third type of reasoning is *mathematical induction*, which is one of the most powerful and common methods for proving theorems and solving mathematical problems, which are based on the well-ordering principle of integers. This method in classical logic means to reach the whole from the part.

If we want to prove the correctness of a specific property that we call $p(n)$, where n is any positive integer number, we first show that this property is true for n, or in other words, $p(1)$ holds, then by accepting the property for $n=k$, we prove that $p(k+1)$ also holds. So, three steps are necessary in the proof by induction method. The first step is to show that $p(1)$ is correct, the second step is to assume the correctness of $p(k)$ and the third step is to prove the correctness of $p(k+1)$ using the second step or both steps. The correctness of $p(k+1)$ results in $p(n)$ will hold for every positive integer.

Example 3: Show $1 + 2 + 3 + \ldots + n = \frac{n(n+1)}{2}$.

Solution: For $n=1$: $1 = \frac{1(1+1)}{1} = 1$. So $p(1)$ holds. Suppose $p(k)$ holds. i.e.,

$$1 + 2 + 3 + \ldots + k = \frac{k(k+1)}{2}.$$

We prove that $p(k+1)$ also holds. For this purpose, we add $(k+1)$ to both sides of this relationship. We will obtain

$$1 + 2 + 3 + \ldots + k + (k+1) = \frac{k(k+1)}{2} + (k+1).$$

We can write the right side of equality as $\frac{(k+1)(k+2)}{2}$. That is, we write

$$1 + 2 + 3 + \ldots + k + (k+1) = \frac{k(k+1)(k+2)}{2},$$

which shows that $p(k+1)$ is also true. In this way $p(n)$ will hold for all n.

***Remark 1*:** The sum of a year's digits method, uses the expected life and adds the digits for every year to give the final depreciation expense amount. For a machine that has a long-life expectancy, it is much simpler to use $S = \frac{n(n+1)}{2}$ where S is the sum of the year's digits and n is life expectancy.

Example 4: Find the sum of year's digits of a machine with a life expectancy of 22 years.

Solution: We have n=22, so $S = \frac{22(22+1)}{2} = 253.$

Example 5: Show

$$1 + a + a^2 + \ldots + a^{n-1} = \frac{a^n - 1}{a - 1}, (a \neq 1).$$

Solution: For $n = 1 : 1 = \frac{a-1}{a-1} = 1$. So $p(1)$ holds. Suppose $p(k)$ holds. i.e.,

$$1 + a + a^2 + \ldots + a^{k-1} = \frac{a^k - 1}{a - 1}.$$

We prove that $p(k+1)$ also holds. For this purpose, we add a^k to both sides of this relationship. We will get

$$1 + a + a^2 + \ldots + a^{k-1} + a^k = \frac{a^k - 1}{a - 1} + a^k.$$

We simplify the right side of this relation and get

$$\frac{a^k + a^{k+1} - a^k - 1}{a - 1} = \frac{a^{k+1} - 1}{a - 1}.$$

That is,

$$1 + a + a^2 + \ldots + a^{k+1} = \frac{a^{k+1} - 1}{a - 1},$$

which shows that is also true. In other words, $p(n)$ holds for all n.

If we pay attention to the inequalities $2^n < n!$ or $2^n > n^3$, it can be seen that when n=1, n=2 and n=3, these inequalities do not hold, and they hold for $n \geq 4$. So, in these problems, we must first specify a number such as m that is correct for $m>1$ attributes $p(m)$. Then we determine the correctness of the feature $p(n)$ for $n \geq m$. This induction method is called *modified induction.*

Example 6: Use the modified induction to show that $2^n > 2n+1$.

Solution: For n=1 we have 2>2+1 and for n=2 also 4>4+1. But for n=3, this inequality holds. So $p(3)$ holds. Now we assume that $p(k)$ holds, that is, $2^k > 2k+1$. To show that the property of $p(k+1)$ is also valid, we multiply the sides of equality by the number 2. We get

$$2^{k+1} > 2(2k+1) = 4k+2 = 2k+(2k+2) > 2k+3.$$

Since $k \geq 3$, therefore, $p(k+1)$ also holds and, as a result $p(n)$ will hold for all $n>2$.

Due to the importance of this method, we divide it into two types of *weak induction* and *strong induction.*

The previous examples were of weak induction type. But sometimes it is not possible to conclude $p(k+1)$ only by using $p(k)$, but it is possible to conclude from establishing $p(m)$ to $p(k)$ that $p(k+1)$ is also true. In such cases, we use the principle of strong induction, which states that if $p(n)$ is a specific property of the integer n with the following conditions

(a) $p(m)$ holds
(b) $p(n)$ holds for $n=k+1$

assuming that $p(n)$ holds for $m \leq n \leq k$ then $p(n)$ holds for all positive integer numbers $n \geq m$.

Example *7*: Show that any integer $n \geq 2$ can be written as a product of prime numbers.

Solution: For $n=2$, $p(2)$ holds. Now suppose we can write any k where $2 \leq k \leq l$ as a product of prime numbers. We prove that the number $k+1$ can also be written as a product of primes. For this purpose, if $k+1$ is prime, the proof is complete, but if it is not prime, so $k+1=(m,n)$ that $k+1>n$, $m>1$ or $n \geq m$, $m \geq 2$. According to the hypothesis of induction, n and m are decomposable into the product of prime factors, that is, $m= p_1p_2 \ldots p_s$, $n= q_1q_2 \ldots q_t$ where $p_1,p_2,\ldots,p_s$ and $q_1,q_2,\ldots,q_t$ are prime numbers. Therefore: $mn= p_1,p_2, \ldots p_s, q_1,q_2, \ldots q_t$..

In the next chapter, we introduce more mathematical proofs to deal with examples which cannot be considered by induction.

1.4 THE COUNTING RULES

The counting rules which contain permutations and combinations are branches of mathematics which are appertained to find the number of ways can be done in a specific process. We start our studies of counting with two basic rules of counting principles.

With 5 letters a, b, c, d and e, and 3 Greek letters α,β and γ, it is obvious that in 5+3=8 ways you can choose a letter that is Latin or Greek letters. Also, if we want to choose two letters, one of which is Latin and the other is Greek, we will have 5×3=15 choices. These examples guide us to the rules of sum and product.

1.4.1. Rule of Sum

Suppose A and B are two separate tasks. If you can do one task in m ways and another task in n ways and you cannot do these two tasks simultaneously, then each of these two tasks can be done in any one of $m+n$ ways.

For example, if there are 22 male staff and 13 female staff in a factory, then by using the addition rule, we can have 22+13=35 choices.

Example 8: How many times is the *xnew=xnew*+1 command executed in the following program segment?

```
For i:=1 to 16 do
   xnew=xnew+1
For j:=1 to 12 do
   xnew=xnew+1.
```

Solution: In the first loop, the above command is executed 16 times. After this loop ends, in the second loop, this command is executed 12 more times, and since these two loops do not interfere, then according to the rule of sum, this command is executed 16+12=28 times.

The rule of sum can be generalized. In such a way that if it is possible to do one task in n_1 different ways the second task in n_2 different ways and the third task in n_3 different ways and, ..., and task k in n_k different ways such that none of these tasks are done simultaneously, then by the rule of sum, each of these tasks can be done in any one of $n_1+n_2+\ldots+n_k$ ways.

1.4.2. Rule of Product

If event A can be done in m different ways, and after that, event B can be done in n different ways then, these two events can be done in $m\times n$ different ways.

Example 9: The association is holding a seminar in an office out of 12 men and 8 women needs a male and female couple to receive guests. How many ways can the community management choose this couple?

Solution: According to the rule of product since $m=12$ and $n=8$ there are 12×8=96 selections to choose a couple between them.

The rule of product can also be generalized. In such a way that if an event takes place in n_1 different ways and the second event in n_2 different ways, ..., and kth in n_k different ways and the number of each event does not depend on how the previous event took place, then the number of ways the events can be done in is $n_1, n_1, \ldots, n_k$ ways.

Example 10: How many ways can you choose a 6-letter password consisting of 3 letters, two digits and a letter so that repetition of letters is allowed?

Solution: The first letter may be chosen as one of 26 letters and so may the second and third letters. The fourth and fifth letters can be chosen from 10 digits, and the last letter is chosen from the 26 letters. Therefore, according to the generalization of the rule of product principle, we get: 26× 26× 26× 10× 10× 26= 45697600 ways to choices such password.

Remark 2: Sometimes the sum and product rules are used together.

Example 11: Suppose we have 26 workers in a factory and one of the Latin letters plus a number from 0 to 9 is chosen to issue an ID card for each worker. How many ways can an ID card been issued?

Solution: Since we have 26 letters of the alphabet and 10 numbers, by using the rule of product 26×10=260 ways, you can issue ID cards that include the letters of the alphabet and the second letter of the number. Moreover, because there are 1×26=26 ways to select the variable with one letter of the Latin alphabet, then, in total, there are 260+26=286 ways to issue an ID card.

In the continuation of our work, we will focus our study on the issues related to counting the members of sets that are grouped in a certain order so that we have less need to use the principles of rules of sum and product directly.

1.5 PERMUTATIONS AND COMBINATIONS

Firstly, we turn our attention to the counting of distinct objects that are located in a certain order. Suppose we have a collection of $x_1, x_2, \ldots, x_n$ objects and we want to select r objects from this collection. In addition, we would like to know how many different ways there are. Does the order of selection matter? Is the repetition of objects allowed or not?

For n=3 and r=2 we will have the following table of states:

(i) $(x_1,x_2), (x_1,x_3), (x_2,x_3), (x_3,x_1), (x_3,x_2), (x_2,x_1)$
(ii) $(x_1,x_1), (x_1,x_2), (x_1,x_3), (x_2,x_3), (x_2,x_2), (x_3,x_1), (x_3,x_2), (x_2,x_1), (x_3,x_3)$
(iii) $(x_1,x_2), (x_1,x_3), (x_2,x_3)$
(iv) $(x_1,x_1), (x_1,x_2), (x_1,x_3), (x_2,x_2), (x_2,x_1), (x_3,x_3)$

In this way, the initial question has turned into four different issues. The first two are called *permutations* of the collections without and with repetition, respectively. The other two, which are called *combinations,* are also without and with repetition, respectively.

1.5.1. Permutation

Let A be a collection of n members $\{x_1,x_2,\ldots,x_n\}$ and $n\geq r\geq 0$. We denote the number of n-permutations of A by, $P(n,r)$.

Theorem 1. The number of permutations of size r from a collection of n distinct elements is

$$P(n,r) = \frac{n!}{(n-r)!} \tag{22}$$

Example 12: In how many ways can three people be selected among eight people, to take a position as President, Vice President and Secretary?

Solution: For the first one, we have 8 choices. Now, when the President is selected, we have 7 choices for the latter, and in this way, we have 6 choices for the Secretary. According to the rule of product, we will have 8×7×6=336 choices. If we show this choice with $p(8,3)$, we get

$$P(8,3) = \frac{8!}{(8-3)!} = \frac{8!}{5!} = \frac{1\times 2\times 3\times 4\times 5\times 6\times 7\times 8}{1\times 2\times 3\times 4\times 5} = 6\times 7\times 8 = 336.$$

Example 13: Out of the 12 rooms in the university, 4 are reserved for deputies and 8 are reserved for group managers. How many ways can we choose the deputy's rooms?

Solution: Since we don't have repetitions, the number of selections according to r=4 and n=7 will be

$$P(7,4) = \frac{7!}{(7-4)!} = \frac{7!}{3!} = \frac{1\times 2\times 3\times 4\times 5\times 6\times 7}{1\times 2\times 3} = 4\times 5\times 6\times 7 = 840.$$

***Remark* 3:** In the case that repetition is allowed, i.e. we have r- permutations with Repetition, the number of choices will be n^r.

Example 14: The personal employee number is a sequence of 9 digits that is not necessarily distinct. How many ways can you make 9-digit sequences?

Solution: Because repetition is allowed here, and n=10, r=9, then we will have 10^9 number of choices.

Example 15: The telephone numbers of the cities of country A are made up of seven digits such that none of the numbers start with 0 or 1.

(i) How many seven-digit numbers will we have?
(ii) How many of these numbers do not contain the digit 0?
(iii) How many of these numbers include at least one 0?

Solution: Let's assume that the digits 0 and 1 are among our selected digits, so according to Remark 3, we will have 10^7=10000000 choices. Now, suppose that 0 and 1 are not among the seven digits of the telephone number. In this case, there are as many as 2×10^6=2000000 numbers that include at least one of these digits. Therefore, the answer (i) is equal to the difference of this number from the total result, which is 8000000. For part (ii), if 0 is included, the number of numbers will be 9^7=4782969. The difference between answer in part (i) and the number of remaining numbers, i.e. 4251528, is the desired answer. To answer part (c), it is enough to subtract the number of numbers that do not contain 0 from the total numbers that contain 0, i.e., 8,000,000. The answer will be 3748472.

***Remark 4*:** The number of permutations of the n objects that are considered together (i.e. $n=r$) is equal to $n!$.

Example 16: How many words can be made with the word FACTORY? How many of these words start with the letter "R"? How many words can be made which contain the vowel letters next to each other?

Solution: The number of permutations of the letters in the word FACTORY is 7!=5040. If we leave the letter R as the first letter, we can make a 6-letter word 6!=620 from the rest of the letters and then add the letter R to them. The word FACTORY has two vowels. With these two letters, we can write *2* words and with the remaining five letters, we can write 5!=120 words. If we consider a 5-letter word including non-vowels marked with x's, as follows:

x[] x[] x[] x[] x[]x

Each of the words written with the two letters a and o can be placed in any of the six places marked with squares to make a seven-letter word. Therefore, according to the principle of rule product, the required number of words is $2!\times5!\times6=1440$.

Now, if we consider the word BOSS, the number of permutations is 12, not 4!, because the four letters are not distinct. This leads us to introduce a modified permutation.

Suppose we have n objects that are not necessarily distinct and consist of k categories such that n_1 objects are in the first category, n_2 objects are in the second category, ..., and n_k objects are in the category k. In this case, a permutation of these objects is called a *modified permutation,* and it is represented by $P(n; n_2,\ldots,n_k)$, so that

$$P(n;n_1,n_2,\ldots,n_k) = \frac{n!}{n_1!n_2!\ldots n_k!} \qquad (23)$$

where $n_1+n_2+\ldots+n_k=n$.

Remark 5: If $n!$, objects be in i categories, i=1,2,…,k and $r = \sum_{i=1}^{k} r_i$, then these r objects can be placed in $P(n; n_1,n_2,\ldots,n_k)$ ways, where

$$P(n;n_1,n_2,\ldots,n_k) = \frac{P(n,r)}{n_1!n_2!\ldots n_k!} \tag{24}$$

Note that if n=r, then we will have the formula (23).

Example 17: A one-row parking lot for cars produced in a factory has 75 parking spaces. We want to park 18 cars, 22 jeeps and 25 vans in this parking lot. How many ways is this possible?

Solution: When the cars are parked, the total r= 18+22+25+65 cars are parked and there are 10 empty spaces. So, according to the modified permutation formula, we get

$$P(75;18,22,25) = \frac{p(75,65)}{18!22!25!}.$$

The permutations that we have reviewed so far have been of the linear type because we usually put the objects in a line (or row). Now suppose that several people are sitting around a table and form a circle. We want to know how many ways they form a circular ring. The permutations that are made in this way are called *circular permutations*. It is shown that the number of r-permutations derived from n distinct objects is equal to $\frac{n!}{r(n-r)!}$. If n=r, then the number of circular permutations is $(n–r)!$. In this type of permutation, we make a kind of movement direction on the circle.

Example 18: If five people marked with letters A, B, C, D and E sit around a table. How many different distance arrangements are possible, provided that we take the arrangements that can be obtained from others as the same one?

Solution: Here n=r=*6*, so the number of arrangements is equal to $\frac{6!}{6(6-6)!}$ = 5!= 120.

For this example, or in other words, for circular permutations, we provided some kind of direction.

Remark 6: If two committees, each with n members, want to sit on the chairs around the same table so that the people next to them do not belong to the same committee (that is, they are one in the middle), this work is possible in $n!(n–1)!$ ways.

1.5.2. Combination

Suppose we choose r objects from n distinct objects regardless of the order in which they are placed. We call each of these selections a combination of r objects of n objects and display them with $C(n,r)$ or $\binom{n}{r}$.

Theorem 2. The number of combinations of size r from a set of n distinct elements is

$$C(n,r) = \frac{n!}{r!(n-r)!} \tag{25}$$

Note that the difference between a combination and a permutation is that in the permutation the order is desired, while in the combination we ignore the order of placing the objects.

Example 19: We throw a coin 10 times. How many ways can 6 heads and 4 tails appear?

Solution: This example is equivalent to the question of how many different ways we can have 6 heads out of 10 throws. Hence, the answer is

$$\binom{10}{6} = \frac{10!}{6!4!} = 410.$$

Example 20: If a person has to answer three of the first five questions and four of the second five questions to get hired, how many choices will she have?

Solution: In the case of the first three questions, there are several $\binom{5}{3}$ choices and for the next four questions, there are several $\binom{5}{4}$ choices for him, which, according to the rule of product, the number of question choices will be equal to

$$\binom{5}{3} \times \binom{5}{4} = 50.$$

Example 20: How many times is the *xnew=xnew+*1 command executed in the following program segment?

```
For i:=1 to 12 do
For j:=i+1 to 12 do
For k:=j+1 to 12 do
   xnew=xnew+1
```

Solution: According to these three nested loops, for every three (i,j,k) that applies to the $1 \leq i<j<k \leq 12$ condition, the desired command is executed once, so to count the number of executions, it is enough to find the number of these threes. It is possible to choose three numbers from among 12 numbers through $C(12,3)=220$.

Example 21: How many groups of at least 16 people can be formed out of 18 people?

Solution: The groups should be 16, 17, or 18 people. Then, we will get:

$$\binom{18}{16} + \binom{18}{17} + \binom{18}{18} = 165.$$

Now the question is, if we have repeated elements in the composition, what will the formula of the composition be?

For example, the number of binary combinations of three letters A, B and C is equal to $\binom{3}{2} = 3$. But if repetition is also allowed, then combinations of two of AA, BB and CC will be added to this set, which will have six modes in total. That's mean, $\binom{4}{2}$.

In a more general case, if we want to select r objects from n distinct objects despite repeating elements, the number of ways will be $C(n+r-1,r)$.

Example 22: A factory produces 8 types of chocolate. This factory wants to produce packages containing 12 chocolates of these 8 types. How many packages of 12 different chocolates will be prepared?

Solution: Because repetition is allowed and $n=8$, $r=12$, as a result, the number of choices is equal to $C(8+12-1,12)= C(19,12)= 50388$.

One important application of combination is given by the following theorem.

Theorem 3. The number of the integer and positive solutions of the equation $x_1+x_2+\ldots+x_n=r$ is $C(n+r-1,r)$.

Example 23: Find the number of integer solutions of the equation

$$x1 + x2 + x3 + x4 + x5 = 24, xi \geq 0, 1 \leq i \leq 5.$$

Solution: Obviously, one of the solutions is $x_1=5, x_2=6, x_3=10, x_4=0, x_5=3$, which is different with the solution $x_1=6$, $x_2=4$, $x_3=7$, $x_4=6$, $x_5=1$. It is possible to say that, e.g., we have placed 24 file books in 5 shelves and observe that every correct non-negative answer observed this equation corresponds to a selection with repetition of size 24 from a set of size 5. Therefore, the number of solutions will be

$$C(5+24-1,24) = C(28,24) = 28!\_24!(4)! = 28 \times 27 \times 26 \times 25 \_\_\_\_\_ \_\_\_\_\_\_\_\_ 1 \times 2 \times 3 \times 4 = 20475.$$

Remark 7: In general, the following statements are equivalent.

(a) The number of the non-negative integer solutions of the equation $x_1+x_2+\ldots+x_n=r$.
(b) The number of selections with repetition of size r from a set of size n.
(c) The number of ways in which r identical objects can be distributed in n distinct containers.

Example 24: Five people intend to choose the system they need from a company from among three types of introductory, intermediate, and professional. If everyone insists on buying, how many different requests will the company face?

Solution: It is not important to the company who buys the systems, only the amount of sales of the systems is considered. Let x_1, x_2 and x_3 be the sales volume of introductory, intermediate and professional systems, respectively. Because five purchases are made, then $x_1+ x_2+ x_3= 5$.

Therefore, the number of different requests is equal to the number of non-negative integer solutions of this equation, i.e., $C(3+5–1,5)=21$.

Remark 8: The number $C(n,r)$ appears in many algebraic equations. One of these equations is *Newton's binomial expansion*, i.e.

$$(x + y) n = C(n,0)x\,n + C(n,1)x\,n{-}1\,y + \ldots + C(n,n-1)xy\,n{-}1 + C(n,n)y\,n$$

where n is a positive integer and, $y \in \mathbb{R}$.

According to this formula, $C(n,r)$ is the coefficient of $x^{n-r}y^r$.

Example 25: Determine the coefficient of x^5y^2 in $(x+y)^7$. What do you say about the coefficient of x^5y^2 of the binomial expansion $(2x+3y)^7$?

Solution: In this example, $n=7$ and $n=5$, so the coefficient of x^5y^2 is $C(7,5)=21$. But for the next state, if we consider the general state of $(ax+by)^n$, we find that this coefficient depends on both a and b. In other words, both a^5 and y^2 will be involved in the result of our work. This coefficient is in the form of $C(7,5)a^5b^2$. So, for the given binomial, the coefficient of x^5y^2 will be $C(7,5)2^5.3^2=6048$.

It can be proved that for a positive integer n, the coefficient of $x_1^{\,n_1}x_2^{\,n_2}\ldots x_k^{\,n_k}$ in $(x_1+x_2+\ldots+x_k)^n$ is

$$\frac{n!}{n_1!n_2!\ldots n_k!}. \tag{25}$$

where $0 \le n_i \le n$, for all $1 \le i \le k$ and $n_1+n_2+\ldots+n_k=n$. See, e.g. (Grimaldi, 1989).

If we go back to Ex. 1.12, we observe that we can also use (5) with $n_1=6$, $n_2=4$, and $n=10$ to get $\frac{10!}{6!4!} = 410$.

Example 26: Find the coefficient of xy^2z^3 in $(x+y–z)^6$.

Solution: In this example, $n^1=1$, $n_2=2$, $n_3=3$ and $n=6$, so the coefficient of xy^2z^3 is $\frac{6!}{1!2!3!} = 60$.

Example 27: How many ways can 9 speakers in a conference are accommodated in 2 different rooms, with 6 and 3 beds, respectively?

Solution: Here, $n_1=6, n_2=3$, and $n=9$, thus the number of ways will be $\frac{9!}{6!3!} = 84$.

In Remark 1, if we assume $S_n = \frac{n(n+1)}{2}$, then, $S_{n+1} = \frac{(n+1)(n+2)}{2}$, we can combine these two relations to obtain $S_{n+1} - S_n = n + 1$.

This relation is known as a *recurrence relation*, which has many applications in counting. In Chapter 9, we describe such relations because sometimes we come to problems that cannot be solved by counting methods such as permutations or combinations. These relations are called the *difference equations*, which are power tolls in counting.

More discussions and methods of counting can also be read in most Discrete Mathematics textbooks. For example, (Grimaldi, 1989) (Liu, 2002) (Grossman, 1995) (Beckenbach, 1964) (Riordan, 1958) (Stanat, 1977) (Stone, 1973) (Sahni, 1981) (Tucker, 1980).

CONCLUSION

In this chapter, we start with some basic concepts of mathematics, which could be helpful for the whole of the book. After introducing marginal discussion about reasoning, we introduce some methods of reasoning, including the induction method. By induction, we can obtain the solution of some summation by an induction method. By introducing some counting, we could apply them to get different formulas for permutations and combinations. By using these formulas, we could solve several problems with counting which we encounter in discrete mathematics.

1.6 Exercises

1. Prove by reasoning of situations that the product of three consecutive natural numbers is divisible by 6.
2. Prove the following relations by mathematical induction method.
   (i) $1^2 + 2^2 + 3^2 + \ldots + n^2 = \frac{n(n+1)(2n+1)}{6}$
   (ii) $1^3 + 2^3 + 3^3 + \ldots + n^3 = \left[\frac{n(n+1)}{2}\right]^2$
   (iii) $1+3+5+\ldots+(2n-1)=n^2$
   (iv) $\frac{1}{1\times 2} + \frac{1}{2\times 3} + \ldots + \frac{1}{n\times(n+1)} = \frac{n}{n+1}$
   (v) $\left(1-\frac{1}{2}\right)\left(1-\frac{1}{3}\right)\left(1-\frac{1}{4}\right)\ldots+\left(1-\frac{1}{n}\right) = \frac{1}{n}$
   (vi) $1\times 2 + 2\times 3 + 3\times 4 + \ldots + n(n+1) = \frac{n(n+1)(n+2)}{3}$
   (vii) $1 + x + x^2 + \ldots + x^{n-1} = \frac{x^n - 1}{x-1}; x \neq 1$
   (viii) $a + (a+d) + (a+2d) + \ldots + (a+nd) = \frac{(n+1)(2a+nd)}{2}$
   (ix) $2^n > n^2$

(x) $n!>2^n(n\geq)$

(xi) $(2n)!<2^{2n}(n!)^2$

(xii) $(n)!< \left(\frac{n+1}{2}\right)^2$

(xiii) $2^{n-1}(3^n+5^n) \geq 8^n$

(xiv) $\frac{1}{1^2}+\frac{1}{2^2}+\ldots+\frac{1}{n^2} < 2$

(xv) $\frac{1}{n+1}+\frac{1}{n+2}+\ldots+\frac{1}{2n} > \frac{13}{24}, (n \geq 2)$

(xvi) $1+\frac{1}{\sqrt{2}}+\frac{1}{\sqrt{3}}+\ldots+\frac{1}{\sqrt{n}} > 2(\sqrt{n+1}-1)$

(xvii) $(1+x)^n\geq 1+nx,\ x\in(-1,\infty)$

(xviii) 9^n-8^n-1 is divisible by 8

(xix) $3^{2n+1}+2^{n+2}$ is divisible by 7

(xx) $n(n\pm 1)(2n\pm 1)$ is divisible by 6.

3. The life expectancy for three different machines is (*a*) 20 years (*b*) 35 years (*c*) 47 years, respectively. Find the sum of the year's digits for these machines.
4. How many ways can two people be selected from a 5-member board and a 4-member board, each of which is separate from the two boards?
5. We want to divide the number of 25 employees into 5 groups of 5 people. How many ways is this division possible?
6. A strike has 16 workers. In how many ways can he choose 4 people to do something?
7. If 6 out of 10 workers in a factory are men, in how many ways can 8 people be selected from among them so that at most one of them is a woman?
8. How many ways can a committee of 5 people be selected from among 4 doctors and 3 nurses so that: (i)-There is no difference between the presence of doctors and nurses? (ii)- The committee should include two doctors. (iii)-The committee should include two nurses.
9. We want to choose 6 factories from 4 government factories and 8 private factories. In each of the following situations, in how many ways can 6 factories be selected?

   (i)-Include only one state factory. (ii)-Be at least a government factory.
10. At a party, guests shake hands. If they shake hands 105 times in total, how many guests are there?
11. We want to group the fourteen people into three different committees so that each of these committees is responsible for examining one issue and the number of its members is at least four. In how many ways can these fourteen people be distributed on these committees with the condition that four on certain people are always on these committees?
12. Determine the coefficients x^3y^4 and x^4y^3 in the binomial expansion $(3x-4y)^7$. Specify whether they are equal or not. In general, if we have $(ax+by)^n$, in what case is the coefficient of $x^r y^{n-r}$ equal to the coefficient of $x^{n-r}y^r$?

13. Five people intend to choose the system they need from a company from among three types of introductory, intermediate and professional systems. If everyone insists on buying, how many different requests will the company face?
14. If 10 people order food in a restaurant that has chicken, fish and meat kebab, in how many ways can they order 4 chicken dishes, 3 fish dishes and 2 meat kebab dishes?
15. In how many ways can 8 girls and 12 boys sit in a row if there is no restriction on sitting? What would be the answer if the girls sat together?
16. How many ways can 15 people be transported from one place to another using two vehicles with a capacity of 3 and 4 people?
17. The telephone numbers of the cities of an American state consist of ten digits, such that none of the numbers start with a zero or a digit.
    (a)- How many eight-digit numbers will we have? (b)- How many of these numbers do not contain zero? (c)- How many of these numbers include at least one zero?
18. With ten flags, 5 of which are green, 3 blue, and 2 red colors, how many different symbols can be made?
19. Among 6 male and 4 female students, in how many ways can 5 people be selected so that two of them are male and three of them are female students?
20. How many ways can a group of 20 people be divided into three groups of 2, 4 and 5 people?
21. A company wants to select four members to take positions as President, Assistant, Treasurer and Secretary. (a)- Find the number of ways in which these four positions can be selected. (b)- If we have to select four members among 12 members, how many selections we may have? (c)- Determine the number of ways without regard to different orders.
22. In how many ways can the manager of a television program schedule 8 commercials if the producer has three different commercials and each message is shown four times?
23. Show that the number of ways that m copies of every n book can be placed in a row is equal to $\frac{(mn)!}{(m!)^n}$.
24. Find the coefficient of
    (i) x^5y^3 in $(x-y)^8$
    (ii) x^3y^2 in $(3x+2y)^5$
    (iii) xy^3z^4 in $(x-3y-2z)^8$
    (iv) $x^3y^2z^2$ in $(2x-y+3z)^7$
    (v) $x^2y^3z^2w^2$ in $(2x-y+3z+2w)^9$
    (vi) $x^3y^2z^2w^3$ in $(x+2y-z+3w)^{10}$.
25. Prove that
    (i) $C(n,0)+C(n,1)+\ldots+C(n,n) = 2^n$

(ii) $C(n,0) - C(n,1) + \ldots + (-1)^n C(n,n) = 0$

(iii) $C(n,r) = C(n,n-r)$.

26. Find the value of r if $C(20,r)=C(n,20-r)$.
27. Find the number of integer solutions of the equation $x_1+x_2+x_3+x_4=42$, in the following cases:

(i) $x_i \geq 0, 1 \leq i \leq 4$.

(ii) $x_i \geq 0, x_i \geq 9$

(iii) $x_i \geq 0, x_1, x_3 \geq 8, x_2, x_4 \geq 8$

(iv) $x_i \geq 0, x_1, x_2, x_3 \geq 12, x_4 \geq 2$

(v) $x_i \geq 0, 6 \leq x_2, x_3 \leq 10, 8 \leq x_1, x_4 \leq 14$.

REFERENCES

Beckenbach, E. F. (1964). *Applied Combinational Mathematics*. John Wiley & Sons.

Grimaldi. Ralph, P. (1989). *Discrete and Combinatorial Mathematics* (2nd ed.). Addison-Wesley Publishing Company.

Grossman, P. (1995). *Discrete Mathematics for Computing*. MACMILLAN PRESS LTD. DOI: 10.1007/978-1-349-13908-8

Kline. Morris. (1964). Mathematics in Western Culture, Oxford University Press.

Liu, C. L. (2002). *Elements of Discrete Mathematics*. TATA McGraaw-Hill Edition.

Riordan, J. (1958). *An Introduction to Combinational Analysis*. John Wiley & Sons.

Sahni, S. (1981). *Concepts in Discrete Mathematics*. Camelot Press.

Stanat, D. F. (1977). *Discrete Mathematics for Compuer Science*. Prentice-Hall.

Stone, H. S. (1973). *Discrete Mathematical Structures and Their Applications, Science Research Associate*. Cliffs.

Tucker, J. P. (1980). *Applied Combinatories*. John Wiley & Sons.

Chapter 2
Sets and Propositions

ABSTRACT

This chapter is devoted to an elementary introduction to sets theory and propositions. We define some fundamental concepts of sets and introduce several types of sets. We study the algebra of sets and define the cardinal number, which is the number of elements of a finite set and its applications. We presented some results related to the cardinality of a finite set by the principle of inclusion and exclusion. We will also consider a related subject to the theory of sets, namely the theory of propositions. After an introduction to propositions and predicate logic, we discuss operations on propositions by using truth tables and their applications on mathematical problems through different mathematical proofs.

2.1 INTRODUCTION

The basis of all fields of mathematics in the present era is the concept of the set, which provides for the concise formulation of topics that are examined in mathematics. Trying to define a work set is difficult, but we can have an intuitive understanding of it. For example, in mathematics, the concept of "numbers" is not defined, but despite this, they all understand about numbers. Here, we present an intuitive definition of the set that was first presented by Georges Cantor in 1895, and then relying on it, we will achieve several algebraic relations by defining some other terms related to the sets.

In many daily tasks, data can be defined as a set, and if the data types are different, several sets can be used to distinguish them. An applied example of set theory is in the field of computer science, particularly in database management. For example, in the database of students, a set can be used to represent the collection of students who are enrolled in a particular course. Some instructive examples of sets application in management are project, inventory, and risk management.

DOI: 10.4018/979-8-3693-3657-1.ch002

In this chapter, in addition to explaining the basic concepts of sets, we will examine some applications, and the rules related to sets by including some different examples.

2.2 FUNDAMENTAL CONCEPTS OF SETS

A set is a collection of distinct objects with the condition that each object in question belongs to this set or is not a member of it. The meaning of being specific is to be able to specify its members exactly. For example, effective management is not a set because its members are not clear. The big factories are not also a set, but even if we just say natural numbers or English alphabets, both represent a set. The objects that make up a set are called the *members* or *elements* of that set, and we use the symbol $\in$ to show the membership, and the uppercase letters A, B, C,... and members of a set by lowercase letters. For example, $x \in A$ is interpreted to mean x is a member of A, or $x \notin B$ means x is not a member of B.

Likewise, we use the following three methods to display each set.

1. Using the Symbol {}

For example, a set of positive integer numbers which we used in the previous chapter is an example of a set. This set is known as *Natural Numbers* denoted by $\mathbb{N}$ such that,

$$\mathbb{N} = \{1,2,3,\dots\}.$$

We remind you of sets that will be used throughout the whole book given by:

(i) $\mathbb{N}^* = \{0,1,2,3,\dots\}$;*Arithmetic numbers*

This set contains all positive integer numbers, and it also has the element '0'. We beware that the set of natural numbers does not contain this element.

(ii) $\mathbb{Z} = \{0,\pm1,\pm2,\pm3,\dots\}$;*Integer numbers*

This set contains all positive and negative integer numbers, and it is denoted by $\mathbb{Z}$.

(iii) $\mathbb{Q} = \left\{\frac{p}{q}, p,q \in \mathbb{Z}; q \neq 0\right\}$;*Rational numbers*

This set is a collection of numbers which can be written as the ratio of two integer numbers. We denote it by $\mathbb{Q}$.

(iv)$\mathbb{R} = \{Asetofnumbersfrom - \infty \text{ to} + \infty\}$;*Real numbers*

This is a set of all numbers that exist. We can represent these numbers on a line such that '0' is chosen as the *origin* and the right side of origin represents positive numbers and the left side of origin as negative numbers.

(v) $\mathbb{Q}^* = \{\mathbb{R} - \mathbb{Q}\}$;*Irrational numbers*

This is a set of rea numbers which are not rational numbers. For example,

$\pi = 3.1415926536\ldots$, and $e = 2.718281285\ldots.$

2. We Can Write a Set by Using Mathematical Symbols

$A = \{x|x = 2k, k \in \mathbb{N}\}$,

which is, a set of positive even numbers.

The set of all Apple stock-holders can be written as:

$A = \{x|x \text{ is an Apple stockholder }\}$

which is read as the set of all x such that x is an Apple stockholder.

3- Using a closed curve. For example, the following form represents a set of 6 members. That is, $A = \{a, b, k, y, m, w, 3, 5, 7, 11, 13, 17\}$.

Figure 1. A set of 12 members in a closed curve

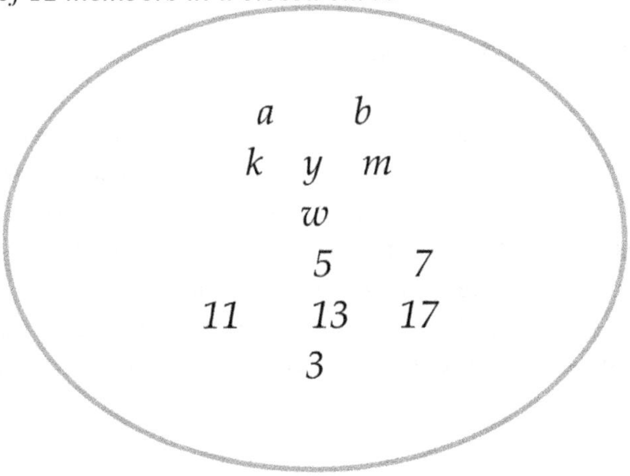

A set can be *finite* or *infinite*. For example, the first two sets are infinite

The other infinite sets that were introduced here, are the set of rational numbers, the set of irrational numbers and the set of real numbers.

We call set A, an *empty set* if it has no members. This set is also called the *null set*. We display this set as $\{\,\}$or $\varnothing$.

Note that $\{0\}$ or $\{\varnothing\}$ are sets with a single member. Even a set of the form $\{\{\,\}\}$ is not a null set. For example, consider an empty box that contains another empty box as a member in it.

Let's consider two sets A and B. If every member of B is a member of A, we say that B is a *subset* of A and we write it as $B \subset A$.

Two sets A and B are said to be equal, i.e. A=B, if and only if, $B \subset A$ and $A \subset B$. In other words

$$A = B \leftrightarrow B \subset A, A \subset B.$$

Remark 1: The null set is a subset of every set.

Remark 2:$\mathbb{N} \subset \mathbb{Z} \subset \mathbb{Q} \subset \mathbb{R}$.

It can be shown that the number of subsets of each set with n members is 2^n. For example, the set $A\{3,8\}$ has 4 subsets $\varnothing, \{3\}, \{8\}$ and $\{3,8\}$.

If a member is repeated in the set, it will not affect the number of members or the number of subsets. In other words, two sets are equal. For example, the sets {M, E, Ms} and {M, M, Ms, E, E, E} are equal.

The set of all subsets of a set A is called the *power set* of that set and is represented by the symbol $P(A)$.

According to the set $A = \{3,8\}$, we have

$$P(A) = \{\varnothing, \{3\}, (8\}, \{3,8\}\}.$$

Example 1: Determine the number of three-membered subsets of the set $A = \{a,b,c,d,e\}$.

Solution: If we count the number of subsets of three-membered subsets of this set, it is like trying to get the number of ways of three objects out of five different objects, i.e., $C(5,3)$. So, the number of ways is $\frac{5!}{3!(5-3)!} = 10$.

We call two sets are *disjointed* if they do not have a common member.

For example, A=$\{1,2,3\}$ and B=$\{a,b,c\}$ are disjoint sets.

We consider a set called the *reference set* or the *universal set* and consider all the other sets as subsets of this set. We show this set with U. So, for every set A, we have $A \subset U$.

Figure 2. Universal set with a subset A

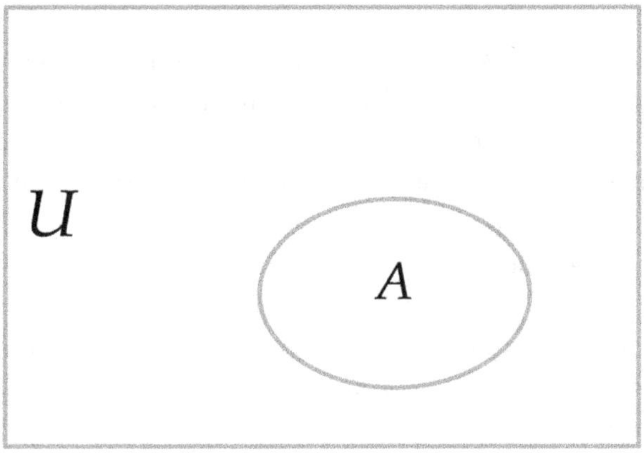

We define the *complement* of the set A, which is denoted by A', as a set that is all the members of the set U except for the members of the set A. In mathematical language

$$A' = \{x|x \in U, x \notin A\}.$$

Example 2: Suppose A is the reference set of a Ministry of Oil, write a reference set for it and then determine its complement.

Solution: We can choose the set of government employees as the reference set because the employees of the oil ministries are subsets of this set. The complement of this set is the set of government employees who are not employees of the Ministry of Oil.

We put in mind the following remarks about the supplement set.

Remark 3: The complement of a set A is equal to A. More briefly $(A')' = A$.

Remark 4: If two sets are equal, then their complements are also equal; that is,

$$A = B \rightarrow A' = B'.$$

Remark 5: The complement of the null set is equal to the reference set and the complement of the reference set is equal to the null set, so that

$$U' = \emptyset, \emptyset' = U.$$

2.3 SET OPERATIONS

In the previous section, we have familiarized ourselves with the basic concepts of sets. In this section, we turn our attention to algebraic operations related to them. These operations are completely different from algebraic operations related to natural numbers or real numbers. But many of their properties, such as *commutative*, *associative* and *distributive* properties, are preserved here as well. Here, we discuss three operations on sets and then we try to illustrate their applications.

1. The *union* of two sets A and B, which we denote by $A \cup B$, is a set whose members exist in A, B, or both. That is,
2. $A \cup B = \{x | x \in A \quad \text{or} \quad x \in B\}$.
   According to this definition, if $A \subset B$ then $A \cup B = B$.
3. The *intersection* of two sets A and B, denoted by $A \cap B$, is a set whose members exist in A and B, or both. Concisely
4. $A \cap B = \{x | x \in A \quad \text{and} \quad x \in B\}$.

For example, if $A = \{a,b,c,d\}$and$B = \{c,d,e,f\}$ then, $A \cap B = \{c,d\}$.

Figure 3. Intersection of two sets A and N, that is A ∩ B

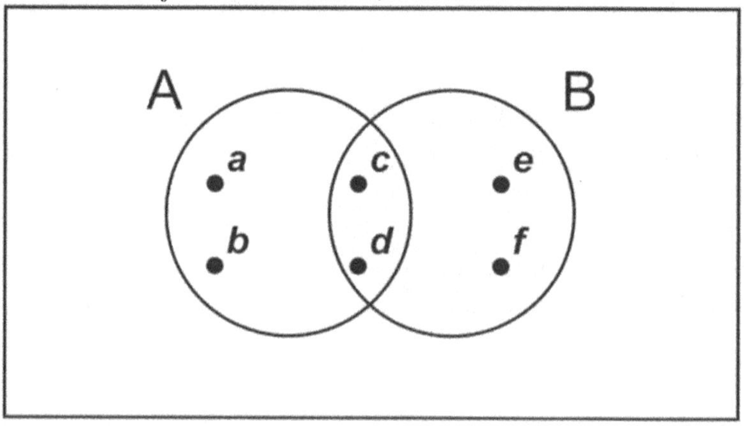

Similarly, if, $A \subset B$ then $A \cap B = A$.

Example 3: If $A = \mathbb{N}^*, B = \mathbb{Z}$ and C are the set of non-negative integers, determine

$A \cup B, A \cap B, B \cup C, B \cap C, A \cup C, A \cap C$.

Solution: Since $A \subset B$ and two sets A and C are distinct, then

$$A \cup B = B, A \cap B = A, B \cup C = B, B \cap C = C, A \cup C = B \text{and} A \cap C = \varnothing.$$

The following properties hold for sets under the operations of union, intersection and complement.

(i) Commutative Laws

$$\{A \cup B = B \cup A \quad A \cap B = B \cap A$$

(ii) Associative Laws

$$\begin{cases} (A \cup B) \cup C = A \cup (B \cup C) \\ (A \cap B) \cap C = A \cap (B \cap C) \end{cases}$$

(iii) Distributive Laws

$$\begin{cases} A \cup (B \cap C) = (A \cup B) \cap (A \cup C) \\ A \cap (B \cup C) = (A \cap B \cup (A \cap C) \end{cases}$$

(iv) Complement Laws

$$\begin{cases} A \cup A' = U \\ A \cap A' = \varnothing \end{cases}$$

Remark 6: $(A')' = A, U' = \varnothing, \varnothing' = U$.
Example 4: Show that $(A \cup B) \cap (A \cup B') = A$.
Solution: Due to the Distributive Laws, we have

$$(A \cup B) \cap (A \cup B') = A \cup (B \cap B').$$

But $B \cap B' = \varnothing$ and $A \cup \varnothing = A$, thus

$$(A \cup B) \cap (A \cup B') = A \cup \varnothing = A.$$

3- The Difference Between Sets *A* and *B*

It is a Set With Members That Belong to A Such That These Members Do Not Belong to B. It is Denoted by the Symbol A–B. That is,

$A - B = \{x | x \in A \quad \text{and} \quad x \notin B\}.$

Therefore, by using this definition, we have $A - B \subset B$. We also have $A - B = A \cap B'$. Because,

$\forall x \in (A - B) \rightarrow x \notin B, x \in A \rightarrow x \in B', x \in A \rightarrow x \in (A \cap B').$

Figure 4. Set of operation A–B

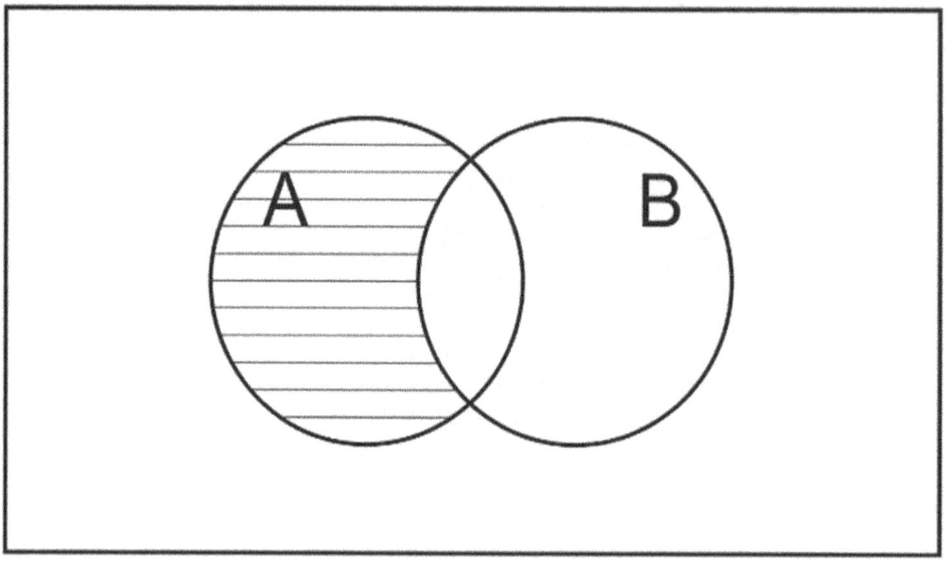

Example 5: Verify the set $A \cap B \cap (A - B)$.
Solution: Since we have $A - B = A \cap B'$, then

$A \cap B \cap (A - B) = A \cap B \cap A \cap B' = A \cap B \cap B' = A \cap \emptyset = \emptyset.$

Before we go further about operations in the algebra of sets, we introduce another difference called *symmetric difference*, which has the properties of commutability and associability. It is represented by the symbol $A\Delta B$ and is defined as follows.

$A\Delta B = A \cup B - A \cap B.$

In other words,

$A\Delta B = (A - B) \cup (B - A).$

That is,

$$A\Delta B = \{x \in A \cup B\Delta x \notin (A - B).$$

Two important formulas that are used to prove algebraic relations related to sets are the following formulas, which are also known as *De Morgan's laws*;

(i) $(A \cup B)' = B' \cap A'$
(ii) $(A \cap B)' = B' \cup A'$.

Example 6: Prove that $B - (A - B) = B$.
Solution: We use the difference formula and De Morgan's law. We will obtain

$$B - (A - B) = B \cap (A - B)' = B \cap (A \cap B')' = B \cap (A' \cup B) = B.$$

Because $B \subset (A' \cup B)$.
Sometimes, it is convenient to use the sets as the interior of some closed curves. For this purpose, any closed curve can be used as a representation of a set. For example, suppose the combination of two sets A and B are given in the following forms and the hatched part of the set is acceptable (see Figure 5).

Figure 5. Graphs of two operations $A \cap B$, $A \cup B$, and complement of B

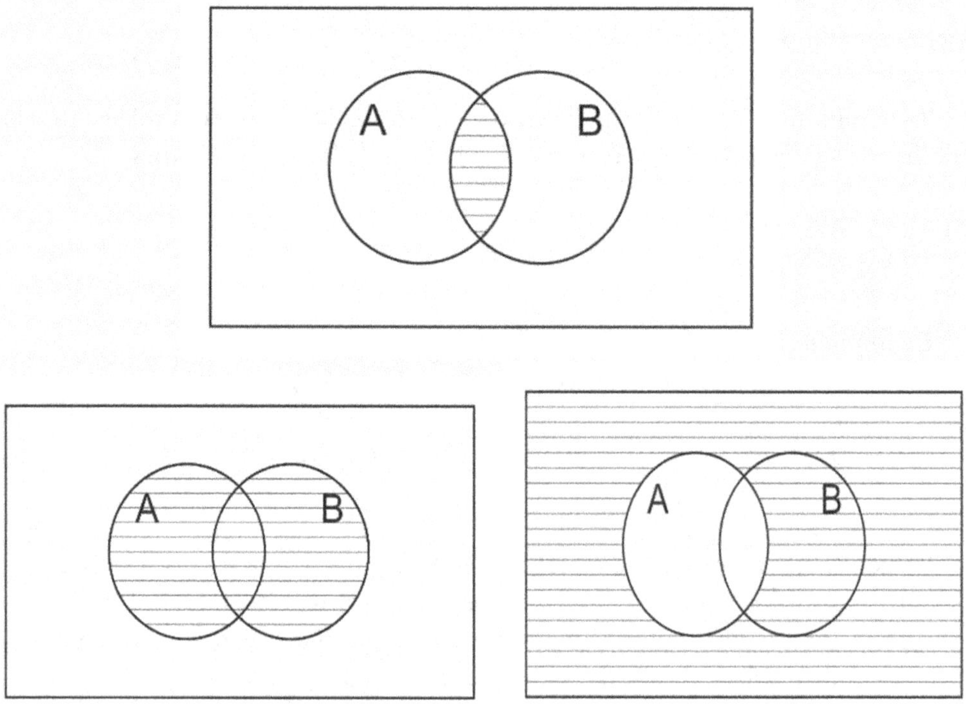

The given shapes are called *Venn diagrams*. In the Venn diagram, a rectangle can be used as a reference set and closed curves can be used as a representation of the sets inside this rectangle.

2.4 NUMBER OF ELEMENTS

The number of elements of a finite set such as A is called the *cardinal number* or *size* of that set and is represented by the symbol $n(A)$. For example, the cardinal numbers of the English and Persian alphabets are 26 and 32, respectively.

The following formulas related to the cardinal numbers can be used in solving problems.

(i) $n(A \cup B) = n(A) + n(B) - n(A \cap B)$

(ii) $n(justA) = n(A) - n(A \cap B)$

(iii) $n(A \cup B \cup C) = n(A) + n(B) + n(C) - n(A \cap B) - n(A \cap C) - n(B \cap C) + n(A \cap B \cap C)$

(iv) $n(justA) = n(A) - n(A \cap B) - n(A \cap C) + n(A \cap B \cap C)$.

As we mentioned, sets can be used in database management. For example, in a database of students, a set can be the collection of students who enrolled in a particular course. Set operations can then be used to find students who are enrolled for both course A and B (intersection), all students enrolled in either course A or course B (union), or students who are only enrolled in course A and not in course B (difference).

Example 7: From a class of 38 students, 16 students have chosen Math, 17 Accountings and 19 Financial Management for the first semester. If 6 students have written names in Math and Accounting, 8 students in Math and Financial Management, and 9 students in Accounting and Financial Management, how many of them have chosen all three subjects? How many people have only one subject?

Solution: Let A, B and C represents Math, Accounting and Financial Management, respectively. We have:

$$n(A \cup B \cup C) = 38, n(A) = 18, n(B) = 18, n(C) = 19, n(A \cap B) = 6,$$

$$n(A \cap C) = 8, n(B \cap C) = 9.$$

Thus,

$$38 = 18 + 18 + 19 - 6 - 8 - 9 + n(A \cap B \cap C) \rightarrow n(A \cap B \cap C) = 6.$$

So, 6 students have chosen all three courses together this semester. Now, the students who have written their names on only one course are those who have chosen the course of Mathematics, Accounting or Financial Management. As a result, we obtain

$$n(justA) = 18 - 6 - 8 + 6 = 10$$

$$n(justB) = 18 - 6 - 9 + 6 = 9$$

$$n(justC) = 19 - 8 - 9 + 6 = 8.$$

Hence, 27 of them have chosen only one course.

We end this section with the following example.

Example 8: The Department of Education School of Management of Shomal University announced the list of exams for 60 participants to the director of the school as follows:

12 passed, 15 failed in Math and Management, 10 in English and Management, and 5 in all three. In addition, none of the students failed math and English courses together. The faculty administration returned the report to education as a protest. Education realized that it had made a mistake in its report. Determine how to make this mistake.

Solution: Let A, B and C represents Math, English and Management. We have

$$n(A \cup B \cup C) = 60, n(A) = 25, n(B) = 18, n(C) = 21, n(A \cap B) = 0$$

$$n(A \cap C) = 15, n(B \cap C) = 10, n(A \cap B \cap C) = 5.$$

It is easy to specify that these results cannot be true because

$$60 \neq 25 + 18 + 21 - 0 - 15 - 10 + 5.$$

We may wonder why we ignored 12 students who passed. Even if we want to consider this number, the training report is still not correct.

To have more information about the sets, readers may refer to (Halmose, 1998) (Enderton, 1977) (Pinter, 1971) (Kunen, 2014) (Jech., 2013) (Kunen, 1980) (Lévy, 1978).

One of the results related to the cardinality of finite sets is derived from a principle called, the *principle of inclusion and exclusion,* which stated that:

If X is a finite set such that $n(X)=N$ and conditions C_i, $1 \leq i \leq m$ hold for some of elements of X. The number of elements of X that do not satisfy these conditions, denoted by $\overline{N} = N(\overline{C_1 C_2 \ldots C_m})$ is

$$\overline{N} = = N - \sum_{1 \leq i \leq m} n(C_i) + \sum_{1 \leq i,j \leq m} n(C_i C_j) + \sum_{1 \leq i,j,k \leq m} n(C_i C_j C_k) + \ldots + (-1)^m n(C_i C_j \ldots C_m).$$

Example 9: Suppose $X=\{1,2,\ldots,600\}$. Find the numbers $1 \leq n \leq 600$ such that is not divisible by 3,5,7 or 11.

Solution: Let's A, B, C and D are those subsets of X not divisible by 3,5,7 or 11 respectively. Here $N=600$ and for $n \in N$, we assume: C_1 is the condition that if n is divisible by 3, C_2 is the condition that if n is divisible by 5, C_3 is the condition that if n is divisible by 7 and C_4 is the condition that if n is divisible by 11, then $\overline{N} = N(\overline{C_1 C_2 C_3 C_4})$ is right answer to this problem. We have

$$N(C_1) = \left[\frac{600}{3}\right] = 200, N(C_2) = \left[\frac{600}{5}\right] = 120, N(C_3) = \left[\frac{600}{7}\right] = 85 \text{and} N(C_4) = \left[\frac{600}{11}\right] = 54.$$

Similarly,

$N(C_1C_2) = N(C_1 \cap C_2) = \left[\frac{600}{15}\right] = 40, N(C_1C_3) = N(C_1 \cap C_3) = \left[\frac{600}{21}\right] = 28,$
$N(C_1C_4) = N(C_1 \cap C_4) = \left[\frac{600}{33}\right] = 18, N(C_2C_3) = N(C_2 \cap C_3) = \left[\frac{600}{35}\right] = 17,$
$N(C_2C_4) = N(C_2 \cap C_4) = \left[\frac{600}{55}\right] = 10, N(C_1C_2C_3) = N(C_1 \cap C_2 \cap C_3) = \left[\frac{600}{105}\right] = 5,$
$N(C_1C_2C_4) = N(C_1 \cap C_2 \cap C_4) = \left[\frac{600}{165}\right] = 3, N(C_2C_3C_4) = N(C_2 \cap C_3 \cap C_4) = \left[\frac{600}{385}\right] = 1$
and$N(C_1C_2C_3C_4) = N(C_1 \cap C_2 \cap C_3 \cap C_4) = \left[\frac{600}{1155}\right] = 0.$

Therefore,
$N(\overline{C_1C_2C_3C_4}) = 600 - (200 + 120 + 85 + 54) + (40 + 28 + 18 + 17 + 10) - (5 + 3 + 1) + (0) = 245.$

In the previous chapter we considered the number of the integer solutions of the equation

$$x_1 + x_2 + \ldots + x_n = r, x_i \geq 0.$$

By the principle of inclusion and exclusion, we can solve such equations with more restrictions.

Example 10: Find the numbers of nonnegative integer solutions in the following equation.

$$x_1 + x_2 + x_3 = 20, x_i \leq 8(i = 1,2,3).$$

Solution: Here X is the set of solutions of this equation, then $n(x) = C(3 + 20 - 1, 12) = C(22, 20)$. If we assume, we are looking for solution x_i>8 ie., x_i≥9 then the answer is $N(\overline{C_1C_2C_3})$. We have $N(C_1) = N(C_2) = N(C_3)$. To find $N(C_1)$ we look to find the number of nonnegative integer solutions to

$$x_1 + x_2 + x_3 = 12, x_i \geq 0(i = 1,2,3).$$

It will be $N(C_i) = C(3 + 12 - 1, 12) = C(14, 12)$. Similarly, the number of nonnegative integer solutions to

$$x_1 + x_2 + x_3 = 4, x_i \geq 0(i = 1,2,3)$$

is $N(C_iC_j) = C(3 + 4 - 1, 4) = C(6, 4)$. It is clear that $N(C_1C_2C_3) = 0$.
Therefore,

$$N(\overline{C_1C_2C_3}) = C(22, 20) - 3C(14, 12) + 3C(6, 4) - (0) = 231 - 273 + 45 = 3.$$

To read more about the principle of inclusion and exclusion, the readers may refer to (Grimaldi, 1989) (Liu, 2002) (Grossman, 1995) (Stanat, 1977) (Stone, 1973) (Sahni, 1981).

2.5 PROPOSITIONS

A proposition is a statement that is either true or false, although its correctness or incorrectness has not yet been known to us. The reason why we choose the proposition as a news sentence is that in the wording of interrogative, imperative or exclamation sentences, it is not possible to judge their correctness or incorrectness.

Example 11: Which of the following statements is proposition?

(i) $cos^2x + sin^2x = 1, \forall x \in \mathbb{R}$.
(ii) $x^3 - 4x^2 + 6x = 4, \forall x \in \mathbb{R}$
(iii) Does the register increase the speed of program execution on the computer?
(iv) Jack London is a writer.
(v) The thousandth digit of the number $\pi = 3.1415926536...$ after the decimal point is 4.

Solution: The statements (i) and (iv) are true propositions. (iii) is not a proposition because speed is relative and its meaning changes with time.

(ii) For x=2 is a proposition. (v) It can be a proposition, but for the time being we do not know about its correctness.

The truth or falsity of a statement is called the value of the statement and is represented by T and F respectively, and the letters $p,q,r,...$ are usually used for statements.

The *contradiction* of a statement like *p,* is the statement itself is opposite to the value of the given statement, and it is represented by the symbol *~p,* and read "not *p*". It should be noted that in describing the contradiction of a proposition, there is no need to take any action on the proposition except that the verb of the proposition is negated. For example, in the case of the contradiction of the statement that "the registry with the volume of 3 is large", it cannot be said that "the registry with the volume of 3 is small", but it can be stated that "the registry with the volume of 3 is not large".

2.5.1 Connective and Truth Tables

Logic is not only concerned with the true values of statements. Consider the following examples:

(i) London is the capital of UK and Texas is the capital of USA.
(ii) If Mr. Biden and Mrs. Harris do not want to be president, so either Mr. Biden does not want to be, or Mrs. Harris does not want to be president.

The first sentence consists of two propositions that are related by the letter "and". In a natural language, the value of a sentence cannot be determined precisely because part of the sentence is true and part is false.

In the second sentence, it is not necessary to know whether Mr. Biden or Mrs. Harris wants to become the president and vice versa. To determine whether this statement is true or not, we specify a criterion that does not face these ambiguities.

The mentioned statements are examples of compound prepositions that are composed of the words, "*and*", "*or*", "*not*", "*if...then*".A combination with "*and*" is an *injunction combination*, with "*or*" is a *disjunction combination*, and with "*if... then*" is called a *conditional combination*. In the following parts, we will evaluate these combinations by some *truth tables*.

(a) **Injunction Combination**

We denote the injunction combination of statements p and q with p^q. This combination is true when p and q are both true. Its truth table is given in Table 1.

Table 1. Injunction combination

p	q	p^q
⋮	⋮	⋮
T	T	T
T	F	F
F	T	F
F	F	F

As you can see, according to the definition of the truth table, the proposition in (i) is not true because the truth of both propositions does not occur at the same time.

(b) **Disjunction Combination**

We denote this combination of statements p and q with $p\vee q$. This combination is true when one of statements p or q is true. Its truth table is given in Table 2.

Table 2. Disjunction combination

p	q	$p\vee q$
⋮	⋮	⋮
T	T	T
T	F	T
F	T	T
F	F	F

Obviously, according to the definition of the truth table, the proposition in (ii) is true because the truth of one of the statements occurs.

(c) **Conditional Combination**

The statement $p\rightarrow q$, reads " if p then q" (or p implies q) is a conditional combination. Before we state its truthful, we consider the following statement.

If she gets a score higher than 12 in the applied math subject, then she can choose the operation research subject.

Suppose p means that we got a score higher than 12 in the math subject and q means that we chose the operations research subject. We examined the following four cases:

1. p is true; she got a score higher than 12 in the math.
   q is true; she chose the operation research.
2. p is true; she got a score higher than 12 in the math.
   q is not true; she chose the operation research.
3. p is not true; she got a score higher than 12 in the math.
   q is true; she chose the operation research.
4. p is not true; she got a score higher than 12 in the math.
   q is not true; she chose the operation research.

It is clear that in case (1), we accept that the student tells true. But in case (2) it can easily be find that the student lies. In case (3), it is not fair to say the student lies because although she chose the operation research subject, she did not get a score of more than 12. The same happens for case (4). It means we cannot claim that she lies.

Therefore, we can have the following truth table (Table 3).

Table 3. Conditional combination

p	q	$p \to q$
⋮	⋮	⋮
T	*T*	*T*
T	*F*	*F*
F	*T*	*T*
F	*F*	*T*

In Table 3, we conclude that when *p* is true but *q* is false, then the conditional combination is not true.

Remark 7: This condition appears in languages of computer science.

In our study of algorithms when "if…then" is used as a control structure, *p* acts when *q* is true. If *p* is false, the operation goes to another line.

(d) **Biconditional Combination**

Any statement in the form of $p \leftrightarrow q$, reads "*p* if and only if *q*" is called a *biconditional combination*. It is true when the two propositions have the same truth table. That is, both are true or false. Its truth table is shown in Table 4.

Table 4. Biconditional combination

p	q	$p \leftrightarrow q$
⋮	⋮	⋮
T	*T*	*T*
T	*F*	*F*
F	*T*	*F*
F	*F*	*T*

Example 12: Write truth table for r^$(p \leftrightarrow q)$.

Solution: We use the following truth tables given statement.

Table 5. Truth table for r^(p q)

p	q	r	p↔q	r^(p↔q)
T	F	T	F	F
T	F	F	F	F
T	T	T	T	T
T	T	F	T	F
F	F	T	T	T
F	F	F	T	F
F	T	T	F	F
F	T	F	F	F

Example 13: Write the truth table for $p\vee(\sim r\rightarrow q)$.
Solution: With the same operation we get the following results Table 6.

Table 6. Truth table for p (~r q)

p	q	r	~r	~r→q	p∨(~r→q)
T	F	T	F	T	T
T	F	F	T	F	T
T	T	T	F	F	T
T	T	F	T	T	T
F	F	T	F	T	T
F	F	F	T	F	F
F	T	T	F	F	F
F	T	F	T	T	T

Example 14: Examine the truth table for the following component statements.

(i) If two sections A and B of a system do not work, then part A or part B does not work.
(ii) The computer is on and working and it is not on.

Solution: *(i)*- If p and q denote, respectively, sections A and the section B work, then the statement can be expressed as $\sim(p \wedge q) \rightarrow (\sim p \vee \sim q)$. Its truth table is given in Table 7.

Table 7. Truth table for tautology

p	q	$p \wedge q$	$\sim(p \wedge q)$	$\sim p$	$\sim q$	$\sim p \vee \sim q$	$\sim(p \wedge q) \rightarrow (\sim p \vee \sim q)$
T	*F*	*F*	*T*	*F*	*T*	*T*	*T*
T	*T*	*T*	*F*	*F*	*F*	*F*	*T*
F	*T*	*F*	*T*	*T*	*F*	*T*	*T*
F	*F*	*F*	*T*	*T*	*T*	*T*	*T*

The last column of the truth table contains only That is, the statement is always true. Such statement is called *tautology.*

(ii) For this case, let's p and q denote "the computer is on" and "the computer works", respectively. Thus, we have the expression given by $(p \wedge q) \wedge \sim p$. We write the truth table, which is given in Table 8.

Table 8. Truth table for contradiction

p	q	$p \wedge q$	$\sim p$	$(p \wedge q) \wedge \sim p$
T	*F*	*F*	*F*	*F*
T	*T*	*T*	*F*	*F*
F	*T*	*F*	*T*	*F*
F	*F*	*F*	*T*	*F*

In this table, the last column contains only *F*. That is, the statement is always false. Such statement is called a *contradiction*

Example 15: Verify whether the component statement given by $(p \rightarrow q) \leftrightarrow (\sim q \rightarrow \sim p)$is tautology or not.

Solution: By constructing the truth table, we get Table 9.

Table 9. Truth table for tautology

p	q	$\sim p$	$\sim q$	$p \rightarrow q$	$\sim q \rightarrow \sim p$	$(p \rightarrow q) \leftrightarrow (\sim q \rightarrow \sim p)$
T	*T*	*F*	*F*	*T*	*T*	*T*
T	*F*	*F*	*T*	*F*	*F*	*T*
F	*T*	*T*	*F*	*T*	*T*	*T*
F	*F*	*T*	*T*	*T*	*T*	*T*

Since the last column of the truth table contains only T, hence the statement is a tautology.

Let's consider the following statement:

"It is not that the entry and exit of staff in the office is not checked".

We could say:

"The entry and exit of staff in the office is checked".

The second statement is simpler than the first statement. If we write these two statements symbolically, we will see that these two statements are the same.

If we assume that p and q are the statements "Staff enter to office" and "Staff leave the office" respectively, then its truth table will be given by Table 10.

Table 10. Truth table for two equivalent statements

p	q	$\sim p$	$\sim q$	$\sim p \wedge \sim q$	$\sim(\sim p \wedge \sim q)$	$p \vee q$
T	T	F	F	F	T	T
T	F	F	T	F	T	T
F	T	T	F	T	T	T
F	F	T	T	T	F	F

As you can see, the last two columns are the same. In this case, two propositions are *equivalent*. In the general case, two given expressions S_1 and S_2 with the same variables are called logical equivalent if the two propositions are equivalents and we write $S_1 \equiv S_2$.

Example 16: Show that $(p \rightarrow q) \wedge (q \rightarrow p) \equiv p \leftrightarrow q$.

Solution: We construct the truth table given by Table 11.

Table 11. Truth table for two two equivalent statements

p	q	$p \rightarrow q$	$q \rightarrow p$	$p \leftrightarrow q$	$(p \rightarrow q) \wedge (q \rightarrow p)$
T	T	T	T	T	T
T	F	F	T	F	F
F	T	T	F	F	F
F	F	T	T	T	T

Since the last two columns of the truth table are the same, thus these two statements are equivalent.

Although the correctness of many relationships related to propositions can be proven using the truth tables, as in many scientific topics, we use special relationships and formulas or rules to prove a given result or theorem. In mathematical logic, there are rules that are similar in many ways to the rules we have already met. In the following, by mentioning these rules, we will explain their applications with some examples. More about mathematical logic can be read in (Supess, 1957) (Delong, 1970) (Stoll, 1963) (Ederton, 2001) (Mendelson, 2015) (Koslow, 1992) (Kriesel & Krivine, 1967) (Kunen, 1980) (Priest, 2001) (Gibson, 1981).

2.5.2 Logical Laws

We know that multiplication has the properties of commutative, associative and distribute laws (rules) that can be extended to mathematical logic and obtain other types of laws whose correctness can be proven using truth tables. These rules help us to deduce other logical relationships from them.

Laws of the Algebra of Propositions

1. Commutative Laws:
   (i) $p \vee q \equiv q \vee p$
   (ii) $p \wedge q \equiv q \wedge p$
2. Associative Laws:
   (i) $(p \vee q) \vee r \equiv p \vee (q \vee r)$
   (ii) $(p \vee q) \vee r \equiv p \vee (q \vee r)$
3. Distributive Laws:
   (i) $p \vee (q \wedge r) \equiv (p \vee q) \wedge (p \vee r)$
   (ii) $p \wedge (q \vee r) \equiv (p \wedge q) \vee (p \wedge r)$
4. Idempotent Laws:
   (i) $p \vee p \equiv p$
   (ii) $p \wedge p \equiv p$
5. Complement Laws:
   (i) $p \vee {\sim}p \equiv T$
   (ii) $p \wedge {\sim}p \equiv F$
   (iii) ${\sim}{\sim}p \equiv p$
   (iv) ${\sim}T \equiv F, {\sim}F \equiv T$
6. DeMorgan's Laws:
   (i) ${\sim}(p \vee q) \equiv {\sim}p \wedge {\sim}q$
   (ii) ${\sim}(p \wedge q) \equiv {\sim}p \vee {\sim}q$
7. Absorption Laws:
   (i) $p \wedge (p \vee q) \equiv p$
   (ii) $p \vee (p \wedge q) \equiv p$
8. Annihihilation Laws:
   (i) $p \wedge F \equiv F$
   (ii) $p \vee T \equiv T$

9. Inverse Laws:
   (i) $p \wedge {\sim}p \equiv F$
   (ii) $p \vee {\sim}p \equiv T$
10. Identity Laws:
   (i) $p \wedge T \equiv p$
   (ii) $p \vee F \equiv p$
11. Implication Laws:
   (i) $p \wedge T \equiv p$
   (ii) $p \vee F \equiv p$
12. Biconditional Laws:
   (i) $p \leftrightarrow q \equiv (q \rightarrow p) \wedge (p \rightarrow q) \equiv (p \vee q) \rightarrow (p \wedge q)$.

Example 17: By using the logical laws, show that

(i) $(p \vee q) \wedge {\sim}({\sim}p \wedge q) \equiv p$
(ii) ${\sim}[{\sim}[(p \wedge q) \wedge r] \vee {\sim}q] \equiv q \wedge r$.

Solution: We use step by step the logical laws. We get

(i) Complement law: $(p \vee q) \wedge {\sim}({\sim}p \wedge q) \equiv (p \vee q) \wedge (p \vee {\sim}q)$
Distributive Law $\equiv p \vee (q \wedge {\sim}q)$
Inverse Law $\equiv p \vee F$
Identity Laws $\equiv p$.
(ii) DeMorgan's Law: ${\sim}[{\sim}[(p \wedge q) \wedge r] \vee {\sim}q] \equiv {\sim}{\sim}[(p \vee q) \wedge r] \wedge ({\sim}{\sim}q)$
Complement law$\equiv [(p \vee q) \wedge r] \wedge q$
Distributive Law$\equiv (p \vee q) \wedge (r \wedge q)$
Commutative Law$\equiv (p \vee q) \wedge (q \wedge r)$
Distributive Law$\equiv [(p \vee q) \wedge q] \wedge r$
Absorption Law $\equiv q$^r.

Example 18: Prove that the following statement is a tautology.

$[[(p \rightarrow q \wedge {\sim}q)] \rightarrow {\sim}p]$.

Solution: We do the same as previous example. We get
Implication Laws: $[[(p \rightarrow q \wedge {\sim}q)] \rightarrow {\sim}p] \equiv {\sim}[{\sim}(p \vee q) \wedge {\sim}q] \vee {\sim}p$

Commutative Law$\equiv {\sim}[{\sim}q \wedge {\sim}(p \vee q)] \vee {\sim}p$
Distributive Law$\equiv {\sim}[({\sim}q \wedge {\sim}p) \vee ({\sim}q \wedge q)] \vee {\sim}p$
Commutative Law$\equiv {\sim}[({\sim}q \wedge {\sim}p) \vee (q \wedge {\sim}q)] \vee {\sim}p$

Inverse Law≡ $\sim[(\sim q \wedge \sim p) \vee F] \vee \sim p$
Identity Law≡ $\sim[(\sim q \wedge \sim p)] \vee \sim p$
DeMorgan's Law ≡ $(\sim\sim q \vee \sim\sim p) \vee \sim p$
Complement Law≡ $(q \vee p) \vee \sim p$
Associative Law≡ $q \vee (p \vee \sim p)$
Inverse Law ≡ $q \vee T$
Annihihilation Law ≡ T.

Although propositional logic provides useful expressions to analyze many logical statements, but some time we encounter with statements so that we cannot deal with algebraic of propositions. For example, consider the following propositions:

1. There exists a number x such that $\cos x+\sin x=1$.
2. For all number of x we have $x + \frac{1}{x} > 2$.

The first statement is true. For example, suppose $x=0$, but the second statement cannot be true. For example, let put $x= -1$.

As we see, the correctness of statements depends on the value of x.

These statements are known as *open statements*. The expressions "for all' and "there exists" are called *quantifiers* and denoted by $"\forall" and "\exists"$.

A statement containing one or more variables is called a *predicate* and denoted by $P(x)$.

Example 19: What is the truth value of the statement given by:

$$\forall x \in \mathbb{R}^+, x + \frac{1}{x} \geq 2.$$

Solution: The value of this statement is true, because since $x>0$ then, we can write

$$x + \frac{1}{x} \geq 2 \Rightarrow x^2 + 1 \geq 2x \Rightarrow x^2 - 2x + 1 \geq 0 \Rightarrow (x-1)^2 \geq 0.$$

Therefore, this expression holds $\forall x \in \mathbb{R}^+$.

Example 20: What is the truth value of the statement given by:

$$\forall x \in \mathbb{R}, 3x^2 - 2x - 1 = 0.$$

Solution: The value of this statement is not true, because let $x=2$ then, we get

$$3(2)^2 - 2(2) - 1 = 1 \neq 0.$$

But, this expression holds if $x = 1$ or $x = -\frac{1}{3}$

Example 21: What is the truth value of the statement given by:

$$\forall x \in \{-1,0,1\}, \exists y \in \mathbb{R}, x^2 + y^2 = xy.$$

Solution: The value of this statement is not true, because if we choose x=1, we will obtain

$$1 + y^2 = y \Rightarrow y^2 - y + 1 = 0.$$

This equation has not real solutions because $\Delta = b^2 - 4ac = 1 - 4 = -3 < 0.$

Example 22: Write the following two propositions in symbolic forms:

(i) For all x there exists a number y such that $x^2+y^2=3xy$.
(ii) There exist x and y such that $x^2+y^2=0$.

Solution: (i)-Assume $P(x,y)$ denotes the predicate "$x^2+y^2=3xy$", then we write

$$\forall x \exists y P(x,y).$$

(ii) Similarly, for this proposition we can write

$$\forall x \exists y P(x,y).$$

We end this chapter by introducing some methods of proving things which are related to propositions.

How to prove theorems and solve mathematical problems is called *mathematical proof*. Knowing the rules and different methods of argument increases the student's ability to solve problems. Tautology is an important category of these rules.

Here we introduce some examples of mathematical proofs, even though most of them have been used directly or indirectly without knowing their names. In previous chapter, we met one of these methods namely, mathematical induction or *inductive proof*. Here we introduce some more methods.

(a) ***Analogy proof***: Analogy is finding similarities between different concepts. In the terms of classical logic, it is to understand one part from another. For example, "A calculator is a computing computer that performs at least four basic operations, is a true statement. Or as another example:

$$[(p \rightarrow q) \wedge (q \rightarrow r)] \equiv p \rightarrow r.$$

(b) ***Direct proof***: In this method, a statement is required with a given assumption, using concepts and propositions that have already been proven or accepted to prove the correctness of the statement.

Example 23: Prove that

$$\forall x \in \mathbb{R}, x^2 + \frac{1}{x^2} \geq 2.$$

Solution: We e write

$$x^2 + \frac{1}{x^2} \geq 2 \Rightarrow x^4 + 1 \geq 2x^2 \Rightarrow x^4 - 2x^2 + 1 \geq 0 \Rightarrow (x^2 - 1)^2 \geq 0.$$

Since $x \in \mathbb{R}$, then this relation holds.

(c) ***Contra-contradictory proof***: In this method, we assume the contradiction of the statement, and we will arrive at the contradiction of the premise in a direct way, because, we have already shown that $p \rightarrow q \equiv {\sim}q \rightarrow {\sim}p$.

Example 23: Prove that if the square of a number is odd, then this number is odd.
Solution: This statement is equivalent to the statement "If a number is even, then its square is even". This statement is the opposite of the first statement, which is easier to prove. Let's $x = 2k, x \in \mathbb{R}$, thus

$$x = 4k = 2(2k) = 2k, k \in \mathbb{Z}.$$

That is, x is also an even number.

(d) ***Reductio ad absurdum***: A method of proof which proceeds by assuming the falsity of what we wish to prove and showing that it leads to contradiction, (Ederton, 2001). Hence, the statement whose falsity we assumed must be true.

Example 22: Prove that $\sqrt{3}$ is an irrational number.
Solution: Assume $\sqrt{3}$is not an irrational number, then we can write

$$\sqrt{3} = \frac{a}{b}, (a,b) = 1 \rightarrow 3 = \frac{a^2}{b^2} \rightarrow a^2 = 3b^2.$$

That is a is divisible by 3. Therefore, $3^2 = 3b^2 \rightarrow b^2 = 3k'$. But, $(a,b)=1$, hence our assumption is not true. That is $\sqrt{3}$ cannot be a rational number.

(e) ***Contradictory proof***: If it seems that a statement is not correct in general, taking an example violates the statement and makes us reach the desired result faster.

Example 24: Prove that if P is a prime number, then P^2+P+1 is also a prime number.

Solution: let's $p=7$. We get, $7^2+7+1=57$ which is not a prime number and this result violates the statement.

(f) ***Inference proof***: The inference method is a kind of *implication method* whose premise consists of one or more propositions. In other words,

$$(p_1 \wedge p_2 \wedge \ldots \wedge p_n) \rightarrow q,$$

where, $p_1, p_2, \ldots, p_n$ are implications.

Example 25: Let's p_1, p_2, p_3 and q are the following propositions:

p_1: If A studies, then he will pass math.
p_2: If A doesn't play soccer, then he will study.
p_3: A failed the math lesson.
q: A has played football.

We want to know whether the correctness of the propositions p_1, p_2, p_3 leads to the correctness of the proposition q or not?

Solution: let's p:A studies math, r:A passed math, s:A plays football, then

$$q{:}s, p_3{:}\sim r, p_2{:}\sim s \rightarrow p, p_1{:}p \rightarrow r.$$

Now we can determine whether the proposition given by

$$[(p \rightarrow r) \wedge (\sim s \rightarrow p) \wedge \sim r] \rightarrow s$$

is true or not by using the truth table. For this purpose, we specify the truth table (see Table 12).

Table 12. Truth table for tautology

p	q	$p \rightarrow r$	$\sim r$	$\sim s$	$\sim s \rightarrow p$	$[(p \rightarrow r) \wedge (\sim s \rightarrow p) \wedge \sim r] \rightarrow s$
T	T	T	F	F	T	T
T	T	T	F	T	T	T
T	F	F	T	F	T	T

p	q	$p \to r$	$\sim r$	$\sim s$	$\sim s \to p$	$[(p \to r) \land (\sim s \to p) \land \sim r] \to s$
T	F	F	T	T	T	T
F	T	T	F	F	T	T
F	T	T	F	T	F	T
F	F	T	T	F	T	T
F	F	T	T	T	F	T

According to this table, we have a tautology statement. In other words, the above result is true

(g) ***Existence or Unique existence proof***: The existence of existential quantifiers in some problems leads to proof of existence. We complete this chapter by citing an example.

Example 26: Prove that there is another rational number between two rational numbers.

Solution: Suppose these two rational numbers are a and b where $b>a$. From this inequality we get $2b > a + b$, i.e, $b > \frac{a+b}{2}$. Similarly, from $a<b$, we obtain $a < \frac{a+b}{2}$. Therefore, $a < \frac{a+b}{2} < b$. that is, there exists a rational number between a and b, which is the arithmetic mean of a and b.

In the end, we remind you that the induction method mentioned in the previous chapter is a type of proof.

CONCLUSION

In this chapter, after introducing the sets and set algebra and Venn diagrams, we could solve some problems related to counting problems. Moreover, by the principle of inclusion and exclusion, we could deal with more problems with counting. We also introduced propositions and the algebra of propositions and their applications. We found how important they are, in particular the use of

them on computers. Most of the time, they are used in the control structure of the algorithm. By introducing truth tables we could solve most of problems related to propositions. By discussing some methods of proving we could also deal with more problems.

2.6 Exercises

1. Which of the following statements is correct?
   (i) $\{\varnothing\} \in \{\varnothing,\{\varnothing\}\}$
   (ii) $\{\varnothing\} \subset \{\varnothing,\{\varnothing\}\}$
   (iii) $\{\{\varnothing\}\} \in \{\varnothing,\{\varnothing\}\}$
   (iv) $\{\varnothing\} \subset \{\varnothing,\{\varnothing,\{\varnothing\}\}\}$
   (v) $\{\{\varnothing\}\} \subset \{\varnothing,\{\varnothing\}\}$
   (vi) $\{\{\varnothing\}\} \subset \{\{\varnothing\},\{\{\}\}\}$
2. Show the correctness of the following equalities using algebra sets.
   (i) $A - (A \cap B) = A - B$
   (ii) $(A \cup B)' - C = (A \cup B \cup C)'$
   (iii) $(A \cup B) \cup (A - B) = A \cup B$
   (iv) $(A \cup B) - (B \cup C) = (A - B) - C$
   (v) $[(A \cup B) - A'] \cup [(B \cup (A - B')] - A' = A$
   (vi) $(A - B) \cap (C - D) = (A \cap C) - (B \cup D)$
   (vii) $((A \cup B) \cap C) \cap B = B \cap C$.
3. Prove that for both sets A and B we have $P(A) \cap P(B) = P(A \cap B)$. Is this issue also valid for community law? Show whether $P(A) \cup P(B) = P(A \cup B)$ is correct or not.
4. Show with an example that the relation $(A \cap B) \cup C = (A \cup B) \cap C$ does not hold. In which cases the relations $A' \cap B = B$ and $A \cup B' = B'$ are correct. Give an example.
5. If B and C are subsets of A, investigate whether the following relation is true or false. $(A - B) \cap (A - C) = A - (B \cap C)$.
6. Simplify each of the following sets using properties of sets.
   (i) $(A \cap B) \cup (A \cap B \cap C') \cup (A' \cap B)$
   (ii) $(A \cap B) \cup (A \cap B') \cup (A' \cap B) \cup (A' \cap B')$
   (iii) $A' \cup (A \cap B') \cup (A \cap B \cap C') \cup (A \cap B \cap C \cap D') \cup \ldots$
7. Prove the truth or falsity of the following relationships using Venn diagrams or other methods.
   (i) $A \Delta (B \Delta C) = (A \Delta B) \Delta C$
   (ii) $A \Delta (B \cup C) = (A \Delta B) \cup (A \Delta C)$
   (iii) $A \cap (B \Delta C) = (A \cap B) \Delta (A \cap C)$
   (iv) $A \cup (B \Delta C) = (A \cup B) \Delta (A \cup C)$.

8. There are p number of factories in a city. Each of these factories produces wares A or B or both. We know that m and n of these factories produce ware A and B, respectively. By using set theory, determine how many of these factories produce both wares A and B. Obtain the possible condition of the answer.
9. The Faculty of Management has one hundred students who jointly took the exam in three courses, A, B and C. Sixty people have accepted all three courses. Twelve people failed only in A, five people only in A and B, three people together in A, B and C, eight people together in A and C and five people together in B and C courses. The number of failed students was equal only on A and B courses. Determine how many failed only in subject C and how many of them failed in only one subject.
10. In choosing a new computer, a college examines 12 different models according to the following considerations:
    (i) Magnetic rotating tape, A.
    (ii) Terminal for graphical display, B.
    (iii) Semiconductor memory C.
    in addition to nuclear memory. The number of computers that have one or more of these aspects are $n(A) = n(B) = n(C) = 7, n(A \cap B) = n(B \cap C) = 2, n(A \cap C) = 3, n(A \cap B \cap C) = 0$.
    (a) How many models, exactly, have one of the desired aspects?
    (b) How many models do not have any of the desired aspects?
11. In how many ways can the 26 letters of the alphabet be permuted so that the word's boy, girl or young occur?
12. In a survey of 100 consumers, 25 wanted to buy chicken, 36 wanted to buy alcoholic drinks and 42 wanted to buy fruit. If 10 wanted to buy the first two items, 8 wanted to buy the second and the third items and 15 wanted to buy the first and third items. How many do not want to buy any of these items? How many wanted to buy only the third item?
13. Use the principle of inclusion and exclusion to find the number of non-negative integer solutions to the following equations.
    (i) $x_1 + x_2 + x_3 \leq 10, 1 \leq x_i \leq 5 (i = 1,2,3)$.
    (ii) $x_1 + x_2 + x_3 + x_4 \leq 20, x_i \leq 8 (i = 1,2,3), x_4 \geq 4$.
    (iii) $x_1 + x_2 + x_3 + x_4 + x_5 \leq 30, x_i \leq 12 (i = 1,2,3), 2 \leq x_4, x_5 \leq 8$.
14. Out of 15 television sets in a store, 3 are black and white. In how many ways can the hotel owner buy 8 of them so that at least 2 of them are black and white?

15. Write the truth tables of the following expressions. Determine which of them are tautologies or contradictions?
    (i) $\sim(p \vee \sim q) \vee p$
    (ii) $[p \rightarrow (p \wedge q)] \rightarrow \sim q$
    (iii) $(p \wedge q) \leftrightarrow (\sim p \vee \sim q)$
    (iv) $[(p \wedge r) \vee (p \vee r) \rightarrow (p \vee \sim q)$
    (v) $(p \wedge \sim q) \vee (\sim p \vee q)$
    (vi) $[p \rightarrow (q \rightarrow p)] \leftrightarrow (p \wedge \sim q)$
    (vii) $[p \wedge (p \rightarrow q)] \rightarrow p$
    (viii) $[p \rightarrow (q \rightarrow \sim p)] \wedge (q \wedge p)$
    (ix) $[(p \wedge r) \leftrightarrow (p \wedge q) \rightarrow (r \leftrightarrow q)$
    (x) $\{[(p \rightarrow q) \rightarrow r] \rightarrow [(r \rightarrow p) \rightarrow (p \wedge q) \rightarrow (r \rightarrow p) \rightarrow (r \rightarrow q)\}$.
16. Prove.
    (i) $\sim(p \leftrightarrow q) \equiv (\sim p \wedge q) \vee (p \wedge \sim q)$
    (ii) $[(p \rightarrow q) \rightarrow (p \rightarrow r)] \equiv [p \rightarrow (q \rightarrow r)]$
    (iii) $r \rightarrow [p \rightarrow (q \rightarrow s)] \equiv [p \rightarrow (q \rightarrow r)$
    (iv) $p \rightarrow (q \rightarrow r) \equiv q \rightarrow (p \rightarrow r)$
    (v) $(\sim p \wedge q) \wedge [p \wedge (p \wedge q)] \equiv (p \wedge q)$
    (vi) $(\sim p \wedge \sim q) \wedge (\sim p \vee q) \wedge (p \vee q) \equiv \sim(p \rightarrow q)$
    (vii) $p \leftrightarrow q \equiv (p \wedge q) \vee \sim(p \vee q)$
    (viii) $[(p \vee q) \rightarrow \sim p] \wedge [(p \vee q) \rightarrow r] \equiv \sim p \wedge (q \rightarrow r)$
    (ix) $[(p \leftrightarrow q) \wedge (q \leftrightarrow r) \wedge (r \leftrightarrow p)] \equiv [(p \rightarrow q) \wedge (q \rightarrow r) \wedge (r \rightarrow p)]$.
    (x) $[(p \leftrightarrow q) \rightarrow \sim(r \rightarrow p)] \vee (r \rightarrow \sim q) \equiv \sim p \vee \sim q \sim r$.
17. Simplify the following expressions by logical laws.
    (i) $(p \vee \sim q) \wedge (p \vee q)$
    (ii) $\sim[(p \rightarrow (p \wedge q)]$
    (iii) $\sim[(p \vee (q \wedge \sim p)]$
    (iv) $p \wedge (q \wedge r) \wedge (\sim p \vee q \vee r)$
    (v) $[(p \leftrightarrow q) \rightarrow \sim(r \rightarrow p)] \vee (r \rightarrow \sim q)$.
18. Write the contradiction of the following propositions.
    (i) $x \in \mathbb{N}, \exists y \in \mathbb{R}, (x - y > 0 \rightarrow y > 0)$
    (ii) $\forall x, y \in \mathbb{R}, \exists z \in \mathbb{R}, [(x < y) \rightarrow (x < y) \rightarrow (x < y < z)]$
    (iii) $\forall x, y \in \mathbb{R}, xy = 0 \leftrightarrow x = 0 or y = 0$
    (iv) $\forall \epsilon > 0, \exists \delta > 0, 0 < |x - a| < \delta \rightarrow |f(x) - f(a) < \varepsilon|$
    (v) $\forall x, y \in \mathbb{R}, x^2 + y^2 > xy \rightarrow x = y \neq 0$.

19. Give a direct proof for each of the following statements if $x, y \in \mathbb{R} - \{0\}$.

(i) $\frac{x+y}{2} \geq \sqrt{xy}$

(ii) $\frac{x+y}{2} \geq xy$

(iii) $\frac{1}{x} + \frac{1}{y} \geq \frac{2}{\sqrt{xy}}$

(iv) $x \leq y \rightarrow \frac{1}{x} \geq \frac{1}{y}$

(v) $x = 2k \rightarrow x^2 - x = 2k'$.

20. Contradict the following statements with an example.

(i) $\forall x \neq 0, \frac{1}{x} \leq x$

(ii) If P is a prime number then P^2+1 is divisible by 5.

(iii) The equation $x^2+y^2=16$ can only have non-integers answers.

21. Prove the correctness of the following statements by reductio ad absurdum.

(i) $\forall x \neq 0, \sqrt{3} - x$ or $\sqrt{3} + x$ is irrational number.

(ii) If $x \neq 0$ is a rational number and y is irrational then, xy is irrational number.

22. Use contra-contradictory proof and prove the following propositions.

(i) If x^2 is an odd number then, x is an odd number.

(ii) If $n \in \mathbb{Z}$ and is not odd then $1^2+3^2+\ldots+n^2$ is an odd number.

REFERENCES

Delong. Howard. (1970). A Profile of Mathematical Logic. Reading, Mass. Addison Wesley.

Ederton. Helbert, B. (2001). *A Mathematical Introduction to Logic* (2nd ed.). Acedamic Press.

Halmos. Paul, R. (1998). Naïve Set Theory (3rd ed.). Springer. Enderton. Herbert B. (1977). Elements of Set Theory. First Academic Press.

Koslow, A. (1992). *A Structuralist Theory of Logic*. Cambridge University Press. DOI: 10.1017/CBO9780511609206

Kreisel, G., & Krivine, J.-L. (1967). *Elements of Mathematical Logic*. North-Holland.

Kunen, K. (1980). *Set Theory: An Introduction to Independence Proofs*. Elsevier.

Kunen. K. Set Theory. (2014). An Introduction To Independence Proofs. Elsevier Science. Jech. Thomas. (2013). Set Theory. Springer.

Lévy, A. (1978). *Basic Set Theory. Springer. Grimaldi. Ralph P. (1989). Discrete and Combinatorial Mathematics* (2nd ed.). Addison-Wesley Publishing Company.

Liu, C. L. (2002). *Elements of Discrete Mathematics, TATA McGraaw-Hill Edition. Grossman, Peter. (1995). Discrete Mathematics for Computing*. MACMILLAN PRESS LTD.

Mendelson. Elliott. (2015). Introduction to Mathematical Logic, (6th ed). CRC Press, Taylor & Francis Group.

Pinter. Charles, C. (1971). *A book of Set Theory*. Addison-Wesley Publishing Company.

Priest, G. (2001). *An Introduction to Non-Classical Logic. Cambridge University Press. Gibson. Carol. (1981). The facts on File Dictionary of Mathematics*. Charles Letts & Co., Ltd.

Stanat, D. F. (1977). *Discrete Mathematics for Compuer Science*. Prentice-Hall.

Stoll. Robert, R. (1963). *Set Theory and Logic*. Freeman.

Stone, H. S. (1973). *Discrete Mathematical Structures and Their Applications, Science Research Associate, Palo Alto, Cliffs, Sahni, S. (1981). Concepts in Discrete Mathematics*. Camelot Press.

Supess, P. (1957). *Introduction to Logic*. D. Van Nostrand Company.

Chapter 3
Functions

ABSTRACT

This chapter deals more with functions. First, we introduce a Cartesian product and its properties, then define the concept of a relation which is a subset of the Cartesian product of two sets. By defining the concept of function, we introduce dependent and independent variables and domain and range of a function that a function can accept. After introducing two specific types of functions, we are going to be familiar with several functions and their properties throughout this chapter. We also define the inverse of a function, and then we introduce and draw figures of most of them to have more ideas about such functions.

3.1 INTRODUCTION

When we formulate a natural process in mathematical language, we will undoubtedly have a relationship between its members. In mathematics, the word relation is a common term used to indicate a relationship between two members of a set. Relationships occur everywhere. For example, when we say that this person is an employee of Company C, we have established a relationship between the employee and the company. In a database where the data is arranged alphabetically, their relationship is such that one precedes the other. In general, when we say A is a subset of B, we establish a kind of relationship between A and B.

Using the theory of sets, we can present a special type of relationship, which is known as a function, and then introduce several types of them, many of which are used in practical management problems.

In the previous chapter, we learned about three operations, namely, union, intersection and difference of sets. In this chapter, we will get acquainted with another operation called a *Cartesian product* between two sets and use it to define *relations* and *functions*.

DOI: 10.4018/979-8-3693-3657-1.ch003

Functional relationships are related to a specific set and any desired relationship for both selected members must belong to this specific set. We consider these two members as a special pair of this set.

3.2 CARTESIAN PRODUCT

We know that both objects such as x and y form a pair, and if order is considered for them, it is called an *ordered pair* and is represented by (x,y), therefore, $(x,y) \neq (y,x)$. Two ordered pairs are equal when their correspondence components are equal.

We can introduce the ordered 3-tuple (x,y,z), or generalize it as the ordered n-tuple, but here we will deal with the ordered pair (x,y).

The *Cartesian product* of two sets A and B, denoted $A \times B$, is the sets of all ordered pairs of the form (x,y) where $x \in A$ and $y \in B$. According to this definition, $A \times B$ is a set of ordered pairs whose first component belongs to A and the second component belongs to B. For example, if $A = \{a,b\}$ and $B = \{b,c,d\}$ then

$$A \times B = \{(a,b),(a,c),(a,d),(b,b),(b,c),(b,d)\}.$$

It is not difficult to show that $A \times B \neq B \times A$. That is, the Cartesian product does not have commutative property.

It is clear that if A has m members and B has n members, then $A \times B$ has $m \times n$ members.

The Cartesian product has the following properties:

(i) $A \times \varnothing = \varnothing \times A = \varnothing$
(ii) $A \times B = B \times A \leftrightarrow A = B$
(iii) $n(A \times B) = n(B \times A)$
(iv) $A \times (B \cup C) = (A \times B) \cup (A \times C)$
(v) $A \times (B \cap C) = (A \times B) \cap (A \times C)$
(vi) $A \times (B - C) = (A \times B) - (A \times C)$
(vii) $(A \times B) \cap (C \times D) = (A \cap C) \times (B \cap D)$.

The set $A \times B$ can be represented as a set of plane points called the *Cartesian coordinate plane*. In other words, if

$$A \times B = \{(x,y)|x \in B \wedge x \in A\},$$

then $A \times B$ represents the two-dimensional coordinate plane. The ordered paired (x,y) is the coordinate of a point like P which gives information about the location of point P. Thus, we can write $P(x,y)$ as the coordinate of a point P where x and y are the *x-coordinate* and *y-coordinate* of P, respectively.

Let A and B be two arbitrary sets. The subset of the product of $A \times B$ is called a *relation* from A to B and is denoted by $\mathfrak{R}$. Assuming the relation $\mathfrak{R}$ and that ($x,y) \in \mathfrak{R}$ we can use the symbol $x\mathfrak{R}y$.That's, $(x,y) \in \mathfrak{R} \leftrightarrow x\,\mathfrak{R}\,y$.

The set of the first components of the relation $\mathfrak{R}$ is called the *domain* $\mathfrak{R}$ and is represented by $D_{\mathfrak{R}}$, and the set of the second components is called the *range* of the relation $\mathfrak{R}$ and is represented by the symbol $R_{\mathfrak{R}}$. It is obvious that $D_{\mathfrak{R}} \subset A$ and $R_{\mathfrak{R}} \subset B$. For example, if $\mathfrak{R} = \{(1,1),(1,2),(2,3)\}$, then $D_{\mathfrak{R}} = \{1,2\}$ and $R_{\mathfrak{R}} = \{1,2,3\}$.

The *identity relation* on a non-empty set A, which we represent by I, consists of all ordered pairs belonging to $A \times A$, where both components are equal. That's, $I = \{(x,x)|x \in A\}$. For example, if $A= \{a,b,c\}$ then

$$I = \{(a,a),(b,b),(c,c)\}.$$

If x and y are related by the relation $\mathfrak{R}$ so that this relation assigns each element x of the domain to one and only one element y of the range $\mathfrak{R}$, we call this relation a *function* and denote it with f. In other words, we call f a function from A to B, if each element of A corresponds to at most one element of B.

We devote the rest of this chapter to considering the functions more and, in this regard, we will introduce different types of functions.

3.3 CONCEPTS AND TERMINOLOGY OF FUNCTIONS

In the fields of science and technology, a *variable* is a quantity that can be measured according to some procedure. In such ways, we come across variables that change for each other. It means they have changed together. Consider a simple situation in which a variable, we call the *independent variable*, is written in terms of another variable. We call this variable *dependent* on the independent variable a *function* if, for every value that the independent variable takes, only one value corresponds to this dependent variable. As in many cases, the functions are an important part of the mathematical model. They also guide the subsequent analysis and data interpretation.

Let A and B be two sets. The function f from A to B, which we denote as $f{:}A \to B$, is a correspondence that compares each member x of A to a single member of B, denoted by $f(x)$, being called the *image* of x. The sets A and B are called the *domain* and *codomain* of f, respectively. The elements of B that are related to the elements located in A form a set called the *range* of the function f, and we denote it here by R_f such that $R_f = \{f(x), x \in A\}$. Thus, the range of a function is a subset of the codomain. Similarly, we denote the domain of f by D_f. If the range of a function is equal to its codomain, that is $R_f=B$, then we say the function is *onto, surjective.*

Although the idea of a function does not impose any restrictions on the nature of domain and range objects, in calculus we are dealing with functions whose range and domain are subsets of real numbers $\mathbb{R}$, which makes such functions *real-valued functions* of a real variable or, in short, real functions, and we can show the figure of these functions in the coordinate plane. For this purpose, we draw the point (x, y) in the coordinate plane for both x and y, where $y=f(x)$. The set of these points is called the *graph* of the function, which we write with a little carelessness:

$$f = \{(x,y), y = f(x), x \in A\}.$$

Of course, we note that the graph of the function f has the property that each line perpendicular to the x-axis intersects the graph of the function at most one point. With this description, the function is a set of ordered pairs whose first components are distinct. If the first components are the same, the second components must also be equal.

If M and m are two constants such that $m \leq f(x) \leq M$ for all x in an interval I, we say, $f(x)$ is *bounded.* M and m are called the *upper* and *lower bounds* of $f(x)$, respectively. For example, the function $f:\mathbb{N} \Rightarrow \mathbb{R}$ defined by $f(n) = \frac{1}{n}$ is bounded but the function $f:\mathbb{R} - \{0\} \Rightarrow \mathbb{R}$ defined by $f(x) = \frac{1}{x}$ is not bounded.

The real-valued function f is called the *even function* if:

(i) $\forall x \in D_f$, we have $-x \in D_f$, and
(ii) $\forall x \in D_f, f(x) = f(-x)$.

The first condition shows that D_f is symmetric about the origin and the second condition emphasizes that the graph of a function is symmetric about the y -axis.

Similarly, f is called an *odd function* if:

(i) $\forall x \in D_f$, we have $-x \in D_f$, and
(ii) $\forall x \in D_f$, and
(iii) $\forall x \in D_f, f(-x) = -f(x)$.

The second condition shows that the graph of f is symmetric about the origin.

For example, the functions $f(x)=x_2-3$ and $f(x)= x^3+2x$ are even and odd functions, respectively, but $f(x)=x^2+2x$ is neither an even nor odd function.

Remark 1: the function $f(x)=0$ is the only function that is either an even or odd function.

The function f on interval I is *periodic* if there exists a real number $t>0$ such that for any $x \in D_f$, $f(x+t)=f(x)$. The least value of t is called the *period* of f.

The function f from $\mathbb{R}$ to $\mathbb{R}$, given by $f(x)=x$, is called the *identity function*. It is an odd function with $D_f = R_f = \mathbb{R}$.

Two functions f and g with the same domain D are equal if for every $x \in D$ we have $f(x)=g(x)$. If two functions f and g are equal, their graphs coincide.

Example 1: Are the functions defined by $f(x) = x - 1$ and $g(x) = \frac{x^2 - 1}{x + 1}$ equal?

Solution: Although we can write $f(x) = x - 1 = g(x)$ but $D_f = \mathbb{R}$ and $D_g = \mathbb{R} - \{1\}$. It means their domains are not the same. Hence, they are not equal.■

In mathematics, a piecewise function is a function defined by multiple sub-functions where each sub-function is applied to a different interval in the domain. For example, the *absolute value function* is defined by $f(x) = |x| = \begin{cases} x, x \geq 0 \\ -x, x < 0 \end{cases}$, which is a *piecewise function* with two sub-functions.

Figure 1. Graph of absolute value function $f(x)=|x|$

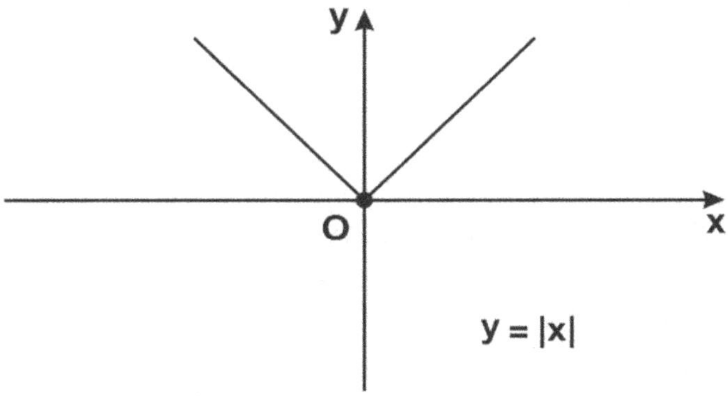

For both real numbers x and y, this function has the following properties:

(i) $|xy| = |x| . |y|$
(ii) $\left|\frac{x}{y}\right| = \frac{|x|}{|y|}, (y \neq 0)$
(iii) $|x + y| \leq |x| + |y|$
(iv) $|x - y| \geq |x| - |y|$

Remark 2: A *step function,* which is a kind of piecewise function, is such that its value jumps from one value to the next. For example, if we consider $C(w)$ the postage cost of a letter of weight w which is given by

$C(w) = 0.15, 1 \geq x > 0\ 0.42, 2 \geq x > 1\ 0.68, 3 \geq x > 2\ 0.95, 4 \geq x > 3\ 1.25 x > 4.$

We define this function as a step function for it.

Here we define other two-step functions, namely sign and greatest integer function.

The *sign function* is denoted by *sgn(x)* is another piecewise function with three sub-functions defined by

$f(x) = sgn(x) = \{ 1, x > 0\ 0, x = 0\ -1, x < 0.$

Figure 2. Graph of sign function f(x)=sgn(x)

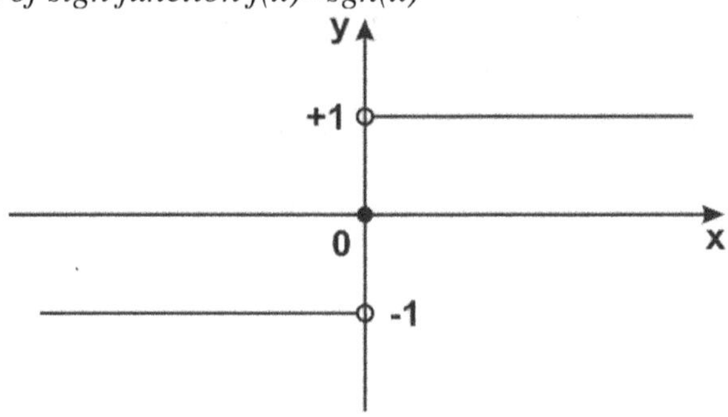

Note that if the function *f*(*x*) is known, then

$sgn(f(x)) = \{ 1, f(x) > 0\ 0, f(x) = 0\ -1, f(x) < 0.$

We know that for any real number *x*, there is a unique largest integer *n* that satisfies the following conditions:

$(n \in \mathbb{Z}), n \leq x < n + 1$

.

This integer is called the greatest integer in *x* and is denoted by the symbol [*x*]=*n*. So, function *y*=[*x*], which is called the *greatest integer function,* is a function that is defined on ℝ and satisfies the following conditions:

$n \leq x < n + 1 \leftrightarrow [x] = n, (n \in \mathbb{Z}).$

Figure 3. Graph of greatest integer function f(x)=[x]

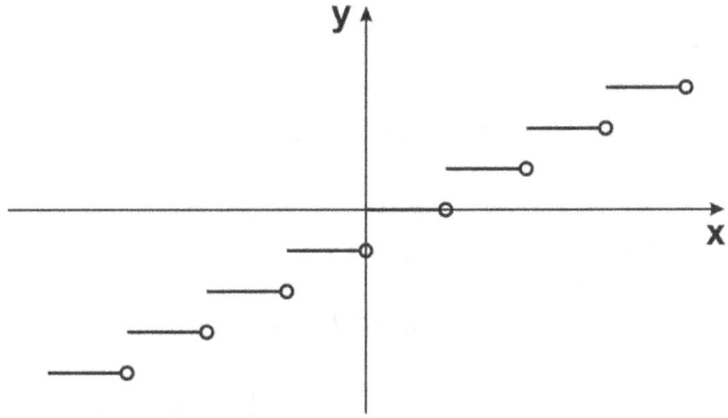

It can be proved that for $x, y \in \mathbb{R}$ and $n \in \mathbb{Z}$.

(i) $[x + n] = [x] + n$
(ii) $x - 1 < [x] \leq x$
(iii) $[x + y] \geq [x] + [y]$
(iv) $[-x] = \{ -[x], n \in Z \ -[x] - 1, n \notin Z.$

Many things around us can be modeled with this function. As we mentioned, the price of priority mail is a function of weight.

For example, let the cost function of postal correspondence within the city be determined by $y = 8\left[\frac{x}{2}\right] + 15$. If the weight of the envelope is 17 grams, then the cost of postage is $8\left[\frac{17}{2}\right] + 15 = 79$.

An application of this function is in computer programming, where it is used to round down a number to the nearest integer. This can be useful when working with data that needs to be converted to whole numbers, such as when calculating the number of items in a shopping cart or determining the number of pages in a document. The greatest integer function ensures that the result is always rounded down, providing an accurate representation of the data.

3.4 ALGEBRAIC OPERATIONS ON FUNCTIONS

If f and g are two functions with the domains D_f and D_g, then the sum, difference, product, and division of these two functions, which are denoted by $f+g$, $f-g$, $f.g$, and $\frac{f(x)}{g(x)}$ respectively, are functions that are introduced as follows:

(i) $(f+g)(x) = f(x) + g(x), x \in Df \cap Dg$
(ii) $(f-g)(x) = f(x) - g(x), x \in Df \cap Dg$
(iii) $(f.g)(x) = f(x).g(x), x \in Df \cap Dg$
(iv) $(f\_g)(x) = f(x)\_g(x), x \in Df \cap Dg - \{x|g(x) = 0\}$.

We denote the function $f+f$ by $2f$ and $f.f$ by f^2. The functions nf and f^n can be deduced by induction, where $n \in \mathbb{N}$. Of course, in general, for any $k \in \mathbb{R}$ we define:

$$kf = \{(x, kf(x))|x \in Df\}$$

$$fk = \{(x, fk(x))|x \in Df\}.$$

Example 2: If $f(x) = \sqrt{x^2 - 1}$ and $g(x) = \begin{cases} 3(x-2), x > 2 \\ -x, x < 1 \end{cases}$. Find f^2, $\frac{f}{g}$ and $\frac{g}{f}$.
Solution: We have

$$Df = (-\infty, -1] \cup [1, +\infty) Dg$$

$$Dg = (-\infty, 1) \cup (2, +\infty)$$

$$Df2 = Df \cap Df = Df = (-\infty, -1] \cup [1, +\infty)$$

$$Df\_g = Df \cap Dg - \{x|g(x) = 0\} = (-\infty, 1] \cup (2, +\infty)$$

$$D_{\frac{g}{f}} = D_g \cap D_f - \left\{x|f(x) = 0\right\} = (-\infty, 1] \cup (2, +\infty).$$

Therefore,

$$(f2)(x) = f(x)2 = x2 - 1, x \in Df$$

$$\left(\frac{f}{g}\right)(x) = \frac{f(x)}{g(x)} = \begin{cases} \frac{\sqrt{x^2-1}}{-x}, x \le 1 \\ \frac{\sqrt{x^2-1}}{3(x-2)}, x > 2 \end{cases} ; x \in D_{\frac{f}{g}}$$

$$\left(\frac{g}{f}\right)(x) = \frac{g(x)}{f(x)} = \begin{cases} \frac{-x}{\sqrt{x^2-1}}, x < 1 \\ \frac{3(x-2)}{\sqrt{x^2-1}}, x > 2 \end{cases} ; x \in D_{\frac{g}{f}}.$$

3.5 COMPOSITION OF TWO FUNCTIONS

Let f and g be two functions with domains D_f and D_g such that f be a function of A in B and g be a function in C. *Composite function* f and g denoted by gof is defined as follows:

$$gof: D_{gof} \rightarrow R_g$$

$$(gof)(x) = g(f(x))$$

$$D_{gof} = \left\{x \in D_f | f(x) \in D_g\right\} \subseteq D_f$$

Look at the following figure for a better understanding of $g(f(x))$.

Figure 4. Graph of composite functions

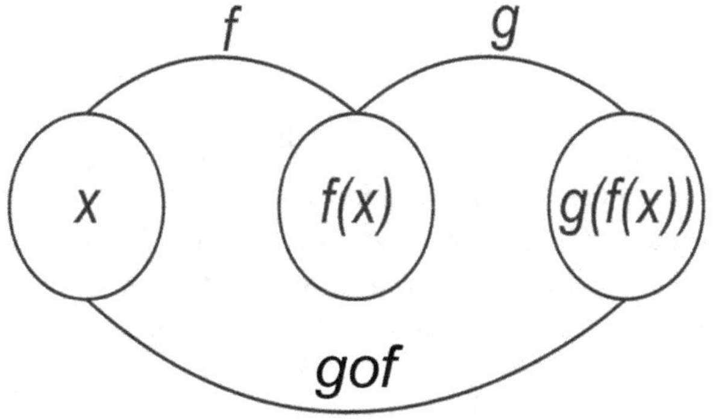

We notice that if $R_f \cap D_g = \varnothing$, then the function gof is null. Also, if $R_f \subseteq D_g$, then $D_{gof} = D_f$.

It can be checked that the following properties are established in the composite of functions:

(i) The associative property of the composite of functions:

(ii) $(fog)oh = fo(goh)$

(iii) The distributive property of the composite of functions compared to the addition or subtraction of functions:

$$fo(g \pm h) = fog \pm foh$$

$$(g \pm h)of = (gof) \pm (hof).$$

3.6 TYPES OF FUNCTIONS

Before we introduced some functions based on the mathematical concepts, we classified them as follows to help with easy understanding and learning.

3.6.1 One-to-One Functions

We have already mentioned that if the range of a function is equal to its co-domain, then the function is onto. A onto function may have the same image in the codomain for two different values of its domain. We define a new terminology for which this does not happen.

Definition 1: The function f is called *one-to-one,* or *injective,* when both distinct members of the domain are mapped to two distinct members of the range. In other words, for both values $x_1, x_2 \in D_f$, we have

$$f(x_1) = f(x_2) \Rightarrow x_1 = x_2.$$

Therefore, the graph of a one-to-one function f has the property that any line parallel to the x-axis intersects the graph of the function at most at one point. If a function f is both one-to-one and onto, we say that f is *bijective.*

Definition 2: The one-to-one and onto function $f{:}A \rightarrow B$ is called a *two-sided function*, and in this case, the two sets A and B are called *equivalent.*

Example 3: Let $f(x) = \begin{cases} x^2 + 2x - 3, x \in R \\ 3x + 1, x \notin R \end{cases}$. Determine whether f is one-to-one, or not.

Solution: Since we can write $f(x) = x^2 + 2x - 3 = (x + 1)^2 - 4$, hence

$\forall x_1, x_2 \in \mathbb{R}{:}f(x_1) = f(x_2) \Rightarrow (x_1 + 1)^2 - 4 = (x_2 + 1)^2 - 4$

$x_1 + 1 = \pm(x_2 + 1) \Rightarrow$ or $x_1 = -(x_2 + 2)$.

Hence, f is not one-to-one. For example, the two values -2 and 0 from the domain of f are mapped to -3 of the range f. ■

3.6.2 Inverse Functions

Definition 3: Function f is called the *inverse* of g if

$(gof)(x) = x, x \in D_f$

$(fog)(x) = x, x \in D_g$.

We note that if f is the inverse of g then, g is also the inverse of f. We show the inverse of f by f^1. We observe that:

$(fof^{-1})(x) = x = (f^{-1}of)(x)$.

Theorem 1. The function f is invertible if and only if it is one-to-one.

To find the inverse of f, if the function $y=f(x)$ is one-to-one, we find the independent variable x in terms of y. That is, we write $x=f(y)$. Then, by changing $x \to y$, $y \to x$,we obtain $y=f^1(x)$, which is inverse of $x=f(y)$. It should be noted that the graphs of f and f^1 are symmetric related to line $y=x$.

Example 4: Let's $f(x)= x^3-3x^2+3x$. Check the invertibility of the function and then find its inverse.

Solution: We write the function $f(x) = x^3 - 3x^2 + 3x$, as $f(x) = (x-1)^3 + 1$. The function f is one-to-one because $\forall x_1, x_2 \in \mathbb{R}$,we have

$f(x_1) = f(x_2) \Rightarrow (x_1 - 1)^3 = (x_2 - 1)^3 \Rightarrow x_1 = x_2$.

Therefore, the function is invertible. To find the inverse of f we write

$y = (x-1)^3 + 1 \Rightarrow x - 1 = \sqrt[3]{y-1} \Rightarrow x = g(y) = \sqrt[3]{y-1} + 1$.

Now, by changing $x \to y, y \to x$ we will get $y=f^1(x) = \sqrt[3]{x-1} + 1$.

3.6.3 Monotonic Functions

Suppose the function f is defined in an interval I. The function f on I is called the *ascending function* if

$$\forall x_1, x_2 \in I: x_1 < x_2 \Rightarrow f(x_1) \leq f(x_2).$$

A function is called a *strictly ascending function* if,

$$\forall x_1, x_2 \in I: x_1 < x_2 \Rightarrow f(x_1) < f(x_2).$$

Similarly, the function f on I is called the *descending function* when

$$\forall x_1, x_2 \in I: x_1 < x_2 \Rightarrow f(x_1) \geq f(x_2),$$

and is a *strictly descending function* if,

$\forall x_1, x_2 \in I : x_1 < x_2 \Rightarrow f(x_1) > f(x_2).$

For example, consider ordered pair functions $f = \{(1,3),(2,1),(3,0)\}$ and $g = \{(0,1),(1,2),(3,2)\}$ then f is strictly descending and g ascending functions. Functions fog and gof both are descending, because $fog = \{(0,3), (1,1),(3,1)\}$ and $gof = \{(1,2),(2,2),(3,1)\}$.

Remark 3: Two important functions in economics are the demand and the supply functions. They are descending and ascending functions, respectively.

Example 5: Suppose $f(x) = \begin{cases} \frac{1}{x-2}, x > 2 \\ \sqrt{2-x}, x \leq 2 \end{cases}$. Check whether it is an ascending or descending function at the given intervals.

Solution: If $x>2$, then for two values x_1 and x_2 where $x_1 < x_2 < 2$, we have

$$0 < x_1 - 2 < x_2 - 2 \Rightarrow \frac{1}{x_1 - 2} > \frac{1}{x_2 - 2} \Rightarrow f(x_1) > f(x_2).$$

Hence, f is strictly an descending function on $(2, \infty)$.

If $x \leq 2$ then for two values x_1 and x_2 where $x_1 < x_2 \leq 2$, we have

$$2x_1 < 2x_2 \leq 4 \Rightarrow 4 - 2x_1 > 4 - 2x_2 \geq 0 \Rightarrow f(x_1) > f(x_2).$$

Hence, f on $(-\infty, 2]$ is strictly descending. ■

3.7 ALGEBRAIC AND NON-ALGEBRAIC FUNCTIONS

The function $y = f(x)$ is called an *algebraic function* when it applies to an indivisible algebraic equation of the form

$$P_0(x)y^n + P_1(x)y^{n-1} + \ldots + P_{n-1}(x)y + P_n(x) = 0$$

where, $n \in \mathbb{N}$ and for $n \geq i \geq 0, P_i(x)$ are the polynomials in terms of x.

Algebraic functions include *polynomial functions*, *rational functions*, which are expressed as the quotient of two polynomials, and *irrational functions*.

Functions that do not have the above conditions are called non-algebraic or transcendental functions. *Trigonometric, Exponential, Logarithmic*, and *Hyperbolic* are *Non-algebraic* or *transcendental functions.*

3.7.1 Trigonometric Functions

The trigonometric functions that we generally met in elementary mathematics are:

(i) $y = sinx$
(ii) $y = cosx$
(iii) $y = tanx$
(iv) $y = cotx$
(v) $y = secx = \frac{1}{\cos x}$
(vi) $y = \csc x = \frac{1}{\sin x}$.

The variable x is expressed in radians. All the enumerated trigonometric functions are periodic. The domain of the functions $sinx$ and $cosx$ is $\mathbb{R}$ with range $[-1, 1]$. Hence they are bounded functions. They are even and odd functions, respectively, with periods $T = 2\pi$.

Figure 5. Graphs of functions f(x) = sinx and f(x) = cosx

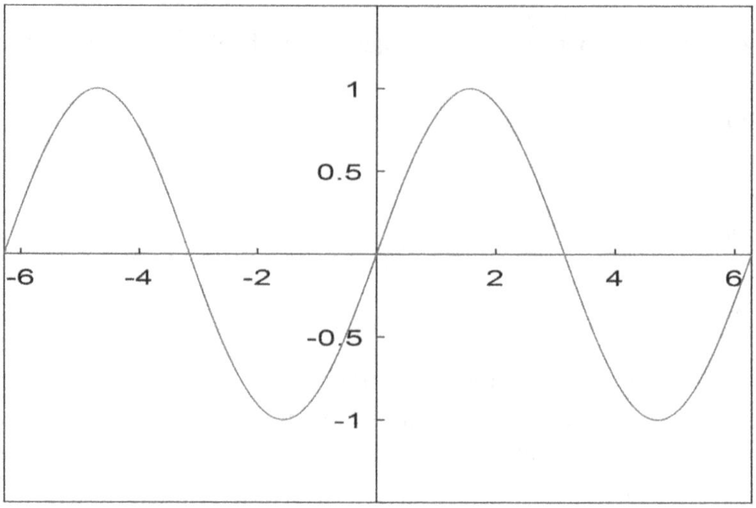

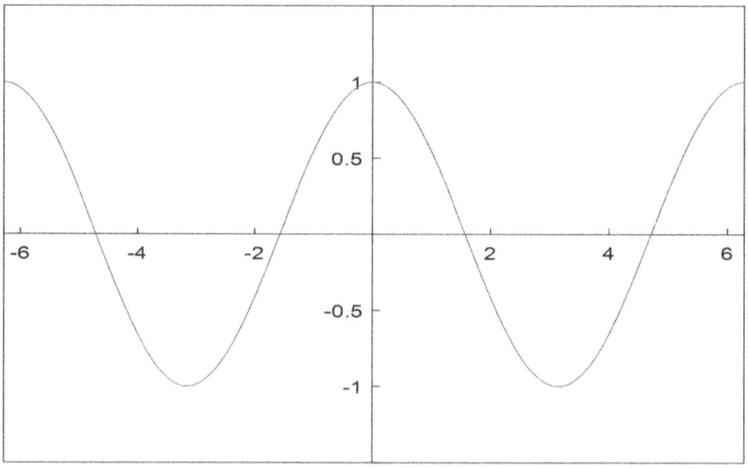

The domain of the functions tan$x$ and sec$x$ is $\mathbb{R} - \left\{ \left(\frac{2n+1}{2}\right) n\pi | n \in \mathbb{Z} \right\}$ and the domain of the functions *cotx* and csc$x$ is $\mathbb{R} - \{(n\pi | n \in \mathbb{Z}\}$. Although they are not bounded and the range of tan$x$ and cot$x$ is $\mathbb{R}$, the range of sec$x$and csc$x$is $(-\infty, -1) \cup (1, +\infty)$. The functions tan$x$ and cot$x$ are odd functions with periods $T = \pi$.

Figure 6. Graphs of functions f(x) = tanx and f(x) = secx

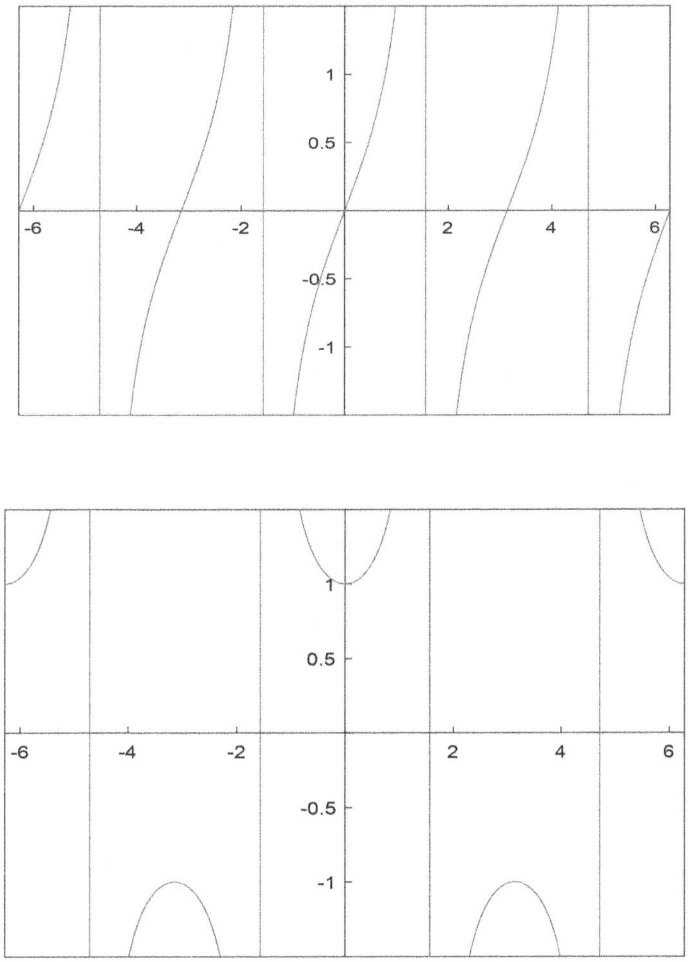

Figure 7. Graphs of functions f(x) = cotx and f(x) = cosecx

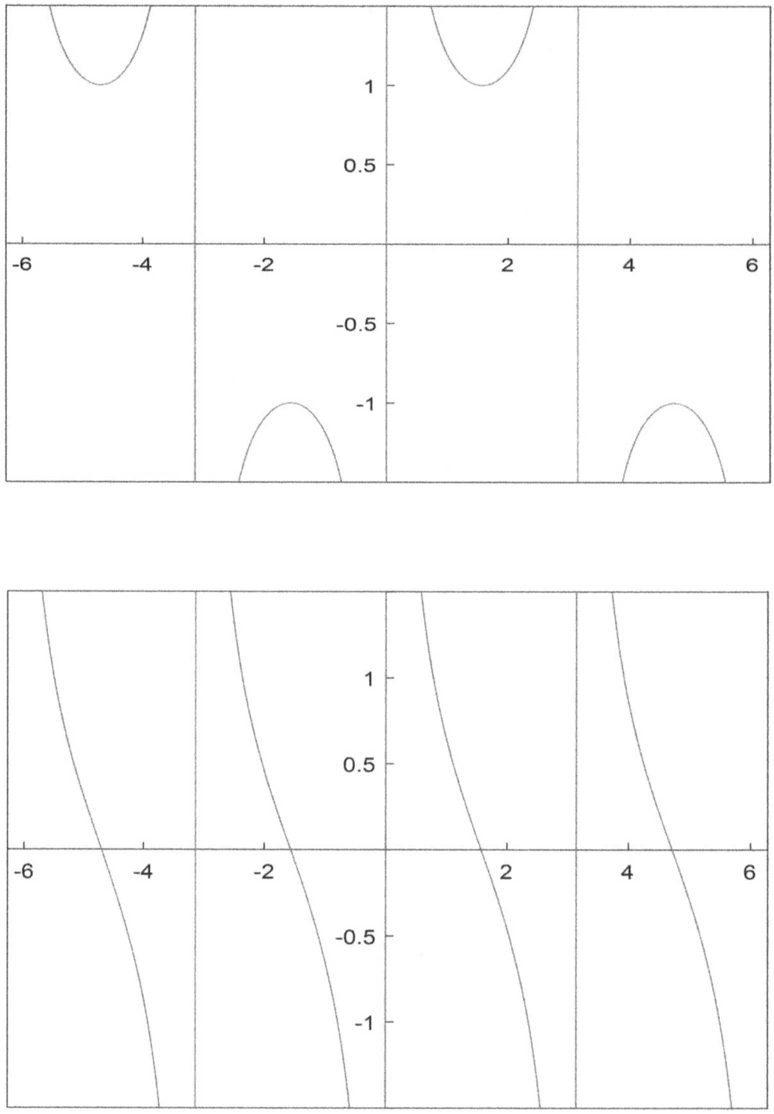

The following properties exist for the trigonometric functions:

(i) $\sin 2x + \cos 2x = 1$
(ii) $\tan x . \cot x = 1$
(iii) $\sec 2x = 1 + \tan 2x$
(iv) $\csc 2x = 1 + \cot 2x$
(v) $tan^2 x = \frac{1 - \cos 2x}{1 + \cos 2x}$
(vi) $\sin(x \pm y) = \sin x . \cos y \pm \sin y . \cos x$
(vii) $\cos(x \pm y) = \cos x . \cos y \mp \sin x . \sin y$
(viii) $\tan(x \pm y) = \frac{\tan x \pm \tan y}{1 \mp \tan x . \tan y}$

Remark 4: The equation $\begin{cases} x = \cos t \\ y = \sin t \end{cases}$ is the parametric equation of the unit circle given by $x^2 + y^2 = 1$.

3.7.2 Inverse Trigonometric Functions

Trigonometric functions are one-to-one in parts of their domain, so they are invertible in these parts. We denote an inverse trigonometric function with the usual symbol (-1) as its exponent. These functions are as follows:

(i) $y = sin^{-1}x, [-1,1] \to \left[-\frac{\pi}{2}, \frac{\pi}{2}\right]; y = sin^{-1}x \leftrightarrow \sin y = x$
(ii) $y = cos^{-1}x, [-1,1] \to [0,\pi]; y = cos^{-1}x \leftrightarrow \cos y = x$
(iii) $y = tan^{-1}x, \mathbb{R} \to \left(-\frac{\pi}{2}, \frac{\pi}{2}\right); y = tan^{-1}x \leftrightarrow \tan y = x$
(iv) $y = cot^{-1}x, \mathbb{R} \to (0,\pi); y = cot^{-1}x \leftrightarrow \cot y = x$
(v) $y = sec^{-1}x, \mathbb{R} - (-1,1) \to [0,\pi] - \left\{\frac{\pi}{2}\right\}; y = sec^{-1}x \leftrightarrow \sec y = x$
(vi) $y = csc^{-1}x, \mathbb{R} - (-1,1) \to \left[-\frac{\pi}{2}, \frac{\pi}{2}\right]; y = csc^{-1}x \leftrightarrow \csc y = x.$

We notice that in the above definitions, we have created restrictions for the functions (values of *y*) because we want only one value for *y* to be obtained for each value of *y*. Of course, we note that the limits of the changes selected for the values of the functions are not unique and other distances can be chosen instead. However, all these functions are bounded and, according to the graph of these functions drawn below, we get complete information about their monotonicity and odd and even status.

Figure 8. Graphs of functions $f(x) = sin^{-1}x$ and $f(x) = cos^{-1}x$

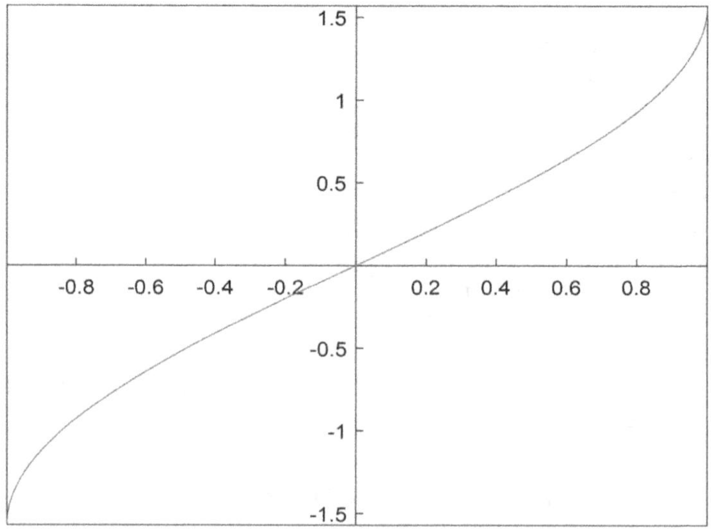

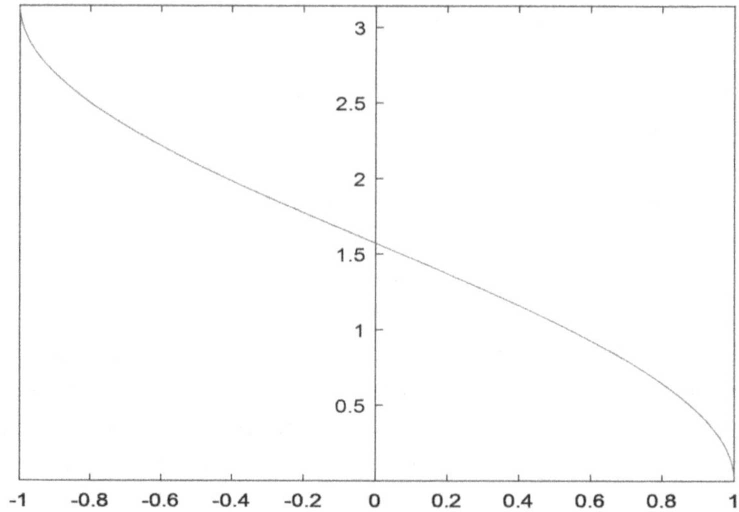

Example 6: Show that $\frac{1}{2}cos^{-1}x = tan^{-1}\sqrt{\frac{1-x}{1+x}}$.

Solution: Let $\frac{1}{2}cos^{-1}x = \alpha$. Thus $cos^{-1}x = 2\alpha \rightarrow x = \cos 2\alpha$.

From identity, $tan^2\alpha = \frac{1-\cos 2\alpha}{1+\cos 2\alpha}$, we get

$\tan\alpha = \sqrt{\frac{1-\cos 2\alpha}{1+\cos 2\alpha}} = \sqrt{\frac{1-x}{1+x}} \Rightarrow \alpha = tan^{-1}\sqrt{\frac{1-x}{1+x}}$. Therefore,

$$\frac{1}{2}\cos^{-1}x = \tan^{-1}\sqrt{\frac{1-x}{1+x}}.$$

Figure 9. Graphs of functions $f(x) = \tan^{-1}x$ and $f(x) = a\,\mathrm{cosec}^{-1}x$

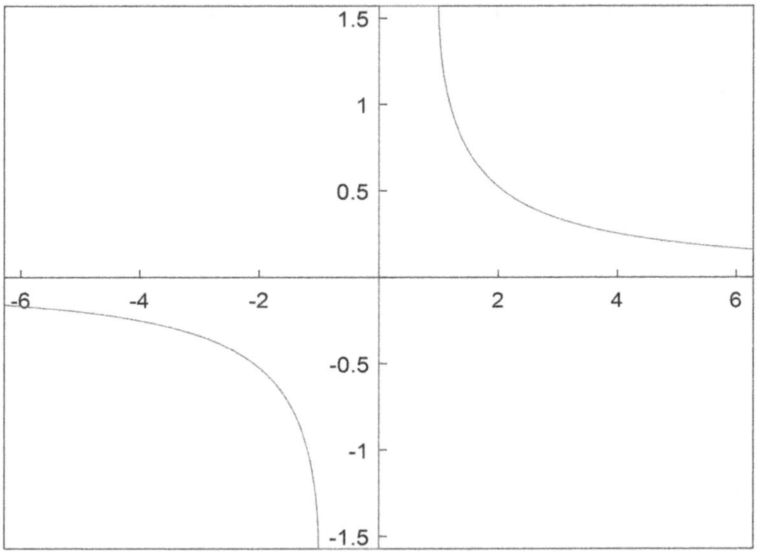

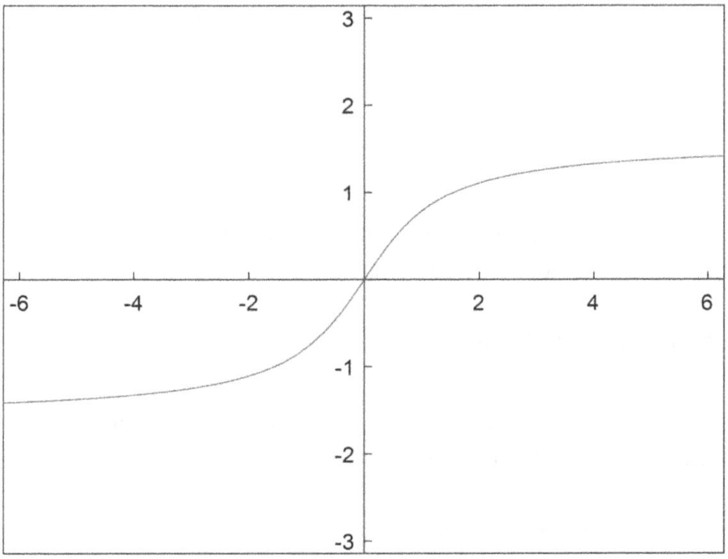

3.7.3 Exponential Functions

The function $y = a^x$, where $a \neq 0$ is a positive real number, is called an *exponential function* with base a. This function is defined on the set of real numbers, which is strictly ascending for $a > 1$ and strictly descending for $a < 1$.

Figure 10. Graphs of function $y = a^x$

For $a > 1$ For $a < 1$

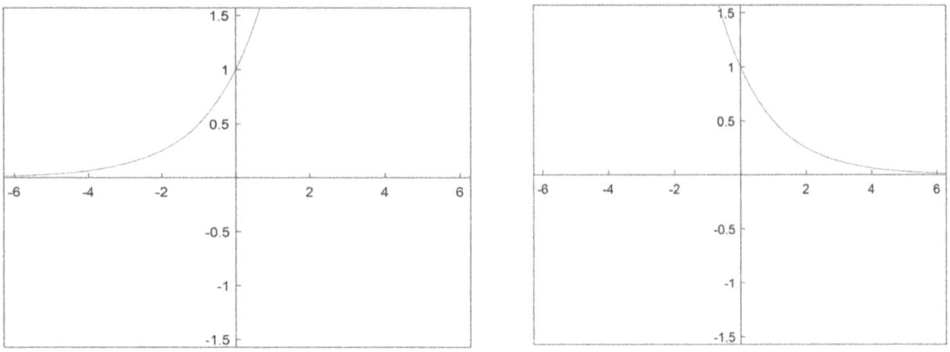

The following properties exist for the exponential functions:

(i) $f(0) = 1$
(ii) $f(x+y) = f(x).f(y)$
(iii) $f(x-y) = \frac{f(x)}{f(y)}$
(iv) $f(xy) = (f(x))^y$

According to the graph of the exponential function, we find that this function is strictly monotonic. Therefore, it is reversible.

3.7.4 Logarithm Functions

The inverse of an exponential function is called a *logarithmic function,* and it is represented as, $y = log_a^x$. That means:

$$y = log_a^x \leftrightarrow a^y = x, (0 < a \neq 1).$$

The range of this function is real numbers, which are strictly ascending for $a > 1$ and strictly descending for $0 < a < 1$.

Figure 11. Graphs of function $y = \log_a^x$

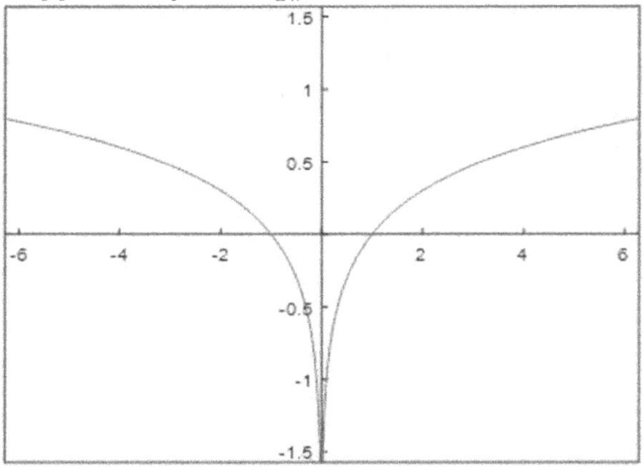

In elementary mathematics, we have become familiar with the properties of exponential and logarithmic functions. Here we only point out that the function $f(x) = \log_a^x, (0 < a \neq 1)$ applies to both positive real values x and y in the following equations:

(i) $f(1) = 0$
(ii) $f(x.y) = f(x) + f(y)$
(iii) $f\left(\frac{x}{y}\right) = f(x) - f(y)$
(iv) $f(x^y) = yf(x)$.

Remark 5: The logarithm that has a base of a=10 is known as a common logarithm (or, *Briggsian logarithm*).

Now, we refer to a special type of exponential function where the base of the exponential function $y = a^x$ is $a = e = 2.71828\ldots$,the *Napier number*.

In next chapter we will show that this number is the limit of the sequence $\left(1 + \frac{1}{n}\right)^n$. But, before that, suppose $a_n = \left(1 + \frac{1}{n}\right)^n$, where, $n \in \mathbb{N}$. For sufficiently large values of n, we calculate values of a_n. We obtain:

$a_{1000} = 2.71692\ldots, a_{10000} = 2.71814\ldots, a_{100000} = 2.71826\ldots,$
$a_{1000000} = 2.71828\ldots, a_{10000000} = 2.71828, \ldots.$

We observe that by making n large, the sequence a_n tends to a constant number between 2.7169 and 2.71829. This number, which we denote by e, is called the *Napier number*. In the more precise sense of mathematics, it is proved that the sequence a_n is convergent and the limit value of this sequence is the irrational number e. The approximate value of e can be calculated with any accuracy. Due to the frequent use of the Napier number in modeling natural phenomena and experimental sciences, if the base of the exponential function is " Napier number", it is called a natural exponential function, which is known by the rule $y = e^x$.

The logarithm function in the base e is called the *natural logarithm function* and is indicated by log_e^x or Lnx, (L for the first letter of the logarithm and n for the first letter of the Napier). Since the natural exponential function and Napier's logarithm are inverses of each other, the graphs of these two functions are symmetric to the line $y = x$.

Figure 12. Graph of exponential function f(x) $= e^x$

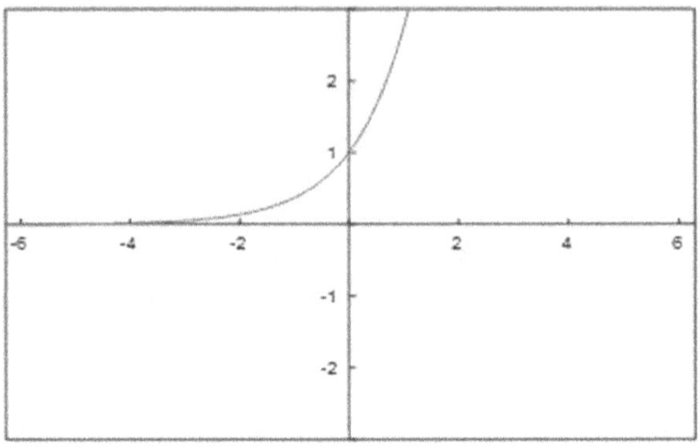

3.7.5 Hyperbolic Functions

In this section, we study special combinations of exponential functions e^x and e^{-x} because of their many applications. These functions, which are known as hyperbolic functions, are defined as follows.

$$y = \text{sinh}x = \frac{e^x + e^{-x}}{2}$$

$$\text{y} = \text{tanh}x = \frac{\text{sinh}x}{\text{cosh}x} = \frac{e^x + e^{-x}}{e^x - e^{-x}}$$

$$y = \text{cosh}x = \frac{e^x - e^{-x}}{2}$$

$$y = \text{coth}x = \frac{\text{cosh}x}{\text{sinh}x} = \frac{e^x - e^{-x}}{e^x + e^{-x}}$$

We note that the domain of functions sinh$x$, *cosh* x and tanh$x$ *is* $\mathbb{R}$. But the domain of coth$x$ is $\mathbb{R} - \{0\}$.

Figure 13. Graphs of hyperbolic functions

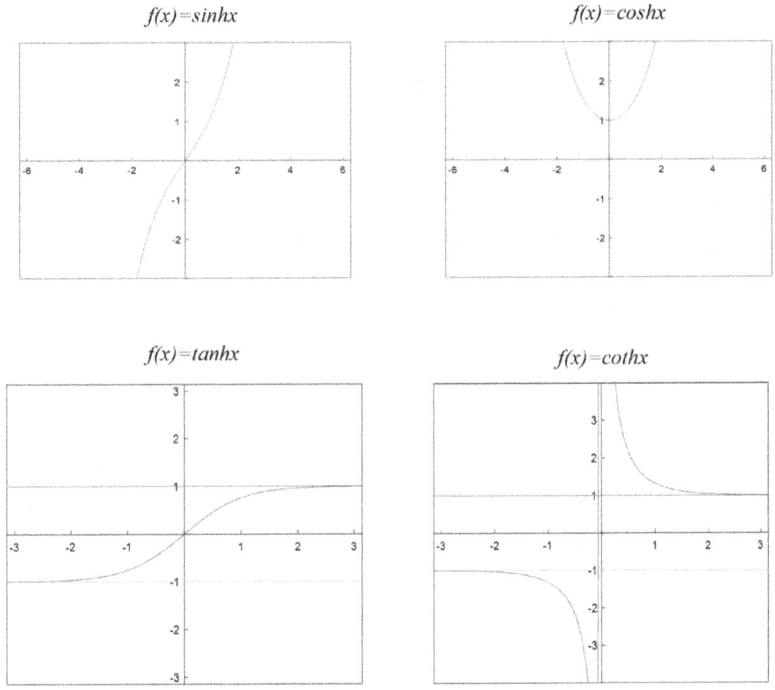

According to these graphs, the range of functions, the state of monotonicity and whether they are odd or even are obtained. For example, the function tanh$x$is strictly descending on $(-\infty\ ,0)$ and $(0,+\infty)$. It is also an odd function, and its range is ($-\infty\ ,-1) \cup (1,+\infty)$.

Similar to trigonometric functions, hyperbolic functions have relationships with each other that can be easily obtained from the definition of these functions. The importance of these relationships is as follows:

(i) $\cosh^2 x - \sinh^2 x = 1$

(ii) $(\cosh x + \sinh x)^n = \cosh nx + \sinh nx$

(iii) $\sinh(x \pm y) = \sinh x . \cosh y \pm \sinh y . \cosh x$

(iv) $\cosh(x \pm y) = \cosh x . \cosh y \pm \sinh x . \sinh y$

(v) $\tanh(x \pm y) = \dfrac{\tanh x \pm \tanh y}{1 \mp \tanh x . \tanh y}$

(vi) $\tanh 2x = \dfrac{2 \tanh x}{1 - \tanh^2 x}$

(vii) $\sinh 2x = 2 \sinh x . \cosh x$

(viii) $\cosh 2x = \cosh^2 x + \sinh^2 x$

(ix) $\cosh 2x - 1 = 2 \sinh^2 x$

(x) $\cosh 2x + 1 = 2 \cosh^2 x.$

Remark 6: The equation $\begin{cases} x = \cosh t \\ y = \sinh t \end{cases}$ is the parametric equation of a hyperbolic given by $x^2 - y^2 = 1$.

3.7.6 Inverse Hyperbolic Functions

According to the graph of hyperbolic functions, we see that the functions $\sinh x$, $\tanh x$ and $\coth x$ are one-to-one. Therefore, they are invertible, and their inverses are indicated by $\sinh^{-1} x$, $\tanh^{-1} x$ and $\coth^{-1} x$ respectively. They are given as follows:

(i) $sinhx{:}\mathbb{R} \rightarrow \mathbb{R}; y = sinh^{-1}x \leftrightarrow \sinh y = x$
(ii) $tanh^{-1}x{:}\mathbb{R} \rightarrow (-1,1); y = tanh^{-1}x \leftrightarrow \tanh y = x$
(iii) $coth^{-1}x, \mathbb{R} \rightarrow (-\infty, -1) \cup (1, +\infty); y = coth^{-1}x \leftrightarrow \coth y = x.$

Since the hyperbolic functions can be expressed in terms of e^x and e^{-x}, it seems that inverse hyperbolic functions can also be written in terms of logarithmic functions. For example, according to the definition of $sinh^{-1}x$, we can write

$$y = sinh^{-1}x \leftrightarrow x = \sinh y = \frac{e^y + e^{-y}}{2} \Rightarrow e^{2y} + 2xe^y - 1 = 0.$$

If we solve this equation for y in terms of x, we obtain

$$e^y = x \pm \sqrt{x^2+1} \Rightarrow y = \text{Ln}(x \pm \sqrt{x^2+1}).$$

Therefore, $\forall x \in \mathbb{R}$

$$sinh^{-1}x = \text{Ln}(x + \sqrt{x^2+1}).$$

Similarly, we can show that

$$tanh^{-1}x = \frac{1}{2}\text{Ln}\left(\frac{1+x}{1-x}\right), x \in (-1,1),$$

$$coth^{-1}x = \frac{1}{2}\text{Ln}\left(\frac{x+1}{x-1}\right), |x| > 1.$$

Figure 14. Graph of $f(x) = sinh^{-1}x$

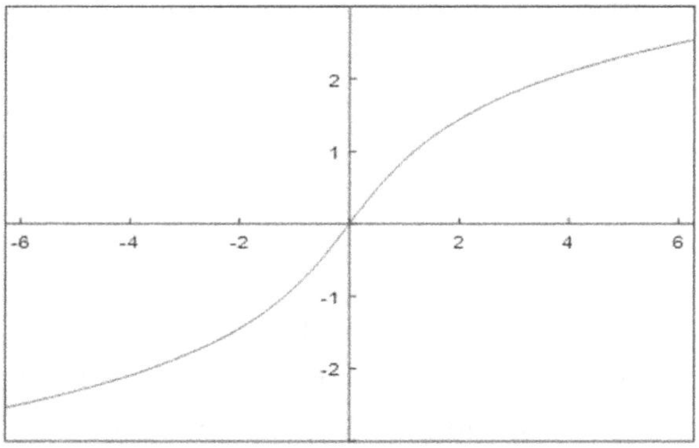

If we limit the domain of the function *coshx* to the interval$[0, +\infty)$, we will have a strictly ascending function, so the function will be invertible. We denote its reverse with $cosh^{-1}x$. Therefore

$coshx{:}[0, +\infty) \ \rightarrow \ [1, +\infty); y \ = \ cosh^{-1}x \ \leftrightarrow \ \text{sinh}y \ = \ x.$

As we mentioned above, the function $cosh^{-1}x$can be expressed in terms of a logarithm function. It can easily be shown that for $x \ \geq \ 1$

$cosh^{-1}x \ = \ \text{Ln}(x + \sqrt{x^2 - 1}).$

Figure 15. Graph of function $f(x)= cosh^{-1}x$

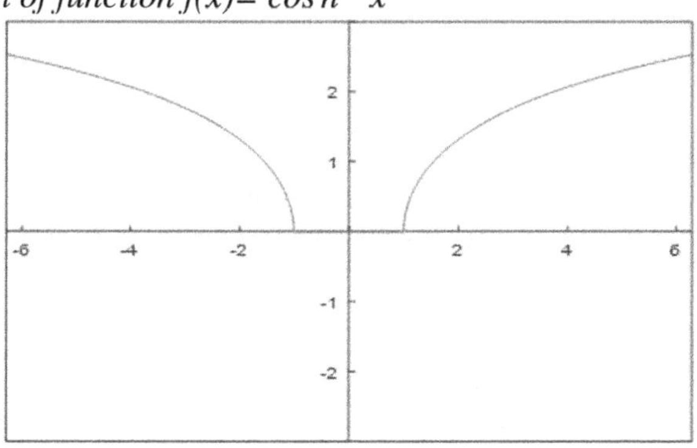

More about functions can be found in most textbooks on Differential and Integral Calculus, e.g., see (Apostol, 1966) (Finey, 1988) (Leithold, 1981) (Rodin, 1970) (Piskunov, 1981) (Siolverman, 1985) (Stewart, 2008) (Thomas, 2014).

CONCLUSION

In this chapter, by defining ordered pairs, we discussed Cartesian product of two sets. This product helped us to define a function which was a correspondence between two sets of numbers. Then, we introduced several types of functions and obtained their inverses. By drawing their figures, we can understand more about them. In particular, concepts of monotonic functions, which are helpful for differential and integral calculus.

3.8 Exercises

1. Which of the following relations, defined on the set of real numbers, are functions?
   (i) $xy = 0$
   (ii) $y = \sqrt{x-1} + \sqrt{1-x}$
   (iii) $x^2 + y^2 = 1$
   (iv) $2x^2 + |y| = y^2$
   (v) $x^2 - 2xy + 3 = 0$
   (vi) $x^2 + y^2 = 1, y \leq 0$
2. Determine the domain and range of the following functions.
   (i) $y = \frac{1}{x} + (-1)^x$
   (ii) $|x^2 - 1| + y^2 = 0$
   (iii) $x^2 + y^2 = 1$
   (iv) $-2x^2 + |y| = y^2$
   (v) $x^2 - 2xy + 3 = 0$
   (vi) $x^2 + y^2 = 1, y \leq 0$
3. Check the equality of each pair of given functions.
   (i) $f(x) = \sqrt{x(x-1)}; g(x) = \sqrt{x}.\sqrt{x-1}$
   (ii) $f(x) = 2; g(x) = \left|\frac{x+2}{x+1}\right|$
   (iii) $f(x) = \sin(x); g(x) = \sqrt{1-\cos^2 x}$
   (iv) $f(x) = \lfloor x \rfloor; g(x) = x sgn x.$
4. State, whether the following functions are; (a)- one-to-one, or (b)-onto.
   (i) $f(x) = \frac{x}{x^2+1}; f:\mathbb{R} \to \mathbb{R}$
   (ii) $f(x) = 3x - 1 - 3[x]; f:\mathbb{R} \to [1,4]$
   (iii) $f(n) = n^2 + 1; f:\mathbb{Z} \to \mathbb{N}$
   (iv) $f(x) = 3x - |2x+1|; f:\mathbb{N}^* \to \mathbb{N}$

(v) $f(x) = \begin{cases} x^2 - 1, x > 1 \\ 2x - 1, x \le 1 \end{cases}; f: \mathbb{R} \to \mathbb{R}$

5. Show that the function $f(x) = \frac{3x+1}{x-2}; f: \{2\} \to \mathbb{R} - \{a\}$ is a one-to-one function. Find the value of a, such that f is an onto function.
6. For what value of a, the function $f(x) = \frac{x+5}{x+a}$ is equal to its inverse?
7. Find the inverse function of the following functions, if it exists.
   (i) $f(x) = \frac{2 - 3x^2}{x^2 - 1}$
   (ii) $f(x) = \frac{1 - 2x}{1 + 3x}, (x > -1/3)$
   (iii) $f(x) = \begin{cases} 3x + 1, x > 1 \\ 2x - 1, x \le 1 \end{cases}$
   (iv) $f(x) = \begin{cases} \frac{1}{x}, x > 0 \\ 0, x \le 0 \end{cases}$
   (v) $f(x) = \sqrt{x^2 - 1} + x$
   (vi) $f(x) = 3x^2 - 4x + 1$
8. Check the following functions to see whether they are ascending or descending at different intervals.
   (i) $f(x) = x^2 + 2^x$
   (ii) $f(x) = \frac{1 - x}{1 + x}, (x > -1)$
   (iii) $f(x) = x + [x]$
   (iv) $f(x) = |\tan x|, (-\frac{\pi}{2} < x < \frac{\pi}{2})$
   (v) $f(x) = \begin{cases} -\sqrt{x}, x > 0 \\ -x, x \le 0 \end{cases}$
   (vi) $(vi) - f(x) = \begin{cases} x - 1, x > 1 \\ x^3 - 1, x \le 1 \end{cases}$
9. Verify whether the following functions are even or odd.
   (i) $f(x) = 2^{sgnx}$
   (ii) $f(x) = x[x^2] - x^3$
   (iii) $f(x) = x - [x]$
   (iv) $f(x) = \cos(Arc \cos x)$
   (v) $f(x) = |x + 1| - |x - 1|$
   (vi) $f(x) = a^x + a^{-x}, (a > 0)$
10. Let's $f(x) = 3x^3 - 1$ and $g(x) = 2x - 3$.
   (i) Find fog and gof
   (ii) Is the equality $fog = gof$ correct?
   (iii) If $h(x) = x - 1$, check the correctness of equality $(fog)oh = fo(goh)$.
11. Determine which of the following functions are periodic. Find the value of their period.
   (i) $f(x) = \sin \sqrt{x}$
   (ii) $f(x) = mx - [mx], (m \in \mathbb{N})$
   (iii) $f(x) = x - [x]$
   (iv) $f(x) = \tan x \,.\, \mathrm{cotg} x$
   (v) $f(x) = \begin{cases} \sqrt{x}, x > 0 \\ x, x \le 0 \end{cases}$
   (vi) $f(x) = \begin{cases} x^{|x|}, x > 0 \\ x^3, x \le 0 \end{cases}$

12. Prove that

(i) $\tanh x = \frac{\sinh 2x}{1 + \cosh 2x}$

(ii) $\sinh 3x = 3\sinh^3 x + 4\sinh x$

(iii) $\sin(x + y)\sin(x - y) = \sin^2 x - \sin^2 y$

(iv) $\cos x \cos 2x \cos 4x \cos 8x \cos 16x = \frac{\sin 32x}{32 \sin x}$

(v) $\tanh \frac{1}{2}(\ln x) = \frac{x - 1}{x + 1}$

(vi) $\frac{\sin 3x - \sin 5x}{\cos 5x - \cos 3x} = \cot 4x$

13. Let $\sinh x = \frac{\pi^x + \pi^{-x}}{2}$ and $\cosh x = \frac{\pi^x - \pi^{-x}}{2}$, prove

(i) $\cosh^2 x - \sinh^2 x = 1$

(ii) $\sinh 2x = 2\sinh x . \cosh x$

(iii) $\cosh 2x = \cosh^2 x + \sinh^2 x$

(iv) $\cosh 2x - 1 = 2\sinh^2 x$

(v) $\cosh 2x + 1 = 2\cosh^2 x.$

REFERENCES

Apostol. Tom, M. (1966). *Calculus* (3rd ed., Vol. 1). JOHN WILEY & SONS.

Finney. Ross, L. (1988). *Calculus and Analytical Geometry* (7th ed.). ADDISON-WESLEY PUBLISHING COMPANY.

Leithold. Louis (1981). The Calculus and Analytical Geometry (4th ed.). Harper & Row.

Piskunov, N. (1981). Differential and Integral, Voume 1 (4th ed.). MIR PUBLISHER, MOSCOW.

Rodin. Burton. (1970). Calculus with Analytical Geometry (4th ed.). Prentice-Hall, Inc., Englewood Cliffs, New Jersey.

Silverman. Richard, A. (1985). *Calculus with Analytical Geometry* (2nd ed.). Prentice-Hall, Inc.

Stewart, J. (2008). *Calculus* (6th ed.). Mc-Graw.

Thomas. George, B. (2014). *Calculus* (13th ed.). Mc-Graw.

Chapter 4
Limits and Continuity

ABSTRACT

This chapter focuses on limits and continuity at a point and on an interval. Infinite limits and the limits at infinity are considered then, concepts of the asymptotes will be declared. Concepts of right and left limits and right and left continuity will be defined. Continuity on an interval will be used to introduce the intermediate value theorem which is also known as Bolzano's theorem. By this theorem we find the interval where the root of an equation may exist. To complete this chapter, we add a section namely Sequences and Series which is optional. After defining the concepts of convergent and divergent for sequences and series we introduce some tests for convergent and divergent.

4.1 INTRODUCTION

Let's consider the function $f(x) = \frac{x^2 - 5x + 6}{x - 2}$. Clearly, $D_f = \mathbb{R} - \{2\}$. In other words, the function is not defined in x=2. What is the value of $f(x)$ when x=2? How do the values of $f(x)$ behave when x is near but different from 2?

We want to consider the behavior of the function near 2. For this purpose, we consider the following table:

Table 1.

x	1 1.5 1.9 1.99 1.999 … 2 … 2.001 2.01 2.1 2.5 3
$f(x)$	-2 -1.5 -1.1 -1.01 -1.001 ? -0.999 -.99 -0.9 -0.5 0

We observe that as x approaches 2, the value of $f(x)$ approaches -1. More precisely, the value of $f(x)$ can be as close to -1 as we want, provided that the value of x is close to 2. That is, we can reduce the difference between $f(x)$ and -1 as much as

DOI: 10.4018/979-8-3693-3657-1.ch004

we want, provided that the difference between x and 2 becomes smaller. Because in the table one of the differences is positive and one is negative, it is better to use the symbol of absolute value.

Thus, if $|x-2|$ is chosen small enough, then $|f(x)+1|$ can be chosen as small as desired. If we use two positive numbers ε and δ for these two differences, we can find some positive number δ such that $|f(x) + 1| < \delta$, whenever $|x - 2| < \varepsilon$.

It should be noted that to define the limit of the function f at a point a, the function f does not need to be defined at this point. Even if the function is meaningful at this point, the limit of the function at this point may not be equal to the value of the function at this point.

Now, according to these contents, we can define the limits of the function and express theorems related to them.

4.2 DEFINITIONS AND THEOREMS OF LIMITS

We assume that the function f is defined near the point a. We say that the limit of the function f when x tends to a is equal to L and we write

$$\lim_{x\to a} f(x) = L,$$

if for every $\varepsilon > 0$, there exists a $\delta > 0$, such that whenever $0 < x - a < \delta$, we have $|f(x) - L| < \varepsilon$.

We call L the *limit* of the function, which must be unique if it exists.

Before continuing to examine the limit problems, we state the theorems related to the limits.

Theorem 1. If $\lim_{x\to a} f(x) = L_1$ and $\lim_{x\to a} g(x) = L_2$ then

(i) $\lim_{x\to a} [f(x) \pm g(x)] = L_1 \pm L_2$
(ii) $\lim_{x\to a} [f(x) . g(x)] = L_1 . L_2$
(iii) $\lim_{x\to a} [f(x)/g(x)] = L_1/L_2$
(iv) $\lim_{x\to a} [\circledast f(x)] = \circledast f(L)$

where $\circledast$ represents an operator such as a radical, logarithm or trigonometric operators.

Example 1: Prove that, $\lim_{x\to 1}(8x - 5) = 3$.

Solution: We must show that $L=3$. For this purpose, we consider $|f(x)-L|$.

We must have

$$|f(x) - L| = |8x - 5 - 3| = 8|x - 1| < \varepsilon \Rightarrow |x - 1| < \varepsilon/8.$$

Hence, by choosing $\delta \leq \varepsilon$, the answer is correct.■

To consider the limit of piecewise functions, one-sided limits, or in other words, right and left-hand limits, are defined.

If you have noticed, at the very beginning of the work, when $x \to 2$, once with values greater than 2, we inclined x towards 2 and once with values smaller than 2. For the first case, we show this state with the $x \to 2^+$, and in the second case, we show it with $x \to 2^-$. In a more general case, when x tends to a with values greater than a that is, $x \to a^+$and if there is a limit, we call it the *right-hand limit* and denote it with L_r. That means

$$\lim_{x \to a^+} f(x) = L_r.$$

Similarly, when x tends to a with values smaller than a that is, $x \to a^-$ and if there is a limit, we call it the *left-hand limit* and denote it with L_l. That means

$$\lim_{x \to a^-} f(x) = L_l.$$

The limit exists, if $L_r = L_l$.

Example 2: Find

$$\lim_{x \to 3^+} \frac{[x^2]-[x]^2}{x^2-9}$$

Solution: Since, $x \to 3^+$, then

$$\lim_{x \to 3^+} [x^2] = [9^+] = 9, \lim_{x \to 3^+} [x]^2 = [3^+]^2 = 3^2 = 9 \text{and} \lim_{x \to 3^+} (x^2-9) = 0^+.$$

Therefore,

$$\lim_{x \to 3^+} \frac{[x^2]-[x]^2}{x^2-9} = \frac{\lim_{x \to 3^+}[x^2] - \lim_{x \to 3^+}[x]^2}{\lim_{x \to 3^+}(x^2-9)} = \frac{0}{0^+} = 0.■$$

Example 3: Show that $\lim_{x \to 0} \operatorname{sgn} x$ does not exist.

Solution: We have

$$\operatorname{sgn} x = \begin{cases} 1, x > 0 \\ 0, x = 0 \\ -1, x < 0. \end{cases}$$

Then, $\lim_{x\to 0^+} \text{sgn}x = 1$, and $\lim_{x\to 0^-} \text{sgn}x = -1$. That is, $L_r \neq L_l$. Hence limit does not exist.

Note that the sign function in the rest of the points belonging to the set $\mathbb{R}$ has a limit.■

Example 4: Does the function f have a limit at x=1?

$$f(x) = \begin{cases} [x] - x, x > 1 \\ 2x + 5, x = 1 \\ sgn(x^2 - 1) + |x|, x < 1. \end{cases} .$$

Solution: We find the right and left-hand limits of f at x=1. We have

$$\lim_{x\to 1^+} f(x) = \lim_{x\to 3^+}([x] - x) = 0,$$

$$\lim_{x\to 1^-} f(x) = \lim_{x\to 1^-}\left(\text{sgn}(x^2 - 1) + |x|\right) = -1 + 1 = 0.$$

Since $\lim_{x\to 1^+} f(x) = \lim_{x\to 1^-} f(x) = 0$, then the function has limit 0 in x=1. ■

Example 5: Find the value of k if the following function has a limit in x=3.

$$f(x) = \begin{cases} x^2 - 2k[x], x \geq 3 \\ \sqrt{18 - x^2} + 12, x < 3. \end{cases}$$

Solution: We have

$$\lim_{x\to 3^+} f(x) = \lim_{x\to 3^+}(x^2 - 2k[x]) = 9 - 6k,$$

$$\lim_{x\to 3^-} f(x) = \lim_{x\to 3^-}\left(\sqrt{18 - x^2} + 12\right) = 15.$$

Since limit exists then $\lim_{x\to 3^+} f(x) = \lim_{x\to 3^-} f(x)$, that is,

$$9 - 6k = 15 \rightarrow k = -1.■$$

One of the theorems that is used in solving limit problems is the *squeeze* (or *sandwich*) *theorem*. It states that, if for all $x \in I$, we have $g(x) \leq f(x) \leq h(x)$ and

$$\lim_{x\to a} h(x) = \lim_{x\to a} g(x) = L,$$

then, $\lim_{x\to a} f(x) = L$.

We can use this theorem to show that, $\lim_{x\to 0} \frac{\sin x}{x} = 1$ by "squeezing" $\frac{\sin x}{x}$ between two functions $h(x)$=1 and $g(x)$=cos$x$ to find the limit at x=0.

In general,

$$\lim_{x\to 0}\frac{\sin^m ax}{(bx)^n} = \begin{cases} 0, m > n \\ \frac{a}{b}, m = n \\ \infty \ , m < n. \end{cases}.$$

These results can be used in many related problems that have the form $\frac{0}{0}$ and cannot be solved using theorems of limit. In this case, we say that the limit has an *ambiguous* shape and the ambiguity must be resolved somehow. The existence of trigonometric functions requires us to use these results.

Example 6: Find

$$\lim_{x\to 0}\frac{1-\cos x}{2x^2}.$$

Solution: For x=0, we obtain, $\frac{0}{0}$, which is an ambiguous number. But, since $1-\cos x = 2\sin^2\left(\frac{x}{2}\right)$, thus,

$$\lim_{x\to 0}\frac{1-\cos x}{2x^2} = \lim_{x\to 0}\frac{2\sin^2\left(\frac{x}{2}\right)}{2x^2} = \frac{1}{4}.\blacksquare$$

Example 7: Determine

$$\lim_{x\to 1}\frac{(3x+1))\sin(x-1)}{(x^2-1)}.$$

Solution: For x=1, we again get $\frac{0}{0}$. We rewrite it as:

$$\frac{(3x+1)\sin(x-1)}{(x^2-1)} = \frac{(3x+1)\sin(x-1)}{(x+1)(x-1)} = \left[\frac{3x+1}{x+1}\right]\cdot\left[\frac{\sin(x-1)}{x-1}\right].$$

Therefore,

$$\lim_{x\to 1}\frac{(3x+1))\sin(x-1)}{(x^2-1)} = \lim_{x\to 1}\left[\frac{3x+1}{x+1}\right].\lim_{x\to 1}\left[\frac{\sin(x-1)}{x-1}\right] = \left[\frac{4}{2}\right].[1] = 2.\blacksquare$$

Remark 1: Let $\lim_{x\to a}\frac{P(x)}{Q(x)} = \frac{0}{0}$, where, $P(x)$ and $Q(x)$ are polynomials of degrees m and n, respectively. Since $P(a)=Q(a)=0$, then $P(x)$ and $Q(x)$ are divisible by $(x-a)$ and we can write

$$\lim_{x\to a}\frac{P(x)}{Q(x)} = \lim_{x\to a}\frac{(x-a)R(x)}{(x-a)S(x)} = \frac{R(a)}{S(a)}.$$

If $\lim_{x\to a}\frac{R(x)}{S(x)} = \frac{0}{0}$, then we repeat the previous procedure.
Example 8: Find

$$\lim_{x\to 2}\frac{2x^3 - 3x^2 + 5x - 14}{x^3 + 7x^2 - 16x - 4}.$$

Solution: We have

$$\lim_{x\to 2}\frac{2x^3 - 3x^2 + 5x - 14}{x^3 + 7x^2 - 16x - 4} = \frac{0}{0}.$$

The numerator and denominator are divisible by $(x-2)$, thus

$$\operatorname{Lim}_{x\to 2}\frac{2x^3 - 3x^2 + 5x - 14}{x^3 + 7x^2 + 16x - 4} = \lim_{x\to 2}\frac{(x-2)(2x^2 + x + 7)}{(x-2)(x^2 + 9x + 2)} = \lim_{x\to 2}\frac{(2x^2 + x + 7)}{(x^2 + 9x + 2)} = \frac{17}{24}. \blacksquare$$

There are other ambiguous forms such as $\frac{\infty}{\infty}$, $\infty - \infty$, $\infty^0, 1^\infty$, and $0 \times \infty$, which we explain by examining the limits of infinity and the limit at infinity in this chapter. We will discuss some of the ambiguous forms in the next chapter.

4.2.1 Infinite Limits

Consider the graph of the function $f(x) = \frac{1}{(x-1)^2}$.

Figure 1. Graph of function $f(x) = \frac{1}{(x-1)^2}$

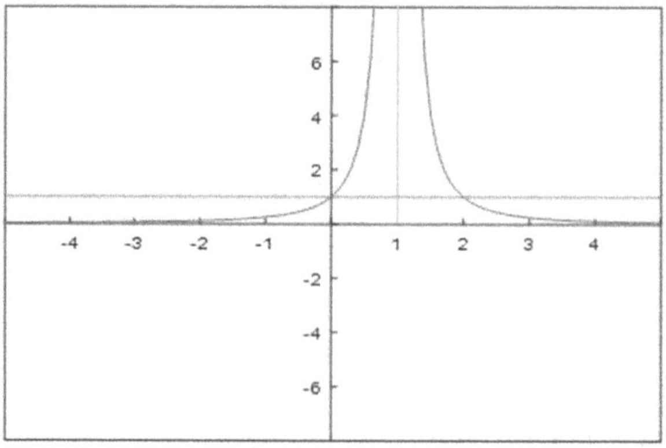

We notice that as the value of x approaches point 1 from the right (or left), it becomes immeasurably larger. More precisely, we can make the value of $f(x)$ as large as we want, provided that the value of x is sufficiently close to 1. We show these concepts with the following symbols:

$$\lim_{x\to1^+}\frac{1}{(x-1)^2} = +\infty \ , \lim_{x\to1^-}\frac{1}{(x-1)^2} = +\infty$$

In other words,

$$\lim_{x\to1}\frac{1}{(x-1)^2} = +\infty \ .$$

In a more general, it can be said that

$$\lim_{x\to a} f(x) = +\infty \ ,$$

if for $M>0$, there exists a number, $\delta > 0$, such that when $|x-a| < \delta$ then $f(x)>M$.

Similarly, when $x \to a$ and $f(x)$ decrease infinitely, we say that if for every $m<0$, there exists a number, $\delta > 0$,such that when $|x-a| < \delta$ then $f(x)<m$.

Example 9: Show that

$$\lim_{x\to3^-}\frac{[x^2]-9}{x^2-9} = +\infty \ .$$

Solution: We have $\lim_{x\to3^-}(x^2-9) = 0$, and also, $x^2-9 < 0$,so the denominator tends to zero with values smaller than zero. In other words, the denominator is 0^-, that is, it is a negative number. We also have $\lim_{x\to3^-}[x^2]-9 = -1$. Thus

$$\lim_{x\to3^-}\frac{[x^2]-9}{x^2-9} = \frac{-1}{0^-} = +\infty \ .$$

Example 10: Find the right-hand limit of $f(x) = e^{\frac{1}{x}}$ at x=0.

Solution: It is clear that $\lim_{x\to0^+}\frac{1}{x} = \frac{1}{0^+} = +\infty$. Then,

$$\lim_{x\to0^+} f(x) = e^{+\infty} = +\infty \ .$$

4.2.2 The Limits at Infinity

Consider the graph of the function $f(x) = \frac{x}{x-1}$.

Figure 2. Graph of function

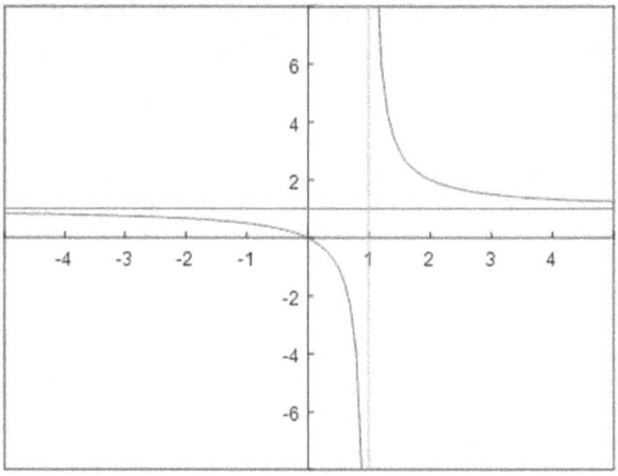

We see that when x increases (or decreases) infinitely, the function $f(x)$ tends to the number 1. In other words,

$$\lim_{x \to \infty} f(x) = 1.$$

This issue can be seen intuitively by writing the result in a table, and claiming that, we can bring the values of $f(x)$ closer to the number 1 as desired with the condition that x is chosen to be large enough. In general, it can be said that if, $x \to +\infty$, then

$$\lim_{x \to +\infty} f(x) = L,$$

If $\forall \varepsilon > 0$, there exists $M>0$, such that when $x>M$ then $|f(x) - L| < \varepsilon$. That is,

$$\lim_{x \to +\infty} f(x) = L \to \forall \epsilon > 0 \exists M > 0 : \forall x > M \to |f(x) - L| < \varepsilon.$$

Similarly, when x decreases infinitely, that is, $x \to -\infty$, we say that if $\forall \varepsilon > 0$, there exists a $m<0$, such that when $x<m$, then $|f(x) - L| < \varepsilon$.

Remark 2: $\operatorname{Lim}_{x \to \infty} \frac{1}{x^n} = 0, n \in \mathbb{N}$.

Example 11: Determine

$$\lim_{x \to \infty} \frac{6x^2 + 4x - 5}{3x^2 - 2x - 1}.$$

Solution: We write,

$$\lim_{x\to\infty}\frac{6x^2+4x-5}{3x^2-2x-1} = \lim_{x\to\infty}\frac{6+\frac{4}{x}-\frac{5}{x^2}}{3-\frac{2}{x}-\frac{1}{x^2}} = \frac{6+0-0}{3-0-0} = 2.$$

Remark 3: Assume $P(x)$ and $Q(x)$ are two polynomials with degree m and n, respectively. That is,

$$P(x) = a_m x^m + a_{m-1}x^{m-1} + \ldots + a_1 x + a_0,\ (a_m \neq 0)$$

$$Q(x) = b_n x^n + b_{n-1}x^{n-1} + \ldots + b_1 x + b_0, (b_n \neq 0).$$

Then,

$$\lim_{x\to\infty}\frac{P(x)}{Q(x)} = \begin{cases} \infty\ , m > n \\ \frac{a_m}{b_n}, m = n \\ 0, m < n \end{cases}.$$

We are back to the previous example. We could say, since $m=n=2$, then,

$$\lim_{x\to\infty}\frac{6x^2+4x-5}{3x^2-2x-1} = \frac{6}{3} = 2.$$

Example 12: Find

$$\lim_{n\to\infty}\frac{1+2+3+\ldots+n}{n!}.$$

Solution: We have,

$$1+2+3+\ldots+n = \frac{n(n+1)}{2}.$$

Then,

$$\lim_{n\to\infty}\frac{1+2+3+\ldots+n}{n!} = \lim_{x\to\infty}\frac{\frac{n(n+1)}{2}}{n!} = 0.$$

Note that the degree of denominator is greater than the degree of the nominator.

The squeeze theorem also holds for infinite limits. We state it by the following theorem for the case $x \to +\infty$.

Theorem 2. Suppose the functions f, g and h are defined in the interval $(a, +\infty)$. For this interval, we also have $h(x) \leq f(x) \leq g(x)$.

If,

$$\lim_{x\to+\infty} h(x) = \lim_{x\to+\infty} g(x) = L,$$

then,

$$\lim_{x\to+\infty} f(x) = L.$$

Example 13: Verify $\lim_{x\to+\infty} \frac{[x]}{x}$.

Solution: Since for $x \in \mathbb{R}$, $x \geq [x] > x - 1$, then $\frac{x-1}{x} < \frac{[x]}{x} \leq 1$. Clearly when

$x \to +\infty$, then $1 < \lim_{x\to+\infty} \frac{[x]}{x} \leq 1$. Hence, $\lim_{x\to+\infty} \frac{[x]}{x} = 1$.

We remind you that the limits of the forms $\frac{0}{0}, \frac{\infty}{\infty}$ or $\infty - \infty$ are ambiguous forms of limits. To overcome these cases, we can use theorems of limits or algebraic identities that we met in Chapters 1 and 3.

Example 14: Show that

$$\lim_{x\to+\infty} \sqrt[3]{8x^3 + x^2 - 6} - 2x = 1/8.$$

Solution: We use the following identity

$$(a - b)(a^2 + ab + b^2) = a^3 - b^3.$$

Let's write

$$= \lim_{x\to+\infty} \frac{x^2 - 6}{\left(\sqrt[3]{8x^3 + x^2 - 6}\right)^2 + 2x\sqrt[3]{8x^3 + x^2 - 6} + 8x^3)} \equiv \lim_{x\to+\infty} \frac{x^2 - 6}{8x^2} = 1/8.$$

4.2.3 The Asymptotes

Suppose the function $f(x)$ has an infinite branch. It means that one of its coordinates tends to infinity. We consider a line such as L to be the *asymptote* of this branch if the distance between the curve and the line approaches zero, as one or both of the x or y coordinates tend to infinity.

If the line of the asymptote is parallel to the y-axis, we call this, the *vertical* asymptote. With this definition, the line $x{=}a$ is a vertical asymptote if

$$\lim_{x\to a^+} f(x) = \pm\infty \text{ or } \lim_{x\to a^-} f(x) = \pm\infty.$$

If the line of the asymptote is parallel to the x-axis, we call this a *horizontal* asymptote. Thus, the line $y=b$ is a horizontal asymptotic if $\lim_{x\to\infty} f(x) = b$.

If $\lim_{x\to\infty} f(x) = \infty$, the line $y=mx+b$ is asymptote if $\lim_{x\to\infty}(mx + b - f(x)) = 0$. We call this asymptote as *slant* (*oblique*). With this definition, we have

$$m = \lim_{x\to+\infty}\frac{f(x)}{x},$$

$$b = \lim_{x\to\infty}(f(x) - mx).$$

Example 15: Find the slant asymptote of $f(x)= x+\cos x$, if it exists.

Solution: We have

$$m = \operatorname{Lim}_{x\to+\infty}\frac{f(x)}{x} = \lim_{x\to+\infty}\frac{1 + \cos x}{x} = \lim_{x\to+\infty}\left(1 + \frac{\cos x}{x}\right) = 1 + \lim_{x\to+\infty}\frac{\cos x}{x} = 1.$$

But $\lim_{x\to\infty}(f(x) - mx) = \lim_{x\to\infty}(x + \cos x - x) = \lim_{x\to\infty}(\cos x)$,does not exist, thus the graph of the function has not any slant asymptote.

Example 16: Verify the slant asymptote of $f(x) = x + \frac{\cos x}{x}$, if it exists.

Solution: We have

$$m = \operatorname{Lim}_{x\to+\infty}\frac{f(x)}{x} = \lim_{x\to+\infty}\left(1 + \frac{\cos x}{x^2}\right) = 1 + \lim_{x\to+\infty}\frac{\cos x}{x^2} = 1.$$

Thus,

$$\lim_{x\to\infty}(f(x) - mx) = \lim_{x\to\infty}\left(x + \frac{\cos x}{x} - x\right) = 0.$$

That is, the line y=x is slant asymptote of function.

Example 17: Verify the asymptotes of $f(x) = \frac{e^x - 1}{e^x + 1}$, if they exist.

Solution: Since $e^x + 1 \neq 0$, hence $f(x)$ has not vertical asymptote. But it has two horizontal asymptotes, because

$$\lim_{x\to+\infty}\frac{e^x - 1}{e^x + 1} \equiv \lim_{x\to+\infty}\frac{e^x}{e^x} = 1,$$

and

$$\lim_{x\to-\infty}\frac{e^x - 1}{e^x + 1} \equiv \lim_{x\to-\infty}\frac{0 - 1}{0 + 1} = -1.$$

Therefore, $y = \pm 1$ are horizontal asymptotes of $f(x)$.

This function has not slant asymptote, because

$$m = \operatorname*{Lim}_{x\to\infty}\frac{f(x)}{x} = \lim_{x\to\infty}\frac{\left(\frac{e^x-1}{e^x+1}\right)}{x} \to \infty \ .$$

Example 18: If $x=1$ is the vertical asymptote of $y = \frac{(m+3)x^2-4}{(m-1)x^2-4}$, find the horizontal asymptote.

Solution: Since $x=1$ is the vertical asymptote, hence $x=1$ must be a root of denominator. That is, $(m-1)(1)^2-4=0$.

This leads to, $m=5$. Thus,

$$y = \frac{8x^2-4}{4x^2-4} = \frac{2x^2-1}{x^2-1}.$$

Therefore, the horizontal asymptotes of y will be

$$y = \lim_{x\to\infty}\frac{2x^2-1}{x^2-1} \to y = 2.$$

To deal with limits, the following results can also be useful.

(i) $\lim_{x\to 0}\frac{1-\cos ax}{bx} = 0,$
(ii) $\lim_{x\to 0^+}(1+kx)^{\frac{1}{x}} = e,$
(iii) $\lim_{x\to\infty}\left(1+\frac{k}{x}\right)^x = e^k.$

4.3 CONTINUITY

In the early days of calculus, almost all the discussed functions were not considered continuous. At that time, there was no need for deep attention in the strict sense of continuity. Until the end of the 18th century, discontinuous functions appeared in connection with various types of physics problems. In particular, regarding the theory of heat, it prompted mathematicians to study the exact meaning of continuity more carefully. From an intuitive point of view, it is felt that the function f can be called "continuous" when its graph can be traced on the paper without removing the tip of the pen. That is, in constructing a graph of a continuous function, the pen never leaves the paper.

In this section, we give a mathematical definition of continuity in a point and continuity in an interval. We start with the definition of continuity in a point.

4.3.1 Continuity in a Point

We start with the definition of continuity in a point.

A function $f(x)$ is said to be continuous at $x=a$, if

$$\lim_{x \to a} f(x) = f(a).$$

Therefore, by this definition, (*i*) the function must be defined at $x=a$, (*ii*) its limit must exist at the point, and (*iii*) the value of the function at that point must equal the value of the limit at that point. If one of these three conditions is not met, we say that the function is not continuous at $x=a$.

Example 19: Check the continuity of function $f(x) = \frac{\sin x}{x}$, at $x=0$, if it exists.

Solution: We obtain, $f(0) = \frac{0}{0}$. That is, the function was not defined at $x=0$. Thus the function is not continuous at this point.

Example 20: Prove that the function $f(x)=[x]$, is not continuous at $x=0$.

Solution: We have, $f(0)=[0]=0$. But, $\lim_{x \to 0}[x]$does not exist, because $\lim_{x \to 0^+}[x]= 0$, and $\lim_{x \to 0^-}[x] = -1$. That is, $L_r \neq L_l$. Hence limit does not exist. That is, this the function is not continuous at $x=0$.

Example 21: Consider the following function for continuity.

$$f(x) = \begin{cases} \frac{\sin x}{x}, x \neq 0 \\ 1, x = 0. \end{cases}$$

Solution: Clearly, $f(0)=1$. By squeeze theorem, we have, $\lim_{x \to 0} \frac{\sin x}{x} = 1$. Then,

$$\lim_{x \to 0} \frac{\sin x}{x} = f(1).$$

That is, the function is continuous at $x=0$.

Similar to the theorem 1, we have the following theorem:

Theorem 3. If the functions $f(x)$ and $g(x)$ are continuous at $x=a$ then,

(i) $f(x) \pm g(x)$

(ii) $f(x) . g(x)$

(iii) $f(x)/g(x), g(a) \neq 0$

are continuous at $x=a$.

Example 22: The cost of transporting goods by truck is based on a formula according to which, as the weight of the goods increases, the cost per kilo of goods decreases. Suppose the weight of a goods is w kilo and the total truckage cost is $C(w)$ dollars and

$$C(w) = \begin{cases} 0.85w, 50 \geq x > 0 \\ 0.75w, 100 \geq x > 50 \\ 0.65w, 150 \geq x > 100 \\ 0.55w, x > 150. \end{cases}$$

Specify the discontinuous points of $C(w)$.

Solution: From the given function, it is obvious that the discontinuous points are x=50, x=100, and x=150. Because $L_r \neq L_l$, at these points.

The following theorems hold for continuity at a point.

Theorem 4. Suppose the functions f, and g are continuous at x=a. Then, $f \pm g, f.g$, and $\frac{f}{g}$, $(g(a) \neq 0)$, are continuous at x=a.

Theorem 5. Let's $\lim_{x \to a} g(x) = L$, and the function $f(x)$ is continuous at the point L. Then, the function fog is continuous at x=a.

Example 23: Assume $f(x) = \frac{x}{x-2}$, and $g(x) = \sqrt{2}$. Is the function fog continuous at x=2?

Solution: We have $fog = f(g(x)) = \frac{g(x)}{g(x)-2} = \frac{\sqrt{2}}{\sqrt{2}-2}$, that is a constant function. Hence, fog is continuous at any point.

In Example 16, although the function has no limit at $x = 50, x = 100$ and $x = 150$, it has a right and left-hand limit at these points. Even the left-hand limit at those points is equal to the value of the function at these points. In such cases, we say the function has left-hand continuity at these points. In general, we say:

The function $f(x)$ has right-hand continuity at x=a if $\lim_{x \to a^+} f(x) = f(a)$.

Similarly, the function $f(x)$ has left-hand continuity at x=a, if $\lim_{x \to a^-} f(x) = f(a)$. If there is continuity, these two must exist.

4.3.2 Continuity on an Interval

Definitions of right and left-hand limits allow us to define continuity for an interval, but it is necessary to separate continuity between two open and closed intervals.

(a) *Continuity at an open interval.* We say that $f(x)$ is continuous in the interval (a,b) if it is continuous for all $x \in (a,b)$.

(b) *Continuity at a closed interval.* We say that $f(x)$ is continuous in the interval $[a,b]$ if it is continuous in (a,b), and also has right-hand continuity in x=a and left-hand continuity in x=b.

Example 24: Check the continuity of the functions, $f(x) = \sqrt{4-x^2}$, and $g(x) = \sqrt{x^2-4}$ on the interval [-2,2].

Solution: The function $f(x)$ is continuous on (-2,2). We have right-hand continuity at x= -2, because $\lim_{x\to-2^+} f(x) = f(-2)$. We also have, left-hand continuity at x=2, because $\lim_{x\to2^-} f(x) = f(2)$, and so the function is continuous on [-2,2].

For the function $g(x)$, we know that $D_g = (-\infty, -2] \cup [2, +\infty)$ and q is continuous on $(-\infty, -2) \cup (2, +\infty)$. In addition, at point 2 it has a right-hand continuity and at -2 it has a left-hand continuity. Thus, the function is continuous on D_g.

Continuity on an interval can be used to introduce a theorem called the *intermediate value theorem.*

Theorem 6. (Intermediate value Theorem). If the function f is continuous on [a, b] and $f(a) \neq f(b)$, then, for any $k \in (f(a), f(b))$ there exists a number $c \in (a,b)$ such that, $f(c)=k$.

This theorem helps to conclude that if f is continuous on [a,b] and $f(a).f(b)<0$, then the equation $f(x)=0$ has at least one root in the interval (a,b).

This result is also known as Bolzano's theorem.

Example 25: Show that the equation, $x - \cos x=0$, has at least a root on the interval $\left(0, \frac{\pi}{2}\right)$.

Solution: The function $f(x)=x - \cos x$ is continuous on $\left(0, \frac{\pi}{2}\right)$Meanwhile, $f(0)=-1<0$, and $f\left(\frac{\pi}{2}\right) = \frac{\pi}{2} > 0$. That is, $f(0).f\left(\frac{\pi}{2}\right) < 0$. Thus, Bolzano's theorem, the given equation has, at least, a root on $\left(0, \frac{\pi}{2}\right)$.

Once more, we emphasis that for more information, the readers can refer to textbooks on Differential and Integral Calculus, e.g., see (Apostol, 1966) (Finney, 1988) (Leithold, 1981) (Rodin, 1970) (Piskunov, 1982) (Silverman, 1985) (Stewart, 2008).

We end this chapter with a brief discussion of the sequences and series which are frequently applied to financial computations.

4.4 SEQUENCES AND SERIES (OPTIONAL)

A function whose domain is the set of natural numbers and its range is the nonzero set is called a *sequence*. We show the value of f for n as a_n and write

$$f(n) = a_n, n \in \mathbb{N}$$

The function f is usually denoted as $\{a_n\}_1^n$ or $\{a_n\}$. For example, if $a_n = \frac{1}{n}$, then

$$\{a_n\}_1^n = 1, \frac{1}{2}, \frac{1}{3}, \ldots.$$

We call the sequence is *convergent* if $\lim_{n\to\infty} a_n$ exists, otherwise we call the sequence is *divergent*. The sequence $a_n = \frac{1}{n}$ is convergent because $\lim_{n\to\infty} a_n = 0$, but the sequence defined by $a_n=(-1)^n$ is divergent because the value of the limit is not unique.

Example 26: Check the convergence of the following sequences:

$$(i) - \left\{\left(1+\frac{1}{n}\right)^n\right\}_1^\infty, (ii) - \left\{\sin\frac{n\pi}{2}\right\}_1^\infty.$$

Solution: *(i)*- We have

$$\lim_{n\to\infty} a_n = \lim_{n\to\infty}\left(1+\frac{1}{n}\right)^n = e.$$

Therefore, the sequence is convergence.

For part *(ii)*, we have $a_1 = \sin\frac{\pi}{2} = 1, a_2 = \sin\pi = 0, a_3 = \sin\frac{3\pi}{2} = -1$, $a_4 = \sin 2\pi = 0$. Since the value of the limit is not unique, then, the sequence is divergent.

We call the sequence $\{a_n\}_1^n$ *non-ascending* if, $a_{n+1} \le a_n, \forall n \in N$ and *non-descending* if, $a_{n+1} \ge a_n, \forall n \in N$. If a sequence is non-ascending, or non-descending we say the sequence is a *monotonic sequence.*

We call the sequence $\{a_n\}_1^n$ a *bounded sequence* if a positive number like M is found such that $|a_n| \le M$. We call this sequence is *bounded above* if $a_n \le M$ and *bounded below* if, $a_n \ge M$.

Example 27: Check the sequences in the previous example, for non-ascending or non-descending and boundless.

Solution: We have, $a_n = \left(1+\frac{1}{n}\right)^n$, whence $a_1 = 2, a_2 = 2.25, a_3 = \frac{64}{27}, \ldots$ That is, the sequence is non-descending. We also have, $2 \le a_n < 3$, hence it is bounded. For the second sequence with, $a_n = \sin\frac{n\pi}{2}$, it is a periodic sequence but since $\left|\sin\frac{n\pi}{2}\right| \le 1$ hence it is a bounded sequence.

Is every bounded sequence convergent? The answer is negative. For example, the sequence with $a_n = (-1)^n$ or $a_n = \sin\frac{n\pi}{2}$ is bounded but is not convergent. For convergence of a bounded sequence we need more conditions.

Theorem 7. Any bounded and monotonic sequence is convergent.

Example 28: Show that the sequence $\left\{\frac{2^n}{n!}\right\}$ is convergent.

Solution: The sequence is a descending sequence because, $a_n = \frac{2^n}{n!} > a_{n+1} = \frac{2^{n+1}}{(n+1)!}$. On the other hand, an upper bound for this sequence is 2 and a lower bound is zero. So according to the above theorem, this sequence is convergent.

Remark 4: One of the properties of convergent sequences is that they are bounded. It can be shown that every convergent sequence is bounded.

The following properties hold for sequences:

If $\lim_{n\to\infty} a_n = a$ and $\lim_{n\to\infty} b_n = b$, then

(i) $\lim_{n\to\infty}(a_n \pm b_n) = \lim_{n\to\infty} a_n \pm \lim_{n\to\infty} b_n = a \pm b,$
(ii) $\lim_{n\to\infty}(a_n . b_n) = \lim_{n\to\infty} a_n \cdot \lim_{n\to\infty} b_n = a.b,$
(iii) $\lim_{n\to\infty}(a_n / b_n) = \lim_{n\to\infty} a_n / \lim_{n\to\infty} b_n = a/b,$
(iv) $a_n \geq b_n \to a \geq b.$

Theorem 8. If $\lim_{n\to\infty} a_n = \lim_{n\to\infty} b_n = l$, and $a_n \leq c_n \leq b_n$ then $\lim_{n\to\infty} c_n = l.$
Example 29: Show that

$$\lim_{n\to\infty} \frac{1}{\sqrt{1+\frac{1}{n}}} = 1.$$

Solution: We have, $1 < \sqrt{1+\frac{1}{n}} < 1+\frac{1}{n} = \frac{n+1}{n}$. Thus, $\frac{n}{n+1} < \frac{1}{\sqrt{1+\frac{1}{n}}} < 1$. But, $\lim_{n\to\infty} \frac{n}{n+1} = 1$. Then according to theorem 8 is the value of the limit is 1.

The property of associativity in the addition operation on the set of real numbers makes the finite sums in the form of $a_1+a_2+a_3+\ldots+a_n$ meaningful. This finite sum can be extended to an infinite sum. We call this sequence a *series*.

One of the famous series in the elementary course is the geometric series, which is given below.

$$a + aq + aq^2 + \ldots = \sum_1^\infty aq^n.$$

This series is convergent for $|q|<1$ and its summation is $\frac{a}{1-q}$. This can be verified by using,

$$1 + a + a^2 + \ldots + a^{n-1} = \frac{a^n - 1}{a - 1}, (a \neq 1), \text{(See Chapter 1, Example 5)}$$

But, calculating the sum of a series is not as simple as geometric series. Sometimes it is even impossible. As sequences, our attempt is to examine the series and discuss briefly their convergence. But firstly, we remind you that the necessary condition for the convergence of series, $\sum_1^\infty a_n$, is, $\lim_{n\to\infty} a_n = 0$.

As we mentioned, it is a necessary condition but remind you that it is not a sufficient condition for a series to be convergent. For example, it can be proved that the series with $a_n = \frac{1}{n}$ is not convergent, although

$$\lim_{n\to\infty} a_n = \lim_{n\to\infty} \frac{1}{n} = 0.$$

Any series of the form $\sum_1^\infty \frac{1}{n}$ is called a *harmonic series.*

Consider the series given by

$$\sum_1^\infty \frac{1}{n^p}.$$

It can be shown that this series is convergent if $p>1$ and is divergent for $p \le 1$.

The following properties hold for series:

(a) If, $\sum_1^\infty a_n$ and $\sum_1^\infty b_n$ are convergent, then the following series are convergent.
   (i) $\sum_1^\infty (a_n \pm b_n)$
(b) If, $\sum_1^\infty a_n$ is convergent and $\sum_1^\infty b_n$ is divergent, then $\sum_1^\infty (a_n + b_n)$ is divergent.

Example 30: Verify that the following series is divergent.

$$\sum_1^\infty \left(\frac{1}{2^n} + \left(1 + \frac{1}{n}\right)^n\right).$$

Solution: Suppose

$$\sum_1^\infty (a_n + b_n) = \sum_1^\infty \left(\frac{1}{2^n} + \left(1 + \frac{1}{n}\right)^n\right)$$

where $a_n = \frac{1}{2^n}$ and $b_n = \left(1 + \frac{1}{n}\right)^n$. The series with $a_n = \frac{1}{2^n}$ is convergent because it is a geometric series with $q = \frac{1}{2} < 1$. Therefore, $\sum_1^\infty a_n$ is convergent. But the series with $b_n = \left(1 + \frac{1}{n}\right)^n$ is divergent, hence by part (b) $\sum_1^\infty (a_n + b_n)$is divergent.

Remark 5: If the series $\sum_1^\infty a_n$and $\sum_1^\infty b_n$ differ only in their m terms, then either both series will converge, or both will diverge.

In the continuation of our work, we first examine the convergence of the series than $\forall n, a_n > 0$

We will introduce the following tests for convergence. You can see their proof in most calculus books. These tests are hold for series with non-negative terms.

(I) Comparison tests
   (a) Let's $b_n \ge a_n$, then $\sum_1^\infty a_n$ is convergent if, $\sum_1^\infty b_n$converges.
   (b) If, $\sum_1^\infty a_n$ is divergent then $\sum_1^\infty b_n$ diverges.
   (c) If, $\lim_{n\to\infty} \frac{a_n}{b_n} \neq 0$, then the both series are either convergent or divergent. But if $\lim_{n\to\infty} \frac{a_n}{b_n} = 0$ and $\sum_1^\infty b_n$ is convergent then $\sum_1^\infty a_n$ is also convergent.

Example 31: Test the series $\sum_1^\infty \frac{1}{\sqrt{n}}$ whether is convergent or not.

Solution: Since, $\frac{1}{\sqrt{n}} > \frac{1}{n}$ and, $\sum_1^\infty \frac{1}{n}$ diverges, hence $\sum_1^\infty \frac{1}{\sqrt{n}}$ diverges too.

Example 32: Verify that the series $\sum_{1}^{\infty}\frac{1}{n^n}$ is convergent.

Solution: We have, $\frac{1}{n^n} \leq \frac{1}{2^n}$. Since, $\sum_{1}^{\infty}\frac{1}{2^n}$ is a geometric series and converges, hence, $\sum_{1}^{\infty}\frac{1}{n^n}$ also converges.

(II) Quotient test (D'Alembert's test)

Let's $\lim_{n\to\infty}\frac{a_{n+1}}{a_n} = L$. If, $L<1$, then $\sum_{1}^{\infty}a_n$ is convergent, and is divergent if, $L>1$. But if, $L=1$, then it is not clear that it is convergent or divergent.

Example 33: Determine if the series $\sum_{1}^{\infty}\frac{a^n}{n!}$ is convergent or divergent

Solution: We have,

$$\lim_{n\to\infty}\frac{a_{n+1}}{a_n} = \lim_{n\to\infty}\frac{a}{n+1} = 0, \forall a.$$

Thus the series $\sum_{1}^{\infty}\frac{a^n}{n!}$ is convergent for all a.

Example 34: Test the series $\sum_{1}^{\infty}\frac{n!}{n^n}$ for convergence.

Solution: We have,

$$\lim_{n\to\infty}\frac{a_{n+1}}{a_n} = \lim_{n\to\infty}\frac{(n+1)n^n}{(n+1)^{n+1}} = \lim_{n\to\infty}\frac{1}{(1+1/n)^n} = \frac{1}{e} < 1.$$

Therefore, the series is convergent.

(III) Root test (Cauchy's test)

Suppose $\lim_{n\to\infty}\sqrt[n]{a_n} = L$. Then the series $\sum_{1}^{\infty}a_n$ is convergent if, $L<1$, and is divergent if, $L>1$ If, $L=1$, then it is not clear that it is convergent or divergent.

Example 35: Determine if the series $\sum_{1}^{\infty}\left(1+\frac{1}{n}\right)^{n^2}$ is convergent or divergent

Solution: We have,

$$\lim_{n\to\infty}\sqrt[n]{a_n} = \lim_{n\to\infty}\left(1+\frac{1}{n}\right)^n = e, > 1.$$

Thus, the series is divergent.

Example 36: Test the series $\sum_{1}^{\infty}\frac{(n+1)^{n^2}}{n^{n^2}.3^n}$ is convergent or divergent

Solution: We have,

$$\lim_{n\to\infty}\sqrt[n]{a_n} = \lim_{n\to\infty}\left(1+\frac{1}{n}\right)^n = 1/e < 1.$$

Therefore, the series is convergent.

The series we have considered since now, are infinite series with positive terms. Now, we are going to consider the series having both positive and negative terms. This type of such a series is called an *alternating series*. This series is convergent if $|a_{n+1}| < |a_n|$.

We say an alternating series is *absolutely convergent* if, $\sum_1^{\infty} |a_n|$ is convergent. The convergent series $\sum_1^{\infty} a_n$ is *conditionally convergent* if, $\sum_1^{\infty} |a_n|$ diverges but $\sum_1^{\infty} a_n$ converges.

A known test so called *Leibniz's test* for convergence of an alternating series states that if:

(i) $a_1 > a_2 > a_3 > \ldots,$

(ii) $\lim_{n\to\infty} a_n = 0$

then the series converges.

For example, by using this test, the series $\sum_1^{\infty} \frac{(-1)^{n+1}}{n}$ is convergent.

Example 36: Test the series $\sum_1^{\infty} \frac{(-1)^n}{\left(1+\frac{1}{n}\right)^{n^2}}$ is convergent or divergent.

Solution: The series is absolutely convergent, because by the Cauchy's ratio test the series $\sum_1^{\infty} \frac{(-1)^n}{\left(1+\frac{1}{n}\right)^{n^2}}$ is convergent. Hence, the series is convergent.

Remark 6: One of the applications of the series is for solving to the limit problems.

Example 37: Find

$$\lim_{n\to\infty} \frac{n!}{n^n}.$$

Solution: In example 34 we have shown that the series $\sum_1^{\infty} \frac{n!}{n^n}$ is convergent. Thus we should have $\lim_{n\to\infty} a_n = 0$. That is, $\lim_{n\to\infty} \frac{n!}{n^n} = 0$.

Any series, of the forms $\sum a_n (x-a)^n$ or $\sum a_n x^n$, is called a *power series* which is very important in solving practical problems.

The series $\sum a_n x^n$ can be convergent for all x or for some values of x. The circle $|x|=R$ is called the *circle of convergence* and R as *radius of convergence*.

Theorem 9. If $\lim_{n\to\infty} \left|\frac{a_{n+1}}{a_n}\right| = L$ then radius of convergence of $\sum a_n x^n$ is $\frac{1}{L}$.

By the quotient test if $\lim_{n\to\infty} \left|\frac{a_{n+1} x^{n+1}}{a_n x^n}\right| < 1$ then the series is absolutely convergent and hence if $|x| < \frac{1}{L}$ the series is convergent. It is clear that if, $|x| > \frac{1}{L}$, then the value of the limit will be more than 1, thus $\lim_{n\to\infty} a_n x^n \neq 0$. In other words, the power series is divergent.

We note that the series $\sum x^n$, $\sum \frac{x^n}{n}$ and $\sum \frac{x^n}{n^2}$ have radius of convergence equal to 1. The series $\sum x^n$ is not convergent on circle $|x|=1$ but the series $\sum \frac{x^n}{n^2}$ is absolutely convergent on all points of circle $|x|=1$. The series $\sum \frac{x^n}{n}$ is divergent at $x=1$, but it converges at all other points.

Remark 7: The series $\sum a_n x^n$ and $\sum n a_n x^{n-1}$ have the same radius of convergence.

In the next chapter, we will come back to discuss more about such series, and we discussing two types of them which are more applicable.

CONCLUSION

In this chapter, using the definitions of limits and continuity, we understood the relationship between limits and continuity. Continuity on an interval has been used to introduce the Intermediate value Theorem. This theorem helps us find where the roots of a nonlinear equation exist. This result is also known as Bolzano's theorem. Discussion of the sequences and series leads us to the power series. We could also have some ideas about the convergence and radius of convergence.

4.5 Exercises

1. Find the following limits.
   (i) $\lim\limits_{x\to 0}[x] + [-x]$
   (ii) $\lim\limits_{x\to 0} x^3 \sin\frac{1}{x}$
   (iii) $\lim\limits_{x\to 2^+}\frac{4 - x^2}{(\cos^{-1}x)^2}$
   (iv) $\lim\limits_{x\to 1}\frac{x^n - 1}{x - 1}$
   (v) $\lim\limits_{x\to -1}\frac{x^2 - 2x - 3}{x^3 + 2x^2 - 1}$
   (vi) $\lim\limits_{x\to 0}\frac{\sqrt{1 + x} - 1}{x}$
   (vii) $\lim\limits_{x\to 1}\frac{x^m - 1}{x^n - 1}$
   (viii) $\lim\limits_{t\to 0}\frac{\sin(x - t) - \sin x}{t}$
   (ix) $\lim\limits_{x\to 0}\frac{\sin x}{\sqrt{1 + \tan x} - \sqrt{1 - \tan x}}$
   (x) $\lim\limits_{x\to 0}\frac{\sin(\sin x)}{x}$
2. Determine the value of a and b such that the following functions have a limit at x=1, and x=2.
   (i) $f(x) = \begin{cases} ax + 1, x < 1 \\ 2[x] + 5b, 1 \le x \le 2 \\ ax^2 + b|x - 1| + 1, x > 2 \end{cases}$

   (ii) $f(x) = \begin{cases} [x] - x, x > 1 \\ 2bx + a - 2, 1 \le x \le 2 \\ sgn(x^2 - 4) + a, x > 2. \end{cases}$
3. Verify whether the following functions are continuous on $(-\infty\ ,+\infty\ )$.
   (i) $f(x) = x^2/(2^x + 1)$
   (ii) $f(x) = \lim\limits_{n\to\infty}\frac{3nx}{nx - 1}$

$$(iii) f(x) = \begin{cases} x + [x], x < -1 \\ 3x, -1 \leq x \leq 1 \\ 4x^2 - 1, x > 1 \end{cases}$$

$$(iv) f(x) = |x + 4| + |x - 4|$$

$$(v) f(x) = \begin{cases} x - [x], x > 1 \\ x - 1, x \leq 1 \end{cases}$$

4. Suppose

$$f(x) = (x^2 + 1)/(x + 1) - ax - b; a, b \in R.$$

Find the value of a, and b such that, $\lim_{x \to +\infty} f(x) = 0.$

5. Find the vertical, horizontal, and oblique asymptotes of the following functions.
   (i) $y = \frac{x^3}{x^2 + x - 2}$
   (ii) $y = \sqrt{x^2 - x^3}$
   (iii) $y = \ln(1 + e^x)$
   (iv) $y = \frac{xe^x}{e^x - 1}$
   (v) $y = \sqrt{x^2 - x + 1}$
   (vi) $y = x - \frac{1}{x}$
6. What choice of the numbers a and b makes the function f continuous everywhere?

$$f(x) = \begin{cases} [x] - a|x|, x < 0 \\ ax^2 + 3bx - 1, 0 \leq x \leq 1 \\ sgn(x^2 - 1) + 2a, x > 1. \end{cases}$$

7. Show that the function $f(x) = \sqrt{x - [x]} + [x]$ is continuous on $\mathbb{R}$.
8. Using the intermediate value theorem, show that the following equations have at least one root in the interval (0,1).
   (i) $x^2 + +\sin x - 1 = 0$
   (ii) $3x^3 + 2x - 4 = 0$
   (iii) $x^3 + +\cos x - 1.2 = 0$
   (iv) $\sinh x + \cosh x - 2 = 0$
9. Prove that the equation $x^{30} + 2x^{20} + x^{12} - 1 = 0$ has two roots on (-1, 1).
10. Assume the function f is continuous on $[a,b]$. Show that there exists a number $c \in [a,b]$ such that $f(c) = \frac{f(a) + f(b)}{2}$.
11. When n is large, we may approximate $n!$ by Striling's formula given by, $n! = \sqrt{2\pi n}\left(\frac{n}{e}\right)^n$. Use this formula to show that

$$\lim_{n \to \infty} \frac{\binom{2n}{n}\sqrt{\pi n}}{2^{2n}} = 1.$$

12. We want to enclose a rectangular area with an area of 2500 square meters with a wall and also build a wall that divides the area into two parts in the middle. We assume the cost of the wall that divides the area is 25 dollars per meter, the wall that surrounds the area is 32 dollars per meter, the length of the middle wall is x meters and the cost of building the wall is assumed to be $C(x)$ dollars. Find the equation that describes $C(x)$ and then find $\lim_{x\to 0} C(x)$ and $\lim_{x\to +\infty} C(x)$ and explain the results.
13. Check the convergence of the following sequences.
    (i) $a_n = \left(\frac{5}{6}\right)^n$
    (ii) $a_n = \left(\frac{6}{5}\right)^n$
    (iii) $a_n = \frac{\sin n}{n}$
    (iv) $a_n = \frac{\sinh n}{n}$,
    (v) $a_n = \frac{1 + 2 + 3 + \ldots + n}{n!}$
    (vi) $a_n = \left(\frac{1}{\ln n}\right)^n$
    (vii) $a_n = \left(1 + \frac{1}{n}\right)^n$.
    (viii) $a_n = \frac{n!}{\cos n}$
    (ix) $a_n = \frac{n!}{e^n}$
    (x) $a_n = \frac{n!}{e^{-n}}$
14. Test the convergence of the following series.
    (i) $\sum\left(\frac{5}{6}\right)^n$
    (ii) $\sum\left(\frac{6}{5}\right)^n$
    (iii) $\sum\frac{\sinh(n + 1)}{n + 1}$
    (iv) $\sum\tan^2\left(\frac{\pi}{6}\right)$
    (v) $\sum\frac{n!}{e^{-n}}$
15. Use the comparison test for the following series.
    (i) $\frac{1}{\ln 2} + \frac{1}{\ln 3} + \frac{1}{\ln 4} + \cdots$
    (ii) $\frac{3}{8} + \frac{6}{50} + \frac{9}{344} + \cdots$.

16. Verify the domain of convergence of the following series.

(i) $\sum \frac{\sin(\frac{\pi}{2^n})}{x^n}$

(ii) $\sum \frac{x^n}{2^{n+1}}$

(iii) $\sum \frac{n}{n+1}\left(\frac{x}{2x+1}\right)^n$

(iv) $\sum 2$ nncos nx

(v) $\sum \frac{n}{(2x-1)^{2n-1}}$

(vi) $\sum \frac{x}{(x+1)^n}$

REFERENCES

Apostol. Tom, M. (1966). *Calculus* (3rd ed., Vol. 1). John Wiley & Sons.

Finney. Ross, L. (1988). *Calculus and Analytical Geometry* (7th ed.). Addison-Wesley Publishing Company.

Leithold. Louis (1981). The Calculus and Analytical Geometry (4th ed.). Harper & Row.

Piskunov, N. (1981). Differential and Integral, Voume 1 (4th ed.). MIR Publisher.

Rodin. Burton. (1970). Calculus with Analytical Geometry (4th ed.). Prentice-Hall, Inc., Englewood Cliffs, New Jersey.

Silverman. Richard, A. (1985). *Calculus with Analytical Geometry* (2nd ed.). Prentice-Hall, Inc.

Stewart, J. (2008). *Calculus* (6th ed.). Mc-Graw.

Chapter 5
Differential Calculus

ABSTRACT

In this chapter, we deal with differential calculus. By definition of differentiation, its interpretations we will derive the differentiations of several functions which are defined in Chapter 3. Besides finding tangent and normal lines, some more applications of differentiation will be given throughout the chapter. Another interpretation of the derivative, which is the instantaneous speed that is observed in physics, will also be considered here and give some examples of its application. After introducing the concept of differential, we introduce chain rules and parametric differentiation. The concepts maxima and minima for functions will be described. We will state Roll's, Lagrange's and Cauchy's theorems as an optional part and then introduce Taylor's formula, which is the most useful one in calculus.

INTRODUCTION

One of the important concepts in differential calculus that is used in many practical and theoretical fields is the concept of derivatives. Most of the relationships between the quantities of the physical world can be expressed using continuous and differentiable functions.

We know that in the function $f{:}A \to B$ when the variable x in A, changes, depending on that variable, the function y in B also changes based on the rule $y=f(x)$. One of the important topics of the function is to determine the number of y changes compared to x changes at any point. This goal is fulfilled by the derivative.

The derivative is one of the basic concepts of mathematics that has many applications in all branches of science. The concept of speed and acceleration of a moving object, the heating and cooling of an object, the reaction speed of a chemical process, the rate of decay of a radioactive process and the growth of a biological organism are among the derivative applications.

DOI: 10.4018/979-8-3693-3657-1.ch005

Derivatives also play a crucial role in managing financial risks, optimizing investment returns, and informing strategic decision-making in the field of management.

5.2 CONCEPT OF DERIVATIVE AND ITS INTERPRETATIONS

Suppose the real function f is defined on the interval (a, b). For $x \in (a,b)$, we form a function of the new variable h with the rule $\frac{f(x+h)-f(x)}{h}$. The limit of this function is called the *derivative* of the function f at the point x when $h \to 0$ (if there is a limit) and is denoted by $f'(x)$. Thus

$$f'(x) = \lim_{h \to 0} \frac{f(x+h)-f(x)}{h} \qquad (1)$$

We call h the *increment* of the independent variable and $\Delta f = f(x+h) - f(x)$ the *increment of the function*. Then, another definition formula for differentiation is

$$f'(x) = \lim_{\Delta x \to 0} \frac{\Delta f}{\Delta x} \qquad (2)$$

The derivative of a function according to the above definition, if it exists, is a real number. If for all the points, in (a,b), there exists a derivative of f then it is said that f has a derivative in (a,b). In this case, a function is defined on (a,b) that for each point $x \in (a,b)$, corresponds to the derivative of f at that point, i.e., $f'(x)$. This function is called the *derivative function* and is denoted by f'. If a function has a derivative at each point $x \in (a,b)$, it is said to be *differentiable* in this interval.

Example 1: Verify that the function $f(x)=x^2$ has a derivative at every point of $\mathbb{R}$. Find its derivative.

Solution: The function $f(x)=x^2$ is continuous on $\mathbb{R}$, and we also have

$$f'(x) = \lim_{h \to 0} \frac{f(x+h)-f(x)}{h} = \lim_{h \to 0} \frac{(x+h)^2 - x^2}{h} = \lim_{h \to 0} \frac{2hx}{h} = 2x$$

Thus, f' exists on $\mathbb{R}$, and $f'(x=2x$.

Remark 1: If $f(x) = x^n, n \in \mathbb{N}$, then $f'(x) = nx^{n-1}$.

Example 2: Prove that the derivative of the function $f(x)=\sin x$ is given by $f'(x)=\cos x$.

Solution: We have,

$$f'(x) = \lim_{h\to 0}\frac{f(x+h)-f(x)}{h} = \lim_{h\to 0}\frac{\sin(x+h)-\sin x}{h} = \lim_{h\to 0}\frac{2\sin\frac{h}{2}.\cos(x+h)}{h}$$

We write:

$$\frac{2\sin\frac{h}{2}.\cos(x+h)}{h} = \frac{\sin\frac{h}{2}}{\frac{h}{2}}.\cos(x+h).$$

Thus,

$$f'(x) = \lim_{h\to 0}\frac{\sin\frac{h}{2}}{\frac{h}{2}}.\cos(x+h) = \lim_{h\to 0}\frac{\sin\frac{h}{2}}{\frac{h}{2}}.\lim_{h\to 0}\cos(x+h) = 1.\cos x = \cos x$$

Since the existence of the derivative in $x=a$ depends on the existence of the limit and the existence of the limit depends on the right and left-hand limits, for this reason, we can define the right and the left-hand derivatives.

Definition 1: Suppose the function f is defined in $x=a$. In this case, we define the right-hand derivative of f at this point, which is denoted by $f'_+(a)$, as follows:

$$f'_+(a) = \lim_{x\to a^+}\frac{f(x)-f(a)}{x-a}$$

Similarly, we define the left-hand derivative of f at this point, denoted by $f'\_(a)$ as follows:

$$f'_-(a) = \lim_{x\to a^+}\frac{f(x)-f(a)}{x-a}$$

Obviously, the function f in $x=a$ is differentiable if $f'_+(a) = f'_-(a)$

Example 3: Check the derivability of function f given by $f(x)=|x|$, at $x=0$.

Solution: According to the definition of right and left derivatives, we have

$$f'_+(0) = \lim_{x\to 0^+}\frac{f(x)-f(0)}{x-0} = \lim_{x\to 0^+}\frac{|x|-0}{x-0} = \lim_{x\to 0^+}\frac{x}{x} = 1,$$

$$f'_{-}(0) = \lim_{x \to 0^-} \frac{f(x) - f(0)}{x - 0} = \lim_{x \to 0^-} \frac{|x| - 0}{x - 0} = \lim_{x \to 0^-} \frac{-x}{x} = -1.$$

Since, $f'_{+}(0) \neq f'_{-}(0)$ then this function is not differentiable in $x=a$.■

Remark 2: If you notice, you find that this function is continuous at $x=a$, but it is not differentiable at this point. In other words, the continuity condition is a necessary but not sufficient condition for derivability. On the contrary, if a function is differentiable at $x=a$, this condition is sufficient for it to be continuous at this point too.

In this section, we provide two interpretations for the derivative. Suppose the function $y=f(x$ is continuous in $P(a,f(a))$, where P is a fixed point located on this curve. Consider the point $Q(b,f(b))$, moving on the curve and approaching point P. The slope of this line is, $\frac{f(x) - f(a)}{x - a}$. When $x \to a$, the point Q tends to the point P, and this secant line approaches the tangent line PT to the curve at the point P. Thus, the limit of $\frac{f(x) - f(a)}{x - a}$ when $x \to a$, will be the slope of the tangent line to the curve representing the function f at a point of length a. We denote the slope of line PT by m_T. Therefore,

$$m_T = \lim_{x \to a} \frac{f(x) - f(a)}{x - a}.$$

Figure 1. Geometric interpretation of derivative

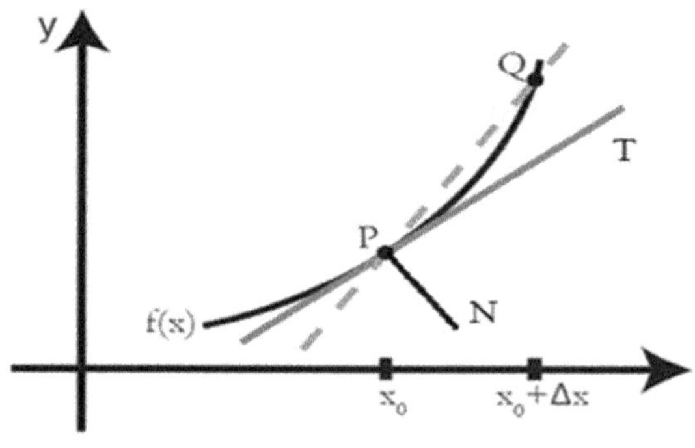

Since the normal line to the curve at this point is perpendicular to the tangent line, if we denote the slope of this line as m_N, according to $m_T.m_N$= -1, we can determine the slope of this line too, and then write the equation of this line.

Example 4: Find the equation of the tangent and normal lines to the curve $y=2x^3-6x+5$ at the point $P(2,9)$.

Solution: We have $y'=6x^2-6$. Then, $m_T=18$, and $m_N = -\frac{1}{18}$. Hence,

$$y - a = m_T(x - b) \rightarrow y - 2 = 18(x - 2) \rightarrow y = 18x - 34,$$

$$y - a = m_N(x - b) \rightarrow y - 2 = -\frac{1}{18}(x - 2) \rightarrow y = -\frac{1}{18}x + \frac{19}{9}$$

Another interpretation of the derivative is the instantaneous speed that is observed in physics. Suppose, $Q=f(t)$ is a quantity function of time. Hence,

$$\Delta Q = f(t + \Delta t) - f(t)$$

shows the change Q from time t to $t + \Delta t$, and $\frac{f(t + \Delta t) - f(t)}{\Delta t}$ is defined as the *average* (or *rate*) *of change* of Q in the unit of time. The relation

$$\lim_{\Delta t \to 0} \frac{f(t + \Delta t) - f(t)}{\Delta t} = f'(t) = Q'(t)$$

is interpreted as the *instantaneous rate of changeQ* in the unit of time. If instead of $Q=f(t)$ we write $S=f(t)$ that S is a directional distance, in this case, the instantaneous speed of a moving object in t which we denote by $V(t)$ is obtained from the relation $V=f'(t)$.

Example 5: The daily production of a coal mine after t hours of working is equal to $Q = 40t + t^2 - \frac{1}{15}t^3$ tons. Find the coal production rate at t=5.

Solution: We know that the rate at t=5 is $Q'(5)$. But $Q'(t) = 40 + 2t - \frac{1}{5}t^2$, thus $Q'(5)=45$.

Example 6: A certain company's annual gross revenue for the t years after January 1, 2020, is P-million dollars, where $P=4t^2+5t+6$. Find the rate according to which the gross income was growing on January 1, 2023.

Solution: January 1, 2023, t=3. Thus, it is enough to find $P'(3)$. We have $P'(3) = (8t + 5)_{t=3} = 29$.

Then, on January 1, 2023, the gross income has been growing at the rate of $29 million per year.

Example 7: The demand equation for a type of product is $y=5p^3+3p+4$, where p represents the price of a commodity in dollars when the 123y commodity is produced. Calculate the average rate of demand relative to price when the price increases from $5 to $8. Find the rate of the instantaneous change in demand relative to price, when the price is $5.

Solution: Since $f(p)= 5p^3+3p+4$, as a result, the average rate changes from 5 to 8 is:

$$\frac{f(5 + 3) - f(5)}{3} = \frac{f(8) - f(5)}{3} = \frac{2588 - 644}{3} = 648.$$

The instantaneous change rate is equal to $f'(5)$. That is, $15(5^2)+3=378$.

As we have seen, the derivative at a point is interpreted as the slope of the tangent line on the curve, which allows us to determine the points where the tangent line is horizontal. Now we would like to use it to check the changes to the function. Suppose the function $f(x)$ is ascending in the interval $[a,b]$. In this case, x and $y=f(x)$ will increase or decrease together. As a result, both $\Delta x = x_2 - x_1$ and $\Delta y = y_2 - y_1$ have the same signs. In other words, the derivative of the function becomes positive, negative or zero in this interval. As a result, if $f(x)$ is continuous in the interval $[a,b]$ and differentiable on the interval (a,b), then the function is ascending if we have for every x belonging to this interval, $f'(x)>0$.

Similarly, if the function $f(x)$ is decreasing in the interval $[a,b]$, it means that when x increases, $y=f(x)$ decreases and vice versa. Now, if $\Delta x$is positive, Δybecomes negative, then we conclude that the derivative is negative in this interval. In other words, if $f(x)$ is continuous in the interval $[a,b]$ and differentiable on the interval (a,b), then the function is descending if for every x belonging to this interval, we have, $f'(x)<0$.

These results help us to know that in drawing the graph in the intervals where the derivative is positive, the function is *ascending* and in the intervals where the derivative is negative, the function is *descending*.

5.3 DIFFERENTIALS

Let's back to (2). We have:

$$f'(x) = \lim_{\Delta x \to 0} \frac{\Delta y}{\Delta x},$$

Where Δy and Δx are increments of the independent and dependent variables respectively. In the limit state, when $|\Delta x|$ is small, then $\frac{\Delta y}{\Delta x} \approx f'(x)$ from which $\Delta y \approx f'(x)\Delta x$. We define the *differential* of the function $y=f(x)$ which we denote by dy as follows:

$$dy = f'(x)\Delta x.$$

In this way, according to the approximate relationship for Δy, conclude that $\Delta y \approx dy$. Now, if, in the definition of dy, we put $y=f(x)=x$, the $f'(x)=1$, and according to the differential definition, we get:

$$dx = dy = f'(x).\Delta x = 1.\Delta x.$$

This helps us to have $dy=f'(x)dx$. In other words

$$\frac{dy}{dx} = f'(x). \tag{3}$$

This will be another symbol to display y'.

Note that, by using the differential, it is possible to obtain suitable approximation values of the function that are not calculated precisely in the given values of x.

Example 8: Find an approximation value for $\sqrt{2}$.

Solution: Suppose $y = \sqrt{x}$. If $x_1=1.96$, then $y_1 = \sqrt{1.96} = 1.4$. Now the question is, if $x_2=2$, what will be the value of y_2? It can be calculated approximately. We have, $\Delta x = x_2 - x_1 = 0.04$. We also have, $\Delta y = y_2 - y_1$.

That is, $y_2 = y_1 + \Delta y$. But we know $\Delta y \approx dy$, i.e. $\Delta y \approx f'(x).\Delta x$. Now, since $f'(x) = \frac{1}{2\sqrt{x}}$, then $\Delta y \approx \frac{1}{2\sqrt{x}}.\Delta x$. By choosing $x=1.96$, and $\Delta x = 0.04$, we get $\Delta y \approx \frac{1}{2\sqrt{x}}.\Delta x = \frac{0.04}{2.8} = \frac{1}{70}$.

So, $y_2 = \sqrt{2} \approx 1.4 + \frac{1}{70}$, that with three decimal places, $\sqrt{2} \approx 1.414$.

If the functions u and v are differentiable, then the following rules are valid.

(i) $d(u \pm v = du \pm dv$

(ii) $d(uv) = vdu + udv$

(iii) $d(\frac{u}{v}) = \frac{vdu - udv}{v^2}, (v \neq 0)$.

We will use these rules later, without proving their correctness here.

5.4 THEOREMS ON DIFFERENTIATION

Theorems on differentiation, specifically the *sum*, *difference*, *product*, and *quotient* rules, are fundamental theorems on differentiation. We can derive these rules using the definition of the derivative and some basic algebraic manipulation. In this section, we will also learn and discuss some other important theorems on differentiation. This will be followed by some solved examples for better understanding and clarity.

Theorem 1. Let's the functions f and g are differentiable on $\mathbb{R}$, then, the functions $f \pm g, f.g$ and $\frac{f}{g}$ are differentiable on $\mathbb{R}$, and the following rules hold:

(i) $(f \pm g)'(x) = f'(x) \pm g'(x)$

(ii) $(f.g)'(x) = f'(x)g(x) + f(x)g'(x)$

(iii) $(\frac{f}{g})'(x) = \frac{f'(x)g(x) + f(x)g'(x)}{[g(x)]^2}, g(x) \neq 0$

Example 9: For $x>1$, find the derivative of the function given by,

$$f(x) = \frac{\sqrt{x}+\frac{1}{\sqrt{x}}}{\sqrt{x}-\frac{1}{\sqrt{x}}}.$$

Solution: To avoid the presence of the radical, first we multiply the numerator and the denominator by the conjugate of the denominator, and then we differentiate the result. We have,

$$f(x) = \frac{\sqrt{x}+\frac{1}{\sqrt{x}}}{\sqrt{x}-\frac{1}{\sqrt{x}}} = \frac{\left(\sqrt{x}+\frac{1}{\sqrt{x}}\right)\left(\sqrt{x}+\frac{1}{\sqrt{x}}\right)}{\left(\sqrt{x}-\frac{1}{\sqrt{x}}\right)\left(\sqrt{x}+\frac{1}{\sqrt{x}}\right)} = \frac{x^2+2x+1}{x^2-1}$$

from which,

$$f'(x) = \frac{(2x+2)(x^2-1)-2x(x^2+2x+1)}{(x^2-1)^2} = \frac{-2x(x+2)}{(x^2-1)^2}.$$

Theorem 2. Suppose the function g is differentiable in x, and f is differentiable in $g(x)$. Then,

$$(fog)'(x) = f'(g(x))g'(x).$$

This type of differentiation is also known as the *chain rule*.

Remark 3**:** (*i*)- If y is a differentiable function of u and u is also a differentiable function of x, such that, $y=f(u)$, and $u=g(x)$, then according to the chain rule we have,

$$(fog)'(x) = f'(g(x))g'(x) \tag{4}$$

(*ii*)- If $y=f(u)$ where $u=g(v)$ and $v=h(x)$, then

$$\frac{dy}{dx} = \frac{dy}{du}\cdot\frac{du}{dv}\cdot\frac{dv}{dx}. \tag{5}$$

Example 10: Find y', if $y = \sqrt{5x^3-3x+2}$.

Solution: Let's $y = f(u) = \sqrt{u}$, and $u=g(x)=5x^3-3x+2$. Therefore, by (4), we get:

$$y' = \frac{dy}{dx} = \frac{dy}{du}\cdot\frac{du}{dx} = \frac{1}{2\sqrt{u}}.(15x^2-3) = \frac{3}{2\sqrt{5x^3-3x+2}}.(5x^2-1).$$

Theorem 3. (*Inverse Function Theorem*). If the function f is continuous and strictly monotonic on the interval $[a,b]$,and the derivative of this function is non-zero at the point x on the interval (a,b), then the inverse function of f, that is, f^1 has a derivative at the point $y=f(x)$ and,

$$(f^{-1})'(y) = \frac{1}{f'(x)}.$$

Remark 4**:** The function $y=f(x)$ and its inverse $y=f^1(x)$ are symmetric to the line $y=x$.

For example, the function $f(x)$ on the interval $\left[-\frac{\pi}{2},\frac{\pi}{2}\right]$ is one-to-one, then it is invertible. We show the inverse of this function by $f(x)$=are sin$x$ or $f(x)=\sin^{-1}x$. We have, $\sin f(x)=x$, then $f'(x).\cos x=1$. That is, $f'(x) = \frac{1}{\cos x}$. But, $\cos^2 f(x)+\sin^2 f(x)=1$. Thus, $\cos f(x) = \pm\sqrt{1-\sin^2 f(x)}$. Since the cosine function is positive on $\left[-\frac{\pi}{2},\frac{\pi}{2}\right]$ then, $\cos f(x) = \sqrt{1-\sin^2 f(x)} = \sqrt{1-x^2}$. That is,

$$f(x) = \sin^{-1}x \to f'(x) = \frac{1}{\sqrt{1-x^2}}.$$

In general, if $u=u(x)$, then

$$f(x) = \sin^{-1}u \to f'(x) = \frac{u'}{\sqrt{1-u^2}}.$$

Similarly, if, $f(x)=\cos^{-1}u$, then $f'(x) = \frac{-u'}{\sqrt{1-u^2}}$.

Remark 5**:** It can be proved that, for $f(x)=\tan^{-1}u$ and, $f(x)=\cot^{-1}u$, then;

(i) $f(x) = \tan^{-1}u \to f'(x) = \frac{u'}{1+u^2}$

(ii) $f(x) = \cot^{-1}u \to f'(x) = \frac{-u'}{1+u^2}$.

Example 11: Find y', if $f(x)=\cot^{-1}(\cos x)$.

Solution: We have $u=\cos x$, then, $f'(x) = \frac{-u'}{1+u^2} = \frac{\cos x}{1+\cos^2 x}$.

Due to the many uses of derivatives in different discussions of differential calculus and for a quick reference to the derivative of functions, most of these derivatives have been discussed in this chapter, but for more derivative formulas, readers may refer to (Apostol, 1966) (Finney, 1988) (Leithold, 1981) (Rodin, 1970).

5.5 FURTHER DIFFERENTIATION METHODS

In addition to differentiations described in previous sections, we introduce some other techniques of differentiation such as *parametric*, *implicit*, and *higher-order differentiations*. We start with the definition of parametric differentiation.

5.5.1 Parametric Differentiation

Parametric differentiation is a type of differentiation in differential calculus and is used when both dependent and independent variables x and y are dependent on a third variable (such as t, which is considered time). For example, consider the set of functions f and g with common interval I, where:

$$\begin{cases} x = f(t) \\ y = g(t) \end{cases} \quad (t \in I).$$

We call these equations the *parametric equations* of the curve C.

If f and g are differentiable on I, then the derivative of the parametric curve C, according to the Inverse Function Theorem, will be defined as follows:

$$\frac{dy}{dx} = \frac{\frac{dy}{dt}}{\frac{dx}{dt}} = \frac{g'(t)}{f'(t)} \tag{6}$$

Cycloid is a curve generated by a point on the circumference of a circle that rolls along a straight line. If a is the radius of the circle and t is the angular displacement of the circle, then its parametric form will be $x=a(t-\sin t)$ and $y=a(1-\cos t)$. Thus, by (6), we get,

$$\frac{dy}{dx} = \frac{\frac{dy}{dt}}{\frac{dx}{dt}} = \frac{a\sin t}{a(1-\cos t)} \Rightarrow \frac{dy}{dx} = y' = \frac{\sin t}{1-\cos t}.$$

One may want to write y' in terms of x and y. we have, $y=a(1-\cos t)$. Whence,

$$1 - \frac{y}{a} = \cos t \Rightarrow t = \cos^{-1}\left(1 - \frac{y}{a}\right).$$

Therefore,

$$y' = \frac{\sin\left[\cos^{-1}\left(1 - \frac{y}{a}\right)\right]}{\frac{y}{a}} = \frac{a\sin\left[\cos^{-1}\left(1 - \frac{y}{a}\right)\right]}{y}.$$

The result is the slope of the tangent to the cycloid at point $T(x, y)$.

5.5.2 Implicit Differentiation

The functions whose derivatives have been examined so far are the functions in which y or in other words, $f(x)$ are given explicitly in terms of x. However, many functional relationships cannot be expressed explicitly. For example, for the relation $yx^3 - \sin xy + 2y^5 - 4y = 0$, we cannot express y explicitly in terms of x. But even though there is no such possibility or it is difficult to find them, there should be one or more ideal functions $y=f(x)$ that hold for the relation $F(x,y)=0$. For example, the functions $y = x, y = 1 - \sqrt{1-x^2}$ and $y = 1 + \sqrt{1-x^2}$ are valid for relation:

$$F(x,y) = y^3 - (x+2)y^2 + xy(x+2) - x^3 = 0.$$

Even, sometimes, it may not be possible to define any function at all. For example, the equation $F(x,y)= x^2+y^2+4=0$, does not define any function.

To find y, we use a process called implicit differentiation. In this way, first, by assuming y to be constant, we differentiate $F(x,y)$ concerning x, and denote the result by F'_x. Once again, by assuming that x is constant, we differentiate $F(x,y)$ concerning y. We denote the result by F'_y. Then, it can be proved that;

$$y' = -\frac{F'_x}{F'_y}. \tag{7}$$

Example 12: Let's assume that the function y in the equation $3y^5 - 2yx^2 + 2xy^3 + 1 = 0$ is a function of the variable x. Find y'.

Solution: We have,

$$F'_x = -4xy + 2y^3$$

$$F'_y = 15y^4 - 2x^2 + 6xy^2$$

$$\therefore\ y' = \frac{4xy - 2y^3}{15y^4 - 2x^2 + 6xy^2}.$$

5.5.3 Higher-Orders Derivative

If the function $y=f(x)$ is differentiable in the interval I, its derivative defines a new function on I which is denoted by f'. This function assigns to each $x \in I$ derivative of f in x that is $f'(x)$. If the function f' is also differentiable in I, we call the function

$$\frac{df'(x)}{dx} = (f'(x)),$$

the *second derivative* of f and denote it with f'. Similarly, if f' is differentiable in I, we call the function

$$\frac{df''(x)}{dx} = (f''(x))'$$

the *third derivative* of f and denote it with $f'''(x)$.

In general, we denote the nth *derivative* of the function f by $f^{(n)}(x)$ and write:

$$f^{(n)}(x) = (f^{(n-1)}(x))'$$

For example, if $f(x) = \frac{1}{1-ax}$, then, $f^{(n)}(x) = \frac{a^n n!}{(1-ax)^{n+1}}$. This can be proved by induction. The statement is true for n=1. Now, suppose the statement is true for k ie., $f^{(k)}(x) = \frac{a^k k!}{(1-ax)^{k+1}}$. We prove it is also true for, n=k+1. For this purpose, we differentiate both sides. We obtain,

$$f^{(k+1)}(x) = \frac{-(k+1)(-a)a^k k!}{(1-ax)^{k+2}} = \frac{a^{k+1}k!(k+1)}{(1-ax)^{k+2}} = \frac{a^{k+1}(k+1)!}{(1-ax)^{k+2}}.$$

That is, the statement is true for n=k+1. Thus, it follows that the statement is true for all positive integers.

Since

$$\frac{d}{dx}(fg) = f\frac{dg}{dx} + g\frac{df}{dx},$$

we can easily show that

$$\frac{d^2}{dx^2}(fg) = f\frac{d^2g}{dx^2} + 2\frac{df}{dx}\frac{dg}{dx} + g\frac{d^2f}{dx^2}.$$

Similarly,

$$\frac{d^3}{dx^3}(fg) = f\frac{d^3g}{dx^3} + 3\frac{df}{dx}\frac{d^2g}{dx^2} + 3\frac{d^2f}{dx^2}\frac{dg}{dx} + g\frac{d^3g}{dx^3}.$$

In general, by induction we can prove that

$$\frac{d^n}{dx^n}(fg) = \sum_{i=0}^{n}\binom{n}{i}\frac{d^if}{dx^i}\cdot\frac{d^{n-i}g}{dx^{n-i}}.$$

5.5.4 Derivatives of Exponential and Logarithm Functions

The most common exponential and logarithm functions in a calculus course are the natural exponential function, $f(x)=e^x$, and the natural logarithm function, $f(x)=\ln x$.

But we will start by looking at the general exponential and logarithm functions, $f(x)=a^x$ and $f(x)=\log_a x$, respectively.

(i) *Exponential Functions*

Let's $f(x)=a^x$.

By the definition of the derivative of $f(x)=a^x$, we have

$$f'(x) = \lim_{h\to 0}\frac{f(x+h)-f(x)}{h} = \lim_{h\to 0}\frac{a^{x+h}-a^x}{h} = a^x\lim_{h\to 0}\frac{a^h-1}{h} = a^x f'(0).$$

So, we need to have $f'(x)$ to get the derivative.

At present, we do not have enough knowledge to get $f'(0)$, but, we will be able to show that for a general exponential function we have,

$$f(x) = a^x \rightarrow f'(x) = a^x \ln a.$$

Since for the natural exponential function we have;

$$\lim_{h\to 0}\frac{e^h-1}{h} = 1,$$

then

$$f(x) = e^x \rightarrow f'(x) = e^x.$$

In general,

$$f(x) = e^u \rightarrow f'(x) = u'e^u.$$

(ii) *Logarithm Functions*

Let's $f(x)=e^x$, and $g(x)=\ln x$. Since $g(x)$ is inverse of $f(x)$, then we have,

$$g'(x) = \frac{1}{f'(g(x))} = \frac{1}{f'(g(x))} = \frac{1}{e^{\ln x}} = \frac{1}{x}.$$

$$\therefore f(x) = \ln x \rightarrow f'(x) = \frac{1}{x}.$$

In general,

$$f(x) = \ln u \rightarrow f'(x) = \frac{u'}{u}.$$

Now, since $\log_a x = \frac{\ln x}{\ln a}$ then,

$$(\log_a x)' = \left[\frac{\ln x}{\ln a}\right]' = \frac{1}{x\ln a}.$$

In some cases, instead of taking the derivative directly, it is better to take the logarithm of the function and then obtain the derivative of the first function from it.

Suppose two functions $f(x)$ and $g(x)$ are differentiable in the interval I and $f(x)>0$. To calculate the derivative of the function,

$$y = [f(x)]^{g(x)},$$

we take the logarithm from the sides of the above equality. We will have:

$$\ln y = g(x)\ln(f(x)).$$

Now we find the derivative of both sides. We get

$$\frac{y'}{y} = g'(x)(x)\ln(f(x)) + g(x)\frac{f'(x)}{f(x)}.$$

Therefore,

$$y' = [f(x)]^{g(x)}\left[g'(x)(x)\ln(f(x)) + g(x)\frac{f'(x)}{f(x)}\right].$$

By this relation, we easily can find the derivative of exponential functions.

Example 13: Find the derivative of the function $f(x)=(\sin x)^{\cos x}$.

Solution: First, we take logarithms from both sides, we obtain

$$\ln(f(x)) = \ln[(\sin x)^{\cos x}] = \cos x.\ln(\sin x).$$

Now, we differentiate both sides, we get, $\frac{f'(x)}{f(x)} = -\sin x\ln(\sin x) + \cos x\frac{\cos x}{\sin x}.$

$$\therefore f'(x) = (\sin x)^{\cos x}[\cos x\cot x - \sin x\ln(\sin x)].$$

5.6 SOME APPLICATIONS OF DERIVATIVES

Previously, in the geometric interpretation of the derivative, we considered the value of the derivative at the point $x=a$ as the slope of the tangent line to the curve $f(x)$ at this point, and by using it, we were able to obtain the equations of the tangent and the normal lines to the curve $f(x)$ at $x=a$. Another interpretation of the derivative has been the physical interpretation, which we call similar to the moving instantaneous speed of a particle M at the moment $t=t_0$. Now we would like to express other uses of derivatives. One of which is determining the maximum and minimum of functions. But firstly, we state the definitions and theorems related to them.

5.6.1 Maxima and Minima

Definition 2: We say that the function f at point c of the open interval I, which is a subset of (a,b), has a *relative maximum* if, for every point of I, we have $f(c) \geq f(x)$.

Similarly, point c of this is the *relative minimum* if for every point of I, we have $f(c) \leq f(x)$.

If the function $f(x)$ in $x=c$ has a relative maximum or minimum point, it is said that $f(x)$ has a relative extremum in c. The following theorem, which is called the *relative extremum theorem*, is used to find the values of c for which there is a relative extremum.

Theorem 4. (*Relative Extremum Theorem*). Suppose that for each x of the interval $I \subseteq (a,b)$, the function $f(x)$ is defined, and if at the point c of this interval, f has a relative extremum and $f'(c)$ exists, then $f'(c)=0$.

Definition 3: We say that the function f at the point $x=c$ of closed interval $[a,b]$, has an *absolute maximum* if, for every point x of this interval, we have $f(c) \geq f(x)$. Similarly, it has an *absolute minimum* if, for all x of this interval, we have, $f(c) \leq f(x)$.

Note that the absolute maximum and minimum are unique if they exist in this interval, but the number of relative maximum and minimum can be non-unique.

The following theorem expresses another property of continuous functions.

Theorem 5. (*Absolute Extremum Theorem*). If the function $f(x)$ is continuous on interval $[a,b]$,then it has an absolute maximum and an absolute minimum.

Note that the presence of continuity is a sufficient but not necessary condition. For example, the function $f(x)=[x]$ is not continuous in $[0, 1]$ but its absolute maximum is at $x=1$. We get the maximum and minimum values of the function $f(x)$ from its values at, $x=a$ and $x=b$, and the points that $f'(x)$ is zero or not defined (known as *critical points*). The largest value of the result is the absolute maximum and the smallest is the absolute minimum. For example, the function f with rule $f(x)=x^2$ in $[1, 2]$, obtains its maximum at $x=2$ and its minimum at $x=1$, not at $x=0$, for which the derivative becomes zero.

Example 14: In the plan of building an amphitheater, it is assumed that if there is room for 50 to 100 people, the net profit for each person will be \$100. But if the seating capacity is more than 100 people, the net profit for each seat will be reduced by \$0.08 multiplied by the number of seats, more than 100, daily. What is the seating capacity to get the highest daily net profit?

Solution: If we consider the seating capacity x and the profit $p(x)$, then according to what was said, $p(x)$ will be defined as follows:

$$p(x) = \begin{cases} 100x, 50 \leq x \leq 100 \\ 108x - 0.08x^2, 100 < x \leq 1350. \end{cases}$$

Since for $x>100$, the daily profit for any seat is equal to $100–0.08(x–100)$, therefore

$$p(x) = (100 - 0.08(x - 100)) - 10x - 0.08x^2.$$

On the other hand, since $p(x)$ should not be negative, as a result, $x=1350$ is the upper limit for $p(x)$. The function $p(x)$ is continuous on [100, 1350] and so has an absolute maximum and minimum. The function is not differentiable at $x=100$ because its right and left-hand derivatives are not equal. For $100 < x \leq 1350$, we have $p'(x)= 108–0.16x$.

Hence, $p'(x)=0$ for $x=675$. For determining the maximum and minimum of $p(x)$, we verify the values of this function at $x=50$, $x=100$, $x=675$, and $x=1350$. We will get $p(50)=5000$, $p(100)=10000$, $p(675)=72900$, $p(1350)=150000$.

Thus, the maximum of the function is 72900, when $x=675$. That is, if the salon has space for 675 people, then the daily net profit will be \$72,900. We note that the points $x=100$, and $x=675$ are critical points.

***Remark* 6:** If there is a derivative at $x=c$, to determine whether this critical point is a relative maximum or relative minimum point, we use the sign of the second derivative of the function at this point, provided that $f'(c)$ exists.

(i)-If $f'(c)<0$, then the function has a relative maximum at $x=c$.

(ii)-If $f'(c)>0$, then f has a relative minimum at $x=c$.

5.6.2 Application in Business and Economics

Economists and business people are frequently interested in how what changes in such parameters as inventory, production, supply, advertising, and price affect other parameters like profit, inflation, demand, and employment, (Anton & Kolman, 1982).

There are three functions that are important to a manufacturer. The cost function, revenue function, and profit function, denoted by $C(x)$, $R(x)$ and $P(x)$, respectively, where $C(x)$ is the total cost function of producing x units of the product, $R(x)$, is the *total revenue* function received from selling x units and $P(x)$ is the *total profit* function obtained from selling x units of the product. If all units produced are sold, then these functions are related by

$$P(x) = R(x) - C(x). \tag{8}$$

In normal cases, x and $C(x)$ are positive. If zero is in domain of C, then $C(0)$ is called the *total cost* production. The derivatives of C(x), R(x), and P(x) are called, the *marginal cost*, the *marginal revenue*, and the marginal profit, respectively. According to this equality, when $p'(x)=0$, we conclude that $R'(x)=C'(x)$.

That is the marginal revenue must be equal to the marginal cost. We also have: $P''(x)= R''(x) - C''(x)$, and this shows that when $R''(x)<C''(x)$, then the profit function will have a relative maximum value.

The marginal cost and marginal revenue are used to determine the level of output for a firm, which will either maximize profit or minimize losses. A firm can operate in perfect competition when other firms cannot influence the price by increasing production. In a situation where there is only one manufacturing company for a particular product, the price and thus the demand can be controlled, which are called *monopoly conditions*.

In the definition of the derivative, we got acquainted with the two concepts of average speed and instantaneous speed. These concepts can also be used for $C(x)$ and $R(x)$. The *average cost* of producing each unit of a commodity is obtained by dividing the total cost by the number of units produced. Let denote it by $AC(x)$, then $AC(x) = \frac{C(x)}{x}$.

A demand function of the form $p=Q(x)$ can be considered as $R(x)=xp$. From this equation, we can have the relation, $p = \frac{R(x)}{x}$, which shows that the average income is the same as the price of each commodity. It is not difficult to show that total revenue is maximized by a linear demand function $p = a - bQ$ at $Q = \frac{a}{2b}$.

For more details, readers may refer to Leithold (1981) and Anton and Kolman (1982). Let's look at some examples.

Example 15: In a monopolistic situation, the demand equation for a particular product is, $x+p=18$. Suppose the total production cost of x unit is given as, $C(x) = \frac{x^3}{3} + \frac{x^2}{2}$.

If we want to maximize the total profit, what should be the price of each unit of goods?

Solution: We have $p=18-x$, thus $R(x)=18x-x^2$. We also have, $P(x)=R(x)-C(x)$, then

$$P(x)= 18x - x^2 - \frac{x^3}{3} - \frac{x^2}{2}$$

Hence, $P'(x)= 18–3x–x^2$. From $P'(x)=0$, we obtain, $x=3$, and $x=-6$ where $x=-6$ cannot be acceptable. We also have, $P''(x)= -3–6x<0$, at $x=3$. Then, $x=3$, shows the maximum point of this function. The price of each product unit is obtained from the relation $P(x)=18–x$. Therefore $p=15$.

The next example was chosen from Leithold (1981).

Example 16: The demand equation for a certain product produced by a monopoly owner is $p=a–bx$ and the total production cost of x unit is obtained from the relation $C(x)=c+dx$. Suppose the government demands a tax based on t dollars for each unit produced by the monopoly owner. Show that to maximize the profits, the monopolist must transfer half of the tax to the consumer's account. That is, the owner of the monopoly should add $\frac{t}{2}$ dollars to the price of each unit.

Solution: We have $p=a–bx$, thus $R(x)= ax–bx^2$. We also have, $P(x)= R(x)–C(x)$, then $P(x)= ax– bx^2– c– dx$.

Hence, $P(x)= ax– bx^2– c– dx$. From $P'(x)=0$, we obtain, $x = \frac{a+d}{2}$.

We also have, $P''(x)= -2b<0$, for every value of x. Thus at $x = \frac{a+d}{2}$ we have the maximum value for $S(x)$. That is, the price of each product unit will be $p(x) = a - \frac{a+d}{2} = \frac{a+d}{2}$. Now, suppose we increase t dollars for each unit produced to the cost, then $C(x)= c+d(x+t)$.

Therefore, $P(x)= R(x)–C(x)= ax– bx^2– c+d(x+xt)$. We have;

$$P'(x) = a - 2bx - d(1 + 2tx) = 0 \rightarrow x = \frac{a-(d+t)}{2b}.$$

Thus, the price of each product unit is $p(x) = a - b\frac{a-(d+t)}{2b} = \frac{a+d}{2} + \frac{t}{2}$. That is, the

The owner must add $\frac{t}{2}$ dollars to the price of each unit to overcome taxes.

Suppose that C(x) dollars is the total cost of producing r units of a commodity. Under the normal circumstances, x and C(x) are nonnegative. If zero is in the domain of C, C(0) is called the *overhead cost* of production.

5.6.3 Concavity and Inflection (Turning) Points

We say that at the point $(c,f(c))$, the curve is concave upwards if there exists an interval I including c, such that for every $x \neq c$ belonging to this interval, the point $(c,f(c))$, located on the curve f is placed below the line tangent to the curve at the point $(c,f(c))$.

Similarly, the concavity of $f(x)$ at this point is downward if, for any $x \neq c$, belonging to this interval, the point $(c,f(c))$ on the curve f lies below the line tangent to the curve at this point.

Figure 2. Graphs of concavity

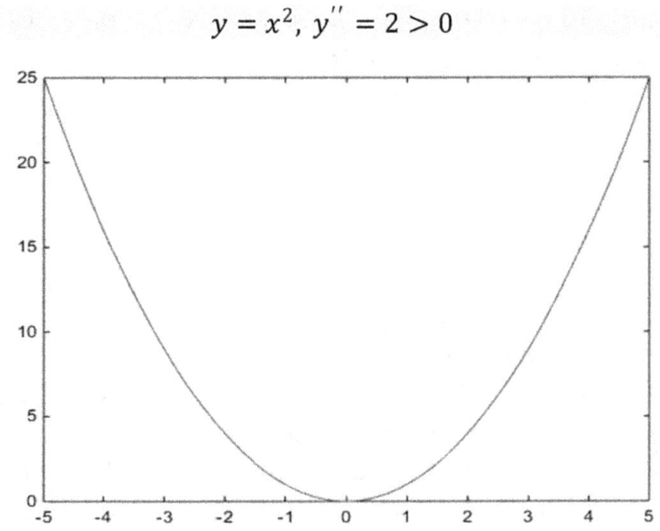

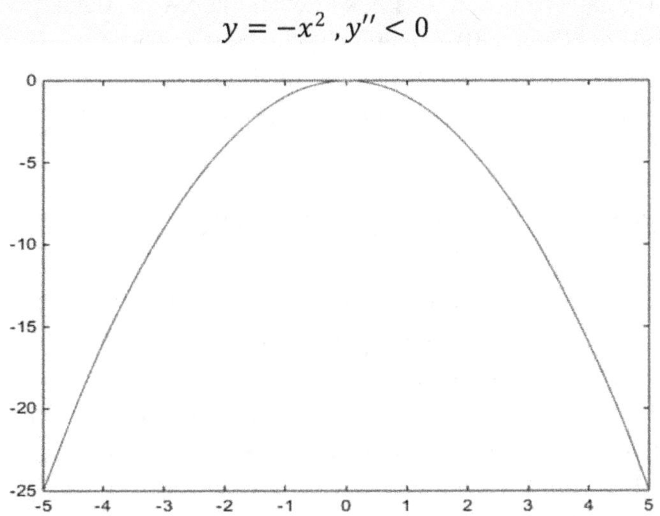

$y = x^2, y'' = 2 > 0$

$y = -x^2, y'' < 0$

It is shown that if, $f''(c)>0$, then the concavity in $(c,f(c))$ is upward, and the concavity will be downward if, $f''(c)<0$. The converse of this statement is not true. We call the point $(c,f(c))$ an *inflection point* of the curve f, if the curve has a tangent line at this point and there is an interval I that contains c, such that for each x of this interval, one of the following two conditions holds:

(i) $f''(x)<0$, for $x<c$
(ii) $f''(x)>0$, for $x>c$

The inflection point theorem states that if the point $(c,f(c))$ is an inflection point of curve f, then, $f''(c)$ is zero if it exists.

The converse of this theorem is not true.

It should be noted that *homographic functions*, whose general form are, $f(x) = \frac{ax+b}{cx+d}$, do not have inflection points. Also, quadratic functions $f(x)=ax^2+bx+c$ do not have inflection points. Tertiary functions may have only one inflection point.

In general, a polynomial of degree n can have up to (n−1) turning points.

Example 17: Find the inflection points of $f(x) = \frac{x^5}{5} - \frac{x^3}{3}$.

Solution: We have $f'(x)=x^4-x^2$. Let's $f'(x)=0$, then, $x = 0$ and $x = \pm 1$. We also have, $f''(x)= 4x^3-2x$. Thus, $f''(0)=0$, and $f''(\pm 1) = \pm 2$. That is, $x=1$, is a minimum relative point of the function, and $x=-1$, is a maximum relative point. The point $x=0$ is an inflection point. The other inflection points are $x = \pm\frac{1}{\sqrt{2}}$.

5.7 MEAN VALUES THEOREMS (OPTIONAL)

In this section, we will state Roll's, Lagrange's and Cauchy's theorems. These theorems can be useful tools for managers to analyze data and make informed decisions in various aspects of business management. Here, we try to get acquainted with their applications by giving some examples. To prove the correctness of these theorems, readers may refer to some calculus. See, e.g., (Apostol, 1966)(Finney, 1988) (Leithold, 1981).

Theorem 6. (*Roll's Theorem*). Let's the function $f(x)$ is continuous in $[a,b]$ and differentiable in (a,b). Moreover, $f(a)=f(b)$, then there exists a point c in (a,b) such that $f'(c)=0$.

The geometric interpretation of this theorem is that there will be at least one point like $c \in (a,b)$ which is tangent to the curve parallel to the x-axis.

We remind you that the point c is not unique, nor is it necessary to have, $f(a)=f(b)=0$. It is sufficient to have $f(a)=f(b)$.

Example 18: Find the points of $f(x)= x^3-3x^2-4x+12$, lie in [-2, 2] such that the tangents to the curve in these points are parallel to the x-axis.

Solution: Roll's theorem is valid for this function, because the function is polynomial and all polynomials with degree $n \geq 0$, are continuous in [-2, 2], and differentiable in (-2,2). We also have, $f(-2)=f(2)$, then there exists, at least, a point c in (-2,2) such that $f'(c)=0$. We have, $f'(x)= 3x^2-6x-4=0$. That is, $x = \frac{3 \pm \sqrt{21}}{3}$. But, $x = \frac{3+\sqrt{21}}{3}$ does not belong to this interval, hence $c = \frac{3-\sqrt{21}}{3}$.

Example 19: Show that for any value of k, the equation, $x^{2025}+2024x-k=0$, has only one real root.

Solution: Since the equation is an odd degree, the existence of a real root is obvious. Now suppose this equation has two real roots in $x=a$ and $x=b$. Then, if we write $f(x)= x^{2025}+2024x-k$ as a result $f(a)=f(b)=0$. Since $f(x)$ is a polynomial, hence it is continuous and differentiable in every real interval. Therefore, the conditions of Roll's theorem are valid for this function and we will have $f'(c)=0$. But for any real value of x, we have $f'(x) = 2025x^{2024} + 2024 \neq 0$, because the function is of even degrees. Thus, one of the conditions of Roll's theorem is not valid. Since the function is continuous and differentiable in $\mathbb{R}$, then the condition $f(a)=f(b)=0$ cannot be true. That is, the equation has only one real root.

Now, we use Rolle's theorem to state one of the basic theorems of differential calculus, which is widely used in solving problems and proving other theorems in differential calculus. For this reason, it is emphasized that you have a proper intuitive understanding of its content.

Theorem 7. (*Lagrange's Theorem*). Suppose the function $f(x)$ is continuous in $[a,b]$ and differentiable in (a,b). Then there exists a point c in (a,b) such that

$$f'(c) = \frac{f(b)-f(a)}{b-a}. \tag{8}$$

The geometric interpretation of this theorem is that, there will be a point at $x=c$ such that the tangent at this point is parallel to the line that passes through the points $A(a,f(a))$ and $A(a,f(a))$.

The converse of Lagrange's theorem may not be true.

Example 20: Prove that for any $x \in \mathbb{R}, e^x \geq 1+x$.

Solution: For $x=0$, equality holds, so we assume $x \neq 0$. By choosing, $f(x)=e^x$, $a=0$, $b=x$, and applying Lagrange's theorem, we get

$$e^c = \frac{f(1)-f(0)}{1-0} = \frac{e^x-1}{x-0} = \frac{e^x-1}{x} > 1 \rightarrow e^x \geq 1+x.$$

Because, $e^c>1$.

One of the results of the previous theorem is the following theorem, from which the l'Hopital's rule can be concluded, which can be used in problems related to the ambiguity of limits.

Theorem 8. (*Cuachy's Theorem*). Suppose the functions $f(x)$ and $g(x)$ are continuous in $[a,b]$ and differentiable in (a,b), and for any x in this interval, $g'(x) \neq 0$, then there exist a point like $c \in (a,b)$ such that $\frac{f'(c)}{g'(c)} = \frac{f(b) - f(a)}{g(b) - g(a)}$.

This relation can be used to develop l'Hopital's rule.

This rule states that, if the functions $f(x)$ and $g(x)$ differentiable in $x=a$, and $\lim_{x \to a} \frac{f(x)}{g(x)} = \frac{0}{0}$, then,

$$\lim_{x \to a} \frac{f(x)}{g(x)} = \lim_{x \to a} \frac{f'(x)}{g'(x)}.$$

This rule can be used even when $\lim_{x \to a} \frac{f(x)}{g(x)} = \frac{\infty}{\infty}$.

Proof of this is shown in advanced calculus books. (See, e.g., Rodin (1970)).

Example 21: Show that $\lim_{x \to 0^+} x^x = 1$.

Solution: Suppose $A = \lim_{x \to 0^+} x^x$.We take the logarithm from both sides. We will get:

$$\ln A = \ln \lim_{x \to 0^+} x^x = \lim_{x \to 0^+} x \ln x = \lim_{x \to 0^+} \frac{\ln x}{1/x} = \frac{-\infty}{\infty}.$$

We use l'Hopital's rule. We obtain

$$\ln A = \lim_{x \to 0^+} \frac{\ln x}{1/x} = \lim_{x \to 0^+} \frac{\frac{1}{x}}{\left(-\frac{1}{x^2}\right)} = \lim_{x \to 0^+} (-x) = 0 \rightarrow \ln A = 0 \rightarrow A = 1.$$

Thus, $\lim_{x \to 0^+} x^x = 1$.

Example 22: Show that

$$\lim_{x \to \infty} \left(1 + \frac{k}{x}\right)^x = e^k.$$

Solution: Let's $A = \lim_{x \to \infty} \left(1 + \frac{k}{x}\right)^x$.Again, we take the logarithm from both sides. We obtain:

$$\ln A = \ln \lim_{x \to \infty} \left(1 + \frac{k}{x}\right)^x = \lim_{x \to \infty} \ln \left(1 + \frac{k}{x}\right)^x = \lim_{x \to \infty} x \ln\left(1 + \frac{k}{x}\right) = \lim_{x \to \infty} \frac{\ln\left(1 + \frac{k}{x}\right)}{\frac{1}{x}} = \frac{0}{0}.$$

We use l'Hopital's rule. We get

$$\ln A = \lim_{x \to \infty} \frac{\ln\left(1 + \frac{k}{x}\right)}{\frac{1}{x}} = \lim_{x \to \infty} \frac{\frac{-k}{x^2}}{\left(-\frac{1}{x^2}\right)} = \lim_{x \to \infty} (k) = k \rightarrow \ln A = k \rightarrow A = e^k.$$

Thus, $\lim_{x\to\infty}\left(1+\frac{k}{x}\right)^x = e^k$.

We end this chapter by stating Taylor's formula, which is widely used in differential and integral calculus.

From (8) we have

$$f(x) = f(a) + (x-a)f'(c).$$

If c is replaced by a, we obtain the tangent line approximation

$$f(x) \approx f(a) + (x-a)f'(a).$$

This leads us to write

$$x \approx a - \frac{f(a)}{f'(a)}$$

if $f(x)=0$ From this relation, we can conclude a recurrence formula, known as *Newton's formula* given by

$$x_{n+1} = x_n - \frac{f(x_n)}{f'(x_n)}, n = 0,1,2,$$

that can be used for approximating the root of equation $f(x)=0$.

An extended formula to (8) that, if the function f has a finite second derivative f'' at every point on an interval I and, a and x be arbitrary points in this interval, then

$$f(x) = f(a) + (x-a)f'(x) + (x-a)^2\frac{f''(c)}{2}. \tag{9}$$

We can also derive another *Newton-like formula* that is a better formula for approximating the root of equation $f(x)=0$, [4].

If we extend in this manner and suppose f has a finite second derivative $f^{(n+1)}$ at

$$f(x) = f(a) + (x-a)f'(a) + (x-a)^2\frac{f''(a)}{2!} + \ldots + (x-a)^n\frac{f^{(n)}(a)}{n!} + R_n. \tag{10}$$

This is known as *Taylor's formula* with *remainder* R_n, where

$$R_n = (x-a)^{n+1}\frac{f^{(n+1)}(c)}{(n+1)!}. \tag{11}$$

If we choose a special case of $a=0$, we obtain the *Maclaurin expansion*

$$f(x) = f(0) + xf'(0) + x^2\frac{f''(0)}{2!} + \ldots + x^n\frac{f^{(n)}(0)}{n!} + \ldots. \quad (12)$$

The formula (12) can be used to write the function $f(x)$ in a polynomial form.

Example 23: Find a polynomial expansion for, $f(x)$=sin$x$. Prove $\lim_{x\to 0}\frac{\sin x}{x} = 1$.

Solution: We have,

$$\sin x = \sin 0 + x\cos 0 - x^2\frac{\sin 0}{2!} - x^3\frac{\cos 0}{3!} + \ldots + x^n\frac{\sin^{(n)}(0)}{n!} + \ldots.$$

Hence

$$\sin x = x - \frac{x^3}{3!} + \ldots + \frac{(-1)^n x^{2n+1}}{(2n+1)!} + \ldots.$$

Using this, we can write

$$\lim_{x\to 0}\frac{\sin x}{x} = \lim_{x\to 0}\frac{x - \frac{x^3}{3!} + \frac{x^5}{5!} - \ldots}{x} = \lim_{x\to 0}\left(1 - \frac{x^2}{3!} + \frac{x^4}{5!} - \ldots\right) = 1.$$

Due to the use of expansion of functions in different discussions of differential and integral calculus, we included here a list of formulas as a quick reference that is obtained using the Maclaurin expansion.

(i) $e^{ax} = 1 + \frac{ax}{1!} + \frac{(ax)^2}{2!} + \frac{(ax)^3}{3!} + \ldots$

(ii) $a^x = 1 + \frac{x\ln a}{1!} + \frac{(x\ln a)^2}{2!} + \frac{(x\ln a)^3}{3!} + \ldots, |ax| < 1$

(iii) $(1 + ax)^{-1} = 1 - ax + (ax)^2 - (ax)^3 + \ldots, |ax| < 1$

(iv) $\ln(1 + x) = x - \frac{x^2}{2} + \frac{x^3}{3} + \ldots, |x| < 1$

(v) $\cos x = 1 - \frac{x^2}{2!} + \frac{x^4}{4!} - \ldots,$

(vi) $\tan x = x + \frac{x^3}{3} + \frac{2x^5}{15} + \frac{17x^7}{315} + \ldots, |x| < \frac{\pi}{2}$

(vii) $\sec x = 1 + \frac{x^2}{2!} + \frac{5x^4}{4!} + \frac{61x^6}{6!} + \ldots, |x| < \frac{\pi}{2}$

(viii) $\operatorname{co\,sec} x = \frac{1}{x} + \frac{x}{6} + \frac{7x^3}{360} + \ldots, |x| < \pi$

(ix) $\tan^{-1}x = x - \frac{x^3}{3} + \frac{x^5}{5} - \frac{x^7}{7} + \ldots,$

(x) $\tanh^{-1}x = x + \frac{x^3}{3} + \frac{x^5}{5} + \frac{x^7}{7} + \ldots.$

More about such series can be seen in most textbook on calculus, for example, (Apostol, 1966) (Finney, 1988) (Leithold, 1981) (Rodin, 1970) (Piskunov, 1981) (Silverman, 1985) (Stewart, 2008).

CONCLUSION

In this chapter, we introduced the concept of derivatives and use them to find the maximum and minimum values of a function. We could use differentiation to introduce the concept of differential. Moreover, after introducing concavity and inflection (turning) points, we come to the inflection point theorem. We stated the mean value theorems and some of their applications. By mean value theorems, we concluded Taylor's formula, which is one of the most applicable formula in calculus.

5.8 Exercises

1. Find the derivative of the following functions using the theorems or differentiation formulas.

$$
\begin{array}{lll}
\text{(i)} & y = & \sqrt{x+\sqrt{x}} \\
\text{(ii)} & y = & \sqrt{x+\sqrt{x+\sqrt{x}}} \\
\text{(iii)} & y = & \ln(\tan x) \\
\text{(iv)} & y = & \ln(\ln(\ln x)) \\
\text{(v)} & y = & \tan(\ln x) \\
\text{(vi)} & y = & \sin(\cos 3x) \\
\text{(vii)} & y = & \sin^{-1}\sqrt{\sin x} \\
\text{(viii)} & y = & \ln(\tan x)+\ln(\cot x) \\
\text{(ix)} & y = & e^{\cosh^2 x+\sinh^2 x}. \\
\text{(x)} & y = & \sqrt{\dfrac{1+\sin e^x}{1-\cos e^x}}
\end{array}
$$

2. Determine the derivative of the following parametric functions by using the theorems and formulas of differentiation.

$$
\text{(i)} \begin{cases} x = a\cos t+\cot t \\ y = a\sin t+\tan t \end{cases}
$$

$$
\text{(ii)} \begin{cases} x = \ln(\tan t)+1 \\ y = \cot t+\tan t \end{cases}
$$

$$
\text{(iii)} \begin{cases} x = e^t\sin t \\ y = e^t\cos t \end{cases}
$$

$$
\text{(iv)} \begin{cases} x = \ln(1+t^2) \\ y = t-\tan^{-1} t \end{cases}
$$

$$
\text{(v)} \begin{cases} x = a(t-\sin t) \\ y = a(1-\cos t). \end{cases}
$$

3. Find the implicit derivative of the following functions.

(i) y 2 – x ln(tanx)= 0
(ii) y 2 + 6xy 3 – 56x 3y + x 4 = 0
(iii) xy – ln(tanx)
(iv) √ _x + √ _y = 1
(v) x y = y x
(vi) e xy + x 2y 3 = sinx – 1

4. Verify that the equation tangent to the following curves at a point on the curve of width y=1.

(i) y 2 = x + ln(y _ x).
(ii) ye y = xe x+1

5. Using the definition of differential, calculate an approximate value for the following data.

(i) tan 44 o
(ii) cos 63 o
(iii) 3 √ _ 127
(iv) 4 √ _ 83

Write the answers to four decimal places.

6. Find the limit of the following functions, if they exist.

(i) $\lim_{x\to 0^+} (\cot x)^{\sin x}$
(ii) $\lim_{x\to 1} (2 - x)^{\tan\frac{\pi x}{2}}$
(iii) $\lim_{x\to 0} (\cos x)^{\operatorname{cosec} x}$
(iv) $\lim_{x\to 1} \frac{x(x-1)}{\sin \pi x}$
(v) $\lim_{x\to 0^+} (\sin x)^{\tanh x}$
(vi) $\lim_{x\to +\infty} \left(1 - \frac{1}{x}\right)^{2x-3}$
(vii) $\lim_{x\to 0^+} x^{x+\tan x}$
(viii) $\lim_{x\to\infty} (x + e^x)^{\frac{1}{x}}$
(ix) $\lim_{x\to 0} \frac{\sin^{-1} x}{\tan^{-1} x}$
(x) $\lim_{x\to\infty} (x)^{\frac{1}{x}}$

7. Find the critical points of the following functions and, if any, determine which one is maximum or minimum.

(i) $y = x(x^3 - 32)$
(ii) $y = xe^x$
(iii) $y = x + \frac{1}{x}$
(iv) $y = \ln x(8 - x)$
(v) $y = e^x - 3$
(vi) $y = \sqrt[3]{x(x+4)^{-2}}$

8. We heated a 5 cm long metal cube. Its side is enlarged by 1/10. What will be the approximate volume after heating?
9. Show that from the parametric equation $x=1/t$ and $y=t$, we get, $y''=2y^3$.
10. Verify that the function $y = c_1e^{-x} + c_2e^{-2x}$ holds for $y''+3y'+2y=0$.
11. Why can we not evaluate $\lim_{x\to\infty}\frac{x\sin x}{x+\cos x}$ by L'Hospital's rule? Find this limit by some other method.
12. Back to exercise 12, from previous chapter. What is the value of x so that the cost of walling is the lowest?
13. The demand equation for a monopolist is $(200-x)^2=80p$ where if the price per unit is p dollars, the quantity demanded is x units. The total cost function is $C(x)= 50x-2x^2$.

(a) What is the price that the monopoly owner should set for each unit to maximize profit?
(b) If the government taxes the monopolist at $4 per unit produced, what should be the total price to maximize profits?
(c) Determine whether the price increase from (*a*) to (*b*) exceeds the tax imposed by the government.

14. A manufacturer can make a profit of $12 per product if he produces 300 or less per week. If he produces more than this amount, the amount of profit will be reduced by 0.05 per item. (*a*)- If the producer produces x units every week, determine his weekly profit as a function of x. (*b*)- Show whether the function defined in part (*a*) is continuous and differentiable at $x=300$.
15. Suppose $f(x)$ is defined as, $f(x)=x^n$. Prove that,

$$f(1) + \frac{f'(1)}{1!} + \frac{f''(1)}{2!} + \ldots + \frac{f^{(n)}(1)}{n!} = 2^n.$$

16. Prove that the equation $x^n + ax + b = 0, n \in \mathbb{N}, a, b \in \mathbb{R}$ cannot have more than three real roots. Similarly, the equation $x^n + ax + b = 0, n = 2k \in \mathbb{N}, a, b \in \mathbb{R}$ cannot have more than four real roots.
17. Use the mean value theorem and find $\lim_{x\to\infty}(\sqrt[3]{n} - \sqrt[3]{n+1})$.
18. Show that

(i) $\sinh x = x + \frac{x^3}{3!} + \frac{x^5}{5!} + \ldots,$
(ii) $\cosh x = 1 + \frac{x^2}{2!} + \frac{x^4}{4!} + \ldots.$

REFERENCES

Anton, H., & Kolman, B. (1982). *Mathematics with Applications for Management, Life, and Social Science*. Academic Press, Inc.

Apostol. Tom M. (1966). Calculus. John Wiley & Sons, Volume 1.

Finney. Ross. L. (1988). Calculus and Analytical Geometry. Addison-Wesley Publishing Company.

Leithold. Louis (1981). The Calculus and Analytical Geometry. Harper & Row.

odin. Burton. (1970). Calculus with Analytical Geometry. Prentice-Hall, Inc., Englewood Cliffs, New Jersey.

Piskunov, N. (1981). Differential and Integral, Vol 1 (4th ed). MIR Publisher.

Saravi. M & Saravi.S. (2011). A New Look at one of The Newton-like Methods for Solving Non-linear Equations, International Journal of Numerical methods and Applications, 5(1), 31-43.

Silverman. Richard, A. (1985). *Calculus with Analytical Geometry* (4th ed.). Prentice-Hall, Inc.

Stewart, J. (2008). *Calculus* (6th ed.). Mc-Graw.

Chapter 6
Integral Calculus

ABSTRACT

This chapter is devoted to integral calculus. This includes two different integrals, namely definite and indefinite integrals. After finding integration of several elementary functions that we met in Chapter 3, we introduce some methods for integrating functions that have wrapped forms. Various applications of integration will be given throughout this chapter in particular, area, volume of a bounded area and length of an arc of a curve. We also call the Mean Values Theorems as an optional part for integration. We define improper integrals which can be used in finance and the continuous random variables in Chapter 12. For evaluating some definite integrals which cannot be evaluated by methods discussed in calculus, we described two numerical methods for such a task.

6.1 INTRODUCTION

In differential calculus, it was intended to investigate the processes of achieving the rate of change of a dependent variable, but in many cases, the rate of change may be certain, and the problem is to find the main value of this variable. This process is called integral calculus, which is the reverse of differential calculus.

Integral calculus includes the study of two different forms of integral called *definite* and *indefinite integrals*. When the general answer to the problem is desired, the indefinite integral is used, while when the problem is for specific limits or a certain range of values, the definite integral is used. We start our work with indefinite integrals and then, when we know the methods of integration to some extent, we will examine the definite integral and its applications. But firstly, we mention the definitions and fundamental theorems related to integral calculus.

DOI: 10.4018/979-8-3693-3657-1.ch006

6.2 FUNDAMENTAL CONCEPTS OF INTEGRAL

Definition 1: The function $F(x)$ is called *antiderivative* or *the primitive function* of $f(x)$ in the interval I if all x belong to this interval, we have $F'(x)=f(x)$

For example, $F(x)=x^2$, is a primitive function of $f(x)=2x$, or $F(x)=\sin x$, is a primitive function of $f(x)=\cos x$,

Since the derivative of $F(x)+c$ is also $f(x)$, then in a more general case, the primitive function of $f(x)$ is, $F(x)+c$.

According to the definition of the primitive function, it can be deduced that the operation of finding the primitive function is a kind of *antiderivative* operation. When the operation of division is the reverse of the operation of multiplication or $\sin^{-1}$ is considered as the reverse of operation of sin operation, we expect to know, what is the reverse of the differential operation? Suppose, $F(x)+c$ is the primitive function of $f(x)$ then

$$d(F(x)+c) = F'(x)dx = f(x)dx,$$

which leads to finding a function such that its differential is $f(x)dx$. That is,

$$f(x)dx = d(F(x)+c).$$

Definition 2: The reverse operation of differential, denoted by "$\int$" is called *integral*.

With this definition, if we apply the operation $\int$ on the sides of the above equality, we get

$$\int f(x)dx = F(x) + c. \tag{1}$$

The function $F(x)+c$ is called the indefinite integral of the function, $f(x)dx$. The component $f(x)$ is called the *integrand* of integral, and $d(x)$ indicates that the integration is achieved with respect to x. We often use the symbol $\int f(x)dx$ to denote any indefinite integral of $f(x)$.

Because integration is the reverse of differentiation, theorems related to integration can be obtained from differential theorems. Therefore, the following theorems can be easily proved by using the corresponding theorems in differential calculus.

Theorem 1. If the functions $f(x)$ and $g(x)$ are integrable and k is a constant number then, the following rules hold:

(i) $\int[f(x) \pm g(x)]dx = \int f(x)dx \pm \int g(x)dx$

(ii) $\int kf(x)dx = k\int f(x)dx$

(iii) $\int[f(a(x))\,g(x)]dx = F(G(x)) + c,$

where $F(x)$ and $G(x)$, are primitive functions of $f(x)$ and $g(x)$, respectively.

Remark 1: The relation (*iii*) is considered as the chain rule for integration.

Now, before explaining some integration methods, we include below a list of elementary integrals in Table 1, obtained directly by referring to the results of the derivative. Using the chain rule for each of them, we give a more general form by assuming $u=f(x)$ and writing each beside them. We remind you that many integrals can be obtained as a combination of these integrals.

Table 1. Some elementary integration formulas

(1)	$\int x^n dx = \frac{x^{n+1}}{n+1} + c,\ \int u' u^n dx = \frac{u^{n+1}}{n+1} + c,\ n \neq -1$
(2)	$\int \frac{dx}{x} = \ln\lvert x\rvert + c,\ \int \frac{u'}{u} dx = \ln\lvert u\rvert + c$
(3)	$\int e^{ax} dx = \frac{1}{a} e^{ax} + c,\ \int u' e^u dx = \ln\lvert u\rvert + c$
(4)	$\int e^{ax} dx = \frac{1}{a} e^{ax} + c,\ \int u' a^u dx = \frac{a^u}{\ln a} + c$
(5)	$\int \cos ax dx = \frac{1}{a} \sin ax + c,\ \int u' \cos u dx = \sin u + c$
(6)	$\int \sin ax dx = -\frac{1}{a} \cos ax + c,\ \int u' \sin u dx = -\cos u + c$
(7)	$\int \tan ax dx = -\frac{1}{a} \ln \cos ax + c,\ \int u' \tan u dx = -\ln \cos u + c$
(8)	$\int \cot ax dx = \frac{1}{a} \ln \sin ax + c,\ \int u' \cot u dx = \ln \sin u + c$
(9)	$\int \sec^2 ax dx = \frac{1}{a} \tan ax + c,\ \int u' \sec^2 u dx = \tan u + c$
(10)	$\int \mathrm{cosec}^2 ax dx = -\frac{1}{a} \cot ax + c,\ \int u' \mathrm{cosec}^2 u dx = -\cot u + c$
(11)	$\int \frac{dx}{\sqrt{a^2 - x^2}} = \sin^{-1}\frac{x}{a} + c,\ \int \frac{u' dx}{\sqrt{a^2 - u^2}} = \sin^{-1}\frac{u}{a} + c$
(12)	$\int \frac{dx}{\sqrt{x^2 - a^2}} = \cosh^{-1}\frac{x}{a} + c,\ \int \frac{u' dx}{\sqrt{x^2 - a^2}} = \cosh^{-1}\frac{u}{a} + c$
(13)	$\int \frac{dx}{\sqrt{x^2 + a^2}} = \sinh^{-1}\frac{x}{a} + c,\ \int \frac{u' dx}{\sqrt{x^2 + a^2}} = \sinh^{-1}\frac{u}{a} + c$
(14)	$\int \frac{dx}{a^2 - x^2} = \frac{1}{a} \tanh^{-1}\frac{x}{a} + c,\ \int \frac{u' dx}{a^2 - u^2} = \frac{1}{a} \tanh^{-1}\frac{u}{a} + c$
(15)	$\int \frac{dx}{a^2 + x^2} = \frac{1}{a} \tan^{-1}\frac{x}{a} + c,\ \int \frac{u' dx}{a^2 + u^2} = \frac{1}{a} \tan^{-1}\frac{u}{a} + c$

Example 1: Evaluate $\int \frac{\cos x}{\sqrt{a + b \sin x}} dx$.

Solution: We write,

$$\int \frac{\cos x}{\sqrt{a + b \sin x}} dx = \int \cos x (a + b\sin x)^{-1/2} dx.$$

Then use (1), we obtain

$$\int\frac{\cos x}{\sqrt{a+b\sin x}}dx = \int\cos x(a+b\sin x)^{-1/2}dx = \frac{(a+b\sin x)^{\frac{1}{2}}}{\frac{1}{2}b}+c = \frac{2}{b}\sqrt{a+b\sin x}+c.$$

Example 2: Integrate, $\int\left(\sqrt{x}+\frac{1}{\sqrt{x}}\right)^2dx.$
Solution: We have,

$$\left(\sqrt{x}+\frac{1}{\sqrt{x}}\right)^2 = x+\frac{1}{x}+2.$$

Thus,

$$\int\left(\sqrt{x}+\frac{1}{\sqrt{x}}\right)^2dx = \int\left(x+\frac{1}{x}+2\right)dx = \frac{x^2}{2}+\ln|x|+2x+c.$$

Example 3: Show that, $\int\frac{\coth(\ln x)}{x}dx = \ln|\sinh(\ln x)|+c.$
Solution: Let's $\ln x=u$, then,

$$\int\frac{\coth(\ln x)}{x}dx = \int\coth u\,du = \int\frac{\cosh u}{\sinh u}du = \ln|\sinh u|+c = \ln|\sinh(\ln x)|+c$$

Now that we know the application of elementary integrals to some extent, we note that even high knowledge of using these types of integrals is necessary but not sufficient to solve any integral. The complexity of solving some integrals forces us to introduce integration methods. However, the integration methods that are introduced in the integral calculus books are not enough to solve the integrals. Unfortunately, many integrals, especially the integrals that are integrals of *error functions* (the functions that cannot be integrated even though they are integrable) cannot be solved with these methods. Only certain cases of them have been solved. The existence of such problems has led to the introduction of numerical methods to solve them. We introduced an example of a numerical method in the previous chapter with Newton's formula for solving non-linear equations. However, although these methods solve the problem of integration to a large extent, every numerical method has an error value. In other words, the problem of integration is still valid. With this explanation, we continue our work by examining some integration methods.

6.3 METHODS OF INTEGRATION

As we mentioned, many problems related to integrals cannot be solved with only elementary integrals. For this reason, in this section, we are going to introduce three integration methods that can be useful in solving many non-elementary integrals.

6.3.1 Integration by Parts

By the product rule for differential, we have, $d(uv)=vdu+udv$, where u and v are functions of x. A rearrangement of this expression gives $vdu=d(uv)-udv$. Integrating both sides of this result leads to the following expression:

$$\int vdu = uv - \int vdu. \tag{2}$$

The relation (2) is the basis of integration by parts method. It is assumed that we choose v and du in the integrand on the left side so that the integral on the right side is simpler than the integral on the left side. Nevertheless, before giving some examples, the question arises that we should choose which one is v and which one is du from the integrand on the left side of (1). We expect that with this selection, the resulting integral on the right side will be elementary, or if we have to integrate from the right side of the equation once more, we will obtain an elementary integral this time. Is there a technique that can be used to have a reason for choosing, for example, v? The answer is yes. Without loss of generality, we assume that the integrand consists of two different functions such as: Algebraic, Tri-geometric, Logarithmic, Exponential and or Inverse functions. Here, the technique of using the word LIATE is that each letter in this word represents the functions Logarithmic, Inverse, Algebraic, Tri-geometric, and Exponential, respectively. Then we act in such a way that which of these two functions under the integrand is the first letter in this word. We choose this function as v and the other as du.

For better understanding, we consider some examples.

Example 4: Integrate, $\int x^{2024} \ln x dx$.

Solution: The integrand consists of two different functions, namely, Algebraic and Logarithmic. Since the Logarithmic function is before the Algebraic function in the word LIATE, hence $v=\ln x$ and $du=x^{2024}dx$. Then $dv = \frac{dx}{x}$ and $u = \frac{x^{2025}}{2025}$. Thus,

$$\int x^{2024} \ln x dx = \frac{x^{2025}}{2025} \cdot \ln x - \int \frac{x^{2025}}{2025} \cdot \frac{1}{x} dx = \frac{x^{2025}}{2025} \cdot \ln x - \frac{1}{2025} \int x^{2024} dx =$$

$$= \frac{x^{2025}}{2025} \cdot \ln x - \frac{x^{2025}}{(2025)^2} + c = \frac{x^{2025}}{2025}(\ln x - \frac{1}{2025}) + c$$

Remark 2: In general,

$$\int x^n \ln x dx = \frac{x^{n+1}}{n+1}(\ln x - \frac{1}{n+1}) + c, \ (n \neq -1).$$

What happens when n=-1? In this case, we have,

$$\int x^{-1}\ln x dx = \int \frac{1}{x}\ln x dx,$$

which is an elementary integral. We have

$$\int x^{-1}\ln x\, dx = \int \frac{1}{x}\ln x\, dx = \frac{(\ln x)^2}{2} + c$$

Example 5: Find $\int \tan^{-1} x dx$.

Solution: Suppose $v=\tan^{-1}x$, and $du=dx$, then $dv = \frac{dx}{x^2+1}$ and $u=x$. Thus,

$$\int \tan^{-1} x dx = x\tan^{-1}x - \int \frac{x}{x^2+1}dx = x\tan^{-1}x - \frac{1}{2}\ln(x^2+1) + c.$$

Example 6: Find $\int x^2 e^{3x} dx$.

Solution: By referring to the word LIATE, we choose $v=x^2$ and $du=e^{3x}dx$, then $dv=2xdx$ and $u = \frac{e^{3x}}{3}$. Thus,

$$\int x^2 e^{3x} dx = \frac{x^2 e^{3x}}{3} - \int \frac{2x e^{3x}}{3} dx.$$

We still have a non-elementary integral on the right side. We impose integral by parts once more. Let's write $v=x^2$ and $du=e^{3x}dx$, we obtain, $dv=dx$, and $u = \frac{e^{3x}}{3}$.

Therefore,

$$\int x^2 e^{3x} dx = \frac{x^2 e^{3x}}{3} - \int \frac{2x e^{3x}}{3} dx = \frac{x^2 e^{3x}}{3} - \frac{2x e^{3x}}{9}$$
$$+ \int \frac{2e^{3x}}{9} dx = \frac{x^2 e^{3x}}{3} - \int \frac{2x e^{3x}}{3} dx = \frac{x^2 e^{3x}}{3} - \frac{2x e^{3x}}{9} + \frac{2e^{3x}}{27} + c.$$

$$\therefore \int x^2 e^{3x} dx = \frac{e^{3x}}{3}\left(x^2 - \frac{2x}{3} + \frac{2}{9}\right) + c.$$

Example 7: Show that, $\int e^{2x} \sin x dx = \frac{e^{2x}}{5}(2\sin x - \cos x) + c$.

Solution: Assume $I = \int e^{2x} \sin x dx$.

Then, by choosing $v=\sin x$ and $du=e^{3x}dx$, we get $dv=\cos.x dx$ and $u = \frac{e^{2x}}{2}$. Thus,

$$I = \int e^{2x} \sin x dx = \frac{\sin x\, e^{2x}}{2} - \int \frac{\cos x\, e^{2x}}{2} dx.$$

We have to apply the part's method to the right-hand side once again. We obtain,

$$I = \int e^{2x}\sin x dx = \frac{\sin x e^{2x}}{2} - \frac{\cos x e^{2x}}{4} - \frac{1}{4}\int \sin x e^{2x} dx.$$

But, $\int e^{2x}\sin x dx = I$. That is,

$$I = \frac{\sin x e^{2x}}{2} - \frac{\cos x e^{2x}}{4} - \frac{I}{4} + c \rightarrow \frac{5I}{4} = \frac{e^{2x}(2\sin x - \cos x)}{4} + c.$$

$$\therefore I = \int e^{2x}\sin x dx = \frac{e^{2x}}{5}(2\sin x - \cos x) + c.$$

Remark 3. In general,

$$\text{(i)} \quad \int e^{ax}\sin bx dx = \frac{e^{ax}(a\sin bx - b\cos bx)}{a^2+b^2}$$

$$\text{(ii)} \quad \int e^{ax}\cos bx dx = \frac{e^{ax}(a\cos bx + b\sin bx)}{a^2+b^2} + c.$$

Integration methods for functions with the degree of natural numbers are simple when this number is small. For example, $\int \text{cox}^2 x dx$ or $\int \cos^4 x dx$, which can be reduced to smaller degrees and then integrated. In cases where this number is large, say n=50, integration will be difficult and time-consuming. In such cases, these types of integrals are checked by a process called a *reduction formula*. We explain it by considering an example.

Example 8: By technique of reduction formula proves that

$$\int \sin^n x dx = \frac{e^{2x}}{5}(2\sin x - \cos x) + c, n \in \mathbb{N}.$$

Use this result and evaluate $\int \sin^6 x dx$.

Solution: Let's $I_n = \int \sin^n x dx$ then, we write,

$$I_n = \int \sin^n xd = \int \sin x \sin^{n-1} x dx = -\cos x \sin^{n-1} x + (n-1)\int \cos\text{: msup}x \sin^{n-2} x dx,$$

where $v=\sin^{n-1}x$, and $du=\sin x dx$. But, $\cos^2 x = 1 - \sin^2 x$, thus,

$$I_n = \int \sin^n xd = \int \sin x \sin^{n-1} x dx = -\cos x \sin^{n-1} x$$
$$+(n-1)\int (1-\sin^2 x)\sin^{n-2} x dx = -\cos x \sin^{n-1} x + (n-1)$$
$$\int \sin^{n-2} x dx - (n-1)\int \sin^n x dx = -\cos x \sin^{n-1} x + (n-1)I_{n-2} - (n-1)I_n.$$

A rearrangement of this expression leads to

$$I_n = -\frac{1}{n}\cos x \sin^{n-1} x + (n-1) I_{n-2}.$$

Now, if we apply this relation to $I_6 = \int \sin^6 x dx$, we get,

$$I_6 = -\frac{1}{6}\cos x \sin^5 x + 5I_4 = -\frac{1}{6} coxx \sin^5 x + 5(-\frac{1}{4}\cos x \sin^3 x + 3I_2)$$
$$= -\frac{1}{6}\cos x \sin^5 x + 5(-\frac{1}{4}\cos x \sin^3 x + 3\left(-\frac{1}{2}\cos x \sin x + I_0\right)\Big).$$

But, $I_0 = \int dx = x + c$. Therefore,

$$\int \sin^6 xd = -\cos x(\frac{1}{6}\sin^5 x - \frac{5}{4}\sin^3 x + \frac{15}{2}\sin x + 15x) + c.$$

6.3.2 Integration by Partial Fractions

Consider the integral given by, $\int R(x)dx$, where $R(x)$ is a rational function given by, $R(x) = \frac{P(x)}{Q(x)}$. Suppose $P(x)$ and $Q(x)$ are polynomials where the degree of $P(x)$ is less than that of $Q(x)$.

If the degree of $P(x)$ is bigger than the degree of $Q(x)$ then by the process of division, this rational function can be as a polynomial plus another rational function such that its numerator has a degree less than the denominator. However, we are considering three cases for:

(i) $Q(x) = a_n(x - x_1)(x - x_2)\ldots(x - x_{n)})$
(ii) $Q(x) = a_n(x - x_1)(x - x_2)\ldots(x - x_{t)})^k\ldots(x - x_{n-t})$
(iii) $Q(x) = a_n(x - x_1)(x - x_2)\ldots(x - x_{n)})\ldots(x^2 + a_k x + b_k)\ldots(x - x_{n-k})$,

where x_i are zeros of $Q(x)$. That is $Q(x_i)=0$. Then, by using these factorizations, $R(x)$ can be written as the partial-fraction expansion. For example, for case (*i*), we write,

$$R(x) = \frac{A_1}{x - x_1} + \frac{A_2}{x - x_2} + \ldots + \frac{A_n}{x - x_n},$$

and for case (*ii*),

$$R(x) = \frac{A_1}{x - x_1} + \frac{A_2}{x - x_2} + \ldots + \frac{A_t}{x - x_t} + \frac{A_{t+1}}{(x - x_{t+1})^2} + \ldots + \frac{A_k}{(x - x_{t+1})^k} + \ldots + \frac{A_{n-k}}{x - x_{n-k}}$$

Similarly, for case (*iii*),

$$R(x) = \frac{A_1}{x - x_1} + \frac{A_2}{x - x_2} + \ldots + \frac{A_t}{x - x_t} + \frac{A_{t+1}}{x^2 + a_k x + b_k} + \ldots + \frac{A_{n-2}}{x - x_{n-2}}.$$

In each case, the integrand has been transferred to a desired form which includes elementary integrals. Our task is to find these coefficients. This can be done by comparing the nominator of the necessary partial-fraction expansion with $P(x)$. In this way, by taking the common denominator from the fraction on the right side of equality, we compare the form of the resulting fraction with $P(x)$ to determine these coefficients. Then integrate the results term by term.

Example 9: Evaluate, $\int \frac{3x - 1}{x^2 - 2x - 3} dx$.

Solution: We have, $x^2 - 2x - 3 = (x+1)(x-3)$. Then,

$$\int \frac{2x - 1}{x^2 - 2x - 3} dx = \int \left(\frac{A}{x + 1} + \frac{B}{x - 3}\right) dx = \int \frac{A(x - 3) + B(x + 1)}{x^2 - 2x - 3} dx$$
$$= \int \frac{(A + B)x - 3A + B}{x^2 - 2x - 3} dx \rightarrow (A + B)x - 3A + B = 3x - 1.$$

Thus $A+B=3$ and $-3A+B=-1$. That is, $A=-1$ and $B=4$. Therefore,

$$\int \frac{3x - 1}{x^2 - 2x - 3} dx = \int \left(\frac{-1}{x + 1} + \frac{4}{x - 3}\right) dx = -\int \frac{dx}{x + 1} + 4\int \frac{dx}{x - 3}$$
$$= -\ln(x + 1) + 4\ln(x - 3) + c = \ln\left[\frac{(x - 3)^4}{x + 1}\right] + c.$$

Example 10: Integrate, $\int \frac{2x - 3}{x^2(x - 1)} dx$.

Solution: In the denominator, we have a repeated zero at $x=0$, thus, we have case (*ii*). We write,

$$\int \frac{2x - 3}{x^2(x - 1)} dx = \int \left(\frac{A}{x} + \frac{B}{x^2} + \frac{C}{x - 1}\right) dx = \int \frac{(A + C)x^2 + (B - A)x - B}{x^2(x - 1)} dx$$
$$\rightarrow (A + C)x^2 + (B - A)x - B = 2x - 3.$$

Hence, $A+C=0$, $B-A=2$, and $B=3$.

Then, $A=-2$, $B=4$, and $C=2$. Therefore,

$$\int \frac{2x - 3}{x^2(x - 1)} dx = \int \left(\frac{-2}{x} + \frac{3}{x^2} + \frac{2}{x - 1}\right) dx = -2\int \frac{dx}{x} + 3\int \frac{dx}{x^2} + 2\int \frac{dx}{x - 1}$$
$$= -2\ln x - \frac{3}{x} + 2\ln(x - 1) + c = 2\ln\left(\frac{x - 1}{x}\right) - \frac{3}{x} + c.$$

Example 11: Find, $\int \frac{3x^2 - 7}{(x - 3)(x^2 + 1)} dx$.

Solution: One term of the denominator cannot be factorized. Then, we have a case (*iii*). We write,

$$\int\frac{3x^2-7}{(x-3)(x^2+1)}dx = \int\left(\frac{A}{x-3}+\frac{Bx+c}{x^2+1}\right)dx$$
$$=\int\frac{(A+B)x^2+(C-3B)x+A-3C}{x^2(x-1)}dx \rightarrow (A+B)x^2+(C-3B)x+A-3C = 3x^2-7.$$

This leads to, $A+B=3$, $C-3B=0$, and $A-3C=-7$. Then, $A=0$, $B=3$, and $C=2$. Therefore,

$$\int\frac{3x^2-7}{(x-3)(x^2+1)}dx = \int\left(\frac{3}{x^2+1}+\frac{2}{x-3}\right)dx$$
$$=3\int\frac{dx}{x^2+1}+2\int\frac{dx}{x-3} = 3\tan^{-1}x+2\ln(x-3)+c.$$

We remind you that if the denominator of the fraction has the factor $(x^2+ax+b)^k$, which cannot be factored, we act like in the case (*ii*). We consider more examples of this type when we discuss definite integrals.

6.3.3 Integration by Change of Variables

In this method, we try to change the integrand in such a way that it is easier to integrate by choosing a suitable value for x as a function of another variable such as t. We can even write the variable t as a function of x provided that integration becomes easier or possible. Unfortunately, the problem of choosing the right variable makes this method difficult or even very difficult in many integrals despite being better than the previous methods, because it does not follow a specific process like the previous two methods. Only our work experience helps us to make such a choice easier. For example, the existence of $\sqrt{a-bx^2}$ in the integral suggests the choice of $x = \sqrt{\frac{a}{b}}\sin t$,although the existence of $\sqrt[n]{f(x)}$ may remind us to choose $f(x)=t^n$.

However, it can be seen that even this type of selection cannot always be appropriate. For this reason, we try not to consider every choice as the right choice and have this feeling that there could be a better choice.

Example 12: Evaluate, $\int\frac{dx}{\sqrt{e^{2x}+1}}$

Solution: Let's $e^{2x}+1=t^2$. We get, $2e^{2x}dx=2tdt$. Hence, $dx = \frac{tdt}{e^{2x}} = \frac{tdt}{t^2-1}$. Then we can write,

$$\int\frac{dx}{\sqrt{e^{2x}+1}} = \int\frac{tdt}{t^2-1} = \frac{\ln(t^2-1)}{2}+c = \frac{\ln(e^{2x}+1)}{2}+c.$$

Example 13: Integrate,

(i) $\int\sqrt{9-x^2}\,dx$

(ii) $\int\sqrt{9+x^2}\,dx$

Solution:

(i) Suppose x=3sin$t$, then, dx=3costdt. Thus,

$$\int\sqrt{9-x^2}\,dx = \int\sqrt{9-9\sin^2 t}\,.3\cos tdt = 9\int\sqrt{1-\sin^2 t}\,.\cos tdt = 9\int\cos^2 tdt =$$
$$=\frac{9}{2}\int(1+\cos 2t)\,dx = \frac{9}{2}\left(t+\frac{\sin 2t}{2}\right)+c = \frac{9}{2}\left(9\sin^{-1}\frac{x}{3}+\frac{\sin 2(\sin^{-1}\frac{x}{3})}{2}\right)+c.$$

(ii) For this integral, we choose x=3sinh$t$, then, dx=3coshtdt. The rest of the calculations are the same as part (i).

Example 14: Evaluate,

(i) $\int\text{cosec}x dx$
(ii) $\int\sec x dx$

Solution:

(i) We have,sin$x$ $= \dfrac{2\tan\frac{x}{2}}{1+\tan^2\frac{x}{2}}$, thus,

$$\int\text{cosec}x dx = \int\frac{dx}{\sin x} = \int\frac{1+\tan^2\frac{x}{2}}{2\tan\frac{x}{2}}dx.$$

By using the substitution $\tan\frac{x}{2} = t$, we get, dx=2(1+t^2)dt. Hence,

$$\int\text{cosec}x dx = \int\frac{dx}{\sin x} = \int\frac{1+\tan^2\frac{x}{2}}{2\tan\frac{x}{2}}dx = \int\frac{dt}{t} = \ln t+c = \ln\left(\tan\frac{x}{2}\right)+c.$$

(ii) Similarly, it can be proved that,

$$\int\sec x dx = \int\frac{dx}{\cos x} = \int\frac{1+\tan^2\frac{x}{2}}{1-\tan^2\frac{x}{2}}dx = \int\frac{2dt}{1-t^2} = \ln(\sec x+\tan x+c.$$

Example 15: Integrate,

$$\int \frac{\sqrt{x-1}}{1+\sqrt[3]{x-1}}dx.$$

Solution: The existence of two radicals with indexes 2 and 3 helps us to assume, $x-1=t^6$. Then $dx=6t^5dt$. Substitute in integral gives

$$\int \frac{1+\sqrt[3]{x-1}}{\sqrt{x-1}}dx = \int \frac{6(1+t^2)t^5}{t^3}dt = 6\int (1+t^2)t^2 dt$$

$$= 2t^3 + \frac{6t^5}{5} + c = 2\sqrt{x-1} + \frac{6\sqrt[6]{(x-1)^5}}{5} + c$$

Now that we are somewhat familiar with the methods of integrations, we will continue our work by considering definite integrals and try to give more examples that are solved by a change of variable method to gain more experience in choosing a suitable substitution.

6.4 DEFINITE INTEGRALS

The concept of the definite integral is often obtained by examining the area bounded by the curve $y=f(x)$, the x-axis and the lines $x=a$ and $y=b$. For this purpose, we need some kind of process so that the calculation of this area can be considered differently. Firstly, we assume the function $f(x)$ is continuous in the interval $[a,b]$. We divide this interval into n sub-intervals separated by $\Delta x_i = x_{i+1} - x_i, i = 1,2,3,\ldots,n$, so that

$$a = x_0 < x_1 < \ldots < x_{i-1} < x_i < \ldots < x_{n-1} < x_n = b.$$

Thus, $x_i = a + \frac{i}{n}(b-a)$, and $\Delta x_i = \frac{b-a}{n}$. We consider the point ξ_i in the sub-interval $[x_{i-1}, x_i]$. Then, $f(\xi_i)(x_i - x_{i-1})$ is the approximate area of the nth rectangle shown in Figure 1. We denote the total area of all such n rectangles with A_n. That is,

$$A_n = \sum_{i=1}^{n} f(\xi_i)(x_i - x_{i-1}),$$

shows an approximation of this area.

Figure 1. Definite integral as a bounded surface

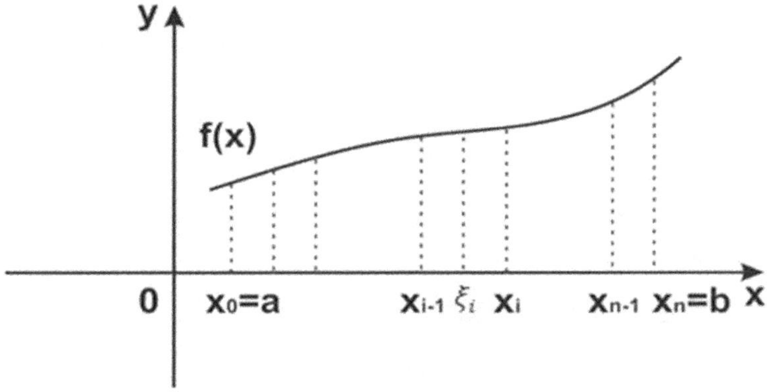

Such a sum is called a *Riemann sum*. In the limit, when $n \to \infty$ or in other words, $\Delta x_i \to 0$, we define the limit value of this sum, which is the area A is called the definite integral of the function $f(x)$ between a and b. That is,

$$\lim_{n\to\infty} A_n = \lim_{n\to\infty} \sum_{i=1}^{n} f(\xi_i)(x_i - x_{i-1}) = A = \int_a^b f(x)dx. \tag{3}$$

The values of a and b, in (3), are called the *lower* and the *upper limits* of integration. According to the above discussion, from the geometrical point of view, the definite integral can be interpreted as the area A.

Example 16: Determine $\int_0^2 x^3 dx$.

Solution: We have, $\Delta x_i = \frac{2-0}{n} = \frac{2}{n}$.Thus, we divide the interval [0,1] to $\frac{2}{n}$ sub-intervals. Choosing, $\xi_i = x_i$ in each interval, the integral can be approximated by using the sum of the areas of n rectangles with a width of $\Delta x_i = \frac{2}{n}$ and a length of $\xi_i^{\,3} = x_i^{\,3}$. We have,

$$A_n = \sum_{i=1}^{n} f(\xi_i)(x_i - x_{i-1}) = \sum_{i=1}^{n} x_i^{\,3}\frac{2}{n} = \left(\frac{2}{n}\right)^4 \sum_{i=1}^{n} i^3 = \frac{4(n+1)^2}{n^2}.$$

Since $\lim_{n\to\infty} A_n = \lim_{n\to\infty} \frac{4(n+1)^2}{n^2} = 4$, then, $\int_0^2 x^3 dx = 4$.

Calculating the area, and therefore the integral, using the limit process is difficult and sometimes impossible. For this reason, we state some of the properties of definite integrals and the basic theorems of these types of integrals so that integration can be done more easily.

6.4.1 Rules of Integration

If the functions $f(x)$ and $g(x)$ are integrable in interval $[a,b]$, then

(i) $\int_a^a f(x)dx = 0$

(ii) $\int_a^b f(x)dx = -\int_b^a f(x)dx$

(iii) $\int_a^b kf(x)dx = k\int_a^b f(x)dx$

(iv) $\left|\int_a^b f(x)dx\right| \leq \int_a^b |f(x)|dx$

(v) $\int_a^b f(x)dx \leq \int_a^b g(x)dx, f(x) \leq g(x)$

(vi) $\int_a^b [f(x) \pm g(x)]dx = \int_a^b f(x)dx \pm \int_a^b g(x)dx$

(vii) $\int_a^b f(x)dx = \int_c^b f(x)dx + \int_a^c f(x)dx, a < c < b$

(viii) $m(b-a) \leq \int_a^b f(x)dx \leq M(b-a), m \leq f(x) \leq M$

(ix) $\int_{-a}^a f(x)dx = 0,$

if $f(x)$ is an odd function and is $2\int_0^a f(x)dx$, if $f(x)$ is even.

The formal proof of each of these rules is done by using the existing properties for finite series, which are simple and some of them can be proved by using some of the previous rules.

Example 17: Show that,

$$\int_{-2}^{2}(x^4+1)e^{x^2}\sin(x\cos x^2)dx = 0.$$

Solution: The integrand is an odd function, hence according to rule (*ix*) the value of the integral is zero.

It should be noted that in indefinite integrals, regardless of whether the function is integrable or not, we obtain the result of the integral. But in definite integrals, since a certain interval is given, the function may not be integrable in that interval. A sufficient condition for the function $f(x)$ to be integrable in the interval $[a,b]$, is that the function is continuous. We note that this condition is sufficient but not necessary. For example, we will show later that even though the greatest integer function is not continuous for integer numbers but $\int_0^n [x]dx$ exists, where $n \in \mathbb{N}$.

Before considering more examples, we state the fundamental theorems of definite integrals, which help us to solve them more easily.

6.4.2 Fundamental Theorems of Integral Calculus

In this part, we mention two of the important fundamental theorems in integral calculus, which are used in dealing with integral problems.

The first fundamental theorem: If the functions $f(x)$ is continuous in interval $[a,b]$ and x is an arbitrary number in this interval such that $F(x) = \int_a^x f(x)dx$, then, $F'(x)=f(x)$.

The second fundamental theorem: If the functions $f(x)$ is continuous in interval $[a,b]$ and $F(x)$ such that $F'(x)=f(x)$, then

$$\int_a^b f(x)dx = F(x)|_a^b = F(b) - F(a). \tag{3}$$

The fundamental theorems establish a link between differential and integral calculus.

Example 18: Find the extreme points of the function, $y = \int_a^x (t^2 + 5t - 6)dt$. Determine which one of these points are maximum and minimum points.

Solution: To find the extreme points, first we differentiate both sides of the given equation and examine $y'=0$. Using the first fundamental theorem, we get, $y'=x^2+5x-6$. Hence, $x^2+5x-6=0$. This leads to $x=2$ and $x=3$. To know which one is maximum, or minimum point, we examine the values of y'' for these points. We have $y''=2x-5$. Thus, $y''(2)<0$ and $y''(3)>0$. That is, $F(x)$ has amaximum at $x=2$ and a minimum at $x=3$.

Example 19: Evaluate,

$$\lim_{x\to 0}\frac{\int_0^x \sin t^4\,dt}{x^5}.$$

Solution: Since, $\lim_{x\to 0}\int_0^x \sin t^4\,dt = 0$, then in limit, we have $\frac{0}{0}$.We use the l'Hospital rule, we obtain

$$\lim_{x\to 0}\frac{\int_0^x \sin t^4\,dt}{x^5} = \lim_{x\to 0}\frac{\sin x^4}{5x^4} = \frac{1}{5}.$$

Example 20: Verify,

$$\int_0^4 [x]dx.$$

Solution: Since, [x] is not continuous in x=0, x=1,…,x=4, then, we write,

$$\int_0^4 [x]dx = \int_0^1 [x]dx = \int_1^2 [x]dx = \int_2^3 [x]dx = \int_3^4 [x]dx = 0 + 1 + 2 + 3 = 7.$$

Example 21: Find the area of an ellipse with diameters $2a$ and $2b$.

Solution: We find area of a quarter of ellipse and then multiply the result by four to get the value of complete area of this ellipse (Figure 2). The equation of ellipse is given by, $\frac{x^2}{a^2} + \frac{y^2}{b^2} = 1$. Then $y^2 = b^2\left(1 - \frac{x^2}{a^2}\right)$. Hence, $y = b\sqrt{\left(1 - \frac{x^2}{a^2}\right)}$. We have,

$$\text{Area}=4\int_0^a f(x)dx = 4b\int_0^a \sqrt{\left(1 - \frac{x^2}{a^2}\right)}\, dx.$$

Figure 2. Area of an ellipse

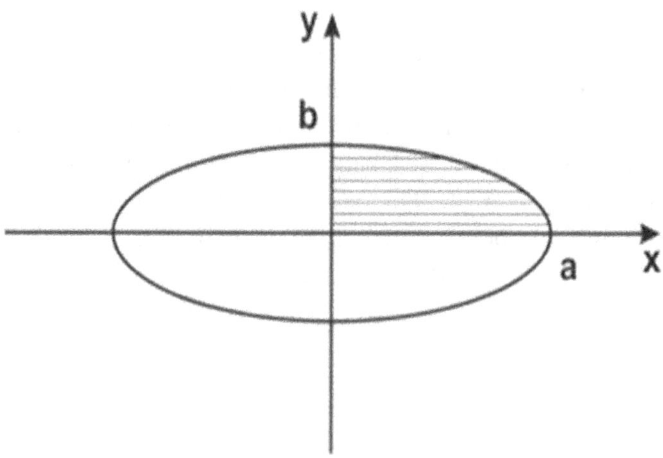

To solve this integration, we choose $x = asin\theta$ where $0 \leq \theta \leq \frac{\pi}{2}$. Thus, $dx = a\cos\theta d\theta$. Substituting in integral, leads to

$$\text{Area} = 4b\int_0^a \sqrt{\left(1 - \frac{x^2}{a^2}\right)}\, dx = 4ab\int_0^{\frac{\pi}{2}} \sqrt{(1 - \sin^2\theta)}\, d\theta$$

$$= 4ab\int_0^{\frac{\pi}{2}} \cos^2\theta d\theta = 2ab\int_0^{\frac{\pi}{2}} (1 + \cos 2\theta)\, d\theta = 2ab\left(\theta + \frac{\sin 2\theta}{2}\right)\Big|_0^{\frac{\pi}{2}} = ab\pi.$$

6.4.3 Mean Values Theorems (Optional)

The *mean* (or *average*) value of a function over an interval $[a,b]$ is defined by

$$AV = \frac{\int_a^b f(x)dx}{b-a}. \quad (5)$$

An application of the average value of a function occurs in economics. It is used to find the average total cost or average total revenue. (See Example 35).

If the function $f(x)$ is continuous in this interval, then it can be proved that there exists a point c in $[a,b]$ such that,

$$\int_a^b f(x)dx = (b-a)f(c). \quad (6)$$

This is known as the *first mean value theorem.*

If in this theorem we choose, $a = x, b = x + \Delta x$, and impose to the right side of (6), we get

$$\frac{F(x+\Delta x) - F(x)}{\Delta x} = f(c).$$

Since,$c \in (x, x+\Delta x)$ then, $\lim_{c \to 0} f(c) = f(x)$. Now, if we apply limits on both sides of (6) when $\Delta x \to 0$, we will get, $F'(x)=f(x)$. This means that, we proved the correctness of the first fundamental theorem.

The first fundamental theorem can be generalized as the following theorem;

Theorem 2. (*Generalized First Mean Value Theorem*). If the functions $f(x)$ and $g(x)$ are continuous in $[a,b]$ and $g(x)$ doesn't change the sign in this interval, then there exists a point c in (a,b) such that

$$\int_a^b f(x)g(x)dx = f(c)\int_a^b g(x)dx.$$

We end this section by stating the following two theorems.

Theorem 3. (*Second Mean Value Theorem*). If the functions $f(x)$ and $g(x)$ are continuous in $[a,b]$ and $g(x)$ is a positive monotone descending function, then there exists a point c in (a,b) such that

$$\int_a^b f(x)g(x)dx = g(a)\int_a^c f(x)dx.$$

But if $g(x)$ is a positive monotone increasing function, then,

$$\int_a^b f(x)g(x)dx = g(b)\int_c^b f(x)dx.$$

Theorem 4. (*Generalized Second Mean Value Theorem*). If the functions $f(x)$ and $g(x)$ are continuous in $[a,b]$ and $g(x)$ is a positive monotone increasing (or descending) function, then there exists a point c in (a,b) such that

$$\int_a^b f(x)g(x)dx = g(a)\int_a^c f(x)dx + g(b)\int_c^b f(x)dx.$$

Note that, $g(x)$ does not always need to be positive.

6.5 IMPROPER INTEGRALS

Suppose we consider the asymptotic area. That is not bounded by the *x-axis* or *y-axis*. In such cases the limit of integrand is infinite. What happens when the integrand is infinite at one or more points in the interval $[a,b]$ These bring in mind whether integrals have finite or infinite values.

Definition 3: We say $\int_a^b f(x)dx$is an *improper integral* if:

(i) One or both upper and lower limits of integration are infinite, or
(ii) The function $f(x)$ is not defined at one or more points of $[a,b]$.

The following integrals are examples of improper integrals.

$$\int_0^\infty e^{-x}dx, \int_{-\infty}^\infty \sin x dx, \int_0^1 \ln x dx, \int_{-1}^1 \frac{1}{\sqrt{x(x^2-1)}}dx.$$

Another kind of these integrals is a combination of the first and second kinds. For example, $\int_0^\infty \frac{\ln x dx}{x}$.

To consider the integrals of the first kind, we assume that the function $f(x)$ is bounded and integrable in the interval $[a,b]$. Then, we define it as follows:

$$\int_0^\infty f(x)dx = \lim_{b\to\infty}\int_0^b f(x)dx$$

$$\int_{-\infty}^b f(x)dx = \lim_{a\to-\infty}\int_a^b f(x)dx$$

$$\int_{-\infty}^\infty f(x)dx = \lim_{a\to-\infty}\int_a^c f(x)dx + \lim_{b\to\infty}\int_c^b f(x)dx.$$

If there is a limit, we say that the integral is *convergent*. Otherwise, we call the integral *divergent*.

Similarly, for the second kind, if the integrand is not finite, but is not defined, at least, at one point, for example at $x=a$, we write:

$$\int_a^b f(x)dx = \lim_{\varepsilon\to 0^+}\int_{a+\varepsilon}^b f(x)dx.$$

Example 22: Check the following integrals for convergence.

(i) $\int_0^\infty e^{-x}dx,$
(ii) $\int_0^\infty e^{-x^2}dx.$

Solution: (i)-We write

$$\int_0^\infty e^{-x}dx = \lim_{b\to\infty}\int_0^b e^{-x}dx = \lim_{b\to\infty}(-e^{-x})\Big|_0^b = \lim_{b\to\infty}(1 - e^{-b}) = 1.$$

Thus this integral is convergent. We write,

$$\int_0^\infty e^{-x^2}dx = \int_0^1 e^{-x^2}dx + \int_1^\infty e^{-x^2}dx.$$

First integral is a proper integral, hence has a constant value, say M. Moreover, for $x > 1, e^{-x^2} < e^{-x}$. Hence,

$$\left|\int_0^\infty e^{-x^2}dx\right| \le \left|\int_0^1 e^{-x^2}dx\right| + \int_1^\infty e^{-x^2}dx\Big| < \int_0^\infty e^{-x^2}dx\Big| + \left|\int_1^b e^{-x}dx\right| \le M + \left|\int_1^b e^{-x}dx\right| = M+$$
$$+\lim_{b\to\infty}\int_1^b e^{-x}dx = M + \lim_{b\to\infty}\int_1^b e^{-x}dx + \lim_{b\to\infty}(-e^{-x})\Big|_1^b = M+\lim_{b\to\infty}(e^{-1} - e^{-b}) = M + e^{-1}.$$

That is, this integral is also convergent.

The following theorem can be useful for convergence.

Theorem 5. Let $\lim_{x\to\infty} x^p f(x) = L$. Then $\int_a^\infty f(x)dx$ converges if $p>1$ and diverges if $p \le 1$.

Example 23: Prove that $\int_1^\infty \frac{dx}{x^p}dx$ converges if, $p>1$.

Solution: Using theorem 5, we have $f(x) = \frac{1}{x^p}$, thus, $\lim_{x\to\infty} x^p f(x) = 1$. Then, the integral is convergent if $p>1$. We also can prove this result by some simple calculations. We have,

$$\int_1^\infty \frac{dx}{x^p}dx = \lim_{b\to\infty}\int_1^b \frac{dx}{x^p} = \lim_{b\to\infty}\left(\frac{x^{1-p}}{1-p}\right)\Big|_1^b = \lim_{b\to\infty}\left(\frac{b^{1-p}-1}{1-p}\right) = \frac{1}{p-1}, \text{ if } p > 1.$$

Example 24: Find,

$\int_0^1 \frac{dx}{x^p} dx$ if $p > 0$.

Solution: We have a second kind improper integral. We write,

$$\int_0^1 \frac{dx}{x^p} = \lim_{\varepsilon \to 0^+} \int_\varepsilon^1 x^{-p} dx = \frac{\lim_{\varepsilon \to 0^+} x^{1-p}}{1-p} = \frac{1}{1-p}, p \neq 1.$$

The integral is divergent if $p>1$.

Improper integrals can be used to answer questions in finance, (Nicholson, 1986). For example, consider the relation given by $P=Se^{-rt}$, where the value of P is an income stream of $\$S$ per year with continuous compounding at r percent per year t. if we integrate $P=Se^{-rt}$ over $(0, \infty)$, it means the continuously compounded flow is perpetual, and then the present value is found as follows:

$$P = \int_0^\infty Se^{-rt} dt = \lim_{b \to \infty} \int_0^b Se^{-rt} dt = \lim_{b \to \infty} \left(-\frac{Se^{-rt}}{r}\right)\Big|_0^b = \frac{S}{r}.$$

That is, the present value of a perpetual stream of $\$S$ is equal to the yearly income stream divided by the annual interest rate.

6.6 APPROXIMATION METHODS FOR EVALUATING DEFINITE INTEGRALS (OPTIONAL)

As we mentioned before, many integrals cannot be solved by direct methods. For this reason, approximation methods are introduced to solve such integrals. Because approximation methods usually produce approximate answers, they contain errors. For this reason, different methods are introduced in numerical analysis so that we can have the least error with a better choice. In this section, we introduce three methods. The last two are numerical methods.

6.6.1 Approximation Using the Expansion of Functions

In this method, we use Taylor's expansion formula for integrand, or parts of integrand, assuming that the integration process becomes possible. For example, consider $\int_0^1 \frac{1-\cos x}{x^2} dx$. Since, $\lim_{x \to 0} \frac{1-\cos x}{x^2} = \frac{1}{2}$, hence we have a proper integral. By the Taylor series of $f(x)=\cos x$ about $c=0$, we have,

$$\cos x = 1 - \frac{x^2}{2!} + \frac{x^4}{4!} - \ldots + \frac{(-1)^n x^{2n}}{(2n)!} + \ldots.$$

That is,

$$\frac{1-\cos x}{x^2} = \frac{1}{2!} - \frac{x^2}{4!} + \ldots + \frac{(-1)^n x^{2n-2}}{(2n)!} + \ldots.$$

Therefore,

$$\int_0^1 \frac{1-\cos x}{x^2} dx = \int_0^1 \left(\frac{1}{2!} - \frac{x^2}{4!} + \ldots + \frac{(-1)^n x^{2n}}{(2n+1)!} + \ldots\right) dx.$$

If we integrate term by term in right-side of the integral, we obtain

$$\int_0^1 \frac{1-\cos x}{x^2} dx = \frac{x}{2!} - \frac{x^3}{3(2!)} + \frac{x^5}{5(4!)} - \ldots + \frac{(-1)^n x^{2n+1}}{(2n+1)(2n)!} + \ldots \Big|_0^1 = \frac{1}{2} - \frac{1}{3(2!)} + \frac{1}{5(4!)} - \ldots.$$

Suppose we use five terms. Thus,

$$\int_0^1 \frac{1-\cos x}{x^2} dx \approx \frac{1}{2} - \frac{1}{3(2!)} + \frac{1}{5(4!)} - \frac{1}{7(6!)} + \frac{1}{9(8!)} \approx 0.341488(6D).$$

6.6.1 Approximation Using the Numerical Rules

There are several numerical methods to approximate definite integrals, in particular when an integrand is an error function. In this section, we introduce two common methods, namely,

(i) The trapezoidal rule,
(ii) Simpson's rule.

To read more about other methods, we refer the readers to numerical analysis textbooks. See, e.g., (Burden, 1989) (Hamming, 1971).

Trapezoidal rule. We divide the interval $[a,b]$ into n sub-intervals separated $\Delta x = h = \frac{b-a}{n}$, so that endpoints are denoted by $x_i=a+ih$, $i=0,1,2,\ldots,n$. That is $x_0=a$, and $x_n=b$. Let's $f_i=f(x_i)$. We choose $(n+1)$ point (x_i,f_i) to approximate the integral. For this purpose, we act the same as we performed for the definition of the definite integral, except that here we use a trapezoid instead of a rectangle (Figure 2).

Figure 3. Graph for trapezoidal rule

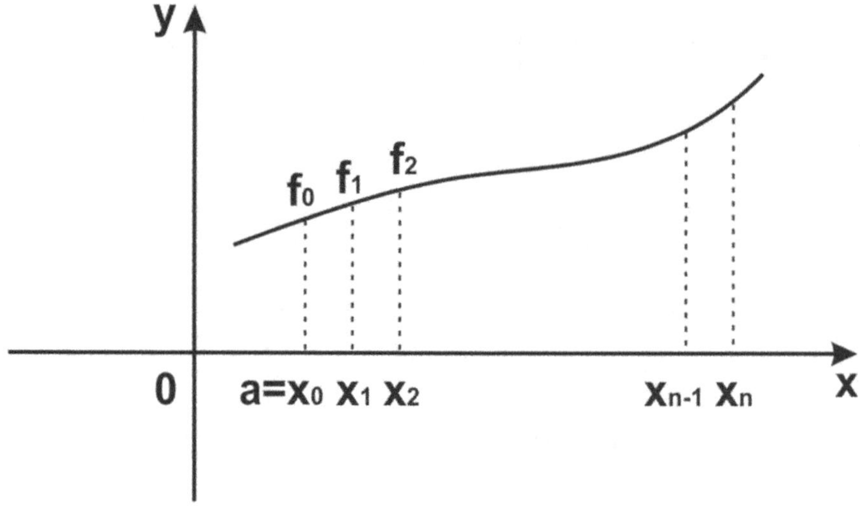

It is obvious that the area under the curve $f(x)$, bounded to the lines $x=a$, $x=b$, and $y=0$ is approximated by using the sum of the areas of these trapezoids. Since, the area of the nth trapezoid is $\frac{h}{2}(f_{i-1}+f_i)$, thus it can be easily concluded that,

$$\int_a^b f(x)dx = \int_{x_0}^{x_n} f(x)dx \approx \frac{h}{2}\left[f_0 + 2(f_1 + f_2 + \ldots + f_{n-1}) + f_n\right]. \tag{7}$$

It is shown that (here we accept without proof) the resulting error value in this method is $\frac{(b-a)h^2}{12}f''(\xi)$, where $\xi \in [a,b]$.

If we want the value of this error to be less than a number like ε, it is enough to find h such that $\frac{(b-a)h^2}{12}M < \varepsilon$, where $M \geq max|f''|$.

Example 25: Use the Trapezoidal rule to approximate, $\int_0^1 e^{-x^2}dx$, with $h = 0.1$.

Solution: We have $h = \frac{b-a}{n}$, hence $n=10$.

Therefore, from (7), we get,

$$\int_0^1 e^{-x^2}dx \approx \frac{0.1}{2}\left[f_0 + 2(f_1 + f_2 + \ldots + f_9) + f_{10}\right]$$

$$= \frac{h}{2}\left[f(0) + 2(f(0.1) + f(0,2) + \ldots + f(0.9)) + f(1)\right]$$

$$= \frac{0.1}{2}\left[1 + 2(e^{-0.01} + e^{-0,04} + \ldots + e^{-0.81}) + e^{-1}\right] \approx 14.924216(6D).$$

Note that, if we choose $h<0.1$, we obtain better approximated values for integral.

Simpson's rule. We divide the interval $[a,b]$ into $\frac{n}{2}$ sub-intervals separated by $\Delta x = 2h$, where n is an even integer, and apply this rule to each subinterval to approximate $f(x)$ by parabola in each interval. We assume that the dividing points on the curve are $P_0(x_0,f_0), P_1(x_1,f_1), \ldots, P_{2n}(x_{2n},f_{2n})$ respectively. It can be shown that any segment of three consecutive points $P_{i-1}(x_{i-1},f_{i-1}), P_i(x_i,f_i), P_{i+1}(x_{i+1},f_{i+1})$ if approximated by a parabola $y=ax^2+bx+c$, then, the area bounded by this parabola, x-axis and lines $x = x_{i-1}$ and $x = x_{i+1}$ will be equal to $\frac{h}{3}(f_{i-1} + 4f_i + f_{i+1})$. Using this result, we write:

$$\int_a^b f(x)dx = \int_{x_0}^{x_{2n}} f(x)dx = \left(\int_{x_0}^{x_2} + \int_{x_2}^{x_4} + \ldots + \int_{x_{2n-2}}^{x_{2n}}\right)f(x)dx$$

$$\rightarrow \approx \frac{h}{3}\left[f_0 + 4(f_1 + f_3 + \ldots + f_{2n-1}) + 2(f_2 + f_4 + \ldots + f_{2n-2}) + f_{2n-2}\right]$$

Therefore,

$$\int_a^b f(x)dx \approx \frac{h}{3}\left[f_0 + 4(f_1 + f_3 + \ldots + f_{2n-1}) + 2(f_2 + f_4 + \ldots + f_{2n-2}) + f_{2n-2}\right] \quad (8)$$

Eq. (8) is known as *Simpson's one-third rule* which can be applied when the interval $[a,b]$ is divided into even subintervals.

Remark 5: It can be proved that if $f^{iv}(\xi)$ exists in then, the error of Simpson's rule is given by

$$-\frac{(b-a)h^4 f^{iv}(\xi)}{180}, a < \xi < b.$$

Note that this error is proportional to h^4, it is therefore better than the trapezoidal rule.

We end this section by considering an example whose value can be obtained by the previous method to have a comparison with approximation methods.

Example 26: Evaluate $\int_0^1 \frac{x^2 dx}{1+x^3}$ to five decimal places with n=8.

Solution: By series method, we get:

$$\int_0^1 \frac{x^2 dx}{1+x^3} = \int_0^1 x^2(1+x^3)^{-1}dx = \int_0^1 x^2(1 - x^3 + x^6 - \ldots)dx$$

$$= \int_0^1 (x^2 - x^5 + x^8 - \ldots)dx = \frac{x^3}{3} - \frac{x^6}{6} + \frac{x^9}{9} - \ldots\Big|_0^1 = \frac{1}{3} - \frac{1}{6} + \frac{1}{9} - \ldots.$$

If we approximate this integral with eight terms, we get,

$$\int_0^1 \frac{x^2 dx}{1+x^3} \approx \frac{1}{3} - \frac{1}{6} + \frac{1}{9} - \frac{1}{12} + \frac{1}{15} - \frac{1}{18} + \frac{1}{21} - \frac{1}{24} \approx 0.21151.$$

The exact value is

$$\int_0^1 \frac{x^2 dx}{1+x^3} = \frac{1}{3}\ln(1+x^3)\Big|_0^1 = 0.23105.$$

Thus, the error is 0.01954. Now, we examine the Trapezoidal rule and Simpson's rule, separately. For Trapezoidal rule, we have

$$\int_0^1 \frac{x^2 dx}{1+x^3} = \frac{1}{3}\ln(1+x^3)\Big|$$

Then $h = \frac{b-a}{n} = 0.125$. Hence,

$$\int_0^1 \frac{x^2 dx}{1+x^3} \approx \frac{0.125}{2}[0 + 2(0.01559 + 0.06154 + 0.13358 + 0.22222$$
$$+ 0.39560 + 45848) + 0.5] = 0.23137.$$

Thus, the error is 0.00032. That is, the Trapezoidal rule produces a better one although it contains more computations. Let's use Simpson's rule, we obtain,

$$\int_0^1 \frac{x^2 dx}{1+x^3} \approx \frac{0.125}{3}[0 + 4(0.01559 + 0.13358 + 0.31397 + 0.45848) + 0.5] = 0.23105.$$

It can be seen that with five decimal places, we have the exact value of the integral. Readers should note that if the computation is performed in more than five decimal places, we may not obtain the exact value of the solution, but it will be much better than the Trapezoidal rule.

6.7 SOME APPLICATIONS OF DEFINITE INTEGRALS

The applications of definite integrals are not limited to the calculation of the area under the curve but are used in many fields of science, technology and engineering.

They enable us to solve many geometric and physical problems. For example, the area between curves, arc length, volumes and the surface of revolution, a moment of inertia, the center of mass, work, etc. They also can be used for analyzing cost, financial and or market in management. In particular, to analysis process data and control charts to monitor the quality of products and processes, helping managers identify areas for improvement and implement corrective actions. We will try to present some examples of applications of definite integrals in economics, business and management, but before that, we apply them to common applications.

6.7.1 Area Bounded by Curves

As we mentioned at the beginning of the definite integral, this integral represents the area bounded by the curve $y=f(x)$ and lines $x=a$, $x=b$ and x-axis. Now, if two continuous functions $f(x)$ and $y=g(x)$ are desired on the interval $[a,b]$ such that on this interval $f(x) \geq g(x)$, then the area bounded by these functions will be expressed by

$$A = \int_a^b (f(x) - g(x))dx.$$

Example 27: Find the area A, bounded by the parabolas $y=2x^2$ and $y=1+x^2$.

Solution: First, we determine the points of intersection of these two parabolas. For this reason, we solve the equation $2x^2=1+x^2$. This gives $x = \pm 1$. Thus,

$$A = \int_{-1}^{1} (f(x) - g(x))dx = \int_{-1}^{1} (x^2 - 1)dx = \frac{x^3}{3} - x \Big|_{-1}^{1} = \frac{4}{3}.$$

Example 28: Find the area A, bounded by, $y=\cos x$, $y=\sin x$ and $x=0$, $x = \frac{\pi}{4}$.

Solution: Since in the given region, $\cos x > \sin x$ then,

$$A = \int_0^{\frac{\pi}{4}} (\cos x - \sin x)dx = \sin x + \cos x \Big|_0^{\frac{\pi}{4}} = \sqrt{2} - 1.$$

6.7.2 Volume of Revolution

If a part of the curve $f(x)$ rotates around a straight line (e.g., the x-axis), the shape of the revolution produced is called a *rotating(solid) body*, which is parallel to that line (Figure 2). We divide this solid into different cross-sections. From these cross-sections, for example, we choose $PQRS$ where $P(x,y)$ (Figure 4).

Figure 4. Graphs of a rotated solid

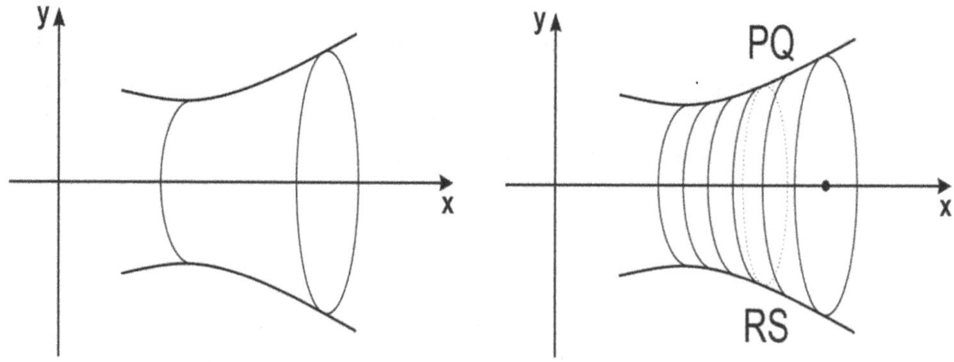

It can be imagined that this section is almost like a cylinder whose radius is y and its height is Δx. Using the formula to calculate the volume of a cylinder, the volume of this section is approximately, $\pi y^2 \Delta x$. Now, if we consider the total volume of the shape V, it is obvious that V will be almost equal to the total volume of such sections. In this way, the volume of the solid becomes:

$$V = \pi \lim_{\Delta x \to 0} \sum_{x=a}^{x=b} y^2 \Delta x = \pi \int_a^b y^2 dx. \quad (9)$$

Example 29: Calculate the volume of revolution formed by the revolution of a part of the curve $f(x)=e^x$ bounded by $x=0$ and $x=1$ about the x-axis.

Solution: By (9) we have,

$$V = \pi \int_a^b y^2 dx = \pi \int_0^1 e^{2x} dx = \frac{\pi}{2} e^{2x} \Big|_0^1 = \frac{\pi}{2}(e^2 - 1).$$

Remark 6: If $f(x)$ and $g(x)$ continuous on the interval $[a,b]$ and on this interval $f(x) \geq g(x)$, then the volume of revolution produced by the area bounded by these functions will be,

$$V = \pi \int_a^b (f^2(x) - g^2(x))\,dx. \quad (10)$$

Example 30: Find the volume of revolution formed by the revolution of curves $y=x^2$, $y = \sqrt{x}$ about the x-axis.

Solution: First we find the points of intersection of these two curves. That is $y=x^2 y = \sqrt{x}$. This leads to $x=0$, $x=1$. Then,

$$V = \pi \int_0^1 (x - x^4)dx. = \pi\left(\frac{1}{2}x^2 - \frac{1}{5}x^5\right)\Big|_0^1 = \frac{3\pi}{10}.$$

Remark 5: If in remark 6 the axis of rotation is chosen as, $y=c$ then the volume of revolution produced is,

$$V = \pi \int_a^b (f(x) - c)^2 - (g(x) - c)^2)dx, \tag{11}$$

where, $x=F(y)$ and $x=G(y)$ and y_1, y_2 are the values of y at the points of intersections.

Example 31: Find the volume of revolution formed by the revolution of curves $y=4x-x^2$ and $y=x^2-6$ about $y+6=0$.

Solution: First, we find the points of intersection of these two curves. Put, $x^2-6=4x-x^2$. Hence $x=-1$, $x=3$. Then,

$$V = \pi \int_{-1}^3 ((4x - x^2 + 6)^2 - (x^2 - 6 + 6)^2)dx = \pi\left(36x + 24x^2 - \frac{4}{3}x^3 - 2x^4\right)\Big|_{-1}^3 = \frac{200\pi}{3}.$$

6.7.3 Arc Length of Curve

There is no simple formula for calculating the length of the curve. For example, a formula for calculating the perimeter of an ellipse has not yet been introduced. We are trying to find a way to calculate the length of the curve using the definite integral.

But, unfortunately, since many of these integrals obtained in these calculations, despite being integrable, cannot be calculated by analytical methods, we can only approximate them with numerical methods. In this section, we introduce the following procedure to find a formula in terms of definite integral. For this purpose, we divide the length AB by the sum of Δl_i such that if l is the length of AB, then

$$l = \sum_{x=a}^{x=b} \Delta l_i.$$

Figure 5. Graph of a part of curve to find its length

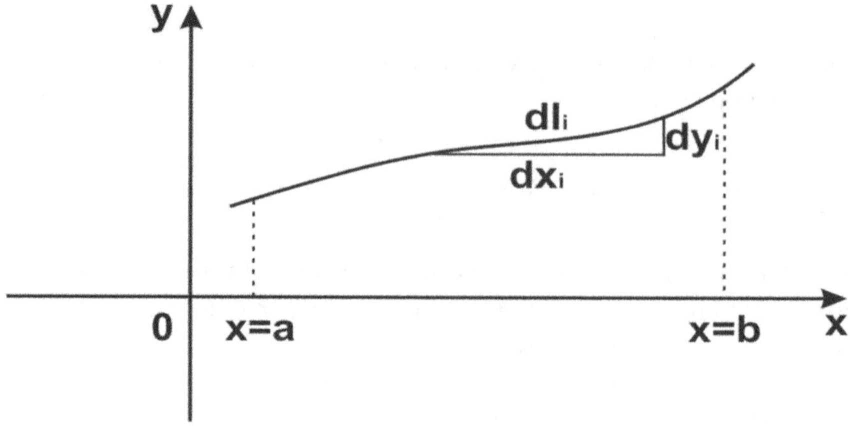

We have, $\Delta l_i \cong \sqrt{\Delta x_i^{\,2} + \Delta y_i^{\,2}}$. That is, $\frac{\Delta l_i}{\Delta x_i} \cong \sqrt{1 + (\frac{\Delta y_i}{\Delta x_i})^2}$. But since $\frac{\Delta y_i}{\Delta x_i} \to \frac{dy}{dx}$ when $\Delta x_i \to 0$ hence,

$$\lim_{\Delta x_i \to 0} \sum_{x=a}^{x=b} \sqrt{1 + (\frac{\Delta y_i}{\Delta x_i})^2} = l = \int_a^b \sqrt{1 + (\frac{dy}{dx})^2}\, dx. \tag{12}$$

Example 32: Find the length of $y = \frac{x^2}{2}$ from x=0 to x=1.

Solution: Since $y = \frac{x^2}{2}$, then, y'=x. Thus, $l = \int_0^1 \sqrt{1 + x^2}\, dx$. Substitute, $x = \sinh t$, we get,

$$l = \int_0^1 \sqrt{1+x^2}\, dx = \int_0^{\sinh^{-1}1} \sqrt{1 + \sinh^2 t}\cosh t dt = \int_0^{\sinh^{-1}1} \cosh^2 t dt$$

$$= \frac{1}{2}\int_0^{\sinh^{-1}1} (1 + \cosh 2t)\, dt = \frac{1}{2}\left(t + \frac{\sinh 2t}{2}\right)\Big|_0^{\sinh^{-1}1} = \frac{1}{2}\left(\sinh^{-1}1 + \frac{\sinh 2\sinh^{-1}1}{2}\right).$$

Remark 6: If the curve is given in parametric form, x=$g(t)$ and y=$h(y)$, then in this case Eq(12) becomes

$$l = \int_{t_1}^{t_2} \sqrt{(\frac{dx}{dt})^2 + (\frac{dy}{dt})^2}\, dt. \tag{13}$$

Example 33: Calculate the arc length of an asteroid given by

$x^{\frac{2}{3}} + y^{\frac{2}{3}} = a^{\frac{2}{3}}$, or $x = a\cos^3\theta,\ y = a\sin^3\theta$

which is a 4- petaled rose,(see Chapter 8).

Solution: We find one part of the asteroid and then multiply it by 4 (Figure 4). Since the asteroid is symmetrical concerning the x and y axes, thus it is enough to calculate one of the four parts of the curve and then multiply it by four (Figure 4). We have,

$$\frac{dx}{d\theta} = -3a\sin\theta\cos^2\theta, \frac{dy}{d\theta} = 3a\cos\theta\sin^2\theta.$$

Therefore,

$$l = 4(l_{AB}) = 4\int_0^{\frac{\pi}{2}} \sqrt{\left(\frac{dx}{d\theta}\right)^2 + \left(\frac{dy}{d\theta}\right)^2}\, d\theta$$

$$= 4\int_0^{\frac{\pi}{2}} \sqrt{9a^2\sin^2\theta\cos^4\theta + 9a^2\cos^2\theta\sin^4\theta}\, d\theta$$

$$= 12a\int_0^{\frac{\pi}{2}} \sqrt{\sin^2\theta\cos^2\theta(\cos^2\theta + \sin^2\theta)}\, d\theta = 12a\int_0^{\frac{\pi}{2}} \sqrt{\sin^2\theta\cos^2\theta}\, d\theta$$

$$= 3a\int_0^{\frac{\pi}{2}} \sin2\theta d\theta = -\frac{3a}{2}\cos2\theta\Big|_0^{\frac{\pi}{2}} = 3a.$$

6.7.4 Application in Business and Economics

According to the definition of marginal cost and marginal revenue functions, we have, $\frac{dC}{dx} = C'(x)$ and $\frac{dR}{dx} = R'(x)$. Therefore, Marginal cost function= $C(x)$= $\int C'(x)dx$ and, Marginal revenue function= $R(x)$= $\int R'(x)dx$.

Example 34: If the marginal revenue is given by xe^x, find the total revenue function by assuming that, $R(1)=1$.

Solution: We have, $R(x) = \int xe^x dx$. Using integration by parts leads to,

$$R(x) = \int xe^x dx = xe^x - \int e^x dx = xe^x - e^x + c.$$

Since, $R(1)=1$,then $e-e+c=1$. That is, $c=1$. Thus, $R(x)=(x-1)e^x+1$.

We have already introduced supply and demand functions. We mentioned that demand functions are descending functions and supply functions are ascending functions. Let Figure 6 represents the demand function.

Figure 6. Graph of demand function

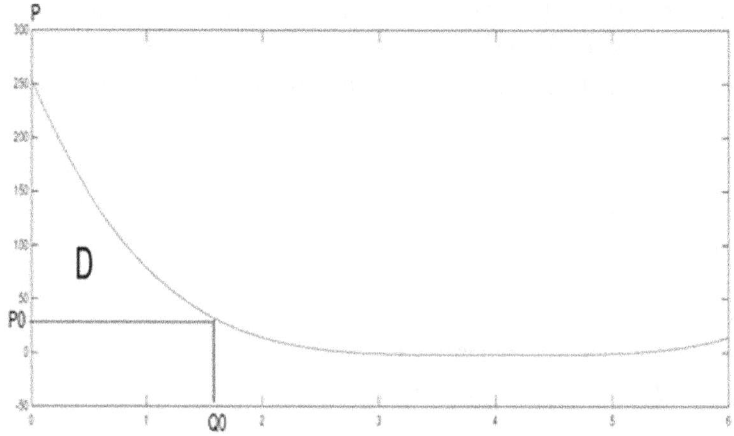

Point E is called the *equilibrium point* in the market if the price P_0 and the corresponding demand in the market are equal to Q_0. So according to Figure 6, consumers who are willing to pay more than price P_0 will benefit. The total benefit for consumers is determined by the area under the curve $f_1(Q)$ and the lines Q=0 and P=Q_0. This area is called *consumer surplus*, which is calculated with the following relationship,

$$consumersurplus = \int_0^{Q_0} f_1(Q)dQ - P_0Q_0.$$

Example 35: Suppose that the demand function is given by P=26–4Q–Q^2. If the equilibrium price is equal to 5, calculate the consumer surplus.

Solution: Since P_0=5, then, 26–4Q–Q^2=5. That is, Q^2+4Q–21=0. From this quadratic equation we obtain, Q=7, Q=3 where Q=3 is acceptable. Thus,

$$consumersurplus = \int_0^3 (26 - 4Q - Q^2)dQ - 15 = 36.$$

Let's consider the supply function P=f(Q), (Figure 7).

Figure 7. Graph of supply function

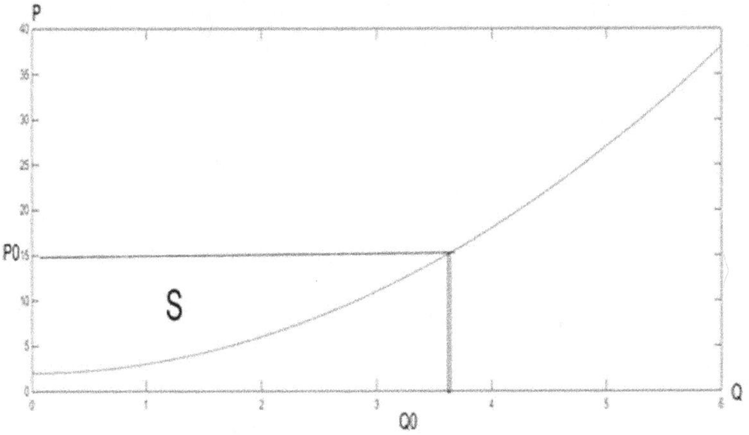

If the equilibrium point in the market is introduced with the coordinate (Q_0,P_0) again, then the producers who produce goods at a price lower than Q_0 will benefit. The total profit of the producer is called the *producer's surplus*, which is equal to the area of the hatched surface. Its value is obtained from the following formula.

$$producer'ssurplus = Q_0 P_0 - \int_0^{Q_0} f_2(Q)dQ.$$

Example 36: Assume the supply function is given by $P=2Q+3$. If $P_0=9$, calculate the producer's surplus.

Solution: If in the supply equation we put $P_0=0$, then $Q_0=3$. Thus,

$$\text{producer's surplus} = 32 - \int_0^3 (2Q + 3)dQ = 14.$$

Recall (5) from section 5.4.3,

$$AV = \frac{\int_a^b f(x)dx}{b - a}.$$

This is the mean (or average) value of a function over an interval $[a,b]$. We mentioned that it is used to find the average total cost or average total revenue in economics.

We end this chapter by considering an example.

Example 37: The demand function is given by $p^2+2x-15=0$, where p is the price of one unit when the demand is for 100 units. Find the average total revenue if the number of units demanded takes on all values from 300 and 500.

Solution: From, $p^2+2x-15=0$, we get $p = \sqrt{15-2x}$. We have $R(x) = xp = x\sqrt{15-2x}$. Since the total revenue of producing $100x$ units, then in the average total revenue, when the number of units takes on all values from 300 to 500, is given by the average value of $R(x)$ on (Burden, 1989) (Kolman & Anton, 1982). Therefore, we can write,

$$AV = \frac{\int_a^b f(x)dx}{b-a} = \frac{\int_3^5 x\sqrt{15-2x}\,dx}{2}.$$

To calculate the integral we assume, $15-2x=t^2$, then $dx=-tdt$. We have $t=3$ and $t = \sqrt{5}$ when $x=3$ and $x=5$. Therefore,

$$AV = \frac{\int_a^b f(x)dx}{b-a} = \frac{\int_3^5 x\sqrt{15-2x}\,dx}{2} = \frac{1}{4}\int_3^{\sqrt{5}} t^2(t^2-15)dt \approx 16.0098.$$

Thus, the average total revenue is 1600.98.

To read more about integral calculus and its applications, the readers may refer to (Apostol, 1966) (Finney, 1988) (Leithold, 1981) (Rodin, 1970) (Piskunov, 1981) (Silverman, 1985) (Thomas, 2014) (Stewart, 2008).

CONCLUSION

In this chapter, we introduced the concept of definite and infinite integrals. We introduce some methods to solve infinite integrals. Using these methods, we can evaluate the definite integrals by two fundamental theorems for integrals. Some applications of definite integral have been discussed and for those definite integrals which cannot be solved by analytical methods, we introduced two approximate methods to approximate their values.

6.8 Exercises

1. Evaluate the following elementary integrals.
   - (i) $\int \frac{4e^{-2x}dx}{5+e^{-2x}}$
   - (ii) $\int \frac{dx}{x(\ln x)^8}$
   - (iii) $\int \frac{dx}{1+\cos 2x}$
   - (iv) $\int \frac{\sin x dx}{2+\cos^2 x}$
   - (v) $\int \frac{(x+1)dx}{5+2x+x^2}$
   - (vi) $\int \frac{\sin x dx}{\sqrt{4+3\cos x}}$
   - (vii) $\int \tan^2 x dx$
   - (viii) $\int \cos^3 x dx$
   - (ix) $\int (\cos^4 x + \sin^4 x)dx$
   - (x) $\int \frac{(1+x)dx}{\sqrt{1+x^2}}$
2. Using integration methods, find the following integrals.
   - (i) $\int x\ 2e\ 4x\, dx$
   - (ii) $\int x \cos 6x dx$
   - (iii) $\int x\ 5 \ln x dx$
   - (iv) $\int \ln x\ 6 dx$
   - (v) $\int \frac{(3x-2)dx}{12-7x+x^2}$
   - (vi) $\int \frac{\sqrt{(1+x^4)}\,dx}{x}$
   - (vii) $\int x \tan -1\, x dx$
   - (viii) $\int \frac{(x-1)dx}{(x+2)x^2}$
   - (ix) $\int e\ -2x \cos 4x dx$
   - (x) $\int \frac{xdx}{\sqrt{1+x}}$
3. Show that
   - (i) $\int_0^{\pi} x \cos x dx = 2$
   - (ii) $\int_0^1 (2x+5)e^x dx = 5e-3$
   - (iii) $\int_0^{\frac{\pi}{2}} x \sin x dx = 1$
   - (iv) $\int_0^2 (x-[x])dx = 1$
   - (v) $\int_0^1 \frac{e^{\sqrt{x}}dx}{\sqrt{x}} = 2(e-1)$
   - (vi) $\int_{\frac{\pi}{4}}^{\frac{\pi}{2}} \cot^2 x dx = \frac{\pi}{4} - 1$
   - (vii) $\int_0^{\frac{\pi}{2}} x^2 \sin x dx = \pi - 2$
   - (viii) $\int_0^{\frac{\pi}{4}} \sec x dx = \ln(1+\sqrt{2})$
   - (ix) $\int_0^1 \sqrt{16-x^2}\, dx = \pi$
   - (x) $\int_0^1 \frac{x \tan^{-1} x dx}{\sqrt{1+x^2}} = \frac{1}{8}(\sqrt{2}+4\pi)$

4. Prove that

(i) $\lim_{x\to 0}\frac{\int_x^{x^2}\sin t dt}{x^2} = -\frac{1}{2}$

(ii) $\lim_{x\to 0}\frac{\int_0^{x^2}\cos^2 t dt}{\sin x^2} = 1$

(iii) $\lim_{x\to 0}\frac{\int_0^{x}\sin t dt}{\int_0^{x} te^t dt} = 1$

(iv) $\lim_{x\to 1}\frac{\int_1^{x} t(t-1) dt}{\sin \pi x} = 0$

5. Find the critical points of the function $y = \int_0^x \frac{\sin t dt}{t^2}$, and then determine which one is maximum and which is minimum.

6. If $I_n = \int_0^1 (1+x^2)^{-n} dx, n \in \mathbb{N}$, prove that$(2n+1)I_n = 2^{-n} + (2n-1)I_{n-1}$. Find $\int_0^1 (1+x^2)^{-3} dx$.

7. If $I_n = \int \frac{\cos^{2n} x dx}{\sin x}, n \in \mathbb{N}$, prove that$(2n+1)I_{n+1} = (2n+1)I_n + \cos^{2n+1} x$. Find $\int_0^{\frac{\pi}{2}} \frac{\cos^6 x dx}{\sin x}$.

8. Find the area of the following given regions.
   (i) The region bounded by $y=x^2$ and $y=4$.
   (ii) The region bounded $y=x^2$ and $y=x^3$.
   (iii) The region bounded by $y=1-x^2$ and x-axis.
   (iv) The region bounded by $y=x^2-4$ and $y=1-2x$.
   (v) The region bounced by $y=\ln x$ and lines $x=1$, $x=e$ and $y=0$.
   (vi) The region bounded by $y = \sqrt{x}$ and lines $x=0$, $x=1$ and $y=0$.
   (vii) The region bounded by $y=\cos x$ and lines $x=0$,$x = \frac{\pi}{2}$ and $y=0$.

9. Prove that the area bounded by the ellipse $\frac{x^2}{4a^2} + \frac{y^2}{9b^2} = 1$ is $6\pi ab$.

10. Find the volume of the region obtained by rotating:
   (i) $y=e^{2x}$ from $x=1$ to $x=2$ about the x axis.
   (ii) $y=\cos x$ from $x=0$ to $x = \frac{\pi}{2}$ about the x-axis.
   (iii) $y=x^2-4x$ from $x=2$ to $x=3$ about the y-axis.

11. Find the volume obtained by rotating the region bounded by curves $y=x^2$ and $x=y^2$about the $x=2$.

12. Find the volume obtained by rotating the region bounded by $y=x^2$ and $y=x+1$ about the $x=2$.

13. Find the volume obtained by rotating the region bounded by $x \geq y^2+1, y \geq 0, x \leq 2$about x-axis.

14. ***(Surface Area)*** The cross-section process enables us to find the area of a rotating surface. It can be shown that the area produced by the rotation about the axis which is located in the upper part of $[a,b]$ is equal to

$$S = 2\pi\int_a^b y\sqrt{1+\left(\frac{dy}{dx}\right)^2}\,dx.$$

(i) Find the surface area obtained by rotating the region bounded by $y=\sin x$ from $x=0$ to $x = \pi$ about the x-axis.

(ii) Find the surface area obtained by rotating the region bounded by $y^2=4x$ from $x=(0,0)$ to $(4,4)$ about the x-axis.

(iii) Find the surface area obtained by rotating the region bounded by the first quarter of the circle $x^2+y^2=1$ about the x-axis.

15. Show that the length of one arc of cycloid $x = \theta - \sin\theta, y = 1 - \cos\theta$ is 8.
16. Find the arc length of curve $y=e^x$ from $x=\ln(\sinh 1)$ to $x=\ln(\sinh 2)$.
17. Calculate the distance traveled by a particle from $t = 0$ to $t = \frac{\pi}{2}$, which at time t its position is described as $x=\cos t+\sin t$, $y=\sin t-\cos t$.
18. The producer of a particular good determines the marginal cost with the rule $C'(x) = x + \pi \cos\frac{\pi x}{80}$, where the total cost of production of x units is $C(x)$ dollars. Assuming that the marginal (total) cost is \$80, what will be the total cost of producing 40 units of goods?
19. The marginal revenue of a particular good is determined by the rule $R'(x)= 3x^2-8x+42$. If, the total revenue of sales of x units is $R(x)$ dollars. Find the total revenue and demand functions.
20. The producer obtains the marginal cost of a certain product from the rule, $C'(x) = \frac{x^2}{1875} + \frac{2x}{9} - 2$. If the selling price per unit is fixed at \$13 and the general cost is \$75 per week, what is the maximum weekly profit?
21. Suppose that the supply function is determined by the rule $P=(Q+1)^2$. Find the producer's surplus if, $P_0=16$.
22. If the demand function is given by $P=20-2Q-3Q^2$ and $P_0=4$, find the consumer surplus.
23. Let the demand and supply functions are given by $P=13-Q-Q^2$ and $P=Q^2+Q+1$, respectively. Determine.
    (i) The coordinates of the equilibrium point when the market is perfectly competitive.
    (ii) The producer's and consumer surplus.
24. ***(work).*** In the definition of the definite integral, if we consider the continuous function $f(x)$ as a force acting on a body that moves to the right of the x- axis from $x=a$ to $x=b$, then the work done by this force in this distance is determined by $\int_a^b f(x)dx$. Find the work done in the following cases:
    (i) A force of $f=m\cos kt$ at time t acts on a particle with mass m in the positive direction of the ox axis. Let's at $x=12$, $t=5$. Calculate the work done up to $t=5$.
    (ii) If a force of 2 kg pulls a spring 20 cm long by 4 cm, find the work done.

REFERENCES

Apostol, T. M. (1966). *Calculus* (2nd ed., Vol. 1). John Wiley & Sons.

Burden, R. L. (1989). Numerical Analysis (4th ed). PWS_KENT Publish Company.

Finney, R. L. (1988). *Calculus and Analytical Geometry* (7th ed.). Addison-Wesley Publishing Company.

Hamming, R. W. (1971). *Introduction to applied and numerical analysis*. Mc Graw-Hill, Inc.

Kolman, H., & Anton, B. (1982). *Mathematics with Applications for Management, Life, and Social Science* (2nd ed.). Academic Press, Inc.

Leithold, L. (1981). *The Calculus and Analytical Geometry* (4th ed.). Harper & Row.

Nicholson, R. H. (1986). *Mathematics for Business and Economics*. McGraw-Hill, Inc.

Piskunov, N. (1981). Differential and Integral, Vol 1 (4th ed). MIR Publisher.

Rodin. Burton Rodin. (1970). Calculus with Analytical Geometry (4th ed). Prentice-Hall, Inc., Englewood Cliffs, New Jersey.

Silverman. Richard, A. (1985). *Calculus with Analytical Geometry* (4th ed.). Prentice-Hall, Inc.

Stewart, J. (2008). *Calculus* (6th ed.). Mc-Graw.

The American Mathematical Monthly (1983). p210, Vol 90, No3.

Thomas. George, B. (2014). *Calculus* (13th ed.). Mc-Graw.

Chapter 7
Differential Calculus of Multivariable Functions

ABSTRACT

This chapter focuses on differential calculus of multivariable functions. We generalize the definition of differentiation to such functions. The limit and continuity in a point on a plane will be defined as we had in Chapter 4. The rules of differentiations of the functions which are introduced in Chapter 5, can also be used for multivariable functions with the difference that we call them partial derivatives. After definition of degree for homogeneity the Euler's Theorem we found a relation between partial derivatives of a multi-valued function and degree of homogeneity. Several applications of partial differentiation will be given through this chapter. We mention that the Taylor's formula for single-valued function can also be generalized to multi-valued functions.

7.1 INTRODUCTION

We know that the area of a rectangle is obtained from the relation $S=ab$, where a and b are the length and width of the rectangle, respectively. To calculate the volume of a rectangular cube, we use the relationship $V=abc$, where a and b are the lengths of the base rectangle, and c is the width of the rectangular cube. The first relation shows that the value of the area depends on a and b. We can consider it as a two-variable function. In the second relation, assuming, for example, $a=x_1$, $b=x_2$ and $c=x_3$, it shows the volume in terms of functions of x_1,x_2 and x_3, i.e. $f(x_1,x_2,x_3)$. These two examples show that in many problems we are dealing with multivariable functions. The function of the total cost of each family depends on incidental expenses

DOI: 10.4018/979-8-3693-3657-1.ch007

such as clothing, food, health care, etc. They are commonly used in management for various purposes, such as optimization, forecasting and decision-making.

In general, a function can be with n variables $x_1,x_2,\dots,x_n$, but in this chapter, we focus on functions with two or three variables.

7.2 MULTIVARIABLE FUNCTIONS

If we write the function f with the rule $w=f(x_1,x_2,\dots,x_n)$, then we have a multivariable function with a set of ordered pairs $((x_1,x_2,\dots,x_n)w)$ that, like a single function, none of the two different ordered pairs have equal members. With this argument, an n-variable function maps the n-dimensional real space, denoted by $\mathbb{R}^n$, to the 1-dimensional real space $\mathbb{R}$, that is, $f:\mathbb{R}^n \rightarrow \mathbb{R}$.

The largest subset of the set $\{(x_1,x_2,...,x_n),x_i \in \mathbb{R}\}$ in which the function f is defined, is called the domain of the function and the set of values that w can take is called the range of the function denoted by D_f and R_f, respectively. The examples we examine in this chapter are mostly for the functions of two variables $z=f(x,y)$ or the functions of three variables, $w=f(x,y,z)$, whose results can be generalized for n-variables functions. Before we go further, let's have a picture about some specific graphs of $f(x,y,z)=0$.

In Chapter 1, we mentioned that a general form for a second-order surface given by

$$Ax^2 + By^2 + Cz^2 + Dxy + Exz + Fyz + Gx + Hy + Iz + J = 0$$

where A,B,C,D,E,F,G,H,I and J are real constant coefficients. The graph of any such equation is called *quadric surface*. Since the coefficients of this equation determine the shape and orientation of the quadric surface in space, hence for the time being we assume $D=E=F=0$. That is, we have the following equation.

$$Ax^2 + By^2 + Cz^2 + Gx + Hy + Iz + J = 0$$

According to this equation, we introduce some types of surfaces that are more well-known forms.

1. If $A=B=C$, then the quadric surface is called a *sphere* with radius r and center (x_0,y_0,z_0) and will be given by

$$(x - x_0)^2 + (y - y_0)^2 + (z - z_0)^2 = r^2$$

If $x_0=y_0=z_0=0$, then the center of sphere is located on origin (Figure 1).

Figure 1. Graph of a sphere

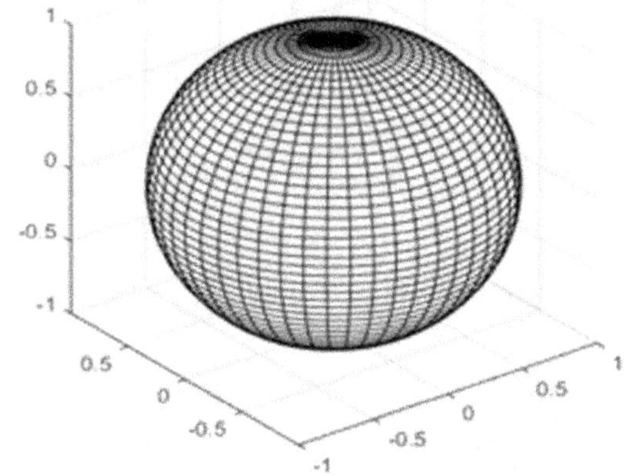

2. If $A>0$, $B>0$, $C>0$, in this case the quadric surface is called an *ellipsoid* with equation

$$\frac{x^2}{a^2}+\frac{y^2}{b^2}+\frac{z^2}{c^2} = 1.$$

Figure 2. Graph of an ellipsoid

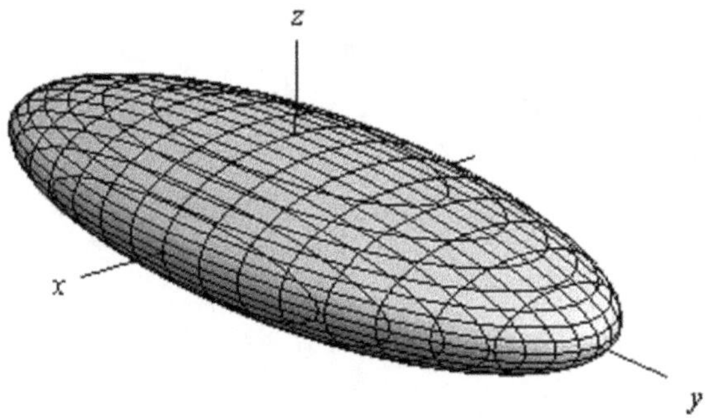

3. If $A>0$, $B>0$, $C<0$, then we will have three following case

(i) $\frac{x^2}{a^2} + \frac{y^2}{b^2} = \frac{z^2}{c^2}$, elliptic cone

(ii) $\frac{x^2}{a^2} + \frac{y^2}{b^2} - \frac{z^2}{c^2} = 1$, hyperboloid of one sheet

(iii) $\frac{x^2}{a^2} + \frac{y^2}{b^2} - \frac{z^2}{c^2} = -1$, hyperboloid of two sheets

Figure 3. Graphs of hyperboloids

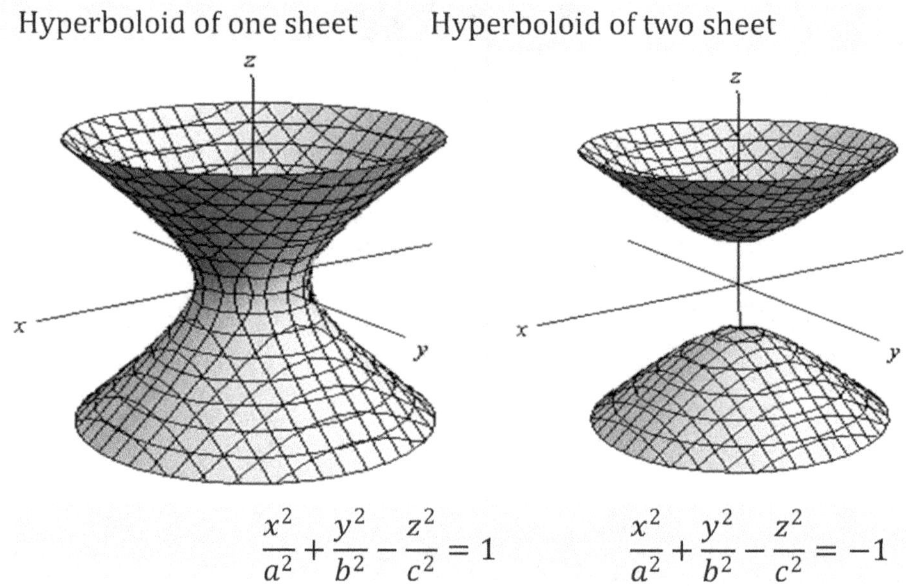

$\frac{x^2}{a^2} + \frac{y^2}{b^2} - \frac{z^2}{c^2} = 1 \frac{x^2}{a^2} + \frac{y^2}{b^2} - \frac{z^2}{c^2} = -1$

Figure 4. Graph of an elliptic cone

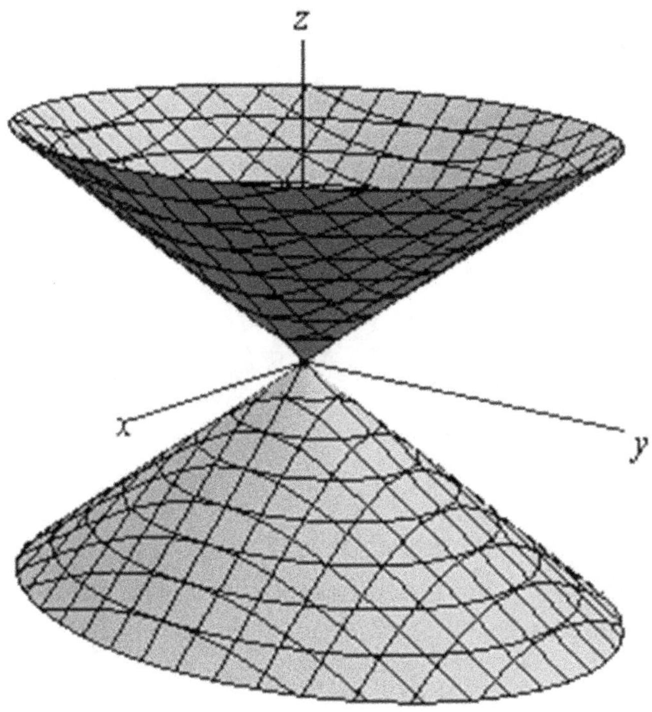

$$\frac{x^2}{a^2} + \frac{y^2}{b^2} = \frac{z^2}{c^2}$$

$$\frac{x^2}{a^2} + \frac{y^2}{b^2} = \frac{z^2}{c^2}$$

4. If $A>0$, $B>0$, $C=0$, in this case the quadric surface is called a *paraboliod* with equation

$$z = \frac{x^2}{a^2} + \frac{y^2}{b^2}.$$

Figure 5. Graph of a paraboliod

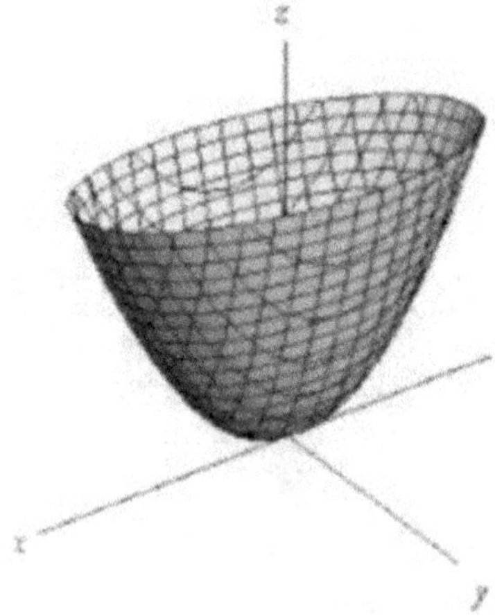

5. If $A>0$, $B<0$, $C=0$, in this case the quadric surface is called a *hyperbolic parabolic* with equation

$$z = \frac{x^2}{a^2} - \frac{y^2}{b^2}.$$

Figure 6. Graph of a hyperbolic parabolic

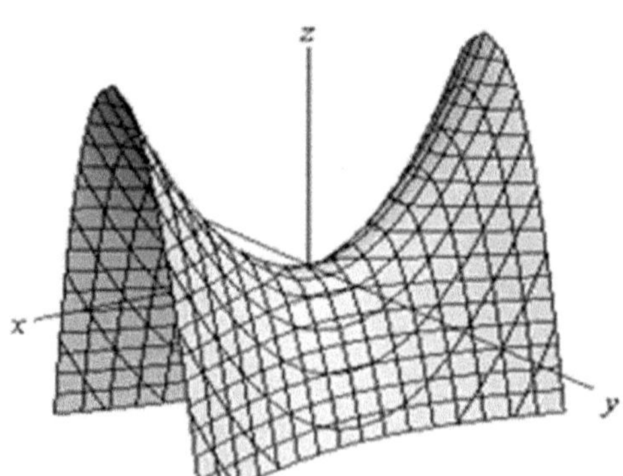

6. If $B>0$, $A=C=0$, in this case the quadric surface is called a *parabolic cylinder* with equation $y^2=az$.

Figure 7. Graph of a parabolic cylinder

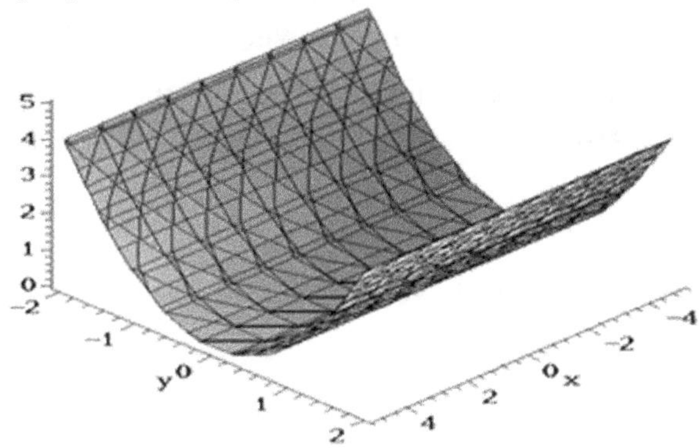

Figure 8. Graph of a cylinder

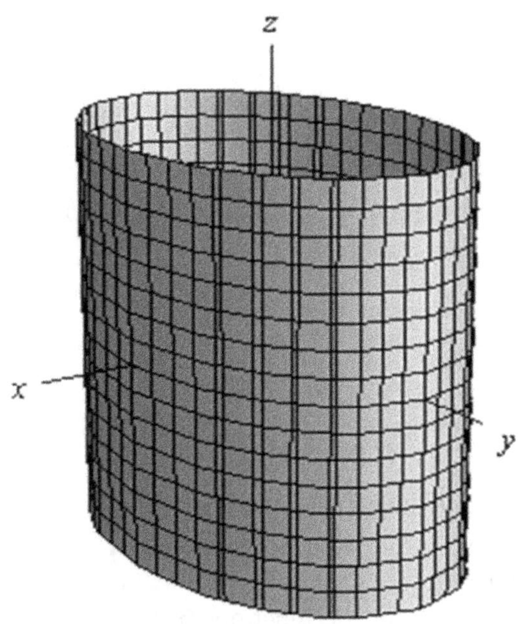

$$\frac{x^2}{a^2}+\frac{y^2}{b^2}=1$$

$\frac{x^2}{a^2} + \frac{y^2}{b^2} = 1$

Let's go back to the general form of a second-order surface and assume D, Eor $F \neq 0$. In this case we may use a change of coordinates so that our new second-order surface does not contain constants *xy, yz,* or *xz*. In the next chapter we will give a brief discussion about this matter when we meet the matrices.

Example 1: Verify the domain and range of the function, $z = \sqrt{1 - \frac{x^2}{4} - \frac{y^2}{9}}$. This relation comprises the surface of a hemi-ellipsoid of diameters 1, 2 and 3 with center at (0,0,0).

Figure 9. Graph of a hemi ellipsoid

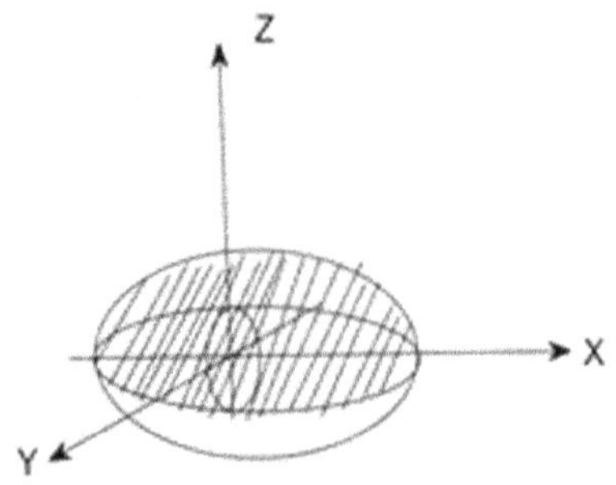

Solution: We should have, $1 - \frac{x^2}{4} - \frac{y^2}{9} \geq 0$. That is, $\frac{x^2}{4} + \frac{y^2}{9} \leq 1$. Therefore, its domain consists of the set of points (x, y) that are inside or on the ellipse, $\frac{x^2}{4} + \frac{y^2}{9} = 1$. That is,

$$D_f = \left\{ (x, y) \middle| \frac{x^2}{4} + \frac{y^2}{9} \leq 1 \right\}.$$

Since according to this set, the largest value of z is 1 and the smallest value is zero then, R_f=[0,1].

Example 2: Determine the domain and range of the function, $z = \frac{2xy - 3}{y^2 + 4}$.

Solution: We have $y^2 + 4 \neq 0$,thus, its domain is, $\mathbb{R}^2$. We do not also have any restrictions for z, then the range of the function will be, $\mathbb{R}$.

The limit and continuity for the functions of two variables are defined in the same way as the single-valued functions. In such a way, we write

$$\lim_{\substack{x \to a \\ y \to b}} f(x, y) = L, \quad (1)$$

if,

$$\varepsilon > 0, \delta > 0, \sqrt{(x-a)^2-(y-b)^2} < \delta| - L| < \varepsilon.$$

The function $f(x,y)$ is continuous at $(x,y)=(a,b)$, if

$$\lim_{\substack{x\to a\\ y\to b}} f(x,y) = f(a,b). \tag{2}$$

For example, the function $f(x,y) = \frac{2xy-3}{y^2+4}$ is continuous on $\mathbb{R}^2$ but the function $f(x,y)= \sqrt{4-x^2-y^2}$ is not continuous outside of the circle $x^2+y^2=4$.

The rules for limit and continuity for the single-valued functions also hold for multivariable functions. For example, if $f(x,y)$ and $g(x,y)$ are continuous at (a,b) then,

$$f(x,y) \pm g(x,y), f(x,y) \cdot g(x,y) \text{ and } \frac{f(x,y)}{g(x,y)}, (g(a,b) \neq 0)$$

are continuous at (a,b).

Regarding the existence of a limit in many fractional functions, we can use the following three techniques for the absence of a limit if $\lim_{\substack{x\to a\\ y\to b}} f(x,y) = \frac{0}{0}$.

1. From (1), we may write

$$\lim_{\substack{x\to a\\ y\to b}} f(x,y) = \lim_{x\to a}\lim_{y\to b} f(x,y)$$

or

$$\lim_{\substack{x\to a\\ y\to b}} f(x,y) = \lim_{y\to b}\lim_{x\to a} f(x,y).$$

If the limit exists, we must have

$$\lim_{y\to b}\lim_{x\to a} f(x,y) = \lim_{x\to a}\lim_{y\to b} f(x,y) = L.$$

Example 3: Show that the function $f(x,y) = \frac{2x-3y}{5x+4y}$ has not limit at (0,0).

Solution: We have $\lim_{y\to 0}\lim_{x\to 0} f(x,y) = -\frac{3}{4}$ and $\lim_{x\to 0}\lim_{y\to 0} f(x,y) = \frac{2}{5}$. Hence the limit does not exist.

2. It is possible that when we use the first technique, the limit values are equal, but despite this, the function does not have a limit. For this purpose, we use polar coordinates, that is, $x = r\cos\theta$, $y = r\sin\theta$. Obviously, when $x \to 0$ and $y \to 0$, then $r \to 0$. There is no limit if $\lim_{r\to 0} f(r,\theta)$ does not exist.

Example 4: Show that the function $f(x,y) = \frac{2xy}{x^2+y^2}$ has not limit at (0,0) even though

$$\lim_{y\to 0}\lim_{x\to 0} f(x,y) = \lim_{x\to 0}\lim_{y\to 0} f(x,y).$$

Solution: We have

$$\lim_{y\to 0}\lim_{x\to 0} f(x,y) = \lim_{y\to 0}\frac{0}{y^2} = 0$$

and

$$\lim_{x\to 0}\lim_{y\to 0} f(x,y) = \lim_{x\to 0}\frac{0}{x^2} = 0$$

But

$$\lim_{x\to 0}\lim_{y\to 0}\frac{2xy}{x^2+y^2} = \lim_{r\to 0}\frac{2r\cos\theta r\sin\theta}{(r\cos\theta)^2+(r\sin\theta)^2} = \lim_{r\to 0}\frac{r^2\sin 2\theta}{r^2} = \sin 2\theta.$$

This means the value of the limit depends on θ. That is, it is not unique. Hence, the limit does not exist.

3. The third technique is path selection. Even with the second technique, we obtain the wrong answer. Hence, we introduce the third technique. In this technique, we choose two paths, like $y=(x)$ and $y=h(x)$, $y=g(x)$ and $y=h(x)$ such that both pass through the point of origin.

Example 5: Prove that the function, $f(x,y) = \frac{2xy}{x+y}$ has no limit at (0,0).
Solution: We have

$$\lim_{y\to 0}\lim_{x\to 0}\frac{2xy}{x+y} = \lim_{x\to 0}\lim_{y\to 0}\frac{2xy}{x+y} = 0,$$

and

$$\lim_{x\to 0}\lim_{y\to 0}\frac{2xy}{x+y} = \lim_{r\to 0}\frac{2r\cos\theta r\sin\theta}{r\cos\theta + r\sin\theta} = \lim_{r\to 0}\frac{r^2\sin 2\theta}{r(\cos\theta + \sin\theta)} = 0.$$

But, if we choose the paths $y=x$ and $y= -x$, we get

$$y = x \to \lim_{x\to 0}\lim_{y\to 0}\frac{2xy}{x+y} = \lim_{x\to 0}\frac{2x^2}{2x} = \lim_{x\to 0} x = 0,$$

$$y = -x \to \lim_{x\to 0}\lim_{y\to 0}\frac{2xy}{x+y} = \lim_{x\to 0}\frac{2x^2}{0} = \infty .$$

That is, the limit does not exist.

Here we remind you that none of these techniques are sufficient for the existence of the limit. They are only suitable for the absence of a limit. To prove the existence of the limit, the definition of the limit in (1) should be used.

Example 6: Verify continuity of the function, $f(x,y) = \frac{xy}{x^2 + y^2 + 4}$.

Solution: Since always $x^2 + y^2 + 4 \neq 0$ hence the function is continuous on $\mathbb{R}^2$.

Example 7: Show that the following function is not continuous at (0, 0).

$$f(x,y) = \begin{cases} \frac{xy^2}{x^2 + y^2}, (x,y) \neq (0,0) \\ 0, (x,y) = (0,0) \end{cases}$$

Solution: The function is defined at (0, 0), but by the second technique it can be seen that the function has no limit at (0, 0). Thus, this function is not continuous at (0, 0).

7.3 PARTIAL DIFFERENTIATIONS

In Chapter 5, we defined the derivative of a single-valued function and examined some of its features. We have considered the geometric interpretation of the derivative at a point and find that the existence of a derivative is equivalent to the existence of the slope of the tangent line on the curve of that function. We used derivatives to determine the maximum and minimum of the functions. We found that if a function is differentiable at a point, it will also be continuous at that point. Now, in this section, we would like to get acquainted with the concept of the partial derivative of multivariable functions, which, despite its high efficiency, cannot take the place of the derivative of single-valued functions. For this reason, we try to add conditions to these types of derivatives to achieve the concept of the derivative of a multivariable function.

Definition 1: We define the partial derivative of the function $z=f(x,y)$ concerning x which is denoted by the symbols, $\frac{\partial f}{\partial x}, \frac{\partial z}{\partial x}, f_x$ or z_x as follows:

$$\frac{\partial z}{\partial x} = \lim_{\Delta x \to 0} \frac{f(x+\Delta x, y) - f(x,y)}{\Delta x} \tag{4}$$

Similarly, the partial derivative of this function concerning y is defined as follows:

$$\frac{\partial z}{\partial y} = \lim_{\Delta y \to 0} \frac{f(x, y+\Delta y) - f(x,y)}{\Delta y} \tag{5}$$

Remark 1: The rules regarding the derivative of single-valued functions are also valid here.

Example 8: Find $\frac{\partial z}{\partial x}$ and $\frac{\partial z}{\partial y}$ if $z=x^2y+e^{xy}$.

Solution: We have,

$$\frac{\partial z}{\partial x} = 2xy + ye^{xy}, \frac{\partial z}{\partial y} = x^2 + xe^{xy}.$$

Example 9: Prove $x\frac{\partial f}{\partial x} + y\frac{\partial f}{\partial y} = 0$ if $f = \frac{x}{y} - \frac{y}{x}, k$ is a real number.

Solution: We have,

$$\frac{\partial f}{\partial x} = \frac{1}{y} + \frac{y}{x^2}, \frac{\partial f}{\partial y} = -\frac{x}{y^2} - \frac{1}{x}.$$

Thus,

$$x\frac{\partial f}{\partial x} + y\frac{\partial f}{\partial y} = \frac{x}{y} + \frac{y}{x} - \frac{x}{y} - \frac{y}{x} = 0.$$

As the single-valued functions, we can find second derivatives of $f(x,y)$ if the functions $\frac{\partial f}{\partial x}$ and $\frac{\partial f}{\partial y}$ are also differentiable. These second derivatives are denoted by

$$\frac{\partial^2 f}{\partial x^2}, \frac{\partial^2 f}{\partial y^2}, \frac{\partial^2 f}{\partial x \partial y} \text{ and } \frac{\partial^2 f}{\partial y \partial x}, \text{ or } f_{xx}, f_{yy}, f_{xy} \text{ and } f_{yx}.$$

It has been proved that if, $\frac{\partial f}{\partial x}$ and $\frac{\partial f}{\partial y}$ are continuous then,

$$\frac{\partial^2 f}{\partial x \partial y} = \frac{\partial^2 f}{\partial y \partial x}.$$

For example, from example 9, we have, $\frac{\partial^2 f}{\partial x \partial y} = -\frac{1}{y^2} + \frac{1}{x^2}$ and $\frac{\partial^2 f}{\partial y \partial x} = -\frac{1}{y^2} + \frac{1}{x^2}$. Thus, $\frac{\partial^2 f}{\partial x \partial y} = \frac{\partial^2 f}{\partial y \partial x}$, if $(x, y) \neq (0,0)$.

Definition 2: We call the functions $f(x,y)$ and $f(x,y,z)$ *homogeneous* of degree k if, in the domain of definition, we have,

$$f(\lambda x, \lambda y) = \lambda^k f(x, y)$$

$$f(\lambda x, \lambda y, \lambda z) = \lambda^k f(x, y, z).$$

For example, the function $f(x,y)=3x^2-5xy+y^2$ is a homogeneous function of degree 2, or the function $f(x,y,y)=4xyz$ is a homogeneous function of degree, and $f(x, y, y) = \frac{4xyz}{x^2 + y^2 - 3z^2}$ is a homogeneous function of degree 1.

The Cobb-Douglas production function given as $Q = A K^{\alpha} L^{\beta}$ is a homogeneous function of degree $\alpha + \beta$, where A is a positive constant and K and L are inputs of capital and labor, respectively.

Theorem 1: (*Euler's Theorem*). If the functions $f(x,y)$ and $f(x,y,z)$ are homogeneous of degree k, then

$$x\frac{\partial f}{\partial x} + y\frac{\partial f}{\partial y} = kf. \tag{16}$$

Remark 2: Eq. 6 shows if f is homogeneous of degree zero then,

$$x\frac{\partial f}{\partial x} + y\frac{\partial f}{\partial y} = 0.$$

Example 10: Show that, $x\frac{\partial f}{\partial x} + y\frac{\partial f}{\partial y} + z\frac{\partial f}{\partial z} = 0$ if, $f(x, y, z) = \frac{x + 2y - z}{\sqrt{x^2 + y^2 + z^2}}$.

Solution: Since the function $f(x, y, z) = \frac{x + 2y - z}{\sqrt{x^2 + y^2 + z^2}}$ is homogeneous of degree zero then by Remark 2, we get,

$$x\frac{\partial f}{\partial x} + y\frac{\partial f}{\partial y} + z\frac{\partial f}{\partial z} = 0$$

Similar to single-valued functions, partial derivatives for functions of two variables $z=f(x,y)$ are interpreted as slopes of tangent lines on the surface of $z=f(x,y)$ at the point (x_0,y_0,z_0). The equations of these tangent lines are given in the following forms:

$$L_1:\begin{cases} z - z_0 = (x - x_0)\frac{\partial z}{\partial x} \\ y = y_0 \end{cases} \quad L_2:\begin{cases} z - z_0 = (y - y_0)\frac{\partial z}{\partial y} \\ x = x_0 \end{cases}$$

Using the equations of these two lines, we can write the equation of the plane that includes these two lines and is tangent to the surface $z=f(x,y)$ at the point (x_0,y_0,z_0). It is given by:

$$z - z_0 = (x - x_0)\frac{\partial z}{\partial x} + (y - y_0)\frac{\partial z}{\partial x}. \tag{7}$$

Figure 10. Graph of tangent lines to surface

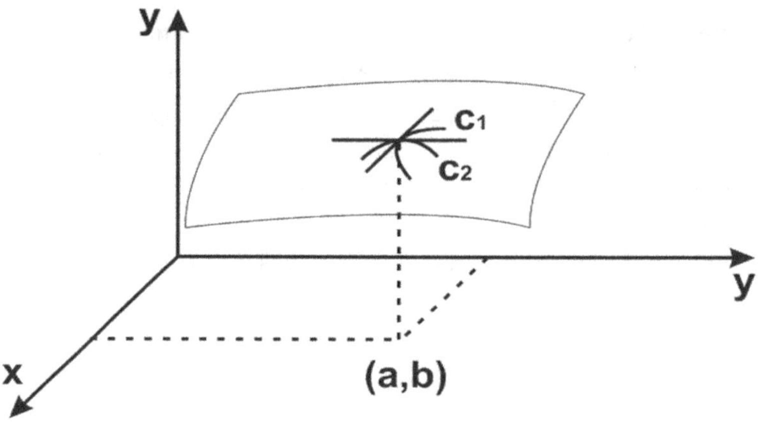

Example 11: Find the equations of lines and plane tangent to the surface $z=x^2-y^2+3xy-4$ at the point (1,1,-1).

Solution: We have, $\frac{\partial z}{\partial x} = 2x + 3y, \frac{\partial z}{\partial y} = -2y + 3x$, then, at (1,1,-1) we get, $\frac{\partial z}{\partial x} = 5 \text{and} \frac{\partial z}{\partial y} = 1$.Thus,

$$L_1:\begin{cases} z = 5(x-1) \\ y = 1 \end{cases} \quad L_2:\begin{cases} z = y-1 \\ x = 1 \end{cases}$$

We write the equation of plane by using (7), we obtain,

$$z + 1 = 5(x-1) + (y-1) \rightarrow 5x + y - z = 7.$$

7.4 TOTAL DIFFERENTIAL

In Chapter 5, we presented an approximate formula in a single-valued function $y=f(x)$ when the small value Δx changes the value of y to $y+\Delta y$ and we observed that $\Delta y = f'(x)\Delta x$. Similar processes can also be applied to multivariable functions. Here, we consider the function $z=f(x,y)$. From the relation $\Delta y = f'(x)\Delta x$ we can guess

$$\Delta z = \frac{\partial z}{\partial x}\Delta x + \frac{\partial z}{\partial y}\Delta y \tag{8}$$

which is often used to calculate change Δz resulting from changes Δx and Δy.

Example 12: Determine an approximate value for $\sqrt{4.01^2 + 2.98^2}$.

Solution: Consider the function, $z = \sqrt{x^2 + y^2}$. This is a semi-elliptic cone. If $x_1=4$ and $y_1=3$ then $z_1=5$. Now, if $x_2=4.01$ and $y_2=2.98$, we want to find the value of z_2. We have,

$$\frac{\partial z}{\partial x} = \frac{2x}{\sqrt{x^2+y^2}}, \frac{\partial z}{\partial y} = \frac{2y}{\sqrt{x^2+y^2}}$$

then, for $x=4$ and $y=3$ we get, $\frac{\partial z}{\partial x} = \frac{8}{5}$ and $\frac{\partial z}{\partial y} = \frac{6}{5}$. We also have, $\Delta x= 4.01–4= 0.01$ and $\Delta y= 2.98–3= -0.02$. Thus, by (8), we get,

$$\Delta z = \frac{\partial z}{\partial x}\Delta x + \frac{\partial z}{\partial y}\Delta y = \frac{8}{5}(0.01) + \frac{6}{5}(-0.02) = -\frac{0.04}{5} = -0.008.$$

Since $\Delta z = z_2 - z_1$, then $z_2 = \Delta z + z_1 = 5 - 0.008 = 4.992$. Thus,

$$\sqrt{4.01^2 + 2.98^2} \approx 4.992.$$

Example 13: The total cost of a manufacturing company is a function of two goods x and y, and is given by, $C(x,y)=(x+y)^2$. If initially there are $x=40$ and $y=60$, the production of commodity x increases by $\Delta x=2$. Find the cost due to this increase.

Solution: We can find this total cost by the total differential. Since, $\Delta x=2$ then,

$$dC = C_x dx = 2(x+y)dx \approx 2(x+y)\Delta x = 2(40+60)\times 2 = 2400$$

Because working with Δz is a little bit difficult, that is why dz is usually used instead of Δz and it is called *total differential* of z. In this case, if we move from point (x,y) to point $(x+\Delta x, y+\Delta y)$, the resulting differential in z is expressed as

$$dz = \frac{\partial z}{\partial x}dx + \frac{\partial z}{\partial y}dy. \tag{9}$$

It can be seen that, the relation (9) is a generalization of the differential for the single-valued function. In more general form, the total differential of the function $f(x_1,x_2,\dots,x_n)$ is given by

$$df = \frac{\partial f}{\partial x_1}dx_1 + \frac{\partial f}{\partial x_2}dx_2 + \dots + \frac{\partial f}{\partial x_n}dx_n. \tag{10}$$

Example 14: If $w=xy^2e^z$, find dw at (2,0,1).

Solution: By (10) we have,

$$dw = \frac{\partial w}{\partial x}dx + \frac{\partial w}{\partial y}dy + \frac{\partial w}{\partial z}dz.$$

But at (0,0,1) we have,

$$\frac{\partial w}{\partial x} = y^2e^z = 0, \frac{\partial w}{\partial y} = 2xye^z = 0, \frac{\partial w}{\partial x} = xy^2e^z = 0.$$

Thus, $dw=0.\ dx+0.\ dy+0.\ dz=0$.

Remark 3: To calculate the total differential of $z=f(x,y)$ with order n, we use the following formula:

$$d^nz = \left(\frac{\partial}{\partial x}dx + \frac{\partial}{\partial y}dy\right)^n z. \tag{11}$$

For example, put $n=2$, we get,

$$d^2z = \left(\frac{\partial}{\partial x}dx + \frac{\partial}{\partial y}dy\right)^2 z = \frac{\partial^2 z}{\partial x^2}dx^2 + 2\frac{\partial^2 z}{\partial x\partial y}dxdy + \frac{\partial^2 z}{\partial y^2}dy^2.$$

Example 15: If $z=x^2+y^2-xy$, find d^2z at (1,1) for $dx=0.1$ and $dy=0.1$.

Solution: At the point (1,1) we have,

$$\frac{\partial z}{\partial x} = 2x-y = 1, \frac{\partial z}{\partial x} = 2y-x = 1, \frac{\partial^2 z}{\partial x^2} = 2, \frac{\partial^2 z}{\partial y^2} = 2, \frac{\partial^2 z}{\partial x\partial y} = -1,$$

with $dx=0.1$ and $dy=0.2$. Therefore,

$$d^2z = \frac{\partial^2 z}{\partial x^2}dx^2 + 2\frac{\partial^2 z}{\partial x\partial y}dxdy + \frac{\partial^2 z}{\partial y^2}dy^2 = 0.02 - 0.04 + 0.08 = 0.06.$$

Assume that the function $z=f(x,y)$ is a constant function, that is, $f(x,y)=k$, then, by (9) we have,

$$0 = \frac{\partial z}{\partial x}dx + \frac{\partial z}{\partial y}dy.$$

Hence, we obtain,

$$\frac{dy}{dx} = -\frac{\frac{\partial z}{\partial x}}{\frac{\partial z}{\partial y}} = -\frac{f_x}{f_y},$$

which is the same formula we obtained in Chapter 4 for implicit differentiation.

The idea of this process can be used when z is given by the relation $F(x,y,x)=0$ so that z is an implicit function of x, y. In this case, according to the above conclusion, we will have the following results:

$$\frac{\partial z}{\partial x} = -\frac{F_x}{F_z}, \frac{\partial z}{\partial x} = -\frac{F_x}{F_z}. \tag{12}$$

Example 16: If $xyz + 1 = e^{2x+y+3z}$, find $\frac{\partial z}{\partial x}$ for $x=y=z=0$.

Solution: Suppose $F(x,y,z) = xyz + 1 - e^{2x+y+3z}$. Then for, $x=y=z=0$,

$$F_x = yz - 2e^{2x+y+3z} = -2 \text{and} F_z = xy - 3e^{2x+y+3z} = -3.$$

Thus,

$$\frac{\partial z}{\partial x} = -\frac{F_x}{F_z} = -\frac{2}{3}.$$

Example 17: If $x^2 + y^2 + z^2 = xy$, find $\frac{\partial z}{\partial x}$ for $2x-y=4$

Solution: Let's $F(x,y,z)= x^2+y^2+z^2-xy$. Then, $F_x=2x-y$ and $F_z=2z$. Thus, for $2x-y=4$, we get,

$$x\frac{\partial z}{\partial x} + y\frac{\partial f}{\partial y} + z\frac{\partial f}{\partial z} = 0$$

Back to (9) and assume that $dz=0$. Thus we get

$$0 = \frac{\partial z}{\partial x}dx + \frac{\partial z}{\partial y}dy$$

Let's $\frac{\partial z}{\partial x} = P(x,y)$ and $\frac{\partial z}{\partial y} = Q(x,y)$. Hence, we can write $P(x,y)dx+Q(x,y)dy=0$.

If the functions $P(x,y)$ and $Q(x,y)$ and their first partial derivatives are continuous in some domain, say D then, we say that $P(x,y)dx+Q(x,y)dy$ is *exact differential* of a function such as $u(x,y)$ in D if,

$$\frac{\partial Q}{\partial x} = \frac{\partial P}{\partial y}.$$

This condition is either a necessary and sufficient condition so that the function $u(x,y)$ to be an exact differential.

For example, we can show that the expression $(2x+y)dx+(x+2y)dy$ is exact differential of a function, and we can find this function. We have, $P(x,y)=2x+y$ and $Q(x,y)=x+2y$. Therefore,

$$\frac{\partial Q}{\partial x} = \frac{\partial P}{\partial y} = 1.$$

Since the differential is exact then we can have a function such as $u(x,y)$. We find this function. Since,

$$(2x + y)dx + (x + 2y) = du = \frac{\partial u}{\partial x}dx + \frac{\partial u}{\partial y}dy,$$

then by comparing both sides of this relation we can write the following relations:

1. $\frac{\partial u}{\partial x} = 2x + y,$
2. $\frac{\partial u}{\partial y} = x + 2y.$

Integration the first relation with respect to x, gives $u(x,y)=x^2+xy+g(y)$. Differentiate both sides with respect to y leads to

$$\frac{\partial u}{\partial y} = x + g'(y).$$

Since from the second relation we have, $\frac{\partial u}{\partial y} = x + 2y$, then

$$x + g'(y) = x + 2y \rightarrow g'(y) = 2y \rightarrow g(y) = y^2 + c.$$

Therefore, $u(x,y)=x^2+xy+y^2+c$.

This idea can be generalized to the functions, $P(x,y)$, $Q(x,y)$ and $R(x,y)$. That is, we say that $P(x,y)dx+ Q(x,y)dy+ R(x,y)dz$ is exact differential of a function $u(x,y,z)$ if

$$\frac{\partial Q}{\partial x} = \frac{\partial P}{\partial y}, \frac{\partial R}{\partial y} = \frac{\partial Q}{\partial z}, \frac{\partial P}{\partial z} = \frac{\partial R}{\partial x}.$$

More applications of this idea can be read in Chapter 9.

7.5 CHAIN RULE

Suppose that the function $z=f(x,y)$ is differentiable and x, y are differentiable functions concerning t. From (9) we can deduce that:

$$\frac{dz}{dt} = \frac{\partial z}{\partial x}\frac{dx}{dt} + \frac{\partial z}{\partial y}\frac{dy}{dt}. \tag{13}$$

The relation (13) is called the *chain rule* for calculating the derivative of z with respect to t.

Example 18: Assume, $x=t+\cos t$, $y=4\ln t-t$, and $z=\sin x+e^y$. Find $\frac{dz}{dt}$.

Solution: We have,

$$\frac{dx}{dt} = 1 - \sin t, \frac{dy}{dt} = \frac{1-t}{t}, \frac{\partial z}{\partial x} = \cos t, \text{and} \frac{\partial z}{\partial y} = e^y.$$

Then,

$$\frac{dz}{dt} = \frac{\partial z}{\partial x}\frac{dx}{dt} + \frac{\partial z}{\partial y}\frac{dy}{dt} = (1 - \sin t)\cos t + \frac{(1-t)e^y}{t}.$$

Remark 4: Suppose the chain rule has been applied when $x=x(u,v)$ and $y=y(u,v)$. Obviously, $z=f(x,y)$ will also be in terms of u and v. If partial derivatives of z exist concerning u or v, then,

$$\frac{\partial z}{\partial u} = \frac{\partial z}{\partial x}\frac{\partial x}{\partial u} + \frac{\partial z}{\partial y}\frac{\partial y}{\partial u}, \frac{\partial z}{\partial v} = \frac{\partial z}{\partial x}\frac{\partial x}{\partial v} + \frac{\partial z}{\partial y}\frac{\partial y}{\partial v}, \tag{14}$$

Note that in relations (14), we cannot eliminate, for example, $\partial x$from the numerator and the denominator of the fraction because their role in the numerator is different from the denominator.

Example 19: Let's $z=x^2+y^2$. This is a paraboloid. If, $x = e^{u^2+v^2}$and$y = \frac{u}{v}$, find $\frac{dz}{du}$ at $u=v=1$.

Solution: At $u=v=1$ we have,

$$\frac{\partial x}{\partial u} = 2ue^{u^2+v^2} = 2e^2, \frac{\partial x}{\partial v} = 1, \frac{\partial z}{\partial x} = 2x = 2e^2$$

and $\frac{\partial z}{\partial y} = 2y = 2$. Thus,

$$\frac{\partial z}{\partial u} = \frac{\partial z}{\partial x}\frac{\partial x}{\partial u} + \frac{\partial z}{\partial y}\frac{\partial y}{\partial u} = 2e^2.2e^2 + 2 = 2(2e^4 + 1).$$

Example 20: Suppose $z=f(x,y)$ where $x = r\cos\theta$ and $y = r\sin\theta$. Prove that,

$$\left(\frac{\partial z}{\partial r}\right)^2 + \frac{1}{r^2}\left(\frac{\partial z}{\partial \theta}\right)^2 = \left(\frac{\partial z}{\partial x}\right)^2 + \left(\frac{\partial z}{\partial y}\right)^2.$$

Solution: We have,

$$\frac{\partial z}{\partial r} = \frac{\partial z}{\partial x}\frac{\partial x}{\partial u} + \frac{\partial z}{\partial y}\frac{\partial y}{\partial u} = \frac{\partial z}{\partial x}\cos\theta + \frac{\partial z}{\partial y}\sin\theta$$

and

$$\frac{\partial z}{\partial \theta} = \frac{\partial z}{\partial x}\frac{\partial x}{\partial \theta} + \frac{\partial z}{\partial y}\frac{\partial y}{\partial \theta} = -r\frac{\partial z}{\partial x}\sin\theta + r\frac{\partial z}{\partial y}\cos\theta.$$

Therefore,

$$\left(\frac{\partial z}{\partial r}\right)^2 + \frac{1}{r^2}\left(\frac{\partial z}{\partial \theta}\right)^2 = \left(\frac{\partial z}{\partial x}\cos\theta + \frac{\partial z}{\partial y}\sin\theta\right)^2 + \frac{1}{r^2}\left(-r\frac{\partial z}{\partial x}\sin\theta + r\frac{\partial z}{\partial y}\cos\theta.\right)^2.$$

After simplifying R.H.S, we get,

$$\left(\frac{\partial z}{\partial r}\right)^2 + \frac{1}{r^2}\left(\frac{\partial z}{\partial \theta}\right)^2 = \left(\frac{\partial z}{\partial x}\right)^2 + \left(\frac{\partial z}{\partial y}\right)^2.$$

7.6 OPTIMIZATION OF MULTIVARIABLE FUNCTIONS

Definition 3: We say that the function $f(x,y)$ at point $(a,b)$of region D has a *relative maximum* if, for every point of D, we have, $f(a,b)\geq f(x,y)$.

Similarly, the point (a,b) is the *relative minimum* if for every point of D, we have $f(a,b)\leq f(x,y)$.

If the function $f(x,y)$ at (a,b), has a relative maximum or minimum, it is said that $f(x,y)$ has a relative extremum at (a,b). The following theorem, which is called the *relative extremum theorem*, is used to find the values of c for which there is a relative extremum.

Theorem 2: (*Relative Extremum Theorem*). If the function $f(x,y)$ in its domain has a relative maximum or minimum at (a,b), and if, in addition, $f(x,y)$ has partial derivatives concerning x and y at (a,b) then, $f_x(a,b)=0$ and $f_y(a,b)=0$.

To determine whether the point (a,b) is a relative maximum or minimum point, we use to test of the second derivatives of the function. In such a way that:

If at (a,b)we have $f_{xx}f_{yy} - f_{xy}{}^2 > 0$, then f at this point has a relative maximum if $f_{xx}<0$.

But if, $f_{xx}>0$, then f has a relative minimum at (a,b).

If at, (a,b), $f_{xx}f_{yy} - f_{xy}^{\ 2} < 0$, then the point (a,b) is neither a relative maximum or minimum point. This point is called a *saddle point.*

When $f_{xx}f_{yy} - f_{xy}^{\ 2} = 0$, then it is not clear whether the point (a,b) is an extremum or saddle point.

Points that satisfy $f_x(x,y)=0$ and $f_y(x,y)=0$, or $f(x,y)$ are not defined, are called *critical points* of $f(x,y)$.

Example 21: Find the critical points of $f(x,y)=x^2+2y^2+2x-4y$.

Solution: We have, $f_x(x,y)=2x+2=0$ and $f_y(x,y)=4y-4=0$. Thus, $x=-1$, $y=1$.

Example 22: Determine the extremum points of $f(x,y)= x^3+3y^2-12x-24y+5$. Which one of these points is a relative minimum point?

Solution: We have, $f_x=3x^2-12=0$ and $f_y=6y-24=0$. Thus, $x=\pm2$, $y=4$. Moreover, $f_{xx}=6x=\pm12$, $f_{yy}=6$ and $f_{xy}=0$. Then we have two extremum points namely, $P_1(2,4)$ and $P_2(-2,4)$. For P_1,

$$f_{xx}f_{yy} - f_{xy}^{\ 2} = (12)(6) > 0, f_{xx} = 12 > 0.$$

Thus, $P_1(2,4)$ is a minimum point. But, for P_2, $f_{xx}f_{yy} - f_{xy}^{\ 2} = (-12)(6) < 0$. Thus, $P_1(2,4)$ is a saddle point.

Remark 5: If the region D is closed, then like the closed interval for single-valued functions, if $f(x,y)$ is continuous on D, then this function has both absolute maximum and absolute minimum, and the extremum points may be located on the boundary of D.

Example 23: Verify the maximum points of $f(x,y)=xy(1-x-y)$ on triangle with vertex (0,0), (1,0) and (0,1).

Solution: We have, $f_x=y-2xy-y^2=0$, $f_y=x-2xy-x^2=0$.

These lead to, (0,0), (1,0), (0,1) and $\left(\frac{1}{3},\frac{1}{3}\right)$. From these four points, only point $\left(\frac{1}{3},\frac{1}{3}\right)$ lies inside the triangle. For the other three points $f(x,y)=0$, and $f\left(\frac{1}{3},\frac{1}{3}\right) = \frac{1}{27}$. Thus, the minimum value of the function is zero and its maximum value is $\frac{1}{27}$.

It is not difficult to show that at $\left(\frac{1}{3},\frac{1}{3}\right)$ $f_{xx}f_{yy} - f_{xy}^{\ 2} > 0, f_{xx} < 0$

This method for obtaining the maximum or minimum value of the function subject to a condition is called the *Lagrange multipliers method.* In general, to find the maximum or minimum of a function $f(x,y)$ subject to a constraint condition given by $g(x,y)=0$, we define the auxiliary function $F(x,y)$ as follows:

$$F(x,y) = f(x,y) + \lambda g(x,y) \tag{16}$$

This function is called the *Lagrange function* and λ is called the *Lagrange multiplier*. We obtain the critical points of this function from the following system.

$$\begin{cases} F_x = 0 \\ F_y = 0 \\ F_\lambda = 0 \end{cases} \quad (17)$$

These points declare the maximum and minimum points of $f(x,y)$.

Example 24: Find the maximum and minimum points of $f(x,y)=2x+y-3$ on $x^2+y^2=4$.

Solution: First, we specify the Lagrange function. So, we write:

$$F = f + \lambda g = 2x + y - 3 + \lambda(x^2 + y^2 - 4).$$

Hence, $F_x = 2 + 2\lambda x = 0$, $F_y = 1 + 2\lambda y = 0$ and $F_\lambda = x^2 + y^2 - 4 = 0$. These lead to, $\pm(2,1)$.

Thus, the extreme points are $\pm(2,1)$. If we substitute them in the function the maximum and minimum of the function will be 2 and -8, respectively.

The relation (16) can be generalized for the function $f(x_1,x_2,\ldots,x_n)$, subject to a constraint condition given by $g(x_1,x_2,\ldots,x_n)=0$ and define F as follows:

$$F(x_1,x_2,\ldots x_n) = f(x_1,x_2,\ldots,x_n) + \lambda g(x_1,x_2,\ldots,x_n) \quad (18)$$

Example 25: When is the product of three numbers maximum if the sum of these three numbers is equal to a fixed number such as k?

Solution: Let x,y and z be these three numbers such that, $x+y+z=k$. We have, $f=xyx$, thus,

$$F(x_1,x_2\ldots,x_n) = f(x_1,x_2\ldots,x_n) + \lambda g(x_1,x_2\ldots,x_n)$$

Then, $F_x = yz + \lambda = 0$, $F_y = xz + \lambda = 0$, $F_z = xy + \lambda = 0$, and $F_\lambda = x^2 + x + y + z - k = 0$.

It would not be difficult to show that, $x = y = z = \frac{k}{3}$.

Remark 6: If a set of constrains such as $g_1(x_1,x_2,\ldots,x_n), g_2(x_1,x_2,\ldots,x_n),\ldots,g_k(x_1,x_2,\ldots,x_n)$ are imposed, then Eq. 17 can be extended by using several multipliers. That is, we can write,

$$F(x_1,x_2\ldots,x_n) = f(x_1,x_2\ldots,x_n) + \lambda_1 g_1(x_1,x_2\ldots,x_n) + \ldots + \lambda_k g_k(x_1,x_2\ldots,x_n) \quad (19)$$

Example 26: Optimize the function $f=x^2+2y^2-z^2+16$ subject to the two constraints $x-3y+z=4$ and $2x+y-z=5$.

Solution: Using Eq. 19, we write,

$F = f + \lambda g_1 + \mu g_2 = x^2 + 2y^2 - z^2 + 16 + \lambda(x - y + z - 4) + \mu(2x + y - z - 5).$

Thus, $F_x = 2x + \lambda + 2\mu = 0, F_y = 4y - \lambda + \mu = 0$ and $F_z = -2z + \lambda - \mu = 0$ and

$F_\lambda = x - y + z - 4 = 0$ and $F_\mu = 2x + y - z - 5 = 0.$

Therefore, we get, x=3, y=1 and z=2. Then, maximum value of f is 23.

7.7 PARTIAL DERIVATIVES AND INTEGRATION (OPTIONAL)

If $z=f(x,y)$ is differentiable related to y then, $\int_a^b f(x,y)dy$ is a single-valued function in terms of x. If we denote this function by $f(x)$ then by the following theorem one can find $f'(x)$ without determining $f(x)$.

Theorem 3: (*Leibnitz's rule with constant limits of integration*). Suppose $f(x,y)$ and $\frac{\partial f(x,y)}{\partial x}$ are continuous for x and y then,

$$\frac{d}{dx}[\int_a^b f(x,y)dy] = \int_a^b \frac{\partial f(x,y)}{\partial x} dy. \tag{20}$$

Example 27: Use

$$\int_0^\pi \frac{dx}{a + bcosx} = \frac{\pi}{\sqrt{a^2 - b^2}}$$

where $a>b$ and find, $\int_0^\pi \frac{dx}{(a + bcosx)^2}$.

Solution: Let's differentiate both sides of $\int_0^\pi \frac{dx}{a + bcosx} = \frac{\pi}{\sqrt{a^2 - b^2}}$ respect to a. We obtain

$$\int_0^\pi \frac{\partial}{\partial a}\left(\frac{1}{a + bcosx}\right)dx = \frac{\partial}{\partial a}\left(\frac{\pi}{\sqrt{a^2 - b^2}}\right) \Rightarrow \int_0^\pi \frac{dx}{(a + bcosx)^2} = \frac{\pi a}{\sqrt{a^2 - b^2}}.$$

Example 28: Evaluate

$$\int_0^\pi \ln(1 + \alpha cosx)dx$$

Solution: Let's,

$$\varphi(\alpha) = \int_0^{\pi} \ln(1 + \alpha cosx)dx.$$

Use (2), we get

$$\varphi'(\alpha) = \int_0^{\pi} \frac{cosxdx}{1 + \alpha cosx} = \tfrac{1}{\alpha}\int_0^{\pi} \left(1 - \frac{1}{1 + \alpha cosx}\right)dx$$
$$= \tfrac{1}{\alpha}\left(x - \frac{1}{\sqrt{1 - \alpha^2}} sin^{-1}\frac{\alpha + cosx}{1 + \alpha cosx}\right)\Bigg|_0^{\pi} = \tfrac{\pi}{\alpha} - \frac{\pi}{\alpha\sqrt{1 - \alpha^2}}.$$

That is,

$$\varphi'(\alpha) = \tfrac{\pi}{\alpha} - \frac{\pi}{\alpha\sqrt{1 - \alpha^2}}.$$

Integrating with respect to α, we obtain,

$$\varphi(\alpha) = \pi\left(\ln\alpha + \ln\frac{1 + \sqrt{1 - \alpha^2}}{\alpha}\right) + c = \pi\ln(1 + \sqrt{1 - \alpha^2}) + c.$$

Since

$$\varphi(0) = \int_0^{\pi} \ln(1 + \alpha cosx)dx = 0$$

then,

$$\varphi(0) = 0 = \pi\ln 2 + c \rightarrow c = -\pi\ln 2.$$

Therefore,

$$\varphi(\alpha) = \pi\left(\ln\alpha + \ln\frac{1 + \sqrt{1 - \alpha^2}}{\alpha}\right) - \pi\ln 2 = \pi\ln\left(\frac{1 + \sqrt{1 - \alpha^2}}{2}\right).$$

Theorem 4: (*Leibnitz's rule with non-constant limits of integration*). Suppose $f(x,y)$ and $\frac{\partial f(x,y)}{\partial x}$ are continuous for x and y then,

$$\frac{d}{dx}\left[\int_{a(x)}^{b(x)} f(x,y)dy\right] = \int_{a(x)}^{b(x)} \frac{\partial f(x,y)}{\partial x}dy + f(x,b(x))\frac{db}{dx} - f(x,a(x))\frac{dx}{dx}. \tag{21}$$

Example 29: Show that

$$\tfrac{d}{da}\int_0^{a^2} tan^{-1}\left(\tfrac{x}{a}\right)dx = 2atan^{-1}(a) - \tfrac{1}{2}\ln(1 + \alpha^2).$$

Solution: By using (21), we get

$$\frac{d}{da}\int_0^{a^2} tan^{-1}(\tfrac{x}{a})dx = = \int_0^{a^2} \frac{1}{1+\frac{x^2}{a^2}}\left(-\tfrac{x}{a^2}\right)dx + 2atan^{-1}a = -\int_0^{a^2} \frac{x}{a^2+x^2}dx + 2atan^{-1}a$$

$$= -\tfrac{1}{2}\ln(a^2+x^2)\Big|_0^{a^2} + 2atan^{-1}a = -\tfrac{1}{2}\ln(\frac{a^2+a^4}{a^2}) + 2atan^{-1}a = 2atan^{-1}(a) - \tfrac{1}{2}\ln(1+\alpha^2).$$

7.8 SOME APPLICATIONS OF PARTIAL DERIVATIVES

In the application of the derivative of single-valued functions in section 4.6, we have expressed some examples of it in economics and business. These types of applications can be extended to two-variable functions. For example, let's assume that $u(x,y)$ is economic savings are the values of x and y of two types of goods, the value of which is \$$a$ for each kilogram of the first product and \$$b$ for each kilogram of the second product, and the total amount allocated for the purchase of both products is a total of c dollars. In this case, we can get the maximum value $u(x,y)$ with the condition: $ax+by=c$.

Example 27: Assume that, $u(x,y)=xy+3y+x$. Find its maximum profit subject to constraint $3x+2y=45$.

Solution: We have,

$$F = f + \lambda g = xy + 3y + x + \lambda(3x + 2y - 45).$$

Then, $F_x = y + 3\lambda = 0$, $F_y = x + 2\lambda = 0$ and $F_\lambda = 3x + 2y - 45 = 0$. These lead to, $x=18$ and $y=27$. Thus, the maximum profit of $u(x,y)$ is \$558.

Example 28: The profit function for producing two goods x and y is given by $p(x,y) = 5xy - 3x^2 - 5y^2 + 15x + 250y - 25$.

What should be the production level of two goods to have the maximum profit?

Solution: First, we find the critical points. We have, $p_x=5y-6x+25=0$, $p_y=5x-10y+250=0$.

This system leads to, $x=40$ and $y=45$. We also have,

$$p_{xx}p_{yy} - p_{xy}^{\ 2} = (-6)(-10) - 25 = 35 > 0.$$

Then the maximum of p at (40, 45) is $p(40, 45)=6600$.

It should be noted that the value of λ is a measure of the sensitivity of $f(x,y)$ to changes in the constraint. Specifically, λ measures the change in the value of the objective function in response to a 1-unit change in the constraint, (Nicholson, 1986). For example, when we consider the cost function $C=f(x,y)$ in such a way that its production quota is $f(x,y)=0$, if in determining the critical points, $\lambda < 0$. If the production quota is reduced by one unit, then the total cost decreases nearly $|\lambda|$ of the unit. But if the production quota increases by one unit, then the cost increases almost by $|\lambda|$ unit. Later, we see a similar analysis between the present interpretation of λ and the interpretation of shadow price in Chapter 11.

Example 29: Minimize the cost of a production company whose function is $C(x,y)= 3x^2+5y^2+4xy+26$ with production quota, $x+y=44$. Estimate the additional marginal cost resulting from a one-unit increase in the production quota.

Solution: The Lagrange function is,

$$F(x,y) = 3x^2 + 5y^2 + 4xy + 26 + \lambda(x + y - 44).$$

Thus, $F_x = 6x + 4y + \lambda = 0$, $F_y = 4x + 10y + \lambda = 0$ and $F_\lambda = x + y - 44 = 0$. Hence, we get, $x=33$, $y=11$ and $\lambda = -242$. Then the lowest cost is, \$5400. Moreover, since $\lambda < 0$, so, with an increase of one unit in the production quota, the additional cost is approximately 242 units.

We end this section by reminding this point that the Mean Value Theorem for multivariable functions can also be extended. In particular, Taylor's expansion formula for two or more variable functions. (See (Leithold, 1981) (Stewart, 2012)). In exercise 19, we mentioned the expansion of some two-variable functions. To have more information about multivariable functions, readers can also see (Apostol, 1966) m (Finney, 1988) (Rodin, 1970) (Piskunov, 1981) (Silverman, 1985) (Thomas, 2014).

7.9 COMPUTER STATION

When working with three-dimensional conic sections and quadratic surfaces in Maple, you'll encounter various shapes, like ellipsoids, hyperboloids, and paraboloids. These surfaces can be analyzed using Maple's algebraic and graphical capabilities. Let's go through definitions, properties, and examples for each of these three-dimensional conic sections.

1. **Ellipsoid**

An ellipsoid is a type of quadratic surface that can be thought of as a three-dimensional analog of an ellipse. It is defined by the equation:

$$\frac{x^2}{a^2} + \frac{y^2}{b^2} + \frac{z^2}{c^2} = 1$$

where a, b, and c are the radii along the x, y, and z axes, respectively. The ellipsoid extends symmetrically from the origin along these axes, and depending on the relative values of aaa, b, and c, it can vary in shape from a flattened disk to a stretched cigar shape.

Here's how you can visualize an ellipsoid in Maple, where we choose a=2, b=3, and c=4 for demonstration purposes:

```
plots[implicitplot3d](x^2/4 + y^2/9 + z^2/16 = 1, x = -2..2, y = -3..3, z = -4..4,
style=surface, axes=normal, grid=[40,40,40], scaling=constrained);
```

Explanation of the Maple Command:

- implicitplot3d: This function is used for plotting surfaces defined by an implicit equation.
- x^2/4 + y^2/9 + z^2/16 = 1: This is the equation of the ellipsoid with a=2, b=3, and c=4.
- x = -2..2, y = -3..3, z = -4..4: These are the plot ranges for the x, y, and z axes. They define the extents of the plot, ensuring the entire ellipsoid is visible.
- style=surface: This option specifies that the plot should visually represent the surface of the ellipsoid.
- axes=normal: This sets the axes in a normal, three-dimensional configuration.
- grid=[40,40,40]: This increases the grid density to improve the resolution of the surface, making it smoother and more detailed.
- scaling=constrained: This ensures that the plot maintains equal scaling in all directions, which helps accurately represent the ellipsoid's true geometric proportions.

This visualization effectively demonstrates the smooth, rounded shape of an ellipsoid, offering a clear view of its symmetric extension in three dimensions.

Properties:

- Symmetric about the x, y, and z axes.
- Resembles a three-dimensional ellipse.

2. Hyperboloid of One Sheet

A **hyperboloid of one sheet** is another type of quadratic surface that is widely used in architectural designs and engineering due to its unique structural properties. It is defined by the equation:

$$\frac{x^2}{a^2} + \frac{y^2}{b^2} + \frac{z^2}{c^2} = 1$$

This surface extends infinitely along the zzz-axis and curves outward, forming a saddle-like shape around the origin. Its distinct feature is that it has only one continuous surface, unlike the two-sheet hyperboloid, which consists of two separate surfaces.

Visualizing a Hyperboloid of One Sheet in Maple

Here's how you can create a 3D plot of a hyperboloid of one sheet in Maple. The command below demonstrates this, with extended plot ranges to illustrate the surface clearly.

Maple Command to Plot a Hyperboloid of One Sheet

```
# Define the hyperboloid
eq2:= (x^2/9) + (y^2/16) - (z^2/4) = 1;
# Plot the hyperboloid
plots[implicitplot3d](eq2, x = -10..10, y = -10..10, z = -10..10,
style = surface, axes = normal);
```

Properties:

- Has two sheets if inverted.
- Hyperboloid cooling towers are familiar examples.

Explanation of the Maple Command:

- **implicitplot3d**: This function is used for plotting three-dimensional surfaces defined by an implicit equation.
- **x^2 + y^2 - z^2 = 1**: This is the equation defining the hyperboloid of one sheet.
- **x = -3..3, y = -3..3, z = -5..5**: These are the ranges for the x, y, and z axes, respectively, chosen to provide a comprehensive view of the hyperboloid's shape over a significant portion of its structure.
- **style=surface**: Specifies that the plot should visually represent the surface of the hyperboloid.
- **axes=normal**: Sets the axes to appear in a normal, three-dimensional configuration, aiding in better spatial understanding.

- **grid=[40,40,40]**: Increases the grid density for a finer, smoother representation of the hyperboloid.
- **scaling=constrained**: Ensures that the scaling is equal in all directions to maintain the correct proportions and symmetry of the hyperboloid.

This visualization will show the characteristic single continuous surface of the hyperboloid of one sheet, which curves outward as it extends infinitely. This Maple plot can help visualize and understand the geometric and structural aspects of such surfaces in mathematical and practical contexts.

3. Hyperboloid of Two Sheets

A **hyperboloid of two sheets** is another type of quadratic surface distinguished by having two disconnected parts, unlike the one-sheet hyperboloid which is a single continuous surface. It is represented by the equation: $-x^2-y^2+z^2=1$.

This equation defines a surface that does not intersect the plane z=0 and instead forms two separate symmetrical sheets, one extending infinitely upward from z=1 and the other downward from z=−1.

Visualizing a Hyperboloid of Two Sheets in Maple

To create a 3D plot of a hyperboloid of two sheets in Maple, you can use the following command, which visually represents the surface and demonstrates its unique double-sheeted structure.

Maple Command to Plot a Hyperboloid of Two Sheets

```
plots[implicitplot3d](-x^2 - y^2 + z^2 = 1, x = -3..3, y = -3..3, z = -5..5,
style=surface, axes=normal, grid=[40,40,40], scaling=constrained);
```

Explanation of the Maple Command:

- **implicitplot3d**: This function is used for plotting three-dimensional surfaces that are defined implicitly.
- **-x^2 - y^2 + z^2 = 1**: This is the equation of the hyperboloid of two sheets.
- **x = -3..3, y = -3..3, z = -5..5**: These plot ranges for the x, y, and z axes cover a sufficient area to clearly display both sheets of the hyperboloid.
- **style=surface**: This option specifies that the plot should visually represent the surface of the hyperboloid.
- **axes=normal**: This sets the axes to appear in a standard, three-dimensional configuration, which helps in understanding the spatial orientation of the surface.

- **grid=[40,40,40]**: This setting increases the grid density for better surface resolution and a smoother visual output.
- **scaling=constrained**: Ensures that the scaling is the same in all directions to accurately represent the geometry of the hyperboloid.

This visualization in Maple clearly shows the disjoint nature of the two sheets, each extending infinitely but never intersecting, characteristic of the hyperboloid of two sheets. Such visualizations are crucial for understanding complex geometric and algebraic properties of quadratic surfaces in both educational and professional contexts.

Equation:

$$\frac{x^2}{a^2} + \frac{y^2}{b^2} - \frac{z^2}{c^2} = 1$$

Maple code:

```
# Define the hyperboloid
eq3:= (x^2/4) + (y^2/4) - (z^2/9) = -1;
# Plot the hyperboloid
plots[implicitplot3d](eq3, x = -10..10, y = -10..10, z = -10..10, style = surface,
axes = normal);
```

4. one-sheet hyperboloid

The one-sheet hyperboloid is a type of quadratic surface characterized by a single connected sheet. It can be represented by the equation: $x^2+y^2-z^2=1$

This equation suggests a surface that extends infinitely in both upward and downward directions, curving outward. The one-sheet hyperboloid is used in various architectural structures and can be defined in Maple using the following command for visualization:

```
plots[implicitplot3d](x^2 + y^2 - z^2 = 1, x = -3..3, y = -3..3, z = -3..3,
style=surface, axes=normal, grid=[30,30,30], scaling=constrained);
```

This Maple command creates a 3D plot of the one-sheet hyperboloid, using the implicitplot3d function from the plots package. The plot ranges for xxx, yyy, and zzz are set to span from −3-3−3 to 333 to provide a clear view of the shape. The style=surface option makes the plot show the surface of the hyperboloid, and scaling=constrained keeps the aspect ratio equal in all dimensions, enhancing the visual representation of the hyperboloid's true geometric proportions.

5. Elliptic Cylinder

An elliptic cylinder is a type of quadratic surface that extends infinitely along one axis (usually the zzz-axis) and has a cross-section shaped like an ellipse. This surface can be defined by the equation:

$$\left(\frac{x}{b}\right)^2 + \left(\frac{y}{b}\right)^2 = 1$$

Where aaa and bbb are the semi-major and semi-minor axes of the ellipse, respectively. For visualization purposes, you might choose specific values for aaa and bbb to see how they affect the shape of the cylinder.

Here's how you can visualize an elliptic cylinder in Maple using specific values for aaa and bbb. Let's say a=2 and b=3:

```
plots[implicitplot3d](x^2/4 + y^2/9 = 1, x = -2..2, y = -3..3, z = -5..5,
style=surface, axes=normal, grid=[30,30,30], scaling=constrained);
```

Explanation of the Maple Command:

- implicitplot3d: This function is used for plotting surfaces defined by an implicit equation.
- x^2/4 + y^2/9 = 1: This is the equation of the elliptic cylinder. Here, a=2 and b=3.
- x = -2..2, y = -3..3, z = -5..5: These are the plot ranges for the xxx, yyy, and zzz axes. They determine how much of the elliptic cylinder is visible in the plot.
- style=surface: This option specifies that the plot should display the surface of the cylinder.
- axes=normal: This sets the axes to appear in a normal, three-dimensional configuration.
- grid=[30,30,30]: This option increases the grid density for better surface resolution.
- scaling=constrained: This ensures that the scaling is the same in all directions, which helps in accurately representing the geometry of the elliptic cylinder.

This Maple visualization provides a clear and accurate depiction of an elliptic cylinder, showcasing its unique geometric properties and infinite extension along the z-axis.

CONCLUSION

In this chapter, we introduced the concept of derivatives for multivariable functions. Similarly, we used them to find extremum points of a function. By introducing the Lagrange function and its multipliers, we could apply them to find the maximum or minimum of a function. Moreover, by defining total differential, we can approximate the value of a function in a given value. By Euler's Theorem, we derived a good relation for a multivariable function to be homogeneous of degree *k*. This relation can be useful for solutions of a linear ordinary differential equation considered in Chapter 9.

7.10 Exercises

1. Find the limit of the following functions at given points.

   (i) $f(x,y) = 2x + 3y - 5; (1,3)$

   (ii) $f(x,y) = \frac{x+y}{x+2}; (2,1)$

   (iii) $f(x,y) = \frac{3xy}{x^2+y^2}; (0,0)$

   (iv) $f(x,y) = \frac{4x^2y}{x^2-16y^2}; (0,0)$

   (v) $f(x,y) = \sin(x+y); (\pi,0)$

   (vi) $f(x,y) = \ln(x+y); (1,0)$

2. Consider the following functions for continuity.

   (i) $f(x,y) = \frac{x^2}{x^2+y^2};\ (x,y) = (0,0)$

   (ii) $f(x,y) = \frac{x+y}{x^2+y^2};\ (x,y) = (0,0)$

   (iii) $f(x,y) = 3x + 4y - 5;\ (x,y) = (2,1)$

   (iv) $f(x,y) = \begin{cases} \frac{x^2y}{x^2+y^2}, (x,y) \neq (0,0) \\ 0, (x,y) = (0,0) \end{cases}$

   (v) $f(x,y) = \begin{cases} \frac{x^2y^2}{x^2+y^2}(x,y) \neq (0,0) \\ 0, (x,y) = (0,0) \end{cases}$

   (vi) $f(x,y) = \begin{cases} \frac{x^2y^2(x^2-y^2)}{x^2+y^2}(x,y) \neq (0,0) \\ 0, (x,y) = (0,0) \end{cases}$

3. Find the total differential for the following functions.
   (i) $z = e^{xy} - 4xy; (0,0), dx = dy = 0.1$
   (ii) $z = (x-y)^3; (1,1), dx = 0.1, dy = -0.2$
   (iii) $z = x + \text{In}y + e^{-x}; (0,1), dx = dy = -0.01$
   (iv) $z = xy - e^{-xy}; (0,0), dx = -0.1, dy = 0.2$
   (v) $z = x^y - y^x; (1,1), dx = dy = 0.01$
   (vi) $z = x^2 + y^2 - xy; (2,1), dx = -0.02, dy = -0.01.$
4. Determine an approximated value for the following expressions.
   (i) $\sqrt[3]{(1.99)^2 + (2.02)^2}$
   (ii) $\sqrt{(0.98)^2 + (1.07)^2 + (2.04)^2}$
   (iii) $\tan 44^o \cos 63^o.$
   (iv) $\sin 88^o \cos 2^o$

   Write your answers to five decimal places.

5. Find x_{xy} for the following functions.
   (i) $z = e^{x^2-y^2} + \text{In}y + e^{-xy}$
   (ii) $z = y\,\text{In}x + xe^y$
   (iii) $z = \text{In}(x^2 + y^2)$
   (iv) $z = \sin(x \cos y)$
   (v) $z = \frac{y}{x}e^{x^2+y^2}$
   (vi) $\lim_{x\to+\infty}\left(1 - \frac{1}{x}\right)^{2x-3}$
   (vii) $z = x^{x+\tan y}$
   (viii) $z = (1 + e^y)^{\frac{1}{x}}$
   (ix) $z = \frac{\sin^{-1}x}{\tan^{-1}y}$
   (x) $z = \frac{e^{x^2y^2}}{xy}$
6. Determine $z_{xx}+z_{yy}$ for the following functions.
   (i) $z = e^{x^2-y^2} + \ln\sqrt{(x-a)^2 + (y-b)^2}$
   (ii) $z = ye^x + xe^y$
   (iii) $z = \sin(x+y) - \cos(x-y)$
   (iv) $z = \tan(x \cot y)$
7. Find xz_x+yz_y for the following functions.
   (i) $z = \frac{2y}{x+y}$
   (ii) $z = e^{\frac{y}{x}}$
   (iii) $z = \frac{x^2}{2y^2} + \frac{2y^2}{2x^2}$
   (iv) $z = \frac{y}{x} + \frac{x}{y}$
   (v) $z = \frac{xy}{x^2+y^2}.$
   (vi) $z = \frac{1}{x} - \frac{1}{y}$
8. Find the equations of the tangent line at the given points on the following surfaces.

(i) $z = x^2 + y^2; (1,1,2)$
(ii) $z = x^2y^2; (1,-1,0)$
(iii) $z = \sqrt{1 - x^2 - y^2}; (1,0,1)$
(iv) $z = \sqrt{4 - 4x^2 - y^2}; (-1,0,0)$

9. Show that if $z=x^2+y^2$ and $x = r\cos\theta, y = r\sin\theta$, then,

$$\left(\frac{\partial z}{\partial r}\right)^2 + \frac{1}{r^2}\left(\frac{\partial z}{\partial \theta}\right)^2 = 4z.$$

10. Find $\frac{\partial z}{\partial x}$ and $\frac{\partial z}{\partial y}$ if:
    (i) $x^2 + y^2 + z^2 = 3xyz$
    (ii) $4x^2 + 3y^2 - 5z^2 - xyz = 1$
    (iii) $e^{xyz} = 1$
    (iv) $xyz(1 + xyz) = 1$
    (v) $x^3 - y^3 + z(x - y) = xyz$
    (vi) $z = \sqrt[3]{x^2 + y^2 - xyz}$
11. Equations $f_{xx}+f_{yy}=0$ or $f_{xx}+f_{yy}+f_{zz}=0$, are known as Laplace's equation. Show that the following functions satisfy the Laplace's equation.
    (i) $f(x,y) = \ln\sqrt{(x-a)^2 + (y-b)^2}$
    (ii) $f(x,y) = \tan^{-1}\left(\frac{x}{y}\right)$
    (iii) $f(x,y,z) = \ln\sqrt{x^2 + y^2 + z^2}$
    (iv) $f(x,y,z) = \cosh 5x \cos 4y \cos 3z$
12. Show that the following expressions are exact differential of a function then, find this function.
    (i) $ydx + xdy$
    (ii) $(\cos x + 3x^2y)dx + (x^3 - y^2)dy$
    (iii) $\frac{1}{y}dy - \frac{x}{y^2}dx$
    (iv) $\frac{(x + 2y)dx + ydy}{(x+y)^2}$
13. Find the critical points of the following functions and verify which of them are maximum or minimum, or saddle points.
    (i) $z = x^2 - y^2$
    (ii) $z = xy$
    (iii) $z = x^3 - y^3$
    (iv) $z = \sqrt[3]{x^2 + y^2 - xyz}$
    (v) $z = e^{xy} - xy$
    (vi) $z = xy(1 - xy) + 2$
    (vii) $z = x(y + x^2 - xy)$
    (viii) $z = xy(y - x) + 4x - 5y$

14. For what values of k, the critical point of the following functions is a saddle point?
   (i) $z = x^2 + ky^2$
   (ii) $z = kx^2 + xy + y^2$
   (iii) $z = x^2 + kxy - y^2$
   (iv) $z = k(x^2 + y^2) - xy$
15. What relation should be established between A and B so that the critical point of the function $z = Ax^2 + xy + By^2$, be a saddle point?
16. What combination of goods x and y should a manufacturing company produce to minimize its joint cost given as, $C(x,y) = 3x^2 - 2xy + 4y^2 + 42$ under the assumption of production quota, $x + y = 36$. If the cost of production is reduced by one unit, examine the effect of this change on costs.
17. Suppose that $w(x, y, z) = x^{\frac{1}{2}} + y^{\frac{1}{3}} + z^{\frac{1}{6}}$ is the amount of demand of a customer for three different types of goods x, y and z. Their prices are \$1, \$2 and \$5 respectively, and the customer has \$60 for the purchase. How much of each product should he buy to maximize his demand?
18. A company can produce 5 radios and 6 televisions with cost, $C(r,t) = 2r^2 + rt + 2t^2$, every month. The selling price of a radio is \$600, and a TV is \$900. First, find the net profit (marginal cost revenue) from the sale of r radio and t TV. Second, find a combination of r and t that maximizes profit.
19. In economics, Wilson's formula about the numbers of goods indicates that the most economical amount of goods that a store can order is obtained by the formula $Q = \sqrt{\frac{2kM}{h}}$, where k is the ordering cost and M is the number of goods sold per week. In the vicinity of the point (2.20, 0.05), the value of Q is more sensitive to which of these three variables? Give reasons for your answer.
20. From the following production function, Find the marginal product of capital, and the marginal product of labor, from the production function given by $Q = 20K^{0.2}L^{0.3}$.
21. The Taylor's expansion formula for the function $f(x,y)$ about $x=a$ and $y=b$ is given by:

$$f(x, y) = f(a, b) + \frac{(x-a)f_x(a, b) + (x-b)f_y(a, b)}{1!}$$

$$+ \frac{(x-a)^2 f_{xx}(a, b) + 2(x-a)(y-b)f_x(a, b) + (y-b)^2 f_{yy}(a, b)}{2!} + \dots.$$

If we choose a special case of $a=b=0$, we get the Maclaurin expansion for $f(x,y)$.

$$f(x, y) = f(0, 0) + \frac{xf_x(0, 0) + yf_y(0, 0)}{1!} + \frac{x^2 f_{xx}(0, 0) + 2xyf_x(0, 0) + y^2 f_{yy}(0, 0)}{2!} + \dots$$

Prove that

(i) $\cos(x+y) = 1 - \frac{(x+y)^2}{2!} + \frac{(x+y)^4}{4!} + \ldots,$

(ii) $\tan^{-1}(x+y) = (x+y) - \frac{(x+y)^3}{3} + \frac{(x+y)^5}{5} + \ldots,$

(iii) $e^x \cos y = 1 + \frac{x}{1!} + \frac{x^2 - y^2}{2!} + \frac{x^3 - 3xy^2}{2!} + \ldots,$

(iv) $\ln(1+x+y) = (x+y) - \frac{(x+y)^2}{2} + \frac{(x+y)^3}{3} + \ldots,$

(v) $\mathrm{x}\,\mathrm{y} = 1 + (\mathrm{x}-1) + (\mathrm{x}-1)(\mathrm{y}-1) + \ldots, (\mathrm{a},\mathrm{b}) = (1,1).$

22. Show that

(i) $\int_0^\infty \frac{e^{-ax} - e^{-bx}}{x} dx = \ln\left(\frac{b}{a}\right), a, b > 0$

(ii) $\int_0^\infty \frac{\sin x}{x} dx = \frac{\pi}{2}$

(iii) $\int_0^\infty e^{-ax} \sin bx dx = \frac{b}{a^2 + b^2}.$

REFERENCES

Apostol, T. M. (1966). *Calculus* (2nd ed., Vol. 1). JOHN WILEY & SONS.

Finney, R. L. (1988). Calculus and Analytical Geometry (7th ed). Addison-Wesley Publishing Company.

Leithold, L. (1981). *The Calculus and Analytical Geometry* (4th ed.). Harper & Row.

Nicholson, R. H. (1986). Mathematics for Business and Economics. McGraw-Hill, Inc.

Piskunov, N. (1981). Differential and Integral, Vol 1 (4th ed). MIR Publisher.

Rodin, B. R. (1970). *Calculus with Analytical Geometry* (4th ed.). Prentice-Hall, Inc.

Silverman, R. A. (1985). *Calculus with Analytical Geometry* (4th ed.). Prentice-Hall, Inc.

Steart, J. (2012). Multivariable Calculus, Brooks.Cole, Cengage Learning, 7th Edition.

Thomas, G. B. (2014). Calculus (13th ed). Mc-Graw, New Jersey.

Chapter 8
Complex Numbers and Polar Coordinates

ABSTRACT

In this chapter, we introduce complex numbers, which are a generalization of real numbers. While explaining some of their applications, we examine the solution of the equations that may have complex roots or complex coefficients by introducing the polar form of a complex number. We will see how the equations of some curves in the polar form are simpler than the Cartesian form. In particular, they make the solution to a given problem easier. Since in practice we encounter certain types of curves in polar form, hence we also consider polar forms of some specific curves and then obtain some formula for calculating the area of a bounded region. We also, like in previous chapter, add Computer Station to help readers to draw the curves in polar forms.

8.1 INTRODUCTION

For a long time, the set of real numbers was considered as the set of whole numbers, but in the early 16th century, when there was a great desire to solve algebraic equations, it was impossible to solve, even, a very simple algebraic equation like $x^2+1=0$. For example, suppose we want to find two numbers whose sum and product are 2. If we assume two numbers are x and y, then we have to solve the following system to find these two numbers.

$$\begin{cases} x+y = 2 \\ xy = 2. \end{cases}$$

DOI: 10.4018/979-8-3693-3657-1.ch008

But by eliminating y from these two equations we get, $x^2+2x+2=0$, from which the solutions will be, $x = 1 \pm \sqrt{-1}$. Mathematicians at that time found that answers like $x = 1 \pm \sqrt{-1}$ do not belong to the set of real numbers because the square of every real number is positive. For this reason, the generalization of the set of real numbers to another set that gives such an answer has become stronger. Fortunately, at the time of Descartes, these numbers, which today are called *imaginary numbers*, were accepted as part of a system of numbers, but Leonardo Euler, a French mathematician, used the sign i to represent, $\sqrt{-1}$ and therefore, the values of $\pm i$ were attributed to the equation, $x^2+1=0$. You can look at 2 as an imaginary number. It doesn't matter what this imaginary number can be, the important thing is that this seemingly imaginary number solves a problem of this type and guides us to a new world of mathematical realities. Something that guides us to reality must be a reality.

8.2 BASIC CONCEPTS AND DEFINITIONS OF COMPLEX NUMBERS

An expression of the form $z=x+iy$ in which $x, y \in \mathbb{R}$ and $i = \sqrt{-1}$ (with, $i^2=-1$) is called a *complex number*. We denote the set of all complex numbers by ¢. Therefore,

$$¢ = \{z = x + iy | x, y \in \mathbb{R},\ i^2 = -1\}.$$

We call x and y the real and imaginary parts of z, respectively, in symbols, $x=Rex, y=Imz$. Then a complex number is an ordered pair of real numbers x and y. Thus, we can write $z=(x,y)$. If $x=0$, we call the number z a *pure imaginary number*.

There is no order property in complex numbers. For example, it cannot be said that the number z_1 is bigger or smaller than the number, z_2. But two numbers $z_1=x_1+iy_1$, and $z_2\text{-}x_2+iy_2$ are said to be equal, if and only if they have equal real parts and the same imaginary parts. That is,

$$z_1 = z_2 \leftrightarrow x_1 = x_2, y_1 = y_2.$$

On the set of complex numbers, operations such as addition, subtraction, multiplication, and division can be defined.

Addition and subtraction of two numbers, $z_1=x_1+iy_1$ and $z_2\text{-}x_2+iy_2$ is defined by:

$$z_1 \pm z_2 = (x_1 \pm x_2) + i(y_1 \pm y_2). \qquad (1)$$

We define the multiplication of two complex numbers z_1=x_1+iy_1 and z_2-x_2+iy_2 as follows:

$$z_1 z_2 = (x_1 + iy_1)(x_2 + iy_2) = (x_1 x_2 - y_1 y_2) + i(x_1 y_2 - x_2 y_1). \qquad (2)$$

The complex number x–iy is called the *conjugate* of the number z, and is denoted by, $\bar{z}$. In other words, we define $\bar{z}$ by changing the sign i of any complex number. Therefore, the coordinate $(z, \bar{z})$ which locates a point is called the *conjugate coordinate*.

Using the definition of multiplication, it is easy to show that

$$z\bar{z} = x^2 + y^2. \qquad (3)$$

Remark 1: Clearly, $z\bar{z}$is a real number.

If z_1, z_2 and z_3 belong to a set of complex numbers, then

(i) $z_1 + z_2 = z_2 + z_1$, Commutative low of addition
(ii) $z_1 + (z_1 + z_3) = (z_1 + z_2) + z_3$ Associative low of addition
(iii) $z_1 . z_2 = z_2 . z_1$ Commutative low of multiplication
(iv) $z_1(z_1 . z_3) = (z_1 . z_2)z_3$ Associative low of multiplication
(v) $z_1(z_2 + z_3) = z_1 . z_2 + z_1 . z_3$, Distributive low.

The division of two complex numbers z_1=x_1+iy_1 and z_2=x_2+iy_2 is defined by

$$\frac{z_1}{z_2} = \frac{x_1 + iy_1}{x_2 + iy_2}.$$

According to (3), we can write

$$\frac{z_1}{z_2} = \frac{x_1 + iy_1}{x_2 + iy_2} = \frac{(x_1 + iy_1)(x_2 - iy_2)}{(x_2 + iy_2)(x_2 - iy_2)} = \frac{(x_1 x_2 + y_1 y_2) + i(x_2 y_1 - x_1 y_2)}{x_2^{\,2} + y_2^{\,2}}$$
$$= \frac{x_1 x_2 + y_1 y_2}{x_2^{\,2} + y_2^{\,2}} + i\frac{x_2 y_1 - x_1 y_2}{x_2^{\,2} + y_2^{\,2}} . \frac{z_1}{z_2} = \frac{x_1 x_2 + y_1 y_2}{x_2^{\,2} + y_2^{\,2}} + i\frac{x_2 y_1 - x_1 y_2}{x_2^{\,2} + y_2^{\,2}}. \qquad (4)$$

Example 1: Show that if z≠(0,0), then there exists a complex number z' such that zz'=1. The number z' is called the inverse of z.

Solution: Let's z'=a+ib, thus according to (2), we have:

$$zz' = (x + iy)(a + ib) = (xa - yb) + i(xb - ay) = 0.$$

By comparing both sides, we get, $xa-yb=0$, $xb-ay=0$. Solving this system of equations for a and b, we obtain: $a = \frac{x}{x^2+y^2}, b = \frac{-y}{x^2+y^2}$. Since $z \neq (0,0)$ hence the existence of z' is obvious.

For every complex number, there is a number $-z$, such that $z+(-z)=0$. We call this number an *additive inverse* for z. Since a complex number is an ordered pair of real numbers, then we can represent such numbers in a xy plane called a *complex plane*. In this plane, we choose the x and y axes as the real and imaginary axes respectively. In this way, every number z is specified by a point $P(x, y)$ in this plane.

The *distance* between two points $z_1=x_1+iy_1$, and $z_2=x_2+iy_2$, in complex plane, denoted by $|z_1-z_2|$, is given by,

$$|z_1 - z_2| = \sqrt{(x_1 - x_2)^2 + (y_1 - y_2)^2}.$$

According to the definition of $\bar{z}$, we have, $x = \frac{z+\bar{z}}{2}$, and $y = \frac{z-\bar{z}}{2i}$. Now, if we replace them in the equation of the line, introduced in Chapter 1, given by $Ax+By+C=0$, we will get,

$$A\left(\frac{z+\bar{z}}{2}\right) + B\left(\frac{z-\bar{z}}{2i}\right) + C = 0.$$

If we rearrange it according to z and $\bar{z}$, we obtain,

$$\bar{E}z + \bar{E}z + C = 0$$

where, $\bar{E} = \frac{A+iB}{2}$.

Example 2: Write the equation of a circle in terms of z and $\bar{z}$.

Solution: The equation of a circle, introduced in Chapter 1, is given by,

$$A(x^2 + y^2) + Bx + Cy + D = 0.$$

If we perform the same calculation as we did for the equation of a line, we will get,

$$Az\bar{z} + \bar{E}z + E\bar{z} + +D = 0,$$

where, $\bar{E} = \frac{B+iC}{2}$.

8.3 POLAR FORM OF COMPLEX NUMBERS

If, $P(x, y)$ is a point in the complex plane corresponding to the complex number $z=x+iy$, then according to Fig 1, we have,

$$x = r\cos\theta, y = r\sin\theta, \tag{5}$$

where $r = \sqrt{x^2+y^2} = |z|$ is called *modulus* or *absolute value* of z. The angle $\theta = \tan^{-1}\frac{y}{x}$ is known as the *argument* of z and dented by, *argz*. Therefore, any complex numbers can be written in the following form,

$$z = r(\cos\theta + i\sin\theta). \tag{6}$$

Figure 1. Graph of a complex number in the complex plane according to x, y and θ

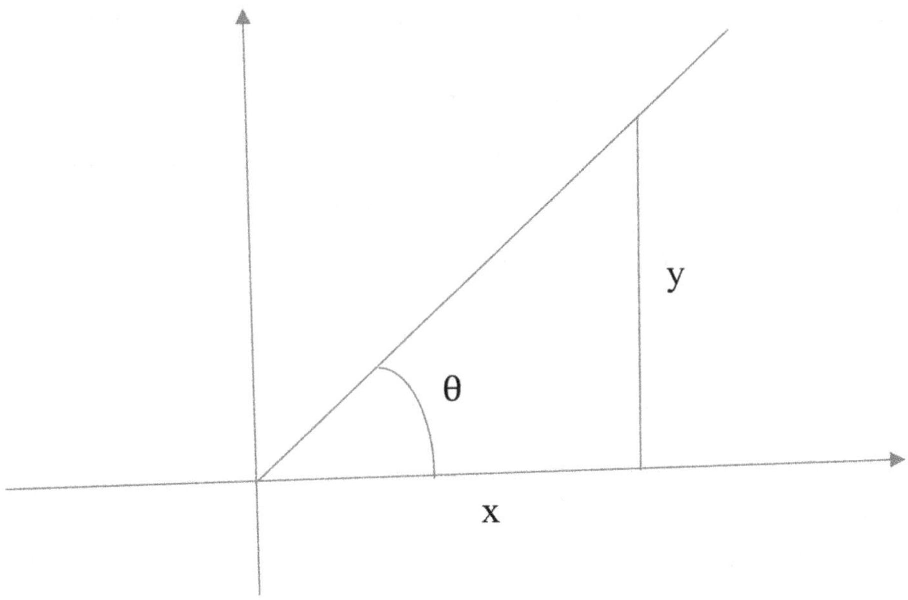

The direction of θ is considered to be anticlockwise. Since cosθ and sinθ are periodic then, the argument of z is multi-valued. The value of θ that lies in the interval (-π,π] is called the *main argument* and denoted by *Argz*. Therefore,

$$argz = Argz + 2k,\ k = 0, k = 0, \pm1, \pm2, ...$$

The following properties hold for modulus and argument.

(i) $|\bar{z}| = |z|$
(ii) $|z|^2 = z\bar{z}$
(iii) $|z_1 z_2| = |z_1||z_2|$
(iv) $\left|\frac{z_1}{z_2}\right| = |z_1|/|z_2|$
(v) $|z_1 + z_2| \leq |z_1| + |z_2|$
(vi) $|z_1 - z_2| \geq |z_1| - |z_2|$
(vii) $\arg(z_1 z_2) = \arg z_1 + \arg z_2$
(viii) $\arg(z_1/z_2) = \arg z_1 - \arg z_2$

Example 3: Prove that, $|z_1 + z_2|^2 + |z_1 - z_2|^2 = 2(|z_1|^2 + |z_2|^2)$.
Solution: According to (*ii*), we have,

$$|z_1 + z_2|^2 + |z_1 - z_2|^2$$
$$= (z_1 + z_2)(\overline{z_1} + \overline{z_2}) + (z_1 - z_2)(\overline{z_1} - \overline{z_2}) = 2z_1\overline{z_1} + 2z_2\overline{z_2} = 2(|z_1|^2 + |z_2|^2).$$

Suppose, $z_1 = r_1(\cos\theta_1 + i\sin\theta_1)$ and $z_2 = r_2(\cos\theta_2 + i\sin\theta_2)$. Then,

$$z_1 z_2 = r_1 r_2(\cos\theta_1 + i\sin\theta_1)(\cos\theta_2 + i\sin\theta_2) = r_1 r_2(\cos\theta_1\cos\theta_2 - \sin\theta_1\sin\theta_2)$$
$$+i(\sin\theta_1\cos\theta_2 + \cos\theta_1\sin\theta_2) = r_1 r_2(\cos(\theta_1 + \theta_2) + i\sin(\theta_1 + \theta_2)).$$
$$\therefore\ z_1 z_2 = r_1 r_2(\cos(\theta_1 + \theta_2) + i\sin(\theta_1 + \theta_2)).$$

Now, if $z_3 = r_3(\cos\theta_3 + \sin\theta_3)$, similarly it can be shown that,

$$z_1 z_2 z_3 = r_1 r_2 r_3(\cos(\theta_1 + \theta_2 + \theta_3) + i\sin(\theta_1 + \theta_2 + \theta_3)).$$

In general, if

$$z_1 = r_1(\cos\theta_1 + i\sin\theta_1), z_2 = r_2(\cos\theta_2 + i\sin\theta_2), \ldots, z_n = r_n(\cos\theta_n + i\sin\theta_n),$$

then,

$$z_1 z_2 \ldots z_n = r_1 r_2 \ldots r_n(\cos(\theta_1 + \theta_2 + \ldots + \theta_n) + i\sin(\theta_1 + \theta_2 + \ldots + \theta_n)).$$

Now, let's $z_1 = z_2 = \ldots = z_n = z = r(\cos\theta + \sin\theta)$. Hence, $z^n = r^n$ $(\cos n\theta + i\sin n\theta)$. That is,

$(\cos\theta + \sin\theta)$ Skipping malformed tag: msup $= \cos n\theta + i\sin n\theta$. (7)

This relation is known as *De Moivre's formula.* By (7) we can prove the correctness of many formulas. For example, if in (6), we put n=2, we get,

$(\cos\theta + i\sin\theta)$ Skipping malformed tag: msup $= (\cos 2\theta + i\sin 2\theta) \rightarrow \cos^2\theta - \sin^2\theta + i(2\cos\theta\sin\theta)$.

By comparing the sides, we obtain the following results.

$$\cos 2\theta = \cos^2\theta - \sin^2\theta, \sin 2\theta = 2\cos\theta\sin\theta.$$

Remark 2: De Moivre's formula is also valid for any negative or fractional number n.

Example 4: Show that,

$$z^n - z^{-n} = 2i\sin n\theta.$$

Then, using this result to show that,

$$\sin^5\theta = \frac{1}{16}(\sin 5\theta - 5\sin 3\theta + 10\sin\theta).$$

Solution: We have, $z - z^{-1} = 2i\sin\theta$. That is, $2i\sin\theta = z - \frac{1}{z}$. Then,

$$(2i\sin\theta)^5 = \left(z - \frac{1}{z}\right)^5 \rightarrow 32i\sin^5\theta = z^5 - 5z^3 + 10z - \frac{10}{z} + \frac{5}{z^3} - \frac{1}{z^5}.$$

We arrange it as,

$$32i\sin^5\theta = (z^5 - \frac{1}{z^5}) - 5(z^3 - \frac{1}{z^3}) + 10\left(z - \frac{1}{z}\right).$$

But $z^n - z^{-n} = 2i\sin n\theta$.

Example 5: Show that,

$$(\sqrt{3} - i)^{24} + (\sqrt{3} + i)^{24} = 2^{25}\cos 4\pi.$$

Solution: We have, $\sqrt{3} - i \rightarrow x = \sqrt{3}$, and

$$y = -1 \rightarrow r = \sqrt{x^2 + y^2} = \sqrt{\sqrt{3}^2 + (-1)^2} = 2, \theta$$
$$= \arctan\left(\frac{-1}{\sqrt{3}}\right) = -\frac{\pi}{6} \Rightarrow \sqrt{3} - i = 2\left(\cos\left(-\frac{\pi}{6}\right) + \sin\left(-\frac{\pi}{6}\right)\right) = 2(\cos\frac{\pi}{6} - isin\frac{\pi}{6}).$$

Then,

$\sqrt{3} - i = 2\left(\cos\frac{\pi}{6} - isin\frac{\pi}{6}\right).$

Similarly, $\sqrt{3} + i \rightarrow x = \sqrt{3}$, and

$$y = 1 \rightarrow r = \sqrt{x^2 + y^2} = \sqrt{\sqrt{3}^2 + 1^2} = 2, \theta$$
$$= \arctan\left(\frac{1}{\sqrt{3}}\right) = \frac{\pi}{6} \Rightarrow \sqrt{3} + i = 2\left(\cos\frac{\pi}{6} + isin\frac{\pi}{6}\right).$$

Thus,

$$\left(\sqrt{3} - i\right)^{24} + \left(\sqrt{3} + i\right)^{24} = \left(2\left(\cos\frac{\pi}{6} - isin\frac{\pi}{6}\right)\right)^{24} + \left(2\left(\cos\frac{\pi}{6} + isin\frac{\pi}{6}\right)\right)^{24}$$
$$= 2^{24}\left(\cos\frac{24\pi}{6} - isin\frac{24\pi}{6}\right) + 2^{24}\left(\cos\frac{24\pi}{6} + isin\frac{24\pi}{6}\right) = 2^{24}\left(2\cos\frac{24\pi}{6}\right) = 2^{25}\cos 4\pi.$$

Example 6: Show that,

$$\left(\frac{\cot\theta + i}{\cot\theta - i}\right)^n = \frac{\cot n\theta + i}{\cot n\theta - i}$$

Solution: We have,

$$\left(\frac{\cot\theta + i}{\cot\theta - i}\right)^n = \left(\frac{\frac{\cos\theta}{\sin\theta} + i}{\frac{\cos\theta}{\sin\theta} - i}\right)^n = \left(\frac{\cos\theta + i\sin\theta}{\cos\theta - i\sin\theta}\right)^n = \frac{(\cos\theta + i\sin\theta)^n}{(\cos\theta - i\sin\theta)^n}$$
$$= \frac{\cos n\theta + i\sin n\theta}{\cos n\theta - i\sin n\theta} = \frac{(\cos n\theta + i\sin n\theta)/\sin n\theta}{(\cos n\theta - i\sin n\theta)/\sin n\theta} = \frac{\cot n\theta + i}{\cot n\theta - i}.$$

A very important application of Moivre's formula is to obtain the nth roots of numbers. Since if we add any integer multiple of 2π to θ, the number z remains unchanged. Therefore, it can be written that,

$$z = \sqrt[n]{r}\left(\cos\left(\frac{\theta + 2k\pi}{n}\right) + i\sin\left(\frac{\theta + 2k\pi}{n}\right)\right), k = 0, 1, \ldots, (n-1). \quad (8)$$

From a geometric point of view, it shows that, the roots are equally spaced on the circle $|z| = z^{\frac{1}{n}}$.

The relation (8) helps us find all roots of polynomial equations.

Example 7: Find the roots of the equation given by, $z^5 - i = \sqrt{3}$.

Solution: We write, $z^5 = \sqrt{3} + i$. Then, $r = \sqrt{1+3} = 2$, and $\theta = \tan^{-1}\left(\frac{1}{\sqrt{3}}\right) = \frac{\pi}{6}$. Thus,

$$z^5 = \sqrt{3} + i = 2(\cos\tfrac{\pi}{6} + i \sin\tfrac{\pi}{6}) = 2(\cos(\tfrac{\pi}{6} + 2k\pi) + i \sin(\tfrac{\pi}{6} + 2k\pi)).$$

Therefore,

$$z = \sqrt[5]{2}(\cos(\frac{\frac{\pi}{6} + 2k\pi}{5}) + i \sin(\frac{\frac{\pi}{6} + 2k\pi}{5})).,k = 0,1,2,3,4.$$

In practice, we may need to find the roots of a polynomial given by

$$a_n z^n + a_{n-1} z^{n-1} + \ldots + a_1 z + a_0 = 0$$

where, $a_n, a_{n-1}, \ldots, a_1, a_0$ can be complex numbers and n is a positive integer. It has been proved that any polynomial equation of degree n, has n roots. If $z_1, z_2, \ldots, z_n$ are the roots of this polynomial then, $(z-z_1)(z-z_2) \ldots (z-z_n)=0$, which is a factor form of a polynomial. These roots may be found by the factor form of polynomial or by some algebraic operations transforming them in simple form so that it can be possible to find these roots. For example, we consider the following example.

Example 8: Solve the equation

$$z^7 + z^6 + z^5 + z^4 + z^3 + z^2 + z + 1 = 0.$$

Solution: Since, $z-1 \neq 0$, (why?), then by multiplying it to both sides of the equation, we get, $z^8-1=0$.

This equation is equivalent to the above equation. Thus, it is enough to solve it and remove, z=-1 from it. We have, $r = \sqrt{1+0}=1$, and $\theta = \tan^{-1}(\frac{0}{1}) = 0$. Hence,

$$z^8 = 1 = (\cos 0 + i \sin 0) = \cos(2k\pi) + i \sin(2k\pi) \rightarrow z = (\cos(2k\pi) + i \sin(2k\pi))^{\frac{1}{8}}.$$

Therefore, by Moivre's formula we obtain

$$z = \cos(\tfrac{k\pi}{4}) + i \sin(\tfrac{k\pi}{4}), k = 1,2,3,4,5,6,7.$$

Note that we did not choose k=0, because $z \neq 1$.

At the end of this section, we mention that we just introduced the complex numbers, not complex variables, or calculus of complex variables. In general, most materials of calculus for real variables can also be used for complex variables. For example, the concepts of limits, continuity, differentiations, and integrations also hold for complex variables. But, since a complex function $f(z)$ can be written in terms of real and imaginary parts, that is $f(z)= u(x,y)+iv(x,y)$, this helps us find more relations for existence of limits and differentiations.

The readers can read more about the calculus of complex variables in (Jameson, 1970) (Churchill & Brown, 1988) (Silverman, 1974) (Tall, 1971) (Albowitz & Fokas, 2003).

8.4 POLAR FORM OF GRAPHS

In this section we are going to use relations in (5) for writing the equation of a curve in polar form. We emphasize that in application we may encounter a graph which its equation is given in a Polar coordinate system rather than a Cartesian coordinate system. Managers can use polar coordinate systems to visualize data that has a circular nature, such as time-based data or directional data. This can help in identifying patterns that might not be visible in the Cartesian coordinate system. Even in many applications, it may be difficult to challenge a Cartesian coordinate system when we are trying to find, for example, a bounded area or length of the following curves:

(i) $(x^2 + y^2)^2 = axy$, (Lemniscate)
(ii) $x^{\frac{1}{2}} + y^{\frac{1}{2}} = a^{\frac{1}{2}}$, (Parabola segment)
(iii) $x^2 + y^2 = a\left(\tan^{-1}\frac{y}{x}\right)^2$, (Archimedean spiral)

As we have seen, it was easier to work with complex numbers and algebraic operations by using these coordinates. For example, we used $x = acos\theta$ or $x = asin\theta$ to evaluate some integrals in Chapter 6 we. Here, we would like to show that the relationships and results in the Cartesian coordinate system are easier to work in the polar coordinate system. But we bear in mind that even though there is a one-to-one correspondence between the points of the plane and its Cartesian coordinate plane, this correspondence will no longer exist in the polar coordinate system.

Previously, we wrote the equations of line and circle in terms of polar coordinates and observed that the number of variables or parameters can be reduced. For example, $r=a^2$ represents circle $x^2+y^2=a^2$ in polar form, or $\overline{E}z + E\overline{z} + C = 0$ represents line $Ax+By+C=0$, where $\overline{E}$ is conjugate of E.

To find the general form for the equation of line given by $Ax+By+C=0$ in polar form, we substitute $x = rcos\theta, y = rsin\theta$ in this equation. We obtain

$$Arcos\theta, +Brsin\theta = C \rightarrow r = \frac{-C}{Acos\theta + Bsin\theta} \rightarrow r = \frac{1}{acos\theta + bsin\theta}. \qquad (9)$$

where $a = -\frac{A}{C}$ and $b = -\frac{B}{C}$.

Example 9: Write the equation $x^2+y^2=ax$ in polar form.

Solution: From (5), we have, $x = r\cos\theta, y = r\sin\theta$, then

$$x^2 + y^2 = ax \rightarrow (rcos\theta)^2 + (rsin\theta)^2 = arcos\theta$$
$$\Rightarrow r^2(\cos^2\theta + \sin^2\theta) = arcos\theta \rightarrow r(r - \mathrm{a}\cos\theta) = 0 \Rightarrow r = 0, r = \mathrm{a}\cos\theta.$$

The graph of r=0 is the pole that lies on $r = \mathrm{a}\cos\theta$, so $r = \mathrm{a}\cos\theta$ is the polar equation of the given equation.

Example 10: Write the equation $r^2 = 4\sin 2\theta$ in Cartesian coordinate form.

Solution: First, we multiply the equation by r^2. We get $r^4 = 4r^2\sin 2\theta$.

Since $r = \sqrt{x^2 + y^2}$ and $\sin 2\theta = 2\sin\theta\cos\theta$, we can write

$$\left(\sqrt{x^2 + y^2}\right)^4 = 8xy \Rightarrow (x^2 + y^2)^2 = 8xy,$$

which is a Lemniscate.

Before we introduce some curves in polar form, it would be better to mention the following points which can be useful in drawing the graph of curves in terms of polar coordinates.

Let's r=f(θ), then

(i) If the equation does not change by converting (r,θ) to $(r, 2k\pi - \theta)$, or $(-r, \pi - \theta + 2k\pi)$, the graph is symmetrical about the polar axis.
(ii) If the equation does not change by converting (r,θ) to $(r, 2k\pi - \theta)$, or $(r, \pi + \theta + 2k\pi)$, the graph is symmetrical about the pole.
(iii) If the equation does not change by converting (r,θ) to $(r, \pi - \theta + 2k\pi)$, or $(-r, 2k\pi - \theta)$, the graph is symmetrical according to $\frac{\pi}{2}$-axis.

In checking whether the curve passes through the pole or not, just put, r=0. If the equation f(θ)=0 has a solution, the curve passes through the pole.

If the curve passes through the pole $\theta=\theta_0$ is the answer to the equation, $f(\theta)=0$, then $\theta=\theta_0$ is the equation of the tangent line to the curve at the pole that must be calculated.

We will describe here the graphs of some special curves. By choosing any of the available functions, you can check the correctness of these graphs as an exercise. We remind you that all the following graphs we use the simplest command given by ezpolar('$f(t)$'). For example,

$$ezpolar\left('\frac{1}{\cos(t) + \sin(t)}'\right),$$

draws the line y=1–x.

In the rest of our work, we will use the same command to draw the given graphs.

(a) Limacon

A graph of equations in the form of $r = \mathrm{a} \pm b\ \sin\theta$ or $r = \mathrm{a} \pm b\ \cos\theta$ is called a *Limacon*, and if *a*=*b* is chosen, it is called a *cardioid*. Consider the equation r=a$\pm b$cosθ.

The equation of $r = a + b\ \cos\theta$ does not change by converting θ to -θ and therefore the polar axis is the axis of symmetry of the curve. For, $r = \mathrm{a} + b\ \cos\theta$ in different situations, we will have the following figures (Figure 2).

Figure 2. Graphs of $r = a + b\ cos\theta$ for three cases a=b, a<b, and a>b

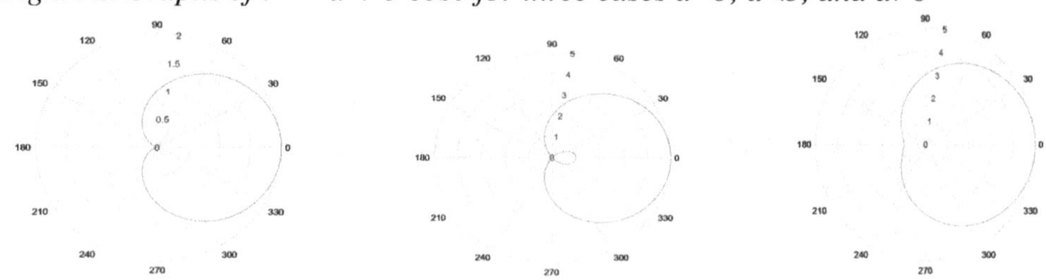

$a = b$ $a < b$ $a > b$

For the case, $r =$ a-b $\cos\theta$, the above graphs are flipped to the right. That is, they will have a rotation of π degree.

In the case of $r = \mathrm{a} \pm b\ \sin\theta$, we will have graphs similar to the graphs in Figure 2, with the difference that in the case of (+), we will have a rotation of $\frac{\pi}{2}$ degree and in the case (-), we will have a rotation of, $-\frac{\pi}{2}$degree (Figure 3).

Note that by converting π to -π, the equation of does not change, so the graph of the curves is symmetrical with according to $\frac{\pi}{2}$-axis.

Figure 3. Graphs of $r = a + b\ sin\theta$ *for three cases a=b, a<b, and a>b*

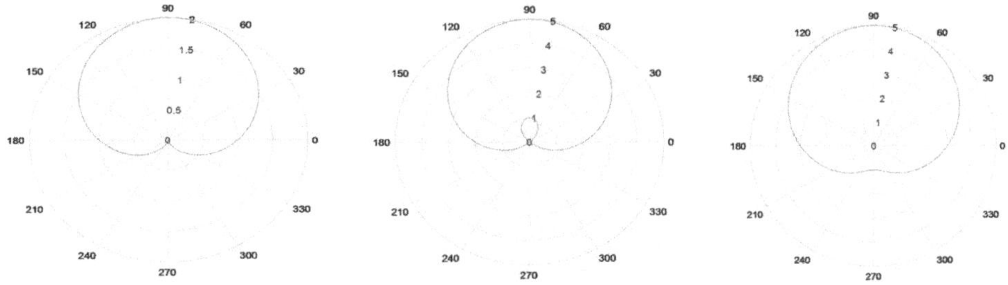

$a = b$ $\qquad$ $a < b$ $\qquad$ $a > b$

(b) n-Petaled Rose

Graph of equation of the forms $r = a\cos n\theta$ or $r = a\sin n\theta$ is a rose which has n petals. This rose has n petals if n is odd and has $2n$ petals if n is even. For example, for n=3, the graph of $r = a\cos 3\theta$ where a>0 is given by Figure 4.

Figure 4. Graph of $r = acos3\theta$ *for case a>0*

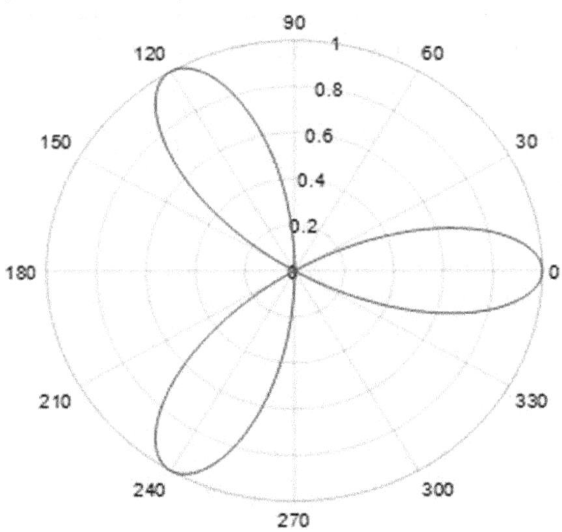

For n=2, the graph of $r = a\cos 2\theta$ is given by Figure 5.

Figure 5. Graph of $r = a\cos 2\theta$ for three case a>0

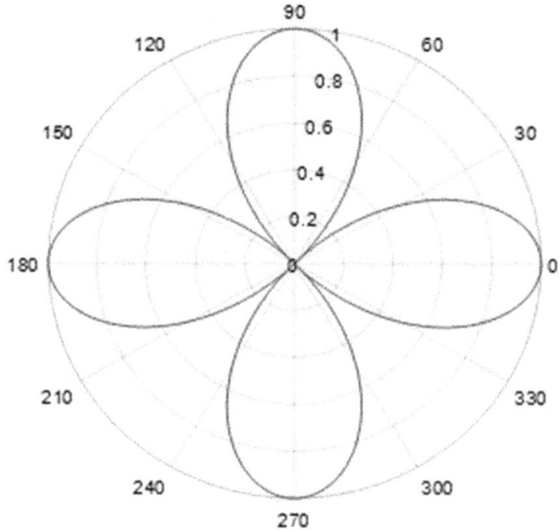

(c) Lemniscate

The equations of the forms $r^2 = a\cos 2\theta$ and $r^2 = a\sin 2\theta$ are called *Lemniscate,* where a is arbitrary. Figure 6 shows graph of $r^2 = a\cos 2\theta$.

Figure 6. Graphs of $r = \sqrt{a\cos 2\theta}$ and $r = \sqrt{a\sin 2\theta}$ for a=1.

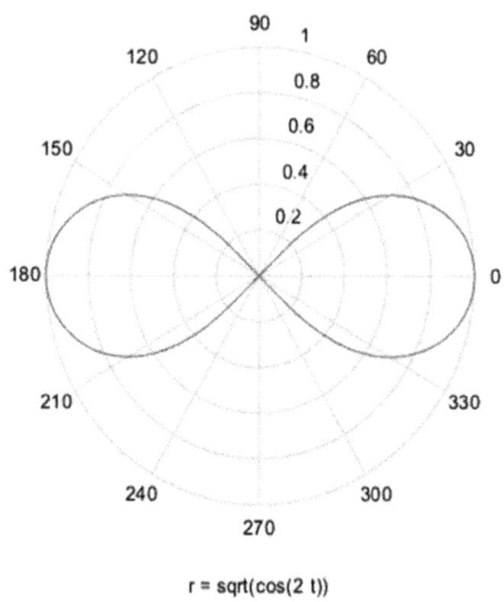

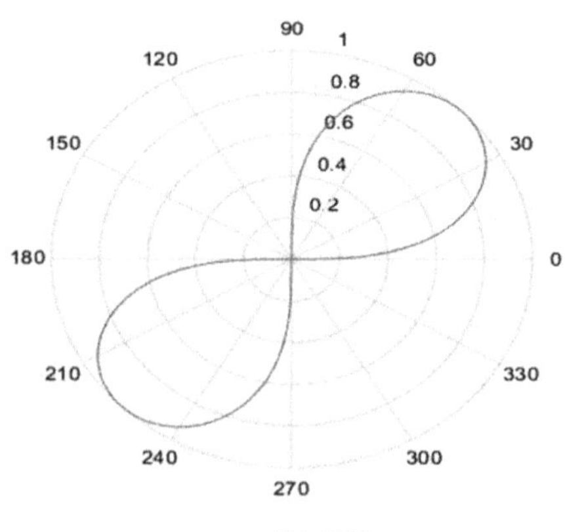

(d) Archimedean spiral

The general form of Archimedean spiral is given by $r=a\theta$ with $a>0$. By converting r to $-r$ the graph does not change, hence the curve is s symmetrical with according to $\frac{\pi}{2}$-axis (Figure 7).

Figure 7. Graph of $r = a\theta$ *for* $a>0$

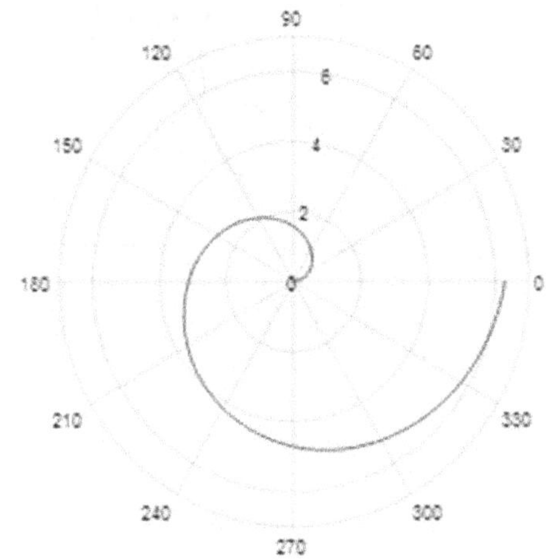

We call the graph given by equation $r = a e^{k\theta}$ a *logarithmic spiral* (Figure 8).

Figure 8. Graph of $r = a e^{k\theta}$ *for* $a=k=1$

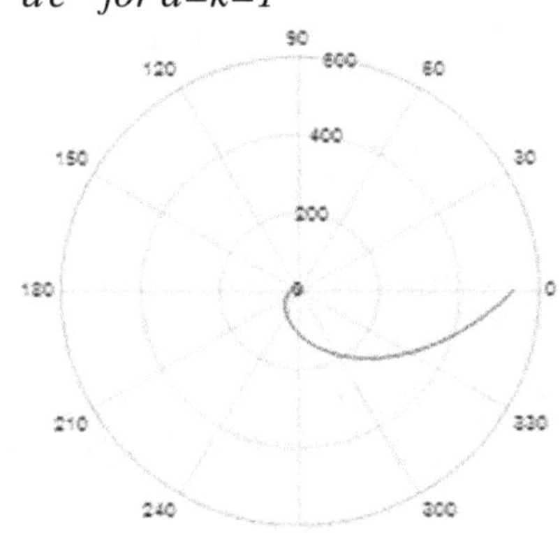

In Cartesian coordinates, the angle α is used to determine the direction of a curve at a point, which is the angle between the tangent line to the curve at this point and the x-axis, but in polar coordinates, for convenience, it is better to use another angle, such as β, which is the angle between the tangent line and the polar axis (Figure 9).

Figure 9. Graph which describes finding the slope of a tangent line

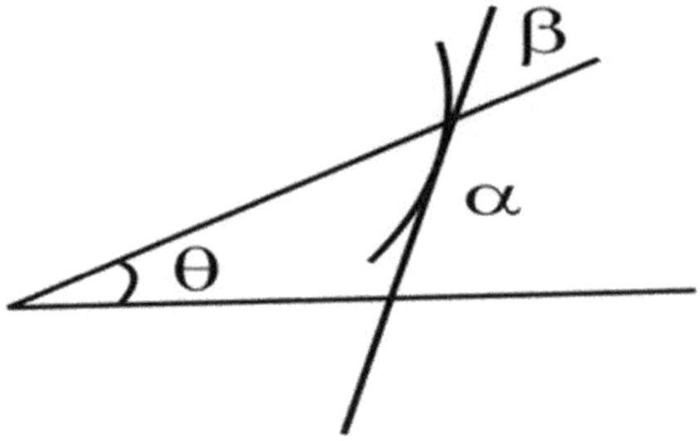

Since $x = r\cos\theta, y = r\sin\theta$, it can be shown that the slope of the curve in terms of polar coordinates will be given by

$$m = \tan\beta = \frac{rd\theta}{dr}. \tag{10}$$

Example 11: Show that the tangent lines are perpendicular to each other at the intersection points of the two curves $r = asec^3\left(\frac{\theta}{2}\right)$ and $r = bcosec^2\left(\frac{\theta}{2}\right)$.

Solution: We must show that, $mm' = -1$. For the first curve, we have,

$$dr = asin\left(\frac{\theta}{2}\right)sec^3\left(\frac{\theta}{2}\right)d\theta \Rightarrow \frac{rd\theta}{dr} = \frac{1}{sin\left(\frac{\theta}{2}\right)sec\left(\frac{\theta}{2}\right)} = m,$$

and for the second curve

$$dr = -bcos\left(\frac{\theta}{2}\right)cosec^3\left(\frac{\theta}{2}\right)d\theta \Rightarrow \frac{rd\theta}{dr} = \frac{-1}{cos\left(\frac{\theta}{2}\right)cosec\left(\frac{\theta}{2}\right)} = m'.$$

It is not difficult to show that $mm'=-1$.

8.5 AREA AND LENGTH OF A POLAR CURVE

(a) Let us the function $r=f(\theta)$ is a continuous function for $\alpha\leq\theta\leq\beta$. We divide region A, bounded by the curve $r=f(\theta)$and lines $\theta=\alpha$, $\theta=\beta$, into n sub-intervals by drawing $\theta = \alpha = \theta_0, \theta = \theta_1, \ldots, \theta = \theta_n = \beta$, and we call the angle between them axis $\Delta\theta_1, \Delta\theta_2, \ldots, \Delta\theta_n$, respectively (Figure10). We choose a sector related to $\Delta\theta_i$. The area of this sector is $\frac{1}{2}r_i^2\Delta\theta_i$. If we add the area of sectors like this sector and call the result A_n, we will have

$$A_n = \sum_{i=1}^{n} \frac{1}{2}r_i^2\Delta\theta_i.$$

when $n\to\infty$ or in other words, $\Delta\theta_i \to 0$, we define the limit value of this sum, as the area of this bounded region and can be found by the following formula:

$$A = \int_\alpha^\beta \frac{1}{2}r^2 d\theta. \quad (11)$$

Figure 10. Graph which describes finding the area of a part of polar curve

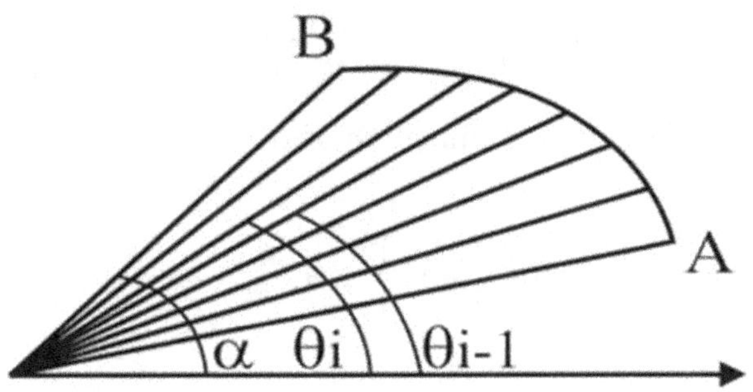

Example 12: Find the area inside a 4-petaled rose $r = \cos 2\theta$.

Solution: Our desired area is from $\theta = -\frac{\pi}{4}$ to $\theta = \frac{\pi}{4}$. Therefore,

$$A = \int_\alpha^\beta \frac{1}{2}r^2 d\theta = \int_{-\frac{\pi}{4}}^{\frac{\pi}{4}} \frac{1}{2}r^2 d\theta = \int_0^{\frac{\pi}{4}} r^2 d\theta = \int_0^{\frac{\pi}{4}} cos^2 2\theta d\theta = \frac{1}{2}\int_0^{\frac{\pi}{4}} (1 + cos4\theta)d\theta = \frac{1}{2}(\theta + sin4\theta)_0^{\frac{\pi}{4}} = \frac{\pi}{8}.$$

Example 13: Find the area A enclosed by one loop of $r = 3\sqrt{\cos 2\theta}$.

Solution: For one loop we have,

$$A = \int_\alpha^\beta \frac{1}{2}r^2 d\theta = \int_{-\frac{\pi}{4}}^{\frac{\pi}{4}} \frac{9}{2}\cos 2\theta d\theta = 9\int_0^{\frac{\pi}{4}} \cos 2\theta d\theta = = \frac{9}{2}(sin2\theta)_0^{\frac{\pi}{4}} = \frac{9}{2}.$$

(b) Let's assume that the calculation of length AB is desired. By drawing the polar axes, we divide the length of AB into the lengths of Δl_i (Figure 11).

Figure 11. Graph which describes finding the area of a part of polar curve

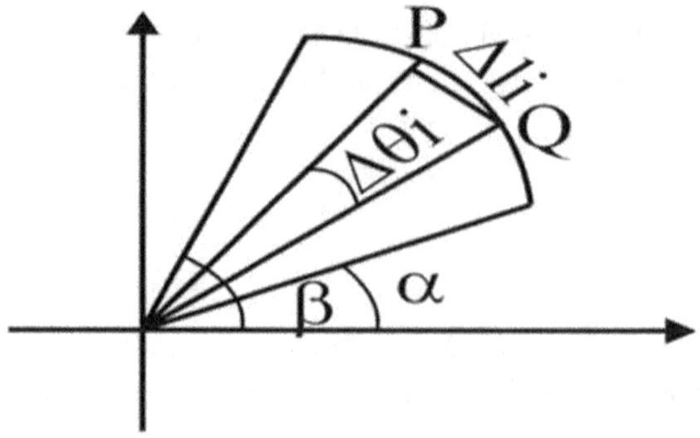

Let us consider one of the resulting lengths. For example, Δl_i. If $OP=r_i$ and $OQ=r_i+dr_i$ then $RQ\cong\Delta r_i$. We also have, $RP = r_i \sin\Delta\theta \cong r_i\Delta\theta_i$. Therefore, from the equality $PQ^2=PR^2+RQ^2$ we conclude from that,

$$\Delta l_i^2 \cong (r_i\Delta\theta_i)^2+(\Delta r_i)^2 \to \left(\frac{\Delta l_i}{\Delta\theta_i}\right)^2 \cong r_i^2+\left(\frac{\Delta r_i}{\Delta\theta_i}\right)^2 \Rightarrow \Delta l_i \cong \left\{r_i^2+\left(\frac{\Delta r_i}{\Delta\theta_i}\right)^2\right\}^{\frac{1}{2}}\Delta\theta_i.$$

Since the length of AB is the summation of Δl_i that is $l = \sum_\alpha^\beta \Delta l_i$, thus

$$l \cong \sum_{\theta=\alpha}^{\theta=\beta}\Delta l_i \cong \sum_{\theta=\alpha}^{\theta=\beta}\left\{r_i^2+\left(\frac{\Delta r_i}{\Delta\theta_i}\right)^2\right\}^{\frac{1}{2}}\Delta\theta_i.$$

In the limit, when $n\to\infty$, this sum tends to a number which is the length of AB and is calculated from the following formula:

$$l = \int_\alpha^\beta\left\{r^2+\left(\frac{dr}{d\theta}\right)^2\right\}^{\frac{1}{2}}d\theta. \qquad (12)$$

Example 13: Find the perimeter of the cardioid $r = a(1+\cos\theta)$.

$$l = 2\int_0^\pi\left\{r^2+\left(\frac{dr}{d\theta}\right)^2\right\}^{\frac{1}{2}}d\theta = 2a\int_0^\pi\left\{(1+\cos\theta)^2+(-\sin\theta)^2\right\}^{\frac{1}{2}}d\theta =$$

$$= 2a\int_0^\pi\{2(1+\cos\theta)\}^{\frac{1}{2}}d\theta = 2a\int_0^\pi 2\cos\left(\frac{\theta}{2}\right)d\theta = 8a.$$

Remark 3: Area of the region $r_1(\theta)$ and $r_2(\theta)$ where $r_1(\theta) \leq r_2(\theta)$ can be found from the following formula:

$$A = \int_{\alpha}^{\beta} \frac{1}{2}(r_2{}^2 - r_1{}^2)d\theta. \tag{13}$$

Example 14: Find the area of the region between inside the cardioid $r = 1 + cos\theta$ and outside the circle r=1.

Solution: The value of θ runs from $-\frac{\pi}{2}$ to $\frac{\pi}{2}$. This can be find by intersecting two curves, i.e., $1 + cos\theta = 1$, which leads to $\theta = \pm\frac{\pi}{2}$. Therefore,

$$A = \int_{\alpha}^{\beta} \frac{1}{2}(r_2^2 - r_1^2)d\theta = \frac{1}{2}\int_{-\frac{\pi}{2}}^{\frac{\pi}{2}}((1+\cos\theta)^2 - 1^2))d\theta = \frac{1}{2}\int_{-\frac{\pi}{2}}^{\frac{\pi}{2}}\left(2\cos\theta + \cos^2\theta\right)d\theta$$

$$= \int_0^{\frac{\pi}{2}}\left(2\cos\theta + \cos^2\theta\right)d\theta = \int_0^{\frac{\pi}{2}}\left(2\cos\theta + \frac{1+\cos 2\theta}{2}\right)d\theta = \left(2\sin\theta + \frac{\theta}{2} + \frac{\sin 2\theta}{4}\right)\Bigg|_0^{\frac{\pi}{2}} = 2 + \frac{\pi}{4}.$$

Remark 4: It can be shown that the resulting surface area of a rotating object is obtained from the following equation:

$$A = 2\pi\int_{\alpha}^{\beta} rsin\theta\left\{r^2 + \left(\frac{dr}{d\theta}\right)^2\right\}^{\frac{1}{2}} d\theta \tag{14}$$

Example 15: Find the area of the surface of revolution generated by rotating the lemniscate, $r = 2\sqrt{cos2\theta}$ about the polar axis.

Solution: We find the values for r such that $cos2\theta \geq 0$, that is $-\frac{\pi}{4} \leq \theta \leq \frac{\pi}{4}$. We have,

$$dl = \sqrt{4cos2\theta + \left(\frac{2sin2\theta}{\sqrt{cos2\theta}}\right)^2}\, d\theta = \frac{2d\theta}{\sqrt{cos2\theta}}.$$

Therefore,

$$A = 2\pi\int_{\alpha}^{\beta} rsin\theta\left\{r^2 + \left(\frac{dr}{d\theta}\right)^2\right\}^{\frac{1}{2}} d\theta$$

$$= 8\pi\int_{-\frac{\pi}{4}}^{\frac{\pi}{4}} \frac{\sqrt{cos2\theta}\,sin\theta}{\sqrt{cos2\theta}}d\theta = 8\pi\int_{-\frac{\pi}{4}}^{\frac{\pi}{4}} sin\theta d\theta = -8\pi(\cos\theta)\Bigg|_{-\frac{\pi}{4}}^{\frac{\pi}{4}} = 8\pi\left(2 - \sqrt{2\pi}\right).$$

Example 16: Find the area of the surface of revolution generated by rotating a part of cardioid $r = a(1 + \cos\theta)$ from $A(0,\pi)$ to $B(2a,0)$ by 2π about the x- axis.

Solution: From $r = a(1 + \cos\theta)$, we obtain $\frac{dr}{d\theta} = -a\sin\theta$. Thus,

$$A = 2\pi\int_0^{\pi} a(1 + cos\theta)\sin\theta(2a\cos\left(\frac{\theta}{2}\right)d\theta = 16\pi a^2\int_0^{\pi}\cos^4\left(\frac{\theta}{2}\right)sin\left(\frac{\theta}{2}\right)d\theta = \frac{32}{5}\pi a^2.$$

More about polar curves can be read from (Leithold, 1981) (Piskunov, 1981) (Silverman, 1985) (Thomas, 2014) (Stewart, 2008).

8.6 COMPUTER STATION

Maple is a comprehensive computer algebra system (CAS) used extensively for mathematical computation, visualization, and programming. It's developed by Maplesoft, a Canadian company, and is widely used by mathematicians, engineers, scientists, and educators for various purposes. Here are some key features and applications of Maple:

1. **Symbolic Computation**: Maple allows users to perform symbolic algebra and calculus. For example, it can simplify expressions, solve equations symbolically, and find limits, derivatives, and integrals.
2. **Numerical Computation**: Beyond symbolic mathematics, Maple can also handle numerical calculations, including numerical solution of equations, optimization, and differential equations.
3. **Visualization**: It includes powerful tools for plotting and graphing a wide array of mathematical functions and data, including 2D and 3D plots.
4. **Programming**: Maple includes a full-featured programming language that supports writing custom functions and developing complete applications within the Maple environment.
5. **Education**: Often used as an educational tool, Maple provides interactive applications and tools to help students learn various mathematical concepts.
6. **Engineering Applications**: Engineers use Maple for control design, signal processing, and simulation.
7. **Document Interface**: Maple offers a document interface that allows users to create technical documents that include live calculations along with text, mathematics, and graphics, making it useful for creating interactive technical reports and educational materials.

Maple's ability to handle complex mathematical problems with symbolic computation and numerical analysis makes it a valuable tool for academic and professional work in science and engineering fields.

Drawing polar diagrams in Maple is a great way to visualize mathematical functions expressed in polar coordinates. A polar diagram represents data or functions in terms of radius and angle and is useful in fields like mathematics, physics, and engineering. Here's a step-by-step guide on how to create polar plots in Maple, complete with example codes.

To draw polar diagrams in Maple, you can use the polarplot function from the plots package. Polar diagrams are often used to represent functions in polar coordinates where the radius r is a function of the angle θ.

Example 1: Simple Polar Plot

Here's a simple example of how to draw a polar plot for the function r=cos (2θ) with(plots):

polarplot(cos(2*theta), theta = 0..2*Pi, title = "Polar Plot of r = cos(2θ)");

To run this in Maple, just paste the code into a Maple worksheet and execute it. Maple will generate the polar plot as specified.

Example 2: Rose Curve

A rose curve is a common polar plot. The function r=cos (kθ) or r=sin (kθ) gives a rose curve with(plots):

polarplot(sin(4*theta), theta = 0..2*Pi, title = "Polar Plot of r = sin(4θ)");

Example 3: Archimedean Spiral

The Archimedean spiral is another interesting polar plot where the radius r is a linear function of θ with(plots):

polarplot(theta, theta = 0..4*Pi, title = "Polar Plot of r = θ");

Example 4: Polar Plot with Multiple Functions

You can also plot multiple functions on the same polar plot with(plots):

polarplot([cos(2*theta), sin(3*theta)], theta = 0..2*Pi, title = "Multiple Polar Plots: r = cos(2θ) and r = sin(3θ)");

Example 5: Cardioid

A cardioid is a heart-shaped curve, which can be plotted using the function r=1−sin (θ) with(plots):

polarplot(1 - sin(theta), theta = 0..2*Pi, title = "Polar Plot of r = 1 - sin(θ)");

Generating All Plots

To generate and view the output of all the above examples in Maple, you can copy the entire code block into your Maple environment. Each plot will be generated separately, and you can view them one by one.

Here's the entire code for all examples: with(plots):

# **Example 1:** Simple Polar Plot
polarplot(cos(2*theta), theta = 0..2*Pi, title = "Polar Plot of r = cos(2θ)");
# **Example 2:** Rose Curve
polarplot(sin(4*theta), theta = 0..2*Pi, title = "Polar Plot of r = sin(4θ)");
# **Example 3:** Archimedean Spiral
polarplot(theta, theta = 0..4*Pi, title = "Polar Plot of r = θ");
# **Example 4:** Polar Plot with Multiple Functions
polarplot([cos(2*theta), sin(3*theta)], theta = 0..2*Pi, title = "Multiple Polar Plots: r = cos(2θ) and r = sin(3θ)");
# **Example 5:** Cardioid
polarplot(1 - sin(theta), theta = 0..2*Pi, title = "Polar Plot of r = 1 - sin(θ)");

Each polarplot command generates a polar diagram based on the provided function and range of θ. You can run this code in Maple, and it will display the corresponding polar diagrams for each example.

CONCLUSION

In this chapter, we introduced the complex numbers and algebraic operations for them. We observed that, by De Moivre's formula, we can prove some trigonometric relationships that we met before in elementary course and can find the roots of some polynomial equations. We wrote the Cartesian coordinates in terms of polar coordinates. With polar coordinates, we introduced some specific curves, and then we found formulas for calculating the area of a bounded region, in particular the area of the surface of revolution generated by resolving a part of a curve. We also obtained a formula to find a length of a curve. We ended the chapter by adding a Computer Station for readers which can help to draw the polar curves.

8.7 Exercises

1. After simplifying the following expressions, write the results in the form of $x+iy$.

   (i) $\left(\frac{1-i\sqrt{3}}{1-i\sqrt{3}}\right)^{60}$

   (ii) $\frac{1+i+i^2+i^3}{i^4+i^5+i^6+i^7}$

   (iii) $1+i+i^2+\ldots+i^{99}$

   (iv) $\frac{(1-i)(2+i)(3-i)}{(4+i)(5-i)(6+i)}$

   (v) $\frac{1+i+i^2-\ldots+i^{99}+i^{100}}{1-i+i^2-\ldots-i^{99}+i^{100}}$

2. Find the roots of given numbers.

   (i) $\sqrt[4]{-1}$

   (ii) $\sqrt[3]{i}$

   (iii) $\sqrt[5]{\frac{1+i}{\sqrt{3}-i}}$

   (iv) $\sqrt[4]{\left(\frac{1+i\sqrt{3}}{2}\right)^3}$

   (v) $\sqrt[6]{(\frac{1-i\sqrt{3}}{1-i\sqrt{3}})^{25}}$

3. Prove that if z_1 and z_2 are roots of equation $z^2+2z+4=0$, then,

$$z_1{}^n + z_2{}^n = 2^{n+1}\cos\frac{n\pi}{3}.$$

4. Prove that,

   (i) $|x| + |y| \leq \sqrt{2}|z|$

   (ii) $|z_1| + |z_2| \leq |z_1 + z_2|$

   (iii) $\arg z + \arg\bar{z} = 2k\pi$

   (iv) $|z_1 + z_2|^2 = |z_1|^2 + 2Re(z_1\bar{z}_2) + |z_2|^2$

   (v) $\arg\left(\frac{z_3 - z_2}{z_3 - z_1}\right) = \arg\left(\frac{z_1}{z_2}\right)$, if $|z_1| = |z_2| = |z_3|$.

5. Solve the following equations.

   (i) $z^3 = 1 + i$

   (ii) $z^5 + 32 = 0$

   (iii) $(z - i)^6 = (z + i)^6$

   (iv) $z^4 + z^3 + z^2 + z + 1 = 0$

   (v) $z^4 - z^3 + z^2 - z + 1 = 0.$

6. Show that,

   (i) $\left(\frac{1 + i\tan n\theta}{1 - i\tan n\theta}\right)^n = \frac{1 + i\tan n\theta}{1 - i\tan n\theta}$

   (ii) $(1 + i)^{20} + (1 - i)^{20} = 2^{11}\cos 5\pi$

   (iii) $\left(\frac{1 + \sin\theta + i\cos\theta}{1 + \sin\theta - i\cos\theta}\right)^n = = \cos(\frac{\pi}{2} - \theta)n + i\sin\left(\frac{\pi}{2} - \theta\right)n$

   (iv) $e^{\pm i\theta} = \cos n\theta \pm i\sin n\theta$, (Formul Euler. Hint: Use Taylor series for $e^{\pm i\theta}$)

   (v) $e^{i\arctan(\frac{1}{2})} = \frac{2 + i}{\sqrt{5}}$.

7. Use identity, $1 + z + z^2 + \ldots + z^n = \frac{1 - z^n}{1 - z}$, and prove that,

$$1 + \cos\theta + \cos 2\theta + \ldots + \cos n\theta = \frac{1}{2} + \frac{\sin(n + \frac{1}{2})\theta}{2\sin\frac{\theta}{2}}.$$

8. Show that the hyperbola $x^2 - y^2 = 1$ can be written as $z^2 + \bar{z}^2 = 2$.
9. Write the expression $(1+a^2)(1+b^2)(1+c^2)$ as the sum of two complete squares.

10. Show that any complex number with modulus 1, except, z=-1, can be written as $z = \frac{1+it}{1-it}$.
11. Prove by method of induction that, $(\cos\theta + i\sin\theta)^n = \cos n\theta + i\sin n\theta$.
12. Show that the equation

$$\left(\frac{1+iz}{1-iz}\right)^n = a + ib, a, b \in \mathbb{R}, n \in \mathbb{N}$$

has real roots if and only if, $a^2+b^2=1$.

13. Suppose, $z = \cos\theta + i\sin\theta$. Show that $z^n + z^{-n} = 2\cos n\theta$, then prove that the equation, $3z^4 - z^3+2z^2 - z=1$ has not real roots.
14. Show that if the real parameter t changes from 0 to 1, then the point $z_1+t(z_2 - z_1)$ describes a line that connects z_1 to z_2.
15. Use De Moivre's formula and show that

$$\cos(n\cos^{-1}x) = \frac{1}{2}[\left(x + \sqrt{x^2-1}\right)^n + \left(x - \sqrt{x^2-1}\right)^n, n \in \mathbb{N}, -1 \leq x \leq 1.$$

16. **(*Optional*).** The *cross product* and the *dot product* of z_1 and z_2, denoted by $z_1 \times z_1$ and $z_1 \odot z_2$ respectively, are defined by

$$z_1 \times z_2 = |z_1||z_2|\sin\alpha = x_1y_2 - y_1x_2$$

$$z_1 \odot z_2 = |z_1||z_2|\cos\alpha = x_1x_2 + y_1y_2$$

Where α is the angle between z_1 and z_2. Show that
(i) $z_1 \times z_2 = Im(\bar{z}_1 z_2)$
(ii) $z_1 \odot z_2 = Re(\bar{z}_1 z_2)$
(iii) if $z_1 \times z_2 = 0$, then z_1 is parall to z_2
(iv) if $z_1 \odot z_2 = 0$, then z_1 is perpendicular to z_2
(v) The area of a parallelgram with sides z_1 and z_2 is $|z_1 \times z_2|$.

17. **(*Optional*).** If A,B and C are the sets of complex numbers, we define $A \cup B$ a set which consists of points belonging either to A or B or both. Similarly, we define $A \cap B$ a set which consists of points belonging to both A and B. If

$$A = \{1+i, 3, 4-i, 2i, 1-i\}, B = \{1-i, 2, 4-i, 2i, 1+3i\}, C = \{1-i, 3, i, 2i, \}.$$

Find $A \cup B, A \cap B, B \cup (A \cap C)$ and $(A \cap B) \cup (A \cap C)$

18. Draw the graphs of the following curves.
    (i) $r sin\theta = a$
    (ii) $r cos\theta = a$
    (iii) $r = 4 + 3\cos\theta$
    (iv) $r = 4\sin 3\theta$
    (v) $r = 4 + 3cos\theta$
    (vi) $r = 4sin3\theta$
    (vii) $r = a^2\sin 2\theta$
    (viii) $r = e^{\theta}$
19. Find the tangent line at point $P\left(6,\frac{3\pi}{2}\right)$ on curve r=-6sinθ.
20. Find slop of the tangent line at point $P\left(a,\frac{\pi}{4}\right)$ on curve $r=a$.
21. Show that the cardioids $r = a(1 + sin\theta)$ and $r = a(1 - sin\theta)$ are perpendicular at each point of intersection.
22. Find the area of 1-petaled rose of $r = 4\sin 3\theta$.
23. Find the area of the region between inside the lemniscate $r^2 = 2sin\theta$ and outside the circle r=1
24. Find the area of the common region between inside the circle $r = acos\theta$ and the cardioids $r = a(1 - cos\theta), a > 0$.
25. Find the area of the region between inside of one loop of $r = a\sin n\theta$, where n is a natural number.
26. Prove the distance between two points $A(r_1,\theta_1)$ and $B(r_2,\theta_2)$ can be obtained by the following formula:

$$\sqrt{r_1^{\,2} + r_2^{\,2} + 2r_1r_2\cos(\theta_2 - \theta_1)}.$$

27. Find the length of the spiral $r = k\theta$ from $A(0,0)$ to $B\left(\frac{\pi}{2},\frac{\pi}{2}\right)$.
28. Find the length of the circle $r=a$ from $A(a,0)$ to $B\left(a,\frac{\pi}{2}\right)$.
29. Find the length of the curve $r = ae^{\theta}$ from θ=0 to $\theta = \frac{\pi}{2}$.
30. Find the area of the surface of revolution generated by reotating $r = 2acos\theta$ from θ=0 to $\theta = \frac{\pi}{2}$ from θ=0 to $\theta = \frac{\pi}{2}$ about the x- axis.

REFERENCES

Ablowitz, Mark J & Fokas, A. S. (2003). Complex Variable: Introduction and Applications.(2nd ed). Cambridge University Press.

Churchill, J., & Ward, B. (1988). *Complex Variables and Applications* (4th ed.). Mc Graw-Hill Co.

Jameson, G. J. O. (1970). *A First Course on Complex Functions*. Chapman and Hall. DOI: 10.1007/978-94-009-5680-3

Leithold, L. (1981). *The Calculus and Analytical Geometry* (4th ed.). Harper & Row.

Piskunov, N. (1981). Differential and Integral, Vol 1 (4th ed). MIR Publisher.

Silverman, Richard A. (1974). Complex Analysis with Applications. Prentice-Hall, INC.

Silverman. Richard, A. (1985). *Calculus with Analytical Geometry* (4th ed.). Prentice-Hall, Inc.

Stewart, J. (2008). *Calculus* (6th ed.). Mc-Graw.

Tall, D. O. (1971). *Functions of a Complex Variable* (1st ed.). Springer.

Thomas. George, B. (2014). *Calculus* (13th ed.). Mc-Graw.

Chapter 9
Differential and Difference Equations

ABSTRACT

This chapter focuses on solutions of linear ordinary differential equations with order one and two. After introducing some basic concepts of ordinary differential equations, we discuss some methods to solve different types of such equations. We apply these methods to solve several problems we encounter in science. To avoid power series methods to solve linear ordinary differential equations, a further analytical method will be offered to solve such equations. We also introduced difference equations and defined some concepts similar to linear ordinary differential equations. After introducing a couple of methods to solve them, we use these methods to solve some applicable problems with discrete variables.

9.1 INTRODUCTION

Differential and difference equations arise in many areas of social science, economics, and management. Most natural laws can be stated in the form of differential equations. Their applications in economics and management allow businesses to analyze complex systems, optimize decision-making processes, and improve overall efficiency and effectiveness in various aspects of business operations.

Differential equations deal with continuous functions while difference equations work on discrete functions. Difference equations are very much analogous to differential equations. Most concepts and methods of solutions for the difference equations are the same for differential equations. Considering that differential equations are more important than difference equations, we start this chapter with a discussion of differential equations.

DOI: 10.4018/979-8-3693-3657-1.ch009

A differential equation is a mathematical equation for an unknown function of one or several variables that relates the values of the function itself and its derivatives of different order. For example,

(i) $y' = ay - by^3$
(ii) $y'' = k\sqrt{1 + y'^2}$
(iii) $\frac{\partial^2 u}{\partial x^2} + \frac{\partial^2 u}{\partial y^2} = 0$
(iv) $\frac{dP}{dt} = m(Q_d - Q_s)$
(v) $\frac{dT}{dt} = rT\left(1 - \frac{T}{k}\right)$,

are examples of differential equations. Eq. (*i*) will be dealt with in the study of population dynamics. Eq.(*ii*) has a wide range of applications in the field of mechanics of simple harmonics. Eq. (*iii*) is the famous Laplace's equation which is found in heat, potential theory, gravitation, and aerodynamics. Eq. (*iv*) arises in economics for the demand function and supply function, where $\frac{dP}{dt}$ is the rate of change of price in the market. Eq. (*v*) is known as the Verhulst equation and occurs in problems of cancer researchers.

We consider some of these equations later and solve them. Of course, many differential equations arise from various fields from which they are taken, but we try to examine a number of them in this book that are in some way representative of real life and can be solved theoretically.

9.2. BASIC CONCEPTS OF DIFFERENTIAL EQUATIONS

If a differential equation contains a single independent variable, the equation is called an *ordinary differential equation* (ODE). If there is more than one independent variable, it is called a *partial differential equation* (PDE). From the above example, (iii) is a PDE and the other are ODEs.

The *order* of a differential equation is the order of the highest derivative occurring in the equation and the *degree* of a differential equation is the highest-ordered derivative that occurs. For example, Eqs (ii) and (iv) are with degree two. The other equations are with degree one.

We say a differential equation is *linear* if the dependent variable and its derivatives are the degree of one. For example, except Eq.(ii) which is nonlinear, the other four equations are linear. Although we mentioned one partial differential equation in our examples, the main target of this chapter is to consider ODEs. Therefore, whenever we talk about differential equations, we mean ordinary differential equations.

In general, any ODE of order n can be written in the form

$$f(x, y, y', y'', \ldots, y^{(n)}) = 0. \tag{1}$$

A *solution* of a differential equation is a relation between dependent and independent variables without the presence of any derivative. The function $y = \phi(x)$ is to be said an *explicit solution* of Eq. (1) on some interval, say, $a < x < b$, if y and its derivatives are substituted into (1), the resulting expression is an identity. An *implicit solution* of Eq. (1) is of the form $G(x,y) = 0$.

A linear differential equation of order n, i.e.,

$$a_n(x)y^{(n)} + a_{n-1}(x)y^{(n-1)} + \ldots + a_2(x)y'' + a_1(x)y' + a_1(x) = 0 \tag{2}$$

has a *family of solutions* in the form of

$$y(x) = c_1y_1 + c_2y_2 + \cdots + c_ny_n \tag{3}$$

where $c_1, c_2, \ldots, c_n$ are arbitrary constants and $y_1, y_2, \ldots, y_n$ are solutions of Eq.(2). We claim that the linear combination of all solutions of a linear ODE is also a solution. This solution is known as a *general solution*.

Example 1: Show that the family of solutions given by

$$y(x) = c_1x + c_2x^3 + \frac{c_3}{x^2},$$

is a general solution of linear ODE given by

$$x^3y''' - 2x^2y'' - 5xy' + 6y = 0.$$

Solution: We have, $y' = c_1 + 3c_2x^2 - \frac{2c_3}{x^3}, y'' = 6c_2x + \frac{6c_3}{x^4}$ and $y''' = 6c_2 - \frac{24c_3}{x^5}$, respectively. By substituting y, y', y'' and y''' in the given equation, it can be seen that the given family of solutions is a general solution for this equation. This is also a closed-form solution for a given equation.

We may wish to seek a solution $y = \phi(x)$ such that $y_0 = \phi(x_0)$. This condition is called an *initial condition*. A differential equation with an initial condition is called an *initial value problem*. An initial value problem for a nth-order differential equation consists of a set of n algebraic conditions at a common point:

$$y(x_0) = y_0, y'(x_0) = y_1, \ldots, y^{(n-1)}(x_0) = y_{n-1}.$$

The conditions are called boundary conditions if they relate to both endpoints $x=a$ and $x=b$. An ODE with boundary conditions is called a *boundary value problem.* If we impose some conditions (such as initial or boundary conditions) on a given differential equation, it leads to one solution, called a *particular solution* (or *specific solution*), from a family of solutions. The linear combination of particular solutions is the general solution. For example, $y_1=x$, $y_2=x^3$ and $y_3 = \frac{1}{x^2}$ are solution functions of the above equation. Thus, they are particular solutions. When we talk about the general solution, it means that any choice of constant gives a specific solution, but for a nonlinear ordinary differential equation, we find a solution that does not arise from a general solution. We call this solution a *singular solution* which is not part of the family of solutions. Since the general solution is a collection of all solutions of differential equations, hence in this book we do not use the term "general solution" for a nonlinear ordinary differential equation. We use the term "singular solution", rather than "general solution".

Example 2: Show that, $y=cx-c^3$, is a family of solutions for $3(y')^3 - xy' + y = 0$, but $y = \frac{2}{9}x^{\frac{2}{3}}$ is a singular solution for this equation.

Solution: From the given equation we obtain $y'=c$. A simple substitution for y and y' in the equation, it can be seen that $y=cx-c^3$, is the family of solutions for this equation. It is easy to show that, $y = \frac{2}{9}x^{\frac{2}{3}}$ is also a singular solution, because this solution cannot be obtained from this family with any choice of c.

In this chapter, we discuss the solutions to first and second-order ODEs. For more information, readers may refer to (Boyce & Diprima, 1977) (Hermann & Saravi, 2014) (Tensnbaum & Pollard, 1964)(Merice & Goldberg, 1978) (Rainville & Bedint, 1974).

9.3. FIRST ORDER ORDINARY DIFFERENTIAL EQUATIONS

If in Eq. (1) we choose, $n=4$, then, we get

$$f(x, y, y') = 0 \tag{4}$$

which is a first-order differential equation.

Since Eq. (4) is order one, then we may guess the solution (if it exists) contains a constant c. That is, the family of solutions will be in the form

$$F(x, y, c) = 0. \tag{5}$$

In other words, if we could write Eq. (2) as $y'=g(x,y)$, then we would search for a family of solutions $y=G(x,c)$. As we mentioned in the previous section, constant c can be specified by a given condition. One way to solve Eq. (4) involves an analytical solution that uses indefinite integration, whereas the second involves computationally intensive numerical methods that approach the problem using easily applied techniques of definite integration. For example, if the changes in a function concerning time are proportional to the function itself, i.e. $\frac{df}{dt} = kf$, then by writing it as $\frac{df}{f} = kdt$ and integrating the sides, we can conclude that,

$$\int\frac{df}{f} = \int kdt \rightarrow \ln f = kt + c.$$

That is, $f = e^{kt+c} = e^c e^{kt} = c_0 e^{kt}$, where $c_0=e^c$ is the initial state of the function at $t=0$.

9.3.1. Solution of First-Order ODEs

The equation we solved was a type of linear ODE. But we always have such a simple one. Our main task is to find analytical solutions of Eq. (4) because there is no general method for writing down solutions of Eq. (4) unless this equation is linear. We are going to introduce some analytical methods, known as elementary methods, based on integration. But first, it is convenient to write Eq. (4) as

$$M(x,y)dx + N(x,y)dy = 0. \tag{6}$$

This equation can be solved in the following cases:

(i) Separable Equations

If Eq. (6) can be put in the form of, $M(x)dx+N(y)dy=0$ we say the variables are separable, and the solution can be obtained by integrating both sides concerning x. That is,

$$\int M(x)dx + \int N(y(x))\frac{dy}{dx}.dx = c,$$

or for simplicity, one can write

$$\int M(x)dx + \int N(y)dy = c$$

.

Example 3: Find the general solution of $xy'+(1+y^2)=0$.
Solution: The given equation can be written as

$$\frac{dy}{1+y^2} = xdx.$$

Integration yields

$$\tan^{-1}y = \frac{x^2}{2} + c,$$

whence

$$y = \tan\left(\frac{x^2}{2} + c\right)$$

Example 4: Find the particular solution of $(1+y)dx+\cot x dy=0$, $y(0)=0$.

Solution: We write, $\frac{dy}{1+y} = \tan x dx$ and integrate. We obtain, $\ln(1+y)=\ln(\cos x-)+c$. Use $y(0)=0$. This leads to $c=0$. Thus, $\ln(1+y)=\ln(\cos x)$. That is, $y=\cos x-1$.

The decay problem occurs in various fields like the decay of radioactive elements in physics and chemistry. Some other typical examples are the human population, certain kinds of investment interest, bacteria in a culture and tumor growth of cancer cells, in particular breast and ovarian cancer cells. Let's consider a quantity $Q=Q(t)$ which Q is the amount of the quantity at time t. If Q has an exponential decay model, then

$$\frac{dQ}{dt} = -kQ, k > 0,$$

where the minus sign shows that Q decreases at a rate proportional to Q. If at the time, say, $t=0$, the amount of Q is Q_0, what relation can be made about the amount available at any time t? If we rewrite the differential equation as

$$\frac{dQ}{Q} = -kdt,$$

hence, the variables are separable. Taking integration, leads to,

$$\ln Q = -kt + \ln c \Rightarrow \ln\frac{Q}{c} = -kt \Rightarrow Q = ce^{-kt}.$$

Initial condition $Q(0)=Q_0$, gives, $c=Q_0$. Thus $Q=Q_0e^{-kt}$.
Later, we will consider more of such equations in applications of ODEs.

(ii) Homogeneous Equations

Definition 1: We call $f(x,y)$ homogeneous of degree k if $f(tx,ty)=t^k f(x,y)$, for some non-zero constant k.

If in Eq. (6), $M(x,y)$ and $N(x,y)$ have the same degree, or $f(x,y)$ is a degree of zero, then substitution $z = \frac{y}{x}$ will reduce the equation to separable form. Let $y=xz$, then $y'=z+xz'$; substituting into equation gives $z+xz'=f(z)$. Now separate the variables, we obtain

$$\frac{dz}{f(z) - z} = \frac{dx}{x}$$

That is, the variables are separable.

Example 5: Solve,

$$y' = \frac{x + 3y}{y + 3x}.$$

Solution: Since degree of $f(x,y) = \frac{x + 3y}{y + 3x}$ is zero, hence substitution $y=xz$ and $y'=z+xz'$ leads to $z + xz' = \frac{1 + 3z}{z + 3}$. Thus, $\left(\frac{3}{1 - z^2} + \frac{z}{1 - z^2}\right)dz = \frac{dx}{x}$. Integrating yields, $\tanh^{-1} z - \frac{3}{2}\ln(1 - z^2) = \ln x + c$.

Since $z = \frac{y}{x}$, then,

$$\tanh^{-1}\left(\frac{y}{x}\right) - \frac{3}{2}\ln\left(1 - \left(\frac{y}{x}\right)^2\right) = \ln x + c.$$

Example 6: Find the general solution of $y' = \frac{xy}{x^2 - y^2}$.

Solution: Since degree of xy and $x^2 - y^2$ are 2, then degree of $f(x,y) = \frac{xy}{x^2 - y^2}$ is zero. Hence substitution $y=xz$ and $y'=z+xz'$ leads to

$$z + xz' = \frac{z}{1 - z^2} \Rightarrow xz' = \frac{z}{1 - z^2} \Rightarrow \left(\frac{1}{z^2} - \frac{1}{z}\right)dz = \frac{dx}{x}.$$

Integrating, yields, $-\frac{1}{z} - \ln z = \ln x + \ln c = \ln cx$. But $z = \frac{y}{x}$, then,

$$\ln cx + \frac{x^2}{y^2} = 0$$

(iii) Exact Equations

Definition 2: We say that the Eq. (6) is exact if,

$$\frac{\partial}{\partial y}M(x,y) = \frac{\partial}{\partial x}N(x,y). \tag{7}$$

By this definition, we say Eq. (7) is *exact* if, $M(x,y)dx+N(x,y)dy$ is the total differential of $z(x,y)$. Therefore, the equation may be written as $dz=0$.

Theorem 1. If $M(x,y)$ and $N(x,y)$ have continuous first partial derivative over some domain D, then Eq. (6) is exact if and only if $M_y=N_x$.

Remark 1: A technique to solve an exact equation is as follows:

(i) Write an equation in three terms. One in terms of x, another one in terms of y, and the last one in terms of x and y. That is

$$A(x)dx + B(y)dy + [C(x,y)dx + D(x,y)dy] = 0.$$

(ii) Integrate term by term concerning x and y, and x or y, respectively. For the last term, it depends on what we choose $C(x,y)dx$ or $D(x,y)dy$. Since the equation is exact, then

$$C(x,y)dx + D(x,y)dy = dF(x,y).$$

Example 7: Find the Solution of the following initial value problem

$$(e^x - y)dx + (y - x)dy = 0, y(0) = 0.$$

Solution: We have, $M(x,y)=e^x-y$ and $N(x,y)=y-x$. Thus, the equation is exact according to the condition $M_y=N_x=-1$. To solve this equation, first, we write it in the form

$$(e^x)dx +)+(y)dy + (-ydx - xdy) = 0,$$

and then, integrate it. We obtain

$$\int(e^x)dx + \int(y)dy - \int(ydx + xdy) = c.$$

We can easily show that the corresponding solution according to this equation is given by

$$e^x + \frac{y^2}{2} - xy = c.$$

To satisfy the initial condition $y(0)=0$, we must choose $c=1$. Hence

$$e^x + \frac{y^2}{2} - xy = 1$$

(iv) Non-Exact Equations

Let's get back to Eq. (6) and assume it is not exact. That is, $M_y \neq N_x$. Finding a solution in this case may be difficult or impossible, even if there exists a solution. But, sometimes Eq. (6) may be made exact by multiplying it by a function $F(x,y)$ ($\neq 0$) called an *integrating factor* that usually is not unique. If such a function exists, then the modified differential equation, that is, $M(x,y)+F(x,y)N(x,y)=0$, will be exact. Therefore, $(FM)_y=(FN)_x$. In other words, $MF_y+FM_y=NF_x+FN_x$. We can rewrite it as

$$(NF_x - MF_y)/F = M_y - N_x. \tag{8}$$

This is a first-order partial differential equation that may have more than one solution. Obtaining such solutions will be more difficult than the original equation (7). Fortunately, if we restrict the integrating factor to a single variable function in terms of x or y, we can find F. Suppose $F=F(x)$ then $F_y=0$ and equation (9) reduces to $dF/F=(M_y-N_x)/N$. Then, in this case

$$F = e^{\int ((M_y-N_x)/N)dx} \tag{9}$$

Similarly, if $F=F(y)$ then, $F_x=0$, and we

$$F = e^{-\int ((M_y-N_x)/M)dy} \tag{10}$$

Thus, we can say that,

(i) $F=F(x)$ if, $(M_y-N_x)/N$ is a function of x and,
(ii) $F=F(y)$ if, $(M_y-N_x)/M$ is a function of y.

Example 8: Determine a particular solution of the differential equation $\sin y \cos x dx+\cos y(\sin y - \sin x)dy=0$.

Solution: We have $M_y=\cos x \cos y$, and $N_x= -\cos x \cos y$, hence equation is not exact but $(M_y-N_x)/M=2\cot y=g(y)$. Thus

$$F(y) = e^{-\int g(y)dy} = e^{\int -2\cot y dy} = e^{-2\ln(\sin y)} = 1/sin^2 y.$$

Multiplying differential equation by $1/\sin^2 y$, we get

$$\frac{\cos x}{\sin y}dx + \frac{\cos y}{\sin^2 y}(\sin y - \sin x)dy = 0.$$

This equation is exact. Rewrite it as

$$\left(\frac{\cos y}{\sin y}dy\right) + \left(\frac{\cos x}{\sin y}dx - \frac{\cos y \sin x}{\sin^2 y}dy\right) = 0,$$

and integrating both sides. The corresponding solution according to this equation will be

$$\ln(\sin y) + \frac{\sin x}{\sin y} = c.$$

To determine the particular solution satisfying the initial value condition we substitute $x=0$ and $y = \pi/2$ into this family of solutions. We obtain $c=0$. Hence the solution will be

$$\ln(\sin y) + \frac{\sin x}{\sin y} = 0$$

Example 9: Determine a particular solution of the following differential equation

$$y(8x - 9y)dx + 2x(x - 3y)dy = 0.$$

Solution: We have, $M=y(8x-9y)$ and $N=2x(x-3y)$, hence $M_y=8x18y$ and $N_x=4x-6y$. The equation is not exact but $(M_y-N_x)/N=2/x=f(x)$.

Thus

$$F(x) = e^{\int f(y)dy} = e^{\int(2/x)dx} = e^{2\ln x} = x^2.$$

Multiplying differential equation by x^2, we get

$$x^2y(8x - 9y)dx + 2x^3(x - 3y)dy = 0.$$

This equation is exact. Rewrite it as

$$(8x^3ydx + 2x^4dy) - (9x^2y^2dx + 6x^3ydy) = 0,$$

and integrating both sides. The corresponding solution according to this equation will be

$$2x^4y - 3x^3y^2 = c$$

(v) Linear Equations

The general form of a first-order linear differential equation is given by

$$y' + p(x)y = q(x). \tag{11}$$

When, $q(x)=0$, then the equation reduces to a separable equation. Assume $q(x)\neq 0$ and consider Eq. (11). This equation is not exact, but it can easily be shown that it has an integrating factor given by

$$F(x) = e^{\int p(x)dx}.$$

Multiply the given equation by this factor, then we get

$$(y' + p(x)y) = e^{\int p(x)dx}.q(x) \tag{12}$$

This equation is exact. Integrate both sides. We get

$$e^{\int p(x)dx}.y = \int e^{\int p(x)dx}.q(x)dx + c.$$

Hence

$$y = e^{-\int p(x)dx}.\int e^{\int p(x)dx}.q(x)dx + c\,e^{-\int p(x)dx}, \tag{13}$$

which is the general solution to Eq. (12).

Remark 2: Always integration of the left-hand side of Eq. (13) will be: $y(x)\times F(x)$.

Example 10: Solve $y'+y\cot x=\operatorname{cosec} x$.

Solution: We have, $p(x)=\cot x$. Hence,

$$F(x) = e^{\int p(x)dx} = e^{\int(\cot x)dx} = e^{\ln x \sin x} = \sin x.$$

We multiply both sides second equation by $\sin x$. We obtain $\sin x(y'+y\cot x)=1$. By a simple integration, we come to $y\sin x=x+c$. Thus, $y = \frac{x+c}{\sin x}$

(vi) Reducible Equations

Some nonlinear differential equations may be reduced to linear or separable equations by forming the dependent variable $z=g(y)$. The most common examples of such equations are Bernoulli and Riccati equations.

(a) Bernoulli Equation

The general form of a Bernoulli equation is given by

$$y' + p(x)y = q(x)y^n, \tag{14}$$

where n is a real number. Applications of this equation are in the study of population dynamics and hydrodynamic stability. When, $n=0$ or 1, this equation reduces to a linear equation. Thus we assume $n\neq 0$, or 1.

If we let $z = y^{1-n}$ then $z' = (1-n)y'y^{2-n}$. That is, $y' = \frac{1-n}{y^{2-n}}z'$. Substituting in Eq. (15). Therefore, in terms of z and x, Eq. 15 reduces to

$$z' + (1-n)p(x)z = (1-n)q(x), \tag{15}$$

which is a first-order linear differential equation.

Example 11: Solve $2xyy'=y^2-2x^3$.

Solution: We write the equation in the form

$$y' - \frac{2}{x}y = -x^2y^{-1}.$$

This is a Bernoulli equation with, n=-1, hence $z = y^{1-(-1)} = y^2$. Substituting in Bernoulli equation, we obtain

$$z' - \frac{1}{x}z = -2x^2.$$

It is not difficult to show that the general solution for this equation is, $\frac{z}{x} = -x^2 + c$. Since $z=y^2$, then, $y^2/x=-x^2+c$,or $y=x(c-x^2)$

(b) *Riccati Equation*

The general form of a Ricatti equation is given by

$$y' + p(x)y = q(x)y^2 + r(x). \tag{16}$$

It is clear that if $r(x)=0$we will have a Bernoulli equation with $n=2$. Therefore, we assume $r(x)\neq 0$. Eq. (16) cannot be solved by elementary methods, but if a particular solution of Eq. (16), call y_1, is known, then the solution of this equation can be obtained through the substitution, $y = y_1 + \frac{1}{z}$, where z is the general solution of $z'+(2qy_1 - p)z=-q$.

Example 12: Show that, $y=\cos x$ is a particular solution to the equation $(1-\sin x \cos x)y'-y+\cos x.y^2= -\sin x$, then, solve this equation.

Solution: We have, $y=\cos x$, hence $y'= -\sin x$. Substituting in equation leads to $(1 - \sin x \cos x)(-\sin x) - \cos x+\cos x.(\cos x)^2= -\sin x+\sin^2 x \cos x - \cos x+\cos x(1 - \sin^2 x)= -\sin x$. Thus, $y=\cos x$ is a particular solution for this equation. Now, let $y = \cos x + \frac{1}{z}$ then $y' = -\sin x - \frac{z'}{z^2}$. Substituting in the equation, we get

$$\left(1 - \sin x \cos x\right)\left(-\sin x - \frac{z'}{z^2}\right) - \left(\cos x + \frac{1}{z}\right)+\cos x\left(\cos x + \frac{1}{z}\right)^2 = -\sin x.$$

By simplifying this expression, we obtain

$$(1 - \sin x \cos x)z' + (1 - 2\cos^2 x)z = \cos x.$$

Since, $(1-\sin x \cos x)' = 1-2\cos^2 x$, then by integrating we get

$$z = \frac{\sin x + c}{1 - \sin x \cos x}.$$

We also have, $y = \cos x + \frac{1}{z}$, that is, $z = \frac{1}{y - \cos x}$. Therefore,

$$y = \frac{c \cos x - 1}{c - \sin x}$$

Remark 3: Another choice for $y(x)$ is to write $y(x)=y_1(x)+z(x)$, where $z(x)$ is the family of solution of the equation $z'+(p - 2qy_1)=qz^2$.

***Example 13*:** Solve $y'+2xy=y^2+x^2+1$, if its particular solution is given by $y_1(x)=x$.

Solution: Let, $y=x+z$ then, $y'=1+z'$. Substituting in the equation we obtain $z'=z^2$.

It is not difficult to show that the family of solution of this equation will be $z = \frac{1}{c - x}$. That is, $y = x + \frac{1}{c - x}$

(vii) Method of Change of Variable

Most of the time a desire to change variables may be useful to solve a differential equation. This choice can be $z=g(x)$ or $z=h(y)$. Although the choice of variables is a little bit difficult most of the time, the presence of variables helps us see what will be better to choose.

Example 14: Solve,

$$y' - \frac{ylny}{x+1} = (x+1)y, y(0) = 1.$$

Solution: Because of ln$y$ one can guess $z=\ln y$ or $y=e^z$. Hence, $y'=e^z z'$. Substituting, y and y' in the differential equation and simplify it. We get

$$z' - \frac{z}{x+1} = x+1.$$

This is a linear equation and can be shown that its particular solution is $z=x(x+1)$. Since $y=e^z$ hence $y = e^{x(x+1)}$

Example 15: Solve $xyy' = 6(3y^2+2) + x(3y^2+2)^2$.

Solution: The presence of $(3y^2+2)$ causes us to choose, $z=3y^2+2$. Hence $z'=6yy'$. If we substitute in differential equation, after simplification, we obtain

$$z' = \frac{z}{x} + \frac{1}{6}z^2,$$

which is a Bernoulli equation with $n=2$. Let $t = z^{1-2} = z^{-1}$ then we get

$$xt' + t = -\frac{1}{6}x.$$

The general solution of this linear equation can easily be found. One can show that $t = \frac{c}{x} - \frac{x}{12}$. Since $t=z^{-1}=(3y^2+2)^{-1}$ then, the required solution is given by

$$(3y^2+2)^{-1} = \frac{c}{x} - \frac{x}{12}$$

9.3.2. Family of Curves. Orthogonal Trajectories

Recall Eq. (5) $F(x,y,x)=0$.

In this equation, for each value of c, it represents a curve in the xy-plane. If for c it represents infinitely many curves, then the totality of these curves is called the *family of curves*. In many engineering applications, we may think of another family of curves that intersect each member of the given family at right angles. We say that these two families are *mutually orthogonal* and the curves of the family to be obtained are called *the orthogonal trajectories*.

For finding orthogonal trajectories of any family of curves given by Eq.(5), we follow the following procedure:

First, we find the differential equation associated with Eq. (3), that is, $y'=f(x,y)$. Let $m=f(x,y)$, then $m'=-1/f(x,y)$, where m and m' are the slope of these two families, respectively. Therefore, we conclude that the differential equation of the orthogonal trajectories will be

$$y' = -1/f(x,y) \tag{17}$$

The solution of Eq. (17) is a family of curves orthogonal to curves given by Eq. (5).

***Example 16*:** Find orthogonal trajectories of $x^2+y^2=c$.

Solution: We have, $x^2+y^2=c$. Differentiate with respect to x, we obtain $m=y'=-x/y$. Then, $m'y'=y/x$. By writing this equation in the form of $dy/y=dx/x$ and integrating it, we get

$$\ln y = \ln x + \ln c = \ln cx \rightarrow y = cx.$$

This is orthogonal trajectories of $x^2+y^2=c$

***Example 17*:** Find orthogonal trajectories of $y=c(\sec x+\tan x)$.

Solution: We write, $\frac{y}{\sec x + \tan x)} = c$. Differentiate with respect to x, we get,

$$\frac{y'(\sec x + \tan x) - y(\sin x \sec^2 x + \sec^2 x)}{(\sec x + \tan x)^2} = \frac{(1 + \sin x)y'\sec x - y\sec^2 x(\sin x + 1)}{\sec^2 x(1 + \sin x)^2}$$

$$= \frac{y'\sec x - y\sec^2 x}{\sec x(1 + \sin x)} = 0 \rightarrow y'\sec x - y\sec^2 x = 0 \rightarrow y' = \frac{\sec x}{y}.$$

Thus, $m' = y' = -\frac{y}{\sec x}$. By writing this equation in the form of $yy'=-\cos x$ and integrating it, we obtain

$$\frac{y^2}{2} = c - \cos x \rightarrow y^2 = 2(c - \cos x).$$

9.4. SECOND ORDER ORDINARY DIFFERENTIAL EQUATIONS

Recall Eq. (1), $f(x,y, y', y'', \ldots, y^{(n)})=0$.

If we choose $n=2$, then the equation

$$f(x,y,y',y'') = 0, \tag{18}$$

is a second-order differential equation. For the first-order differential equation, we found that its solution contains one arbitrary constant, but for the second-order the solution must contain two arbitrary constants because two integrations are required to obtain a solution. In general, finding the family of solutions for Eq. (2) is difficult and in more cases impossible, particularly when the equation is nonlinear. For this reason, in this chapter, we deal with linear ones because of their importance in engineering and applied science.

The general form of any second-order linear ODEs is given by

$$P(x)y'' + Q(x)y' + R(x)y = S(x), \tag{19}$$

where, $P(x)$, $Q(x)$, $R(x)$ and $S(x)$ are given continues functions on $a<x<b$.

Suppose that in this interval $P(x) \neq 0$, then we may write Eq. (5) in the form

$$y'' + p(x)y' + q(x)y = r(x), \tag{20}$$

where $p(x) = \frac{Q(x)}{P(x)}, q(x) = \frac{R(x)}{P(x)}$ and $r(x) = \frac{S(x)}{P(x)}$.

If $r(x)=0$, then we have

$$y'' + p(x)y' + q(x)y = 0, \tag{21}$$

which is a *homogeneous* or *complementary equation*. We set out here that the concept of homogeneous is not related to its use in the previous chapter. To solve Eq. (20), it is necessary to solve its homogeneous one first, given by (21).

The existence and uniqueness theorem for second-order linear differential equations can be stated as follows:

Theorem 2 (*Fundamental theorem*). If the functions $p(x)$, $q(x)$ and $r(x)$ continue on some interval $a<x<b$, then Eq. (6) with initial conditions, $y(x_0)=y_0$ and $y'(x_0)=y_1$ where $x_0 \epsilon (a,b)$ has one, and only one solution, $y=\phi(x)$ satisfies Eq. (21).

If y_1 and y_2 are two solutions of Eq. (21), then,

$$y(x) = c_1y_1 + c_2y_2 \tag{22}$$

is a general solution for Eq. (21). We can prove that y_1 and y_2 constitute a basis of solutions for Eq. (7).

9.4.1 Methods of Solution for Homogeneous Equations

As we mentioned in the previous section, finding the general solution of linear homogeneous differential equations in terms of elementary functions is difficult and most of the time impossible. Fortunately, the general solution of the linear equations with constant coefficients can easily be obtained, and we keep in mind that the linear equations with constant coefficients are of great practical importance as well as of theoretical interest. But for linear equations with variable coefficients, there is no general form of solution. In this section, we try to introduce methods that can be used for second-order linear equations with specific properties. We begin with the homogeneous case with constant coefficients.

(i) Equations with Constant Coefficients

Consider the equation

$$L[y] = ay'' + by' + cy = 0, \tag{23}$$

where a,b and c are real numbers. Since y, y' and y'' differ only by constant multiplicative factors then we seek solutions of the form $y=e^{nx}$. Therefore, $y'=me^{mx}$ and $y''=m^2e^{mx}$. When these results are substituted into Eq. (34), we obtain, e^{mx}-$(am^2+bm+c)=0$.

Thus, e^{nx} is a solution of Eq. (23) if and only if

$$am^2 + bm + c = 0 \tag{24}$$

This equation is called the *characteristic equation* and has two roots, namely, m_1 and m_2. Then $y_1 = e^{m_1x}$ and $y_2 = e^{m_2x}$ are solutions of Eq. (23).

Remark 4: Comparison Eq. (23) with Eq. (24) shows that one can get Eq. (24) directly from Eq. (23) without substitution. The equation itself leads directly to Eq. (24).

Example 18: Find the general solution of $y'' - 3y' - 4y=0$.

Solution: We have $m^2 - 3m - 4=0$, whence m_1=-1 and m_2=4. Hence, $y(x) = c_1 e^{-x} + c_2 e^{4x}$

Remark 5: If $m_2 \neq m_1$, but are complex numbers, that is, $m=M \pm iN$ then the general solution of Eq. (23) may be written in the form

$$y(x) = e^{Mx}(c_1 e^{iNx} + c_2 e^{-iNx}). \tag{25}$$

Using Euler's identities, $e^{\pm iNx} = \cos Nx \pm i\sin Nx$, we may write Eq. (25) in the form of

$$y(x) = e^{Mx}(A\cos Nx + B\sin Nx). \quad (26)$$

where $A=c_1+ic_2$ and $B=c_1-ic_2$.

Example 19: Find the general solution of $y'+y=0$.

Solution: We have $m^2+1=0$, whence $m\pm i$. Thus, $y(x)=e^0(A\cos x+B\sin x)=A\cos x+B\sin x$.

Remark 6: If $m_2=m_1=m$, then $y_1=e^{mx}$ and we may obtain a second solution by the method of reduction of order (we describe this method in the next section). It can be shown that $y_2=xe^{mx}$. Hence $y(x)=(c_1+c_2x)e^{mx}$.

Example 20: Solve $4y''-4y'+y=0$.

Solution: The characteristic equation $4m^2-4m+1=0$ can be written in the form $(2m-1)^2=0$, that is, $m = \frac{1}{2}$. Hence, the solution is,

$$y(x) = (c_1 + c_2x)e^{\frac{x}{2}}$$

Example 21: Find the general solution of $y''' + y''-5y' + 3y = 0$.

Solution: We have

$$m^3 + m^2 - 5m + 3 = 0, \text{or}\,(m-1)^2(m+3) = 0 \rightarrow m_1 = m_2 = 1, m_3 = -3.$$

Thus, the general solution is:

$$y(x)= (c_1 + c_2x)e^x + c_3e^{-3x}$$

Remark 6: The Cauchy-Euler equation given by

$$ax^2y'' + bxy'+c = 0, \quad (26)$$

which is not an equation with constant coefficients. Let $x=e^t$, then $dx=e^t dt$. That is, $y'=\frac{1dy}{xdt}$. Similarly, it can be shown that, $y'' = \frac{1}{x^2}\left(\frac{d^2y}{dt^2} - \frac{dy}{dt}\right)$. Substitute y' and y'' into the Cauchy-Euler equation. We obtain

$$a\frac{d^2y}{dt^2} + (b-a)\frac{dy}{dt} + cy = 0. \quad (27)$$

This is an equation with constant coefficients. A more general form is

$$a(Ax+B)^2y'' + b(Ax+B)y' + cy = 0.$$

This equation can be transformed into one having constant coefficients by letting $ax+b=e^x$.

Example 22: Find the general solution of $x^2y'' - 4xy' + 6y = 0$.

Solution: Let $x=e^t$,then, we obtain

$$\frac{d^2y}{dt^2} - 5\frac{dy}{dt} + 6y = 0.$$

The characteristic equation is, $m^2 - 5m+6=0$. Thus, we get, $m_1=2$ and $m_2=3$. Thus, the general solution is,

$$y(x) = c_1e^{2t} + c_2e^{3t} = c_1x^2 + c_2x^3$$

(ii) Method of Reduction of Order

Recall Eq. (21), $y'' + p(x)y' + q(x)y = 0$ and suppose one of its solutions, namely, y_1 is known. Let's $y_2=uy_1$. It can be shown that

$$u = \int\left\{\exp\left[-\int^x p(t)dt\right]/y_1{}^2\right\}dx \tag{28}$$

Therefore, the general solution will be

$$y(x) = y_1\left\{c_1 + c_2\int\left\{\exp\left[-\int^x p(t)dt\right]/y_1{}^2\right\}dx\right\}. \tag{29}$$

Example 23: Show $y_1=e^x$ is a solution for

$$(x+1)y'' - (2x+3)y' + (x+2)y = 0.$$

Find the general solution.

Solution: We have $y_1 = y'_1 = y''_1 = e^x$. Substitute in the equation, we obtain

$$(x+1)e^x - (2x+3)e^x + (x+2)e^x = xe^x + e^x - 2xe^x - 3e^x + xe^x + 2e^x = 0.$$

Since $p = \frac{-(2x+3)}{x+1}$ then

$$u = \int\left\{\exp\left[-\int^x p(t)dt\right]/y_1{}^2\right\}dx = \int\frac{e^{\int\frac{2x+3}{x+1}dx}}{e^{2x}}dx = \int\frac{e^{2x+\ln(x+1)}}{e^{2x}}dx = \int(x+1)dx = \frac{(x+1)^2}{2}.$$

Using Eq. (28), we come to

$$y(x) = e^x[c_1 + c_2(x+1)^2]$$

Example 24: If $y_1=x^2$ is given for

$$x^2y'' + xy' - 4y = 0, x > 0,$$

find the general solution of this equation.
Solution: Since $p(x)=\frac{1}{x}$ then we get

$$u = \int \frac{\exp\left[-\int^x \frac{1}{t}dt\right]}{x^4}dx = \int \frac{1}{x^5}dx = -\frac{4}{x^4}.$$

Hence, $y_2 = uy_1 = -\frac{4}{x^2}$. That is,

$$y = c_1x^2 + c_2x^{-2}$$

We remind you that this equation is a Cauchy-Euler equation hence it can be solved as like a previous procedure. This means, some examples may also be solved by two or more, different methods.

(iii) Exact Equations

The concept of exactness in first-order differential equations can be extended to second-order linear ordinary differential equations. We call the equation

$$P(x)y'' + Q(x)y' + R(x)y = 0, \tag{30}$$

exact if,

$$P''(x) - Q'(x) + R(x) = 0. \tag{31}$$

If the equation is exact, then it can be proved that Eq. (22) may be written in the form

$$[P(x)y']' + [f(x)y]' = 0, \tag{32}$$

where $f(x)=Q(x) - P'(x)$.
Integrating Eq. (24) gives $f(x)=Q(x) - P'(x)$. That is,

$$P(x)y' + [Q(x) - P'(x)]y = c_1. \tag{33}$$

This is a first-order linear ordinary differential equation and can be easily solved.

Example 25: Find the general solution of

$$x(x-2)y''+4(x-1)y'+2y=0, x\neq 0,2.$$

Solution: We have,

$$P''(x)-Q'(x)+R(x)=2-4+2=0.$$

Therefore, the equation is exact. By Eq. (25), we have

$$x(x-2)y'+2(x-1)y=c_1.$$

By integration, we obtain $x(x-2)y=c_1x+c_2$. Hence

$$y=(c_1x+c_2)/x(x-2)$$

The idea of exactness can be extended to any order linear ordinary differential equation and prove that necessary and sufficient conditions for the equation

$$p_0(x)y^{(n)}+p_1(x)y^{(n-1)}+p_2(x)y^{(n-2)}+\ldots+p_{n-1}(x)y'+p_n(x)y=0$$

to be exact is

$$p_n(x)-p'_{n-1}(x)+p''_{n-2}(x)+\ldots+(-1)^n p_0{}^{(n)}(x)=0. \quad (34)$$

Example 26: Solve

$$xy'''+(x^2+x+3)y''+2(1+2x)y'+2y=0.$$

Solution: We have

$$p_0(x)=x, p_1(x)=x^2+x+3, p_2(x)=2(1+2x) \text{and} p_3(x)=2,$$

hence

$$p_3(x)-p'_2(x)+p''_1(x)+p'''_0(x)=2-4+2-0=0.$$

The equation is exact, so we can write

$$(xy'')' + [(x^2 + x + 3)y']' + [(1 + 2x)y]' = 0.$$

By integration, we get

$$xy'' + (x^2 + x + 3)y' + (1 + 2x)y = c_1.$$

This is a non-homogeneous equation which we will consider later. But if we choose $c_1=0$ then the equation

$$xy'' + (x^2 + x + 2)y' + (1 + 2x)y = 0,$$

is also an exact equation. Did we accidentally reach an exact equation? It was not an accident. When we reduce an order in any exact equation, the result is itself an exact equation. Therefore, we can use this property and solve inhomogeneous equations. First, we write an inhomogeneous equation as,

$$(xy')' + [(x^2 + x + 1)y]' = c_1.$$

Integrating this equation, we obtain

$$xy' + (x^2 + x + 1)y = c_1 x + c_2.$$

This is a first-order linear differential equation and can easily be solved.

9.4.2 Methods of Solution for Inhomogeneous Equations

Recall Eq. (20), $y'' + p(x)y' + q(x)y = r(x)$, where $p(x)$, $q(x)$ and $r(x)$ are continues functions on $a<x<b$. Let y_c denote the solution of the homogeneous equation reduced by Eq. (20). We call, henceforth, this solution a *complementary solution.* Furthermore, let y_p be any particular solution of Eq. (20), then it can be proved that $y=y_c+y_p$ is the solution of Eq. (20). We call this solution the general solution of Eq. (20).

Suppose we have a complementary solution. How can we find a particular solution? In this section, we introduce two common general methods for finding particular solutions, but the first one can be used just for equations with constant coefficients. The second method is a more general one for any form of Eq. (20).

(i) Method of Undetermined Coefficients

Let's, $r(x)$ is strictly limited to be

$$r(x) = e^{ax}\left(a_0x^n + a_1x^{n-1} + \ldots + a_n\right)\begin{cases} b_1 cos\beta x \\ b_2 sin\beta x. \end{cases} \tag{35}$$

Consider

$$ay'' + by' + cy = r(x), a, b, c \epsilon R. \tag{36}$$

We guess the particular solution has the form

$$y_p = e^{ax}\left(A_0x^n + A_1x^{n-1} + \ldots + A_n\right)(Acos\beta x + Bsin\beta x), \tag{37}$$

then, substituting y_p, y'_p and y''_p in given equation and compare the terms with those of $r(x)$. In this process, different possibilities may occur. We discuss them with the help of some solved examples.

Example 27: Find the particular solution of $y'' - 3y' - 4y = 5e^{-4x}$.

Solution: A reasonable guess would be, $y_p = Ae^{-4x}$, because $r(x) = 5e^{-4x}$ .Then, $y'_p = -4Ae^{-4x}$and $y''_p = 16Ae^{-4x}$. Substitute them in the equation, leads to

$$16Ae^{-4x} + 12Ae^{-4x} - 4Ae^{-4x} = 24Ae^{-4x} \rightarrow 24Ae^{-4x} = 5e^{-4x}.$$

Hence, we obtain $A = \frac{5}{24}$. That is, $y_p = \frac{5}{24}e^{-4x}$.

Now we reconsider this example with a small change.

Example 28: Find the particular solution of $y'' - 3y' - 4y = 5e^{4x}$.

Solution: Again, we guess, $y_p = Ae^{4x}$. Then, $y'_p = 4Ae^{4x}$and $y''_p = 16Ae^{4x}$. Substitute them in the equation, leads to

$$16Ae^{4x} - 12Ae^{4x} - 4Ae^{4x} = 24Ae^{4x} \rightarrow 0 = 5e^{4x}.$$

Hence, we cannot find A in this process. Where does it come to such difficulty? The difficulty arises from this fact that e^{4x} is a solution of its homogeneous equation. That is, $y'' - 3y' - 4y = 0$. To ignore this difficulty we guess, y_p=Axe^{4x} rather than y_p=Ae^{4x}. Why? We may claim that $r(x)$ and $y_1(x)$ are not linearly independent. Thus, to overcome this difficulty, we do as we did in the case that m_1=m_2, for solving a homogeneous equation. Therefore, let y_p=Axe^{4x}, then

$$y'_p = A(4x+1)e^{4x} \text{and} y''_p = 8A(2x+1)e^{4x}.$$

Substituting y_p, y'_p and y''_p in equation, we obtain

$$8A(2x+1)e^{4x} - 3A(4x+1)e^{4x} - 4Axe^{4x} = 5e^{4x} \rightarrow A = 1.$$

Thus, $y_p = xe^{4x}$

Remark 7: If the characteristic equation has multiple roots then one may guess that $y_p = Ax^2e^{ax}$.

Example 29: Find the general solution of $y'' - 4y' + 4y = 3e^{2x}$.

Solution: The corresponding characteristic equation has roots $m_1 = m_2 = 2$. Hence we guess $y_p = Ax^2e^{2x}$. If we substitute y_p, y'_p and y''_p in the equation and compare both sides, we obtain $A=3$. Thus, $y(x) = (c_1 + c_2x)e^{2x} + 3x^2e^{2x}$

Example 30: Find the general solution of $y'' + 9y = 2cos3x$.

Solution: Clearly, $y_1 = \cos 3x$ and $y_2 = \sin 3x$ are two independent solutions of the corresponding homogeneous equation. Since $y_1 = \cos 3x$ and $r(x) = 2 = \cos 3x$ are linearly dependent then we guess $y_p = x(A\cos 3x + B\sin 3x)$. Thus,

$$y''_p = (6B - 9Ax)cos3x - (6A + 9Bx)sin3x.$$

Substitute y_p and y''_p in the equation and compare both sides. We come to $A = 0$ and $B = \frac{1}{3}$. Hence $y_p = \frac{1}{3}xsin3x$. The corresponding general solution will be

$$y(x) = y_c + y_p = c_1 cos3x + c_2 sin3x + \frac{1}{3}xsin3x$$

Remark 8: As we mentioned in (45), if $r(x)$ is a linear combination of terms, then y_p will also be a linear combination of the terms in $r(x)$.

Example 31: Find the particular solution of $y'' - 4y = 8x^2 - 4e^{-2x}$.

Solution: Since $r(x)$ contains a polynomial with degree 2 and an exponential function which is a solution to the corresponding homogeneous equation, then we have

$$y_p = Ax^2 + Bx + C + Dxe^{-2x} \rightarrow y''_p = 2A - 4D(1 - x)e^{-2x}.$$

Substituting in the equation, leads to $A=-2$, $B=0$, $C=-1$ and $D=1$. Thus, $y_p = -2x^2 - 1 + xe^{-2x}$

Remark 9. If inhomogeneous equation is given by

$$a_0y^{(n)} + a_1y^{(n-1)} + a_2y^{(n-2)} + \ldots + a_{n-1}y' + a_ny = c,$$

Where $a_0, a_1, \ldots, a_n$ and $c \epsilon R$, then $y_p = \frac{c}{a_n}$. But, if $a_n = 0$, then $y_p = \frac{cx}{a_{n-1}}$. In general, if $a_n = a_{n-1} = \ldots = a_{n-k+1} = 0$, then $y_p = \frac{cx^k}{k!a_{n-k}}$.

(ii) Method of Variation of Parameters

Consider Eq. (20). Let y_1 and y_2 be two linearly independent solutions to the corresponding homogeneous equation reduced by Eq. (20). Then the general solution of this homogeneous equation is given by $y=c_1y_1+c_2y_2$. This solution may bring this suggestion to our mind that we let $y_p=u_1y_1+u_2y_2$, be the particular solution of Eq. (20). If so, then, it can be proved that,

$$u_1 = \int \frac{-y_2 r(x)}{y_1 y_2' - y_1' y_2} dx, u_2 = \int \frac{y_1 r(x)}{y_1 y_2' - y_1' y_2} dx. \tag{38}$$

Hence,

$$y_p = y_1 \int \frac{-y_2 r(x)}{y_1 y_2' - y_1' y_2} dx + y_2 \frac{y_1 r(x)}{y_1 y_2' - y_1' y_2} dx. \tag{39}$$

Example 32: Find the particular solution of the following differential equation

$$y'' - 2y' + y = e^x \tan x . \sec^2 x.$$

Solution: It is not difficult to show that $y_c=(c_1+c_2x)e^x$, Let $y_1=e^x$ and $y_2=xe^x$, then $y_1y_2'-y_1'y_2 = e^{2x}$. We have

$$u_1 = \int \frac{-x \tan x . \sec^2 x e^{2x}}{e^{2x}} dx = -\int x \tan x . \sec^2 x dx = -\frac{1}{2}(x \tan^2 x - \tan x + x)dx,$$

$$u_2 = \int \frac{\tan x . \sec^2 x e^{2x}}{e^{2x}} dx = \int \tan x . \sec^2 x dx = \frac{\tan^2 x}{2}.$$

Therefore,

$$y_p = u_1 y_1 + u_2 y_2 = -\frac{e^x}{2}(x \tan^2 x - \tan x + x) + \frac{x e^x \tan^2 x}{2} = \frac{e^x}{2}(\tan x - x).$$

Example 33: Find the general solution of $(1 - x)y'' + xy' - y = 2(x-1)^2 e^{-x}$.
Solution: Clearly, $y_1=x$ and $y_2=e^x$, hence, $y_1y_2'-y_1'y_2 = (x-1)e^x$. We have

$$u_1 = \int \frac{-2(x-1)e^x e^{-x}}{(x-1)e^x} dx = \int 2e^{-x} dx = -2e^{-x},$$

$$u_2 = \int \frac{-2x(x-1)e^{-x}}{(x-1)e^x} dx = \int -2e^{-2x} dx = \left(x + \frac{1}{2}\right) e^{-2x}.$$

Therefore, $y_p = u_1 y_1 + u_2 y_2 = \left(\frac{1}{2} - x\right) e^{-x}$, then the general solution will be

$$y(x) = y_c + y_p = c_1 x + c_2 e^x + \left(\tfrac{1}{2} - x\right) e^{-x}$$

Remark 10: In the method of variation of parameters, if we let, $y_p = uy_1$, then we have a method of reduction of order. That is, the method of reduction of order can also be used for inhomogeneous equations.

Example 34: Find the general solution of $xy'' - y' + (1 - x)y = 1$.

Solution: We know (See Ex.7) $y_c = c_1 x + c_2 e^x$. Choose, $y_1 = e^x$. We assume $y = uy_1 = ue^x$, then

$$y' = (u' + u)e^x \rightarrow y'' = (u'' + 2u' + u)e^x.$$

Substituting y, y' and y'' into the given equation, we obtain

$$u'' + \left(1 - \frac{1}{x-1}\right)u' = \frac{1}{x-1}.$$

Suppose $u' = z$, then we have $z' + \left(1 - \frac{1}{x-1}\right)z = \frac{1}{x-1}$, which is a linear first-order differential equation. One can see that

$$z = 1/(x-1) + c_1(x-1)e^{(-x)} \rightarrow u' = 1/(x-1) + c_1(x-1)e^{(-x)}.$$

Integrating both sides leads to $u = \ln(x-1) - c_1 x e^{-x} + c_2$. Hence

$$y = uy_1 = e^x \ln(x-1) + c_1 x + c_2 e^x$$

An interesting point in this solution is that $y_c = c_1 x + c_2 e^x$ appears in the general solution, hence we may guess $e^x \ln(x-1)$ is a particular solution.

9.5. A FURTHER METHOD FOR SOLUTION OF LINEAR ODES (OPTIONAL)

As we know, many linear ODEs may have solutions which can be expressed explicitly or implicitly in terms of elementary functions, even if their coefficient functions are not analytical functions. Such solutions are called closed-form solutions. Since linear order ODEs, in particular second order, arise frequently in science and engineering, hence the exploitation of analytical methods for solving such equations becomes a main subject of considerable interest in most textbooks (Boyce & Diprima, 1977) (Hermann & Saravi, 2014) (Tensnbaum & Pollard, 1964) (Merice & Goldberg, 1978) (Rainville & Bedint, 1974). In most cases, it is difficult to obtain the closed-form solutions for a given ODE. Although in some specific cases we could find such solutions, all the methods are really the exception rather than the rule, (Merice & Goldberg, 1978) (Rainville & Bedint, 1974). At present, the power series methods are used to find solutions, even in series form. In this manner, if there is a closed-form solution it can be found by these methods. The methods will be more applicable if the coefficient functions are polynomials. In particular, they are well suited for finding a solution of a general linear ODE given by

$$P_k(x)\,y^{(n)} + P_{k-1}(x)\,y^{(n-1)} + \ldots + P_1(x)y' + P_0(x)y \;=\; 0, k \;\leq\; n \tag{40}$$

where $P_i(x)$, i=0,1,…,k are known real polynomials.

We remind you that if the polynomials have no common factor, then Eq. (40) has an *ordinary point* if $P_k(x)\neq 0$ and a *singular point* if $P_k(x)=0$. We also recall that the singular points, if there are, can be subdivided into two classes called *regular* and *irregular* singularities.

In case n=2, the power series method leads to introducing some other methods in several books or papers. Actually, it seems we must still seek other means of expression for solution if, at least, it has fewer computations.

In the next section we use another strategy by which one can attempt to determine the closed-form solutions in polynomial form, if they exist, which do not have many computations, even when we have singular points.

The main idea for manipulation through this strategy comes from the fact that the Cauchy-Euler equation of any order can be solved by choosing $y=x^m$, as its solution.

The procedure includes two steps. First, we construct characteristic equations by substituting y and its necessary derivatives in the equation. Then, using values of m obtained from this equation, we try to find a polynomial that will be the polynomial form solution of the given ODE.

We consider the procedure for n=2 and, in this manner we try to test some examples, even for n>2.

It is better to emphasize that the situation for non-linear cases is more difficult than linear ones if we utilize the power series method because, in practice, we may be faced with difficult computations, (Rainville & Bedint, 1974) (Saravi & Zareenkham, 2021) Nevertheless, it can be seen that a remarkably large number of ODEs with specific physical applications could be solved if we replace $y=ax^m$ in lieu of $y=x^m$ (Elyadi, 2000).

We describe the method and consider some examples that have already been solved by the power series methods.

Recall Eq. (40) with n=2,

$$P_2(x)y'' + P_1(x)y' + P_0(x)y \;=\; 0. \tag{41}$$

As we mentioned, at first step we search for characteristic equations by setting

$$y=x^m. \tag{42}$$

We have, $y' = mx^{m-1}$, and$y'' = m(m-1)x^{m-2}$.We substitute y, y' and y'' into Eq. (41) to obtain values of m from these characteristic equations produced by this substitution.

A reliable procedure for obtaining the polynomial solutions may be done by using a special ansatz given by

$$y=P(x), \tag{43}$$

where $P(x)$ will be specify by values of m obtained in first step.

At second step, we substitute Eq. (43) into Eq. (41) and concentrate on finding coefficients of this polynomial. In general, the method works well for Eq. (41) in particular, when the coefficients of Eq. (40) match with orders of equation.

Unfortunately, the method cannot be useful when we have an ODE with constant coefficients or those equations that their series solutions can be written in closed-form solutions. One may transfer such equations into the Cauchy-Euler equation, and then, solve the equation by this procedure. Of course, this is not a good way to do, because, it comprises more computations. It is merely offered for comparison.

First, we consider the existence of solution for Eq. (40) by following theorem.

Theorem 3: Consider the ODE given by:

$$Ly = \sum_{i=0}^{n} P_i(x) D^i y = 0. \tag{44}$$

where $P_i(x)$, $i=0,1,\ldots,n$, are known real polynomials, D^i denotes ith order of differentiation with respect to x. Suppose

$$P_i(x) = A_{i,i}x^i + A_{i,i-1}x^{i-1} + \ldots + A_{i,1}x + A_{i,0}. \tag{45}$$

Then Eq. (44) has, at least, a polynomial solution such that its degree is biggest value of following equation

$$A_{n,n}m(m-1)\ldots(m-n+1) + A_{n-1,n-1}m(m-1)\ldots(m-n+2) + \ldots + A_{1,1}m + A_{0,0} = 0.$$

For example, for $i=2$,we have

$$(A_{2,2}x^2 + A_{2,1}x + A_{2,0})y'' + (A_{1,1}x + A_{1,0})y' + A_{0,0}y = 0.$$

Hence, we obtain

$$A_{2,2}m(m-1)+A_{1,1}m+A_{0,0} = 0.$$

That is

$$A_{2,2}m^2+(A_{1,1}-A_{2,2})m+A_{0,0} = 0. \tag{46}$$

In case of an ODE of third order it is enough to add term $m(m-1)(m-2)A_{33}$ to Eq. (43) to obtain

$$A_{3,3}m^3+(A_{2,2}-3A_{3,3})m^2+(A_{1,1}-A_{2,2}+2A_{3,3})m+A_{0,0} = 0, \tag{47}$$

and so on.

***Remark* 11**: If two roots of Eq. (43) are m_1 and m_1+1, then we obtain $y = c_1 y_1 + c_2y_2$, where y_1 and y_2 are closed polynomial-form solutions of degree m_1, m_1+1, respectively. This idea can be extended to Eq. (44). That is, if its roots are m_1, m_1+2 and m_1+3 then we get $y = c_1y_1 + c_2y_2 + c_3y_3$, where y_1, y_2 and y_3 are closed polynomial-form solutions of degree m_1, m_1+1 and m_1+2 respectively.

The rest of this section is devoted to considering some examples which are taken from several textbooks. All of them have been considered by power series methods. Bear in mind that in all examples the series solutions achieved about the point $x=0$.

Example 35: Solve $(1+x^2)y''-8xy'+20 = 0$.

Solution: This equation has ordinary points. Since $A_{2,2} = 1, A_{1,1} = -8$and $A_{0,0} = 20$, then

$$A_{2,2}m^2+(A_{1,1}-A_{2,2})m+A_{0,0} = m^2-9m+20 = 0.$$

Hence, $m=4$ and $m=5$. By Remark 1, we expect to get $y = c_1y_1 + c_2y_2$, where y_1 and y_2 are polynomial-form solutions of degree 5 and 4 respectively. Let

$$y = P(x) = c_1x^5+c_2x^4+c_3x^3+c_4x^2+c_5x+c_6.$$

By substitution in equation and rearrange it in terms of $x^5, x^4, x^3, x^2, x, 1$ gives

$$(20c_1-40c_1+20c_1)x^5+(12c_2-32c_2+20c_2)x^4$$
$$+(20c_1+2c_3)x^3+(12c_2+6c_4)x^2+(6c_3+12c_5)x+2c_4+20c_6 = 0.$$

Whence $c_1 = c_1, c_2 = c_2, c_3 = -10c_1, c_4 = -2c_2$ and $c_6 = -\frac{1}{10}c_4 = \frac{1}{5}c_2$. Thus

$$y = c_1\left(x^5 - 10x^3 + 5x\right) + c_2\left(x^4 - 2x^2 + \frac{1}{5}\right)$$

Example 36: Solve the following ODE

$$x^2(x+3)y''' - 3x(x+2)y'' + 6(x+1)y' - 6y = 0, |x| < 3.$$

Solution: Since $A_{3,3} = 1, A_{2,2} = -3, A_{1,1} = 6$ and $A_{0,0} = -6$, hence

$$A_{3,3}m^3 + (A_{2,2} - 3A_{3,3})m^2 + (A_{1,1} - A_{2,2} + 2A_{3,3})m + A_{0,0} = m^3 - 6m^2 + 11m - 6 = 0.$$

Therefore, m=1,2, and 3. By remark 2 we expect to get $y = c_1y_1 + c_2y_2 + c_3y_3$, Where y_1, y_2 and y_3 are polynomial-form solutions of degree 3, 2 and 1. Suppose

$$y = P(x) = c_1x^3 + c_2x^2 + c_3x + c_4.$$

By the same substitution as previous example, one can show that,

$$c_1 = c_1, c_2 = c_2, c_3 = c_3 \text{ and } c_4 = c_3.$$

Hence, $y = c_1x^3 + c_2x^2 + c_3(x+1)$

***Remark* 12:** In case of ordinary points, at least one part of the solution will be series form if some values of m are negative integers or non-integers. In particular, if all roots are complex or negative then we would not have any closed polynomial form solution. Even if all the coefficients of $P(x)$ found to be zero, this means, Eq. (41) has only series solutions.

Example 37: Consider $(x^2 + 4)y'' + 2xy' - 12 = 0$.

Solution: We have $A_{2,2} = 1, A_{1,1} = 2$ and $A_{0,0} = -12$. Therefore,

$$A_{2,2}m^2 + (A_{1,1} - A_{2,2})m + A_{0,0} = m^2 + m - 12 = 0.$$

Hence m=3 – 4. Existence of m=-4, it shows that we have a series solution. Since we have ordinary point then we can ignore m=-4, and set $y = c_1x^3 + c_2x^2 + c_3x + c_4$ to declare the solution. Finding y' and y'' and substitute into the equation leads to

$$(12c_1 - 12c_1)x^3 - 6c_2x^2 + (12c_1 - 5c_3)x + (8c_2 - 12c_4) = 0.$$

This gives; $c_1 = c_1, c_2 = c_4 = 0$ and $c_3 = \frac{12}{5}c_1$.
Hence,

$$y_1 = c_1\left(x^3 + \frac{12}{5}x\right).$$

In this example we could not find another solution. In fact, the second solution is in series form and one may wish to find it by reduction of order method.

***Remark* 13:** It easily can be shown that, about $x=0$ the well-known equations such as; *hermite, Laguerre, Chebyshev*, and *Legendre* equation, that is,

(i) $y'' - 2xy' + 2\lambda y = 0,$
(ii) $xy'' + (1 - x)y' + \lambda y = 0,$
(iii) $(1 - x^2)y'' - xy' + \lambda^2 y = 0,$
(iv) $(1 - x^2)y'' - 2xy' + \lambda(\lambda + 1)y = 0.$

respectively, have always polynomial solutions when their index, λ, is a non-negative integer, apart of what kind points they have. In such cases we may write,

$$y(x) = a_\lambda x^\lambda + a_{\lambda-1}x^{\lambda-1} + \dots + a_1 x + a_1 = 0. \tag{47}$$

That is, $m=\lambda$.

***Example 38*:** Solve $y'' - 2xy' + 8y = 0$..

Solution: This is a Hermite equation with index $\lambda=4$. This means, $m=4$. Thus, we have a polynomial solution. Set

$$y = P(x) = c_1x^4 + c_2x^3 + c_3x^2 + c_4x + c_5.$$

Find y' and y'', then substitute y, y' and y'' in equation and rearrange it. We obtain

$$(8c_1 - 8c_1)x^4 + (6c_2 - 8c_2)x^3 + (12c_1 + 4c_3)x^2 + 7c_4x + (2c_3 + 8c_1) = 0.$$

This leads to,

$$c_1 = c_1, c_2 = 0, c_3 = -3c_1, c_4 = 0 and c_5 = -\frac{1}{4}c_3 = \frac{3}{4}c_1.$$

Thus,

$$y = c_1x^4 - 3c_1x^2 + \frac{3}{4}c_1 = c_1\left(x^4 - 3x^2 + \frac{3}{4}\right)$$

***Example 39*:** Consider

$$xy'' + (1 - x)y' + 2y = 0.$$

Solution: This is Laguerre equation with. Since λ=2 then, using Remark 3, we have m=2. We set $y = c_1x^2 + c_2x + c_3$. By substituting y, y' and y'' in equation we obtain,

$$(2c_1 - 2c_1)x^2 + (4c_1 + c_2)x + (c_2 + 2c_3) = 0.$$

This leads to,

$$c_1 = c_1, c_2 = -4c_1, c_3 = -c_2/2.$$

Hence,

$$y_1 = c_1(x^2 - 4x + 2)$$

Note that this equation has a regular singular point at x=0. This strategy can be generalized to singular points too. According to what type of roots obtained from the indicial equation, the procedure works for all kind of singular points. Here it is not necessary to determine an indicial equation because its roots are those we find by coefficients of characteristic equation which has smaller degree. Rather than this fact, the roots of characteristic equations help us to have an understanding of the choice of $P(x)$. For example, if the values of m are negative or fractional numbers, then we use them as degrees of $P(x)$. In the case of repeated roots, we would not have any logarithm terms if the indicial equation has not negative root. For example, see the example 39.

***Example 40*:** Solve $2x(x + 1)y'' + 3(x + 1)y' - y = 0.$

Solution: This equation has two regular singular points at x=0, -1. If, we solve it by power series method we find that its indicial equation has two distinct roots that do not differ by an integer. Because, if we set, $y=x^m$, then by substituting y, y' and y'' we get

$$(2m - 1)(m + 1)x^m + m(2m + 1)x^{m-1} = 0.$$

From the coefficient of x^{m-1} we obtain, m=0 and $m = -\frac{1}{2}$, which are roots of indicial equation and do not differ by an integer. Actually, we do not need to determine indicial equation at all, and can use directly Eq. (44) to find the solution, but values of these roots help us to know what kind solution we have.

Now, since

$$A_{2,2}m^2 + (A_{1,1} - A_{2,2})m + A_{0,0} = 2m^2 + m - 1 = 0,$$

then, m=-1 and $m = \frac{1}{2}$. Thus,

$$y = c_1 x^{1/2} + c_2 x^{-1/2} + c_3 x^{-1} + c_4.$$

By substituting y, y' and y'' in equation we will have

$$(c_1 - c_1)x^{1/2} + (c_1 - c_2)x^{-1/2} + (4c_3 - 3c_3)cx^{-1} + c_4 = 0.$$

This gives,

$$c_1 = c_1, c_2 = c_1, c_3 = c_{41} = 0.$$

Hence,

$$y_1 = c_1(x^{1/2} + x^{-1/2})$$

For the cases that the indicial equation have two distinct roots such that they differ by an integer, we split the solution into two parts;

1. Solution with logarithm term
2. Solution without logarithm term

In both cases, we set, $P(x)=P_M(x)+Q_N(x)$, where, M and N are positive and negative, respectively.

Note that for example 40, we do not have any logarithm term because the indicial equation has not negative root.

Example 41: Consider $x(x + 1)y'' + (x + 5)y' - 4y = 0$.

Solution: This equation has regular singular points at x=0, -1 and the indicial equation produces by this equation has two roots which differ by in integer. Let $y=x^m$. We simply obtain $m=\pm 2$, 0, -4. Thus M=2 and N=-4. Then,

$$y = c_1 x^2 + c_2 x + c_3 + c_4 x^{-1} + c_5 x^{-2} + c_6 x^{-3} + c_7 x^{-4}.$$

By substituting y, y' and y'' in equation we obtain,

$$c_1 = c_1, c_2 = 4c_1, c_3 = 5c_1, c_4 = 0, c_5 = c_5, c_6 = \frac{4}{5}c_5, c_7 = \frac{1}{5}c_5.$$

Replacing these results into y leads to

$$y = c_1(x^2 + 4x + 5) + c_5(x^{-2} + \frac{4}{5}x^{-3} + \frac{1}{4}x^{-4}).$$

***Example* 42:** Solve

$$x(x - 1)y'' + 2(x - 1)y' - 2y = 0.$$

Solution: This equation has regular singular points at x=0,1 and it can be shown that its indicial equation produces by this equation has two roots, 1 and -2, respectively, which differs by three. That is, it can have polynomial solution. From the characteristic equation we have m=0, ±1, -2. Thus, M=1 and N=-2. Thus,

$$y = c_0 + c_1 x + c_2 x^{-1} + c_3 x^{-2}.$$

By substituting y, y' and y'' in equation we obtain

$$c_1 = c_1, c_0 = -c_1 \text{ and } c_2 = c_3 = 0.$$

Hence $y_1 = c_1(x - 1)$

***Remark* 14:** The procedure also is applicable even if we have a polynomial recursion formula.

We end this section by considering an equation which, by the power series method, leads to a recursion formula.

Example 43: Consider the equation

$$x(x - 2)^2y'' - 2(x - 2)y' + 2y = 0.$$

Find its general solution.

Solution: This equation has a polynomial recursion formula in terms of a_n, a_{n-1} and a_{n-2}. If we let,

$$y = \sum_{n=0}^{\infty} a_n x^{n+r},$$

where, r is roots of indicial equation. By our procedure, we set $y=x^m$ and find m=0, 1, -1/2. Thus

$$y = c_1 + c_2 x + c_3 x^{-1/2}.$$

Substitute y, y' and y'' in this equation, we get

$$c_2 = -\frac{c_1}{2} \text{and} \, c_3 = 0.$$

Hence,

$$y_1 = c_1\left(1 - \frac{x}{2}\right).$$

9.6. SOME APPLICATIONS OF ORDINARY DIFFERENTIAL EQUATIONS

Earlier, we explained an application of differential equations, which was to find the paths perpendicular to the given paths. Another geometrical application is to determine the equation of a curve that has a slope $y' = f(x,y)$ and passes through a point (a,b). For this purpose, we solve the equation to determine the curve.

Example 44: Find the equation of the curve that passes through (0,1) and its slope is given by the particular solution of $y' = \cos x + y\tan x$.

Solution: We rewrite the equation as, $y' + y\tan x = \cos x$. This is a linear first-order ODE with $p(x) = \tan x$. Thus, $F(x) = e^{\int \tan x dx} = e^{\ln\cos x} = \cos x$. We multiply it in the equation, and we get, $\cos x(y' + y\tan x) = \cos^2 x$.

Integrating both sides leads to,

$$y\cos x = \int \cos^2 x dx = \int \frac{1 + \cos 2x}{2} dx = \frac{x}{2} + \frac{\sin 2x}{4} + c.$$

$$y = \left(\frac{x}{2} + \frac{\sin 2x}{4} + c\right)\sec x.$$

Now, we apply $y(0)=1$. This gives $c=1$. Thus, the equation of the curve will be,

$$y = \left(\frac{x}{2} + \frac{\sin 2x}{4} + 1\right)\sec x.$$

Usually, the supply and demand functions in the market are affected by the price. Therefore, an economist needs information such as the current price: we denote it by $P(t)$. Suppose the first and second derivatives of supply and demand are given as follows:

$$Q_s = a_1 P'' + b_1 P' + c_1 P + d_1, Q_d = a_2 P'' + b_2 P' + c_2 P + d_2.$$

In the equilibrium state, we have $Q_s = Q_d$ which is an inhomogeneous second-order differential equation with constant coefficients. That is,

$$(a_1 - a_2)P'' + (b_1 - b_2)P' + (c_1 - c_2)P = -(d_1 - d_2).$$

By Remark 9, its particular solution is,

$$P_p = -\frac{(d_1 - d_2)}{(c_1 - c_2)}.$$

If $P_p > 0$, then P_p is called the equilibrium price. Thus, the equilibrium price is the same particular solution of the differential equation obtained. The equilibrium is said to be *dynamically stable* if and only if, $\lim_{t\to\infty} P(t) = P_p$, where $P(t) = P_c + P_p$.

Therefore, the stability depends on the roots of the characteristic equation given by

$$(a_1 - a_2)P'' + (b_1 - b_2)P' + (c_1 - c_2)P = 0.$$

To know more about the dynamic stable, the reader may refer to Chang (1967).

Example 45: If,

$$Q_d = 2P'' + 3P' + P + 5,$$

$$Q_s = P'' + 4P' + 3P + 1,$$

find the equilibrium price and verify that the equilibrium is dynamically stable.

Solution: We set, $Q_d = Q_s$. This leads to $P - P' - 2P = -4$. The particular solution is, $P_p = \frac{-4}{-2} = 2$. Thus, the equilibrium price is 2. To find whether the equilibrium is stable or not, we find P_c. We have, $P'' - P' - 2P = 0$. This yields that, $m^2 - m - 2 = 0$. That is, $m=2$ and $m=-1$. Hence, $P_c = c_1 e^{2t} + c_2 e^{-t}$. Then,

$$P(t) = P_c + P_p = c_1 e^{2t} + c_2 e^{-t} + 2.$$

But $\lim_{t\to\infty} P(t) = \lim_{t\to\infty}\left(c_1 e^{2t} + c_2 e^{-t} + 2\right) = \infty$. That is, the equilibrium is not dynamically stable.

In relatively small populations, if evolutionary transformations do not occur, according to Malthus' law, the time rate of growth is proportional to the existing population, that is, $\frac{dy}{dt} = ky$ which is a first-order differential equation with separable variables. If we assume the number of the population in t_0 is y_0, it can be shown that $y = y_0 e^{kt}$ with $k > 0$.

At the beginning of this chapter, we mentioned that the decay problem occurs in the tumor growth of cancer cells. Simple models of tumor growth and treatment based on a single nonlinear ODE are given by $\frac{dN}{dt} = \lambda N$, where, λ is a constant and $N(t)$ is the number of clonogenic cells in a tumor and can be treated as a continuous, deterministic function of the time t (Saravi & Saravi, 2020). This equation is often generalized to a nonlinear first order (ODE) which incorporates growth deceleration of the form,

$$\frac{dN}{dt} = f(N),$$

where $f(N)$ is an appropriate function. For example, the equation given by

$$\frac{dN}{dt} = aN - bN^2, a > 0, b > 0$$

is called *logistic growth.* The model represented by this equation is referred to as *Verhulst- Pierre model.*

Example 46: Suppose $S(t)$ is the number of supermarkets throughout the country that are using a computerized checkout system. If this system is described by

$$\frac{ds}{dt} = S - 0.001\,S^2, S(0) = 1,$$

Solve this equation and determine how many supermarkets are using the computerized method when t=5.

Solution: We rewrite the equation in the following form:

$$\frac{ds}{S - 0.001\,S^2} = dt.$$

The variables are separated, then integrate. We get

$$\int \frac{ds}{S - 0.001\,S^2} = \int dt \to \int\left(\frac{1}{S} + \frac{0.001}{1 - 0.001S}\right)dS = \int dt.$$

Thus,

$$\ln S - \ln(1 - 0.001S) = t - \ln c \to \ln\frac{S}{c(1 - 0.001S)} = t \to \frac{S}{(1 - 0.001S)} = ce^t.$$

If we apply $S(0)$=1, we obtain, $c = \frac{1}{0.999}$. Therefore,

$$S = \frac{1}{(0.001 + 0.999\,e^{-t})}.$$

To find the number of supermarkets use the computerized method when t=5 we put t=5 in the solution. This leads to,

$$\frac{1}{(0.001 + 0.999e^{-5})} = 129.$$

The Gompertz model exhibits an exponential decay of the growth rate, given by following nonlinear ODE

$$\frac{dV}{dt} = V(a - b\ln V),$$

where a and b are constants. It has been successfully used to model breast and lung cancer growth. This nonlinear equation can be solved by changing the variable given by $V=e^u$ to get linear ODEs. (See Ex 8.12).

More discussions about solutions of linear and even non-linear ODEs can be seen in most textbooks of ODEs. But, before ending this chapter, we discuss briefly the Difference Equations of first and second which are applicable for discrete variables.

9.7. DIFFERENCE EQUATIONS

As we mentioned in Chapter 1, sometimes, we come across counting problems that cannot be solved by permutation or combination methods. But they can be solved for smaller sizes and the answer can be found from the information obtained. In such a way that if the numerical function $a(n)$, which we prefer to write as $a_n (n \geq 0)$ is the number of combinations of the n objects, and it can be found from the values of a_0, a_1, ..., a_{n-1} by having a relationship. Such relationships between a_n and previous numerical values are called *recurrence relations*.

This type of recurrence relation is a powerful tool used in counting, structuring new combinations, and analyzing algorithms. The complexity of the algorithms and the counting required to execute them can be simplified with the help of the computer by writing recurrence commands available in most programming languages. For example, one way to sort a series of numeric data is a method known as "bubble sort". In this method, the input is an array $A[1]$, $A[2]$, ..., $A[n]$ of n real numbers, which must be sorted in ascending order. If a_n represents the number of comparisons required to sort n numbers in this way, it can be shown that the recurrence relation related to this sort will be given by

$$a_n = a_{n-1} + n - 1, n \geq 2 \text{with} a_1 = 0.$$

It can be observed that we have numerical functions a_n and a_{n-1}.

One of the famous recurrence relations called the *Fibonacci sequence* attributed to the Italian mathematician, which is related to the generation of rabbits, is introduced as follows.

$$f_n = f_{n-1} + f_{n-2}, n \geq 3 \text{with } f_1 = f_2 = 1.$$

In this relation, we have three numerical functions.

These examples lead us to differential equations. The definitions and methods of solving such equations are the same for recurrence relations.

Differential equations are used to model systems that are continuously changing, but if the change happens discretely instead of continuously, then we use difference equations that are some kind of recurrence sequence. In many cases, it is of interest to model the evolution of some systems over time as a discrete variable.

A difference equation is an equation that contains a sequence of differences, that is, an equation that expresses the value of a sequence as a function of the other terms. Therefore, it can be solved by finding a sequence that satisfies the equation. Difference equations are equivalent to differential equations and arise whenever an independent variable can have only discrete values. For example, in engineering, in view of their applications in discrete time-systems, used in association with microprocessors. Many problems in probability give rise to difference equations. By analogy with differential equations, we define a difference equation as a relationship given by

$$f\left(x, y, \frac{\Delta y}{\Delta x}, \frac{\Delta^2 y}{\Delta x^2}, \ldots, \frac{\Delta^n y}{\Delta x^n}\right) = 0 \tag{48}$$

where $\Delta y = y(x+h) - y(x)$ and $\Delta x = h$.

The operator Δ has the following properties:

(i) $\Delta k = 0, k$ is a constant

(ii) $\Delta ky = k\Delta y$

(iii) $\Delta(af(x) \pm b(g(x)) = a\Delta f(x) \pm b\Delta g(x)$.

Example 47: Find $\Delta^2 e^{-x}$.

Solution: We have,

$$\Delta e^{-x} = e^{-(x+h)} - e^{-x} = (e^{-h} - 1)e^{-x}.$$

Therefore,

$$\Delta^2 e^{-x} = \Delta(\Delta e^{-x}) = \Delta((e^{-h} - 1)e^{-x}) = (e^{-h} - 1)\Delta e^{-x} = (e^{-h} - 1)^2 e^{-x}.$$

Back to (48). We can equivalently define the following relation as a general form of a difference equation.

$$F(x, y, y(x + h), y(x + 2h), \ldots, y(x + nh)) = 0. \quad (49)$$

If we use subscript notation, the equation (49) can be written as

$$F(n, y_n, y_{n+1}, y_{n+2}, \ldots, y_{n+m}) = 0. \quad (50)$$

with $x=a+nh$ and $y_n=f(a+nh)$.

Similar to differential equations, one can define the order of a difference equation and note whether it is linear or non-linear and whether it is homogeneous or inhomogeneous.

We define the order of a difference equation as the difference between the largest and the smallest argument occurring in the difference equation. For example, $y_n = y_{n-1} + y_{n-2}$ is a homogeneous difference equation with order, $n-(n-2)=2$, and the equation $5y_{n+1} - 3y_n = (8n - 3)2^n$ is inhomogeneous with order, $(n+1)-n=1$.

In general, any difference equation of order one, and two can be written in the following forms respectively.

$$y_{n+1} = f(n, y_n), n = 0, 1, \ldots \quad (51)$$

$$y_{n+2} = f(n, y_{n+1}, y_n), n = 0, 1, \ldots \quad (52)$$

which can be linear or nonlinear. In this section, we will focus more exclusively on linear first and second-order difference equations both homogeneous and inhomogeneous.

9.8. SOLUTION OF LINEAR DIFFERENCE EQUATIONS WITH CONSTANT COEFFICIENTS

The method of solving difference equations is analogous to that of solving differential equations as demonstrated in previous sections. Although the solution of differential equations are even supposedly elementary examples can be hard to solve, by contrast, elementary difference equations are relatively easy to deal with. Since difference equations are readily handled by the program, a standard approach to solving a nasty differential equation is to convert it to an approximately equivalent difference equation. To have an idea of how we should solve such equations, we start with a simple example.

Suppose a bank pays an annual interest equal to $i\%$ in the form of monthly compound interest to savings. If a person deposits \$$S$ in his account on the first day of August, what amount will he have in his account after one year?

Because the annual interest rate is $i\%$, then the annual interest rate will be, $\frac{i\%}{12} = \frac{i}{1200}$. Suppose that for $0 \le n \le 12$, the amount of this person's savings at the end of the nth month is equal to a_n, then

$$a_{n+1} = a_n + \frac{i}{1200}a_n,$$

where $\frac{i}{1200}a_n$ is the profit from a_n during month $n+1$ for $0 \le n \le 11$, and $a_0 = \$S$. Therefore, the difference equation to determine the amount available in a person's account after one year becomes $a_{n+1} = (1 + \frac{i}{1200})a_n$. This is a difference equation with order one. It is not difficult to show that its solution is $a_n = S\left(1 + \frac{i}{1200}\right)$ if we start with $a_0 = S$ and find a_1 and $a_2, \ldots, a_n$.

Back to the equation related to bubble sorting, that is,

$$a_n - a_{n-1} = n - 1, n \ge 2, a_0 = 0.$$

It is a non-homogeneous linear one-order equation, which is not difficult to solve, but time-consuming if it is done step by step. For this reason, we provide a more general solution method for solving such equations here, even with higher order.

The general form of a linear difference equation in one variable is given by

$$y_n + a_0 y_{n-1} + a_1 y_{n-2} + \ldots + a_{m-1} y_{n-m} = f(n), n \ge m \tag{53}$$

where $a_0, a_1, \ldots, a_{m-1}$ are real numbers.

We concentrate on second-order linear equations with constant coefficients, which take the form

$$y_n + a_0 y_{n-1} + a_1 y_{n-2} = f(n). \tag{54}$$

We assume that $a_1 \ne 0$, otherwise we have the first-order difference equation. If $f(n)=0$ then we have a homogeneous difference equation. To find a general solution for (54), it is necessary to solve its homogeneous one given by

$$y_n + a_0 y_{n-1} + a_1 y_{n-2} = 0. \tag{55}$$

We seek a solution of the form $y_n = r^n$. Substituting into (55), leads to

$$r^n + a_0 r^{n-1} + a_1 r^{n-2} = (r^2 + a_0 r + a_1) r^{n-2} = 0 \rightarrow r^{n-2} \neq 0,$$

then,

$$r^2 + a_0 r + a_1 = 0. \tag{56}$$

Equation (56) is a quadratic equation called a *characteristic equation*. This equation will have two roots r_1 and r_2.

The following three cases can be established regarding these roots:

(i) $r_1 \neq r_2$, both are real numbers,
(ii) $r_1 = r_2$,
(iii) $r_1 \neq r_2$, both are complex numbers.

These three cases lead to two linearly independent solutions. The linear combination of these two solutions is called the *general solution*. By using two initial values, we can find a solution which is called a *particular solution*.

(a) For the first case, we will have two solutions $r_1^{\ n}$ and $r_2^{\ n}$, which are linearly independent, so the general solution will be:

$$y_n = c_1 r_1^{\ n} + c_2 r_2^{\ n} \tag{57}$$

where c_1 and c_2 are two arbitrary constants.

Example 48: Find linearly independent solutions of the difference equation given by,

$$y_n + 8y_{n-1} + 15y_{n-2} = 0.$$

Solution: We choose a solution of the form $y_n = r^n$. Substituting into equation gives

$$r^n + 8r^{n-1} + 15r^{n-2} = (r^2 + 8r + 15) r^{n-2} = 0 \rightarrow r^2 + 8r + 15 = 0.$$

The roots are $r_1 = 3$ and $r_2 = 5$. Thus,

$$y_n = c_1 3^n + c_2 5^n.$$

Remark 15: As linear ordinary equations, we can directly write the characteristic equation without substituting $y_n = r^n$ in the equation. It is enough to use.

$$r^2 + a_0 r + a_1 = 0.$$

Example 49: Solve the difference equation resulting from the Fibonacci sequence.
Solution: We have,

$$f_n = f_{n-1} + f_{n-2} \text{ with } f_1 = f_2 = 1.$$

We write, $f_n - f_{n-1} - f_{n-2} = 0$, whence $r^2 - r - 1 = 0$.
By solving this equation, we will have two solutions, $r_1, r_2 = (1 \pm \sqrt{5})/2$.
Therefore, the general solution is:

$$f_n = c_1 \left(\frac{1+\sqrt{5}}{2}\right)^n + c_2 \left(\frac{1-\sqrt{5}}{2}\right)^n.$$

Applying the two conditions $f_1=1$ and $f_2=1$ leads to the following particular solution.

$$f_n = \frac{1}{\sqrt{5}}\left(\frac{1+\sqrt{5}}{2}\right)^n - \frac{1}{\sqrt{5}}\left(\frac{1-\sqrt{5}}{2}\right)^n.$$

(b) For the second case, we will have two solutions, $r_1^{\ n} = r_2^{\ n} = r^n$, which are not linearly independent. According to our experience in solving linear ordinary differential equations, we can write the general solution as follows:

$$y_n = (c_1 + c_2 n) r^n. \tag{58}$$

Remark 16: In general, for a homogeneous difference equation with a characteristic equation that has k repeated roots, its general solution is written as follows:

$$y_n = \left(c_1 + c_2 n + c_3 n^2 + \ldots + c_k n^k\right) r^n. \tag{59}$$

Example 50: Find the general solution of the following difference equation.

$$y_n - 6y_{n-1} + 12y_{n-2} - 8y_{n-3} = 0.$$

Solution: The characteristic equation of this difference equation is, $r^3 - 6r^2 + 12r - 8 = 0$.
This equation can be written as $(r-2)^3=0$. Thus, we will have three roots which are equal to 2. According to (59), the general solution will be:

$$y_n = (c_1 + c_2 n + c_3 n^2)\, 2^n.$$

(c) For the third case, we have two complex roots, namely, $r_1=a+ib$ and $r_2=a-ib$, which lead to two linearly independent solutions $r_1^{\ n}$ and $r_2^{\ n}$. Thus, the general solution is:

$$y_n = c_1 (a + ib)^n + c_2 (a - ib)^n. \tag{60}$$

To have a different form solution to this form, we perform the same manipulation as we did for such a case in the differential equation. Let's write, $a \pm ib = R(\cos\theta \pm i\sin\theta)$, then, (60) can be written as

$$y_n = c_1 (a + ib)^n + c_2 (a - ib)^n = c_1 [R(\cos\theta + isin\theta)]^n + c_2 [R(\cos\theta - isin\theta)]^n.$$

Now if we imply De Moivre's formula, we obtain

$$y_n = R^n(Acosn\theta + Bsinn\theta), \tag{61}$$

where $A = c_1 + ic_2$ and $B = c_1 - ic_2$.

Example 51: Find the general solution of the following difference equation,

$$y_{n+2} - 2y_{n11} + 4y_n = 0.$$

Solution: The characteristic equation is $r^2-2r+4=0$.

The roots are given by $r = 1 \pm i\sqrt{3}$.We have, $R = \sqrt{1+3} = 2$, and $\theta = \tan^{-1}\sqrt{3} = \frac{\pi}{3}$.

Therefore, $y_n = 2^n\left(Acos\frac{n\pi}{3} + Bsin\frac{n\pi}{3}\right)$.

Back to (53),

$$y_n + a_0 y_{n-1} + a_1 y_{n-2} + \ldots + a_{m-1} y_{n-m} = f(n), n \geq m$$

where $a_0, a_1, \ldots, a_{m-1}$ are real numbers. We turn our attention to solve second-order difference equations. That is, the equation given by (54). The result can be generalized for any order higher than two. The method which we use to obtain the general solution is the same as the method we used for linear second-order differential equations with constant coefficients. First, we obtain the general solution of the homogeneous difference equation as the complementary solution from this equation, and then we find a solution as a particular solution using the method of undetermined coefficients. We denote these two solutions with symbols $y_n^{(h)}$ and $y_n^{(P)}$, respectively. It can be shown that $y_n = y_n^{(h)} + y_n^{(P)}$ applies to the inhomogeneous difference equation. This will be the general solution of the inhomogeneous equation. But how can we find $y_n^{(P)}$ by the method of undetermined coefficients? In this method, depending on what function $f(n)$ is, we use trial solutions in the following ways:

(a) If $f(n)=ca^n$, then we assume $y_n^{(P)} = Ar^n$ with the condition that a^n is not one of the homogeneous solutions.
(b) If $f(n) = c_n r^n + c_{n-1} r^{n-1} + \ldots + c_1 r + c_0$, then we choose, $y_n^{(P)} = A_n r^n + A_{n-1} r^{n-1} + \ldots + A_1 r + A_0$
(c) If $f(n)=c\sin bn$, or $f(n)=c\cos bn$ then we take, $y_n^{(P)} = A\sin bn + B\cos bn$.
(d) If $f(n)$ is a combination of these functions, then we also consider $y_n^{(P)}$ to be a combination of them. For example, if $f(n)= a\sin bn+ca^n$, then $y_n^{(P)} = A\sin bn + B\cos bn + Ca^n$.

In all cases, by substituting $y_n^{(P)}$in the inhomogeneous equation and then comparing the equality, the undetermined coefficients can be obtained to determine $y_n^{(P)}$.

Example 52: Find the general solution of the following difference equation.

$$5y_n - 8y_{n-1} + 3y_{n-2} = 12\left(-\tfrac{3}{5}\right)^n.$$

Solution: The homogeneous equation is $5y_n - 8y_{n-1} + 3y_{n-2} = 0$. Its characteristic equation is $5r^2 - 8r+3=0$. The roots are $r_1=1$, and $r_2 = \frac{3}{5}$. Thus,

$$y_n^{(h)} = c_1(1)^n + c_2\left(\tfrac{3}{5}\right)^n = c_1(1)^n + c_2\left(\tfrac{3}{5}\right)^n.$$

Let's $y_n^{(P)} = c\left(-\frac{3}{5}\right)^n$. Substitute in the equation. We get,

$$5c\left(-\tfrac{3}{5}\right)^n - 8c\left(-\tfrac{3}{5}\right)^{n-1} + 3c\left(-\tfrac{3}{5}\right)^{n-2} = 12\left(-\tfrac{3}{5}\right)^n \to \tfrac{48c}{5} = \tfrac{108}{25} \to c = \tfrac{9}{20}.$$

Then, $y_n^{(P)} = \frac{9}{20}\left(-\frac{3}{5}\right)^n$. Therefore,

$$y_n = y_n^{(h)} + y_n^{(P)} = c_1 + c_2\left(\tfrac{3}{5}\right)^n + \tfrac{9}{20}\left(-\tfrac{3}{5}\right)^n.$$

Let's back to this example and consider it with, $f(n) = 12\left(\frac{3}{5}\right)^n$. If we do the same procedure as we did to find $y_n^{(P)}$, we obtain,

$$5c\left(\tfrac{3}{5}\right)^n - 8c\left(\tfrac{3}{5}\right)^{n-1} + 3c\left(\tfrac{3}{5}\right)^{n-2} = 12\left(\tfrac{3}{5}\right)^n \to 0 = \tfrac{108}{25}.$$

Thus, it is impossible to find c. where does it come such a difficulty? It is because $\left(\frac{3}{5}\right)^n$ is a solution of the resulting homogeneous equation. To overcome this difficulty, we choose $y_n^{(P)} = cn\left(\frac{3}{5}\right)^n$. Substituting this choice leads to

$$5cn\left(\frac{3}{5}\right)^n - 8c(n-1)\left(\frac{3}{5}\right)^{n-1} + 3c(n-2)\left(\frac{3}{5}\right)^{n-2} = 12\left(\frac{3}{5}\right)^n \Rightarrow -\frac{6c}{5} = \frac{108}{25} \to c = \frac{-48}{5}.$$

Thus, $y_n^{(P)} = -\frac{48}{5}\left(\frac{3}{5}\right)^n$. Then,

$$y_n = y_n^{(h)} + y_n^{(P)} = c_1 + c_2\left(\frac{3}{5}\right)^n - \frac{48}{5}\left(\frac{3}{5}\right)^n.$$

We end this section with one more example, and in the next chapter, we give some examples of the application of difference equations in the calculation of determinants and eigenvalues of specific matrices.

Example 53: Find the sum of $1^2+2^2+3^2+\ldots+n^2$.

Solution: Suppose $S_n=1^2+2^2+3^2+\ldots+n^2$. Then, $S_{n-1} = 1^2 + 2^2 + 3^2 + \ldots + (n-1)^2$.

Thus, $S_n - S_{n-1} = n^2$. This is a linear first-order inhomogeneous equation. It is not difficult to show that the difference equation $S_n - S_{n-1} = 0$ has a solution given by $S_n^{(h)} = C$. Assume

$$S_n^{(P)} = n(an^2 + bn + c).$$

Substitute in equation, yields

$$n(an^2 + bn + c) - (n-1)(a(n-1)^2 + b(n-1) + c) = n^2.$$

This leads to $a = \frac{1}{3}, b = \frac{1}{2}$ and$c = \frac{1}{6}$. Therefore,

$$S_n^{(P)} = n\left(\frac{1}{3}n^2 + \frac{1}{2}n + \frac{1}{6}\right) = \frac{n}{6}(2n^2 + 3n + 1).$$

Then,

$$S_n = S_n^{(h)} + S_n^{(P)} = C + \frac{n}{6}(2n^2 + 3n + 1).$$

We have, $S_1=1$. Then $1 = C + \frac{1}{6}(2(1)^2 + 3(1) + 1) \to C = 0$. Hence,

$$S_n = \frac{n}{6}(2n^2 + 3n + 6) = \frac{n(n+1)(2n+1)}{6}.$$

Note that, since $S_n = C$, was also a solution of the homogeneous equation, to avoid difficulty, we selected $S_n^{(p)} = n(an^2 + bn + c)$ rather than $S_n^{(p)} = an^2 + bn + c$.

More about the difference equations are discussed in Elyadi (2000).

CONCLUSION

In this chapter, we introduced the concepts of order and degree of the differential and differenc equations. By introducing different ordinary differential and difference equations, we could manage to solve several applications of them.

We could easily solve the well-known equations such as: Hermite, Lagureee, Chebyshev and Legendre equation by a new method given by author. By constructing some relations called, recurrence relations, we could easily solve several problems in applied mathematics.

9.9. Exercises

1. Verify the degree and the order of the following differential equations.
   (i) $xy'' - y' = \sqrt{y^4 - 1}$
   (ii) $e^x y''' - y' = x\cos x$
   (iii) $y' + xy^3 = e^x$
   (iv) $x^3 (y'')^3 - (y')^5 = x - 3x^2$
   (v) $y' + 3x^2 y^4 = e^{2x} \sin 4x$
   (vi) $(x^2 + y^2)dx - 2xydx = 0$
2. Find the general solution of the following differential equations.
   (i) $yy' = e^{x-y}$,
   (ii) $y' - e^{-x} y = x$
   (iii) $\sqrt{x^2 + y^2}\, dx = ydy$,
   (iv) $xy^2 dx + e^x dy = 0$
   (v) $y' + 3x^2 y^4 = e^{2x} \sin 4x$,
   (vi) $(x^2 + y^2)dx + 4xydx = 0$
   (vii) $(e^x - xy^2)dx + (y^3 - yx^2)dy = 0$,
   (viii) $xy^2 dx + (x^3 + y^3)dy = 0$
   (ix) $y'\cos x + y = 1 - \sin x$,
   (x) $xy' + (1 + x\cot x)y = x$
   (xi) $y' = y - xy^3$
   (xii) $2 \tan y \sin 2x dx + (\sin y - \cos 2x) dy = 0$
   (xiii) $y(e^x + y)dx + (e^x + 2xy)dy = 0, (ivx) - xy' - y = (xy)^k$
   (xiv) $y(2x^2 - xy + y^2)dx - x^2(2x - y)dy = 0$
   (xv) $x(3xy - 4y^3 + 6)dx + (x^3 - 6x^2 y^2 - 1)dy = 0$
   (xvi) $y(\ln x - \ln y) dx + (y - x\ln x + x\ln y)dy = 0$.

3. Use the change of variable z=sin$x$ to convert the equation,

$$(3\ \text{sin}y - 5x)dx + (2x^2\text{coty})dy = 0$$

to Bernullie's equation, and then solve it.

4. Find the family of solutions of each of the following Riccati equations.
   (i) $xy' = y + x^3(y^2 - x^2), y_1 = x$
   (ii) $xy' - y = y^2 - x^4, y_1 = x^2$
5. Find the orthogonal trajectories of the following family of curves.
   (i) $e^x + e^{-y} = c$
   (ii) $y = 3x - 1 + ce^{-3x}$
   (iii) $3x^2 + y^2 = cx,$
   (v) $x^n + y^n = c$
6. Verify the curves which pass through the point (0,1), and their slope is given by the following ordinary differential equations.
   (i) $y' = \frac{xy}{3x + 4y}$
   (ii) $y' = 3x - 2y$
   (iii) $y' = \cos x + y \sec x$
   (iv) $y' = \frac{2x + y - 3}{x + 2y - 1}$
7. Solve the following differential equations.
   (i) $y'' - 13y' + 36y = 0$
   (ii) $y'' + 4y'' - 5y = 2$
   (iii) $9y'' + 12y' + 4y = 0$
   (iv) $y^{(4)} + y = 2cosx - sin2x$
   (v) $y'' - 6y' + 10y = 0$
   (vi) $y'' + 9y = 2\sin 3x$
   (vii) $y'' - 4y = e^{-3x}$
   (viii) $y'' - 7y' + 12y = 4 - 3x^2$
   (ix) $y''' + y'' - 4y' + 2y = 0$
   (x) $2x^2y'' - 5xy' + 8y = 0$
   (xi) $y'' - 16y = 2$
   (xii) $x^2y'' - 2xy' + 2y = 0$
   (xiii) $y'' - y = e^{2x}$
   (xiv) $y'' - y = 2e^{-x}$
   (xv) $y'' + 2y' + y = 3e^x - 2e^{-x}$
   (xvi) $y'' + 9y = sin2x$
8. Solving the nonlinear second-order ODEs is difficult, and most of the time is impossible. We consider two special cases of such nonlinear equations.

(1) Suppose Eq. (2) does not contain y hence we have $f(x, y', y'')=0$. The substitution $y'=p$ can be used to reduce the order of the equation to the equation of the first order. Because, let $y''=p'$ then we get $f(x,p,p')=0$.

(2) Suppose Eq. (2) does not contain x, hence we have. So we have $f(y, y', y'')=0$. Let $y'=p$ then $y'' = p\frac{dp}{dy}$. Therefore, Eq. (4) can be written as $f(y,p,p')=0$. These two equations are a first-order ODE and may be solved for p. Solve the following nonlinear differential equations.

(i) $y'' + 2x(y')^2 = 0$

(ii) $y'' + (y')^3 = 0$

(iii) $y'' + (y')^2 = 2y$

(iv) $yy'y'' = 1 - (y')^3 = 0$

9. A differential equation for a hormone secretion model is given by $h'(t)=1-\cos 2\pi t-h(t)$, $h(0)=1$, where $h(t)$ is the amount of a certain hormone in the blood at any time t. Solve this equation and find $h(t)$. What happens to the level of hormone in the blood as $t\to\infty$.

10. In fluid flow, the path of a particle of fluid is called *streamlines* and the orthogonal trajectories of these lines are called *equipotential lines.* If we assume that streamline is $xy=c$ find equipotential lines.

11. A bacteria culture is known to grow at a rate proportional to the amount present. After one hour, 500 strands of the bacteria are observed, and after three hours 2500 strands. Find an expression for the approximate number of strands of bacteria at any time t. Approximate the number of strands of the bacteria originally in the culture.

12. The Gompertz growth model for a population may be written as $x'(t) = -kx\ln\left(\frac{x}{N}\right)$, where $x(t)$ is the population at any time t, and k and N are positive constants. This model has been employed quite successfully in the modeling of the growth of animal tumors. Solve this equation if $x(t)$.

13. In actuarial science, a commonly used model for the growth of a population $P(t)$ is the general Gompertz equation given by $P'(t)=P(a-b\ln P)$, where a and b are constants. Solve this equation such that $P(0)=P_0$. What is the long-term behavior of $P(t)$?

14. (Temperature field): Curves of constant temperature $T(x,y)=c$ in a temperature field are called *isotherms.* Their orthogonal trajectories are the curves along which heat will flow (in regions that are free of sources or sinks of heat and are filled with homogeneous medium). If the isotherms are given by $y^2+2xy-x^2=c$, what is the heat of flow?

15. A student of Shomal University carries Coronavirus at the university that has 5000 students. Suppose the rate at which the virus spreads is proportional not only to the number N of infected students, but also to the students not infected. If the following initial value problem governs such a problem, it shows that

the number of infected students after 20 days will be 833 students when it is observed that $N(5)=10$.

$$\frac{dN}{dt} = kN(a - N), a(0) = 1 = kN(5000 - N).$$

16. It has been found that if there is no control, the rate of growth of the bacteria population B is proportional to itself. If between 12:00 noon and 2:00 p.m., the number of B becomes a hundred times the number at noon.
17. Consider the tumor cell population by a DE of the form $\frac{dX}{dt} = aX - bX^2$, $X(t_0)=X_0$, where $a>0$. Choose $b>0$ to inhibit the growth of x as demanded by reality. This equation is termed as a logistic equation and growth governed by it is called the logistic law of cancer tumor growth. As we mentioned in example 46, the model represented by this equation is referred to as *Verhulst- Pierre model*.

    Solve this equation by the separation of variables method.
18. Find the equilibrium price and verify whether the equilibrium is dynamically stable or not.
    (i) $Q_d = 2P'' + 5P' + 3P + 6, \quad Q_s = P'' + 2P' + P + 12,$
    (ii) $Q_d = 3P'' + P' + 3P + 2, \quad Q_s = P'' + 3P' + P + 4,$
    (iii) $Q_d = P'' + 3P' + 5P + 8, \quad Q_s = 2P'' + 3P' + P + 9$
    (iv) $Q_d = 2P'' + 3P' + 2P, \quad Q_s = P'' + P' + 2P + 2.,$
19. In a model of the changing population $P(t)$ of a community, it is assumed that $\frac{dP}{dt} = \frac{dB}{dt} - \frac{dD}{dt}$ where $\frac{dB}{dt}$ and $\frac{dD}{dt}$ are the birth, and death rates, respectively, solve it for $P(t)$ if

$$\frac{dB}{dt} = aP, \frac{dD}{dt} = bP \text{ and } P(0) = P_0$$

Show that $P(t) = P_0 e^{(a-b)t}$. Analyze the cases and $b=a$.

20. Find the general solution of the following difference equations.
    (i) $y_{n+1} - 2y_n + 4y_{n-1} = 0$
    (ii) $y_n - 8y_{n-1} + 12y_{n-2} = 0$
    (iii) $4y_n - 6y_{n-1} + 9y_{n-2} = 0$
    (iv) $y_{n+1} - 2y_n + 4y_{n-1} = 2n - 1$
    (v) $y_{n+1} - 6y_n + 10y_{n-1} = 5 \sin\frac{n\pi}{2}$
    (vi) $y_{n+3} - 8y_{n+2} - 3y_{n+1} + 10y_n = 0$
    (vii) $y_{n+3} - 8y_{n+2} - 3y_{n+1} + 10y_n = 0$
    (viii) $y_{n+1} - 14y_n + 36y_{n-1} = 2n^2 - 3n + 1$
    (ix) $y_{n+2} - 6y_{n+1} + 9y_n = 2(5^n) - 2n^2 + 5n + 4$
    (x) $y_{n+2}{}^2 - 4y_{n+1}{}^2 + 3y_n{}^2 = 2(5^n) - 2n^2 + 5n + 4.$

21. Find the sum of $1^3 + 2^3 + 3^3 + \ldots + n^3$.
22. In a win-lose game, a person starts the game with \$$M$ and decides to exit the game when he reaches \$$N$≥\$$M$ (or lose all his money). If we consider the probability of his winning and losing $\frac{1}{2}$ and one dollar is added to his money for each win and subtracted if he loses, what is the probability that he will lose all his money?
23. If L_n represents the number of areas resulting from drawing n straight lines on the plane, write a difference equation for L_n and specify this number.
24. A student borrows \$5000 from the university with a monthly compound interest of 12%. If he is to pay this loan in two years, how much will be the monthly payment?
25. Find a particular or the general solution of the following equations, if it exists, by the method which is described in section 9.5.
    (i) $(1 - 4x^2)y'' + 6xy' - 4y = 0$
    (ii) $(1 + 2x^2)y'' + 3xy' - 3y = 0$
    (iii) $2xy'' + (1 + 2x)y' - 5y = 0$
    (iv) $x^2y'' + x(x - 1) + (1 - x)y = 0$
    (v) $x^2y'' + 3x(x + 1) + (1 - 3x)y = 0$
    (vi) $x^2y'' + x(2 + 3x)y' - 2y$

REFERENCES

Boyce, W. E., & Diprima, R. C. (1977). *Elementary Differential Equations and Boundary Value Problems* (3rd ed.). John-Wiley& Sons.

Hermann, M & Saravi, M. (2014). A First Course in Ordinary Differential Equations, Springer-book company.

M. Tensnbaum, T, & Pollard. H. (1964). Differetial Equations. Harper & How.

Saravi, S., & Saravi, M. (2020). A Short Survey in Application of Ordinary Differential Equations on Cancer Research. *American Journal of Computational and Applied Mathematics*, 10(1), 1–5. DOI: 10.5923/j.ajcam.20201001.01

Chang, A. c. (1967). *Fundamental Methods of Mathematical Economics*. McGraw Hill.

Porter, M. C., & Golberg, J. (1978). *Mathematical Methods* (2nd ed.). Prentice-Hall International Inc.

Rainville, E. D., & Bedint, P. A. (1974). *Elementary Differential Equations*. Mac. Millan Publishing.

Saravi, M., M & Zareenkhan. N. (2021). A note on Generalizatio to Method of Reduction of solving Second Order Linear Ordinary Differential Equations. *Further Applied Mathematics*, 2(2), 28–32.

Elyadi, S. (2000). *An Introduction to Difference Equations* (3rd ed.). Springer.

Chapter 10
Matrix Algebra and System of Linear Equations

ABSTRACT

This chapter deals with an elementary introduction to matrix algebra. First, we give a brief introduction to vectors and vector operations, then we discuss basic materials on matrices, determinants, their properties and the solution of linear system of equations. We also consider the solution of the systems of linear equations by using the inverse of the coefficient matrix of the given system of equations. We introduce the Gaussian method based on a series of algebraic operations which are compatible with computer software. Regarding the importance of eigenvalues, the eigenvalues and eigenvectors, which are numbers and vectors associated with square matrices. The last section of this chapter considers some applications of matrices to several examples we encounter in industry or applied mathematics.

10.1 INTRODUCTION

The matrices play a very important role in practical issues and are widely used in various fields of science and engineering. The general purpose of this chapter is to familiarize with the basic concepts and definitions of matrices and related algebraic operations and to define the determinants of a matrix and its related features. We start with a simple example. Suppose we want to specify a polynomial of the degree 2, i.e., $P(x)=ax^2+bx+c$ so that, $P(1) = 2, P'(1) = 0 \text{and} P''(1) = -2$. According to this data, we have,

$$P(1) = a + b + c = 2$$

DOI: 10.4018/979-8-3693-3657-1.ch010

$$P'(1) = 2a + b = 0$$

$$P''(1) = 2a = -2.$$

From the third equation, we get a=-1. We substitute it in the second equation, we obtain b=2. If we put the values of a and b in the first equation, we will have c=-1. Therefore, we could simply solve this system of equations. Nevertheless, we are going to introduce some materials for solving such a system with other methods.

From these equations, we can have the following arrangements.

$$\begin{bmatrix} 1 & 1 & 1 \\ 2 & 1 & 0 \\ 2 & 0 & 0 \end{bmatrix}, \begin{bmatrix} a \\ b \\ c \end{bmatrix}, \begin{bmatrix} 2 \\ 0 \\ -2 \end{bmatrix}.$$

Each of these arrangements is called a *matrix*, which consists of several rows and columns. Two of these matrices, which have only one column, are formally called *vectors*.

The main subject of this chapter devoted to the concept of a matrix and matrix algebra will enable us to consider the solution of such a system of linear equations more systematically and to express the result more compactly. In this chapter, our main goal is to consider two fundamental problems, which are: (i)-The solution of a linear system. (2)- The calculation of eigenvalues and eigenvectors of a matrix. But first, we mention a brief introduction to vectors which may be useful in this book. In general, a quantity that is defined by both magnitude and direction is a vector. Many physical quantities such as force, speed, and acceleration are vector quantities.

By a vector $\boldsymbol{a}$, we mean a list of numbers which are called the *components* of $\boldsymbol{a}$. That is, $\boldsymbol{a}= (a_1,a_2,\ldots,a_n)$.

The length or *norm* of $\boldsymbol{a}$ denoted by $\|\boldsymbol{a}\|$ is a positive quantity defined by

$$\|a\| = \sqrt{a_1{}^2 + a_2{}^2 + \ldots + a_n{}^2}.$$

A vector with length unity is called a *unit vector.*

We usually represent a vector with three components a_1, a_2 and a_3 in terms of three unit vectors $\boldsymbol{i,j}$, and $\boldsymbol{k}$ having the directions of the positive x, y and z axes of a three- dimensional rectangular coordinate system and denoted by

$$a = \mathrm{a}_1 i + a_2 j + a_3 k.$$

From the following figure, vectors $\boldsymbol{OC}$ and $\boldsymbol{OM}$ can be denoted by:

$OC = 2i + 3j, OM = 2i + 3j + 5k.$

Figure 1.

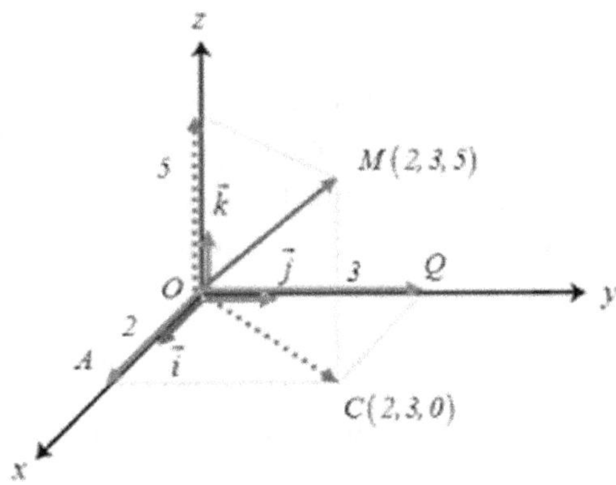

Two vectors ***a*** and ***b*** are equal, if they have the same components and if the corresponding components are equal.

Addition or subtraction of two vectors ***a*** and ***b*** with the same number of components, written $a \pm b$, is a vector obtained by adding (subtracting) corresponding components from ***a*** and ***b***.

The product of a vector ***a*** by a scalar *k* is a vector *k***a,** is obtained by multiplying each component of ***a*** by *k*.

Two types of multiplications can be defined for two vectors, depending on whether the result is a scalar or a vector. We represent these two types of multiplications by ***a.b*** and $a \times b$ and defined respectively by

$$a.b = a_1 b_1 + a_2 b_2 + a_3 b_3,$$

$$a \times b = (a_2 b_2 - a_3 b_3)i + (a_3 b_3 - a_1 b_1)j + (a_1 b_1 + a_2 b_2)k.$$

These two relations can also be written by

$$a.b = ab\cos\theta,$$

$$a \times b = ab\sin\theta.n,$$

where θ is the angle between two vectors ***a*** and ***b***, and ***n*** is a perpendicular vector to $a \times b$.

Another type of product is called *triple products* is denoted by $a.(b \times c)$ which is a scalar and is in absolute value equal to the volume of a parallelepiped with sides ***a, b*** and ***c***. We can prove that

$$a.(b \times c) = b.(c \times a) = c.(a \times b).$$

Now we are back to discussing matrices because the main subject of this chapter is devoted to the concept of a matrix and matrix algebra, which will enable us to consider the solution of a system of linear equations more systematically and to express the result more compactly. Our main goal is to consider two fundamental problems, which are:

(1) The solution of a linear system.
(2) The calculation of eigenvalues and eigenvectors of a matrix.

But first, we introduce mathematical expressions of matrices.

10.2 BASIC CONCEPTS

A rectangular array of the form

$$\begin{bmatrix} a_{11}\ldots a_{1j}\ldots a_{1n} \\ \vdots \\ a_{i1}\ldots a_{ij}\ldots a_{in} \\ \vdots \\ a_{m1}\ldots a_{mj}\ldots a_{mn} \end{bmatrix}$$

where elements a_{ij}; $i=1,2,\ldots,m$ and $j=1,2,\ldots,n$ are real or complex numbers or variables is called a *matrix*. For $i=1,2,\ldots,m$, let $r_i = [a_{i1}\, a_{i2} \ldots a_{in}]$ and $c_j = \begin{bmatrix} a_{1j} \\ a_{2j} \\ \vdots \\ a_{mj} \end{bmatrix}$. They are known as *rows* and *columns* of matrix respectively. A matrix of m rows and n columns is called an $m \times n$ matrix with *order* or *size* $m \times n$. Matrices are usually shown by capital letters such as ***A,B,…***, and squared-off brackets. It is convenient to write $A = [a_{ij}]_{m \times n}$, or simply $\boldsymbol{A}=a_{ij}$.

Definition 1: A $n \times n$ matrix is called a *square matrix.*

In a square matrix, the *diagonal* (or *main diagonal*) of the matrix $\boldsymbol{A}$ are elements a_{ii}; $i=1(1)n$ which are called diagonal elements. The sum of the diagonal elements of $\boldsymbol{A}$ is called the *trace* of $\boldsymbol{A}$ and is denoted by $tr(\boldsymbol{A})$. Hence, $tr(A) = \sum_{i=1}^{n} a_{ii}$.

Remark 1: It can be shown that $\text{tr}(\boldsymbol{AB})=\text{tr}(\boldsymbol{BA})$.

If all elements above or below of main diagonal are zero, the result is called a *Diagonal matrix* and is denoted by D. Thus,

$$D = \begin{bmatrix} a_{11}00\ldots0 \\ \vdots \\ 00\ldots a_{ii}\ldots0 \\ \vdots \\ 00\ldots0a_{nn} \end{bmatrix}.$$

If a_{ii}; $i=1,2,\ldots,n$ then the diagonal matrix is called the *identity matrix* and is denoted by $\boldsymbol{I}_n$ or $\boldsymbol{I}$.

Remark 2: A=IA=AI.

Matrices $\boldsymbol{A}=[a_{ij}]$ and $\boldsymbol{B}=[b_{ij}]$ are equal if their corresponding elements are equal.

If we interchange rows and columns of a matrix $\boldsymbol{A}$, we obtain a matrix called *transpose* of $\boldsymbol{A}$ and denoted by $\boldsymbol{A}^T$. That is, if $\boldsymbol{A}=[a_{ij}]$ then $\boldsymbol{A}^T=[a_{ji}]$.

Example 1: Consider the matrix $\boldsymbol{A}$ given by

$$\begin{bmatrix} 1 & 6 & 2 \\ 3 & -4 & 0 \\ 1 & 3 & 5 \end{bmatrix}.$$

Find $\text{tr}(\boldsymbol{A})$ and transpose of $\boldsymbol{A}$.

Solution: We have, $tr(A) = \sum_{i=1}^{3} a_{ii} = a_{11} + a_{22} + a_{33} = 2$. By the definition of the transpose of a matrix, we interchange the rows with corresponding columns. We get

$$A^T = [a_{ji}] = \begin{bmatrix} 1 & 3 & 1 \\ 6 & -4 & 3 \\ 2 & 0 & 5 \end{bmatrix}.$$

Remark 3: We have $(\boldsymbol{AB})^T=\boldsymbol{B}^T\boldsymbol{A}^T$.

The square matrix $\boldsymbol{A}$ is said to be *orthogonal* if $\boldsymbol{A}^T\boldsymbol{A}=\boldsymbol{A}\boldsymbol{A}^T=\boldsymbol{I}$.

For example, the matrix $\frac{1}{3}\begin{bmatrix} 0 & 2 & 5 \\ -2 & 0 & -3 \\ -5 & -3 & 0 \end{bmatrix}$ is an orthogonal matrix.

If all elements below the main diagonal of a square matrix are zero, the matrix is called an *Upper triangular matrix* and it is denoted by ***U***. Symbolically, $\boldsymbol{U}=[a_{ij}]$, $a_{ij}=0$ for $i>j$.

Similarly, if all elements below the diagonal are zero, then the matrix is called a *Lower triangular matrix,* denoted by ***L***. That is, $\boldsymbol{L}=[a_{ij}]$, $a_{ij}=0$ for $i<j$.

For example, the following matrices are upper and lower matrices, respectively.

$$\begin{bmatrix} 1 & 3 & 1 & 2 \\ 0 & 4 & 0 & 1 \\ 0 & 0 & 5 & 4 \\ 0 & 0 & 0 & 3 \end{bmatrix}, \begin{bmatrix} 2 & 0 & 0 & 0 \\ 2 & 4 & 0 & 0 \\ 1 & 0 & 2 & 0 \\ 4 & 5 & 2 & 3 \end{bmatrix}.$$

These two matrices show that some elements above the diagonal of upper triangular or below the diagonal of lower triangular matrices can also be zero.

Remark 4: Some matrices can be written in product forms of ***L*** and ***U***. That is, ***A=LU.***

An $n \times n$ matrix of the following form is called a *common tridiagonal matrix*

$$\begin{bmatrix} a & c & 0 & 0 & \cdots & 0 & 0 \\ b & a & c & 0 & \cdots & 0 & 0 \\ 0 & b & a & c & 0 & \cdots & 0 \\ & & & \vdots & & & \\ 0 & 0 & 0 & \cdots & 0 & b & a \end{bmatrix}$$

We come back to such matrices in the later sections.

A *conjugate transpose* of matrix ***A***, denoted by $\overline{A}$ is a matrix such that $\overline{A} = [\overline{}$ $a_{Jl}]$. A square matrix ***A*** such that $\overline{A}^T = A$ is called *Hermitian* and denotes it by A^H. It can be shown that

$$(AB)^H = B^H A^H.$$

The square matrix ***A*** is called *symmetric* if $\boldsymbol{A}^T=\boldsymbol{A}$. If $\boldsymbol{A}^T=-\boldsymbol{A}$ then, matrix ***A*** is known as *skew-symmetric.*

For example, $\begin{bmatrix} 2 & 3 & 5 \\ 3 & 1 & -4 \\ 5 & -4 & 6 \end{bmatrix}$ is a symmetric matrix and $\begin{bmatrix} 0 & 2 & 5 \\ -2 & 0 & -3 \\ -5 & -3 & 0 \end{bmatrix}$ is a skew-symmetric matrix.

Remark 5: Any square matrix can be written as the sum of a symmetric and a skew-symmetric matrix.

A square matrix ***A*** is called *idempotent* if, $\boldsymbol{A}^2=\boldsymbol{A}$.

If $\boldsymbol{A}$ is a matrix and k is the least positive integer such that $A^{k+1} = A$, then $\boldsymbol{A}$ is called *periodic* with period k.

If $\boldsymbol{A}^k=0$, $\boldsymbol{A}$ is called *nilpotent.*

In the next section, we define the addition, subtraction, and multiplication of matrices. These operations are governed by certain rules which will be discussed in this section.

10.3 MATRICES ALGEBRA

Assume $\boldsymbol{A}$ and $\boldsymbol{B}$ are two matrices with m rows and n columns, then

Matrix Addition: $A + B = [a_{ij}]_{m\times n} + [b_{ij}]_{m\times n} = [a_{ij} + b_{ij}]_{m\times n}$.

Matrix Subtraction: $A - B = [a_{ij}]_{m\times n} - [b_{ij}]_{m\times n} = [a_{ij} - b_{ij}]_{m\times n}$.

Example 2: Let

$$A = \begin{bmatrix} 1 & 3 & 5 & 2 \\ 4 & 4 & 2 & 1 \\ 2 & -3 & 1 & 4 \\ -1 & 0 & 2 & 3 \end{bmatrix} \text{and } B = \begin{bmatrix} 2 & -2 & 4 & 6 \\ 2 & 4 & 3 & 0 \\ 1 & 0 & 2 & 0 \\ 4 & 5 & -2 & 3 \end{bmatrix}$$

Find $\boldsymbol{A+B}$, $\boldsymbol{B+A}$, $\boldsymbol{A-B}$ and $\boldsymbol{B-A}$.

Solution: We have,

$$A + B = \begin{bmatrix} 3 & 1 & 9 & 8 \\ 6 & 8 & 5 & 1 \\ 3 & -3 & 3 & 4 \\ 3 & 5 & 0 & 6 \end{bmatrix}, \quad B + A = \begin{bmatrix} 3 & 1 & 9 & 8 \\ 6 & 8 & 5 & 1 \\ 3 & -3 & 3 & 4 \\ 3 & 5 & 0 & 6 \end{bmatrix}.$$

Therefore, $\boldsymbol{A+B=B+A}$.

$$A - B = \begin{bmatrix} -1 & 5 & 1 & -4 \\ 2 & 0 & -1 & 1 \\ 1 & -3 & -1 & 4 \\ -5 & -5 & 4 & 0 \end{bmatrix}, \quad B - A = \begin{bmatrix} -1 & 5 & 1 & -4 \\ 2 & 0 & -1 & 1 \\ 1 & -3 & -1 & 4 \\ -5 & -5 & 4 & 0 \end{bmatrix}$$

That is, $\boldsymbol{A-B= -(B-A)}$.

Matrix Multiplication: If $AB = [a_{ij}]_{m\times p} \times [b_{ij}]_{p\times n} = [c_{ij}]_{m\times n} = C$, where

$$c_{ij} = [a_{i1}\, a_{i2} \ldots a_{1n}] \begin{bmatrix} b_{1j} \\ b_{2j} \\ \vdots \\ b_{nj} \end{bmatrix} = \sum\nolimits_{k=1}^{n} a_{ik} b_{kj}.$$

Example 3: Let $A = \begin{bmatrix} 2 & 3 & 1 \\ 5 & 4 & 2 \end{bmatrix}$ and $B = \begin{bmatrix} 1 & 3 \\ 4 & 5 \\ 2 & 1 \end{bmatrix}$. Find ***AB*** and ***BA***.
Solution: We have ***AB*** and ***BA***. respectively

$$AB = \begin{bmatrix} 2 & 3 & 1 \\ 5 & 4 & 2 \end{bmatrix}\begin{bmatrix} 1 & 3 \\ 4 & 5 \\ 2 & 1 \end{bmatrix} = \begin{bmatrix} 16 & 22 \\ 25 & 37 \end{bmatrix}.$$

$$BA = \begin{bmatrix} 1 & 3 \\ 4 & 5 \\ 2 & 1 \end{bmatrix}\begin{bmatrix} 2 & 3 & 1 \\ 5 & 4 & 2 \end{bmatrix} = \begin{bmatrix} 17 & 15 & 7 \\ 33 & 32 & 14 \\ 7 & 10 & 4 \end{bmatrix}.$$

We see that, $\boldsymbol{AB} \neq \boldsymbol{BA}$. Note that tr($\boldsymbol{AB}$)=tr($\boldsymbol{BA}$)=53.

It should be noted that

If $\boldsymbol{AB}=0$, then it is not necessary that $\boldsymbol{A}=0$ or $\boldsymbol{B}=0$

If $\boldsymbol{AB}=\boldsymbol{AC}$, then it not necessary that $\boldsymbol{B}=\boldsymbol{C}$

Multiplication by Scalar: $\alpha A = \alpha[a_{ij}] = [\alpha a_{ij}]$.

Definition 2. Inverse matrix of a $n \times n$ matrix $\boldsymbol{A}$ is a matrix denoted by $\boldsymbol{A}^{-1}$ such that $\boldsymbol{A}^{-1}\boldsymbol{A}= \boldsymbol{A}\boldsymbol{A}^{-1}= \boldsymbol{I}$.

Remark 6: $(\boldsymbol{AB})^{-1}=\boldsymbol{B}^{-1}\boldsymbol{A}^{-1}$. In general, if $\boldsymbol{A}_1,\boldsymbol{A}_2,\ldots,\boldsymbol{A}_k$ are invertible, then

$$(A_1.A_2,\ldots.A_k)^{-1} = A_k^{-1}.A_{k-1}^{-1}.\ldots.A_2^{-1}.A_1^{-1}.$$

The division of two matrices, $\boldsymbol{A}$ and $\boldsymbol{B}$ that is $\frac{B}{A}$, cannot be directly defined. But, since we have $\boldsymbol{AA}^{-1}=\boldsymbol{I}$ according to the inverse definition, then we can write

$$\frac{B}{A} = \frac{BA^{-1}}{AA^{-1}} = \frac{BA^{-1}}{I} = BA^{-1},$$

with a condition that $\boldsymbol{A}$ is invertible. Apart from this condition, when division is possible that if $\boldsymbol{A}$ is a square matrix and the multiplication of two matrices $\boldsymbol{B}$ and $\boldsymbol{A}^{-1}$ is also possible. In other words, $\boldsymbol{A}$ is a $n \times n$ matrix and $\boldsymbol{B}$ is a $m \times n$ matrix.

Determining the inverse of a matrix requires some more definitions, in particular the *determinant of a matrix*, which plays an important role in the theory of matrices. Therefore, in the next section, we will define the determinant and its properties. Then we introduce the *congruent* and *adjoint matrices*, and then we introduce the following relation to specify $\boldsymbol{A}^{-1}$,

$$A^{-1} = \frac{adj(A)}{\det(A)}, \tag{1}$$

provided, $\det(\boldsymbol{A})\neq 0$.

Remark 7: If $\det(\boldsymbol{A})\neq 0$. we say the matrix is *invertible*.

Definition 3: We say the matrix $\boldsymbol{A}$ is *singular* if, det($\boldsymbol{A}$)≠0.

Remark 8: There exists $\boldsymbol{A}^{-1}$ iff, $\boldsymbol{A}$ is non-singular.

The rest of this section is optional and can be useful for readers to have more knowledge about some other operation matrices.

Definition 4: **(Optimal)** Two matrices $\boldsymbol{A}$ and $\boldsymbol{B}$ are *similar* if there exists a non-singular matrix P such that $\boldsymbol{PAP^{-1}=B}$.

Remark 9: If $\boldsymbol{A}$ is similar to $\boldsymbol{B}$ and $\boldsymbol{B}$ is similar to $\boldsymbol{C}$, then $\boldsymbol{A}$ is similar to $\boldsymbol{C}$.

Remark 10: If $\boldsymbol{A}$ is similar to $\boldsymbol{B}$, then $\boldsymbol{A}^{-1}$ is similar to $\boldsymbol{B}^{-1}$ and also $\boldsymbol{A}^k$ is similar to $\boldsymbol{B}^k$.

Remark 11: (*Power expansion*). If $\boldsymbol{A}$ and $\boldsymbol{B}$ commute then

$$(A+B)^n = \sum_{k=0}^{n}\binom{n}{k}A^{n-k}\,B^k.$$

Remark 12: If $\boldsymbol{A}$ is similar to $\boldsymbol{B}$, then, $\boldsymbol{A}^k$ is similar to $\boldsymbol{B}^k$.

Remark 13: We know that for any real value of x,

$$e^x = 1+\frac{x}{1!}+\frac{x^2}{2!}+\frac{x^3}{3!}+\dots.$$

Hence, the powers of matrices can be calculated like powers of real numbers so that e^A can be defined with the following formula:

$$e^A = 1+\frac{A}{1!}+\frac{A^2}{2!}+\frac{A^3}{3!}+\dots.$$

Example 4: Assume $A = \begin{bmatrix} x & 0 \\ 0 & y \end{bmatrix}$. Prove that and $e^A = \begin{bmatrix} e^x & 0 \\ 0 & e^y \end{bmatrix}$.

Solution: We have

$$e^A = 1+\frac{A}{1!}+\frac{A^2}{2!}+\frac{A^3}{3!}+\dots = \begin{bmatrix} 1 & 0 \\ 0 & 1 \end{bmatrix} + \begin{bmatrix} x & 0 \\ 0 & y \end{bmatrix} + \frac{1}{2!}\begin{bmatrix} x^2 & 0 \\ 0 & y^2 \end{bmatrix} + \frac{1}{3!}\begin{bmatrix} x^3 & 0 \\ 0 & y^3 \end{bmatrix} + \dots$$

$$= \begin{bmatrix} 1+x+\frac{x^2}{2!}+\frac{x^3}{3!} = \dots & 0 \\ 0 & 1+x+\frac{x^2}{2!}+\frac{x^3}{3!} = \dots \end{bmatrix} = \begin{bmatrix} e^x & 0 \\ 0 & e^y \end{bmatrix}.$$

Let elements of matrix $\boldsymbol{A}$ be a function of t. Then

$$DA = \lim_{\Delta t\to 0}\frac{\Delta A}{\Delta t} = \frac{dA}{dt}.$$

If $\boldsymbol{A}$ and $\boldsymbol{B}$ are differentiable, then the following properties hold:

(i) $\frac{d}{dt}(A + B) = \frac{dA}{dt} + \frac{dB}{dt}$

(ii) $\frac{d}{dt}(AB) = \frac{dA}{dt}B + A\frac{dB}{dt}$

(iii) $\frac{d}{dt}(A_1A_2\ldots A_n) = \frac{dA_1}{dt}(A_2\ldots A_n) + A_1\frac{dA_2}{dt}(A_3\ldots A_n) + \ldots + A_1A_2\ldots A_{n-1}\frac{dA_n}{dt}.$

10.4 DETERMINANT

We assign a number to each matrix like $\boldsymbol{A}$, which is called the *determinant* of the matrix. We show it with the symbol det($\boldsymbol{A}$) or $|\boldsymbol{A}|$. A general formula to determine the determinant of $\boldsymbol{A}$ is given by

$$\begin{aligned}\det(A) = |A| &= \sum_{j=1}^{n}(-1)^{i+j}a_{ij}M_{ij};\text{(expansion by } i\text{th row)}\\ &= \sum_{i=1}^{n}(-1)^{i+j}a_{ij}M_{ij};\text{(expansion by } j\text{th column)},\end{aligned} \tag{2}$$

where the M_{ij} called the *minor* of element a_{ij}, which is the determinant of $(n - 1) \times (n - 1)$ matrix is obtained by deleting the ith row and the jth column of $\boldsymbol{A}$.

Theorem 1. The row (or column) expansion in (2) gives the same result for det($\boldsymbol{A}$).

Proof: See, e.g., Anton (1977).

These two expansions in (2) are known as *Laplace expansions*.

From (2), for n=2 and n=3 we have,

$$|A| = \begin{vmatrix} a_{11} & a_{12} \\ a_{21} & a_{22} \end{vmatrix} = a_{11}a_{22} - a_{12}a_{21}$$

$$|A| = \begin{vmatrix} a_{11} & a_{12} & a_{13} \\ a_{21} & a_{22} & a_{23} \\ a_{31} & a_{32} & a_{33} \end{vmatrix} = a_{11}\begin{vmatrix} a_{22} & a_{23} \\ a_{32} & a_{32} \end{vmatrix} - a_{12}\begin{vmatrix} a_{21} & a_{23} \\ a_{31} & a_{33} \end{vmatrix} + a_{13}\begin{vmatrix} a_{21} & a_{22} \\ a_{31} & a_{32} \end{vmatrix}.$$

For n=3, we also can directly use the following relation:

$$|A| = \begin{vmatrix} a_{11} & a_{12} & a_{13} \\ a_{21} & a_{22} & a_{23} \\ a_{31} & a_{32} & a_{33} \end{vmatrix} = \begin{matrix} a_{11} & a_{12} & a_{13} \\ a_{21} & a_{22} & a_{23} \\ a_{31} & a_{32} & a_{33} \end{matrix}\begin{vmatrix} a_{11} & a_{12} \\ a_{21} & a_{23} \\ a_{31} & a_{32} \end{matrix}$$

$$= (a_{11}a_{22}a_{33} + a_{12}a_{23}a_{32+}a_{13}a_{21}a_{33}) - (a_{13}a_{22}a_{31} + a_{11}a_{23}a_{32+}a_{12}a_{21}a_{33})$$

This method is known as the *Sarrus rule*.

Example 5: Find $\begin{vmatrix} 2 & 1 & 5 \\ 3 & 0 & 4 \\ 0 & 6 & 2 \end{vmatrix}$ by Sarrus rule.

Solution: We have $\begin{vmatrix} 2 & 1 & 5 \\ 3 & 0 & 4 \\ 0 & 6 & 2 \end{vmatrix} = \begin{matrix} 2 & 1 & 5 \\ 3 & 0 & 4 \\ 0 & 6 & 2 \end{matrix}\begin{vmatrix} 2 & 1 \\ 3 & 0 \\ 0 & 6 \end{matrix}$= (0+0+90) – (0+48+6)=36.

Let $A_{ij} = (-1)^{i+j}M_{ij}$, then $\det(A) = \sum a_{ij}A_{ij}$. The quantity A_{ij} is known as a *cofactor*. The *Adjoint Matrix*, denoted by adj(**A**), is defined by the following expression,

$$\text{adj}(A) = \begin{bmatrix} A_{11}\cdots A_{ji}\cdots A_{n1} \\ \vdots \\ A_{1i}\cdots a_{ji}\cdots a_{ni} \\ \vdots \\ A_{1n}\cdots A_{jn}\cdots A_{nn} \end{bmatrix}.$$

Now, we are able to find $\boldsymbol{A}^{-1}$ by (1). That is,

$$A^{-1} = \frac{adj(A)}{\det(A)} \text{ provided that } \det(A) \neq 0.$$

Determinants have the following properties that can be used in calculations.

(i) If all the elements in a row (or in a column) of **A** are zero, then, det(**A**)=0.
(ii) If the matrix **A** has two identical rows (or columns), then, det(**A**).
(iii) If all the elements in a row (or in a column) of **A** are multiplied by a number k, then the value of the determinant of a resultant matrix is k det(**A**).
(iv) If a row (or a column) of **A** is multiplied by a number k and be added to another row (or a column), then the value of the det(**A**) does not change.
(v) If we transpose two adjacent rows (or columns), it will change the sign in the value of the determinant. That is, is det(**A**) becomes -det(**A**).
(vi) det(**U**)= det(**L**)= $a_{11}a_{22}\cdots a_{m}$.
(vii) det(**A**)=det($\boldsymbol{A}^T$).

Example 6: Show that,

$$\begin{vmatrix} 1 & 2 & 3 & 4 \\ 5 & 6 & 7 & 8 \\ 9 & 10 & 11 & 12 \\ 13 & 14 & 15 & 16 \end{vmatrix} = 0.$$

Solution: If we subtract the first row from the third row, and the second row from the fourth row, we get

$$\begin{vmatrix} 1 & 2 & 3 & 4 \\ 4 & 4 & 4 & 4 \\ 9 & 10 & 11 & 12 \\ 4 & 4 & 4 & 4 \end{vmatrix} = 0.$$

Because two rows are identical.

Example 7: Show that,

$$\begin{vmatrix} 1 & 3 & -2 & 4 \\ 2 & -3 & 1 & 12 \\ 3 & 9 & 0 & -3 \\ 2 & 6 & -4 & 13 \end{vmatrix} = -270$$

.

Solution: If we subtract the first row twice from the fourth row and three times from the third row, we will get

$$\begin{vmatrix} 1 & 3 & -2 & 4 \\ 0 & -9 & 5 & 2 \\ 0 & 0 & 6 & -15 \\ 0 & 0 & 0 & 5 \end{vmatrix}.$$

Since this is an upper triangular matrix then the determinant is $1 \times (-9) \times 6 \times 5 = -270$

Now that we are familiar with the determinant and its properties, we will continue our discussion about determining the inverse of $\boldsymbol{A}$.

Determinants of common tridiagonal matrices $n \times n$ can be obtained by converting them into differential equations. Here we explain how to calculate with an example.

Suppose

$$D_n = \begin{vmatrix} a & b & 0 & 0 & \cdots & 0 & 0 \\ c & a & b & 0 & \cdots & 0 & 0 \\ 0 & c & a & b & 0 & \cdots & 0 \\ & & & \vdots & & & \\ 0 & 0 & 0 & \cdots & 0 & c & a \end{vmatrix}.$$

Expanding by the first row leads to the following recurrence relation $D_n - a D_{n-1} + bcD_{n-2} = 0, n>2$.

This is a homogeneous equation with $r^2 - ar+bc=0$, $n>2$. Then,

$$r = a \pm \sqrt{b^2 - 4ac} = a \pm i\sqrt{4ac - b^2} \text{ if } b^2 - 4ac<0.$$

It is not difficult to show that the general solution to this equation is

$$D_n = (\sqrt{bc})^n (Acosn\theta + Bsinn\theta).$$

We have, $D_1 = a$ and $D_2 = a^2 - bc$, then $A=1$ and $B=\cot\theta$. Thus

$$D_n = \frac{(\sqrt{bc})^n \sin(n+1)\theta}{\sin\theta},$$

where, $\cos\theta = \frac{a}{2\sqrt{bc}}$ and $\sin\theta \neq 0$. If, $\sin\theta=0$, then we use

$$\lim_{\theta \to 0} \frac{\sin(n+1)\theta}{\sin\theta} = n+1.$$

That is,

$$D_n = (n+1)(\sqrt{bc})^n.$$

Example 8: Find,

$$\begin{vmatrix} 4 & 2 & 0 \\ 2 & 4 & 2 \\ 0 & 2 & 4 \end{vmatrix}.$$

Solution: We have, $D_1 = a = 4$ and $D_2 = a^2 - bc = 0$, then,

$$\cos\theta = \frac{4}{2\sqrt{4}} = 1, i.e., \theta = 0. \text{ Thus}, D_3 = (3+1)(\sqrt{4})^3 = 32.$$

As we have already mentioned, the covariance matrix $\boldsymbol{A}$ is a matrix whose members are composed of its cofactors. If we denote this matrix by $\boldsymbol{N}$, then the adjoint matrix of $\boldsymbol{A}$ is the transpose of the matrix $\boldsymbol{N}$. That is N^T. Now, according to this information, we can obtain the inverse of $\boldsymbol{A}^{-1}$ using Eq. (1).

***Example* 9:** Determine the inverse of the matrix $\boldsymbol{A}$ in example 4.

Solution: We have,

$$A = \begin{bmatrix} 2 & 1 & 5 \\ 3 & 0 & 4 \\ 0 & 6 & 2 \end{bmatrix}, |A| = 36.$$

To find adj($\boldsymbol{A}$) we verify $\boldsymbol{N}$ because adj($\boldsymbol{A}$)=$\boldsymbol{N}^T$. We have,

$$N = \begin{bmatrix} \begin{vmatrix} 0 & 4 \\ 6 & 2 \end{vmatrix} & -\begin{vmatrix} 3 & 4 \\ 0 & 2 \end{vmatrix} & \begin{vmatrix} 3 & 0 \\ 0 & 6 \end{vmatrix} \\ -\begin{vmatrix} 1 & 5 \\ 6 & 2 \end{vmatrix} & \begin{vmatrix} 2 & 5 \\ 0 & 2 \end{vmatrix} & -\begin{vmatrix} 2 & 5 \\ 0 & 2 \end{vmatrix} \\ \begin{vmatrix} 1 & 5 \\ 0 & 4 \end{vmatrix} & -\begin{vmatrix} 1 & 5 \\ 0 & 4 \end{vmatrix} & \begin{vmatrix} 2 & 1 \\ 3 & 0 \end{vmatrix} \end{bmatrix} = \begin{bmatrix} -24 & -6 & 18 \\ 28 & 4 & -12 \\ 4 & -7 & -3 \end{bmatrix}.$$

Therefore,

$$N^T = \begin{bmatrix} -24 & 28 & 4 \\ -6 & 4 & -8 \\ 18 & -7 & -3 \end{bmatrix} = adj(A).$$

Using Eq. (1), we get

$$A^{-1} = \frac{adj(A)}{\det(A)} = \frac{\begin{bmatrix} -24 & 28 & 4 \\ -6 & 4 & -7 \\ 18 & -12 & -3 \end{bmatrix}}{36} = \begin{bmatrix} \frac{-2}{3} & \frac{7}{9} & \frac{1}{9} \\ \frac{-1}{6} & \frac{1}{9} & \frac{-7}{36} \\ \frac{1}{2} & \frac{-1}{3} & \frac{-1}{12} \end{bmatrix}.$$

To check that the inverse of $\boldsymbol{A}$ is correct, we should have $\boldsymbol{AA^{-1}=I}$. We have,

$$AA^{-1} = \begin{bmatrix} 2 & 1 & 5 \\ 3 & 0 & 4 \\ 0 & 6 & 2 \end{bmatrix} \begin{bmatrix} \frac{-2}{3} & \frac{7}{9} & \frac{1}{9} \\ \frac{-1}{6} & \frac{1}{9} & \frac{-7}{36} \\ \frac{1}{2} & \frac{-1}{3} & \frac{-1}{12} \end{bmatrix} = \begin{bmatrix} 1 & 0 & 0 \\ 0 & 1 & 0 \\ 0 & 0 & 1 \end{bmatrix} = I.$$

We note that to know that the matrix $\boldsymbol{N}$ is correct, the product of each row (or column) in the same row (or column) of the matrix $\boldsymbol{A}$ should be equal to the determinant of the matrix, which is 36. This is a good test to even know if the determinant $\boldsymbol{A}$ is correct or not. We can also obtain det($\boldsymbol{A}$) in this way, without calculating it first.

Example 10: If

Solution: First, we find $\boldsymbol{B}^{-1}$. We have

$$N = \begin{bmatrix} \begin{vmatrix} 2 & 1 \\ -1 & 1 \end{vmatrix} & -\begin{vmatrix} 3 & 1 \\ 0 & 1 \end{vmatrix} & \begin{vmatrix} 3 & 2 \\ 0 & -1 \end{vmatrix} \\ -\begin{vmatrix} 1 & 0 \\ -1 & 1 \end{vmatrix} & \begin{vmatrix} 2 & 0 \\ 0 & 1 \end{vmatrix} & -\begin{vmatrix} 2 & 1 \\ 0 & -1 \end{vmatrix} \\ \begin{vmatrix} 1 & 0 \\ 2 & 1 \end{vmatrix} & -\begin{vmatrix} 1 & 0 \\ 2 & 1 \end{vmatrix} & \begin{vmatrix} 2 & 1 \\ 3 & 2 \end{vmatrix} \end{bmatrix} = \begin{bmatrix} 3 & -3 & -3 \\ -1 & 2 & 2 \\ 1 & -2 & 1 \end{bmatrix}.$$

Clearly, $|B|=3$. Check it. Thus,

$$N^T = \begin{bmatrix} 3 & -1 & 1 \\ -3 & 2 & -2 \\ -3 & 2 & 1 \end{bmatrix} = adj(B).$$

Using Eq.1, we get

$$B^{-1} = \frac{adj(B)}{\det(B)} = \frac{\begin{bmatrix} 3 & -1 & 1 \\ -3 & 2 & -2 \\ -3 & 2 & 1 \end{bmatrix}}{3} = \begin{bmatrix} 1 & \frac{-1}{3} & \frac{1}{3} \\ -1 & \frac{2}{3} & \frac{-2}{3} \\ -1 & \frac{2}{3} & \frac{1}{3} \end{bmatrix}.$$

Therefore,

$$\frac{A}{B} = \frac{AB^{-1}}{BB^{-1}} = \frac{AB^{-1}}{I} = AB^{-1} = \begin{bmatrix} 1 & -2 & 3 \\ 0 & 2 & 4 \\ -5 & 1 & 0 \end{bmatrix} \begin{bmatrix} 1 & \frac{-1}{3} & \frac{1}{3} \\ -1 & \frac{2}{3} & \frac{-2}{3} \\ -1 & \frac{2}{3} & \frac{1}{3} \end{bmatrix} = \begin{bmatrix} 0 & \frac{1}{3} & \frac{8}{3} \\ -6 & 4 & 0 \\ -6 & \frac{7}{3} & \frac{-7}{3} \end{bmatrix}.$$

10.5 SYSTEM OF LINEAR EQUATIONS

We started this chapter by specifying a polynomial of the degree 2, i.e., $P(x)=ax^2+bx+c$ so that, $P(1)=2$, $P'(1)=0$ and $P''(1)=-2$. According to this data, we can have the following arrangements.

$$\begin{bmatrix} 1 & 1 & 1 \\ 2 & 1 & 0 \\ 2 & 0 & 0 \end{bmatrix}, \begin{bmatrix} a \\ b \\ c \end{bmatrix}, \begin{bmatrix} 2 \\ 0 \\ -2 \end{bmatrix}.$$

If we assume $A = \begin{bmatrix} 1 & 1 & 1 \\ 2 & 1 & 0 \\ 2 & 0 & 0 \end{bmatrix}$, $x = \begin{bmatrix} a \\ b \\ c \end{bmatrix}$ and $b = \begin{bmatrix} 2 \\ 0 \\ -2 \end{bmatrix}$, where $\boldsymbol{A}$, is a coefficient matrix, $\underline{x}$,. an unknown column vector and $\underline{b}$ a known column vector. This leads to writing this system of equations in the following form:

$$A\underline{x} = \underline{b}, \tag{2}$$

In general, any standard linear equation problem is given by

$$\begin{aligned} a_{11}x_1 + a_{12}x_2 + a_{13}x_3 + \ldots.+a_{1n}x_n &= b_1 \\ a_{21}x_1 + a_{22}x_2 + a_{23}x_3 + \ldots.+a_{2n}x_n &= b_2 \\ &\vdots \\ a_{n1}x_1 + a_{n2}x_2 + a_{n3}x_3 + \ldots.+a_{nn}x_n &= b_n, \end{aligned} \tag{3}$$

n be written in the following form:

$$\begin{bmatrix} a_{11}\ldots a_{1j}\ldots a_{1n} \\ \vdots \\ a_{i1}\ldots a_{ij}\ldots a_{in} \\ \vdots \\ a_{n1}\ldots a_{nj}\ldots a_{nn} \end{bmatrix} \begin{bmatrix} x_1 \\ \vdots \\ x_j \\ \vdots \\ x_n \end{bmatrix} = \begin{bmatrix} b_1 \\ \vdots \\ b_j \\ \vdots \\ b_n \end{bmatrix} \tag{4}$$

where the coefficients a_{ij} and $b_i(i=1(1)n, j=1(1)n)$ are constants. In this section, we introduce three methods to solve (4).

A linear system that has no solutions is said to be *inconsistent*. If it has at least one solution, then the system is called *consistent*. For example, the following system is inconsistent.

$$x + y + z = 3$$

$$5x + y + z = 2$$

$$3x + y + z = 4.$$

Given a system of linear equations, we shall want to decide whether the system is consistent or not. If it is consistent, we will find its solutions. In Section 2.3 we discussed methods for solving systems of two linear equations in two unknowns. We shall now develop a method that can be used to solve any linear system. The following methods have been introduced in most textbooks on Linear Algebra. For example, see (Anton, 2977) (Hoffman & Kunze, 1971).

10.5.1 Solving the System of Linear Equations with the Inverse

As we mentioned, this kind of linear system of equations can be written in the form given by Eq. (2). That is,

$$A\underline{x} = \underline{b}$$

Theoretically, Eq. (2) has a solution given by

$$\underline{x} = A^{-1}\underline{b}. \tag{5}$$

Therefore, to find the solution of this system of linear equations, one of the techniques is to find the inverse of the coefficient matrix. Now, if we apply (5) to the above system, we get,

$$\begin{bmatrix} x_1 \\ x_2 \\ x_3 \end{bmatrix} = \begin{bmatrix} 1 & 1 & 1 \\ 2 & 1 & 0 \\ 2 & 0 & 0 \end{bmatrix}^{-1} \begin{bmatrix} 2 \\ 0 \\ -2 \end{bmatrix}.$$

Let's find the inverse matrix. We have,

$$N = \begin{bmatrix} \begin{vmatrix} 1 & 0 \\ 0 & 0 \end{vmatrix} & -\begin{vmatrix} 2 & 0 \\ 2 & 0 \end{vmatrix} & \begin{vmatrix} 2 & 1 \\ 2 & 0 \end{vmatrix} \\ -\begin{vmatrix} 2 & 1 \\ 2 & 0 \end{vmatrix} & \begin{vmatrix} 1 & 1 \\ 2 & 0 \end{vmatrix} & -\begin{vmatrix} 1 & 1 \\ 2 & 0 \end{vmatrix} \\ \begin{vmatrix} 1 & 1 \\ 1 & 0 \end{vmatrix} & -\begin{vmatrix} 1 & 1 \\ 2 & 0 \end{vmatrix} & \begin{vmatrix} 1 & 1 \\ 2 & 1 \end{vmatrix} \end{bmatrix} = \begin{bmatrix} 0 & 0 & -2 \\ 0 & -2 & 2 \\ -1 & 2 & -1 \end{bmatrix}.$$

Clearly, $|A|=-2$. Thus,

$$N^T = \begin{bmatrix} 0 & -1 & 1 \\ 0 & -2 & 2 \\ -2 & 2 & -1 \end{bmatrix} = adj(A).$$

Using Eq. (1), we obtain

$$A^{-1} = \frac{adj(A)}{\det(A)} = \frac{\begin{bmatrix} 0 & -1 & 1 \\ 0 & -2 & 2 \\ -2 & 2 & -1 \end{bmatrix}}{-2} = \begin{bmatrix} 0 & \frac{1}{2} & \frac{1}{-2} \\ 0 & 1 & -1 \\ 1 & -1 & \frac{1}{2} \end{bmatrix}.$$

Therefore,

$$\begin{bmatrix} x_1 \\ x_2 \\ x_3 \end{bmatrix} = \begin{bmatrix} 0 & \frac{1}{2} & \frac{1}{-2} \\ 0 & 1 & -1 \\ 1 & -1 & \frac{1}{2} \end{bmatrix} \begin{bmatrix} 2 \\ 0 \\ -2 \end{bmatrix} = \begin{bmatrix} -1 \\ 2 \\ 1 \end{bmatrix} \Rightarrow x_1 = -1, x_2 = 2 \text{and} x_3 = 1.$$

Example 11: Use $\underline{x} = A^{-1}\underline{b}$and solve $\begin{cases} x + 2y + 3z = 1 \\ x + 3y + 4z = 1 \\ x + 4y + 4z = 2. \end{cases}$

Solution: We have, $A = \begin{bmatrix} 1 & 2 & 3 \\ 1 & 3 & 4 \\ 1 & 4 & 4 \end{bmatrix}, \underline{b} = \begin{bmatrix} 1 \\ 1 \\ 2 \end{bmatrix}$ and $\begin{bmatrix} x \\ y \\ z \end{bmatrix}$. Thus

$$\underline{x} = A^{-1}\underline{b} \Rightarrow \begin{bmatrix} x \\ y \\ z \end{bmatrix} = \begin{bmatrix} 1 & 2 & 3 \\ 1 & 3 & 4 \\ 1 & 4 & 4 \end{bmatrix}^{-1} \begin{bmatrix} 1 \\ 1 \\ 2 \end{bmatrix}.$$

It is not difficult to show that $A^{-1} = \begin{bmatrix} 4 & -4 & 1 \\ 0 & -1 & 2 \\ -1 & 2 & -1 \end{bmatrix}$. Hence

$$\begin{bmatrix} x \\ y \\ z \end{bmatrix} = \begin{bmatrix} 4 & -4 & 1 \\ 0 & -1 & 2 \\ -1 & 2 & -1 \end{bmatrix} \begin{bmatrix} 1 \\ 1 \\ 2 \end{bmatrix} = \begin{bmatrix} 2 \\ 1 \\ -1 \end{bmatrix} \rightarrow x = 2, y = 1, z = -1.$$

10.5.2 Solving the System of Linear Equations with Cramer's Rule

This is a simple method using just a series of determinants to find $\underline{x}$ by

$$\underline{x} = \frac{|A_i|}{|A|}, \tag{6}$$

where A_i is a matrix formed from A by replacing the ith column of A with $\underline{b}$. That is,

$$x_1 = \frac{|A_1|}{|A|}, x_2 = \frac{|A_2|}{|A|}, \ldots, x_n = \frac{|A_n|}{|A|}.$$

Example 12: Solve $\begin{cases} x + 2y + z = 6 \\ x + 3y + 4z = 5 \\ 2x + 2y + z = 8. \end{cases}$

Solution: We have, $A = \begin{bmatrix} 1 & 2 & 3 \\ 1 & 3 & 4 \\ 1 & 4 & 4 \end{bmatrix}, \underline{b} = \begin{bmatrix} 1 \\ 1 \\ 2 \end{bmatrix}$ and $\underline{x} = \begin{bmatrix} x \\ y \\ z \end{bmatrix}$. Thus

$$x = \frac{\begin{vmatrix} 1 & 2 & 3 \\ 1 & 3 & 4 \\ 2 & 4 & 4 \end{vmatrix}}{\begin{vmatrix} 1 & 2 & 3 \\ 1 & 3 & 4 \\ 1 & 4 & 4 \end{vmatrix}} = 2, y = \frac{\begin{vmatrix} 1 & 1 & 3 \\ 1 & 1 & 4 \\ 1 & 2 & 4 \end{vmatrix}}{\begin{vmatrix} 1 & 2 & 3 \\ 1 & 3 & 4 \\ 1 & 4 & 4 \end{vmatrix}} = 1 \text{and } z = \frac{\begin{vmatrix} 1 & 2 & 1 \\ 1 & 3 & 1 \\ 1 & 4 & 2 \end{vmatrix}}{\begin{vmatrix} 1 & 2 & 3 \\ 1 & 3 & 4 \\ 1 & 4 & 4 \end{vmatrix}} = 2.$$

10.5.3 Solving the System of Linear Equations with Gaussian Method

The method is based on the fact that the interchanging of two equations or the addition of a multiple of one equation to another does not change the solutions. These operations reduce the system to an upper triangular (lower triangular) system of equations which can be solved by backward (forward) substitution. To have a triangular system, we introduce a matrix $A|\underline{b}$by using the matrix of coefficients and the vector. This matrix is called an *augmented matrix*. Then, with a series of algebraic operations called the *row operations*, we convert the matrix $\boldsymbol{A}$ into an upper triangular matrix. That's, $U|\underline{b}'$. Then we obtain $x_n, x_{n-1}, \ldots, x_1$ respectively. For example, in step k, eliminates the coefficients $a^{(k)}_{ik}$ with the following row operations:

$$rowi - m_{ik} \times rowk, i = k + 1, \ldots, n.$$

where $m_{ik} = \frac{a^{(k)}_{ik}}{a^{(k)}_{kk}}$.

This is a numerically stable algorithm used in computer software. We can, in general, use the following algorithm as a part of our program implementation as an optional task:

for k=1,..,n–1 (step counter)
for i=k+1,…,n (row counter)

$$m_{i2} = \frac{a_{ik}^{(k)}}{a_{kk}^{(k)}}$$

for j=k+1,…,n (column counter)

$$a_{ij}^{(k+1)} = a_{ij}^{(k)} - m_{ik} * a_{kj}^{(k)} j$$

end j

$$b_i^{(k+1)} = b_i^{(k)} - m_{ik} * b_k^{(k)}$$

end i
end k.

We describe this method by considering the following example.

Example 13: Solve the following system by the Gauss elimination method.

$$2x_1 - x_2 + 3x_3 + 2x_4 = -2$$
$$x_1 + x_2 - 4x_3 + x_4 = 2$$
$$3x_1 + 2x_2 + x_3 - 6x_4 = 1$$
$$x_1 + 3x_2 + 2x_3 - x_4 = 0.$$

Solution: In the first step, we must eliminate $a_{i1}^{(1)}, i = 2,3,4$, with following row operation,

$$Rowk - m_{k1} * Row1, k = 2,3,4.$$

This leads to

$$2x_1 - x_2 + 3x_3 + 2x_4 = -2$$

$$1.5x_2 - 5.5x_3 = 3$$

$$0.5x_2 + 5.5x_3 - 3x_4 = -2$$

$$5.5x_2 - 5.5x_3 - 6x_4 = 5.$$

In the next step, we should eliminate $a_{i2}^{(1)}, i = 3,4$, with

$$Rowk - m_{k2} * Row2, k = 3,4.$$

We obtain,

$$2x_1 - x_2 + 3x_3 + 2x_4 = -2$$

$$1.5x_2 - 5.5x_3 = 3$$

$$7.3333x_3 - 3x_4 = -3$$

$$14.6667x_3 - 6x_4 = -6.$$

The last step is to eliminate $a_{k3}^{(2)}$, with

$$Rowk - m_{k3} * Row3, k = 4.$$

This leads to

$$2x_1 - x_2 + 3x_3 + 2x_4 = -2$$

$$1.5x_2 - 5.5x_3 = 3$$

$$7.3333x_3 - 3x_4 = -3$$

$$-6x_4 = -6.$$

It is clear that by backward substitution we obtain, x_4=1, x_3=0, x_2=2 and x_1=-1, respectively.

The algorithm breaks down if $a_{kk}^{(k)} = 0$. Also, a small $a_{kk}^{(k)}$ gives large m_{ik} and instability occurs in the algorithm. For example, consider

$$0.0002x_1 + 1.3241x_2 = 2.6512$$

$$x_1 - x_2 - 13.$$

By the elementary elimination method, we get x_1=15 and x_2=2. However, the Gaussian elimination with four decimal figures in the calculations leads to

$$0.0002x_1 + 1.3241x_2 = 2.6512$$

$$-6621.5000x_2 = -13269.0000,$$

whence x_2=2.0039 and x_1=11. The actual value is not correct due to the large multiple m_{21}=5000. The error in the value of x_1 arises because of a round-off error in the calculations. Here this difficulty can be removed by interchanging two rows. That is to write

$$x_1 - x_2 - 13$$

$$0.0002x_1 + 1.3241x_2 = 2.6512.$$

Now in the first step, we obtain

$$x_1 - x_2 - 13$$

$$-1.3241x_2 = -2.6486,$$

whence, x_2=2, x_1=15.

In general, a procedure called *partial pivoting* can be used to overcome the difficulty that may arise in each step. The strategy is to select the element with the largest magnitude (so-called *pivotal element*) in the first column of the matrix, $A^{(k)}$, then interchange row k with the first row (Golub & Van, 1996) (Maron & Lopez, 1991). This ensures that $|m_{ik}| \leq 1$.

Example 14: Solve the following system by the Gauss elimination method.

$$x_1 - x_2 + 2x_3 - x_4 = -8$$
$$2x_1 - 2x_2 + 3x_3 - 3x_4 = -20$$
$$x_1 + x_2 + x_3 = -2$$
$$x_1 - x_2 + 4x_3 + 3x_4 = 4.$$

Solution: Since m_{21}=2, hence there is no necessary to use partial pivoting, but after the first step we obtain

$$x_1 - x_2 + 2x_3 - x_4 = -8$$

$$-x_3 - x_4 = -4$$

$$2x_2 - x_3 + 2x_4 = 6$$

$$2x_3 + 4x_4 = 12.$$

Since $a^{(2)}{}_{22} = 0$ therefore, we interchange the second row with the third row. We get,

$$x_1 - x_2 + 2x_3 - x_4 = -8$$

$$2x_2 - x_3 + x_4 = 6$$

$$-x_3 - x_4 = -4$$

$$2x_3 + 4x_4 = 12.$$

Second-row operation leads to

$$x_1 - x_2 + 2x_3 - x_4 = -8$$

$$2x_2 - x_3 + x_4 = 6$$

$-x_3 - x_4 = -4$

$2x_4 = 4.$

By backward substation, we obtain x_4=2, x_3=2, x_2=4 and x_1=-7, respectively.

Theorem 2. Gaussian elimination is equivalent to an **LU** decomposition of ***A*** where **L** is a unit lower triangular and **U** is upper triangular.

Proof See, e.g., Maron and Lopez (1991).

Remark 14: Solving a system of linear equations by use of inverse or Cramer's rule is useless when n is large. In particular, they are difficult for numerical work. But in such cases, Gaussian elimination method is useful because it is compatible with computer software.

10.6. INTERPRETATION OF THE SOLUTION OF LINEAR EQUATIONS

Recall Eq. (2). $A\underline{x} = \underline{b}$

If $\underline{b} = \underline{0}$,then the system of equations is called *homogeneous*. The system of homogeneous equations has an obvious solution $\underline{x} = \underline{0}$. Can this system have other answers? The answer is positive. This system has many solutions if |***A***|=0. If, |***A***|≠0, the system has only unique solution, namely, $\underline{x} = \underline{0}$.

Example 15: What should be the value of m so that the following system has more than one solution?

$$\begin{cases} 2x - 3y + mz = 0 \\ 8x + 4y - z = 0 \\ 3x - y + 5z = 0. \end{cases}$$

Solution: We must have |***A***|=0. That is, $\begin{vmatrix} 2 & -3 & m \\ 8 & 4 & -1 \\ 3 & -1 & 5 \end{vmatrix} = 0$. Using Sarrus's rule gives (40+9–8m) – (12m+2–120)=0 → m=8.35.

If $\underline{b} \neq 0$,then, the system is called *inhomogeneous*. In this case if, |***A***|≠0, the system has only one unique solution. But if |***A***|=0 then the system can have many solutions or even no solution at all. If |***A***|=0, then the system can have no solution unless each row of the augmented matrix is a combination of two other rows. For example, although the determinant of the following coefficient matrix of the system is zero but has no solution because any row of the augmented matrix is not a combination of the other two rows,

$$\begin{cases} 3x + 2y + z = 1 \\ 4x - 3y - 2z = 3 \\ x + 5y + 3z = 2. \end{cases}$$

But

$$\begin{cases} 3x + 2y + z = 1 \\ 4x - 3y - 2z = 3 \\ x - 5y - 3z = 2. \end{cases}$$

has many solutions because the first row of the augmented matrix is a combination of the second and third rows.

Consider a collection of vectors $\{\underline{v}_1, \underline{v}_2, \ldots, \underline{v}_m\}$

Definition 5: If

$$c_1\underline{v}_1 + c\underline{v}_2 + \ldots + c_m\underline{v}_m = \underline{0}$$

Then the vectors $\{\underline{v}_1, \underline{v}_2, \ldots, \underline{v}_m\}$ is said to *linearly independent* if

$$c_1 = c_2 = \ldots = c_m = 0.$$

If there exist α_i not all zero, such that, $\sum_{i=1}^{m} c_i\underline{v}_i = \underline{0}$, then vectors are *linearly dependent*.

For example, the vectors

$$\left\{ \begin{bmatrix} 0 \\ 1 \\ 0 \end{bmatrix}, \begin{bmatrix} 0 \\ 1 \\ 0 \end{bmatrix}, \begin{bmatrix} 0 \\ 0 \\ 1 \end{bmatrix} \right\}$$

are linearly independent but the vectors

$$\left\{ \begin{bmatrix} 2 \\ -3 \\ 3 \end{bmatrix}, \begin{bmatrix} 5 \\ -1 \\ 3 \end{bmatrix}, \begin{bmatrix} 3 \\ 2 \\ 1 \end{bmatrix} \right\}$$

are linearly dependent.

Note that for any matrix of order $m \times n$, if $m>n$ then vectors must be linearly dependent and the maximum number of linearly independent rows equals the maximum number of linearly independent columns.

One may write

$$x_1\underline{a}_1 + \ldots + x_j\underline{a}_j + \ldots + x_n\underline{a}_n = \underline{b} \tag{7}$$

where $\underline{a}_j = \begin{bmatrix} a_{1j} \\ \vdots \\ a_{nj} \\ \vdots \\ - \end{bmatrix}$. Then,

(i) If $\{\underline{a}_j\}_{j=1}^{n}$ are linearly independent, then there exists a unique solution for any $\underline{b}$.

(ii) If $\{\underline{a}_j\}_{j=1}^{n}$ are linearly dependent, then there does not exist a solution unless $\underline{b}$ is linearly dependent on the $\underline{a}_j$s when the solution is not unique.

(iii) $A\underline{x} = \underline{e}_i$ has solution $\underline{x} = A^{-1}\underline{e}_i$, i.e., ith column of inverse.

Example 16: Show that the following system has a unique solution.

$$\begin{cases} 2x - 3y + z = 1 \\ x + 2y - 3z = 3 \\ 4x - 5y + z = -4. \end{cases}$$

Solution: If we consider each column of the matrix as a vector, we must obtain c_1,c_2 and c_3 from the following equation,

$$c_1\begin{bmatrix} 2 \\ 1 \\ 4 \end{bmatrix} + c_2\begin{bmatrix} -3 \\ 2 \\ -5 \end{bmatrix} + c_3\begin{bmatrix} 1 \\ -3 \\ 1 \end{bmatrix} = 0.$$

We get,

$$\begin{aligned} 2c_1 - 3c_2 + c_3 &= 0 \\ c_1 + 2c_2 - 3c_3 &= 0 \rightarrow c_1 = c_2 = c_3 = 0. \\ 4c_1 - 5c_2 + c_3 &= 0 \end{aligned}$$

Since they form linear independent vectors, then the system has only one solution.

Definition 6: The *rank* of a matrix $\boldsymbol{A}$ is the number of linearly independent column vectors (or row vectors) of $\boldsymbol{A}$.

Remark 15: For a square $n \times n$ matrix $\boldsymbol{A}$, then the matrix is nonsingular if, *Rank* ($\boldsymbol{A}$)=n and it is singular if, *Rank* ($\boldsymbol{A}$)<n.

According to this remark, if the rank of the matrix is less than the number of rows, the system of equations will have an infinite number of solutions.

Example 17: Determine the rank of the matrix $A = \begin{bmatrix} 1 & 2 & 3 \\ -1 & 4 & -6 \\ 2 & -2 & 9 \end{bmatrix}$.

Solution: If we add the third row to the second row we get, $\begin{bmatrix} 1 & 2 & 3 \\ 1 & 2 & 3 \\ 2 & -2 & 9 \end{bmatrix}$. We have two identical rows, thus $|A|=0$. This indicates we have many solutions.

Remark 16: In the case of a homogeneous one, i.e., $A\underline{x} = \underline{0}$ there exist non-trivial solutions if and only if $\{\underline{a}_j\}_{j=1}^{n}$ are linearly dependent.

In the introduction of this chapter, we were able to solve the example by a method so-called the *elimination method*. It may be questioned that the method was simple, but why should we solve a system of linear equations in other ways by using what we learned about matrices? It should be remembered that when the number of unknowns increases, it is tedious to solve them, or directly conclude about the uniqueness of the solution. The methods presented using matrices are also compatible with computers. That is, when the number of equations is large, which is very time-consuming with manual operations, the solutions can be obtained with one programming program, and this would be possible when using the rules that follow the matrices.

10.7. EIGENVALUES AND EIGENVECTORS

The eigenvalues and eigenvectors are numbers and vectors associated with square matrices. The basic concepts of the eigenvalues and eigenvectors are given in most textbooks on linear algebra, in particular, from the computational methods written on eigenvalue problems (Gerald, 1972) (Gourlay & Watson, 1973). From the application point of view, they are useful throughout science and engineering. The solution of an inhomogeneous system of ODEs can be considered by determining the eigenvalues and eigenvectors of the coefficient matrix, in particular when we have a large system of equations, (Hermann & Saravi, 2014).

Let $\boldsymbol{A}$ be a square real matrix of order n. A nonzero vector $\underline{x}$ is called an *eigenvector* of $\boldsymbol{A}$ if there exists a scalar λ such that

$$A\underline{x} = \lambda\underline{x} \tag{8}$$

The scalar λ is called an *eigenvalue* of $\boldsymbol{A}$.

If $\boldsymbol{A}$ has n distinct eigenvalues, then it has n linearly independent eigenvectors, (Gourlay & Watson, 1973).

Theorem 3. Let λ_1 be an eigenvalue of multiplicity m, then, there exists at most m linearly independent eigenvectors associated with this eigenvalue. In particular, if λ_1 is distinct then there exists exactly one eigenvector $\underline{x}_1$ associated with λ_1.

Proof See, e.g., (Gerald, 1972).

To determine λ, we write Eq. (8) in the form $(A - \lambda\mathbf{I})\underline{x} = 0$. This system has a nontrivial solution if

$$|A - \lambda \mathbf{I}| = 0. \tag{9}$$

The relation (9) leads to an algebraic polynomial equation in λ of degree n given by

$$\lambda^n + a_1\lambda^{n-1} + a_2\lambda^{n-2} + \ldots + a_n = 0. \tag{10}$$

This is known as the *characteristic equation* of the matrix $\boldsymbol{A}$.

If we can find all eigenvalues, λ_i, $i=1,2,\ldots,n$, then all eigenvectors can be determined by

$$A\underline{x}_i = \lambda_i \underline{x}_i. \tag{11}$$

Example 18: Find the eigenvalues and corresponding eigenvectors of the following matrix.

$$A = \begin{bmatrix} 1 & 2 \\ 3 & 2 \end{bmatrix}.$$

Solution: We have

$$|A - \lambda \mathbf{I}| = \begin{vmatrix} 1 & -\lambda & 2 \\ 3 & 2 & -\lambda \end{vmatrix} = 0 \Rightarrow (1-\lambda)(2-\lambda) - 6 = 0 \rightarrow \lambda_1 = 4, \lambda_2 = -1.$$

To find corresponding eigenvectors we set, $A\underline{x}_i = \lambda_i \underline{x}_i$. With $\lambda_1=4$, we get

$$\begin{bmatrix} 1 & 2 \\ 3 & 2 \end{bmatrix}\begin{bmatrix} x_1 \\ x_2 \end{bmatrix} = 4\begin{bmatrix} x_1 \\ x_2 \end{bmatrix} \Rightarrow \begin{cases} x_1 + 2x_2 = 4x_1 \\ 3x_1 + 2x_2 = 4x_2 \end{cases} \Rightarrow \begin{cases} -3x_1 + 2x_2 = 0 \\ 3x_1 - 2x_2 = 0 \end{cases} \Rightarrow x_1 = c_1, x_2 = \tfrac{3}{2}c_1.$$

Therefore, $\underline{x}_1 = \begin{bmatrix} x_1 \\ x_2 \end{bmatrix} = \begin{bmatrix} c_1 \\ \frac{3}{2}c_1 \end{bmatrix} = \frac{c_1}{2}\begin{bmatrix} 2 \\ 3 \end{bmatrix}$. Similarly, with $\lambda_2=-1$, we get

$$\begin{bmatrix} 1 & 2 \\ 3 & 2 \end{bmatrix}\begin{bmatrix} x_1 \\ x_2 \end{bmatrix} = -1\begin{bmatrix} x_1 \\ x_2 \end{bmatrix} \Rightarrow \begin{cases} x_1 + 2x_2 = -x_1 \\ 3x_1 + 2x_2 = -x_2 \end{cases} \Rightarrow \begin{cases} 2x_1 + 2x_2 = 0 \\ 3x_1 + 3x_2 = 0 \end{cases} \Rightarrow x_1 = c_1, x_2 = -c_1.$$

Thus, $\underline{x}_2 = \begin{bmatrix} x_1 \\ x_2 \end{bmatrix} = \begin{bmatrix} c_1 \\ -c_1 \end{bmatrix} = c_1\begin{bmatrix} 1 \\ -1 \end{bmatrix}$.

Example 19: Find the eigenvalues and corresponding eigenvectors of the matrix given by

$$A = \begin{bmatrix} 1 & 2 & -1 \\ 2 & 1 & 1 \\ 1 & 1 & 0 \end{bmatrix}.$$

Solution: We have

$$|A - \lambda \mathbf{I}| = \det\begin{bmatrix} 1-\lambda & 2 & -1 \\ 2 & 1-\lambda & 1 \\ 1 & 1 & -\lambda \end{bmatrix} = 0 \Rightarrow \lambda^3 - 6\lambda^2 + 11\lambda - 6 = 0.$$

That is, $(\lambda - 1)(\lambda - 2)(\lambda - 3) = 0 \Rightarrow \lambda = 1, \lambda = 2, \lambda = 3.$

To find corresponding eigenvectors we set, $A\underline{x}_i = \lambda_i \underline{x}_i$. With $\lambda=1$, we get

$$\begin{bmatrix} 1 & 2 & -1 \\ 2 & 1 & 1 \\ 1 & 1 & 0 \end{bmatrix}\begin{bmatrix} x_1 \\ x_2 \\ x_3 \end{bmatrix} = 1\begin{bmatrix} x_1 \\ x_2 \\ x_3 \end{bmatrix}$$

$$\Rightarrow \begin{cases} x_1 + 2x_2 - x_3 = x_1 \\ 2x_1 + x_2 + x_3 = x_2 \\ x_1 + x_2 + 0 = x_1 \end{cases} \Rightarrow \begin{cases} 2x_2 - x_3 = 0 \\ 2x_1 + x_3 = 0 \\ x_1 + x_2 = x_3 \end{cases} \Rightarrow x_1 = c_1, x_2 = -c_1, x_3 = -2c_1.$$

Therefore, $\underline{x}_1 = \begin{bmatrix} x_1 \\ x_2 \\ x_3 \end{bmatrix} = c_1\begin{bmatrix} 1 \\ -1 \\ 2 \end{bmatrix}$. With similar manipulations, we obtain

$\underline{x}_2 = c_2\begin{bmatrix} 1 \\ -1 \\ 1 \end{bmatrix}$ and $\underline{x}_3 = c_3\begin{bmatrix} 1 \\ 1 \\ 0 \end{bmatrix}$.

It is difficult to solve the Eq. (10) equation for $n \geq 3$ so we may use numerical methods to find one or more roots of Eq. (10), for example, Newton's method is discussed in Chapter 5. Nevertheless, numerical methods for approximating roots of polynomial equations of high degree are sensitive to rounding errors, (Gerald, 1972) (Gourlay & Watson, 1973). However, in this section, we summarize some of the properties of eigenvalues that may be useful for determining one or all eigenvalues.

(i) If $\boldsymbol{A}$ is an upper (or lower) triangular matrix then $\lambda_i = a_{ii}, i = 1(1)n$.

(ii) If the sum of elements of each row (or column) is a then one of the eigenvalues is a.

(iii) If rank $(\boldsymbol{A}) < n$, that is $|\boldsymbol{A}|=0$, then one of the eigenvalue is zero

(iv) $\prod^n \lambda_i = |A|$.

(v) $\sum_1^n \lambda_i = \sum_1^n a_{ii}$

(vi) All eigenvalues of a symmetric matrix are real.

(vii) If λ is an eigenvalue of $\boldsymbol{A}$ then λ^k is also one of the eigenvalues of $\boldsymbol{A}^k$, in particular if k=-1 then $\frac{1}{\lambda}$ is an eigenvalue of the inverse matrix of $\boldsymbol{A}$.

(viii) and $\boldsymbol{A}^T$ has the same eigenvalues.

(ix) If λ is an eigenvalue of $\boldsymbol{A}$ and $f(\boldsymbol{A})$ is a polynomial, then $f(\lambda)$ is an eigenvalue of $f(\boldsymbol{A})$.

Example 20: Determine the eigenvalues of matrix $A = \begin{bmatrix} 2 & -2 & 2 \\ 3 & 5 & 3 \\ -1 & 1 & -1 \end{bmatrix}$.

Solution: We have

$$|A - \lambda \mathbf{I}| = \begin{vmatrix} 2 & -2 & 2 \\ 3 & 5 & 3 \\ -1 & 1 & -1 \end{vmatrix} = 0.$$

If we multiply the third row by 2 and then add it to the first row, we obtain all elements zero on the first row. Thus, the determinant is zero. That is one of the eigenvalues is zero. By property (iii), The sum of elements of each column is 4 then, another eigenvalue is 4. By (*vi*), $\sum_1^n \lambda_i = \sum_1^n a_{ii}$. That is, $0+4+\lambda_3 = 2+5-1$. Thus $\lambda_3=2$.

Example 21: Find one of the eigenvalues of $\boldsymbol{A}^{-1}$ if $A = \begin{bmatrix} 1 & 3 & 1 \\ 2 & 1 & 2 \\ 1 & 1 & 3 \end{bmatrix}$.

Solution: The sum of elements of each row is 5 then one of eigenvalues is 5. Thus by property (*vii*) one of the eigenvalues of A^{-1} is $\frac{1}{5}$.

As we mentioned in the previous chapter, difference equations can be used on the theory of linear algebra. We have already used them to find the determinant of common tridiagonal matrices. Now we use the same procedure to find eigenvalues of such matrices.

In section 10.4, we used differential equations to find determinants of a triangular matrix. Here, we come back to discuss once more finding eigenvalues of triangular matrices too.

Suppose,

$$D_n = \begin{vmatrix} a & b & 0 & 0 & \cdots & 0 & 0 \\ c & a & b & 0 & \cdots & 0 & 0 \\ 0 & c & a & b & 0 & \cdots & 0 \\ & & & \vdots & & & \\ 0 & 0 & 0 & \cdots & 0 & c & a \end{vmatrix}. \tag{12}$$

Expanding by the first row leads to the following recurrence relation $D_n - a D_{n-1} + bc D_{n-2} = 0, n>2$.

This is a homogeneous equation with $D_1=a$ and $D_2=a^2-bc$. It is not difficult to show that the general solution to this equation is

$$D_n = (\sqrt{bc})^2 (A cos n\theta + B sin n\theta).$$

We have, $D_1=a$ and $D_2=a^2-bc$, then $A=1$ and $B=\cot\theta$. Thus

$$D_n = \frac{(\sqrt{bc})^2 \sin(n+1)\theta}{\sin\theta},$$

where $\cos\theta = \frac{a}{2\sqrt{bc}}$ and $\sin\theta \neq 0$. Now if replace a by $a-\lambda$ into (12), we get

$$D_n = \frac{(\sqrt{bc})^2 \sin(n+1)\varnothing}{\sin\varnothing} = 0$$

where $\cos\varnothing = \frac{a-\lambda}{2\sqrt{bc}}$ and $\sin\varnothing \neq 0$. Hence

$$\lambda = a - 2\sqrt{bc}\cos\varnothing \text{ where } sin(n+1)\varnothing = 0, \text{i.e.}, \varnothing = \frac{k\pi}{n+1}, \quad k = 1,2,\ldots,n. \quad (13)$$

Example 22: Find all eigenvalues of matrix $\boldsymbol{A}$.

$$A = \begin{bmatrix} 3 & 4 & 0 & 0 & 0 \\ 1 & 3 & 4 & 0 & 0 \\ 0 & 1 & 3 & 4 & 0 \\ 0 & 0 & 1 & 3 & 4 \\ 0 & 0 & 0 & 1 & 3 \end{bmatrix}.$$

Solution: Using the relations in (13), we obtain $\varnothing = \frac{k\pi}{6}$, k=1,2,3,4,5 and

$$\lambda = a - 2\sqrt{bc}\cos\varnothing = 3 - 4\cos\frac{k\pi}{6}, \quad k = 1,2,3,4,5.$$

This leads to

$$\lambda_1 = 3 - 2\sqrt{3}, \lambda_2 = 1, \lambda_3 = 3, \lambda_4 = 4, \lambda_5 = 3 + 2\sqrt{3}.$$

Definition 7: A square matrix $\boldsymbol{A}$ with order n is said to be *non-defective* (*non-deficient*) if, it has n linearly independent eigenvectors, otherwise is called *defective* (*deficient*).

Remark 17: If Hermitian matrix is non-defective then, it contains a set of mutually orthonormal eigenvectors $x_1, x_2, \ldots, x_n$. That is, $x_i^H x_j = \delta_{ij}$.

Remark 18: The Hermitian matrix has real eigenvalues.

Theorem 4. (*Transformation to Diagonal* Form) The matrix $\boldsymbol{A}$ is non-defective if and only if there exists a non-singular matrix $\boldsymbol{X}$, such that $\boldsymbol{X^{-1}AX=D}$, where $\boldsymbol{D}$ is a diagonal matrix.

Theorem 5. There exists a non-defective matrix $\mathbf{P}$ such that, $\mathbf{P^{-1}AP=J}$.

Proof: See Gourlay and Watson (1972).

Definition 8. If square matrix $\boldsymbol{A}$ is not singular and $\boldsymbol{A}^H=\boldsymbol{A}^{-1}$, then $\boldsymbol{A}$ is said to be a *unitary matrix.*

Theorem 6. (*Shur theorem*). There exists a non-defective matrix **P** such that $\mathbf{P}^{-1}\mathbf{AP}=\mathbf{U}$, in particular, there exists unitary matrix **P** such that $\boldsymbol{P}^H\boldsymbol{AP}=\boldsymbol{U}$.

Proof: See Horn and Johnson, 1996).

In Chapter 7, we mentioned that the quadratic surfaces with terms *xy, xz* and *yz* cannot be specified by values of the coefficients of x^2, y^2 and y^2. In this section, by using eigenvalues and corresponding eigenvectors to them and changing their coordinates, we will write them in a form that does not contain terms *xy, xz* and *yz*, and then, with the same procedure as before, the type of the quadratic surfaces can be determined.

Consider $ax^2+bxy+cxz+dy^2+eyz+fz^2$.

From this expression we can drive the following symmetric matrix:

$$A = \begin{pmatrix} a & \frac{b}{2} & \frac{c}{2} \\ \frac{b}{2} & d & \frac{e}{2} \\ \frac{c}{2} & \frac{e}{2} & f \end{pmatrix}.$$

Let's λ_1, λ_2 and λ_3 be eigenvalues of this matrix with corresponding eigenvectors, X_1, X_2 and X_3, respectively. First, we find the unit vectors corresponding to vectors, X_1, X_2 and X_3 then we define the coordinate change matrix denoted by M as follows: $M= (u_1, u_2, u_3)$.

It can be shown that with the coordinate change given by

$$\begin{pmatrix} x \\ y \\ z \end{pmatrix} = M\begin{pmatrix} x' \\ y' \\ z' \end{pmatrix},$$

a quadratic surface is obtained, which is without the constraints of the terms x', y' and z'. This quadratic surface is equivalent to the given quadratic surface.

Example 23: Specify the type of quadratic surface given by $z=xy$.

Solution: From xy we can drive the following symmetric matrix:

$$A = \begin{pmatrix} 0 & \frac{1}{2} & 0 \\ \frac{1}{2} & 0 & 0 \\ 0 & 0 & 0 \end{pmatrix}.$$

We find eigenvalues of this matrix from $|A-\lambda I|=0$. We obtain

$$\begin{vmatrix} -\lambda & \frac{1}{2} & 0 \\ \frac{1}{2} & -\lambda & 0 \\ 0 & 0 & -\lambda \end{vmatrix} = 0 \Rightarrow \lambda\left(\lambda^2 - \frac{1}{4}\right) = 0 \rightarrow \lambda_1 = 0, \lambda_2 = \frac{1}{2} \text{and} \lambda_3 = -\frac{1}{2}.$$

From $AX_1=\lambda_1X_1$, we get

$$\begin{pmatrix} 0 & \frac{1}{2} & 0 \\ \frac{1}{2} & 0 & 0 \\ 0 & 0 & 0 \end{pmatrix}\begin{pmatrix} a_1 \\ a_2 \\ a_3 \end{pmatrix} = 0\begin{pmatrix} a_1 \\ a_2 \\ a_3 \end{pmatrix} \Rightarrow a_1 = a_2 = 0, a_3 = c.$$

$$\therefore X_1 = c\begin{pmatrix} 0 \\ 0 \\ 1 \end{pmatrix} \rightarrow X_1 = \begin{pmatrix} 0 \\ 0 \\ 1 \end{pmatrix}, \text{with} c = 1.$$

Similarly, from $AX_2=\lambda_2X_2$, we get,

$$\begin{pmatrix} 0 & \frac{1}{2} & 0 \\ \frac{1}{2} & 0 & 0 \\ 0 & 0 & 0 \end{pmatrix}\begin{pmatrix} b_1 \\ b_2 \\ b_3 \end{pmatrix} = \frac{1}{2}\begin{pmatrix} b_1 \\ b_2 \\ b_3 \end{pmatrix} \Rightarrow b_1 = b_2 = c, b_3 = 0.$$

$$\therefore X_2 = c\begin{pmatrix} 1 \\ 1 \\ 0 \end{pmatrix} \rightarrow X_2 = \begin{pmatrix} 1 \\ 1 \\ 0 \end{pmatrix}, \text{with} c = 1,$$

and from $AX_3=\lambda_3X_3$, we obtain

$$X_3 = \begin{pmatrix} 1 \\ -1 \\ 0 \end{pmatrix}.$$

From vectors, X_1, X_2 and X_3, we get the following unit vectors

$$u_1 = \begin{pmatrix} 0 \\ 0 \\ 1 \end{pmatrix}, u_2 = \frac{1}{\sqrt{2}}\begin{pmatrix} 1 \\ 1 \\ 0 \end{pmatrix}, u_3 = \frac{1}{\sqrt{2}}\begin{pmatrix} 1 \\ -1 \\ 0 \end{pmatrix}.$$

Therefore,

$$M = (u_1 u_2 u_3) = \frac{1}{\sqrt{2}}\begin{pmatrix} 0 & 1 & 1 \\ 0 & 1 & -1 \\ \sqrt{2} & 0 & 0 \end{pmatrix}.$$

By this coordinate change matrix we get

$$\begin{pmatrix} x \\ y \\ z \end{pmatrix} = \frac{1}{\sqrt{2}}\begin{pmatrix} 0 & 1 & 1 \\ 0 & 1 & -1 \\ \sqrt{2} & 0 & 0 \end{pmatrix}\begin{pmatrix} x' \\ y' \\ z' \end{pmatrix} = \frac{1}{\sqrt{2}}\begin{pmatrix} y' + z' \\ y' - z' \\ \sqrt{2}x' \end{pmatrix},$$

$$\therefore\ x = \frac{1}{\sqrt{2}}(y' + z'), y = \frac{1}{\sqrt{2}}(y' - z'), z = x'.$$

Substituting in $z=xy$ leads to

$$x' = \frac{y'^2 - z'^2}{2},$$

which is a parabolic cylinder.

10.8. SOME APPLICATION OF MATRICES

A system of linear equations in n variables can be used to solve a practical problem with n equations, thus the matrices can be widely used in science and engineering. In this section, we are going to discuss a few of the applications of matrices. We put some more in the exercises section. We start with a geometric example.

Example 24: Show that the points, (1,0), (2,3), (-1,1) and (0,1) do not lie on a circle.

Solution: Previously in example 2 of Chapter 7, the equation of a circle was introduced by $A(x^2+y^2)+ Bx+Cy+D=0$.

This circle passes through the points (1,0), (2,3), (-1,1) and (0,1) thus,

$$\begin{aligned} A + B + D &= 0 \\ 13A + 2B + 3C + D &= 0 \\ 2A - B + C + D &= 0 \\ A + C + D &= 0. \end{aligned}$$

The matrix of coefficients of this system is:

$$\begin{bmatrix} 1 & 1 & 0 & 1 \\ 13 & 2 & 3 & 1 \\ 2 & -1 & 1 & 1 \\ 1 & 0 & 1 & 1 \end{bmatrix}.$$

It is not difficult to show that the determinant of this matrix is not zero. That is, this system of equations has a unique solution given by $A=B=C=D=0$. This means that we have not any circle such that these points lie on it.

Example 25: In the Faculty of Management, B.Sc and M.Sc students for boys and girls are given the following matrix:

$$A = \begin{matrix} \text{Boys} \\ \text{Girls} \end{matrix} \begin{bmatrix} 150 & 50 \\ 120 & 60 \end{bmatrix}$$

Tuition, housing, and food expenses for students of these courses are given by:

$$B = \begin{matrix} \text{B.Sc} \\ \text{M.Sc} \end{matrix} \begin{bmatrix} 450 & 700 & 600 \\ 650 & 850 & 500 \end{bmatrix}$$

Find the matrix ***AB*** and explain what the elements of ***AB*** mean.

Solution: We have,

$$AB = \begin{bmatrix} 150 & 50 \\ 120 & 60 \end{bmatrix} \begin{bmatrix} 450 & 700 & 600 \\ 650 & 850 & 500 \end{bmatrix} = \begin{bmatrix} 100000 & 147500 & 115000 \\ 93000 & 133000 & 102000 \end{bmatrix}.$$

Each element of the matrix ***AB*** represents the total cost in the tuition, housing, and food sections, respectively. The first row is related to male students and the second row is for female students.

Example 26: A company produces 50 goods of type A, 30 goods of type B and 40 goods of type C. The price of each unit is 60, 80 and 100 dollars respectively. If the cost per unit to produce A is \$55, for B is \$70 and for C is \$90, find the weekly profit in terms of 1- Total sales, 2- Sales per unit.

Solution: If we consider the number of goods sold with Q and the selling price of each unit p and the cost of each unit C, as a result, we have in the form of a matrix given by:

$$Q = \begin{bmatrix} 50 \\ 30 \\ 40 \end{bmatrix}, p = \begin{bmatrix} 60 \\ 80 \\ 100 \end{bmatrix}, C = \begin{bmatrix} 55 \\ 70 \\ 90 \end{bmatrix}.$$

Therefore, the total income will be as follows,

$$\text{Total income} = p^T Q = [60 \quad 80 \quad 100] \begin{bmatrix} 50 \\ 30 \\ 40 \end{bmatrix} = 3000 + 2400 + 4000 = 9400,$$

and

$$\text{Total cost} = C^T Q = [55 \quad 70 \quad 90] \begin{bmatrix} 50 \\ 30 \\ 40 \end{bmatrix} = 2750 + 2100 + 3600 = 8450,$$

Then

1- The weekly profit $=P^TQ-C^TQ=$ 9400–8500=950.
2- The profit per unit is $P-C$, i.e.,

$$\begin{bmatrix} 5 \\ 10 \\ 10 \end{bmatrix}.$$

Therefore,

$$\text{Total profit} = (p - C)^T Q = [51010] \begin{bmatrix} 50 \\ 30 \\ 40 \end{bmatrix} = 250 + 300 + 400 = 950.$$

We end this section by considering another example, but we will put more practical examples in the exercises section.

Example 27: A transport company has three types of trucks. This company has contracted to move three types of cargo A, B and C. The following table shows how many units of each type of cargo can carry:

Cargo	1 2 3	Truck
A	2 1 3	
B	4 2 3	
C	3 1 1	

Let's assume that the transport order is 20 units from A, 26 units from B and 15 units from C. How many trucks of each type should we have so that they are all fully loaded?

Solution: If we consider the trucks for each type in the order of x,y and z, according to the data of the problem, we will have the following system of equations:

$$\begin{cases} 2x + y + 5z = 20 \\ 4x + 2y + 3z = 26 \\ 3x + y + z = 15 \end{cases}$$

We apply Cramer's rule to this system. We get,

$$x = \frac{\begin{vmatrix} 20 & 2 & 3 \\ 26 & 3 & 4 \\ 15 & 4 & 4 \end{vmatrix}}{\begin{vmatrix} 2 & 1 & 5 \\ 4 & 2 & 3 \\ 3 & 1 & 1 \end{vmatrix}} = \frac{-21}{-7} = 3, y = \frac{\begin{vmatrix} 2 & 20 & 5 \\ 4 & 26 & 3 \\ 3 & 15 & 1 \end{vmatrix}}{\begin{vmatrix} 2 & 1 & 5 \\ 4 & 2 & 3 \\ 3 & 1 & 1 \end{vmatrix}} = \frac{-28}{-7} = 4, z = \frac{\begin{vmatrix} 2 & 1 & 20 \\ 4 & 2 & 26 \\ 3 & 1 & 15 \end{vmatrix}}{\begin{vmatrix} 2 & 1 & 5 \\ 4 & 2 & 3 \\ 3 & 1 & 1 \end{vmatrix}} = \frac{-14}{-7} = 2.$$

Therefore, we need 3 trucks from the first type, 4 trucks from the second type, and 2 trucks from the third type.

CONCLUSION

In this chapter, after introducing vectors and matrices we obtained the solutions of a system of linear equations by considering some methods to solve them, and then we presented the Gauss elimination method which will be used when the numbers of equations are high.to. We observed how important this method is. The eigenvalues and eigenvectors problems have been discussed, and some procedures have been introduced for determining eigenvalues. In the next chapter, we see how we can use this method for linear programming problems. In fact, many of the ideas in this chapter are used in later sections.

10.9 Exercises

1. Find $\mathrm{tr}(\boldsymbol{A}^2)$
2. for the following matrices.

(i) $\begin{bmatrix} 12 \\ 34 \end{bmatrix}$

(ii) $\begin{bmatrix} 21 \\ 12 \end{bmatrix}$

(iii) $\begin{bmatrix} -35 \\ -14 \end{bmatrix}$

(iv) $\begin{bmatrix} 2 & 6 & 5 \\ 0 & 1 & 1 \\ 4 & 0 & 3 \end{bmatrix}$

(v) $\begin{bmatrix} 1 & 2 & 3 \\ 2 & 1 & 3 \\ 1 & 1 & 1 \end{bmatrix}$

(vi) $\begin{bmatrix} 1 & 2 & 3 \\ 2 & 1 & 3 \\ 3 & 2 & 1 \end{bmatrix}$

3. Find the determinant of the following matrices.

(i) $\begin{bmatrix} 2 & 1 & -4 \\ 1 & 2 & -1 \\ 3 & 1 & -3 \end{bmatrix}$

(ii) $\begin{bmatrix} 2 & -1 & 4 \\ 1 & -2 & 2 \\ 3 & -1 & 0 \end{bmatrix}$

(iii) $\begin{bmatrix} 1 & -1 & 0 \\ 0 & 1 & -1 \\ -1 & 0 & 1 \end{bmatrix}$

(iv) $\begin{bmatrix} a-b & b-c & c-a \\ b-c & c-a & a-b \\ c-a & a-b & b-c \end{bmatrix}$

(v) $\begin{bmatrix} m & a-d & md \\ m & b-d & md \\ m & c-d & m \end{bmatrix}$

(vi) $\begin{bmatrix} a & b & -c \\ a & -b & c \\ -a & b & c \end{bmatrix}$

4. Prove that $a.(a \times c) = 0$.

5. Show that if $A = \begin{bmatrix} 4 & 3 & 3 \\ -1 & 0 & -1 \\ -4 & -4 & -3 \end{bmatrix}$, then $\boldsymbol{A}^{-1} = \boldsymbol{A}$.

6. For what value of a, the following matrices are invertible?

(i) $\begin{bmatrix} a & 2 & 1 \\ 2 & a & 0 \\ 1 & 1 & 1 \end{bmatrix}$

(ii) $\begin{bmatrix} 1 & 3 & 0 \\ 2 & a & 1 \\ 1 & 2 & 4 \end{bmatrix}$

(iii) $\begin{bmatrix} a & b & -c \\ a & -b & c \\ -a & b & c \end{bmatrix}$

7. Find $x+y+z$, from the following matrices.

(i) $\begin{cases} x + y - z = 0 \\ x - y - 2z = 0 \\ -x + y + z = 0 \end{cases}$

(ii) $\begin{cases} 3x + 2y + z = 0 \\ 4x - 5y + 2z = 0 \\ -x + y + 8z = 0 \end{cases}$

8. For what value of k the following system of equations has a non-zero solution?

(i) $\begin{cases} x + ky - z = 0 \\ x - y - z = 0 \\ x + 2y + z = 0 \end{cases}$

(ii) $\begin{cases} x + y + z = 0 \\ x - 2y + z = 0 \\ 4x + y + kz = 0 \end{cases}$

(iii) $\begin{cases} x + 2y - z = -1 \\ 4x + 3y - 2z = 3 \\ 3x + y + kz = 4 \end{cases}$

(iv) $\begin{cases} 5x - 2y - 3z = 2 \\ kx + y + 2z = 3 \\ 9x - 5y - 8z = 1 \end{cases}$

9. Find one of the eigenvalues of the following matrices.

(i) $\begin{bmatrix} 2 & 1 & -4 \\ -3 & 1 & 2 \\ 1 & -2 & 2 \end{bmatrix}$

(ii) $\begin{bmatrix} 2 & 3 & -2 \\ -2 & -4 & 3 \\ 1 & 2 & 0 \end{bmatrix}$

(iii) $\begin{bmatrix} a & 2 & 3 \\ 0 & 1 & 6 \\ 0 & 4 & 5 \end{bmatrix}$

10. Find rank of the following matrices.

(i) $\begin{bmatrix} 1 & 2 & 2 \\ 0 & 0 & 1 \\ 2 & 1 & 1 \end{bmatrix}$

(ii) $\begin{bmatrix} 1 & 0 & 0 \\ 3 & 2 & 0 \\ -1 & 3 & 3 \end{bmatrix}$

(iii) $\begin{bmatrix} 2 & 2 & 3 \\ 0 & 1 & -1 \\ 2 & -1 & -5 \end{bmatrix}$

(iv) $\begin{bmatrix} 1 & 2 & 1 & 2 \\ 2 & 1 & 2 & 1 \\ 3 & 3 & 3 & 3 \\ 6 & 6 & 6 & 6 \end{bmatrix}$

(v) $\begin{bmatrix} 2 & 2 & 2 & 2 \\ 1 & 1 & 1 & 1 \\ 4 & 4 & 4 & 4 \\ 3 & 3 & 3 & 3 \end{bmatrix}$

(vi) $\begin{bmatrix} 1 & 3 & 2 & 1 \\ 0 & 2 & 1 & 3 \\ 0 & 0 & 3 & 1 \\ 0 & 0 & 0 & 4 \end{bmatrix}$

11. Prove, in general, the identity $(\boldsymbol{A}+\boldsymbol{B})^2=\boldsymbol{A}^2+2\boldsymbol{AB}+\boldsymbol{B}^2$ cannot be true. For what nonzero matrix $\boldsymbol{B}$ does identity exist?

12. If $A = \begin{bmatrix} 1 & 2 \\ 3 & 4 \end{bmatrix}$ and $B = \begin{bmatrix} 2 & 1 \\ 1 & 2 \end{bmatrix}$, show that $(\boldsymbol{A}+\boldsymbol{B})^2=\boldsymbol{A}^2+\boldsymbol{B}^2$.

13. Let $A = \begin{bmatrix} 1 & 1 & 1 \\ a & b & c \\ a^2 & b^2 & c^2 \end{bmatrix}$. Show that det($\boldsymbol{A}$)= $(a - b)(b - c)(c - a)$.

14. Let $C = \begin{bmatrix} -11 & -9 & 6 \\ 20 & 16 & -10 \\ 8 & 6 & -3 \end{bmatrix}$, $N = \begin{bmatrix} -22 & -3 & -25 \\ 40 & 6 & 44 \\ 16 & 3 & 16 \end{bmatrix}$. Show that;

(i) $\boldsymbol{C}^k=C$,

(ii) $\boldsymbol{N}^3=(0)$.

15. Prove that

(i) $\begin{vmatrix} x^2 & (x+1)^2 & (x+2)^2 & (x+3)^2 \\ y^2 & (y+1)^2 & (y+2)^2 & (y+3)^2 \\ z^2 & (z+1)^2 & (z+2)^2 & (z+3)^2 \\ v^2 & (v+1)^2 & (v+2)^2 & (v+3)^2 \end{vmatrix} = 0$

(ii) $\begin{vmatrix} 010\ldots0 \\ 001\ldots0 \\ \vdots \end{vmatrix} = (-1)^{n-1}$

(iii) $$\begin{vmatrix} 1+x_1y_1 & 1+x_1y_2 & \ldots & 1+x_1y_n \\ 1+x_2y_1 & 1+x_2y_2 & \ldots & 1+x_2y_n \\ \vdots \\ 1+x_ny_1 & 1+x_ny_2 & \ldots & 1+x_ny_n \end{vmatrix} = 0$$

(iv) $$\begin{vmatrix} a+b & a & a & \ldots & a \\ a & a+b & a & \ldots & a \\ \vdots \\ a & a & a & \ldots & a+b \end{vmatrix} = (a+b)b^{n-1}$$

16. Assume $\boldsymbol{A}^2=\boldsymbol{A}$. Prove, if $\lambda \neq 1$, then $\boldsymbol{A}-\lambda\boldsymbol{I}$ is invertible and $(A-\lambda I)^{-1} = I + \frac{\lambda}{1-\lambda}A$. Show also that if $\boldsymbol{A}\neq\boldsymbol{I}$, then $|\boldsymbol{A}|=0$.

17. Prove that

(i) $|B^{-1}AB| = |A|$

(ii) $|A^n| = |A|^n$

(iii) $|AB| = |A||B|$

(iv) $|A+B| \neq |A| + |B|$

18. Suppose $A = \begin{bmatrix} \cos\frac{\pi}{n} & -\sin\frac{\pi}{n} \\ \sin\frac{\pi}{n} & \cos\frac{\pi}{n} \end{bmatrix}$, where n is a natural number. Prove that $A^{2n} = I$.

19. Find the eigenvalues and eigenvectors of matrix $A = \begin{bmatrix} 2 & 1 & 1 \\ 2 & 3 & 2 \\ 1 & 1 & 2 \end{bmatrix}$ Determine a matrix P such that $P^{-1}AP$. is a diagonal matrix.

20. Show that the following system is consistent if $2a-b-c=0$.

$$\begin{bmatrix} 1 & 1 & -1 \\ 3 & -1 & 2 \\ 1 & -3 & 4 \end{bmatrix}\begin{bmatrix} x_1 \\ x_2 \\ x_3 \end{bmatrix} = \begin{bmatrix} a \\ b \\ c \end{bmatrix},$$

21. For what values of k the following system has a unique solution?

$$\begin{bmatrix} -1 & 1 & 1 \\ -3 & 8 & 4 \\ 7 & 1 & 9 \end{bmatrix}\begin{bmatrix} x_1 \\ x_2 \\ x_3 \end{bmatrix} = k\begin{bmatrix} x_1 \\ x_2 \\ x_3 \end{bmatrix}.$$

22. For what values of a,b and c the following systems have many solutions?

(i) $$\begin{bmatrix} 1 & -2 & 1 \\ -1 & 1 & 3 \\ -2 & 3 & 2 \end{bmatrix}\begin{bmatrix} x_1 \\ x_2 \\ x_3 \end{bmatrix} = \begin{bmatrix} a \\ b \\ c \end{bmatrix}$$

(ii) $$\begin{bmatrix} a & 1 & 1 \\ 1 & b & 1 \\ 1 & 1 & c \end{bmatrix}\begin{bmatrix} x_1 \\ x_2 \\ x_3 \end{bmatrix} = \begin{bmatrix} a \\ b \\ c \end{bmatrix}$$

23. Solve the following systems by Cramer's rule or using the inverse of the coefficient matrix.

(i) $$\begin{bmatrix} -1 & 2 & 1 \\ -1 & 1 & 3 \\ -2 & 3 & 2 \end{bmatrix} \begin{bmatrix} x_1 \\ x_2 \\ x_3 \end{bmatrix} = \begin{bmatrix} 1 \\ 3 \\ 5 \end{bmatrix}$$

(ii) $$\begin{bmatrix} 2 & -1 & 1 \\ 1 & -3 & 1 \\ 1 & -1 & 4 \end{bmatrix} \begin{bmatrix} x_1 \\ x_2 \\ x_3 \end{bmatrix} = \begin{bmatrix} 2 \\ 3 \\ 1 \end{bmatrix}$$

24. Find eigenvalues and corresponding eigenvectors of the following matrices.

(i) $$\begin{bmatrix} 2 & 1 \\ 0 & 3 \end{bmatrix}$$

(ii) $$\begin{bmatrix} 1 & 2 \\ 2 & 1 \end{bmatrix}$$

(iii) $$\begin{bmatrix} 1 & 2 \\ 3 & 4 \end{bmatrix}$$

(iv) $$\begin{bmatrix} 3 & -2 \\ 4 & -1 \end{bmatrix}$$

(v) $$\begin{bmatrix} 3 & -1 & 1 \\ 7 & -5 & 1 \\ 6 & -6 & 2 \end{bmatrix}$$

(vi) $$\begin{bmatrix} 2 & -1 & 1 \\ 3 & -2 & 1 \\ 5 & -4 & 1 \end{bmatrix}$$

(vii) $$\begin{bmatrix} 1 & 1 & -1 \\ 1 & 2 & -2 \\ 3 & 2 & 8 \end{bmatrix}$$

(viii) $$\begin{bmatrix} -1 & 1 & 0 \\ 1 & 1 & 2 \\ 3 & 2 & 2 \end{bmatrix}$$

25. Find determinant and eigenvalues of the following matrices.

(i) $$\begin{bmatrix} 3 & 4 & 0 & 0 & 0 \\ 2 & 3 & 4 & 0 & 0 \\ 0 & 2 & 3 & 4 & 0 \\ 0 & 0 & 2 & 3 & 4 \\ 0 & 0 & 0 & 2 & 3 \end{bmatrix}$$

(ii) $$\begin{bmatrix} 1 & 4 & 0 & 0 & 0 \\ 4 & 1 & 4 & 0 & 0 \\ 0 & 4 & 1 & 4 & 0 \\ 0 & 0 & 4 & 1 & 4 \\ 0 & 0 & 0 & 4 & 1 \end{bmatrix}$$

(iii) $$\begin{bmatrix} 1 & 1 & 0 & 0 & 0 \\ 1 & 1 & 1 & 0 & 0 \\ 0 & 4 & 1 & 1 & 0 \\ 0 & 0 & 1 & 1 & 1 \\ 0 & 0 & 0 & 1 & 1 \end{bmatrix}$$

(iv) $\begin{bmatrix} 2 & 3 & 0 & 0 & \cdots & 0 \\ 1 & 2 & 3 & 0 & \cdots & 0 \\ 0 & 1 & 2 & 3 & \cdots & 0 \\ & & \vdots & & & \\ 0 & 0 & \cdots & 1 & 2 & 3 \\ 0 & 0 & \cdots & 0 & 1 & 2 \end{bmatrix}$

(v) $\begin{bmatrix} 0.1 & 0.2 & 0 & 0 & \cdots & 0 \\ 0.3 & 0.1 & 0.2 & 0 & \cdots & 0 \\ 0 & 0.3 & 0.1 & 0.2 & \cdots & 0 \\ & & \vdots & & & \\ 0 & 0 & \cdots & 0.3 & 0.1 & 0.2 \\ 0 & 0 & \cdots & 0 & 0.3 & 0.1 \end{bmatrix}$

(vi) $\begin{bmatrix} 2 & \frac{1}{2} & 0 & 0 & \cdots & 0 \\ \frac{1}{2} & 2 & \frac{1}{2} & 0 & \cdots & 0 \\ 0 & \frac{1}{2} & 2 & \frac{1}{2} & \cdots & 0 \\ & & \vdots & & & \\ 0 & 0 & \cdots & \frac{1}{2} & 2 & \frac{1}{2} \\ 0 & 0 & \cdots & 0 & \frac{1}{2} & 2 \end{bmatrix}$

26. Consider the problem $\boldsymbol{Ax}=\boldsymbol{e}_k$ where $\boldsymbol{e}_k$ is a vector with elements zero except kth element with unity. Theoretically, $\boldsymbol{x}=\boldsymbol{A}^{-1}\boldsymbol{e}_k$. Thus $\boldsymbol{x}$ is a kth element of the inverse matrix. Use this procedure to find the inverse of the following matrices.

(i) $\begin{bmatrix} 1 & 2 & 1 \\ 0 & 2 & 3 \\ 0 & 1 & 2 \end{bmatrix}$

(ii) $\begin{bmatrix} 2 & 4 & -1 \\ 1 & -3 & 2 \\ 3 & 2 & 4 \end{bmatrix}$

(iii) $\begin{bmatrix} 4 & 1 & 0 & 0 & 0 \\ 1 & 4 & 1 & 0 & 0 \\ 0 & 1 & 4 & 1 & 0 \\ 0 & 0 & -1 & 4 & 1 \\ 0 & 0 & 0 & 1 & 4 \end{bmatrix}$

(iv) $\begin{bmatrix} 1 & 2 & 0 & 0 & 0 \\ 3 & 1 & 2 & 0 & 0 \\ 0 & 3 & 1 & 2 & 0 \\ 0 & 0 & 3 & 1 & 2 \\ 0 & 0 & 0 & 3 & 1 \end{bmatrix}$

27. (*Over-determined system of linear systems*) Let us consider the linear system given by

$$A_{mn}x_{n1=}b_{m1}, m > n.$$

Define the residual vector $\boldsymbol{r}=\boldsymbol{Ax}-\boldsymbol{b}$. By least square, we seek a solution that minimizes $r^T r = \sum r_i^{\,2}$. This leads to $\boldsymbol{A}^T\boldsymbol{Ax}=\boldsymbol{A}^T\boldsymbol{b}$. This is a symmetric and positive definite system. This system gives an appreciated solution. Find appreciative solutions for the following systems.

(i) $2x + 3y = 1, x - y = -2, x + 2y = 0$

(ii) $x - y = -1, x + 3y = -2, x + y = -1.$

28. *Show that three points (x1,y2), (x2,y2) and (x3,y3) lie on a line if*

$$\begin{vmatrix} x_1 y_1 1 \\ x_2 y_2 1 \\ x_3 y_3 1 \end{vmatrix} = 0.$$

29. Show that if, $\boldsymbol{a}=a_1, \boldsymbol{i}+a_2, \boldsymbol{j}+a_3, \boldsymbol{k}$ and $\boldsymbol{b}=b_1, \boldsymbol{i}+b_2, \boldsymbol{j}+b_3, \boldsymbol{k}$ then

$$a \times b = \begin{vmatrix} ijk \\ a_1 a_2 a_3 \\ b_1 b_2 b_3 \end{vmatrix}.$$

30. (i) Show that if $\boldsymbol{a}=a_1, \boldsymbol{i}+a_2, \boldsymbol{j}+a_3, \boldsymbol{k}$, $\boldsymbol{b}=b_1, \boldsymbol{i}+b_2, \boldsymbol{j}+b_3, \boldsymbol{k}$ and $\boldsymbol{c}=c_1, \boldsymbol{i}+c_2, \boldsymbol{j}+c_3, \boldsymbol{k}$ then,

$$a.(b \times c) = \begin{vmatrix} a_1 a_2 a_3 \\ b_1 b_2 b_3 \\ c_1 c_2 c_3 \end{vmatrix}.$$

(ii) As we mentioned the value of $|a.(b \times c)|$ is equal to volume of a parallelepiped with sides **a,b** and **c**. Find volume of a parallelepiped with sides $a = -3i + 2j + 4k, b = 2i - 3j - k$ and $c = 3i - j + 2k$.

(iii) Let's $a = i + 4j + 7k, b = 2i - j + 4k$ and $c = -9j + 18k$. Prove that they lie in a plane.

31. Find the types of the following quadratic surfaces.

(i) $z^2 + xy = x + z$

(ii) $2x^2 - 4xy + y^2 - 4yz = z$

(iii) $5x^2 + 6y^2 + 3z^2 = 4xy + 4xz$

(iv) $x^2 - 4xy + 2y^2 - 4yz + 3z^2 = 1$

(v) $3x^2 - 4xy - 8xz + 6y^2 - 4yz - 3z^2 = 4.$

32. Find the equilibrium solution (D=S) of a single product market specified by the following linear model using the matrix inversion method of coefficients D, S, and p. where, D,S,p are demand, supply, and price of goods, respectively.

$$D = 12 - p$$
$$S = 4p - 6.$$

33. Find the equilibrium solution (D_1=S_1, D_2=S_2) of a two-product market specified by the following linear model using Cramer's rule of coefficients $D,S,$ and p where, D_i, S_i, p_i, i=1,2 are demands, supplies and prices of goods, respectively.

$$D_1 = 20 - 2p_1 - p_2, D_2 = 8 + 5p_1 - 2p_2$$

$$S_1 = 2 + 4p_1 - p_2, S_1 = 2 + 4p_1 - p_2$$

34. A firm produces three kinds of products x,y and z. The total time spent for producing these products is 20 hours. If it spent time as much as z as y and x together, and time spent on y and z combined equals four times that spent on x, what is the time to be spent on each type of product?

35. The University of Shomal has 130 staff at a total of \$328000 per month. The number of staff who are assistant professors is, 85 and the rest are full professors. The president of the university decided to increase an additional amount to the monthly wage to give the staff who are assistant professors 3% and the rest %4 per month raise. If the amount increased is \$11505, what was the average monthly wage for the assistant professors and the full professors?

36. In a country, there are two types of parties, D and R. Every person is a member of one of these parties conducts an election period every year. During one year, $\frac{4}{5}$ of the members of D remain in this party and $\frac{1}{5}$ of them become members of R. Also, $\frac{3}{5}$ of the members of R stay in R and the remaining $\frac{2}{5}$ become members of party D. Despite all the membership changes every year at the time of voting, the ratio of D and R members to the total population remains constant. What proportion of voters belong to D?

REFERENCES

Anton, H. (1977). *Elementary Linear Algebra* (2nd ed.). Wiley.

Hoffman, K., & Kunze, R. (1971). Linear Algebra. (2nd ed). Englewood Cliff, N. J. Prentice- Hall.

Golub, G. H., & Van, C. F. (1996). *Matrix Computations* (3rd ed.). The Johns Hopkins University Press.

Maron, M. J., & Lopez, R. J. (1991). *Numerical Analysis; A practical Approach.* Wadsworth, Inc.

Gerald, J. T. (1972). Applied Numerical Analysis. (2 nd ed). (Reading, Mass. Addison-Wesley.

Gourlay, A. R., & Watson, G. A. (1973). *Computational Methods for Matrix Eigen-problems*. John Wiley and Sons.

Hermann, M., & Saravi, M. (2014). A First Course in Ordinary Differential Equations, Springer-book company.

Horn, R. A., & Johnson, C. R. (1996). *Matrix Analysis*. Cambride University Press.

Chapter 11
Linear Programming

ABSTRACT

This chapter delves into the realm of linear programming, emphasizing its geometric perspective. We will explore the simplex method, a pivotal linear programming technique, offering a detailed discussion of its principles and computational steps. The chapter will illustrate various applications of linear programming methods across science and industry, demonstrating their pivotal role in optimizing decisions and solving complex problems. Through real-world examples, we aim to highlight the effectiveness and versatility of linear programming in addressing practical challenges, thereby bridging the gap between theoretical mathematics and practical implementation. Since manipulation of a Simplex method takes time to obtain right answer, we added some of the most popular LP software to overcome this problem.

11.1 INTRODUCTION

As the decision-making process becomes increasingly intricate with the expansion of organizations and the evolution of technology, managers are compelled to navigate a complex mesh of internal and external variables that impact their operations. This growing complexity highlights the necessity for powerful analytical tools that can help dissect these variables and provide actionable insights.

Linear programming, with its origins in the practical needs of the military during the mid-20th century, was conceived by George B. Dantzig. This mathematical strategy was initially used to optimize resources and logistics in a structured and quantifiable manner. Since its inception, linear programming has evolved into a critical tool across various sectors.

Today, the relevance of linear programming extends beyond its military applications into the realms of marketing, where it helps in maximizing exposure and minimizing costs; production, where it ensures optimal use of resources and minimizes waste; and operational management, where it assists in streamlining processes and

DOI: 10.4018/979-8-3693-3657-1.ch011

improving efficiency. Its adaptability and precision make it invaluable not only in these areas but also in accounting, where it aids in budgeting and financial planning; economics, where it helps in forecasting and market analysis; and industrial engineering, where it supports system optimization and process improvement.

Linear programming serves as a cornerstone in the development of management science, offering a clear, methodical approach to solving problems that are characterized by multiple influencing factors and constraints. It is a testament to the power of simple, robust mathematical frameworks in tackling complex, dynamic challenges in modern organizational settings.

Linear programming earns its name due to its exclusive handling of linear relationships among variables. The theoretical framework and solution methodologies associated with linear programming are inherently simpler when compared to those of other mathematical branches. This field focuses on optimizing (either maximizing or minimizing) a dependent variable that is linearly influenced by a set of independent variables, known as decision variables. These decision variables are bound by numerous linear constraints, which shape the feasible solutions.

While differential calculus proves beneficial for many optimization challenges, linear programming problems necessitate a distinct approach due to their unique structure. This chapter will begin by outlining two primary forms of the linear programming model. Following this, we will delve into the graphical method, an intuitive and straightforward technique suitable for solving linear programming problems involving just two variables.

However, as the number of variables and constraints expands, the graphical method becomes impractical. In such cases, we turn to the simplex method, a robust, non-graphical technique that efficiently navigates through multiple dimensions to find the optimal solution. This method, developed for more complex scenarios, demonstrates the scalability and adaptability of linear programming in handling a broad spectrum of real-world problems.

11.2 LINEAR PROGRAMMING FORMS

Linear programming is one of the most powerful techniques that managers can use in solving their various problems according to the conditions of the problem. If we consider the three tasks of providing financial resources, production, and sales as the main tasks of every production company, linear programming has demonstrated its ability to solve problems well in the second task (i.e., production) and presented its capabilities in the other two tasks.

In this section, we introduce two forms of linear programming, namely, *algebraic form* and *matrix form*. We start with an algebraic form.

Its general forms with n decision variables subject to m constraints for maximization and minimization cases, respectively, are:

$$\text{Maximize: } Z = c_1X_1 + c_2X_2 + \ldots + c_nX_n$$

Subject to:

$$\begin{aligned} a_{11}X_1 + a_{12}X_2 + \ldots + a_{1n}X_n &\leq b_1 \\ a_{21}X_1 + a_{22}X_2 + \ldots + a_{2n}X_n &\leq b_2 \\ &\vdots \\ a_{m1}X_1 + a_{m2}X_2 + \ldots + a_{mn}X_n &\leq b_m \\ X_i \geq 0; i = 1,2,\ldots,n, & \end{aligned} \tag{1}$$

and

$$\text{Minimize: } Z = c_1X_1 + c_2X_2 + \ldots + c_nX_n$$

Subject to:

$$\begin{aligned} a_{11}X_1 + a_{12}X_2 + \ldots + a_{1n}X_n &\geq b_1 \\ a_{21}X_1 + a_{22}X_2 + \ldots + a_{2n}X_n &\geq b_2 \\ &\vdots \\ a_{m1}X_1 + a_{m2}X_2 + \ldots + a_{mn}X_n &\geq b_m \\ X_i \geq 0; i = 1,2,\ldots,n. & \end{aligned} \tag{2}$$

In many linear programming problems, it will be better to express problems in matrix form. According to (1) or (2), four matrices ***A, B, C*** and ***X*** can be developed, where

$$A = \begin{bmatrix} a_{11}\,a_{12}\ldots a_{1n} \\ a_{21}\,a_{22}\ldots a_{2n} \\ \vdots \\ a_{m1}\,a_{m2}\ldots a_{mn} \end{bmatrix}, B = \begin{bmatrix} b_1 \\ b_2 \\ \vdots \\ b_m \end{bmatrix}, C = \begin{bmatrix} c_1 \\ c_2 \\ \vdots \\ c_n \end{bmatrix} \text{ and} X = \begin{bmatrix} x_1 \\ x_2 \\ \vdots \\ x_n \end{bmatrix}.$$

These matrices lead to $\boldsymbol{Z=C^TX}$, as the *objective function* which defines the criterion for evaluating the solution, and

$$AX \leq B \tag{3}$$

$$AX \geq B \tag{4}$$

as the system of constraints on the objective function with $X \geq 0$.

After modeling the problem, it is time to solve it. For convenience, we consider two main forms. A linear programming in (1) or (2), is said to be in *standard form* if all restrictions are equal and all variables are nonnegative. That is, it has the sign = instead of ≤ and ≥, and the *canonical form* which has the sign ≤ or ≥.

Later we will see that for applying the *simplex method,* the given problem must be put in standard form. The canonical form is also useful, especially in exploiting duality relationships.

Before considering an example, we note that different forms of linear programming can be converted by using simple relationships in basic mathematics, such as:

(i) $x \leq y \leftrightarrow -x \geq -y$
(ii) $x \leq y \leftrightarrow x + S = y$
(iii) $x \geq y \leftrightarrow x - S = y$

where $S>0$ is called an *auxiliary variable.*

Example 1: Find the standard form of the following model.

Maximize: $Z = 4X_1 + X_2 + 3X_3$

Subject to: $3X_1 + 5X_2 + 2X_3 \leq 25$

$2X_1 + X_2 + 4X_3 \geq 32$

$X_1 + 4X_2 + 6X_3 = 40.$

$X_i \geq 0; i = 1,2,3.$

Solution: To obtain the standard form, it is enough to add an auxiliary variable to the first constraint and subtract another auxiliary variable from the second constraint. We get:

Maximize: $Z = 4X_1 + X_2 + 3X_3$

Subject to: $3X_1 + 5X_2 + 2X_3 + S_1 = 25$

$$2X_1 + X_2 + 4X_3 - S_2 = 32$$

$$X_1 + 4X_2 + 6X_3 = 40.$$

$$X_i \geq 0; i = 1,2,3.$$

Notice that the third constraint does not need any auxiliary variable s.

Remark 1**:** To differentiate S_1 and S_2, we call them the *slack* and the *surplus variables*, respectively.

11.3 METHODS OF SOLUTION FOR LINEAR PROGRAMMING

Before introducing some methods, it is better to introduce some common terms in linear programming.

- **Solution:** A set of values assigned to the decision variables is called a solution, whether this solution is desirable or not, and whether this set of values applies within the constraint or not.
- **Feasible Solution:** This is a solution that applies to all constraints.
- **Optimal Solution:** The best feasible solution or the solution is feasible for which the objective function becomes the most favorable state
- **Feasible Region:** A region with a set of feasible solutions is called a feasible region.
- **Boundary Equation:** The boundary equation of each constraint is obtained by replacing the sign$\leq$ or $\geq$ and or =.
- **Corner Point Solution:** The values assigned to the decision variables resulting from the intersection of the boundary equations are called corner point solutions.
- **Basic Feasible Solution:** Each solution at feasible corner points is called a basic feasible solution.

11.3.1 Graphical Method

The graphical method is one of the simple methods for solving two-dimensional linear programming problems, that is, problems that consist of only two decision variables X_1 and X_2. We should find the decision variables in such a way that they give the best objective value in addition to satisfying the given constraints. For this purpose, we take the following steps:

In the first step, we consider the constraints by replacing inequality signs with equality signs for drawing their graphs, which are straight lines.

In the next step, we determine each of the regions of feasible solutions, which can be located on a line or one side of the line. In the third step, by combining the regions of the solutions, a common region is created, which is a feasible region. We shade this region. In the last step, we find corner points, and then we evaluate the objective function at each corner (or extreme) points to determine where the largest or smallest values occur. Ordinarily, one of the solutions will be optimal.

Let us for a better understanding, illustrate these steps by considering some examples.

Example 2: Solve the following model by graphical method.

Maximize: $Z = 3X_1 + 2X_2$

Subject to: $2X_1 + 3X_2 \leq 80$

$X_1 + X_2 \leq 30$

$X_i \geq 0; i = 1,2.$

Solution: First we draw the lines $2X_1+3X_2=80$ and $X_1+X_2=30$, Figure 1.

In this figure, we declare the regions that $X_1 \geq 0$ and $X_2 \geq 0$. We have four corner points $O(0, 0)$, $A(30, 0)$, $B(10,20)$ and $C(0, \frac{80}{3})$ which are extreme points. Substitute them in objective function. It yields, $Z_O=0$, $Z_A=90$, $Z_B=70$ and $Z_C = \frac{160}{3}$. Thus, the corner point A is a desired point for Z.

Figure 1. With feasible region

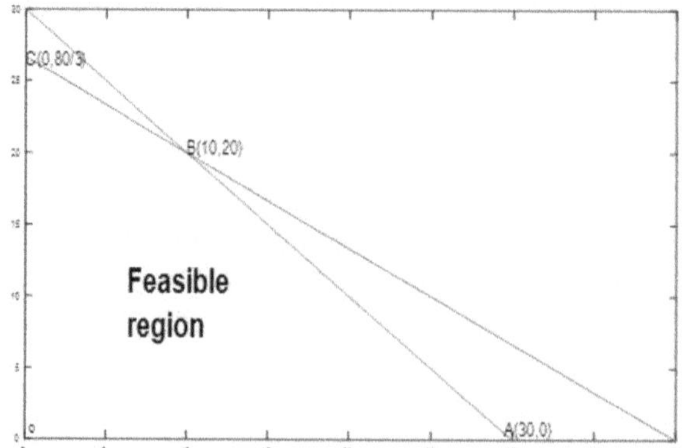

Example 3: Solve the following linear programming problem by graphical method.

Minimize: $Z = 5X_1 + 3X_2$

Subject to: $X_1 + X_2 \leq 9$

$4X_1 + X_2 \geq 24$

$3X_1 + 2X_2 \geq 18$

$X_i \geq 0; i = 1,2.$

Solution: Let us draw the lines $X_1+X_2=9$, $4X_1+X_2=24$ and $3X_1+2X_2\mp18$, Figure 2.

We have five corner points $A(9, 0)$, $B(6, 0)$, $C(0, 24)$, $D(0, 9)$ and $E(5, 4)$. The points B, D and E can be extreme points. We substitute them in the objective function. It yields $Z_B=30$, $Z_D=27$ and $Z_E=37$. Thus the corner point D is the desired extreme point for Z (Figure 2).

Figure 2. With feasible region

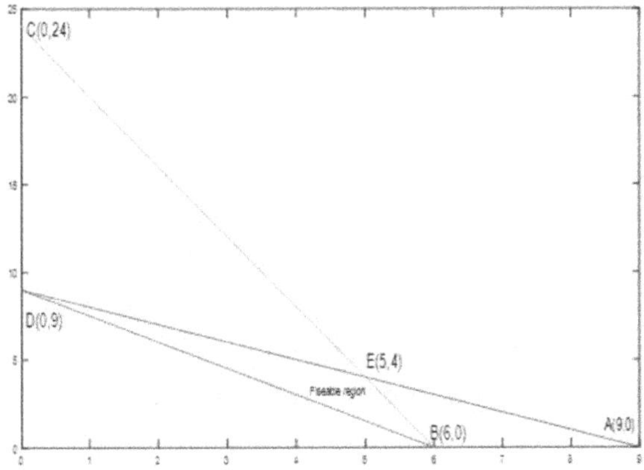

Theorem 1. (*The extreme point theorem*). Let$R$ be the most feasible region. If R is bounded, then the optimal feasible value of the objective function must occur at one of the extreme (or corner) points of the boundary.

***Remark 2*:** The maximum number of extreme points is $\binom{m+n}{n}$ where m is the number of constraints and n is the number of variables.

In example 2, we have m=n=2, thus $\binom{m+n}{n} = \frac{4!}{2!2!} = 6$. That is, we have 6 extreme points. Four of these points are optimal points.

Theorem 2. Let R be the most feasible region. If R is unbounded, then the optimal feasible value of the objective function may not exist. However, if it exists, it must occur at a corner point of R.

Remark 3: If we reverse the directions of the inequalities in the constraints, we obtain a linear programming problem that has no feasible solution, and hence no optimal solution either. Such a linear program is called *infeasible*.

Before we go further, it would be better to have a short interpretation of the solutions. In solving a linear programming problem, we may have the following optimal solutions in a feasible region or no solution.

(i) *A unique optimal solution*. See, for example, the optimal solution in examples 1 and 2.

(ii) *Alternate or multiple optimal solutions*. This happens when the parallel objective function is one of the given constraints. Consider the following example.

Example 4: Solve the following linear programming problem by graphical method.

Maximize: $Z = X_1 + 3X_2$

Subject to: $3X_1 + 4X_2 \leq 12$

$X_1 + 3X_2 \leq 6$

$X_i \geq 1; i = 1,2.$

Solution: For any value of Z, the objective function is parallel with $X_1+3X_2=6$. Thus, we have an alternate optimal solution. We draw the lines, $3X_1+4X_2=12$, $X_1+3X_2=6$, Figure 3. The points $A(4, 0)$, $B(6, 0)$, $C(2.4, 1.2)$, $D(0, 2)$ and $E(0, 3)$ are corner points. We substitute in the objective function. It yields, $Z_A=3$, $Z_B=6$, $Z_C=6$, $Z_D=2$ and $Z_E=9$. Thus, the corner point E is corner point solution.

Figure 3. Graph of lines $3X_1+4X_2=12$ and $X_1+3X_2=6$

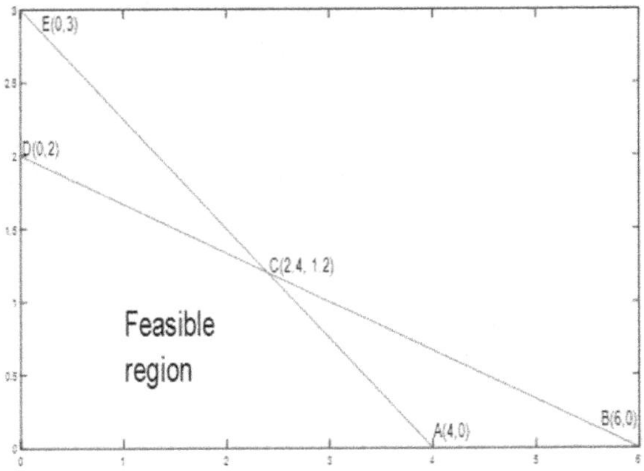

(iii) *Degenerate solution.* Sometimes, we encounter a kind of solution when there is a corner point which is the intersection of more than two lines. For example, the graph related to the following example has four corner points, $A(4, 0)$, $B(4, 0)$, $C(0, 3)$ and $D(0, \frac{16}{3})$, respectively. It can be seen that the points A and B coincide. The maximum value of Z happens on A and B.

Maximize: $Z = 12X_1 + 17X_2$

Subject to $3X_1 + 4X_2 \leq 12$

$4X_1 + 3X_2 \leq 16$

$X_i \geq 0; i = 1, 2.$

A corner point may be corrupted but not optimal. For example, in the following linear programming problem, the point (0, 2) is a degenerated point but the point (8, 0) is the optimal point.

Maximize: $Z = X_1 + X_2$

Subject to: $X_1 + 4X_2 \leq 8$

$X_1 + 2X_2 \geq 4$

$X_i \geq 0; i = 1, 2.$

(iv) *Unbounded optimal region.* Sometimes, an optimal solution may not exist even when there are feasible solutions. This happens when the objective function can attain arbitrarily large values. In this case, we say that linear programming is unbounded. (see Figure 4)

Remark 4: We may have an unbounded optimal region with definite and bounded optimal solutions. (see Figure 5).

Figure 4. With feasible region

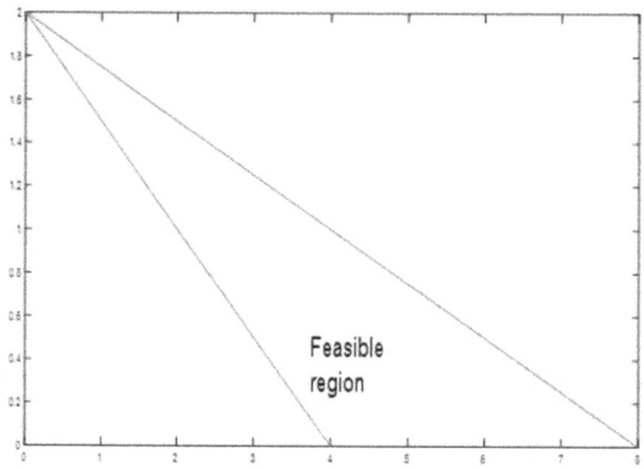

Figure 5. With feasible region

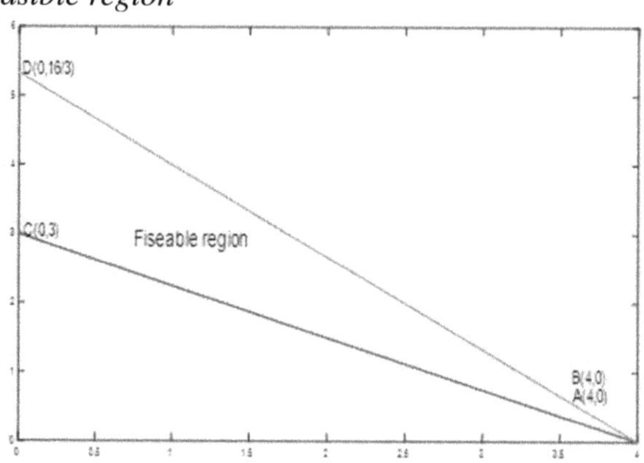

If there is no feasible solution, it may be because the problem is not formulated correctly and, or it has inconsistencies in the constraints. It means that one or more constraints violate other constraints. For example, consider the following example.

Maximize: $Z = 3X_1 + 2X_2$

Subject to: $X_1 + X_2 \leq 4$

$2X_1 - X_2 \leq 4$

$10 \geq X_1 \geq 5, X_2 \geq 0.$

It can be seen that no point can be found that applies within the given constraints, hence the problem is without a feasible region, and hence no feasible and optimal solution, Figure 6.

Figure 6. With infinite feasible region

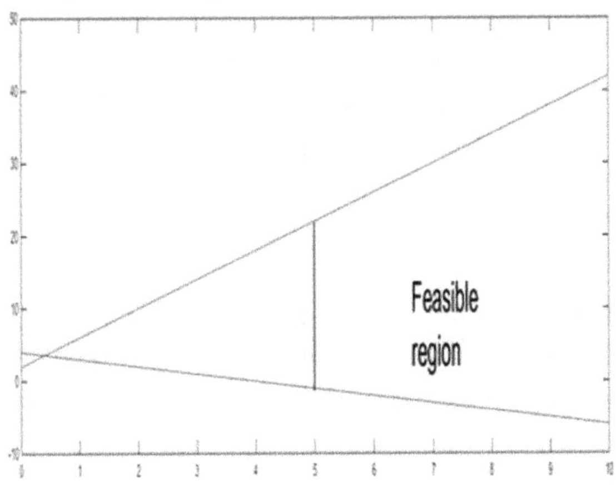

It makes sense to explain why the extreme point must be at a corner of the region of feasible solutions. This leads us to introduce the concept of a convex set.

Definition 1: A *convex set* is a set of points where, when we connect any two arbitrary points of this set with a straight line, the connecting line is also complete in the set.

The previous example shows why these sorts of conditional constraints do not occur in linear programming. A constraint cannot be valid in one region and invalid in another. For example, from Figure 6, we have $y \leq ax+b$ for $0 \leq x \leq x_1$ and $y \leq y_1$ for $x_1 \leq x \leq x_2$. The constraint $y \leq ax+b$ does not hold for $x_1 < x \leq x_2$ and similarly, the constraint

$y \leq y_1$ does not hold for $0 < x \leq x_1$. The same discussion can be used for the constraint $y \leq cx+d$. These sorts of conditional constraints do not occur in linear programming.

Figure 7. Graph of lines $y=ax+b$, $y=y_1$ and $y=cx+d$

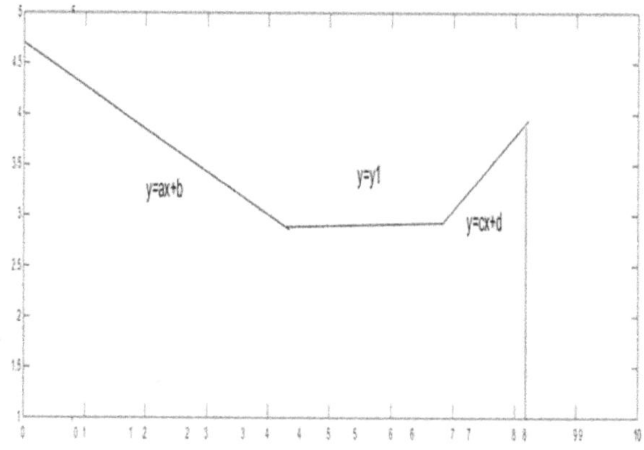

Remark 5. It can be demonstrated that the feasible region of linear programming is always a convex set and a linear objective function is also a convex set.

Since it takes time to find the feasible solution, in this section we introduce MATLAB Code for Graphical Method of Linear Programming in last section later.

Computer Station

To illustrate the graphical method of solving linear programming problems using MATLAB, we'll use a simple example involving two decision variables. The graphical method can be effectively utilized when dealing with two-variable linear programming problems because it allows for visualization of the feasible region and objective function.

Example Problem

Let's consider a problem where we want to maximize the objective function:

$$z = 3x_1 + 5x_2$$

Subject to the constraints:

$$x_1 + 2x_2 \leq 20$$

$$ 3x_1 + x2 \leq 30 $$

$$ x_1, x_2 \geq 0 $$

MATLAB Code

Here's a MATLAB code snippet that uses the `fill` function to plot the feasible region and `fplot` to display the objective function lines:

```matlab
% Define the variables
x1 = linspace(0, 20, 400); % Range for x1
% Constraints
x2_constr1 = (20 - x1) / 2; % x1 + 2x2 <= 20
x2_constr2 = 30 - 3 * x1; % 3x1 + x2 <= 30
% Non-negativity constraints
x2_constr1(x2_constr1 < 0) = NaN; % Adjusts values outside the constraints
x2_constr2(x2_constr2 < 0) = NaN;
% Plot feasible region
figure;
hold on;
fill([0, 0, min(x1(~isnan(x2_constr1))), min(x1(~isnan(x2_constr2)))],...
     [0, min(x2_constr2), min(x2_constr1(~isnan(x2_constr1))), 0], 'g');
% Add labels and titles
title('Feasible Region for Linear Programming Problem');
xlabel('x_1');
ylabel('x_2');
xlim([0 15]);
ylim([0 15]);
% Plot the constraints and the axes
plot(x1, x2_constr1, 'b', 'LineWidth', 2);
plot(x1, x2_constr2, 'r', 'LineWidth', 2);
line(xlim, [0,0], 'Color', 'k');
line([0,0], ylim, 'Color', 'k');
% Plotting the objective function lines
z = @(x1, x2) 3 * x1 + 5 * x2;
fplot(@(x1) (20 - 3*x1)/5, [0, 10], 'k--');
```

```
  % Find the maximum of the objective function
  optimal_x1 = fminbnd(@(x1) -z(x1, (20 - x1)/2), 0, 10);
  optimal_x2 = (20 - optimal_x1) / 2;
  max_z = z(optimal_x1, optimal_x2);
  scatter(optimal_x1, optimal_x2, 'filled');
  text(optimal_x1, optimal_x2, sprintf('  Max z=%.2f at
(%.2f,%.2f)', max_z, optimal_x1, optimal_x2));
  hold off;
```

Explanation of the Code

1. **Define Variables and Constraints**: `x1` is defined over a possible range and `x2` constraints are calculated based on the provided inequalities.
2. **Plot Feasible Region**: Uses the `fill` function to create the feasible region, defined by the intersection of the constraints.
3. **Plot Constraints**: Uses `plot` to draw the constraint lines on the graph.
4. **Objective Function Line**: Plots a representative line of the objective function (`fplot`) and moves it to show maximization.
5. **Optimization**: `fminbnd` is used in a way to find the maximum value by turning the maximization problem into a minimization problem (by using negative sign).
6. **Results**: The optimal values for `x1` and `x2` are calculated and displayed, along with the maximum value of the objective function.

This MATLAB code provides a visual and analytical solution to the example linear programming problem using the graphical method.

11.3.2 Simplex Method

In the previous section, we examined the graphical method for solving linear programming problems with two decision variables. But in the real world, we encounter problems that have more than two decision variables and are consequently too large to be solved by the graphical method. Also, this method does not indicate if the feasible region is unbounded or empty without first going through the whole set of extreme points, which, by remark 2, can be quite large. For these reasons, it is no longer possible to use this method to solve them. Such problems are usually solved by the simplex method. The simplex method, which is an iterative procedure, was developed in 1947 by George B. Dantzig to solve any linear programming problem in a finite number of steps, and finally, the maximum or minimum values of the objective function are attained. Simplex algorithm is a general technique for solving linear programming problems. In this method, first, the model is entered into a table, and then a series of mathematical steps are performed on the table. In the simplex method, it always moves better from one corner to another to find the best corner. Simplex starts its operation to search for the optimal solution from the origin of the coordinates, except for the cases where it is clearly stated that the operation starts from a point other than the origin. The Gaussian elimination described in the previous chapter has a fundamental theoretical and didactic significance, as a starting point for further developments. In the first step, we convert the model into standard form. Before presenting the simplex method, it is necessary to understand the following concepts.

Let us assume we have m variables.

- **Basic Variable:** The n variables $S_i > 0$; $i=1,2,\dots,n$ are called basic variables.
- **Non-Basic Variable:** The $m-n$ variables $X_i = 0$; $i=1,2,\dots,m-n$ are called non-basic variables.
- **Basic Solution:** Any solution is obtained from solving our system of equations is called a basic solution.
- **Basic Feasible Solution:** Any nonnegative basic solution is called a basic feasible solution. In general, the number of basic feasible solutions is less than or equal to C^{m}_{m-n} where m is a number of constraints and n is the number of variables (including the slack variables).

Theorem 3. For every extreme point, there is a basis (not necessarily unique), and, conversely, for every basis, there is a (unique) extreme point. Moreover, if an extreme point has more than one basis representing it, then it is degenerate. Conversely, a degenerate extreme point has more than one set of basic variables representing it if and only if the system Ax=b itself does not imply that the degenerate basic variables corresponding to an associated basis are identically zero, (Jarvis, Bazaraa, & Sherali, 1990).

The best way to implement the simplex algorithm by hand is through tableau form. A linear program can be put in tableau format by creating a matrix with a column for each variable. We intentionally do not take a linear program in the equational form: The variables are non-negative, but to apply the simplex method, the inequalities have to be converted into equations, by adding the new variables, namely, *auxiliary variables*. Three types of auxiliary variables can be used to convert the inequalities into equality equations. They are *slack*, *surplus,* and *artificial variables*. The artificial variables are used temporarily and will be removed later. After that the equational form is declared, we declare the augment matrix for this system of equations. This matrix is called the *initial simplex tableau* for the problem, Table 1.

Table 1.-

$X_1X_2...X_nS_1S_2...S_mA_1A_2...A_pZ$	***b***
Coefficients of the first equation	b_1
Coefficients of the second equation	b_2
.	...
.	b_n
Coefficients of objective function	0

From this tableau, we can read the first basic feasible solution by setting $X_1=X_2=...=X_n=0$. We emphasize that, in the last tableau all coefficients of objective function must be positive and also $b_i \geq 0$.

Example 5: Write the augmented matrix of the following system of equations.

Maximize: $Z = 4X_1 + 5X_2$

Subject to: $2X_1 + X_2 \leq 5$

$3X_1 + 2X_2 \leq 6$

$0 \leq X_1 \leq 3, X_2 \geq 0.$

Solution: The equational form is

$-4X_1 - 5X_2 + Z = 0$

$2X_1 + X_2 + S_1 = 5$

$3X_1 + 2X_2 + S_2 = 6$

$X_1 + S_3 = 3,$

with the matrix form

The augmented matrix for this system is,

$$\begin{array}{cccccc|c} X_1 & X_2 & S_1 & S_2 & S_3 & Z & \\ \hline 2 & 1 & 1 & 0 & 0 & 0 & 5 \\ 3 & 2 & 0 & 1 & 0 & 0 & 6 \\ 1 & 0 & 0 & 0 & 1 & 0 & 3 \\ \hline -4 & -5 & 0 & 0 & 0 & 1 & 0 \end{array}$$

In the first step, we have Z=0. To increase the value of Z, we have to move to a new basic feasible solution. The simplex method consists of moving from one basic feasible solution to another until the optimal solution. Those values in the final tableau under each slack value are called the *shadow prices*, which is referred to as the economic value of resources, and it is the marginal value of the resources used in production. We declare it when we describe an example later. But, before solving some examples, we have to know about the *pivot operation*. We already met the concepts of partial pivoting and pivot elements in the previous chapter. We call the column that the pivot element is located as the *pivot column*. In the simplex algorithm, the pivot element is replaced by a 1 by dividing all other elements in this row by the pivot element and making 0's other elements on this column by row operations. The second simplex tableau can have the optimal solution if the objective row has non-negative elements and $b_i \geq 0$. If not we do the same process for another column. But how will the pivot element be chosen? First, we select the negative element with the largest absolute value in the objective row. For example, in the previous example, -5 is the one we are looking for. The pivot column is one where -5 is located. Then, by dividing each element of the last column by the corresponding entry in the pivot column, the smallest ratio is the pivot element. Here the pivot element is 2 which lies in the second row and column, i.e., $a_{22}=2$. We divide the second row by the pivot element and by some row operations, we reduce the pivot column to $\begin{bmatrix} 0 \\ 1 \\ 0 \\ 0 \end{bmatrix}$.

We examine the optimal solutions. If not, we will continue the same process for another column until we arrive at an optimal solution.

To have a better understanding of the simplex method, we describe its algorithm step by step by resolving example 2 using the simplex method. We have

$$\text{Maximize: } Z = 3X_1 + 2X_2$$

$$\text{Subject to: } 2X_1 + 3X_2 \leq 80$$

$X_1 + X_2 \le 30.$

Then, the equational form is

$2X_1 + 3X_2 + S_1 = 80$

$X_1 + X_2 + S_2 = 30$

$-3X_1 - 2X_2 + Z = 0.$

Therefore, the augmented matrix is

$$\begin{array}{ccccc} X_1 & X_2 & S_1 & S_2 & Z \end{array}$$
$$\left[\begin{array}{ccccc|c} 2 & 3 & 1 & 0 & 0 & 80 \\ 1 & 1 & 0 & 1 & 0 & 30 \\ \hline -3 & -2 & 0 & 0 & 1 & 0 \end{array}\right].$$

From this tableau, we can read the first basic feasible solution by setting $X_1=X_2=0$. We obtain $S_1=80$, $S_2=30$ and $Z=0$, respectively. As we mentioned, to increase the value of Z we have to move to a new basic feasible solution. The pivot column is column one because the most negative entry in the objective row is -3.

First, we find the pivot element and then change the basis. This can be done by dividing each element of the last column by the corresponding entry in the pivot column. The smallest ratio indicates that the pivot element is $a_{21}=1$. Since the pivot element is 1, hence we do not need to divide the second row by 1. By the row operations given by R_2-R_1 and R_3+3R_1 we alter

$$\begin{bmatrix} 1 \\ 1 \\ -3 \end{bmatrix} \text{ to } \begin{bmatrix} 1 \\ 0 \\ 0 \end{bmatrix}.$$

We get,

$$\begin{array}{ccccc} X_1 & X_2 & S_1 & S_2 & Z \end{array}$$
$$\left[\begin{array}{ccccc|c} 0 & 1 & 1 & -1 & 0 & 20 \\ 1 & 1 & 0 & 1 & 0 & 30 \\ \hline 0 & 1 & 0 & 0 & 1 & 90 \end{array}\right].$$

We have no negative entries in the objective row and the last column, thus, we have arrived at an optimal solution now. This simplex tableau yields, X_1=30, X_2=0 and Z=90. This is the same value for *Z* we obtained in example 2.

Remark 6: For calculating possible solutions with *m* equations and *m+n* variables we have several combinations which can be determined by $\binom{m+n}{m}$. One of these solutions is optimal.

For example, for previous example, we have *m*=2 and *m+n*=4 variables, thus

$$\binom{m+n}{m} = \binom{4}{2} = \frac{4!}{2!2!} = 6.$$

These 6 solutions can be derived by imposing the following choices;
$X_1 = X_2 = 0, X_1 = S_1 = 0, X_1 = S_2 = 0, X_2 = S_1 = 0, X_2 = S_2 = 0, \text{and} S_1 = S_2 = 0.$

If we refer to figure in example 2, we will find that there are also 6 extreme points.

Example 6: Solve the following linear programming.

Maximize: $Z = 7X_1 + 5X_2 + 2X_3$

Subject to: $2X_1 + X_2 + 2X_3 \leq 8$

$X_1 + 2X_2 + X_3 \leq 10$

$2X_1 + X_2 + 4X_3 \leq 40$

$X_i \geq 0; i = 1,2,3.$

Solution: The equational form of this program is,

$$2X_1 + X_2 + 2X_3 + S_1 = 8$$

$$X_1 + 2X_2 + X_3 + S_2 = 10$$

$$2X_1 + X_2 + 4X_3 + S_3 = 40$$

$$-7X_1 - 5X_2 - 2X_3 + Z = 0.$$

The augmented matrix for this system is,

$$\begin{array}{ccccccc|c} X_1 & X_2 & X_3 & S_1 & S_2 & S_3 & Z & \\ \hline 2 & 1 & 2 & 1 & 0 & 0 & 0 & 8 \\ 1 & 2 & 1 & 0 & 1 & 0 & 0 & 10 \\ 2 & 1 & 4 & 0 & 0 & 1 & 0 & 40 \\ \hline -7 & -5 & -2 & 0 & 0 & 0 & 1 & 0 \end{array}.$$

The negative value with the largest absolute value in the objective row is -7. Then the pivot element is located on the first column. We do the same as we did for the previous example to find which one is the pivot element. Therefore, we divide each element of the last column by the corresponding entry in this column. These quotients lead us to find the pivot element, which is 2. We divide the first row by the pivot element. We obtain

$$\begin{array}{ccccccc|c} X_1 & X_2 & X_3 & S_1 & S_2 & S_3 & Z & \\ \hline 1 & \frac{1}{2} & 1 & \frac{1}{2} & 0 & 0 & 0 & 4 \\ 1 & 2 & 1 & 0 & 1 & 0 & 0 & 10 \\ 2 & 1 & 4 & 0 & 0 & 1 & 0 & 40 \\ \hline -7 & -5 & -2 & 0 & 0 & 0 & 1 & 0 \end{array}$$

We perform the following row operations to reduce $\begin{bmatrix} 1 \\ 1 \\ 2 \\ -7 \end{bmatrix}$ to $\begin{bmatrix} 1 \\ 0 \\ 0 \\ 0 \end{bmatrix}$.

$R_2 - R_1, R_3 - 2R_1, R_4 + 7R_1$.

These operations lead us to the second tableau. That is,

$$\begin{array}{ccccccc|c} X_1 & X_2 & X_3 & S_1 & S_2 & S_3 & Z & \\ \hline 1 & \frac{1}{2} & 1 & \frac{1}{2} & 0 & 0 & 0 & 4 \\ 0 & \frac{3}{2} & 0 & -\frac{1}{2} & 1 & 0 & 0 & 6 \\ 0 & 0 & 2 & -1 & 0 & 1 & 0 & 32 \\ \hline 0 & -\frac{3}{2} & 5 & \frac{7}{2} & 0 & 0 & 1 & 28 \end{array}$$

We again have a negative element in the objective row, which is $-\frac{3}{2}$. Thus, the pivot element lies in the second column. It is not difficult to show that the pivot element is $\frac{3}{2}$. dividing the second row by this number we get the following tableau:

$$\begin{array}{ccccccc|c} X_1 & X_2 & X_3 & S_1 & S_2 & S_3 & Z & \\ \hline 1 & \frac{1}{2} & 1 & \frac{1}{2} & 0 & 0 & 0 & 4 \\ 0 & 1 & 0 & -\frac{1}{3} & \frac{2}{2} & 0 & 0 & 4 \\ 0 & 0 & 2 & -1 & 0 & 1 & 0 & 32 \\ \hline 0 & -\frac{3}{2} & 5 & 3 & 0 & 0 & 1 & 28 \end{array}$$

The row operations given by $R_1 - \frac{1}{2}R_2$ and $R_4 + \frac{3}{2}R_2$,yield,

$$\begin{array}{ccccccc|c} X_1 & X_2 & X_3 & S_1 & S_2 & S_3 & Z & \\ \hline 1 & 0 & 1 & \frac{2}{3} & \frac{1}{3} & 0 & 0 & 2 \\ 0 & 1 & 0 & -\frac{1}{3} & \frac{2}{3} & 0 & 0 & 4 \\ 0 & 0 & 2 & -1 & 0 & 1 & 0 & 32 \\ \hline 0 & 0 & 8 & 5 & 1 & 0 & 1 & 34 \end{array}$$

There is no negative entry in the objective row and the last column, hence we can read the optimal solution through this simplex tableau. We have, X_1=2, X_2=4, X_3=0 and Z=34.The basic solutions are S_1=0, S_2=0 and S_3=32. This optimal solution can be checked by substituting the values we have in the constraint equations and the objective function. We have

$$2X_1 + X_2 + 2X_3 + S_1 = 2(2) + 4 + 0 + 0 = 8$$

$$X_1 + 2X_2 + X_3 + S_2 = 2 + 2(4) + 0 + 0 = 10$$

$$2X_1 + X_2 + 4X_3 + S_3 = 2(2) + 4 + 32 + 0 = 40$$

$$Z = 7X_1 + 5X_2 + 2X_3 = 7(2) + 5(4) + 2(0) = 34.$$

We have already mentioned, those values in the final tableau, under each slack value are the shadow prices. The shadow price of a constraint is the amount by which the objective function value will change if the right-hand side of the constraint is increased or decreased by one unit, (Winston, 1997). **It tells you how much more profit you would get by increasing the amount of that resource by 1-unit.** We declare it by describing an example.

Example 7: Solve the following linear programming.

Maximize: $Z = 4X_1 + 2X_2$

Subject to: $5X_1 + X_2 \leq 35$

$4X_1 + 4X_2 \leq 39$

$X_1 + 3X_2 \leq 27$

$X_i \geq 0; i = 1,2.$

Solution: First, we write the equational form of this program. We get,

$5X_1 + X_2 + S_1 = 35$

$4X_1 + X_2 + S_2 = 39$

$X_1 + 3X_2 + S_3 = 27$

$-4X_1 - 2X_2 + Z = 0.$

The initial simplex tableau is,

$$\begin{array}{cccccc|c} X_1 & X_2 & S_1 & S_2 & S_3 & Z & \\ \hline 5 & 1 & 1 & 0 & 0 & 0 & 35 \\ 4 & 4 & 0 & 1 & 0 & 0 & 39 \\ 1 & 3 & 0 & 0 & 1 & 0 & 27 \\ \hline -4 & -2 & 0 & 0 & 0 & 1 & 0 \end{array}$$

The negative value with the largest absolute value in the objective row is -4. Then the pivot element is located on the first column. We do the same as we did for the previous example to find which one is the pivot element. We divide each element of the last column by the corresponding entry in this column. We find that the pivot element is 5. By dividing the first row by the pivot element, we obtain

$$\begin{array}{cccccc|c} X_1 & X_2 & S_1 & S_2 & S_3 & Z & \\ 1 & \frac{1}{5} & \frac{1}{5} & 0 & 0 & 0 & 7 \\ 4 & 4 & 0 & 1 & 0 & 0 & 39 \\ 1 & 3 & 0 & 0 & 1 & 0 & 27 \\ \hline -4 & -2 & 0 & 0 & 0 & 1 & 0 \end{array}.$$

By the following row operations, we reduce $\begin{bmatrix} 1 \\ 4 \\ 1 \\ -4 \end{bmatrix}$ to $\begin{bmatrix} 1 \\ 0 \\ 0 \\ 0 \end{bmatrix}$.

$R_2 - 4R_1, R_3 - R_1, R_4 + 4R_1$.

We obtain the second simplex tableau.

$$\begin{array}{cccccc|c} X_1 & X_2 & S_1 & S_2 & S_3 & Z & \\ 1 & \frac{1}{5} & \frac{1}{5} & 0 & 0 & 0 & 7 \\ 0 & \frac{16}{5} & \frac{-4}{5} & 1 & 0 & 0 & 11 \\ 0 & \frac{14}{3} & \frac{-1}{5} & 0 & 1 & 0 & 20 \\ \hline 0 & \frac{-6}{5} & \frac{4}{5} & 0 & 0 & 0 & 28 \end{array}.$$

The negative element in the objective row is $-\frac{6}{5}$. Thus, the pivot element lies on the second column. The pivot element is $\frac{16}{5}$. We divide the second row by $\frac{16}{5}$. We obtain the following tableau:

$$\begin{array}{cccccc} X_1 & X_2 & S_1 & S_2 & S_3 & Z \end{array}$$

$$\left[\begin{array}{cccccc|c} 1 & \frac{1}{5} & \frac{1}{5} & 0 & 0 & 0 & 7 \\ 0 & \frac{16}{5} & \frac{-4}{5} & 1 & 0 & 0 & \frac{55}{16} \\ 0 & \frac{14}{3} & \frac{-1}{5} & 0 & 1 & 0 & 20 \\ \hline 0 & \frac{-6}{5} & \frac{4}{5} & 0 & 0 & 0 & 28 \end{array}\right].$$

The row operations given by $R_1 - \frac{1}{5}R_2, R_3 - \frac{14}{3}R_2$ and $R_4 + \frac{6}{5}R_2 X_3=0$ and $Z = \frac{257}{8}$. The basic solutions are $S_1=0$, $S_2=0$ and $S_3 = \frac{95}{24}$. This optimal solution can be checked, as in the previous example. By looking at the final simplex tableau, one can express the shadow price to find how much the objective function will be changed as a result of a 1-unit increase in the set. In this example, Z would increase by $\frac{1}{2}$ unit for a 1-unit change in the first constraint and increases by $\frac{3}{8}$ unit for a 1-unit change in the second constraint, and by 0 for a 1-unit change in the third constraint. We must note that since the third constraint has a positive slack variable, hence its shadow price is zero because it is not fully been used in the optimal solution.

Now, we will explain what to do when the initial tableau does not contain an identity matrix. This happens when we use the simplex algorithm to find the minimal value. The algorithm is nearly the same as the one we used to find the maximal value. But since the initial tableau does not contain an identity matrix, we have to add an artificial variable to each constraint to generate an initial basic feasible solution. There are two main methods for dealing with such cases: The Two-Phase method and the Big-M method. Both of these methods involve adding artificial variables. We describe in this chapter only the Big-M method with the help of a numerical example and then introduce the *dual problem* which is easier to solve than the optimal problem.

Example 7: Solve the following problem by the Big-M method.

Minimize: $Z = 5X_1 + 3X_2$

Subject to: $X_1 + X_2 \geq 9$

$4X_1 + X_2 \geq 24$

$X_i \geq 0; i = 1,2.$

Solution: The equational form of this program is

$$X_1 + X_2 - S_1 = 9$$

$$4X_1 + X_2 - S_2 = 24$$

$$-5X_1 - 3X_2 + Z = 0.$$

Therefore,

$$\begin{array}{c} \begin{array}{ccccc} X_1 & X_2 & S_1 & S_2 & Z \end{array} \\ \left[\begin{array}{ccccc|c} 1 & 1 & -1 & 0 & 0 & 9 \\ 4 & 1 & 0 & -1 & 0 & 24 \\ \hline -5 & -3 & 0 & 0 & 0 & 0 \end{array}\right], \end{array}$$

From this tableau, we can read the first basic feasible solution by setting, X_1=X_2=0. We get S_1=-9, S_2=-4. Since basic feasible solutions must be non-negative, or we can claim that the initial tableau does not contain an identity matrix, hence we have to add an artificial variable to each constraint to generate an initial basic feasible solution. Therefore, we write

$$X_1 + X_2 - S_1 + A_1 = 9$$

$$4X_1 + X_2 - S_2 + A_2 = 24$$

$$-5X_1 - 3X_2 + Z = 0.$$

The augmented matrix for this system is,

$$\begin{array}{c} \begin{array}{ccccccc} X_1 & X_2 & S_1 & S_2 & A_1 & A_2 & Z \end{array} \\ \left[\begin{array}{cccccc|c} 1 & 1 & -1 & 0 & 1 & 0 & 9 \\ 4 & 1 & 0 & -1 & 0 & 1 & 24 \\ \hline -5 & -3 & 0 & 0 & -M & -M & 0 \end{array}\right], \end{array}$$

where M is a large number to ensure that artificial values will be excluded from the optimal solution. In the first step, we must remove each M from columns of artificial variables by multiplying each constraint row by M and adding these rows to the objective row. We get

$$\begin{array}{ccccccc} X_1 & X_2 & S_1 & S_2 & A_1 & A_2 & Z \end{array}$$
$$\left[\begin{array}{cccccc|c} 1 & 1 & -1 & 0 & 1 & 0 & 9 \\ 4 & 1 & 0 & -1 & 0 & 1 & 24 \\ \hline 5M & -5 & 2M & -3 & -M & -M00 & 33M \end{array}\right]$$

The value with the largest positive value in the objective row is located in the first column. To find the pivot element, we divide each element of the last column by the corresponding entry in this column. The pivot element is 4 which lies in the second row. We divide this row by the pivot element. We obtain

$$\begin{array}{ccccccc} X_1 & X_2 & S_1 & S_2 & A_1 & A_2 & Z \end{array}$$
$$\left[\begin{array}{cccccc|c} 1 & 1 & -1 & 0 & 1 & 0 & 9 \\ 1 & \frac{1}{4} & 0 & -\frac{1}{4} & 0 & \frac{1}{4} & 6 \\ \hline 5M & -5 & 2M & -3 & -M & -M00 & 33M \end{array}\right].$$

We perform the following row operations to reduce $\begin{bmatrix} 1 \\ 1 \\ 5M-5 \end{bmatrix}$ to $\begin{bmatrix} 0 \\ 1 \\ 0 \end{bmatrix}$. $R_1 - R_2$ and $R_3 - (5M-5)R_2$. We get,

$$\begin{array}{ccccccc} X_1 & X_2 & S_1 & S_2 & A_1 & A_2 & Z \end{array}$$
$$\left[\begin{array}{cccccc|c} 0 & \frac{3}{4} & -1 & \frac{1}{4} & 1 & -\frac{1}{4} & 3 \\ 1 & \frac{1}{4} & 0 & -\frac{1}{4} & 0 & \frac{1}{4} & 6 \\ \hline 0 & \frac{3M-7}{4} & -M & \frac{M-5}{4} & 00 & \frac{5(1-M)}{4} & 3M+30 \end{array}\right].$$

We again have a positive element in the objective row, which is $\frac{3M-7}{4}$. Thus, the pivot element lies on the second column. It is not difficult to show what the pivot element is $\frac{3}{4}$. Dividing the first row by this number, we get the following tableau:

$$\begin{array}{ccccccc} X_1 & X_2 & S_1 & S_2 & A_1 & A_2 & Z \end{array}$$

$$\left[\begin{array}{cccccc|c} 0 & 1 & -\frac{4}{3} & \frac{1}{3} & \frac{4}{3} & -\frac{1}{3} & 4 \\ 1 & \frac{1}{4} & 0 & -\frac{1}{4} & 0 & \frac{1}{4} & 6 \\ \hline 0 & \frac{3M-7}{4} & -M & \frac{M-5}{4} & 00 & \frac{5(1-M)}{4} & 3M+30 \end{array}\right]$$

The row operations, $R_2 - \frac{1}{4}R_1$ and $R_3 - \frac{(3M-7)}{4}R_1$, yield

$$\begin{array}{ccccccc} X_1 & X_2 & S_1 & S_2 & A_1 & A_2 & Z \end{array}$$

$$\left[\begin{array}{cccccc|c} 0 & 1 & -\frac{4}{3} & \frac{1}{3} & \frac{4}{3} & -\frac{1}{3} & 4 \\ 1 & 0 & \frac{1}{3} & -\frac{1}{3} & -\frac{1}{3} & \frac{1}{3} & 5 \\ \hline 0 & 0 & -\frac{7}{3} & -\frac{2}{3} & \frac{7-M}{3} & \frac{2-3M}{3} & 37 \end{array}\right]$$

There is no positive entry in the objective row, thus we can read the optimal solution through this simplex tableau. We have, X_1=5, X_2=4 and Z=37.

As can be seen, the *M*-method is an effective method with functional limitations, but it contains more operations than a maximum problem, and by using a computer, the rounding error hurts the accuracy of the method.

Fortunately, the minimum problem can be solved by converting it to a related maximum problem. What does it mean we convert a minimum problem to a maximum problem? Among several methods, rather than the Big-*M* method, one is called the *dual method*. By this method, first, the original problem converts to the corresponding problem known as a *dual problem* and then solves it.

The Von Neumenn Duality principle states that: the optimal solution of the original problem has the same value as its dual problem.

How can we convert our original problem into a dual problem?

First, we write our problem in standard form and construct the augmented matrix. We interchange the rows and columns to form the augmented matrix of the dual problem. We transpose the matrix form of the original problem to find the matrix of the dual problem. If our original problem is a minimum problem, for the dual problem we have a maximum problem. For example, if our original problem is

Minimize: $Z = 4X_1 + 5X_2 + 2X_3$

Subject to: $X_1 + 2X_2 + 2X_3 \geq 20$

$X_1 + 2X_2 + X_3 \geq 30$

$2X_1 + X_2 + 4X_3 \geq 12$

$X_1, X_2 \text{ and } X_3 \geq 0,$

then its matrix form is:

$$\left[\begin{array}{ccc|c} 1 & 2 & 2 & 20 \\ 1 & 2 & 1 & 30 \\ 2 & 1 & 4 & 12 \\ 4 & 5 & 2 & 0 \end{array}\right].$$

By interchanging the rows and columns, we get:

$$\left[\begin{array}{ccc|c} 1 & 1 & 2 & 4 \\ 2 & 2 & 1 & 5 \\ 2 & 1 & 4 & 2 \\ 20 & 30 & 12 & 0 \end{array}\right].$$

Therefore, our dual problem will be:

Maximize:

$Z = 20Y_1 + 30Y_2 + 12Y_3$

Subject to: $Y_1 + Y_2 + 2Y_3 \geq 4$

$2Y_1 + 2Y_2 + Y_3 \geq 5$

$2Y_1 + Y_2 + 4Y_3 \geq 2$

$Y_1, Y_2 \text{ and } Y_3 \geq 0.$

We return to example 7 and solve it by the dual method. We had

Minimize: $Z = 5X_1 + 3X_2$
Subject to: $X_1 + X_2 \geq 9$
$4X_1 + X_2 \geq 24$
$X_i \geq 0, i = 1,2$

Its dual is:

Maximize: $Z = 9Y_1 + 24Y_2$
Subject to: $Y_1 + Y_2 \leq 5$
$4Y_1 + Y_2 \leq 3$
$Y_i \geq 0, i = 1,2$

The equational form of this problem is

$Y_1 + Y_2 + S_1 = 5$

$4Y_1 + Y_2 + S_2 = 3$

$-9Y_1 - 24Y_2 + Z = 0.$

The augmented matrix for this system is

$$\begin{array}{ccccc|c} Y_1 & Y_2 & S_1 & S_2 & Z & \\ \hline 1 & 4 & 1 & 0 & 0 & 5 \\ 1 & 1 & 0 & 1 & 0 & 3 \\ \hline -9 & -24 & 0 & 0 & 1 & 0 \end{array}$$

The negative value with the largest absolute value in the objective row is -24, hence the pivot element located on the second column. We divide each element of the last column by the corresponding entry in this column. These quotients show that the pivot element which is located in the first row is 4. We divide the elements of the first by 4. We get

$$\begin{array}{ccccc}Y_1 & Y_2 & S_1 & S_2 & Z\end{array}$$

$$\left[\begin{array}{ccccc|c} \frac{1}{4} & 1 & \frac{1}{4} & 0 & 0 & \frac{5}{4} \\ 1 & 1 & 0 & 1 & 0 & 3 \\ \hline -9 & -24 & 0 & 0 & 1 & 0 \end{array}\right]$$

We do the following row operations to alter $\begin{bmatrix} 1 \\ 1 \\ -24 \end{bmatrix}$ to $\begin{bmatrix} 1 \\ 0 \\ 0 \end{bmatrix}$.

$R_2 - R_1, R_3 + 24R_1$.

We obtain,

$$\begin{array}{ccccc}Y_1 & Y_2 & S_1 & S_2 & Z\end{array}$$

$$\left[\begin{array}{cccccc|c} \frac{1}{4} & 1 & \frac{1}{4} & 0 & 0 & & \frac{5}{4} \\ \frac{3}{4} & 0 & -\frac{1}{4} & 1 & 0 & & \frac{7}{4} \\ \hline -3 & 0 & 6 & 0 & 1 & 0 & 30 \end{array}\right].$$

We have a negative element in the third row, hence the pivot element is located in the first column. We divide each element of the last column by the corresponding entry in this column. The pivot element which is located in the second row is $\frac{3}{4}$. We divide the elements of the second by $\frac{3}{4}$. This gives

$$\begin{array}{ccccc}Y_1 & Y_2 & S_1 & S_2 & Z\end{array}$$

$$\left[\begin{array}{cccccc|c} \frac{1}{4} & 1 & \frac{1}{4} & 0 & 0 & & \frac{5}{4} \\ 1 & 0 & -\frac{1}{3} & \frac{4}{3} & 0 & & \frac{7}{3} \\ \hline -3 & 0 & 6 & 0 & 1 & 0 & 30 \end{array}\right].$$

By row operations given by $R_1 - \frac{1}{4}R_2$ and $R_3 + 3R_2$, we reduce $\begin{bmatrix} \frac{1}{4} \\ 1 \\ -3 \end{bmatrix}$ to $\begin{bmatrix} 0 \\ 1 \\ 0 \end{bmatrix}$.

$$\begin{array}{ccccc} Y_1 & Y_2 & S_1 & S_2 & Z \end{array}$$

$$\left[\begin{array}{cccccc|c} 0 & 1 & \frac{1}{3} & -\frac{1}{3} & 0 & & \frac{2}{3} \\ 1 & 0 & -\frac{1}{3} & \frac{4}{3} & 0 & & \frac{7}{3} \\ \hline 0 & 0 & 3 & 0 & 5 & 0 & 37 \end{array}\right].$$

Remark 7: We point out that by duality, if our original problem has three variables will be reduced to two variables which can be solved by the graphical method.

Example 8: Solve the following problem.

Minimize: $Z = 6X_1 + 2X_2 + 3X_3$

Subject to: $3X_1 + 2X_2 + X_3 \geq 36$

$2X_1 + X_2 + 3X_3 \geq 24$

$X_i \geq 0; i = 1,2,3.$

Solution: The dual to this problem is

Maximize: $Z = 36Y_1 + 24Y_2$

Subject to: $3Y_1 + 2Y_2 \leq 6$

$2Y_1 + Y_2 \leq 2$

$Y_1 + 3Y_2 \leq 3.$

$Y_i \geq 0; i = 1,2.$

This can be solved by a graphical method. It would not be difficult to show that Max Z=38 for dual and happens for $Y_1 = \frac{5}{6}$ and $Y_2 = \frac{1}{3}$. Therefore, the minimum value of the original problem is 38.

11.4 SENSITIVITY ANALYSIS

When we solve a system of linear equations by the Gauss elimination method, we should bear in mind that a small change, even in one of the coefficients of the system, for example a_{ij} or b_i causes a big change on exact solutions. It means the system is usually sensitive to such changes. This fact brings in mind a hypothetical question about whether changing in the objective function by increasing or decreasing one of the objective coefficients by a small change how much would it change the optimality? In general, by solving a linear programming problem, we may encounter the following changes:

- Changes in one or more components of a constant matrix ***B*.**
- Changes in one or more coefficients of a constant matrix ***A*.**
- Adding or removing a new constraint.
- Adding or removing a new variable.

Basically, the meaning of sensitivity analysis is the effect of changes in model parameters on the optimal solution. In such cases, some parameters may have different values so that there is no change in the optimal solution, but some other parameters may affect the optimal solution with a slight change and obtain a new optimal solution, or it may even be rejected as an unfeasible solution.

Let us have a change on one element of the right-hand side. We denote it by B^*. Therefore, $Z^*=a^*B^*, X^*=A^*B^*$, where a^* is the coefficient vector of S_i in final objective function, and A^* is a matrix with elements of S_i in final tableau.

As an example, we go back to example 7, where we had the following initial and final simplex tableaus:

$$\left[\begin{array}{cccccc|c} 5 & 1 & 1 & 0 & 0 & 0 & 35 \\ 4 & 4 & 0 & 1 & 0 & 0 & 39 \\ 1 & 3 & 0 & 0 & 1 & 0 & 27 \\ \hline -4 & -2 & 0 & 0 & 0 & 1 & 0 \end{array}\right], \left[\begin{array}{cccccc|c} 1 & 0 & \frac{1}{4} & \frac{-1}{16} & 0 & 0 & \frac{101}{26} \\ 0 & 1 & \frac{-1}{4} & \frac{5}{16} & 0 & 0 & \frac{55}{16} \\ 0 & 0 & \frac{29}{30} & \frac{35}{25} & 1 & 0 & \frac{95}{24} \\ \hline 0 & 0 & \frac{1}{2} & \frac{3}{8} & 0 & 0 & \frac{257}{8} \end{array}\right],$$

and change the first component of the initial tableau to the following form and continue to consider the results.

$$\left[\begin{array}{cccccc|c} 5 & 1 & 1 & 0 & 0 & 0 & 35.5 \\ 4 & 4 & 0 & 1 & 0 & 0 & 39 \\ 1 & 3 & 0 & 0 & 1 & 0 & 27 \\ \hline -4 & -2 & 0 & 0 & 0 & 1 & 0 \end{array}\right].$$

We have,

$$Z^* = \begin{bmatrix} \frac{1}{2} & \frac{3}{8} & 0 \end{bmatrix} \begin{bmatrix} 35.5 \\ 39 \\ 27 \end{bmatrix} = \frac{1}{2} \times 35.5 + \frac{3}{8} \times 39 + 0 = \frac{259}{8},$$

$$X^* = \begin{bmatrix} \frac{1}{4} & \frac{-1}{16} & 0 \\ \frac{-1}{4} & \frac{5}{16} & 0 \\ \frac{29}{30} & \frac{35}{24} & 1 \end{bmatrix} \begin{bmatrix} 35.5 \\ 39 \\ 27 \end{bmatrix} = \begin{bmatrix} X_1 \\ X_2 \\ S_3 \end{bmatrix} \rightarrow \begin{bmatrix} X_1 \\ X_2 \\ S_3 \end{bmatrix} = \begin{bmatrix} \frac{103}{16} \\ \frac{43}{16} \\ \frac{14183}{120} \end{bmatrix}.$$

$$\therefore\ Z^* = \frac{259}{8}, X_1 = \frac{103}{16}, X_2 = \frac{43}{16}, S_3 = \frac{14183}{120}.$$

Since all elements of X^* are nonnegative, thus, the new solution is optimal.

Remark 8: If we get a solution with negative elements, then the solution is not feasible, and we should carry on the solution the simplex method.

We offer the readers who wish to have more information about such sensitivities, refer to Winston (1997), which has a valuable discussion about this matter.

11.5 SOME APPLICATIONS OF LINEAR PROGRAMMING

Liner programming is one of the most powerful methods that managers can use to solve their various problems according to the conditions of the problem.

Linear programming models are used for resource allocation, air routing, design and use of communication networks, transportation issues and many other issues. Some of these issues include hundreds of restrictions and thousands of variables.

It has many applications in the military, industry, and urban engineering. Maximizing income or minimizing production costs is mainly used in macroeconomics and business management. For example, inventory management, asset and stock management, allocation of human resources and non-human resources, and planning promotional trips. Many companies and government institutions have saved millions of dollars with the successful use of linear programming, and examples of these successes can be named the scheduling of police officers in San Francisco designed by Taylor and Huxley in 1989.

Using network models, Powell and others in 1988 developed a model for allocating loads for truck drivers in North American Lines. Using this model has provided better services to customers and reduced annual costs.

In 1989, Vasgo and others assisted Bethelm Steel in designing an ingot mold facility that resulted in annual operating cost savings.

***Example* 9:** In a manufacturing company, two types of goods are produced using two materials *A* and *B*. The first product consists of 2 units of *A* and 3 units of *B*, and the second product consists of 4 units of *A* and 1 unit of *B*. The maximum inventory of *A* and *B* per week is 60 units respectively. If the profit per unit of these two goods is 5 and 7 dollars, respectively, how much of each product should be produced to maximize the profit?

Solution: According to the given data, we need to solve the following linear programming problem.

Maximize: $Z = 7X_1 + 9X_2$

Subject to: $2X_1 + 3X_2 \leq 60$

$4X_1 + X_2 \leq 80$

$X_i \geq 0; i = 1, 2.$

We use a graphical method. First, we draw easily lines $2X_1+3X_2=60$ and $4X_1+X_2=80$, we will get four corner points $O(0, 0)$, $A(20, 0)$, $B(0, 15)$ and $C(18, 8)$. We substitute in the objective function. It yields $Z_O=0$, $Z_A=140$, $Z_B=135$ and $Z_C=198$. Thus 18 units of *A* and 8 units of *B* produce maximum profit

***Example* 10:** An industrial company plans to produce three types of washing machines. For this purpose, it uses two human resources and raw materials. For the first, second, and third types, 1, 5, and 3 people require, respectively, a maximum of 150 Man-hours, and raw materials 2, 4, and 1 kg, with a maximum amount of 200 kg. If the profit per unit is 100, 50 and 150 dollars respectively, find the maximum amount of the final revenue.

Solution: According to the given data, we need to solve the following linear programming problem.

Maximize: $Z = 100X_1 + 50X_2 + 150X_3$

Subject to: $X_1 + 5X_2 + 4X_3 \leq 150$

$2X_1 + 4X_2 + X_3 \leq 200$

$X_i \geq 0; i = 1,2,3.$

For simplicity, we convert this problem to its dual one and then solve it by the graphical method. It is not difficult to show that the dual to this problem is

Minimize: $Z = 150Y_1 + 200Y_2$

Subject to: $Y_1 + 2Y_2 \geq 100$

$5Y_1 + 4Y_2 \geq 50$

$4Y_1 + Y_2 \geq 150$

$Y_i \geq 0; i = 1,2.$

By drawing the lines $Y_1+2Y_2=100$, $5Y_1+4Y_2=150$ and $4Y_1+Y_2=200$, we get three corner points $A(100, 0)$, $B(0, 150)$, and $C(\frac{200}{7}, \frac{250}{7})$. If we substitute these values in the objective function, we come to $Z_c=50000$. Thus, the maximum profit 50000.

Example* 11*: A company is attempting to maximize Z from the production of three products X_1, X_2 and X_3 according to the following table.

Table 2.

Product	R_1	R_2	R_3
X_1	4	2	2
X_2	2	5	3
X_3	2	4	5

The company has available 1600 units of R_1, 1000 units of R_2 and 1200 units of R_3.the company makes a profit of \$4, \$1, and \$3, respectively on its product. Find X_1, X_2 and X_3 so that Z is maximum.

Solution: According to the given data, we have to solve the following linear programming problem.

Maximize: $Z = 4X_1 + X_2 + 3X_3$

Subject to: $4X_1 + 2X_2 + 2X_3 \leq 1600$

$2X_1 + 5X_2 + 3X_3 \leq 100$

$$2X_1 + 4X_2 + 5X_3 \leq 1200$$

$$X_i \geq 0; i = 1,2,3.$$

We use simplex method to solve it. The equational form is

$$4X_1 + 2X_2 + 2X_3 + S_1 = 1600$$

$$2X_1 + 5X_2 + 3X_3 + S_2 = 1000$$

$$2X_1 + 4X_2 + 5X_3 + S_3 = 1200$$

$$-4X_1 - X_2 - 3X_3 + Z = 0.$$

Thus, the initial tableau is

$$\begin{array}{ccccccc} X_1 & X_2 & X_3 & S_1 & S_2 & S_3 & Z \end{array}$$
$$\left[\begin{array}{ccccccc|c} 4 & 2 & 2 & 1 & 0 & 0 & 0 & 1600 \\ 2 & 5 & 3 & 0 & 1 & 0 & 0 & 1000 \\ 2 & 4 & 5 & 0 & 0 & 1 & 0 & 1200 \\ \hline -4 & -1 & -3 & 0 & 0 & 1 & & 0 \end{array}\right].$$

The pivot element is located on the first column because the negative value with the largest absolute value in the objective row is -4. We divide each element of last column by the corresponding entry in this column. These quotients lead us to find pivot element which is 4. We divide the first row by the pivot element. We obtain

$$\begin{array}{ccccccc} X_1 & X_2 & X_3 & S_1 & S_2 & S_3 & Z \end{array}$$
$$\left[\begin{array}{ccccccc|c} 1 & \frac{1}{2} & \frac{1}{2} & \frac{1}{4} & 0 & 0 & 0 & 400 \\ 2 & 5 & 3 & 0 & 1 & 0 & 0 & 1000 \\ 2 & 4 & 5 & 0 & 0 & 1 & 0 & 1200 \\ \hline -4 & -1 & -3 & 0 & 0 & 0 & 1 & 0 \end{array}\right]$$

We perform the following row operations to reduce $\begin{bmatrix} 1 \\ 2 \\ 1 \\ -4 \end{bmatrix}$ to $\begin{bmatrix} 1 \\ 0 \\ 0 \\ 0 \end{bmatrix}$.

$R_2 - 2R_1, R_3 - 2R_1, R_4 + 4R_1.$

These operations lead us to the second tableau. That is,

$$\begin{array}{ccccccc|c} X_1 & X_2 & X_3 & S_1 & S_2 & S_3 & Z & \\ \hline 1 & \frac{1}{2} & \frac{1}{2} & \frac{1}{4} & 0 & 0 & 0 & 400 \\ 0 & 4 & 2 & -\frac{1}{2} & 1 & 0 & 0 & 200 \\ 0 & 3 & 4 & -\frac{1}{2} & 0 & 1 & 0 & 400 \\ \hline 0 & 1 & -1 & 1 & 0 & 0 & 1 & 1600 \end{array}$$

We have again a negative element in the objective row, which is -1. It is not difficult to show that the pivot element is $-\frac{1}{2}$. Here we have two choices because we have two pivot elements. We choose one which is located in the third row. Dividing the third row by this number we get the following tableau:

$$\begin{array}{ccccccc|c} X_1 & X_2 & X_3 & S_1 & S_2 & S_3 & Z & \\ \hline 1 & \frac{1}{2} & \frac{1}{2} & \frac{1}{4} & 0 & 0 & 0 & 400 \\ 0 & 4 & 2 & -\frac{1}{2} & 1 & 0 & 0 & 200 \\ 0 & \frac{1}{4} & 1 & -\frac{1}{8} & 0 & \frac{1}{4} & 0 & 100 \\ \hline 0 & 1 & -1 & 1 & 0 & 0 & 1 & 1600 \end{array}$$

The row operations given by $R_1 - \frac{1}{2}R_3$, $R_2 - 2R_3$ and $R_4 + R_3$, yield

$$
\begin{array}{ccccccc|c}
X_1 & X_2 & X_3 & S_1 & S_2 & S_3 & Z & \\
1 & \frac{1}{8} & 0 & \frac{5}{16} & 0 & 0 & 0 & 350 \\
0 & \frac{9}{2} & 0 & -1 & \frac{1}{4} & 0 & 0 & 0 \\
0 & \frac{3}{4} & 1 & \frac{1}{8} & 0 & \frac{1}{8} & 0 & 100 \\
\hline
0 & \frac{3}{4} & 0 & \frac{7}{8} & 0 & 0 & 1 & 1700
\end{array}.
$$

There is no negative entry in the objective row and the last column hence we can read the optimal solution through this simplex tableau. We have, X_1=350, X_2=0, X_3=100 and Z=1700. The shadow prices are zero.

To read more about linear programming readers may refer to (Smythe, Anderson, & Williams, 1974) (Kim, 1971) (Vajda, 1962) (Heady & Candler, 1958) (Driebeek, 1969) (Simonnard, 1966).

11.6 COMPUTER STATION

Linear programming (LP) is a mathematical technique for optimization in which a linear objective function is maximized or minimized subject to linear constraints.

There are several suitable and well-known Python tools for linear programming and mixed-integer linear programming. Some of them are open source, while others are proprietary. Whether you need a free or paid tool depends on the size and complexity of your problem as well as on the need for speed and flexibility.

It's worth mentioning that almost all widely used linear programming and mixed-integer linear programming libraries are native to and written in Fortran or C or C++. This is because linear programming requires computationally intensive work with (often large) matrices. Such libraries are called solvers. The Python tools are just wrappers around the solvers.

Several software tools are available for solving linear programming problems, each offering various features and capabilities. Here are some of the most popular LP software:

IBM ILOG CPLEX Optimization Studio

IBM ILOG CPLEX Optimization Studio is a comprehensive suite for optimization modeling and solution development. It includes the CPLEX Optimizer, which is renowned for its ability to solve large-scale linear programming (LP), mixed-integer programming (MIP), and quadratic programming (QP) problems efficiently.

- Key Features:
  - **High-Performance Solvers:** Solves LP, MIP, QP, and quadratically constrained programming (QCP) problems. Advanced algorithms for simplex, barrier, and network flow optimization.
  - **Interactive Development Environment (IDE):** Provides an intuitive graphical user interface for model development. Features debugging, profiling, and visualization tools to assist in model creation and analysis.
  - **Extensive API Support:** Supports multiple programming languages including C++, Java, Python, .NET, and MATLAB. Facilitates integration into various application environments and custom workflows.
  - **Advanced Presolve Techniques:** Reduces problem size and complexity before applying optimization algorithms, improving performance.
  - **Parallel Processing:** Utilizes multi-core processors to solve problems faster by performing parallel computations. Includes deterministic parallel optimization to ensure reproducible results.
  - **Constraint Programming:** Incorporates a robust constraint programming solver for solving combinatorial problems and scheduling.
  - **Real-Time Optimization:** Supports real-time decision-making applications with its ability to handle dynamic data and provide rapid solutions.
  - **Data Integration:** Integrates with various data sources such as databases, spreadsheets, and enterprise applications. Facilitates easy data import and export.
  - **Sensitivity Analysis:** Provides tools for performing sensitivity analysis to understand the impact of changes in model parameters.
  - **Scenario Analysis:** Supports scenario analysis to evaluate different scenarios and their impacts on the optimization model.
  - **User-Friendly Modeling Language (OPL):** The Optimization Programming Language (OPL) is a high-level language designed for expressing optimization models. OPL enables concise and readable model formulations.
- Advantages:
  - **Performance:** Known for its speed and robustness, especially in solving large and complex problems.

- **Flexibility:** Extensive API support allows for integration into various environments and custom solutions.
- **Scalability:** Can handle very large datasets and complex models with millions of variables and constraints.
- **Support and Documentation:** Comprehensive documentation, tutorials, and customer support ensure users can effectively leverage the software's capabilities.

Gurobi Optimizer

Gurobi Optimizer is a state-of-the-art mathematical optimization solver designed for solving various types of optimization problems, including linear programming (LP), mixed-integer programming (MIP), quadratic programming (QP), and second-order conic programming (SOCP). It is known for its high performance, reliability, and ease of integration with numerous programming environments.

- Key Features:
  - **High-Performance Solvers:** Solves LP, MIP, QP, and SOCP problems with cutting-edge algorithms. Advanced pre solve techniques, heuristics, and cutting planes to improve solver efficiency. Parallel algorithms that leverage multi-core processors for faster solutions.
  - **Wide Range of APIs:** Extensive API support for Python, C, C++, Java, MATLAB, and .NET. Integration with popular modeling languages such as AMPL, GAMS, and R.
  - **Multi-Objective Optimization:** Supports multi-objective optimization, allowing users to optimize multiple objectives simultaneously and explore trade-offs.
  - **Distributed Optimization:** Distributed algorithms to solve large problems across multiple machines.
- Features like Compute Server, Cloud, and Instant Cloud for Scalability and Flexibility:
  - **Barrier Solver:** Highly efficient interior-point methods for solving large-scale and complex problems. Ideal for continuous optimization problems with many constraints.
  - **Presolve and Tuning Tools:** Extensive presolve routines to simplify and reduce problem size before applying the main solver.
- Automatic and Manual Tuning Tools to Adjust Solver Parameters for Optimal Performance:
  - **Solution Pool and Scenario Analysis:** Maintains multiple solutions for MIP problems, allowing users to analyze different optimal or near-

optimal solutions. Scenario analysis tools to evaluate the impact of parameter changes on the solutions.

- **Detailed Documentation and Support:** Comprehensive documentation, including user manuals, quick start guides, and example code.

- Active User Community and Responsive Technical Support Team:
- Advantages:
  - **Performance:** Renowned for its speed and ability to solve very large and complex optimization problems efficiently.
  - **Flexibility:** Wide range of API support makes it easy to integrate into various applications and programming environments.
  - **Scalability:** Distributed optimization and cloud capabilities allow it to handle large-scale problems and scale with user needs.
  - **Ease of Use:** User-friendly interface and extensive documentation make it accessible to both beginners and experienced users.
  - **Support:** Excellent customer support and active community provide valuable resources for troubleshooting and optimization.
- Use Cases:
  - **Supply Chain and Logistics:** Optimizing distribution networks, vehicle routing, inventory management, and warehouse operations.

    Example: A global retailer uses Gurobi to optimize its supply chain network, reducing transportation costs and improving delivery times.
  - **Finance and Investment:** Portfolio optimization, risk management, asset allocation, and financial planning.

    Example: An investment firm uses Gurobi to optimize its portfolio, maximizing returns while minimizing risk based on market scenarios.
  - **Manufacturing and Production:** Production planning, scheduling, resource allocation, and process optimization.

    Example: A manufacturing company uses Gurobi to optimize its production schedule, balancing workload and minimizing production costs.
  - **Energy Sector:** Power generation planning, grid optimization, energy trading, and resource allocation.

    Example: An energy provider uses Gurobi to optimize the dispatch of power plants, minimizing operational costs while ensuring supply meets demand.
  - **Telecommunications:** Network design, traffic routing, capacity planning, and resource allocation.

    Example: A telecom operator uses Gurobi to design an efficient network topology, optimizing data flow and reducing latency.

- **Transportation:** Airline scheduling, fleet management, public transportation planning, and logistics optimization.

  Example: An airline uses Gurobi to optimize its flight schedule, improving profitability while maintaining service quality and regulatory compliance.

- Getting Started with Gurobi:
  - **Installation:** Gurobi can be installed on Windows, Linux, and macOS. It is available as a standalone solver or can be integrated with various development environments.
  - **Licensing:** Gurobi offers free academic licenses for students and researchers, making it accessible for educational purposes.
  - **Learning Resources:** Gurobi provides extensive resources, including tutorials, example models, webinars, and an active user community.

Example Python Code Using Gurobi

Here is a simple example of solving an LP problem using the Gurobi Python API:

```
import gurobipy as gp
from gurobipy import GRB
# Create a new model
model = gp.Model("example_model")
# Define decision variables
x = model.addVar(name="x")
y = model.addVar(name="y")
# Set the objective function
model.setObjective(2 * x + 3 * y, GRB.MAXIMIZE)
# Add constraints
model.addConstr(x + y <= 10, "c1")
model.addConstr(x - y >= 3, "c2")
# Optimize the model
model.optimize()
# Print the solution
if model.status == GRB.OPTIMAL:
    print(f"x = {x.x}")
    print(f"y = {y.x}")
    print(f"Objective value = {model.objVal}")
else:
    print("No optimal solution found")
```

LINDO/LINGO

LINDO and LINGO are software tools used for solving optimization problems, offering a range of solvers and an intuitive way to model problems using algebraic formulations.

LINDO stands for "Linear, Integer and Nonlinear Optimizer." It is a powerful tool for building and solving linear, nonlinear (convex & nonconvex), and integer optimization models. LINDO provides APIs for several programming languages, including C, C++, and Java, allowing it to integrate seamlessly into various applications.

LINGO is a comprehensive tool designed to make building and solving Linear, Nonlinear (convex & nonconvex), Quadratic, Quadratically Constrained, Second Order Cone, Stochastic, and Integer optimization models simpler and more efficient. LINGO uses a modeling language to describe the optimization problem, which helps in understanding and formulating complex models conveniently.

These tools are used across diverse fields such as logistics, finance, energy management, and manufacturing for optimizing various processes and decision-making scenarios. They are particularly useful in operations research, helping to find the best possible solution or feasible solutions to decision problems under the given constraints.

AMPL (A Mathematical Programming Language)

AMPL (A Mathematical Programming Language) is a high-level language designed specifically for describing and solving large, complex problems in mathematical programming and operations research. It's particularly well-suited for linear programming, nonlinear programming, integer programming, and complex optimization problems involving multiple objectives and constraints.

- Key Features of AMPL:
  - **Modeling Flexibility:** AMPL allows you to express optimization models that closely resemble the way they are mathematically described in textbooks and scientific papers. This makes it easy for experts to translate mathematical models into executable code.
  - **Data Separation:** One of AMPL's strengths is its separation of the model description from the data. This means you can change data without rewriting the model, facilitating scenario analysis and parametric studies.

- **Solver Integration:** AMPL interfaces with a wide range of solvers, including popular ones like CPLEX, Gurobi, and MINOS, as well as specialized solvers for particular types of optimization problems.
- **Scalability:** It is effective for both small classroom models and large-scale problems involving millions of constraints and variables.

- Common Uses:
  - **Supply Chain Optimization:** Designing efficient supply chains to minimize costs or maximize service levels.
  - **Financial Planning:** Asset allocation, portfolio optimization, and risk management.
  - **Manufacturing:** Production planning, scheduling, and resource allocation.
  - **Energy:** Optimizing power generation and distribution networks.

AMPL is widely used in academia for teaching optimization concepts as well as in industry for developing robust decision support systems. Its ability to articulate complex optimization problems clearly and its robust solver integrations make it a preferred choice among researchers and practitioners in operations research and industrial engineering.

GAMS (General Algebraic Modeling System)

GAMS (General Algebraic Modeling System) is a high-level modeling system for mathematical programming and optimization. It is designed for modeling and solving linear, nonlinear, and mixed-integer optimization problems. The system is particularly useful in handling large, complex problems, making it a popular choice among researchers and industry professionals across various fields such as economics, finance, energy planning, and environmental management.

- Key Features of GAMS:
  - **Algebraic Formulation:** Like AMPL, GAMS allows you to formulate problems in a way that is close to their algebraic representation. This makes the model easier to read and understand for those familiar with mathematical formulations.
  - **Solver Integration:** GAMS supports numerous solvers, including CPLEX, Gurobi, BARON, and more. It can automatically select the appropriate solver based on the problem type (LP, NLP, MIP, etc.), or users can specify their preferred solver.
  - **Modularity and Scalability:** GAMS models can be built in a modular fashion, where different model components are developed independent-

ly and integrated seamlessly. This makes it scalable for very large and complex models.

- **Data Management:** GAMS has powerful data management capabilities, allowing for efficient handling of large datasets and scenario management. This is particularly useful in applications like energy system modeling where multiple scenarios must be evaluated.

- Common Uses:
  - **Economic Modeling:** Macro-economic forecasting, policy analysis, and financial risk assessment.
  - **Energy Sector:** Planning and optimization of generation and distribution, including renewable energy integration.
  - **Environmental Science:** Ecosystem modeling, pollution control, and resource management.
  - **Supply Chain Management:** Network design, logistics planning, and inventory control.

Educational and Professional Application:

GAMS is widely used in both academic settings for teaching concepts of optimization and in professional environments to develop decision support systems that require robust and efficient handling of complex models. Its comprehensive documentation and extensive library of model examples also make it a valuable learning tool for students and new users in the field of operations research.

Overall, GAMS provides a flexible and powerful platform for formulating, solving, and analyzing optimization problems, making it an essential tool in the arsenal of operations researchers and decision-makers.

MATLAB Optimization Toolbox

The MATLAB Optimization Toolbox is an excellent tool for addressing various management problems using linear programming and other optimization techniques. It offers a wide range of functions to solve linear, integer, and quadratic programming problems, among others. Here's a brief overview of how you could use this toolbox for linear programming in management scenarios:

- Key Functions in the Optimization Toolbox for Linear Programming:

  linprog: This function is specifically used for linear programming. You can define your objective function, constraints, and bounds to find the optimal solution. It's suitable for tasks like resource allocation, cost minimization, and production planning in management.

intlinprog: For integer linear programming problems, where the decision variables are integers, which is common in scenarios like scheduling, staffing, and other discrete optimization problems in management.

lsqlin: This function solves linear least squares problems with constraints, which can be useful for data fitting and statistical models in management.

- Applications in Management

  Supply Chain Management: Optimize logistics, distribution networks, and inventory management.

  Financial Planning: Asset allocation, portfolio optimization, and risk management.

  Operations Management: Workforce scheduling, facility location decisions, and production planning.

The Optimization Toolbox also includes tools for sensitivity analysis and post-optimization analysis, which can help managers understand the impact of changes in input parameters on the optimal solution. This can be crucial for making informed decisions in a dynamic management environment.

SciPy (Python)

SciPy is a popular Python library that provides many user-friendly and efficient numerical routines, including solvers for linear programming problems. It's often used in management for optimizing resources, scheduling tasks, and other decision-making processes that can be modeled as linear programming problems.

- **Using SciPy for Linear Programming:** SciPy's *linprog* function is part of the optimize module and can solve linear programming problems using different methods. Here's a brief overview of how you might use it:
  - Define the Problem: Identify your objective function, constraints, and bounds for your variables.
  - Setup the Parameters:
    - Objective function coefficients: This is usually a one-dimensional array.
    - Constraint matrix: A matrix representing the coefficients in the linear constraints.
    - Constraint bounds: An array of bounds for each constraint (either as equalities or inequalities).
    - Variable bounds: Each variable's lower and upper bounds.
    - Call the Solver: Use the linprog function to solve the problem.

        - Interpret Results: The solver returns an object with the optimal value, the solution for the variables, and other diagnostic information.
- Tips for Using SciPy in Management:
    - **Data Integration**: Ensure that the data used for constraints and objectives is up-to-date and accurately reflects real-world conditions.
    - **Solver Choice**: The default solver in newer versions of SciPy uses the HiGHS solvers, which are efficient and robust for large-scale problems.
    - **Post-optimization Analysis**: Always analyze the results in the context of the problem to ensure they make practical sense.

This tool can be highly effective for various management scenarios, especially in operations research, resource allocation, and logistics planning.

8. GLPK (GNU Linear Programming Kit)

- Features:
    - Open-source software for solving LP, MIP, and other related problems.
    - Provides a callable library and standalone solver.
    - Supports the GNU Math Programming Language (GMPL), a modeling language similar to AMPL.
    - Includes primal and dual simplex methods, branch-and-bound, and cutting planes.
- Advantages:
    - Free and open-source.
    - Suitable for small to medium-sized problems.
- Use Cases:
    - Academic research, teaching, small-scale industrial applications.

9. Excel Solver

- Features:
    - Built-in add-in for Microsoft Excel for optimization.
    - Supports LP, nonlinear, and integer programming.
    - User-friendly interface with integration directly in Excel.
    - Suitable for small to medium-sized problems.
- Advantages:
    - Easy to use for non-experts.
    - Widely accessible and integrated into a common software platform.
- Use Cases:

- Business modeling, financial planning, resource allocation, and scheduling.

10. OR-Tools (Google Optimization Tools)

- Features:
  - Open-source software suite for optimization provided by Google.
  - Supports LP, MILP, CP (Constraint Programming), and routing problems.
  - APIs for C++, Python, Java, and .NET.
  - Highly performant with support for large-scale problems.
  - Integrates with Google's infrastructure for large-scale and cloud-based solutions.
- Advantages:
  - Free and open-source with extensive documentation.
  - Highly scalable and performant.
- Use Cases:
  - Logistics, supply chain optimization, routing, and scheduling problems.

Each of these tools has its own strengths and is suited to different types of linear programming problems. The choice of software depends on the specific requirements of the problem, the user's familiarity with the tool, and any budget constraints.

To illustrate the graphical method of solving linear programming problems using MATLAB, we use a simple example involving two decision variables. The graphical method can be effectively utilized when dealing with two-variable linear programming problems because it allows for visualization of the feasible region and objective function.

Example Problem

Let's consider a problem where we want to maximize the objective function:

$$z = 3x_1 + 5x_2$$

Subject to the constraints:

$$x_1 + 2x_2 \leq 20$$

$$3x_1 + x2 \leq 30$$

\[x_1, x_2 \geq 0 \]

MATLAB Code

Here's a MATLAB code snippet that uses the `fill` function to plot the feasible region and `fplot` to display the objective function lines:

````
```matlab
% Define the variables
x1 = linspace(0, 20, 400); % Range for x1
% Constraints
x2_constr1 = (20 - x1) / 2; % x1 + 2x2 <= 20
x2_constr2 = 30 - 3 * x1; % 3x1 + x2 <= 30
% Non-negativity constraints
x2_constr1(x2_constr1 < 0) = NaN; % Adjusts values outside
the constraints
x2_constr2(x2_constr2 < 0) = NaN;
% Plot feasible region
figure;
hold on;
fill([0, 0, min(x1(~isnan(x2_constr1))), min(x1(~isnan(x2_
constr2)))],...
     [0, min(x2_constr2), min(x2_constr1(~isnan(x2_con-
str1))), 0], 'g');
% Add labels and titles
title('Feasible Region for Linear Programming Problem');
xlabel('x_1');
ylabel('x_2');
xlim([0 15]);
ylim([0 15]);
% Plot the constraints and the axes
plot(x1, x2_constr1, 'b', 'LineWidth', 2);
plot(x1, x2_constr2, 'r', 'LineWidth', 2);
line(xlim, [0,0], 'Color', 'k');
line([0,0], ylim, 'Color', 'k');
% Plotting the objective function lines
z = @(x1, x2) 3 * x1 + 5 * x2;
fplot(@(x1) (20 - 3*x1)/5, [0, 10], 'k--');
% Find the maximum of the objective function
optimal_x1 = fminbnd(@(x1) -z(x1, (20 - x1)/2), 0, 10);
````
````

```
optimal_x2 = (20 - optimal_x1) / 2;
max_z = z(optimal_x1, optimal_x2);
scatter(optimal_x1, optimal_x2, 'filled');
text(optimal_x1, optimal_x2, sprintf('  Max z=%.2f at
(%.2f,%.2f)', max_z, optimal_x1, optimal_x2));
hold off;
```

Explanation of the Code

1. **Define Variables and Constraints**: `x1` is defined over a possible range and `x2` constraints are calculated based on the provided inequalities.
2. **Plot Feasible Region**: Uses the `fill` function to create the feasible region, defined by the intersection of the constraints.
3. **Plot Constraints**: Uses `plot` to draw the constraint lines on the graph.
4. **Objective Function Line**: Plots a representative line of the objective function (`fplot`) and moves it to show maximization.
5. **Optimization**: `fminbnd` is used in a way to find the maximum value by turning the maximization problem into a minimization problem (by using negative sign).
6. **Results**: The optimal values for `x1` and `x2` are calculated and displayed, along with the maximum value of the objective function.

This MATLAB code provides a visual and analytical solution to the example linear programming problem using the graphical method.

CONCLUSION

As we observed, this chapter presented two elementary methods for linear programming problems. Although these treatments are elementary, the materials are intrinsically technical.

11.7 Exercises

1. Solve the following models by the graphical method.

   (i) Maximize: $Z = 2X_1 + 3X_2$

   Subject to: $2X_1 + 3X_2 \leq 20$

   $X_1 + X_2 \leq 40$

   $X_i \geq 0; i = 1,2.$

(ii) Minimize: $Z = 6X_1 + 5X_2$
Subject to: $4X_1 + X_2 \le 20$
$3X_1 + 4X_2 \le 40$
$X_i \ge 0; i = 1,2.$

(iii) Minimize: $Z = 100X_1 + 90X_2$
Subject to: $X_1 + X_2 \ge 100$
$4X_1 + 5X_2 \ge 50$
$4X_1 + 3X_2 \ge 80$
$X_i \ge 0; i = 1,2,3.$

(iv) Maximize: $Z = 12X_1 + 16X_2$
Subject to: $X_1 + 2X_2 \le 10$
$3X_1 + 2X_2 \le 30$
$4X_1 + X_2 \le 20$
$X_i \ge 0; i = 1,2,3.$

(v) Maximize:$Z = 12X_1 + 16X_2$
Subject to: $X_1 + 2X_2 \le 10$
$3X_1 + 4X_2 \le 30$
$4X_1 + X_2 \le 20$
$X_i \ge 0; i = 1,2.$

(vi) Minimize: $Z = X_1 + 3X_2$
Subject to: $X_1 - X_2 \le 24$
$2X_1 + 3X_2 \le 12$
$X_i \ge 0; i = 1,2.$

(vii) Minimize: $Z = 10X_1 + 16X_2$
Subject to: $X_1 + X_2 \ge 10$
$2X_1 + 3X_2 \le 20$
$4X_1 + 3X_2 \ge 30$
$X_i \ge 0; i = 1,2,3.$

2. Write the dual of linear programming problems in Ex 1.
3. By writing the dual of the following problems, solve them graphically.

(i) Minimize: $Z = 18X_1 + 12X_2 + 16X_3$
Subject to: $X_1 + 2X_2 + 3X_3 \ge 40$
$2X_1 + 3X_2 + X_3 \ge 30$
$X_i \ge 0; i = 1,2,3.$

(ii) Maximize: $Z = 12X_1 + 10X_2 + 20X_3$
Subject to: $X_1 + X_2 + X_3 \le 45$
$3X_1 + 4X_2 + 2X_3 \le 30$
$X_i \ge 0; i = 1,2,3.$

(iii) Minimize: $Z = 8X_1 + 3X_2 + 6X_3$
Subject to: $X_1 - X_2 + X_3 \ge 12$

$X_1 + 2X_2 - X_3 \geq 16$
$X_i \geq 0; i = 1,2,3.$

(iv) Maximize: $Z = 12X_1 + 10X_2 + 10X_3$
Subject to: $X_1 - 2X_2 - 3X_3 \leq 30$
$X_1 - 2X_2 - 3X_3 \leq 30$
$X_i \geq 0; i = 1,2,3.$

(v) Maximize: $Z = 12X_1 + 10X_2 + 10X_3$
Subject to: $X_1 + 6X_2 + 3X_3 \leq 30$
$4X_1 + 5X_2 + 2X_3 \leq 25$
$X_i \geq 0; i = 1,2,3.$

4. A company produces two types of a product, A and B. The product A requires 3 hours of grinding and 2 hours of finishing, and the product B needs 4 hours of grinding and 3 hours of finishing. The company has 3 grinders and 4 finishers, each of whom works 60 hours per week. The products A and B bring a profit of $4 and $5, respectively. Assuming that all products made will be sold, how many of each should be made to maximize profits?
5. A company manufactures two types of goods. The production time of the first product is twice that of the second product. If all the goods are only of the second type, the company can produce a total of 800 goods. Suppose that the maximum daily sales of first and second type goods in the market are 400 and 300 and the profit from their sale is $6 and $4, respectively. Find the number of goods that should be produced of both types to maximize total profit.
6. A company produces two types of products *A* and *B*. The profit margin for *A* is 45 and for *B* is 30. Type *A* takes 5 hours of processing, 4 hours of assembly, and 2 hours of packaging, and type *B* takes 4 hours of processing, 5 hours of assembly, and 3 hours of packaging. Suppose 60 hours are available for processing, 50 hours for assembly, and 40 hours for packaging. Find the maximum profit.
7. A cloth manufactures three types of clothes. For such products, there are three manufacturing phases. For the first phase there are 80 hours and for another two phases there are 75 and 90 hours respectively. If the company makes a profit of $5 on the first type of close it makes and $4 for another two types, determine the number of each type of clothes each day to maximize its profits.
8. A company sends a product from three cities of origin *A*, *B* and *C* to three cities of destination *D*, *E* and *F* according to the following table. The sending amount of each destination is included in this table. Find the minimum cost to demand for the above cities.

Table 3.

d / *o*	***D***	***E***	***F***	supply
A	**12**	**18**	**20**	200
B	**10**	**20**	**30**	**500**
C	**24**	**18**	**12**	**300**

REFERENCES

Driebeek, N. J. (1969). *Applied Linear Programming*. Addison-Wesley Publishing Company, Inc.

Gass, S. I. (1975). *Linear Programming: Methods and Applications* (4th ed.). McGraw-Hill Book Company.

Heady, E. O., & Candler, W. (1958). *Linear Programming methods*. Iowa State College Press.

Jarvis, J. J., Bazaraa, M. S., & Sherali, H. D. (1990. Linear Programming and Network. (2nd ed). Flows. John Wiley & Sons.

Kim, C. (1971). *Linear Programming*. Holt, Rinehart and Winston, Inc.

Lewis, C. (2008). Linear Programming: Theory and Applications, Text paper.

Simonnard, M. (1966). *Linear Programming*. Prentice-Hall, Inc.

Smythe, W. R., Anderson, D. J., & Williams, T. A. (1974). *Linear Programming for Decision Making*. West publishing Company.

Vajda, S. (1962). Reading in Linear Programming, John Wiley & Son, Inc., New York.

Winston, C., & Wayene, L. (1997). *Introduction to Mathematical Programming Applications and Algorithms*. Duxbury Press.

Chapter 12

Probability and Statistics

ABSTRACT

This chapter contains two parts. The first part is devoted to probability and the second part discusses briefly the statistics for finite sample spaces. First, we define the basic concepts and definitions of probability, then we introduce conditional probability. We discuss several applicable examples and talk more about applications of probability in different fields. The second part contains the concepts and materials of statistics such as Mathematical averages, which are arithmetic, geometric and harmonic means, and Positional averages, which are median and mode. It has been tried to explain about them such that the readers understand the relationship between the model and the corresponding real-world problem.

12.1 INTRODUCTION

In our normal life, we often talk about the probability of the occurrence of some events. For example, "Barcelona will probably win the match", or "The chance of the Democratic candidate to win the election is 58%", and or "They would probably not be there at the right time". Now let's see what we mean by these statements and how we express a statement with a coefficient like 58%. If we pay attention to the above statements, each of them represents a random experiment, and since their answer is not known, therefore, with our guesses or the information that we already have about such experiments, we express such statements. We may assign a number to each of our guesses. However, in general, our knowledge is not sufficient to make such predictions. For example, when we throw a fair coin, we cannot predict the results. We can just say that in one of two cases, a head or tail is equally likely

DOI: 10.4018/979-8-3693-3657-1.ch012

(i.e., events with the same probability) to occur, and we assign a probability, $\frac{1}{2}$ for getting a head or tail.

For most people, the probability of an event happening in the future is used to determine the size, and we accept this interpretation as a meaningful and practical interpretation, but we will seek a better understanding of the measurement method and how to use it in decisions.

The concept of probability as an application to physical, biological, and social mechanisms that cannot be predicted with certainty, but about which observations are available, is necessary.

To develop the theory of probability, it is not essential to clarify the practical meaning of probability. In addition, since philosophically it can lead to an endless discussion, there is no need for more than this discussion in this case. For this reason, we accept the concept of probability based on relative frequency, and in this chapter, we discuss the relationship between observation and judgment through probability. But before going through, we introduce some concepts and definitions of probability in the next section.

12.2 BASIC CONCEPTS AND DEFINITIONS OF PROBABILITY

Any result of an experiment is called an *event*. Here, the term event refers to any occurrence of our interest. All possible results of this experiment make the *sample space*, denoted by S. For example, the sample space for getting a head or tail is $S=\{H,T\}$. Therefore, an event is a subset of the sample space of an experiment.

A sample space S is called *discrete* if the number of its members is finite or countable. Like the sample space of throwing a coin or a die.

We attribute a number to each point of the finite sample space, which is called the *weight* of that point. This weight is usually indicated by ω if it changes from 0 to 1, and each value determines the probability of an event in a random experiment, and the total weights of all points in the sample space is always equal to 1.

In many experiments, the probability of the occurrence of all events in the sample space is assumed to be the same, and therefore equal weights are considered for them, and zero weight is considered for the events outside the sample space.

According to the introduction mentioned above, we define the probability of each event as below.

Definition 1: We call the sum of all the weights in the event A, the probability of the event A and denote it by $P(A)$.

By this definition, we have:

(i) $P(\phi)=0$, (The probability of an impossible event is zero.)

(ii) $P(S)=1$, (The probability of a certain event is 1.)
(iii) $0 \leq P(A) \leq 1$.

It should be noted that in practice, there is no impossible event, and events whose probability of occurrence is close to zero are considered as impossible events. In this way, events whose probability of occurrence is close to 1 will be considered as certain events. For example, if, in practice, the probability of the occurrence of an event is calculated and this probability is equal to $\left(\frac{1}{2}\right)^{500}$,this event, it can be ignored and it is considered an impossible event. In the following parts, we will discuss more about negligible events and their complements, certain events, and their relationships.

Suppose we did an experiment, and its possible events are $A_1, A_2, \ldots, A_n$.

Definition 2: The events $A_1, A_2, \ldots, A_n$ are called *mutually exclusive*, or *disjoint* if they cannot occur together. In other words,

$$A_i \cap A_j = \varnothing, i \neq j, 1 \leq i,j \leq n.$$

Hence,

$$P(A_i \cap A_j) = 0.$$

Definition 3: If an experiment contains N simple events, and all are equally likely events, then the probability of each occurrence A in this experiment can be determined as

$$P(A) = \frac{n(A)}{n(S)} = \frac{n}{N}, \tag{1}$$

where n is the number of favorable states of the event of A.

This is the *classical approach* to probability, based on the assumption that each event is equally likely.

Example 1: We toss a fair coin 2 times. What is the probability of observing a head twice?

Solution: Since the coin is fair, we assign weight w to every point of the sample space, $S_1=\{H,T\}$. We have, $P(S_1)=1$

$$P(H) + P(T) = 1 \rightarrow w + w = 1 \rightarrow w = \frac{1}{2}.$$

That is, for a fair coin, the probability of having a head or a tail is 1/2. Now, if we throw this coin 2 times, according to the principle of counting the sample space of this experiment, there will be 4 sample states as follows:

$S = \{TT, TH, HT, HH\}$.

Now, if we define A as the occurrence of only one head, then we get $A=\{HH\}$, and if we use relation 1, we obtain

$$P(A) = \frac{n(A)}{n(S)} = \frac{1}{4}.$$

***Example* 2:** We throw a toss once. What is the probability that the number on the square will be divisible by 3?

Solution: If we assign weight w to any point of the test sample space, we get $S = \{1,2,3,4,5,6\}$

$$\therefore\ P(S) = 1 \rightarrow w + w + w + w + w + w = 1 \rightarrow w = \frac{1}{6}.$$

As a result, the probability of each point of the sample space is $\frac{1}{6}$. If we define A as an occurrence such that the number is perfect, then

$$A = \{3,6\}, P(A) = \frac{1}{6} + \frac{1}{6} = \frac{1}{3}.$$

We get the same result if we use relation 1,

$$P(A) = \frac{n(A)}{n(S)} = \frac{2}{6} = \frac{1}{3}$$

***Example* 3:** From a box containing 4 red balls and 6 blue balls, we take out 2 balls randomly one after another without placement find: (a) The probability that both of them are red? (b) The probability that both are the same color?

Solution: The box contains 8 balls, and two balls are randomly drawn out without placement. So

$$n(S) = C_2^6 = \frac{10!}{2!8!} = 45.$$

Because the number of red balls is 4, then

$$n(A) = C_2^4 = \frac{4!}{2!2!} = 6.$$

Therefore,

$$P(A) = \frac{n(A)}{n(S)} = \frac{6}{45} = \frac{2}{15}.$$

To calculate that both are the same color, the number of states in the sample space where both are red balls or both are blue balls must be counted. We have:

$$n(B) = C_2^4 + C_2^6 = 6 + 15 = 21.$$

Thus,

$$P(B) = \frac{n(B)}{n(S)} = \frac{21}{45} = \frac{7}{15}$$

In many cases, we will come across unequally likely events. In such problems, relation 1 is not applied to them. Let's consider one example.

Example 4: The dice is made in such a way that the probability of odd numbers occurring in it is twice that of even numbers. If we throw this dice once, what is the probability that a perfect square will appear?

Solution: If we indicate the weight of even numbers with, ω, the weight of odd numbers will be 2ω. Since $S=\{1,2,3,4,5,6\}$ and $P(S)=1$, thus

$$2\omega + \omega + 2\omega + \omega + 2\omega + \omega = 1 \rightarrow \omega = \frac{1}{9}$$

If we consider A as the occurrence of perfect square, we get $A=\{1,4\}$, thus

$$P(A) = 2\omega + \omega = \frac{1}{9} \rightarrow \omega = \frac{1}{3}$$

It should be noted that if the experiment cannot be expressed in a classical approach, the use of equation (1) is not correct. For example, consider throwing an unfair dice. The probability of each of the events 1 to 6 is not, $\frac{1}{6}$. The question is how to determine the probability of this type of incident. In fact, what should be done to determine the weight of these incidents? To answer this question, we provide another definition of probability, and that concept of probability is the theoretical limit of the relative frequency of an event.

Definition 4: If an experiment is repeated N times and the number of occurrences A in this N experiment is of order m, then the *relative frequency* of the event A is

$$P_r(A) = \frac{m}{N} = \frac{\text{The number of occurrence frequency } A}{\text{The total frequency}} \quad (2)$$

Remark 1: The frequency of an event is also called the *statistical probability* of that event. Formulas 1 and 2 are different from each other. Formula 1 is used in the theoretical calculation of the probability of event A, while Formula 2 is used for the empirical calculation of the probability of event A. Of course, we note that there is a clear relationship between the relative frequency of an event and its probability. This relationship is such that when the number of repetitions of experiments tends to infinity, the relative frequency balances and approaches a constant value, and this constant value is exactly the probability of an occurrence. In other words, probability is the theoretical limit of relative frequency when the repetition of experiments tends to infinity. That is,

$$P(A) = \lim_{n\to\infty}\left(\frac{m}{n}\right).$$

This approach is called the *empirical approach*. The probability obtained in this way is known as *empirical probability*.

For example, if we have tossed a fair coin 10 times and 4 heads have appeared, the relative frequency of the event is A equal to $\frac{4}{10}$, which is different from the probability of the event A i.e., $\frac{5}{10} = \frac{1}{2}$. But if we increase the number of throws, we will see that the relative frequency fluctuates around the number $\frac{1}{2}$ until it approaches the constant number $\frac{1}{2}$.

Karl Pearson, a famous English statistician who has many studies in descriptive statistics, tossed a coin 24,000 times and observed 12,012 heads, which is very close to the probability $\frac{1}{2}$ for the number of heads because $\frac{12012}{24000} \cong \frac{1}{2}$.

Now, we will state some theorems and use them to determine the probability of compound events with the help of the known probability of simple events.

Theorem 1. If A_1 and A_2represent two events, then

$$P(A_1 \cup A_2) = P(A_1) + P(A_2) - P(A_1 \cap A_2) \tag{3}$$

This theorem can be generalized to n events, $A_1, A_2, \ldots, A_n$. For example, for n=3, we get

$$P(A_1 \cup A_2 \cup A_3) = P(A_1) + P(A_2) + P(A_3)$$
$$-P(A_1 \cap A_2) - P(A_1 \cap A_3) - P(A_2 \cap A_3) + P(A_1 \cap A_2 \cap A_3).$$

Proof See Mendenhall, Beaver, and Beaver (2003).

Remark 2: If A_1 and A_2 are two mutually exclusive events, then

$$P(A_1 \cup A_2) = P(A_1) + P(A_2).$$

This result can also be generalized to n events, $A_1, A_2, \ldots, A_n$. We write

$$P(A_1 \cup A_2 \cup \ldots \cup A_n) = P(A_1) + P(A_2) + \ldots + P(A_n).$$

***Example* 5:** We draw a card randomly from a pack of playing cards. What is the probability that the selected card is an ace or a club?

Solution: Suppose A and C represent two events such that, A=an ace and C=a club. Then

$$P(A) = \tfrac{4}{52} = \tfrac{1}{13}, P(C) = \tfrac{13}{52} = \tfrac{1}{4} \text{and} P(A \cap C) = \tfrac{1}{52}.$$

Therefore,

$$P(A \cup C) = P(A) + P(C) - P(A \cap C) = \tfrac{1}{13} + \tfrac{1}{4} - \tfrac{1}{52} = \tfrac{4}{13}.$$

Definition 4: Suppose A is an event. The complement of A, denoted by A', is the set of events in sample space that are not contained in A.

Remark 3: If event A' is the complement of event A, then

$$P(A') = 1 - P(A) \tag{4}$$

***Example* 6:** From ten cards with the numbers 1 to 15, we will choose a card randomly. Find the probability that it is a number not divisible by 3 or 4?

Solution: Suppose A_1 and A_2 represent two events defined that are divisible by 3 or 4, respectively. Then

$$P(A_1) = \tfrac{5}{15} = \tfrac{1}{3}, P(A_2) = \tfrac{3}{15} = \tfrac{1}{5} \text{and} P(A_1 \cap A_2) = \tfrac{1}{15}.$$

Hence,

$$P(A_1 \cup A_2) = P(A_1) + P(A_2) - P(A_1 \cap A_2) = \tfrac{1}{3} + \tfrac{1}{5} - \tfrac{1}{15} = \tfrac{7}{15}.$$

Therefore, the probability that the selected card number is not divisible by 2 or 5 will be

$$P(A_1 \cup A_2)' = 1 - \tfrac{7}{15} = \tfrac{8}{15}$$

***Example 7*:** From a container containing 7 red beads and 8 blue beads, we randomly remove 5 beads. What is the probability that all three are the same color? What is the probability that they are not the same color?

Solution: Let us A_1 and A_2 are the two events we defined, then

$$P(A_1) = \frac{C_5^7}{C_5^{15}} = \frac{21}{3003} \text{and} P(A_2) = \frac{C_5^8}{C_5^{15}} = \frac{56}{3003}.$$

Therefore,

$$P(A_1 \cup A_2) = P(A_1) + P(A_2) = \frac{21}{3003} + \frac{56}{3003} = \frac{1}{39}.$$

According to relation 4, we get

$$P(A_1 \cup A_2)' = 1 - P(A_1 \cup A_2) = 1 - \frac{1}{39} = \frac{38}{39}$$

***Example 8*:** A male and a female appear in an interview for two roles in the same film. Suppose that the probability of this selection for male and female is $\frac{1}{2}$ and $\frac{1}{3}$, respectively. What is the probability that: (a) only one of them will be selected? (b) None of them will be selected?

Solution: (a) We define M and F are two events then, the probability that only one of them can be selected is:

$$P(M)P(F') + P(M')P(F) = \frac{1}{2}\left(1 - \frac{1}{3}\right) + \left(1 - \frac{1}{2}\right)\frac{1}{3} = \frac{1}{18}.$$

(b) Similarly, we have

$$P(M')P(F') = \left(1 - \frac{1}{2}\right)\left(1 - \frac{1}{3}\right) = \frac{1}{3}$$

12.3 CONDITIONAL PROBABILITY

In many cases, we wish to find the probability of an event A related to another event, both of the same sample space. The events A and B are said to be *dependent* if the occurrence of event A effects the probability of the occurrence of another event. In this section, we introduce the conditional probability, and then we will discuss and show how one event that occurred affects the probability of another event. Suppose you roll a fair die and assume you throw a healthy dice, and you ask your friend, what is the probability of getting 3, he will say $\frac{1}{6}$. Now tell him that the number that appeared is odd. In this case, what is the probability of getting 3, he will definitely say $\frac{1}{3}$.

Definition 5: The probability of the occurrence of event B, provided that we know that event A has occurred, is called *conditional probability* and is denoted by the symbol $P(B|A)$. The value of the conditional probability is calculated using the following equation:

$$P(B|A) = \frac{P(A \cap B)}{P(A)} \tag{5}$$

where $P(A)>0$.

It should be noted that in the definition of conditional probability, it is not mentioned that the occurrence of event A effects the occurrence of event B. In the continuation of our work, we will examine this important matter.

***Example* 9:** We throw two tosses. If we know that the first toss showed the number 6, what is the probability that the sum of them is at least 10?

Solution: The test sample space has 36 sample points. We define the occurrences of A and B as follows:

A: The event that the first dice is the number 6.
B: The event is that the total is at least 10.

Therefore,

$$A = \{(6,1),(6,2),(6,3),(6,4),(6,5),(6,6)\}$$

$$B = \{(4,6),(5,5),(5,6),(6,4),(6,5),(6,6)\}$$

$$\therefore\ A \cap B = \{(6,4),(6,5),(6,6)\}.$$

We also have

$$P(A) = \frac{n(A)}{n(S)} = \frac{6}{36} = \frac{1}{6}.$$

$$P(A \cap B) = \frac{n(A \cap B)}{n(S)} = \frac{3}{36} = \frac{1}{12}.$$

Thus,

$$P(B|A) = \frac{P(A \cap B)}{P(A)} = \frac{\frac{1}{12}}{\frac{1}{6}} = \frac{1}{2}$$

Example 10: We throw two tosses. If we know that the sum of the numbers appearing is equal to 6, what is the probability that one of the tosses is 2?

Solution: We define the occurrences of A and B as follows:

A: The event that the total sum is 6.
B: The event is that one of the tosses shows the number 2.

We have,

$$A = \{(1,5),(2,4),(3,3),(4,2),(5,1)\}$$

$$B = \{(1,2),(2,2),(3,2),(4,2),(5,2),(6,2),(2,1),(2,3)\}$$

$$\therefore A \cap B = \{(2,4),(4,2)\}.$$

Then

$$P(A) = \frac{n(A)}{n(S)} = \frac{5}{36}.$$

$$P(A \cap B) = \frac{n(A \cap B)}{n(S)} = \frac{2}{36} = \frac{1}{18}.$$

Thus,

$$P(B|A) = \frac{P(A \cap B)}{P(A)} = \frac{\frac{1}{18}}{\frac{5}{36}} = \frac{2}{5}$$

Theorem 2. If the events A and B occur simultaneously, then

$$P(A \cap B) = P(B|A)P(A) \tag{6}$$

Theorem 2 can be generalized for n events $A_1, A_2, \ldots, A_n$ as follows:

$$P(A_1 \cap A_2 \cap \ldots \cap A_n)$$

$$= P(A_1)P(A_2|A_1)P(A_3|A_1 \cap A_2)\ldots P(A_n|A_1 \cap A_2 \cap \ldots \cap A_{n-1}). \tag{7}$$

Example 11: From the box containing 5 blue and 4 red beads, we remove two beads at a time without placement. What is the probability that the second selected bead is blue? What is the probability that both are not the same color?

Solution: For the first case, we need to find the probability of the event $A_1 \cap A_2$. According to (6), we have

$$P(A_1 \cap A_2) = P(A_2|A_1)P(A_1).$$

We have,

$$P(A_1) = \frac{5}{9}, P(A_2|A_1) = \frac{3}{6}$$

Thus,

$$P(A_1 \cap A_2) = P(A_2|A_1)P(A_1) = \frac{5}{8} \times \frac{3}{6} = \frac{2}{7}.$$

For the second case, we have to find the probability of the event $(A_1 \cap B_2) \cup ($ $B_1 \cap A_2)$. Because the occurrences of $A_1 \cap B_2$ and $B_1 \cap A_2$ are incompatible, so

$$P((A_1 \cap B_2) \cup (B_1 \cap A_2)) = P(A_1 \cap B_2) + P)\cup(B_1 \cap A_2).$$

Since

$$P(A_1 \cap B_2) = P(B_2|A_1)P(A_1) = \frac{4}{7} \times \frac{3}{6} = \frac{2}{7}$$

$$P(B_1 \cap A_2\ ) = P(A_2|B_1)P(B_1) = \frac{3}{7} \times \frac{4}{6} = \frac{2}{7}$$

$$\therefore \frac{2}{7} + \frac{2}{7} = \frac{4}{7}$$

Example 12: From the box containing 5 white beads and 2 black beads, we remove one bead and put it aside without observing its color and then, remove another bead. What is the probability that this bead is white?

Solution: We define the following events:

A: The event that the first bead is a white one.
B: The event that the first bead is a black one.
C: The event that the second bead is a white one

We must determine the conditional probability given by

$$P(C|A \cup B) = \frac{P(C \cap (A \cup B))}{P(A \cup B)}.$$

We have, $C \cap (A \cup B) = (C \cap A) \cup (C \cap B)$, thus,

$$P(C \cap (A \cup B)) = P(C \cap A) + P(C \cap B),$$

because $C \cap A$and$C \cap B$ are mutually exclusive, and

$$P(A \cup B) = \frac{5}{7} + \frac{2}{7} = 1.$$

Therefore,

$$P(C|A \cup B) = P(C|A)P(A) + P(C|B)P(B) = \frac{5}{7} \times \frac{4}{6} + \frac{2}{7} \times \frac{5}{6} = \frac{5}{7}$$

As you can see, this probability is equal to the probability that the first bead is white. If you leave the second bead aside and remove the third die, the probability that this bead is white is still equal to 5, and if you remove the 6 beads, the probability that the seventh die is white is still equal to 6, i.e., it is equal to the probability of the first bead.

Example 13: From the box containing 12 lamps, 4 of which are defective, we remove 3 lamps one after the other without replacing them. What is the probability that all 3 bulbs are fair?

Solution: Let's suppose the event the ith fair bulb is denoted by A_i (i=1,2,3). According to relation 3, we get, the number A_i (i=1,2,3). Since these events are incompatible, therefore

$$P(A_1 \cap A_2 \cap A_3)$$
$$= P(A_1)P(A_2|A_1)P(A_2|A_1 \cap A_3)P(A_3|A_1 \cap A_2) = \frac{8}{12} \times \frac{7}{11} \times \frac{6}{10} = \frac{14}{55}$$

Definition 6: Two events are called *independent* if and only if

$$P(A \cap B) = P(A)P(B). \tag{8}$$

If we compare relation (8) with relation (5), the condition of independence of two events A and B can also be written as, $P(B|A)=P(B)$.

In other words, if event A, does not coincide with event B, then we call the two events A and B independent.

Example 14: Suppose that 40% of university employees are over 30 years old. Also, suppose that 50% of the employees who are over 30 years old are married and 30% of the employees who are under 30 years old or younger are married. We choose an employee at random, and it turns out that he is married. What is the probability that the age of the employee is more than 30?

Solution: We define the occurrences of A, B and C as follows:

A: The event when the employee is more than 30 years old
B: The event when the employee is 30 or less than 30 years old.
C: The event when the employee is married.

According to three events A, B and C, we have

$$P(A) = 0.4, P(B) = 0.6, P(C|A) = 0.5 \text{and} P(C|B) = 0.3.$$

We must calculate $P(A|C)$. Since $C = (A \cap C) \cup (B \cap C)$, thus

$$P(C) = P(A \cap C) + P(B \cap C)$$
$$= P(A)P(C|A) + P(B)P(C|B) = 0.4 \times 0.5 + 0.6 \times = 0.38.$$

Therefore,

$$P(A|C) = \frac{P(A \cap C)}{P(C)} = \frac{0.2}{0.38} \cong 0.53$$

In the Bayes theorem, which will be stated in the next part, we will see a more general state of the above example.

Definition 7: The events $A_1, A_2, \ldots, A_n$ are called *independent* if and only if

$$P(A_i \cap A_j) = P(A_i)P(A_j), i \neq j$$

$$P(A_i \cap A_j \cap A_k) = P(A_i)P(A_j)P(A_k), i \neq j \neq k$$

$$P(A_1 \cap A_2 \cap \ldots \cap A_n) = P(A_1)P(A_2)\ldots P(A_n).$$

Example 15: From a box containing 9 zippers, where 4 of them are defective. We draw 3 zippers at random, one at a time without replacement. What is the probability that none of them are detectives?

Solution: Let us A and B are first and second events where the zipper is non-defective. Thus, $P(A) = \frac{5}{9}$, because 5 of them are non-defective. Each zipper has the same probability ($\frac{1}{9}$) to be selected. At the beginning, $P(B) = \frac{5}{9}$. The events are independent, thus

$$P(A \cap B) = P(A)P(B) = \frac{5}{9} \times \frac{5}{9} = \frac{25}{81}.$$

If A has occurred, then there are 8 zippers left in the box. Thus, $P(B|A) = \frac{4}{8} = \frac{1}{2}$. Hence,

$$P(A \cap B) = \frac{5}{9} \times \frac{1}{2} = \frac{5}{18}$$

Example 16: Show that if A and B are two independent events, then the A' and B' are also two independent events.

Solution: We have,

$$P(A' \cap B') = P(A \cup B)' = 1 - P(A \cup B) = 1 - P(A) - P(B) + P(A \cap B)$$
$$= -P(A) - P(B) + P(A)P(B) = (1 - P(A))(1 - P(B)) = P(A')P(B')$$

Theorem 3 (*Bayes theorem*). Suppose that the set $\{B_1, B_2, \ldots, B_n\}$ is a subset of the sample space S. If C is an arbitrary event of S and $P(C) \neq 0$, then for $k=1,2,\ldots,n$ we have:

$$P(B_k|C) = \frac{P(B_k \cap C)}{\sum_1^n P(B_i \cap C)} = \frac{P(B_k)P(C|B_k)}{\sum_1^n P(B_i)P(C|B_i)}.$$

Proof See Hance (1977).

Example 17: We have three boxes numbered 1, 2, and 3, each of which contains white, blue, and red cards. Let's say there are 3 white cards, 2 blue cards, and 4 red cards in the second box. 4 white cards, 3 blue cards and 5 red cards, and in the third box there are 7 white cards, 5 blue cards and 3 red cards. We choose one of the boxes randomly and remove two cards from it. If these cards are blue and red, what is the probability that this box is number 1, or number 2, or number 3?

Solution: We define the following events:

E: The blue and red event.

E_i: The event of the selected box.

Therefore, $P(E_i) = \frac{1}{3}$ and

$$P(E|E_1)=\frac{4}{9}\cdot\frac{2}{8}+\frac{2}{9}\cdot\frac{4}{8}=\frac{2}{9}$$

$$P(E|E_2)=\frac{5}{12}\cdot\frac{3}{11}+\frac{3}{12}\cdot\frac{5}{11}=\frac{5}{22}$$

$$P(E|E_3)=\frac{3}{15}\cdot\frac{5}{14}+\frac{5}{15}\cdot\frac{3}{14}=\frac{2}{7}.$$

According to Bayse formula, we have

$$P(E_1|E)=\frac{\frac{1}{3}\cdot\frac{2}{9}}{\frac{1}{3}\cdot\frac{2}{9}+\frac{1}{3}\cdot\frac{5}{22}+\frac{1}{3}\cdot\frac{2}{7}}=\frac{308}{1019}$$

$$P(E_2|E)=\frac{\frac{1}{3}\cdot\frac{5}{22}}{\frac{1}{3}\cdot\frac{2}{9}+\frac{1}{3}\cdot\frac{5}{22}+\frac{1}{3}\cdot\frac{2}{7}}=\frac{315}{1019}$$

$$P(E_3|E)=\frac{\frac{1}{3}\cdot\frac{2}{7}}{\frac{1}{3}\cdot\frac{2}{9}+\frac{1}{3}\cdot\frac{5}{22}+\frac{1}{3}\cdot\frac{2}{7}}=\frac{396}{1019}.$$

Note that the sum of these probabilities is 1.

12.4 SOME APPLICATIONS OF PROBABILITY

We usually remember probabilities with math lesson problems about dice or coin flips. What is the probability that two dice will turn even at the same time or similar questions? But more and more we realize that we need a more concrete and practical understanding of possibilities. Probability is not just a tool with which we get part of a high school math grade, but a key tool with which we look at the whole world.

Applications of probability theory in everyday life are applied in risk assessment and trading in the commodity market. Governments typically apply probabilistic methods to environmental regulation, to analyze the path.

Let's say that, as a freelancer, you have offered prices for four different projects, or you are negotiating with four different clients in your small and compact company. In each of these situations, you have limited time and energy to meet and talk with customers. How much should I spend on which project or client? After all, spending time is also a cost. How much should I count on each project or client? Should I put most of my energy into the most expensive project?

An important influence of probability theory in everyday life is in the assessment of risk-taking and in business in the case of buying and selling goods. Governments specifically apply probabilistic methods to the regulation of societies, known as "policy analysis," and often measure the level of welfare using methods that are stochastic and select programs based on their probabilistic effects on the population. Evaluate statistically in general.

A good example is the assumed probabilistic effect of Middle East conflicts on oil prices, which have statistically significant ripple effects on the overall economy. An assessment by one business unit about whether a war is more or less likely causes prices to fluctuate and encourages other traders to do the same. According to this principle, probabilities are not evaluated independently and are not necessarily dealt with rationally. The theory of behavioral credits has been created to explain the effect of these group thoughts on prices, policies, peace, and conflict.

Another important application of probability theory in everyday life is reliability. Most consumer products such as cars and electronic devices use credit theory in their design to reduce the possibility of their defects. The probability of a defect is usually closely related to the warranty period of the product. In this section, we examine some practical examples and in the exercise section, we leave several practical examples to the reader to solve them.

Example 18: The janitor of the residential complex has 8 keys to open all the doors of this complex. If we know that only one of the keys can open the door of any house and usually 40% of the doors are open. If a raider only has three keys with him, what is the probability that he will be able to enter an apartment?

Solution: We define events A and B as follows:

A: The event that the door of the apartment is open.
B: The event that the janitor has the key that opens all the doors.

According to the defined events, we must find $P(A \cup B)$. Since, the two events are independent, then we have

$$P(A \cup B) = P(A) + P(B) - P(A \cap B) = P(A) + P(B) - P(A)P(B).$$

But $P(A)$=0.4 and $P(B) = \frac{C_1^1 C_2^7}{C_3^8} = \frac{3}{8}$. Hence,

$$P(A \cup B) = \frac{4}{10} + \frac{3}{8} - \frac{4}{10} \times \frac{3}{8} = \frac{5}{8}$$

Example 19: An employee uses a bus or private car to go to her office. To go to work, she uses her car $\frac{3}{4}$ times and the bus $\frac{1}{4}$ times. When she uses her car, she arrives at her office at the right time, and when she uses the bus, she arrives at her office 60% of the time at the right time. What is the probability that she used her car?

Solution: We define the following events.

A: The event when the employee uses her car.
A': The event when the employee uses the bus.
B: The event when the employee arrives at her office at the right time
B': The event when the employee does not arrive at her office at the right time.

According to the defined events, we must calculate $P(A|B')$. We have,

$$P(A|B') = \frac{P(A \cap B')}{P(B')} = \frac{P(B'|A)}{P(A)P(B'|A) + P(A')P(B'|A')}$$

We have, $P(A) = \frac{3}{4}, P(A') = \frac{1}{4}, P(B|A) = \frac{3}{4}$. Hence, $P(B'|A) = \frac{3}{5}$. Then

$$P(B'|A') = 1 - P(B|A') = \frac{2}{5},$$

$$P(A|B') = \frac{\frac{3}{4} \times \frac{1}{4}}{\frac{3}{4} \times \frac{1}{4} + \frac{1}{4} \times \frac{2}{5}} = \frac{15}{23}$$

More about applications of probability can be seen in Fellere (1957).

12.5 A SHORT INTRODUCTION TO STATISTICS

Statistics refer to a set of scientific methods that are used to collect information, classify, analyze, and interpret refer. Suppose we get information about the lifespan of lamps made by a factory, or about the income of people in a city, or the blood type of workers in a company. These collections, each of which has a specific characteristic, are called *statistical population*.

The part of statistics that discusses the estimation of community parameters from sample parameters is called *inferential statistics* and the part that discusses summarizing and describing the important characteristics of the data set without statistical inference is called *descriptive statistics*, which includes summary. It is to put the data in the form of tables, to display them graphically by means of diagrams and to calculate the numerical data. In this section, we only consider descriptive statistics.

Every day, many of us talk about average height, average income, average grades, or such averages. These averages are called *measures of central tendency*. In general, we have two types of averages:

1- *Mathematical averages,* which are *arithmetic, geometric* and *harmonic, means*
2- *Positional averages,* which are *median.* and *mode.*

In this section, we focus more on the three most common measures of central tendency, namely, the arithmetic mean, median and mode.

Definition 8: Let's $x_1, x_2, \ldots, x_n$ represent a set of numbers. The arithmetic mean, or simply, mean, of this set denoted by $\bar{x}$ is defined as

$$\bar{x} = \frac{x_1 + x_2 + \ldots + x_n}{n} \tag{9}$$

Remark 6: Usually, the symbol μ is used for the average of the population.

Example 20: Find the mean of 500 even integers from 1 to 1000.

Solution: We must find

$$\bar{x} = \frac{2 + 4 + \ldots + 1000}{500}.$$

But, for example 3 in Chapter 1, we have

$$1 + 2 + 3 + \ldots + n = \frac{n(n+1)}{2}.$$

$$\therefore\ 2 + 4 + \ldots + 1000 = 2(1 + 2 + 3 + \ldots + 500) = 500 \times 501.$$

Thus,

$$\therefore\ 2 + 4 + \ldots + 1000 = 2(1 + 2 + 3 + \ldots + 500) = 500 \times 501$$

Example 21: The monthly income of 100 people in a city of the USA are \$52000, \$63000, \$70000, \$72500, \$68000, \$58500, \$48000, \$52000, \$48500 and \$68500. Determine the mean income for the people of this city.

Solution: We have n=10, then

$$\bar{x} = \frac{\begin{array}{c}52000 + 63000 + 70000 + 72500 + 68000\\ +58500 + 48000 + 52000 + 48500 + 68500\end{array}}{10} = 60100.$$

Therefore, the mean income for the people of this city is \$60100

Note that the sum of data differences is zero. That is, $\sum_1^n (x_i - \bar{x}) = 0.$

If the x_i data has f_i repetitions, then relation 5 is written as follows

$$\bar{x} = \frac{x_1 f_1 + x_2 f_2 + \ldots + x_n f_n}{N}. \tag{10}$$

where, N is the total number of values being averaged.

***Example* 22:** The frequency distribution of monthly income of N people is given in the following table. Find its mean average.

Table 1.

x_i	f_i
$4200	9
$4800	8
$5400	6
$6300	4
$6900	3

Solution: We have, $N= 9+8+6+4+3=30$, then

$$\bar{x} = \frac{4200 \times 9 + 4800 \times 8 + 5400 \times 6 + 6300 \times 4 + 6900 \times 3}{30} = 5150.$$

Thus, the mean average monthly income for 30 people is $5150.

Although the average relies on all the data, it has one deficiency. For example, suppose the following amounts were collected by 15 people to help a charity:

80, 90, 150, 240, 240, 360, 420, 480, 540, 600, 620, 650, 650, 650, 9500

The mean of these numbers is 15300/15=1020. Now, if it is announced that each person contributed $1020 on average, it is not true for any of those 15 people. To have a more accurate summary, the median is often given to describe the data.

Definition 9: If the data $x_1,x_2,\ldots,x_n$ are arranged in ascending order, then the middle data is called the median, with the condition that the number of data is odd. But, if the number of data is even, the median is the average two middle data.

If we calculate the median for the previous example, we get 480, and if we announce this value, it is an acceptable value for the majority and is more reasonable than the previous value.

Example 23: According to the doctor's request, the patient should measure his heart rate at 12 noon for ten consecutive days and inform the doctor of the results. If the results are 77, 75, 82, 69, 82, 84, 66, 82, 65, 75, find the mean and median of these results.

Solution: We have n=10, then

$$\bar{x} = \frac{77 + 75 + 82 + 69 + 82 + 84 + 66 + 82 + 65 + 75}{10} = 75.8.$$

To find the median we record as 65, 66, 69, 75, 75, 77, 82, 82, 82, 84. Since the numbers of data are even, then the median is $\frac{75+77}{2} = 76$.

Definition 10: The mode of a set of the data $x_1, x_2, \ldots, x_n$ is the value of data that occurs at the highest frequency.

In the previous example, the most common number is 82, thus mode=82.

Suppose the production rate of a factory in five consecutive years is 2, 4, 8, 12, or 20 times compared to the previous year, and we want to find the average increase in production. If we use the arithmetic, we get 7.2 and this means that we had an increase of 7.2 times every year, and this is not correct. Because in this case, the amount of increase in the fifth year is, $(7.2)^5 \cong 19349$ times to the first year. The increase in the fifth year is 15360 times the increase in the first year. This example shows that we need another type of average which is stated below.

Definition 11: If the data x_i is positive, the geometric mean denoted by G is defined as

$$G = \sqrt[n]{x_1 \times x_2 \times \ldots \times x_n}.$$

According to this definition, the average increase in the above example is:

$$G = \sqrt[5]{2 \times 4 \times 8 \times 12 \times 20} = \sqrt[5]{15360} \cong 6.875.$$

Thus, the amount of increase in the fifth year is $(6.875)^5 \cong 15359$.

***Example* 24:** The capital of a factory increases by 12% after one year compared to the previous year, and also increases by 15% in the third year and 18% in the fourth year compared to the previous year. What will be the average increase in the last three years?

Solution: We have $x_1=1.12$, $x_2=1.15$ and $x_3=1.18$, then

$$G = \sqrt[3]{1.12 \times 1.15 \times 1.18} \cong \sqrt[3]{1.51984} \cong 1.14974.$$

Therefore, the average increase is 0.14974.

Although the meaning gives an indication of the “center” of a collection of numbers, it does not give the information as to how far apart it is spread. Here we define the concept of *deviation,* which tells us how far the number x_i is from the mean, and on which side of the mean x_i lies.

Definition 12: If $\bar{x}$ is the mean of the set of numbers, x_i, $i=1(1)n$, then the data $x_i - \bar{x}$ is called the deviation from the mean.

Remark 7: Since the value of $x_i - \bar{x}$ can be negative, to eliminate negative deviations, we use the number $(x_i - \bar{x})^2$rather than $x_i - \bar{x}$ It is called *squared deviation* from the mean.

Definition 13: The average of the squared deviation is called *variance* of the data, and is represented by V,

$$V = \frac{\sum(x_i - \overline{x})^2}{n} = \frac{(x_1 - \overline{x})^2 + (x_2 - \overline{x})^2 + \ldots + (x_n - \overline{x})^2}{n} \tag{11}$$

Unfortunately, squaring also exaggerates the values of the deviations, making the variance an unrealistic measure. We compensate by taking the square root of the variance. This number is called the *standard deviation* and is represented by σ. Thus $\sigma = \sqrt{V}$.

***Example* 25:** Find the variance of the following data.

1, 2, 3, 4, 5, 6, 7, 8, 9, 10.

Solution: We have,

$$\overline{x} = \frac{1+2+3+4+5+6+7+8+9+10}{10} = 5.5.$$

Therefore,

$$V = \frac{\sum(x_i - \overline{x})^2}{10} = \frac{(1-5.5)^2 + (2-5.5)^2 + \ldots + (10-5.5)^2}{10} = 8.25.$$

$$\sigma = \sqrt{V} = \sqrt{8.25}.$$

***Example* 26:** If the variance of 10 data in ascending order is zero, find the mean of the first data, 5 times of the middle data, and 4 times the last data.

Solution: Suppose these ten data are, $x_1, x_1, x_2, x_3, x_4, x_5, x_6, x_7, x_8, x_9, x_{10}$.

Since the variance is zero, then these ten data are equal. That is, $x_i = x_1$, $i = 1,2,\ldots,10$. Then,

$$\overline{x} = \frac{x_1 + 5x_1 + 4x_1 + 5x_1}{10} = x_1.$$

Variance and Standard Deviation are the two important measurements in statistics. Variance is the measure of how the data points vary according to the mean, while standard deviation is the measure of the central tendency of the distribution of the data. The basic difference between variance and the standard deviation is in their units. The standard deviation is represented in the same units as the mean of data, while the variance is represented in squared units.

12.6 THE CONTINUOUS RANDOM VARIABLES (OPTIONAL)

A random variable is a function based on which a number is assigned to each point of the sample space, and we indicate it with X and specify its value with x. That is, $X(e)=x$, with each possible event in S.

When the random variable can accept any real number in a continuous interval, this random variable is of continuous type. For example, weight, height, and time are continuous random variables. We call a random variable is continues if its set of possible values is an entire interval of numbers. In this case, the concepts that exist in the case of discrete random variables are defined similarly here.

We devote here a short discussion to such variables which are related to definite integrals.

Definition 14: We call the function $f(x)$ a *probability density or frequency function* for the random variable X over all real numbers if:

1. $f(x) \geq 0, \forall x \in \mathbb{R}.$
2. $\int_{-\infty}^{\infty} f(x)dx = 1$
3. $P(a < x < b) = \int_a^b f(x)dx.$

By this definition, the probability that an event may occur can be measured by the corresponding area under a probable function.

Example 27: The random variable X has a probability density function of the form

$$f(x) = \begin{cases} \sin\pi x - 2k & 0 \leq x \leq 1 \\ \cos\frac{\pi x}{2} + k^2 & 1 < x \leq 2 \\ 0 & \textit{other}. \end{cases}$$

Find the value of k.

Solution: We have,

$$\int_{-\infty}^{\infty} f(x)dx = 1 \rightarrow \int_0^1 (\sin\pi x - 2k)dx + \int_1^2 \left(\cos\frac{\pi x}{2} + k^2\right)dx$$

$$= -\frac{\cos\pi x}{\pi} - 2kx\Big|_0^1 + \frac{2\sin\frac{\pi x}{2}}{\pi} - k^2x\Big|_1^2 = (k+1)^2 = 0 \rightarrow k = -1$$

Example 28: The time in minutes between cars passing on a street is given by the frequency function $f(t)=e^{-t}$ for $t \geq 0$. Find the probability of a car passing in 0.45 minutes.

Solution: We have,

$$P = \int_a^b f(x)dx = \int_0^{0.45} e^{-t}dt = -e^{-t}\Big|_0^{0.45} = 1 - e^{-0.45} \cong 0.3624$$

***Example* 29:** The proportion of assignments completed a given day is described by the probability density function $f(x)=12(x^2 - x^3)$ for $1 \geq x \geq 0$. What is the probability that (a) 50 percent or less of the assignments will be completed within the day, and (b) 50 percent or more will be completed?

Solution: We have,

$$\text{(a) } P = \int_0^{0.5} 12(x^2 - x^3)dx = 12\left[\frac{x^3}{3} - \frac{x^4}{4}\right]\Big|_0^{0.5} = 0.3125.$$
$$\text{(b) } P = \int_{0.5}^{1} 12(x^2 - x^3)dx = 12\left[\frac{x^3}{3} - \frac{x^4}{4}\right]\Big|_{0.5}^{1} = 0.6875.$$

As expected, $P_a+P_b= 0.3125+0.6875=1$.

Two measurements of the continuous random variables are the *expected value,* or mean, and the variance.

Definition 15: If the continuous random variable X has a probability function $f(x)$, the expected value, or mean, of X is

$$E(X) = \int_{-\infty}^{\infty} xf(x)dx.$$

The following properties hold for the expected value:

(a)- $E(C)=C,$

(b)- $E(CX)=CE(X), C$ is a constant number.

***Example* 30:** The random variable X has the following probability density function.

$$f(x) = \begin{cases} 4x^2 - e^{x^2}, & 0 \leq x \leq 1.5 \\ 0, & otherwise \end{cases}$$

Calculate the value of (a) $E(X)$ and (b) $E(2X - 2)$.

Solution: We have,

$$\text{(a) } -E(X)_5 = \int_{-\infty}^{\infty} xf(x)dx = \int_0^{1.5} x(4x^2 - e^{x^2})dx = 4\int_0^{1.5} x^3dx - \int_0^{1.5} xe^{x^2}dx = \left(x^4 - \frac{e^{x^2}}{2}\right)\Big|_0^{1.5} \cong 0.8811.$$

$$\text{(b) } -E(3X - 2) = 3E(X) - E(2) = 3(0.8811) - 2 = 0.6433$$

Remark 8: If the random variable is discrete, then

$$E(X) = \sum xf(x).$$

***Example 31*:** A game of chance is based on tossing 4 fair coins. If we get 4, 3, or 2 heads, we win \$100, \$50, or \$25 respectively. Otherwise, we lose \$80. Let X be the amount won in this game. Find the expected value of winning this game.

Solution: We have 16 cases such that

$$P(X = \$100) = \frac{1}{16}, P(X = \$50) = \frac{4}{16}, P(X = \$25) = \frac{6}{16} \text{and} P(X = -\$75) = \frac{5}{16}.$$

Therefore,

$$E(X) = \sum xf(x) = \frac{100}{16} + \frac{200}{16} + \frac{150}{16} - \frac{400}{16} = \frac{50}{16} = 3.125.$$

That is, in each game we can win \$3.125.

Definition 16: The variance of a continuous random variable X, denoted by $V(X)$ is

$$V(X) = E(X - E(X))^2.$$

But

$$E(X - E(X))^2 = E(X^2 - 2XE(X) + E(X)^2) = E(X^2) - E(X)^2,$$

thus,

$$V(X) = E(X - E(X))^2 = E(X^2) - E(X)^2.$$

From the definition of the standard derivation for a discrete variable, the standard derivation of a continuous random variable X is also square roots of variance, i.e., $\sqrt{V(X)}$.

***Example* 32:** The random variable X has the following probability density function.

$$f(x) = \begin{cases} 3x - 1, & 0 \leq x \leq 1 \\ 0, & otherwise \end{cases}$$

Determine the variance and the standard derivation.

Solution: We have,

$$E(X) = \int_{-\infty}^{\infty} xf(x)dx = \int_0^1 x(3x - 1)dx = \left(x^3 - \frac{x^2}{2}\right)\Big|_0^1 = \frac{1}{2}.$$

$$E(X^2) = \int_{-\infty}^{\infty} x^2 f(x)dx = \int_0^1 x^2(3x - 1)dx = \left(\frac{3x^4}{4} - \frac{x^3}{3}\right)\Big|_0^1 = \frac{5}{12}.$$

Therefore,

$$V(X) = E(X^2) - E(X)^2 = \frac{5}{12} - \frac{1}{4} = \frac{1}{6} \rightarrow \sigma = \sqrt{V(X)} = \frac{1}{\sqrt{6}} = \frac{\sqrt{6}}{6}$$

Although we had an introduction about statistics, this is not sufficient to know about it. We offer readers the chance to refer to Freund (1992), which is a magnificent textbook about statistics.

CONCLUSION

In this chapter, we discussed basic concepts in probability and statistics. Some solid, realistic applications of the material have been used throughout the chapter. The examples in this chapter demonstrate that in studying a sequence of random experiments, it is not possible to forecast individual results. We understood that the method of selecting the sample is extremely important if we want the conclusions to be reliable.

To read more about statistics, readers may refer to (Mendenhall, Beaver, & Beaver, 2003) (Hance, 1977) (Freund, 1992).

12.7 Exercises

1. A container contains 20 cards in four different colors so that 5 cards of each color and cards of the same color are numbered from 1 to 5. We take out 2 cards randomly and without placement. What is the probability that both cards have the same number?
2. One card is drawn randomly from the well-shuffled pack of 52 cards in each of the following cases. Find the probability of getting: (a) An ace of red color (b) A jack, queen, or king card.
3. Assume we have a bag containing 16 blue and 14 yellow balls. Further, assume that we randomly draw two balls, one after the other, without replacement. Let's define:

Event *A*: The first ball is blue. Event *V*= The second ball is blue. What will be the joint probability of *A* and *B*?

4. From a three-child family, we want to select one of them. What is the probability of our choice to be exactly one girl?
5. We threw three tosses. What is the probability that the sum of the faces is more than 15?
6. We threw a toss once. What is the probability that the number on the square will be perfect?
7. We threw a coin once. If, $P(H)=3P(T)$ what is the probability that the head will appear?
8. We toss a coin five times. What is the probability that the tail will appear at least once?
9. A dice is made in such a way that the probability of odd numbers occurring in it is twice that of even numbers. If we throw this dice, what is the probability that the number on the square will be a perfect?
10. In a meeting of 10 people, assuming that different months of the year can be the birth month of each of these people with the same probability, calculate the probability that at least three of them were born in the same month.
11. 35% of the students of the Faculty of Management have failed the math course, and 20% have failed the finance course. We will have the following three situations: 1- The student has failed both courses. 2- Have failed the maritime course but passed the finance course. 3- Have failed the finance course but passed the math course.

Calculate $P(B|A)$ if $A \subset B$. If two sets are mutually exclusive.

12. Suppose the probability of an aircraft engine failure is $\frac{1}{10000}$. If this aircraft has another similar engine that operates independently, so if the first engine fails, this engine will automatically take control of the aircraft. How likely is this aircraft to be reliable?
13. We randomly selected five numbers from the set $\{1,2,3,\ldots,30\}$. What is the probability that their sum is an even number?
14. From a production pile containing 15 pieces, 10 of which are healthy, we took a random sample of 5 with replacements. What is the probability that the fifth piece removed is fair, given that the sample contains 4 fair pieces? What is the probability that the sample is selected without being replacement?
15. In a company, there are three types of automatic machines, M_1, M_2 and M_3 under the control of one worker. The probability that these machines will work without problems for 3 hours is $\frac{1}{5}, \frac{2}{5}$ and $\frac{3}{5}$ respectively. Assuming independence of operation, what is the probability that at least two machines will work without worker control?

16. The manager responsible for the quality department of a company intends to control the quality of parts of a box of 60 pieces. If he has enough reason that 15% of the parts of the box are broken, he will not allow the box to pass to the next stage. To obtain sufficient evidence, he decides to select a random sample of 15 without replacement from the box and test them. If at least one broken piece is found in the sample, do not allow the box to pass. Find the probability that the box is accepted.
17. A company produces three types of mobiles. The company produces 40%, 25% and 35% for types A, B and C, respectively. If the percentage of defective cars of these three types of mobiles is 2%, 4% and 6% respectively, what is the probability that we will choose randomly a mobile from this company that is defective? What is the probability that the selected mobile is defective in the first type?
18. According to previous records, the probability of victory, draw and defeat of Team A against Team B is $\frac{3}{5}$, 1 and $\frac{2}{5}$ respectively. In next year's competition, these two clubs have four games against each other. What is the probability that Team A will have at least three wins? What is the probability that there will be two wins, one draw and one loss?
19. Consider three boxes, each containing two mobiles. One of these boxes contains two fair mobiles, another one contains both defective mobiles, and the third box contains one defective mobile. Suppose we randomly select one of the boxes and try one of the mobiles in it. Assuming that this mobile is fair, what is the probability that the second mobile is also fair?
20. In a survey of 54 men, 36 men are native and 18 are non-native. If half of them are single, and we choose one randomly, what is the probability that he is native or single?
21. Consider three boxes, each containing two mobiles. One of these boxes contains two fair mobiles, another one contains both defective mobiles, and the third box contains one defective mobile. Suppose we randomly select one of the boxes and try one of the mobiles in it. Assuming that this mobile is fair, what is the probability that the second mobile is also fair?
22. In a survey of 54 men, 36 men were native and 18 are non-native. If half of them are single and we choose one randomly, what is the probability that he is native or single?
23. From the box containing 5 blue and 4 red beads, we remove two beads at a time without placement. What is the probability that the second selected bead is blue?
24. A company hired 124 workers for a project, paying 50 of them $40 an hour, 30 $30 an hour, and the rest $25 an hour. What is the average hourly wage?

25. We draw two cards from a pack of playing cards. What is the probability of getting an ace and a king?
26. From a container containing 4 white beads and 5 black beads, we randomly remove 4 beads. What is the probability that all three are the same color? What is the probability that it is not the same color?
27. A company produces an article which consists of three parts, A, B and C. In the process of A and B, 10 out of 100 are likely to be defective and for part C, 8 out of 100 are likely to be detective. What is the probability that the assembled part will not be detectives?
28. In building a construction complex, the delivery of the complex may be delayed due to the high cost of building materials. The probability that the construction materials will not be raised, and the complex will be delivered on time is 70%. The probability that the construction materials will be raised, and the complex will not be delivered on time is 50%, and the probability that the construction materials will be raised, and the complex will be delivered on time is 30%. What is the probability that the complex will be delivered on time?
29. Show that the minimum value of the function $f(x) = \sum_{1}^{n} (x - x_i)^2$ occurs at $x = \bar{x}$ where $\bar{x}$is the mean of points $x_1,x_2,\ldots,x_n$.
30. The average of 25 numbers is 15.5. If we exclude one number, the average of the remaining 24 numbers is equal to 15. What is the omitted number?
31. Suppose the life in hours of a tube has the density $f(x) = xe^{-x^2}$ when $x \geq 5000$ and zero, when $x<150$. What is the probability that none of four such tubes for a car will have to be replaced during the first 5000 hours of operations?
32. The sum of 15 numbers is equal to 35. If we multiply each of these numbers by 4 and add 2.5 units to each of them, what will be the sum of the new numbers?
33. The random variable X has the following probability density function. Find the value of $P(X \leq 1.5)$.

$$f(x) = \begin{cases} 2x - 1, & 0 \leq x \leq 1 \\ e^{2x} - x, & 1 < x \leq 2 \\ 0, & otherwise \end{cases}$$

34. Find the value of k if the random variable X has a probability density function of the form $f(x) = e^{-k(x^2 - 6x)}$.
35. The score of five subjects of a student with a factor of 2 is equal to 16. What should the grade of the sixth subject be, which is meant by the coefficient of 3 so that the average of his 6 subjects is 17?

36. A bomb-plane from a country I_1 carrying three bombs to attack a specific factory of a city in the country I_2. If a bomb falls within 70 feet of the city, the factory will be sufficiently damaged to disrupt traffic. With a certain bomb sight, the density of the points of impact of a bomb is

$$f(x) = \begin{cases} \frac{152 + 3x^2}{15}, -15 \leq x \leq 0 \\ \frac{152 - 3x^2}{15}, 0 \leq x \leq 15 \end{cases}$$

If all three bombs are used what is the probability that the factory will be damaged where x represents the vertical deviation from the aiming point which is the factory in this case.

REFERENCES

Fellere, W. (1957). *An Introduction to Probability and Its Applications* (2nd ed., Vol. 1). John Wiley & Sons.

Freund, J. E. (1992). *Mathematical Statistics* (5th ed.). Prentice- Hall.

Hance, El. (1977). *Practical Problems in Statistics.* Kitab Mahal Pubication.

Mendenhall, W., & Beaver, R. J., & Beaver, B. M. (2003). Introduction to Probability and Statistics. (11th ed). Thomson Brooks/Cole.

Compilation of References

Ablowitz, Mark J & Fokas, A. S. (2003). Complex Variable: Introduction and Applications.(2nd ed). Cambridge University Press.

Anton, H. (1977). *Elementary Linear Algebra* (2nd ed.). Wiley.

Anton, H., & Kolman, B. (1982). *Mathematics with Applications for Management, Life, and Social Science*. Academic Press, Inc.

Apostol. Tom M. (1966). Calculus. John Wiley & Sons, Volume 1.

Apostol. Tom, M. (1966). *Calculus* (3rd ed., Vol. 1). JOHN WILEY & SONS.

Beckenbach, E. F. (1964). *Applied Combinational Mathematics*. John Wiley & Sons.

Boyce, W. E., & Diprima, R. C. (1977). *Elementary Differential Equations and Boundary Value Problems* (3rd ed.). John-Wiley& Sons.

Burden, R. L. (1989). Numerical Analysis (4th ed). PWS_KENT Publish Company.

Chang, A. c. (1967). *Fundamental Methods of Mathematical Economics*. McGraw Hill.

Churchill, J., & Ward, B. (1988). *Complex Variables and Applications* (4th ed.). Mc Graw-Hill Co.

Delong. Howard. (1970). A Profile of Mathematical Logic. Reading, Mass. Addison Wesley.

Driebeek, N. J. (1969). *Applied Linear Programming*. Addison-Wesley Publishing Company, Inc.

Ederton. Helbert, B. (2001). *A Mathematical Introduction to Logic* (2nd ed.). Acedamic Press.

Elyadi, S. (2000). *An Introduction to Difference Equations* (3rd ed.). Springer.

Fellere, W. (1957). *An Introduction to Probability and Its Applications* (2nd ed., Vol. 1). John Wiley & Sons.

Finney, R. L. (1988). Calculus and Analytical Geometry (7th ed). Addison-Wesley Publishing Company.

Finney. Ross. L. (1988). Calculus and Analytical Geometry. Addison-Wesley Publishing Company.

Finney. Ross, L. (1988). *Calculus and Analytical Geometry* (7th ed.). ADDISON-WESLEY PUBLISHING COMPANY.

Freund, J. E. (1992). *Mathematical Statistics* (5th ed.). Prentice- Hall.

Gass, S. I. (1975). *Linear Programming: Methods and Applications* (4th ed.). McGraw-Hill Book Company.

Gerald, J. T. (1972). Applied Numerical Analysis. (2 nd ed). (Reading, Mass. Addison-Wesley.

Golub, G. H., & Van, C. F. (1996). *Matrix Computations* (3rd ed.). The Johns Hopkins University Press.

Gourlay, A. R., & Watson, G. A. (1973). *Computational Methods for Matrix Eigenproblems*. John Wiley and Sons.

Grimaldi. Ralph, P. (1989). *Discrete and Combinatorial Mathematics* (2nd ed.). Addison-Wesley Publishing Company.

Grossman, P. (1995). *Discrete Mathematics for Computing*. MACMILLAN PRESS LTD. DOI: 10.1007/978-1-349-13908-8

Halmos. Paul, R. (1998). Naïve Set Theory (3rd ed.). Springer. Enderton. Herbert B. (1977). Elements of Set Theory. First Academic Press.

Hamming, R. W. (1971). *Introduction to applied and numerical analysis*. Mc Graw-Hill, Inc.

Hance, El. (1977). *Practical Problems in Statistics*. Kitab Mahal Pubication.

Heady, E. O., & Candler, W. (1958). *Linear Programming methods*. Iowa State College Press.

Hermann, M & Saravi, M. (2014). A First Course in Ordinary Differential Equations, Springer-book company.

Hermann, M., & Saravi, M. (2014). A First Course in Ordinary Differential Equations, Springer-book company.

Hoffman, K., & Kunze, R. (1971). Linear Algebra. (2nd ed). Englewood Cliff, N. J. Prentice- Hall.

Horn, R. A., & Johnson, C. R. (1996). *Matrix Analysis*. Cambride University Press.

Jameson, G. J. O. (1970). *A First Course on Complex Functions*. Chapman and Hall. DOI: 10.1007/978-94-009-5680-3

Jarvis, J. J., Bazaraa, M. S., & Sherali, H. D. (1990. Linear Programming and Network. (2nd ed). Flows. John Wiley & Sons.

Kim, C. (1971). *Linear Programming*. Holt, Rinehart and Winston, Inc.

Kline. Morris. (1964). Mathematics in Western Culture, Oxford University Press.

Koslow, A. (1992). *A Structuralist Theory of Logic*. Cambridge University Press. DOI: 10.1017/CBO9780511609206

Kreisel, G., & Krivine, J.-L. (1967). *Elements of Mathematical Logic*. North-Holland.

Kunen. K. Set Theory. (2014). An Introduction To Independence Proofs. Elsevier Science. Jech. Thomas. (2013). Set Theory. Springer.

Kunen, K. (1980). *Set Theory: An Introduction to Independence Proofs*. Elsevier.

Leithold. Louis (1981). The Calculus and Analytical Geometry (4th ed.). Harper & Row.

Leithold. Louis (1981). The Calculus and Analytical Geometry. Harper & Row.

Leithold, L. (1981). *The Calculus and Analytical Geometry* (4th ed.). Harper & Row.

Lévy, A. (1978). *Basic Set Theory. Springer. Grimaldi. Ralph P. (1989). Discrete and Combinatorial Mathematics* (2nd ed.). Addison-Wesley Publishing Company.

Lewis, C. (2008). Linear Programming: Theory and Applications, Text paper.

Liu, C. L. (2002). *Elements of Discrete Mathematics, TATA McGraaw-Hill Edition. Grossman, Peter. (1995). Discrete Mathematics for Computing*. MACMILLAN PRESS LTD.

Liu, C. L. (2002). *Elements of Discrete Mathematics*. TATA McGraaw-Hill Edition.

M. Tensnbaum, T, & Pollard. H. (1964). Differetial Equations. Harper & How.

Maron, M. J., & Lopez, R. J. (1991). *Numerical Analysis; A practical Approach*. Wadsworth, Inc.

Mendelson. Elliott. (2015). Introduction to Mathematical Logic, (6th ed). CRC Press, Taylor & Francis Group.

Mendenhall, W., & Beaver, R. J., & Beaver, B. M. (2003). Introduction to Probability and Statistics. (11th ed). Thomson Brooks/Cole.

Nicholson, R. H. (1986). Mathematics for Business and Economics. McGraw-Hill, Inc.

Nicholson, R. H. (1986). *Mathematics for Business and Economics*. McGraw-Hill, Inc.

odin. Burton. (1970). Calculus with Analytical Geometry. Prentice-Hall, Inc., Englewood Cliffs, New Jersey.

Pinter. Charles, C. (1971). *A book of Set Theory*. Addison-Wesley Publishing Company.

Piskunov, N. (1981). Differential and Integral, Vol 1 (4th ed). MIR Publisher.

Piskunov, N. (1981). Differential and Integral, Voume 1 (4th ed.). MIR PUBLISHER, MOSCOW.

Piskunov, N. (1981). Differential and Integral, Voume 1 (4th ed.). MIR Publisher.

Porter, M. C., & Golberg, J. (1978). *Mathematical Methods* (2nd ed.). Prentice-Hall International Inc.

Priest, G. (2001). *An Introduction to Non-Classical Logic. Cambridge University Press. Gibson. Carol. (1981). The facts on File Dictionary of Mathematics*. Charles Letts & Co., Ltd.

Rainville, E. D., & Bedint, P. A. (1974). *Elementary Differential Equations*. Mac. Millan Publishing.

Riordan, J. (1958). *An Introduction to Combinational Analysis*. John Wiley & Sons.

Rodin. Burton Rodin. (1970). Calculus with Analytical Geometry (4th ed). Prentice-Hall, Inc., Englewood Cliffs, New Jersey.

Rodin. Burton. (1970). Calculus with Analytical Geometry (4th ed.). Prentice-Hall, Inc., Englewood Cliffs, New Jersey.

Sahni, S. (1981). *Concepts in Discrete Mathematics*. Camelot Press.

Saravi. M & Saravi.S. (2011). A New Look at one of The Newton-like Methods for Solving Non-linear Equations, International Journal of Numerical methods and Applications, 5(1), 31-43.

Saravi, M., M & Zareenkhan. N. (2021). A note on Generalizatio to Method of Reduction of solving Second Order Linear Ordinary Differential Equations. *Further Applied Mathematics*, 2(2), 28–32.

Saravi, S., & Saravi, M. (2020). A Short Survey in Application of Ordinary Differential Equations on Cancer Research. *American Journal of Computational and Applied Mathematics*, 10(1), 1–5. DOI: 10.5923/j.ajcam.20201001.01

Silverman, Richard A. (1974). Complex Analysis with Applications. Prentice-Hall, INC.

Silverman. Richard, A. (1985). *Calculus with Analytical Geometry* (2nd ed.). Prentice-Hall, Inc.

Smythe, W. R., Anderson, D. J., & Williams, T. A. (1974). *Linear Programming for Decision Making*. West publishing Company.

Stanat, D. F. (1977). *Discrete Mathematics for Compuer Science*. Prentice-Hall.

Steart, J. (2012). Multivariable Calculus, Brooks.Cole, Cengage Learning, 7th Edition.

Stoll. Robert, R. (1963). *Set Theory and Logic*. Freeman.

Stone, H. S. (1973). *Discrete Mathematical Structures and Their Applications, Science Research Associate, Palo Alto, Cliffs, Sahni, S. (1981). Concepts in Discrete Mathematics*. Camelot Press.

Stone, H. S. (1973). *Discrete Mathematical Structures and Their Applications, Science Research Associate*. Cliffs.

Supess, P. (1957). *Introduction to Logic*. D. Van Nostrand Company.

Tall, D. O. (1971). *Functions of a Complex Variable* (1st ed.). Springer.

The American Mathematical Monthly (1983). p210, Vol 90, No3.

Thomas, G. B. (2014). Calculus (13th ed). Mc-Graw, New Jersey.

Tucker, J. P. (1980). *Applied Combinatories*. John Wiley & Sons.

Vajda, S. (1962). Reading in Linear Programming, John Wiley & Son, Inc., New York.

Winston, C., & Wayene, L. (1997). *Introduction to Mathematical Programming Applications and Algorithms*. Duxbury Press.

About the Author

Masoud Saravi started off academic studies in UK's Dudley Technical College. He received his first degree in Mathematics and Statistics from Polytechnic of North London, and his second degree in Numerical Analysis from Brunel University. After obtaining an MPhil in Applied Mathematics from Iran's Polytechnic University, he was appointed Lecturer of Mathematics. In 2000, he applied at UK's Open University, acquiring a Ph.D. in Numerical Analysis. His research interests include numerical solution of ODE's, differential equations and integral equations as well as DAE and spectral methods. Dr. Saravi has published 8 successful titles in the area of mathematics. The immense popularity of his books is deemed as a reflection of more than 30 years of educational experience, and a result of his accessible style of writing, as well as a broad coverage of well laid out and easy to follow subjects. His books on Calculus, Differential Equations and Engineering Mathematics, are recommended coursebooks in several renowned universities in Iran. As of May 2012, Professor Saravi is a Guest Researcher in the faculty of mathematics and informatics at the Friedrich-Schiller-University of Jena, Germany.

About the Author

Index

www.ingramcontent.com/pod-product-compliance
Lightning Source LLC
LaVergne TN
LVHW080609300926
849162LV00005B/1091